EXCEEDING EXPECTATIONS:

A USER'S GUIDE TO IMPLEMENTING

BRAIN RESEARCH IN THE CLASSROOM

by Susan J. Kovalik
and
Karen D. Olsen

Exceeding Expectations:

A User's Guide to Implementing Brain Research in the Classroom

by Susan J. Kovalik and Karen D. Olsen

Edited by Jane McGeehan and Kathleen Wolgemuth
Graphics by Lanitta Jaye Delk   Cover design by Marni Erwin

Published by Susan Kovalik & Associates, Inc.

© 2001 Susan Kovalik

Distributed by Books for Educators, Inc.
17051 SE 272nd Street, Suite 18
Covington, WA 98042
888/777-9827, FAX 253/630-7215
E-mail: books4@oz.net
www.books4educ.com

ISBN # 1-878631-55-1

Printed in the United States of America

Dedication

To my parents

Malcolm and Josephine Jafferies

Who taught me that making a positive difference in the world

is the highest goal one can attain and that it demands courage, integrity, and perseverance.

And to my grandchildren

Kendra, Serena, Austin, Katrina, Kendall, Jack, and Ashley

who must continue the effort.

Susan J. Kovalik

Acknowledgements

"The very least you can do in your life is to figure out what you hope for.
And the most you can do is live inside that hope."

— Barbara Kingsolver

The "hope" of Susan Kovalik and Associates is to facilitate learning communities that are dynamic environments for teaching and learning and that successfully "grow responsible citizens."

The Associates of Susan Kovalik and Associates, all classroom teachers or administrators, are responsible for the training and coaching of thousands of educators in the United States and around the world. They are "on the road" at least 50% of the year, guiding and supporting educators who are committed to creating a true learning community. The Associates' contributions to the development of the ITI model are many and varied. and as more and more of the bodybrain research is known the model becomes bedrock solid. The following associates are currently working throughout the United States and the world.

Karen Olsen, who has held the intellectual conscience and integrity of the ITI model since 1987. She is author, co-author, and contributing editor of all our publications.

Barbara Pedersen whose vision, leadership, and statewide support of ITI efforts in Indiana, has carried ITI to over 400 schools throughout Indiana under the name of C.L.A.S.S. Program (Connecting Learning Assures Successful Students).

Jo Gusman, who early on recognized the power ITI had for ESL students and knew the importance of the affective filter/domain in the classroom.

Ann Ross, who believed that ITI could work in middle school, no matter what the neighborhood, and wrote the ITI middle school book, *The Way We Were, The Way We CAN Be* with Karen D. Olsen.

Sister Patt Walsh, whose insight took us into the world of technology and developed our on-line network for answering pressing questions about ITI implementation and keeping teachers in touch with each other.

Patty Harrington who patiently guided us in the understanding of TRIBES and the need for a solid foundation for building classroom community.

Jane McGeehan, who had the courage to take ITI into the high school, was the contributing editor of the ITI book for administrators, *Transformations: Leadership for Bodybrain-Compatible Learning*, and is now the CEO of Susan Kovalik and Associates, guiding us to the next level of development.

Kari Kling, whose initiative and perseverance produced the ITI math book, *It's Not About Math, It's About Life,* and *The Only Being There Experience Guide Students Ever Need: Connect Learning, Trips, Kids, and School.*

Judy Eacker whose talent and spirit gave the LIFESKILLS a voice through song and a sensitive ear to the needs of students.

Sue Pearson whose efforts and commitment produced the LIFESKILL book, *Tools For Citizenship and Life: Using the ITI Lifelong Guidelines and LIFESKILLS in Your Classroom.*

Nicole Miller, whose enlightened teaching in an inner city middle school was documented in the video, *ITI in the Urban Middle School.*

Linda Jordan, using initiative and problem solving, co-developed an exceptional teacher training program at the college level to prepare graduating students with the ITI tools necessary to be successful.

Jill Hay, a special education educator used integrity when she adopted a class and taught one day a week for a year to understand the power of the ITI model for special education students in to provide better leadership through her staff development role.

Jean Blaydes, who early on understood the connection between movement and learning and has travelled the world sharing that message with humor and perseverance.

To the associates who are no longer "on the road" but have influenced the model: Dean Tannewitz,, Joy Raboli, Pattie Mills, Kathy Theuer, Sally Johnson, Martha Kaufeldt, Robert Ellingsen, Jacque Melin, and Ventura Lopez.

None of this is possible without the support of the people "back home." A big thank you to all the families out there who realize the power of knowledge and commitment and who share those they love with other people's children.

Two families that went above and beyond were the Helman family and the Milhous family. Each family spent one year in Slovakia, formerly part of Czechoslovakia, with only reimbursement for expenses, to train and coach teachers in ITI, allowing them to move from a communist educational system to education for freedom. Today there are 27 ITI teacher centers in Slovakia and two universities provide ITI certification for new teachers. Additional SKA staff also went back and forth during our seven year experience and in 1999 Susan Kovalik received a medal of honor from the Minister of Education for providing an alternative education model to their country.

To the people who answer the phone at Susan Kovalik & Associates and make it all happen: Jane McGeehan, Debora Schweikl, Denny Peace, Vivienne Lietz, Lori Ann Moos-Albuquerque, and Judy Notti and Eve Sayers

To all the teachers who have worked with us during model teaching weeks and summer institutes: Gary Allers (MI), Rosalie Alexander (IN), Ginger Andersen (CA), Cathy Barron, Esther Bench (CA), Diane Berry (CA), Cinthy Black, Karen Bogan (IN), Carolyn Boyd (CA), Dottie Brown (SC), Cheryl Canfield (NY), Shan Carlson (CA), Gail Chambers (CA), Pat Champion, Julie Cox (MI), Lois Craig (WA), Diane della Maggiore (CA), Molly Doherty (MO), Jean Floyd (SC), Shirley Franck (IN), Belinda Garza (CA), Julita Galleguillos (CA),Vickie Hogan (CA), Marsha Isaacson (CA), Sylvia Kahn (CA), Marilyn Kelly (CA), Kris Kennedy (CA), Karen Kindrick (CA), Lauren Kirk (TX), Karen Kraai (MI) Edger Lampkin (CA), Cheryl Larison (CA), Barbara Lindrup (MI), Carol Lippert (AZ), Julie Lovell (SC), Alissa Braddy (SC), Debby Meyer (NY),

Lisa Muff (NE), Jackie Munoz (CA), Michael Nauss (MI), Art Nemitz (MI), Barbara Norris (FL), Olga O'Brien (CA), Diana O'Bryan (OR), Sheryl O'Connor (MI), Jeanne Olovson (MI), Florence Paulson (MI) Jeannine Poole (IN), Sue Price (IN), Wilma Ramirez (CA), Inga Randle (IN) Joan Reinkemeyer (MO), Brenda Russell (FL), Patty Simis (CA), Jean Spanko (AZ), Linda Steel (FL), Dolphus Stephens (IN), Paula Tielsch (CA), Barbara Till (MI), Colleen Uhl (UT), Susan Voorhees (AZ), Lorrie Webb (TX), Denise White (OK), Diane Williams (CA), Jeannie Williams (OR), Brenda Wykoff (AZ).

To the courageous administrators who understand the value and integrity of implementing a model that benefits all children: Terry Chandler (SC), Francie Summers (NV), Cathey Frederick (OK), Donna Cranswick (AZ), Ken Horn (MI) Terri Patterson (TX), Linda Kondris (CO), Tom Padalino (OK), Dennis Mah (CA), Maureen Ferrie (FL), Jeanne Herrick (CA), Margie Bickerstaff (GA), Dee Oakes (NY), Mary Ellen Bluem (MI), Marjorie Bowers (KY), Ursula Silwka (MI), Larry Holt (TN), Rick Prunty (MI), Allison Marks (CA), Orlo Knight (UT), Sr. Mariam Kaeser (OK), Anna Warren (TX), Mary Brandt (OK), Greg Webster (MI), Judy Lynn (Japan), Kay Dyer (MI), Ed Baldwin (FL), Bobbie Beckman (TN), Nancy Sisung (MI), Pete Carter (TN), Sr. Mary Clare (OK), Sherry Grate (IN), Beverly Nichols (KS), Vince Ontiveros (AZ), Johnny Calder (SC), Brent Palmer (IA), Sandra Kovatch (MN), Kathy Maisonville (MI), Ellen Hancock (CA), Mecheall Giombetti (FL), Barbara Klimek (MI), Karen Schulte (MI), Steve Waterman (CA), Gregg Petersen (IA), Marilyn Junk (OK), Becky Greer (KS), Kay Schultz (KS), Sandy McClelland (AZ), Kaethe Perez (FL), Joetta Surace (NJ), Linda Plante (MN), Warren Smith (FL), Marci Smith (FL), Linda Lewis (FL), Marion Gundling (FL), Marilyn Jones (FL), E.A. Murray (FL), Peggy Randle (MI), Cheri Meyer (MI), Anita Molsted (OR), Dick Molsted (OR), Janet Nash (FL), Diedre Zockheem (MI), Debbie Minch (FL), Richard Kunzi (MI), Maree Price (SC), Jane Veirs (AZ), Peggy Warren (AZ), Dennis Joyce (MI), Eula Baumgarner (AZ), Santo Pino (FL), Harriet Maclean (CA), Sharon Collins (IA), Becci Rutledge (GA), Jill Fuss (AZ), Randy Moffitt (IA), Sharon Brewer (TX), Ines Schmook (FL), Sharon Searson (WA), Scott Dodson (NE), Bob Abaya (CA), Robin Lynch (IN), Susan Jordan (IN), Dolores Sapp (FL), Syd Dickson (UT), Karl Klimek (MI), Ray Conti (CA), Martin Meyer (OR), Anne Sardeson (OH), Shelley Schurch (WA), Wilma White (CA), Patricia Martin (FL), Carol Husk (CO), Beverly Kempley (AZ), Barry Liebovitz (FL) ,Cookie Green (TN), and Bob McDonald (OR).

Thousands of students and teachers go to school each day with excitement and anticipation of the possibility ahead of them. Each of you has, in countless ways during untold hours, contributed to that possibility.

Thank you isn't a big enough phrase, but I do thank each and every one of you for allowing me to "live inside my hope." For in the end.

> "We will conserve only what we love.
> We will love only what we understand.
> We will understand only what we are taught."
> Baba Dioum

Table of Contents

Part B: *Stages of Implementation: 1—Getting Started*

Part C: *Stages of Implementation: 2—First Steps to Integrating Curriculum*

Part D: *Stages of Implementation: 3-5—Working Toward Total Integration in a Fully Bodybrain-Compatible Learning Environment*

Preface

> " This is a "must read" book for every educator who would like practical methods for applying brain research. Throughout the world, international and national schools are using the ITI conceptual framework to develop responsible citizens. The ITI model is applicable to any classroom and applies well to all cultures. At our school in Kobe, Japan, we have found that the nomenclature is easy to teach to children of all nationalities. LIFESKILL are the cornerstone for our program of character/values education and parents are able to understand the concepts and reinforce these values at home. But more important, the ITI model gives our multinational teaching staff common language to use in their professional day-to-day life. "
>
> —David Ottaviano, Ed.D.
> *Headmaster*
> Canadian Academy
> Kobe, Japan

> " After visiting an ITI middle school, I realized again that Susan Kovalik's ITI model is doing nothing less than <u>developing greatness in young human beings</u> . . . responsible, respectful, and creative citizens who can contribute to society. Why do we ever wonder what American education should be about! "
>
> —Jeanne Gibbs, *author*
> *TRIBES: A New Way of Learning and Being Together*
> TRIBES Learning Communities
> CenterSource Systems, LLC

This book is a labor of love. It represents a lifetime of thinking and teaching and it holds forth the hope that we will find the political will to use brain research to transform our schools and, in so doing, transform our world. It is heartening to hear from those implementing ITI that this hope is taking wing and that, in ways big and small, ITI is contributing to making the world a better place. We invite you to join with us.

The Authors

Introduction

Origins of the ITI Model

As a new sixth grade teacher, I worked my intuition overtime to come up with the best ways to teach my students. As an Italian, that meant providing plenty of enthusiasm, exuberant gestures, laughs, hugs, and food. My formula worked; my students loved school and loved learning. Then I became a K-6 science teacher for 1,200 students. To my basic Italian instructional strategies, I added lots of hands on of real things—your basic nightmare for a custodian and for the music teacher with whom I shared space. Snakes, rats, chickens, you name it. More good results with kids. Then one day the custodian told me he had seen a notice for a new job opening—teacher for the gifted and talented (GT). He told me I should apply! Whether it was because he had noticed the enthusiasm of my students or hoped longingly for a more traditional science teacher with fewer critters and exploratory items, I'll never know. But I took his suggestion. My work with GT students led me to giving workshops, in the course of which I was noticed by a talent scout for an organization that sponsored conferences across the country. Fully convinced that we needed to save students from the boredom and tedium of textbooks and worksheets—so why not start with the gifted!—I hit the road.

As I'd promised my three teenage children that I would take each of them on the road with me for a week, I soon found myself in Indiana with my youngest son, Marshall. The GT coordinator, our dinner hostess, was very enthusiastic about her mission, effusive about the needs and achievements of GT students. As the testimonials rolled on, my son spun his corner-fold napkin to make a loop and pretended to hang himself, gagging for added effect. As I stared in disbelief at my son, I was further shocked as he burst out: "Do you really believe that the only students who want a good teacher and something interesting to learn are the ones that score high on a one-hour test?" In response our dinner hostess said he seemed a little hostile. "Yes," he said, "my brother and sister [who were in a GT program] get all the good teachers and I get the left-overs. And no one ever asked me what I wanted."

Marshall was right. Every kid deserves a good teacher. I left the field of gifted education and turned my attention to learning for all students.

The most important lessons in life often come from our own family experiences.

Three years later, Marshall came home from high school in January of his senior year and said to me, "I know what you believe and I know what you stand for, but I'm quitting school. Before you say anything, you go sit in my classes for a day and at the end of the day if you can look me in the eye and tell me that six more months of this will really enhance who I am as a person, then we'll talk about it." After sitting through his classes, I could not look him in the eye and say, "Yes, it would." Marshall left school.

Marshal was right again.

My quest for answers intensified. I scoured bookstores for books about learning and happened upon Leslie Hart's *Human Brain and Human Learning* in 1983. At last . . . an explanation about how the brain learns from a scientific perspective. New doors began to open. To my wonderment, many of my earlier intuitions about instructional strategies and curriculum development were confirmed by brain research. I was ecstatic! I began to analyze my teaching strategies. They worked not because I was an extroverted Italian but because they allowed students' brains to work the way they naturally work; the strategies were, as Hart coined the term, "brain-compatible." In fact, anyone could learn the techniques and they worked for all students—not just GT, not just reluctant learners, but all students. The ITI model was born. Over the past 18 years, the ITI model has continued to evolve to stay current with emerging brain research and to respond to an on-going search for the best curricular and instructional practices by my associates and I and ITI teachers across the country.

The ITI model reflects another side of my family experience, that of the political activism of my parents, Malcolm and Josephine Jafferies. They imprinted on me early in life that the purpose of an educated life is citizenship—active participation in our democratic processes.

On behalf of all the Marshalls out there who want and deserve good teachers and something interesting to learn and in deep gratitude for my parents who modeled citizenship, knowing how precious and fragile a democratic society is, I welcome you to the ITI model.

Susan J. Kovalik
August, 2001
Covington, Washington

Overview of the ITI Model

The ITI model has two main goals:

- To create participating citizens, willing and able to engage in our democratic processes to improve life now and for future generations

- To help educators translate current brain research into practical strategies for the classroom and schoolwide

Pursuing one goal without the other is an empty activity. The world has urgent problems to solve and we have children waiting to learn and grow and hoping to have meaningful work to do.

The ITI model is based in current brain research. Our knowledge of how the human brain learns—the biology of learning—is used to inform our decision-making about what's worth teaching as we develop curriculum and instructional strategies that will work best.

Few will be surprised by the core concepts summarizing major areas of agreement in brain research; much of the brain biology summarized here rings true with our intuitions. It is our belief that schools of the 21st century must act on best practice for curriculum development and instructional strategies, practice informed by brain research rather than educational tradition and habit.

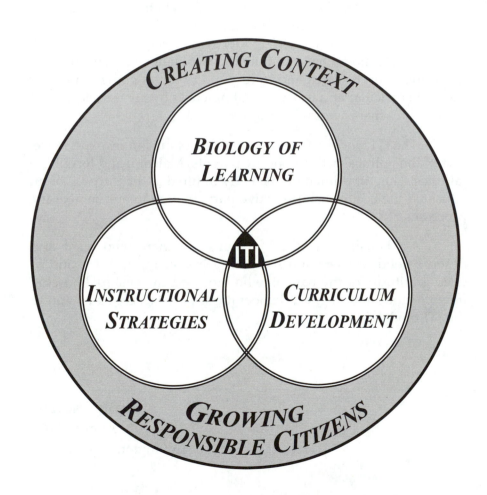

Brain Biology — The Five ITI Learning Principles

The ITI model is based on five basic principles from brain research, each of which is discussed in Part A, Chapters 1-6:

1 *Intelligence* is a function of experience (see Chapter 1)

2 Learning is an inseparable partnership between *brain* and *body* (see Chapter 2)

— Emotion is the gatekeeper to learning and performance

— Movement enhances learning

3 There are *multiple intelligences* or ways for solving problems and producing products (see Chapter 3)

4 Learning is a *two-step process*:

— Step one: Making meaning through pattern seeking (see Chapter 4)

— Step two: Developing a mental program for using what we understand and wiring it into long-term memory (see Chapter 5)

5 *Personality* impacts learning and performance (see Chapter 6)

The Nine Bodybrain-Compatible Elements of Curriculum Development and Instruction

The bodybrain-compatible elements of the ITI model are the primary ways of translating brain research into action in the classroom. These nine elements are:

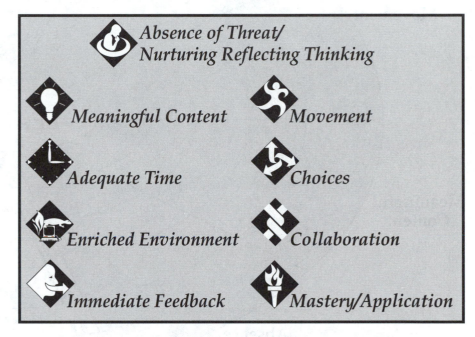

These nine bodybrain-compatible elements appear at the back of each of the six chapters dealing with an ITI Learning Principle (see Chapters 1-6). This intermix of theory—the Learning Principles—and practical applications—the Bobybrain-Compatible Elements—is illustrated on the next page. The concentric circles represent the brain research concepts; the pie wedges represent the bodybrain-compatible elements.

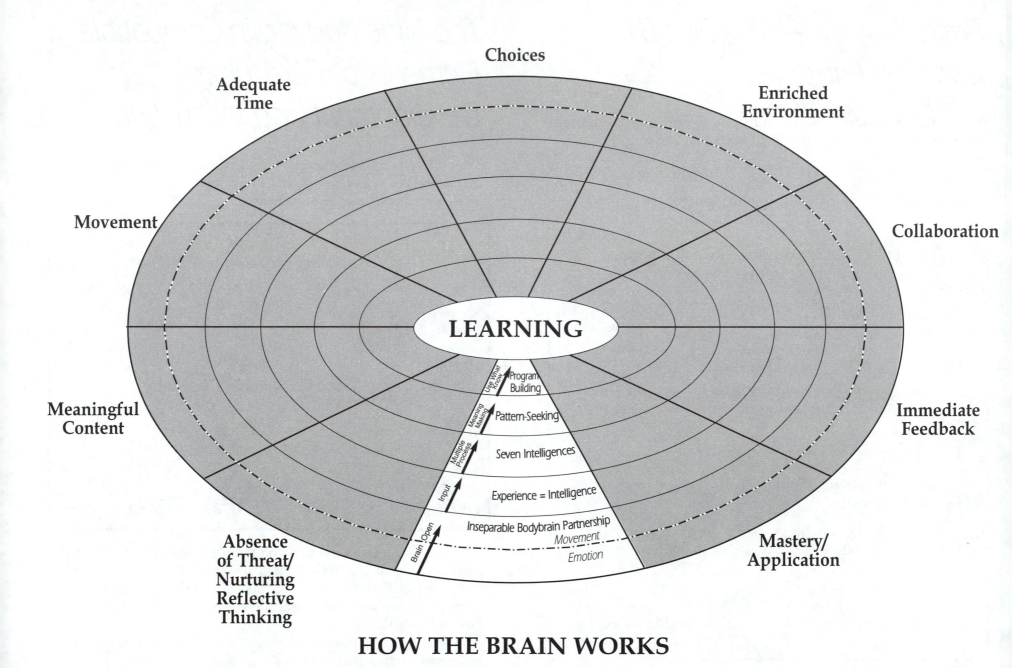

Choices

Adequate
Time

Enriched
Environment

Movement

Collaboration

Meaningful
Content

Immediate
Feedback

Absence
of Threat/
Nurturing
Reflective
Thinking

Mastery/
Application

LEARNING

Use What Know → Program Building

Meaning Making → Pattern-Seeking

Multiple Process → Seven Intelligences

Input → Experience = Intelligence

Brain Open → Inseparable Bodybrain Partnership
Movement
Emotion

HOW THE BRAIN WORKS

Toward Bodybrain-compatible Teaching/Learning

Although much about the five ITI Learning Principles from brain research and their relationship to the nine bodybrain-compatible elements jumps from the page with a sense of déjà vu, implementing them in the face of a system that is brain-antagonistic in so many ways is indeed a challenge.

Coherence, Not Piecemeal. Achieving bodybrain-compatibility for your students is not the result of following a check list. The concepts from brain research cannot be implemented by a few simple strategies. Effective implementation will only come through full understanding of the brain research and the richness of its implications. As you study each of the ITI Learning Principles in Chapters 1-6, do ask yourself, "So what?" What does this mean to my students? What does this suggest that I change about my classroom? What does it mean to base my teaching in brain research rather than traditional practices?

Implementing ITI is not a piecemeal affair in which one picks and chooses what to implement. Perhaps the most important things to say about brain research and its implementation is this: *If even one of the bodybrain-compatible elements is not in place, the learning environment is not bodybrain-compatible.*

Old Yet New. It is important to recognize that the curricular and instructional strategies described in the ITI model are not new. Good teachers have implemented them over the years but did so intuitively. But intuition alone is insufficient when putting together a coherent, comprehensive approach to curriculum and instruction for a schoolwide program improvement effort.

Basing our improvement efforts on brain research urges us to use old tools differently and for new purposes. It would, in fact, be easier to implement brain research if it required all new curricular and instruction strategies. Just throw out everything you're doing now and start fresh. Hardest of all is to use old strategies in new ways for new purposes.

What makes this so hard is that it's extremely difficult to maintain a clear vision of old tools used anew when one lives in an old structure with its old pictures, old habits, old vocabulary with its old ideas, and old pressures. Before we know it, we're back where we started. And old tools used in old ways will not produce the results for students that we desire. When old tools are used in new ways, with the purpose of translating brain research into action, you will be amazed at the changes in student behavior, attitudes, and test scores. You'll also find yourself enjoying teaching more than you ever thought possible.

The Balance Between Curriculum and Instruction

The ITI model is perhaps best known as a curriculum development model with its integrated yearlong theme structure, yet it is first and foremost a means of translating brain research into practical classroom applications. In that endeavor, experience has taught us that creating a bodybrain-compatible teaching/learning environment is a necessary prerequisite before moving on to more traditional aspects of curriculum development. Once these environment and classroom leadership/management elements are in place, the curriculum development aspects of the ITI model then come to the forefront.

How to Use This Book

This is not a book to be read from cover to cover in one swoop. It is designed to be read in stages over a three-to-five year period.

Part A is your touchstone. Read it and re-read it until you feel you have a grasp of the vision it forecasts. Revisit it each time you begin a new part of the book.

Read **Part B** when you're ready to begin implementing. Chapter 7 describes what to do before school starts. Chapter 8 gets you off to a running start with an outline and lesson plan for the first day of school. It models many of the curricular and instructional strategies you'll need during the first year of implementation. The recommendations are based on the experiences of thousands of ITI teachers across the country and proven research.

Once you have your bodybrain-compatible learning environment firmly in place (which typically takes a year of concerted effort), read **Part C.** Part C explains how to begin integrating curriculum.

Part D explains how to achieve full integration of curriculum through Stages 3-5 of the *ITI Classroom Stages of Implementation.* Expect this to take an additional two to three years.

Part E should be read concurrently with Parts B through D. Part E describes the instructional strategies needed every day and those needed when introducing and reteaching a concept or skill.

As you use this book, notice that we have provided quick graphic references for you. The chapters in Parts A-E each have a distinguishing symbol as shown above.

As you read through Parts A and B, keep in mind the following curriculum definitions. Key points and inquiries are fundamental curriculum development structures. You should be familiar with them from the very beginning of your journey into the ITI model. Key points are accompanied by a strip of puzzle pieces along the left margin, symbolic of the brain's pattern-seeking processes as it attempts to make meaning of its surroundings. Inquiries are accompanied by a strip of action elements along the left margin, symbolic of the brain's drive to use what it understands through doing—taking action such as that requested in the inquiries.

ITI CURRICULUM DEFINITIONS

KEY POINTS — The essential concepts, knowledge, skills, and attitudes/values all students are to learn. They are written so as to enhance students' ability to make meaning by detecting patterns. Key points answer the question: "What do we want students to understand?"

INQUIRIES — Opportunities to practice using the essential concepts, knowledge, skills, and attitudes/values of the key points in real-world situations in order to develop mental programs for long-term memory. Inquiries answer the question: "What do we want students to do with what they understand?"

YEARLONG THEME — A yearlong organizational structure consisting of the theme, monthly components, and weekly topics. Its purpose is to provide a mental web or pattern for what is studied.

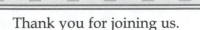

Thank you for joining us.

Part A

Brain Research

And Its Practical Application

Brain Research and the ITI Model

The ITI model starts with brain research to determine best practice—everything from curriculum development to instructional strategies, classroom assessment of student progress to evaluating student achievement program-wide, classroom and school design to budgeting.

The challenges facing students, teachers, and administrators are greater than ever before and are not likely to be solved until we change our ways of thinking about learning and teaching. As Einstein commented: "Problems can't be solved by the same thinking that created them." This is the 21st century. Traditional ways of teaching and the habits of mind that go with them must give way to using best knowledge.

Bodybrain Biology

In 1990, President George Bush proclaimed the final years of the 20th century as the Decade of the Brain. As we enter the 21st century, our public and private school systems still struggle to come to terms with how brain research should be used as a basis for reform efforts. We believe that a significant part of the resistance to using brain research stems from piecemeal views of brain research findings. Teachers need and deserve a comprehensive view of brain research that includes practical applications to the classroom. For others, the source of resistance comes from an awareness that what brain research is telling us suggests a rigorous need to change our 150+ year old practices, a degree of change that may seem overwhelming or outside our level of commitment.

The purpose of Part I is to describe five learning principles from brain research that provide a biology base for a comprehensive view of instructional strategies and curriculum development needed to improve students learning. Embedded in the five concepts is a discussion of the nine bodybrain-compatible elements of the ITI model that translate brain research insights into practical, everyday applications in the classroom and school.

Five Learning Principles from Brain Research

Although the enormous complexity of the brain and the dizzying, science-fiction-like capabilities of today's research technologies can make for heavy treading when reading brain research studies, descriptions of how the human brain learns can be expressed in relatively simple conceptual terms. And although we may not know as much as we will, we certainly know enough to get started.

> "Most school practice arises from tradition, ritual, and the context within which schools are conducted. Only during this century has scientific learning theory had an influence and then only in a minor way. The school is a kind of subculture in which are preserved the relics of former times, with a few practices added or subtracted because of contemporary thought."
>
> Foshay

The learning principles outlined here are, we believe, fundamental to establishing a working theory of human learning for the 21st century. Corroborated by researchers studying the human brain from many different avenues, they provide a powerful template for making decisions about curriculum and instruction and other issues for systemic rethinking of American education.

These five principles defined here are discussed in Chapters 1 through 6. Each chapter describes how the nine bodybrain-compatible elements of the ITI model are used to translate each of these brain principles into practical, and powerful, classroom applications. The bodybrain-compatible elements are described in the order of their power to implement that particular learning principle.

The five ITI Learning Principles about how the human brain learns are:

● *Intelligence as a function of experience*[1]

Intelligence—defined in the ITI model as a problem-solving and/or product-producing capability[1]—is the result of real physiological change in the brain that occurs as a result of sensory input, processing, organizing, and pruning. Genetics is not the immutable determiner of intelligence it is generally believed to be.

● *Emotions as gatekeeper to learning and performance*[2]

Much of the information processed in the brain comes from "information substances" produced throughout the body, many of which are the "molecules of emotion" that drive attention which in turn drives learning and memory.

● *Multiple intelligences*[3]

We have not one generic intelligence but at least seven,[4] each of which operates from a different part of our brain. Intelligence in the ITI model is defined as "a problem-solving or product-producing capability."[5]

● *Learning as a two-step process:*[6]

Step One—The brain makes meaning through **pattern seeking**. As it does so, it is not logical or sequential. **Step one of learning** *is the extraction, from chaos, of meaningful patterns.*[7]

Step Two—Most information we use is embedded in **programs**, a planned sequence to accomplish a purpose or goal; information not embedded in programs is generally unretrievable and thus unusable. **Step two of learning** *is the acquisition of a mental program.*[8]

● *Impact of personality on learning and performance*[9]

Personality preferences, with which we are born, strongly influence how we take in information, organize it, make decisions about it, and interact with others when using it.

Notes

1 Recommended first book to read is *Magic Trees of the Mind* by Marion Diamond (New York: Penguin, 1998).

2 Recommended first books to read are *Molecules of Emotion: Why We Feel the Way We Feel* by Candace Pert (New York: Touchstone, 1997) and *Smart Moves: Why Learning Is Not All in Your Head* by Carla Hannaford (Alexander, NC: Great Ocean Publishers, 1995).

3 Recommended first book to read is *Multiple Intelligences in the Classroom* by Thomas Armstrong (Alexandria, VA: ASCD, 2000).

4 Howard Gardner originally proposed seven intelligences. To qualify, each intelligence had to meet many criteria; key for us was that the intelligence operated from a different part of the brain. Recently, Gardner has proposed an eighth candidate that he explores quite thoroughly (see *Intelligence Reframed: Multiple Intelligences for the 21st Century*, Chapter 4). However, the naturalist intelligence does not appear to operate from a distinct part of the brain and, even more troublesome, its description parallels general functions of the brain as a whole as described by Leslie Hart, pattern seeking, and by Elkhonon Goldberg (*The Executive Brain: Frontal Lobes and the Civilized Mind*. Oxford: University Press, 2001) and others (notably Nobel Prize-winning psychologist Herbert Simon). Another reason we do not address the naturalist intelligence here is that it would add yet another issue for teachers to tussle with, one we feel is best addressed under ITI Learning Principle #4, the first step in learning: pattern seeking.

5 This definition of intelligence was developed by Howard Gardner in the early 1980s. See *Frames of Mind: The Theory of Multiple Intelligences*. He has updated and expanded that definition: "A biopsychological potential to process information that can be activated in a cultural setting to solve problems or create products that are of value in a culture." (See *Intelligence Reframed: Multiple Intelligences for the 21st Century*. New York: Basic Books, 1999, page 33-34.) Says Gardner, "Although we all receive these intelligences as part of our birthright, no two people have exactly the same intelligences in the same combinations. After all, intelligences arise from the combination of a person's genetic heritage and life conditions in a given culture and era." (*Intelligence Reframed*, p. 45.)

6 Recommended first book to read is *Human Brain and Human Learning* by Leslie A. Hart (Covington, WA: Books For Educators, Inc., 1999).

7 This definition of step one of learning comes from the work of Leslie Hart, *Human Brain and Human Learning*, p. 127.

8 This definition of step two of learning comes from the work of Leslie Hart, *Human Brain and Human Learning*, p. 161.

9 Recommended first books to read are *Effective Teaching, Effective Learning: Making the Personality Connection in Your Classroom* by Alice M. Fairhurst and Lisa L. Fairhurst and, for the survey questions to identify personality preferences/temperament, *Please Understand Me: Character and Temperament Type II* by Keirsey and Bates.

Chapter 1: Intelligence As a Function of Experience

In the past two decades, our definition of intelligence has changed dramatically. We used to be told that intelligence was a singular, general characteristic—people were either across the board smart or not so smart. Of course, all of this was determined by a paper-pencil test that distilled human capability down to a single number, an intelligence quotient or IQ number. And, clearly, to have a 120 was far more desirable than 100. However, thanks to Howard Gardner, who synthesized a large body of neuroscience, genetics, cognitive science, psychology, and cross-cultural observations in the early 1980s, we now have a much more useful definition of intelligence: *A problem-solving and/or product-producing capability.*[1] The ITI model uses this definition throughout.

We were also taught that intelligence was immutable—what you were born with was what you would end up with. Yet, our own common sense and experience, personal and professional, tell us that practice solving real problems and creating products of value in the real world does increase capacity to do so. For example, co-author Karen Olsen, having decided at age five that what she would do with her life was become a teacher, hoped desperately to become a vocal music teacher. Her genetic gifts, however, did not include perfect pitch or even an ear that would allow her to play anything but a fixed-pitch instrument such as a piano. Yet, through her thousands of hours of practice, double and triple what students with innate musical talent spent, she did succeed in sig-nificantly increasing her musical intelligence—her problem-solving and product-producing capability in music. However, her product, holding her own in eight-part harmony was accomplished through compensating measures—using the feel of the vibration in her throat (if it was "off," she knew she had either the wrong note or bad tone; in either case, stop for a bar and then pick up again). But she also knew she would never be able to rise to the level of excellence that those with inborn musical intelligence could achieve quite easily. Nor could she rise to a level of adequacy to train and direct musical groups. Thus, she switched her teaching career to a subject of higher innate intelligence, language arts.

> ## ITI Learning Principles
>
> - Intelligence as a function of experience
> - Bodybrain partnership
>   - emotion as gatekeeper
>   - movement to enhance learning
> - Multiple intelligences
> - Learning as a two-step process
> - Impact of personality

The decision to abandon music was deeply disappointing but an important lesson to Karen as a future educator. Even though she couldn't hit the pinnacle of music performance, there wasn't a moment of her musical experiences—singing with community and church groups and as a music minor in college (except perhaps her music history course with its frightfully boring textbook!)—that she doesn't cherish to this day. Although painful, the lesson she learned is that the purpose of public education ought to be that of assisting students to develop all of Howard Gardner's intelligences.[2] Our goal should be giving students options in life—options which make life rich and deeply satisfying both vocationally and avocationally.

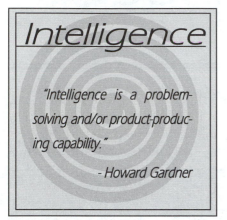

Intelligence

"Intelligence is a problem-solving and/or product-producing capability."

- Howard Gardner

Beyond our own experiences with developing intelligence, personal and professional, the work of Marian Diamond, UC Berkeley, Reuven Feurstein, Israel, and many others refutes the long-held beliefs about intelligence being genetically fixed, singular quality. Feurstein and his associates have even gone so far as to stipulate that "Genetics is no barrier to learning."[3]

Marian Diamond's work[4] shows that an enriched environment results in measurable physiological growth in the brain. In short, if we know how the brain learns—what happens physiologically when learning occurs—we can assist a learner to create new "hard-wiring" in the brain to carry new learnings. Intelligence, the capability to solve problems and create products, is significantly influenced by environment and experience. For example, most "gifted" students in our programs for the gifted and talented are not "gifted" as in the realm of such people as Einstein, Mozart, David Packard, Eleanor Roosevelt, Steve Wozniak, Sacajawea, or Maria Montessori. Rather, they are advantaged; they are students whose parents provided an enriched environment which nurtured a physiological development of neural networks which became long-term memory of knowledge and skills and greatly expanded vocabulary.

An enriched environment spurs brain growth; a sterile and/or hostile environment retards mental growth. Here is the story.

The Biology of Learning

Due to fantastic advances in technology such as PET scans, MRI, and fMRI, our understanding of how learning takes place has radically expanded in the past two decades. While the story is all fantastically more complex than needed for our purposes here or in the classroom, a simplified accounting of the biology of learning provides, we believe, valuable pictures which can help teachers enhance student learning. "Just what does go on in there?" is a question of undeniable human curiosity and one whose answer is critical to improving teaching and learning. As Leslie Hart says, "Although we don't know as much as we may and will, we know sufficient to change our ways."[5] And we can do so without taking "a bridge too far."[6]

An Old Paradigm: Genetics Versus Environment

In the midst of our deepest discouragement over our failures to deliver on the promise that all students can learn, it is easy to fall victim to the old belief that genetics sets intelligence and capability in an immutable way. Today what we know about the genetics versus environment debate is summed up beautifully by Dr. John Ratey: "We are not prisoners of our genes or our environment. Poverty, alienation, drugs, hormonal imbalances, and depression don't dictate failure. Wealth, acceptance, vegetables, and exercise don't guarantee success. Our own free will may be the strongest force directing the development of our brains, and therefore our lives. . . . the brain [child and adult] is both plastic and resilient, and always eager to learn. ***Experiences, thoughts, actions, and emotions actually change the structure of our brains.***"[7] As Ratey says, everything affects brain development and development is a lifelong process. The challenge of educators and parents is to provide the best possible environment for learning—one in which experiences are powerful enough (engaging sensory input, the subject of this chapter), thinking is reflective and analytical not just reactive, actions/movement are used to enhance learning, and emotions open the door to learning and performance (the subject of Chapter 2).

When standing before a group of 30-35 students, we must believe in our hearts and know without a shadow of a doubt in our minds that all students can learn, that all students can succeed and that, with help from brain research and this book, that it is in every-one of us to make such learning happen.

The Basic Building Blocks of Learning

The basic building blocks of learning are: neurons, brain organization, and information substances.

Neurons, Dendrites, and Axons

There are, on conservative estimate, 100 billion brain cells (neurons). Each neuron has one axon and as many as 100,000. The resulting intertwining and forms an interconnected tangle with 100 trillion *constantly changing* connections. There are more possible ways to connect the brain's neurons than there are atoms in the universe.[8]

How neurons organize themselves and how they connect with each other results in the outward manifestations of learning and the quality we call intelligence. For example, the graphic on this page illustrates the increase in complexity of dendrites and axons from birth to age two. As a result, the brain actually becomes denser and heavier (during infancy, the overall size of the skull increases as well, reaching full size by age five).

Such growth—multiple branching of the dendrites, myeli-nation of axons, enlargement of synapses and overall size of the neurons—is the brain's response to rich sensory input from an enriched environment. In contrast, sterile, boring environments not only result in significantly less growth but in actual shrinking of existing dendrites. A period of drastically reduced enrichment, even

Growth in complexity of neurons from birth to age two

| At birth | At 6 months | At 24 months |

Source: *Magic Trees of the Mind: How to Nurture Your Child's Intelligence, Creativity, and Healthy Emotions from Birth Through Adolescence* by Marian Diamond, Ph.D., and Janet Hopson, pp. 106-107.

as short as four days, can result in measurable shrinkage of dendrites.[9] "Use it or lose it"[10] is a universally acknowledged premise among neuroscientists and is powerful advice when it comes to growing and maintaining a healthy brain. Parents and educators alike, take heed. Your job is to help children (and fellow adults) grow dendrites[11] and to nurture continued use of what is grown.

Exactly how learning occurs is still a mystery, hidden at the molecular level. But the story is rapidly unfolding. In simple terms, there are two ways that neurons in the brain communicate with each other. The means of communication that has been understood for decades is an electrical-chemical process. The sending neuron transmits an electrical signal down its axon to its tip which is very close to the bulbous ending on the dendritic spines of the receiving cell. Chemical messengers, neurotransmitters, travel from the axon to the dendrite across the synaptic gap. If the information is compelling enough[12] to the receiving neuron, it in turn will spark an electrical transmission down its axon to the dendrites of another cell and on and on until the communication is complete, all at the rate of up to a billion times a second.[13] This means of communication carries the bulk of academic learning, particularly symbolic and abstract content, but is heavily influenced by emotion. (See the discussion of information substances in Chapter 2)

Enrichment Theory. The story of neurons, axons, and dendrites and how to make them develop and grow leads us to the new field of brain enrichment pioneered by Dr. Marian Diamond. The kinds of questions such researchers ask are closely akin to those which educators raise when they ask the time-worn question, "How can I best help Johnny learn X (math or geography or spelling)?" The work of Dr. Diamond suggests that the question "How can I help Johnny?" should be re-phrased: "How do I best stimulate the brain to make it grow, to increase the number and strength of connections being made, and to "hard-wire" learning into long-term memory?"

In short, learning is the result of actual physical growth in the brain. To talk about learning is to talk about the physiology of the brain and how to enhance its physical growth and thus learning. According to Dr. Diamond, a number of physiological changes occur when the brain is immersed in an enriched environment:[14]

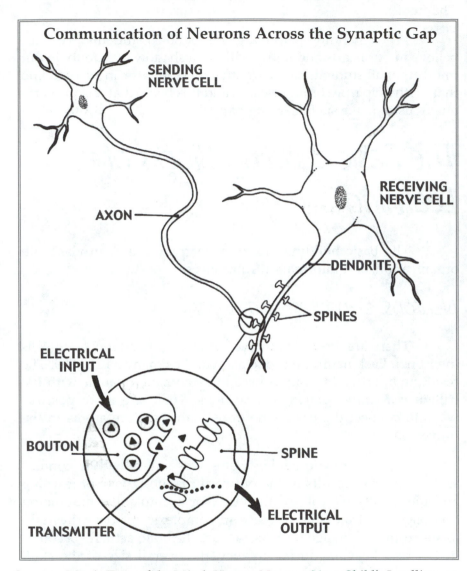

Source: *Magic Trees of the Mind: How to Nurture Your Child's Intelligence, Creativity, and Healthy Emotions from Birth Through Adolescence* by Marian Diamond, Ph.D., and Janet Hopson, p. 26.

1. Dendritic spines grow, change shape, or shrink as we experience the world. Neurons grow larger. The brain becomes denser and heavier. Therefore, choose the types of input that will produce the greatest physiological change in the brain.

2. The stimulation of an enriched environment results in significant physiological change in the brain—as much as 20% compared to brains in sterile, boring environments.

3. There is a correlation between brain structure and what we do in life—what we spend time doing and not doing.[15] In other words, how we spend our time—what we ask our brain to do on a daily basis—actually alters its physical structure. Vast amounts of time spent on television and/or video games (4-6 hours daily) wires the brain to do television and video games and does not wire the brain for other things like physical exploration or high facility for initiating and processing language. If students cannot do what you expect of them, such as learn phonics, take time to build the neural wiring and structures that will enable them to do what is expected of them.

4. Much of the increase in the physical size of the brain (at birth, the brain is one quarter of its eventual adult size) is due to myelination, a process by which fatty tissue forms around the axons of frequently-firing neurons which act like rubber insulation on electrical cords. This allows for speedier and more reliable transmission of electrical impulses thus improving communication among neurons. While much of this process occurs with the unfolding maturation of the brain,[16] much can be deliberately enhanced through ample practice in using the knowledge or skill being learned, particularly in real-world settings which allow for rich sensory input and feedback. See Chapters 4 and 5 for a discussion of developing mental programs.

5. Use it or lose it is a maxim for all ages—birth through old age. "Brains don't just steadily make more and more connections. Instead, they grow many more connections than they need and then get rid of those that are not used. It turns out that deleting old connections is just as important as adding new ones."[17]

Implications: If learning is the result of such physiological changes, then the question for teachers becomes: What should the classroom teacher do to maximize growth in the brain? The answers aren't mysterious or complicated yet they fly in the face of our traditional curricular tools and instructional processes.

1. Eliminate or drastically reduce low-sensory input materials and processes such as textbooks, worksheets, and working in isolation. Provide large amounts of sensory input from *being there* experiences in the real world. Remember, dittos don't make dendrites!

2. Demanding performance when the requisite wiring is not in place is akin to keeping the high jump bar over someone's head when he/she doesn't have the physical skills for jumping it at waist height. In track sports, this would be instantly recognized as both cruel and a foolish waste of time.

3. Design curriculum and instructional strategies that encourage practice and mastery in real-world applications rather than aiming at quick quiz responses that usually stop short at ability to recognize content rather than demanding students understand and and be able to use it. Using knowledge and skills in real-world applications greatly increases development and maintenance of neural connections.

Brain Organization

Our understanding of how the brain organizes itself is currently undergoing a major paradigm shift. In the 1980s and early 1990s, our view was that the brain was modular, that different parts of the brain control different abilities and these parts (or modules) operate independently. In this view, words and their meaning were stored in certain places and functions such as vision and hearing were operated by specific parts of the brain (the occipital and temporal lobes).[18] Such a modular view of the brain may still be accurate for older structures such as the thalamus but not for the neocortex.

In his book, *The Executive Brain: Frontal Lobes and the Civilized Mind,* Elkhonon Goldberg asserts that "the mental representation of a thing is not modular. It is distributed, since its different sensory components are represented in different parts of the cortex. And it is gradiental, since the regions of these partial representations are continuous upon the areas of corresponding sensory modalities." While this may sound a bit like Greek, Goldberg provides a teacher-friendly description of the two models through his discussion of how the brain processes from a word to a thing.[19]

The modular brain view of the brain holds that all word meanings are bundled together and separated from the cerebral representation of the real physical world that they denote.

The gradiental/distributive view of the brain holds that the representation of word meanings is distributed in close neuroanatomical proximity to the cerebral representations of the corresponding aspects of the physical world. This means that the meanings of different types of words are coded in different parts of the cortex.[20] In other words, the knowledge of word meaning is not stored in the brain as a separate, compact module. Different aspects of word meaning are distributed in close relationship to those aspects of physical reality which they denote." In educational terms, ***the meanings are stored close to the sensory and motor areas that participated in acquiring information about these objects.*** For instance, naming animals activates the left occipital areas (name plus picture) whereas naming tools activates the left premotor regions in charge of right hand movements (name plus movement when using the tool). (See illustration.)

This is exciting stuff! It provides hard brain science to back up what teachers know from working with students. Learning the

meanings of 20 vocabulary words a week, when presented for straight memorization, are harder for students to learn and remember than those same 20 words used in real-world conversation at a *being there* location. Why? Because real context and real use invites the brain to associate the meanings in multiple locations in the brain thus making the learning and recall richer and easier.

Novelty and the Brain. This gradiental/distributive view of the brain has other fascinating facets. As teachers, we well know that boredom is deadly. Little or no learning occurs. In brain terms, little is happening inside the brain. Worksheet and novelty are, for the brain, almost mutually exclusive.

In contrast, novelty creates significant brain activity, particularly in the frontal lobes. As illustrated below, the brain is most active when the cognitive task is novel and least active when familiar. Again, the greater the brain activity, the greater the learning.

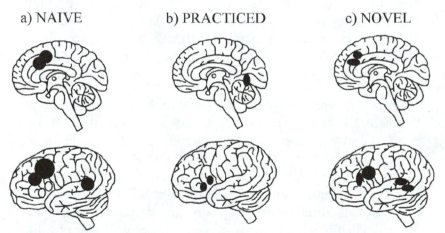

The frontal lobe activity when confronted with novelty. a) The prefrontal cortex is active when the cognitive task is novel. b) Frontal activation drops with task familiarization. c) It becomes partially activated again when a somewhat different task is introduced, similar to the first one but not identical to it.

Source: *The Executive Brain* by Elkhonon Goldberg, page 70. [Adapted from M. E. Raichle, J. A. Fiez, T. O. Videen, A. M. MacLeod, J. V. Pardo, P. T. Fox, S. E. Petersen, "Practice-related changes is human brain functional anatomy during nonmotor learning," *Cerebral Cortex* vol. 4, no. 1 (1994)].

As John Ratey points out in his book, *A User's Guide to the Brain: Perception, Attention, and the Four Theaters of the Brain*, skill acquisition recruits more cortical neurons to master the skill; then, as the skill becomes more automatic, less of the recruited cortex is used and the function is delegated to lower parts of the brain. "Thus, the brain has a tremendous ability to compensate and rewire with practice."[21]

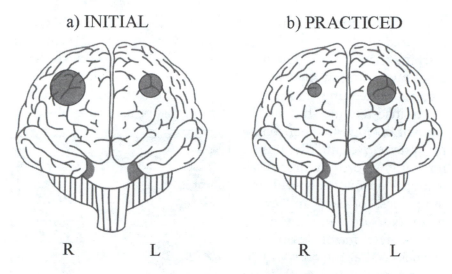

a) INITIAL   **b) PRACTICED**

R   L   R   L

The frontal lobes, hemispheres and novelty. a) A novel task activates predominantly the right prefrontal cortex. b) As the task becomes familiar, the overall level of activation drops and shifts from the right to the left prefrontal regions.

Source: *The Executive Brain* by Elkhonon Goldberg, page 71. [Adapted from J. M. Gold, K. F. Berman, C. Randolph, T. E. Goldberg, D. Wienberger, "PET validation of a novel prefrontal task: delayed response alteration," *Neuropsychology*, vol 10, 3-6, (1996). Reprinted with permission].

Brain Organization and the ITI Definition of Learning

Perhaps the most fascinating aspect of Goldberg's gradiental model with its shifts from right to left frontal and from front to back is that it provides a physiological explanation for Leslie Hart's definition of learning as a two-step process, a definition used in the ITI model (see Chapters 4 and 5). To assist teachers in planning curriculum and instructional strategies, we have broken each of those steps into two phases. The correspondence is striking.

Stages of the process of learning	Part of the brain engaged in learning process
■ **Step One: Pattern-Seeking**	
Identifying patterns....................................	Primarily right frontal lobes shifting to
Making meaning/understanding................	Primarily left frontal lobes
■ **Step Two: Program-Building**	
Able to use learning with support..............	Shift from front toward back of brain
Ability to use the learning becomes automatic and part of long-term memory.......	Shift to back and lower/older brain structures

Knowing that a different part of the brain is being engaged and doing its job helps teachers key in to what students need and the time it takes to make those physiological shifts in the brain. Suddenly, planning curriculum and instructional strategies is no longer a haphazard guessing game.

The underlying factor here, however, is that the input provided must truly engage the brain and *being there* experiences in the real world provide plenty of novelty for each student's brain.

Information Substances

The description of neurons, dendrites, and axons described in pages 1.3-1.5 has been bedrock knowledge for some decades. Recently, however, the story has expanded quite dramatically. In short, it seems that the Greeks were on to something 2,000 years ago when they emphasized the importance of educating and training both mind and body.

Another means of communication among neurons, and one that interconnects the entire body, is wholly chemical. A greatly expanded number of neurotransmitters, often referred to as "information substances" or "molecules of emotion"[22] carry information throughout the body. Some of these substances are created in other organs in the body but wherever they are produced and wherever else they are received (the heart and respiratory center are major "hot spots"), all are received by neurons in the brain. See the discussion of information substances in Chapter 2.

Translating Brain Research into Action Using the Nine Bodybrain-Compatible Elements

Intelligence as a function of experience — active, full-bodied participation in the world — presents a very different picture of learning than the traditional one based on seat time with students quietly working in rows and credits earned for specified hours of lecture and reading of assigned textbooks. Curriculum content cannot be inserted into students' heads but must be assembled by each student through his/her sensory system. Admittedly this is not a tidy or orderly process as it differs dramatically with the uniqueness of each and every brain. Nor are there any guarantees. The major lesson for teachers is that the only way to achieve uniform results is to radically vary the sensory input, giving each student what he/she needs to develop accurate and comprehensive understandings and then learn to apply what they understand.

The ITI model presents nine ways to translate brain research into action in the classroom and school. Each of the nine bodybrain-compatible elements is discussed in the order of their power to translate this body of brain research — intelligence as a function of experience — into practical strategies in the classroom.

Bodybrain-Compatible Elements

- Enriched Environment
- Meaningful Content
- Collaboration
- Movement
- Choices
- Adequate Time
- Immediate Feedback
- Mastery
- Absence of Threat / Nurturing Reflective Thinking

Enriched Environment

Our window on the world is far more powerful than conventional thinking indicates. Human beings have at least 19 senses, not five.[23] And, not surprisingly, there is a direct correlation between the number of senses activated and the amount and locations of brain activity. Quite simply, the greater the range of sensory input, the greater the physiological activity and growth in the brain. The result is more learning and a greater likelihood that such learning will be retained in long-term memory.

While the names of some of these senses may seem foreign, your use of them is not. Consider this story for example, a childhood memory of co-author Karen Olsen that is as vivid today as it was almost half a century ago.

An Example of Vivid Memory Based on High Sensory Input

Age eight, with her older brother, engaged in the thoroughly hopeless but intriguing task of attempting to dam up the creek south of the family home; sunshine on their backs, reflections dancing on the water; bare feet scrunching in the pebbly gravel and gooey mud; the tepid, slow-moving water with darting minnows disturbed by rearranging of rocks and the shovels full of smelly mud; the sweat from their efforts dripping down their faces; their laughter rippling across the creek; her brother's nearness; his patience with a little sister who "never stayed home like the other girls did" …the lessons of that day, the wonder of the creek, the beauty of family relationships.

Such moments of acute sensory awareness stay with us always.[24] To see examples of what information each of the 19 senses processed, see the chart on the following page.

An enriched environment is a learning environment that focuses sensory input—through all 19 senses—on the concept or skill to be learned. Maximizing sensory input is a fundamental ITI

goal when developing curriculum and planning instructional strategies for a number of reasons. First, input through the senses is the brain's only way to bring in information from the outside world; there are no short cuts. Second, large amounts of sensory input enable students to grasp the concepts/information accurately and completely, thereby eliminating misunderstandings. Third, large amounts of sensory input is what causes physiological changes in the brain, resulting in the phenomena of learning.

Lesson Planning for the 19 Senses

A fundamental ITI goal when developing curriculum and planning instructional strategies is to maximize sensory input focusing on the concepts and skills to be taught. When lesson planning, the 19 senses can be grouped into six categories or kinds of input to consider.

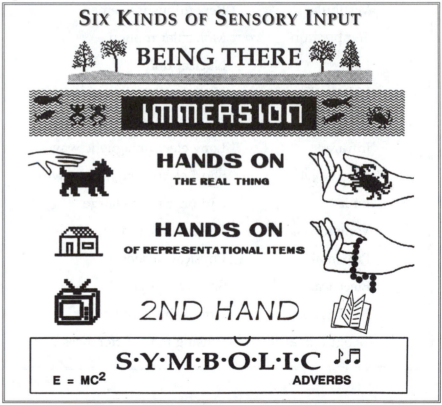

THE 19 SENSES

SENSES	KIND OF INPUT	EXAMPLES OF SENSORY INPUT FROM STORY
Sight	Visible light	Reflections dancing on the water; darting minnows, dams breaking, etc.
Hearing	Vibrations in the air	Laughter, gravel scrunching; mud sucking; rocks clashing, splashing
Touch	Tactile contact	Bare feet scrunching in the pebbly gravel; tepid, slow-moving water
Taste	Chemical molecular	Sweat dripping down their faces; an occasional splash of creek water
Smell	Olfactory molecular	Smelly mud
Balance	Kinesthetic geotropic	Keeping balance wading in the deep gravel; moving rocks/mud
Vestibular	Repetitious movement	Re-arranging rocks and shoveling smelly mud
Temperature	Molecular motion	Warm summer day
Pain	Nociception	Thankfully, none!
Eidetic imagery	Neuroelectrical image retention	The vivid picture of the scene and its details
Magnetic	Ferromagnetic orientation	The location of the creek—south of the family home
Infrared	Long electromagnetic waves	The warmth and power of the sun's rays
Ultraviolet	Short electromagnetic waves	The warmth and power of the sun's rays
Ionic	Airborne ionic charge	The refreshing feeling from being around water
Vomeronasal	Pheromonic sensing	Primal sense of smell—body odors, sweat, rotting vegetation
Proximal	Physical closeness	The nearness of the brother
Electrical	Surface charge	The humidity of the creek eliminated any perceivable static electricity
Barometric	Atmospheric pressure	The steady, unchanging atmospheric pressure of a calm summer day
Geogravimetric	Sensing mass differences	Density (weight to mass) of material—pebbly gravel versus gooey mud

The 19 senses activated by each of these kinds of input are illustrated on pages 1.10 and 1.12.

The two kinds of input **least used** in classrooms, *being there* and *immersion,* provide the **most sensory input.** Conversely, the two *most commonly used, secondhand* and *symbolic,* provide the *least sensory input.* The definitions of these six kinds of input and the senses they feed are described on pages 1.12 and 1.13.

In the typical classroom, 90 percent of the input consists of secondhand and symbolic input and most hands-on experience comes from manipulating representational items. In the ITI classroom, the goal is to flip those percentages so that 90 percent of the sensory input during initial learning (meaning-making and practicing how to use what is learned in real-world ways) is from *being there* and immersion experiences and 10 percent from hands-on experience with the real thing.

Secondhand input—principally reading, Internet, and video—is then a useful way to extend what has been learned through *being there* experiences supplemented with immersion, and hands-on experiences with the real thing.[25]

If this information seems disturbing and too impossible to be true, think back to an attempt to learn something "from scratch" that was fraught with difficulties and failures. For co-author Karen Olsen, it was her first experience trying to "learn" computers. This is her story: A colleague and his wife offered computer literacy classes in their home (at the time, they had more computers in their spare bedroom for such a class than the local university did). I was thrilled at the opportunity, paid my $30 and sat in the front row. Her instructor-friend dove right into "what goes on inside the box." "Wow," I thought, "If I understood how things work, program writing, never mind word processing, would be a piece of cake. This is the class for me!"

The story that unfolded boggled my mind. Whoever thought up this stuff in the first place? If I didn't understand something, I raised my hand and kept it there until I got an explanation I understood. The night was fascinating. I left the class thrilled to my toes! It was, after all, quite understandable conceptually despite its sci-fi veneer.

The next morning, my mother, whom I tried to talk into coming with me during her visit, asked reasonably enough, "Well, what did you learn last night?"

"Holy moley, Mom. You should have come! You would've loved it. It was our kind of workshop. He explained what goes on inside the box. It was fabulous!"

"Oh," she said, "just what does go on in there?"

"Well, when you plug it in and turn it on, it . . . ah, er."

Egad, how is it possible? I couldn't remember a thing except that I remembered that I understood it at the time. But nothing else stuck in my brain. Two things conspired against my getting the information into long-term memory. First, I had no prior experience with what goes on inside the black box, no mental post office box address for the information. Second, the only sensory input for this new learning was auditory and thus provided no context to help learn about the goings on in the box. Consequently, the information evaporated from my short-term memory during the night.

Remember, there is no such thing as by passing the sensory system; it is the bodybrain partnership's[26] way of taking

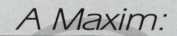

A Maxim:

There is a direct correlation between the number of senses activated and the amount and locations of brain activity. Human beings have at least 19 senses, not five.

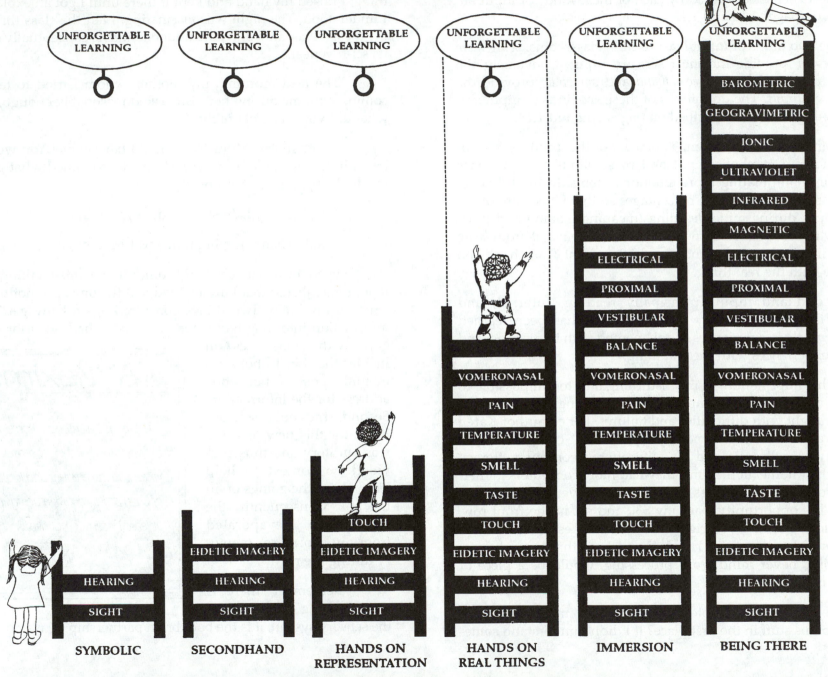

Being there input occurs when real things are studied in their real-world context, such as a pond, lake or wetlands area, a mall, a factory, or a neighbor's backyard—literally *"being there."* All 19 senses are activated, producing maximum electrical and chemical activity in the brain. Input is rich, varied, and plentiful.

Immersion input replicates the real world context of the *being there* experience in the classroom as fully as possible. For example, if a pond is the *being there* site, a classroom pond (a child's swimming pool with a black plastic drape) is created with as many real pond critters and plants as possible. The classroom itself is then made to look like a pond with the water line slightly above the teacher's head when standing. Blue film covers the windows to simulate the water line of the pond. Replicas of animals and plants at the water's edge and underwater cover the walls. The tape deck plays water sounds and pond animal sounds. At least 100 books and other printed materials about ponds, and other multi-media resources fill the room. Models and pictures of pond animals and plants are available for close analysis and exploration. The environment provides input for 13 of the 19 senses.

Hands-on of the real thing provides input through examination of real world things but without the context of *being there* or *immersion*. In the case of the pond, there would be frogs and polliwogs, cattails, and so forth for students to handle and examine closely, engaging 9 of the 19 senses.

Hands-on of representational items provides input from models of real things such as plastic frogs and polliwogs. Without the context of *being there* or *immersion* or the experience of the real items, hands-on of representational items elicits response from only 4 of the 19 senses. Such limited sensory input provides limited brain activation and thus limits pattern-seeking capabilities for many learners. Program-building opportunities are all very limited because real world applications are so difficult to create with only representational items.

Secondhand input can be found in books, computers, videotapes, and other multi-media presentations which can activate only sight, hearing, and eidetic imagery. Such limited input makes pattern-seeking difficult and provides no opportunities for program-building.

Symbolic is the most difficult input to process. Fewer than 20 percent of students can learn well through this type of input which includes such things as mathematical sentences and parts of speech. High linguistic and spatial intelligence is needed to make use of symbolic input, plus prior *being there* experiences related to the new learnings.

Full application of brain research

Higher stages of applying brain research

Middle stages of applying brain research

Early stages of applying brain research

The traditional classroom

in information. We cannot expect to set aside millions of years of evolution in favor of our traditional textbooks, lectures, and worksheets. Again, the moral of the story here is that dittos don't make dendrites!

Even in the area of language arts, sensory input is essential. For example, success in creative writing and poetry, even much of descriptive narrative, depends heavily upon sensory input and reflecting those experiences in words in order to evoke similar feelings and thoughts in the reader. Revisit co-author Karen Olsen's half-century-old memory of playing with her brother in a creek (see page 1.9). It is a vivid descriptive narrative, the stuff from which poetry is written. Interestingly, she wrote this description over 10 years ago, a quick, off the cuff reminiscence. Now, looking back and comparing it to each of the 19 senses, it is startling to see that the fullness of the memory relied on input from each and every sense.

There are many lessons here for teachers. If you want vivid creative writing, edge-to-edge painting with real detail, deep understanding of concepts, and accurate use of skills, to name but a few areas of learning, we must provide students with full sensory input. *Being there* experiences — visits to real-life locations — is the most powerful way to do so.

For example, choose a favorite work of fiction, such as Pat Conroy's *Prince of Tides,* a short story by Hemingway, a poem you memorized long ago and still recall. Analyze it against the 19 senses. If it is powerful enough to make you feel like you're there, looking at or participating in the scene, you're reading language encoded by all 19 senses or piggybacking on input that was. Once the high levels of sensory input have worked their magic, secondhand and symbolic input "makes sense" and can support learning.

USING *ENRICHED ENVIRONMENT* TO ENHANCE DEVELOPMENT OF INTELLIGENCE

Curriculum Development

- Base curriculum planning at the classroom level on *being there* interactions with the real world. Provide them as early in the study of a concept or skill as possible. Then, revisit the location often and go again at the end of study as a means to assess students' ability to apply what they understand and whether the concepts and skills have been wired into long-term memory.

- Based on the *being there* experience, develop lots of group and individual inquiries* that provide opportunities for solving problems and producing real products, including social/political action projects.

- Take time to access prior experiences of students. Tapping existing memory gives a "post office" address in the brain making new learning more efficient and giving the teacher an opportunity to detect and correct misconceptions.

- Develop inquiries for "homework" which ask the student to apply the information/skill in settings relevant to the student's life (home, neighborhood, friends' interests, hobbies and workplaces of parents, extended family, family friends).

---

* Inquiries, or activities, are a key structure for developing curriculum in the ITI model. Inquiries provide opportunities to practice using the concepts and/or skills of the key points. For a discussion of inquiries and key points, see Chapters 15 and 14.

USING *ENRICHED ENVIRONMENT* TO ENHANCE DEVELOPMENT OF INTELLIGENCE

Instructional Strategies

- Make the classroom a complete immersion experience reflecting the *being there* location upon which your curriculum is based.

- Have at least 100 resources (print and nonprint) related to the current topic of student available in the room—real things, models, diagrams, blueprints, sketches, and art objects, as well as the traditional sources such as books, magazines, multimedia, including the Internet.

- Invite guest speakers who are experts on the topics of interest to the classroom.

- Take away all materials—posters, bulletin boards, books, displays, models, etc.—not directly related to the key points and inquiries of the current monthly component or weekly topic.

Meaningful Content

No one—student or teacher—gets up in the morning and says, "Oh, boy, I hope this day is boring!" Quite the opposite; children and adults dread boredom. For the brain, it is the straight-line equivalent of a heart monitor showing no heartbeat . . . death by multiple paper cuts. So what makes content meaningful? For the most part, it is real-life context, richness of sensory input, and relevance to the learner that produces an emotional response of "I care." Context means that the concept to be studied is placed in real-life settings that are experienceable by students. Richness means that the learning experience provides sensory input for all 19 senses. Please note, however, that richness and clutter are the antithesis of each other.

Using the Context of Real Life

Providing input through real-life contexts is important for several reasons:

- The amount and variety of sensory input (discussed in pages 1.9-1.13)
- Demonstration of how and why concepts and skills are used
- Reminding students of previous related experiences and illustrating future possibilities (work or interest)
- Overcoming inequities
- Correcting misconceptions
- Providing a base for second language acquisition

Demonstration of How and Why Concepts and Skills Are Used. Since its inception in the early 1800s, America's public education system has relied on textbooks to convey learning. If students stumbled, no worries. High dropout rates weren't a public concern for over 100 years. After all, there were plenty of jobs that didn't require the ability to read and write and apprenticeships, entry to various fields, were common.

Today, however, the ability to read and write is critical to virtually every job for men and women. We simply must find ways to teach all students to high levels of reading proficiency and writing skills. The key to doing so is massive sensory input.

The need for sensory input as the starting point for learning is well illustrated by the following. As the saying goes, 80 percent of reading comprehension is based on prior knowledge.

"*Cayard* forced *America* to the left, filling its sails with 'dirty air,' then tacked into a right-hand shift. . . .That proved to be the wrong side. *America*, flying its carbon fiber/liquid crystal main and headsails, found more pressure on the left. *Cayard* did not initiate a tacking duel until *II Moro* got headed nearly a mile down the leg. . . . *Cayard* did not initiate a jibbing duel to improve his position heading downwind and instead opted for a more straight-line approach to the finish."[27]

We can assume this paragraph has something to do with sailing and we could answer questions such as these:

1. What kind of air filled America's sail?
2. What kind of sail did America have?
3. How far down the leg did II Moro get before Cayard initiated a tacking duel?
4. What strategy to the finish did Cayard use?

Does answering these questions about Cayard and America really mean you understand what is happening in this race or, even more importantly, could you participate in the race yourself? For over 99 percent of us, the answer is no. Why? Because we have never been sailing. We lack *being there* experiences from which concepts are developed. This passage could be understood with teacher explanation and the use of a dictionary but arrival at a level of comprehension needed to read and understand other short descriptions of sailing would likely not occur.

This statement bears repeating: Understanding of concepts, as opposed to memorizing factoids, requires large amounts of sensory-based; the best source of sensory input (richness and variety) comes from *being there* experiences in real-world settings (see the sensory input ladders on page 1.12). Sensory experience is not a luxury; it is a prerequisite for understanding.

The moral to this story is that it is possible to be an A student because you are a good reader yet not really understand what you've read. Most standardized tests of content, such as science and social studies, are tests of reading ability, not of mastery of content.

Reminding Students of Previous Related Experiences and Illustrating Future Possibilities. Connecting to prior, related experiences is particularly crucial when learning something new. First, it provides a post office box (column of cells) in the brain ready to receive and process related concepts/skills. Second, it heightens emotional response. "This relates to something I already care about."

Students can only dream to the limits of their awareness. *Being there* experiences open new doors and fire off emotions that make the bodybrain attend more carefully and fully to the concepts and skills to be learned. (See Chapter 2 for a discussion of molecules of emotion.)

Overcoming Inequities. Providing students with real-life context for learning is especially critical if students have no prior experience (or no successful experience) with the concept or skill to be learned. The only way to overcome the disparity of experiences that students bring to the classroom is to provide the sensory input that leads to concept development through *being there* and immersion experiences. If we were truly committed to leveling the playing field for students, we would focus time and resources on those subjects that allow us to overcome gaps in students' prior experiences most quickly. Sound hard to do? Not at all.

The subject area in which the gaps among students can most readily be overcome is science, a subject that begs for *being there* experiences, immersion, and hands-on of the real thing. Within minutes, enough sensory input can be provided that students can all be on equal footing.

The subject area in which the gaps among students is the greatest and takes the most time and work to bridge is language arts. Why? Because it trades primarily in second-hand input and symbolic input.

Where does a traditional schedule allocate the most time? Language arts. The least time, science.

If we were serious about learning for all students, we would base our integrated themes in science because most science, particularly at elementary grades, is directly experienceable through the 19 senses.

Correcting Misconceptions. If students hold misconceptions, massive amounts of sensory input is needed to rewire the brain.[28] For example the graduating Harvard students and their faculty, when asked to explain the reasons for the seasons, still applied the "the stove is hot" experiences of their childhood—things are hotter the closer you get (to a hot stove and the earth to the sun in summer) and colder the farther away you get—despite all high school and college courses in between.[29] Lessons about the earth's orbit being round rather than highly elliptical that were based primarily upon secondhand information—lecture and textbooks in high school and university—failed to provide the necessary sensory input to override learning from their infancy about hot objects.

Second Language Acquisition. Sensory experience is also crucial to the learning of a second language because many words do not translate from one language to another as interchangeable pieces.

For example, Eskimos have many words for snow; English but a few. Would one of those English words fully convey the conditions of today's snow to an Eskimo? Probably not. Similarly, the Slovak language has one word for sad, pensive, melancholy, wistful, reflective.[30] Feeling a bit blue? Will just any one of the five English words communicate your feelings to a friend? Probably not.

Words are not learned in isolation; they are learned in context, in real-world settings which contribute to the specific meaning of a word. Without this contextual backdrop, learning a second language is emotionless and flat and difficult.

Learning in the ITI Model: A Definition

Based on the brain research discussed so far, learning is defined in the ITI model as:

> *Being there*
> EXPERIENCE → CONCEPT → LANGUAGE → APPLICATION TO → LONG-TERM
> REAL WORLD   MEMORY

In other words, powerful, bodybrain-compatible learning for students occurs when high levels of sensory input from *being there* experiences are processed by the pattern-seeking brain to construct meaning which can be expressed by language (the attachment of a word to this new understanding). Having language then makes possible further exploration and application (program building for long-term retention and use). The brain readily learns (makes meaning) and applies (builds a program for using) information learned in this sequence.

In contrast, conventional schooling relies heavily on lecture and reading (textbooks/worksheets, Internet, and other second-hand explanations). Beginning with language, definitions of things and processes, whether via lecture or reading, works only with those students who have had prior experience with what is being discussed or who have unusually high linguistic skills. This works only with those students who have had prior experience with what is being discussed and it may, and often does, result in high test scores for highly verbal students but failure at being able to apply knowledge and skills and a remarkable lack of transfer to long-term memory as represented by the fading ink in the graphic below.

LANGUAGE → → → CONCEPT → → → APPLICATION

School As Counter Balance

Every child's brain is unique; a portion of this uniqueness comes from genetic wiring, much is shaped by environment. According to Jane Healy, in her book *Endangered Minds: Why Our Children Don't Think,* "Experience—what children do every day, the ways in which they think and respond to the world, what they learn, and the stimuli to which they decide to pay attention—shapes their brains. Not only does it change the ways in which the brain is used (functional change), but it also causes physical alterations (structural change) in neural wiring systems."[31] What is taken in by the senses makes for profound differences in the structure of the brain. In short, the brain of Video Kid is quite different in structure than that of the Child of Print (the child whose parents have immersed him/her in books, stories, conversation, etc.).

The differences between Video Kid and Child of Print are profound from the teacher's point of view. Whereas Child of Print comes to school with a "well-muscled" left hemisphere and language center, Video Kid, on the other hand, arrives with a Joe Puny

left hemisphere and undeveloped language capacity (albeit an active right hemisphere and visually-oriented brain). In the "use it or lose it" environment of the brain, connections form and rapidly die. If Video Kid watches television an average of 130 minutes seven days a week but spends less than four minutes a day on reading,[32] it is clear that Video Kid's preparation is not only highly language-deficient but, in fact, such a daily diet is also very language-antagonistic in terms of developing needed neural networking for language processing. Numerous studies suggest that the brains of spectators, however rich the visual images, are no different from those brains which live in impoverished environments.[33] In other words, if there is no active involvement, there is minimal activity in the brain.

It is not our purpose here to catalog the impact on the modern brain of TV, computers, and other visual, non-interactive technologies.[34] Our intent is only to make the point that many of today's students come with very little direct experience of the real world and thus with minimal conceptual understanding of what makes the world work. Accompanying this deficit is minimal language development; without receptive and expressive language capability, the seven scientific thinking processes[35] are simply not possible. Thinking demands language; according to Healy, "language is the scaffolding for thought."

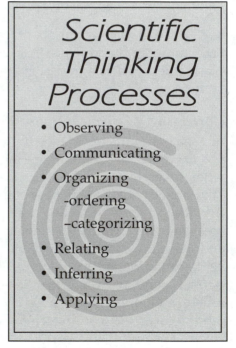

Scientific Thinking Processes

- Observing
- Communicating
- Organizing
  -ordering
  –categorizing
- Relating
- Inferring
- Applying

In the past we could assume that students came to school with a wide range of experience of the real world and the concepts and language that come with such experience. After all, a working farm was a virtual gold mine of real life experience—animal husbandry, crops of all kinds, the economics of supply and demand, problem-solving spurred by equipment that breaks down in a remote field, and the geometry and mathematics involved in building fences and new buildings. City kids who were a part of the street markets and who had family members living in different neighborhoods had a range of firsthand experiences as well—economics, supply and demand, varied forms of transportation. Consequently, schools of the past could use a wide range of "secondhand" sources during instruction—books, textbooks, workbooks, worksheets, dittos,

pictures, models, and, more recently, videos, the internet, etc.—because children came to school possessing a rich tapestry of real experiences to build upon and learning continued apace.

Today's student, on the other hand, comes with a shortage of experiences with the real world and the concepts and language that accompany them because in many areas of the U.S. it is not considered safe to be out exploring the neighborhood. These students arrive at school ill-equipped to learn from our "secondhand" sources. As 80% of reading comprehension is based on prior knowledge, in effect, one can only take from a book what one brings to the book. Books can expand our knowledge but cannot create it from scratch. According to Frank Smith, "...Much of today's school failure results from academic expectations for which students' brains were not prepared—but which were bulldozed into them anyway. Deficits in everything from grammar to geography may be caused by teaching that bypasses the kind of instruction that could help children conceptually come to grips with the subject at hand."[36]

USING *MEANINGFUL CONTENT* TO ENHANCE DEVELOPMENT OF INTELLIGENCE

Curriculum Development

- State curriculum as concepts and base them in real-world locations, situations, and events.

- Ensure that curriculum is age-appropriate—comprehensible by the student given his/her stage of brain development.

- When planning your curriculum and daily lessons, find out what prior experiences students have had. What concepts and skills do they already understand and can apply? Don't assume that students have the necessary conceptual building blocks from prior experience to understand what your curriculum is about. Investing the time to get to know each student pays big dividends.

- Be alert to misconceptions. To correct them, provide massive amounts of sensory input.

USING *MEANINGFUL CONTENT* TO ENHANCE DEVELOPMENT OF INTELLIGENCE

Instructional Strategies

- Provide *being there* interactions with the real world—people, processes, things. Allow students to explore beyond what you envision in order to construct their own meaning-understandings that are accurate, complete, and comprehensive.

- Base second language acquisition on *being there* and immersion experiences which convey the fullness of what the words of the new language mean.

- Use cooperative learning strategies that encourage students to connect prior knowledge with the new.

Collaboration

Research provides a very compelling endorsement of the power of collaboration to increase learning, improve the quality of products, and make the work/learning environment more pleasant and productive. The research over the past 50 years is conclusive. (See *TRIBES: A New Way of Learning* by Jeanne Gibbs, *Designing Groupwork: Strategies for the Heterogeneous Classroom* by Elizabeth Cohen, *Cooperative Learning* by Spencer Kagan, and the pioneering work of Johnson and Johnson.)

Also, from a brain perspective, Leslie Hart, *Human Brain and Human Learning, Updated,* talks about the need for great quantities of input to the brain which collaboration helps provide. Frank Smith, in *Insult to Intelligence: The Bureaucratic Invasion of Our Classrooms*, lists opportunity for manipulation of information as one of the key ingredients for learning. Active learning processes result in active brains. Collaboration is not just a bow to the social needs of students, it is a vital way of enhancing academic learning.

Full understanding of what is being learned and the ability to apply it in real-life settings—creative problem solving and flexible use of what is learned—depends upon ample opportunity to manipulate information in our heads, to test it, expand it, connect it with prior learnings. Collaborating with others allows us to examine our own thinking while expanding our knowledge base. According to both authors, one teacher facing a classroom of thirty brains, each with very different ways of learning, is insufficient to the task. Collaboration—students teaching each other and providing a sounding board for each other—is an essential classroom structure in a bodybrain-compatible learning environment.

Powerful rationales for collaboration come also from business. In 1989, the U.S. Department of Labor released its commission report entitled, *Investing In People.* An entire chapter was devoted to what education needs to do in order to improve the quality of the American work force. This is one of their observations:

"Business can make additional contributions by providing schools with the information that they need to develop course content and instructional methods that meet the current and emerging needs of the work place. Increasingly, employees will have to work in cooperative groups, be able to make decisions about production problems and processes, and develop the ability to acquire new skills and behavior on the job. We urge schools to adjust their instructional methods to match more closely the situation students will later face in the work place."

The requisite skills for running one's own business are and have always been problem-solving, decision-making, and the ability to communicate with peers and adults—be it farmer, homemaker, inventor, engineer, or a businessman (even as a shoeshine boy or delivery girl). However, with the growth of huge, multi-national corporations and large bureaucracies, a significant portion of our population are now employees, not entrepreneurs. Thus, significant numbers of students are growing up in homes where the work of the parents or other adults is not known to them and the standards of successful business (such as the drive to master skills and provide quality customer service) are rarely modeled with a sense of consequence to the survival of the business or to one's personal reputation in the community. Collaboration in the classroom over real problems to be solved and real products to be created goes a long way to filling in that experiential gap for students.

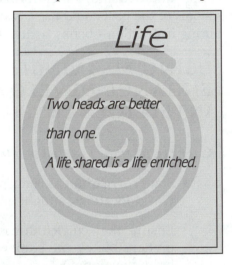

Life

Two heads are better than one.

A life shared is a life enriched.

As previously cited, collaboration increases understanding and improves quality of output. And this brings us back to the classroom. Collaboration dramatically increases opportunities for the bodybrain partnership to play an active rather than passive role in learning thus spurring physiological change in the brain. It is an essential instructional strategy for the classroom and should be used daily. Do note, however, that collaboration needs to be balanced with times for reflective thinking (see Chapter 2).

USING *COLLABORATION* TO ENHANCE DEVELOPMENT OF INTELLIGENCE

Curriculum Development

- The content for good collaboration should be:

  1) A challenge that no one group member working alone can do. Thus, genuine inclusion of all is a must rather than a sociological nicety.

  2) Reflective of real life and engage the 19 senses.

- The content of inquiries assigned for collaborative work should include social/personal skills as well as curriculum content.

- In the ITI model, collaborative groups are called Learning Clubs. The goal of collaborative tasks should always be increased achievement and higher quality products. Collaboration is a means to an end (learning), not an end in itself. Never use collaboration as a social event. If you want to have a party or allow chatting to fill in an odd moment or two, have the party or allow chatting in pairs. Collaboration should be viewed by students as genuine work, serious study. The value of the work should be obvious to all during collaborative work.

USING *COLLABORATION* TO ENHANCE DEVELOPMENT OF INTELLIGENCE

Instructional Strategies

- Change the composition of the "class family group" or Learning Club monthly or at least every six weeks. Getting to know others well accelerates learning, prevents cliques, and increases opportunities to practice applying the Lifelong Guidelines and LIFESKILLS.* Changing group members gives an opportunity for a fresh start for students who get off on the wrong foot with their first Learning Club group. Learning how to get to know others, and be comfortable doing so, is a critical personal/social skill.

- In addition to the ongoing class family group, create groups for skills and interests.

  Skill groups—short-term, ad hoc groups for studying specific skills or concepts among which students shift from group to group as mastery is attained

  Interest groups—opportunities to share/work on a topic of special interest

Again, the primary purpose of collaboration is to increase input to the bodybrain learning partnership and increase emotional engagement and opportunities to apply what is learned.

---

* The Lifelong Guidelines and LIFESKILLS are the agreed upon behaviors guiding both students and adults; they form the basis for classroom leadership and management. See Chapters 9 and 10.

 # Movement

It's humbling to think that our amazing, science fiction-like technology of the 21st century has finally reached a level that it can tell us what the Greeks knew 2,500 years ago. The body and mind are a partnership affair—you can't develop one without the other. They are in fact a single operating system. What took us so long?

The Greeks understood this partnership through observation of the human condition and applied it to the education of their young. We now know from scientific fact that it's true yet seem resistant to applying the implications to our schools and homes. But, I'm getting ahead of myself. For an explanation of the brain research behind movement as a tool for enhancing learning, see Chapter 2. For our purposes here, two things are key:

- Movement is fundamental to the very existence of a brain. In fact, only an organism that moves from place to place even requires a brain.[37]

- The entire front half of the brain is devoted to organizing action, both physical and mental. "Higher" brain functions have evolved from movement and still depend on it.[98]

- Movement is crucial to every brain function, including memory, emotion, language, and learning.[39]

This being the case, it is obvious that having students sit quietly in rows is a worst case scenario for the brain. What it needs is active participation from its partner, the body. In contrast, *being there* experiences are tailored made for the bodybrain partnership. There is action, emotion, and plenty of raw material for cognitive processes.

USING *MOVEMENT* TO ENHANCE DEVELOPMENT OF INTELLIGENCE

Curriculum Development

- Add to your key points an example of how the concept is used so the movement inherent in using the concept is part of the brain's encoding. Do the same with skill key points unless the use of the skill is obvious. Whenever possible, point out applications of the key point that affect students now at home, school, their favorite mall, etc., not just down the road later in life.

- Base your inquiries in *being there* locations. Make them action oriented, requiring that a problem typical of that location be solved or a product needed or sold at that location be produced.

- Code your inquiries according to the multiple intelligences as a way of reminding yourself how well you are including movement. Make sure you develop plenty of inquiries for bodily-kinesthetic, musical, spatial, and interpersonal intelligences, all of which emphasize movement.

USING *MOVEMENT* TO ENHANCE DEVELOPMENT OF INTELLIGENCE

Instructional Strategies

- During direct instruction, illustrate using hands-on of the real thing

- When selecting inquiries for whole class, group, or individual work, assign those that include movement first. Assign linguistic inquiries (e.g., write a paragraph or essay, make a list, look up in the dictionary, write a poem or lyrics for a rap song) only after students have developed a full and accurate understanding of the concept or skill and are able to apply what they understand. In fact, as a rule of thumb, assign last those inquiries that are wholly linguistic.

- Use movement throughout the day to:
  - Reset emotions (to energize or to slow the pace as needed)
  - Pique interest by illustrating how things are used
  - Use the body to do memorable simulations (such as make the shapes of the letter of the alphabet, mimic animal movements, perform plays, skits, and hand signs, and so forth)

Choices

The most mind-numbing quality of bureaucracy is its assembly line sameness. Common sense and brain research to the contrary, "the system" is based on the misguided assumption that the same input (textbook and lecture) will produce the same learning, that the same equals equity, that the same equals fairness, and that because of the misbehavior of a few, all must be restricted from an activity or punished with a blanket treatment.

In reality, nothing could be more unfair than giving two very different brains—and no two brains are alike—the same input and expecting the outcome to be the same. It's not only unfair, it's cruel. If we want the same learning outcomes from different brains, we must provide different input to each—whatever each brain needs to arrive at the standard end point. And given the huge differences in prior experiences, intelligence strengths, personality preferences, and brain processes, reliance on the textbook and lecture are patently ridiculous.

> ## *Choices*
>
> *In reality, nothing could be more unfair than giving two very different brains—and no two brains are alike—the same input and expecting the outcome to be the same. It's not only unfair, it's cruel.*

To some, however, the idea of offering choices to students (and teachers) may seem like warmed-over "Do your own thing" from the 60s. Somehow offering alternatives is viewed as antithetical to high standards or the notion of core curriculum for all. Some might believe that having choices is fluff or, more to the point, that it runs against the grain of having clear standards and high expectations: one can't just go around doing what one wants all the time; learning after all is serious business and therefore should be expected to hurt a little.

But in reality, offering students choices—ones well crafted/selected by the teacher—has enormous power to enhance learning. In addition to its many positive emotional effects, having choices allows students to select the kind of input that they most need in order to understand and apply concepts and skills. Although this demands that teachers develop a rich variety of inquiries in the short run, in the long run it's much more time and energy efficient because it significantly reduces the amount of re-teaching and remedial teaching needed when initial instruction fails.

The choices to be offered vary greatly due to age, ability to stay focused on the task, and experience with making and sticking with decisions.

For example, for the young learner, choice can be as simple as chalk versus crayon or paint and the number of options need to be limited to two or three. Although learning to speak and write standard English is not an item of choice for an educated person, the content of essays could and should take into account student interests. Also, students who have never been to the ocean, need more time exploring tidepools and more time discussing what they find than students who frequently visit the ocean. First timers would also benefit from construction projects creating an immersion experience of the tidepools while the frequent visitor might be ready to move to second-hand resources at the library.

The truth is that offering choices is essential if one's goal is mastery and application of concepts and skills, not to mention creating lifelong learners who possess a passion for learning.

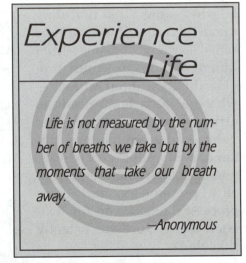

Experience Life

Life is not measured by the number of breaths we take but by the moments that take our breath away.

—Anonymous

USING *CHOICES* TO ENHANCE DEVELOPMENT OF INTELLIGENCE

Curriculum Development

- Develop at least 5-10 inquiries for every key point.
    - Design some for whole class work, some for collaborative choice, and some for individual choice.
    - Make sure that you build in choice based on the multiple intelligences and Bloom's taxonomy (see Chapter 3) plus personality preferences (see Chapter 6).
    - Make them action-oriented requiring students to apply concepts and skills to real-life problems and products.

- Encourage students, after teaching them the format, to write their own inquiries. Select those you think will provide the best application and practice of concepts and skills.

Instructional Strategies

- During meaning-making/gaining an understanding of concepts and skills, invite students to select inquiries that rely on intelligences in which the student is strong; during practice applying what is understood, encourage students to select inquiries requiring intelligences that they wish to strengthen.

- Provide opportunities for students to tutor each other. Looking for ways to explain and demonstrate what one understands to another increases mental processing and creates new " Aha's."

Adequate Time

It was Albert Einstein who said that man invented the concept of time and has spent the rest of his life being controlled by it! It seems all the more true today when technology has literally added 20 percent to our work week, mainly because we take on larger and larger undertakings due to the fabled promise of assistance from our technological helpers—computers, fax machines, cellular telephones, and instantaneous worldwide communication.

In addition, knowledge continues to accumulate daily at an ever-expanding rate. As it does so, it is more essential than ever that

Adequate Time

To everything there is a season, and a time for every purpose under heaven.

we constantly reevaluate what we believe students should know in order to become contributing members of society. As higher expectations—state standards, benchmarks, tests, etc.—wind their political course, too often the result is more of the same—more dates, more facts, more definitions, more homework.

We need to reduce the number of standards by writing them conceptually so they can take us deeper into meaningful content which in turn allows students to immerse themselves in understanding and learning to use what they understand in real-world ways. Skills likewise should be grouped into meaningful wholes. Until then, we need to pull the standards, however fragmented they might be, into real-world settings that can help give them a sense of coherence, relevance, and importance. *Being there* experiences provide a powerful glue. Both understanding and learning to use what we understand require time for the brain to engage and make those mysterious physiological changes that result in long-term memory.

USING *ADEQUATE TIME* TO ENHANCE DEVELOPMENT OF INTELLIGENCE

Curriculum Development

- Reduce the number of things to be learned by teasing out the underlying concepts and presenting them in meaningful chunks. Once students understand the concept, additional related knowledge can be learned much more easily. As Frank Smith says, "Understand-ing takes care of learning." Learning then becomes nearly effortless and automatic.

- Clarify in your own mind exactly what you want students to understand and then what you want them to do with it. Factoids can then easily be left behind.

Instructional Strategies

- Before you begin planning the sensory input students will need, carefully assess the extent of their prior experience and knowledge relevant to the concept or skill. Then allocate the time needed for *being there, immersion* and *hands-on of the real thing* in the initial time block so students move beyond recognition to understanding. For subsequent instruction and inquiries, make sure students can complete their work without interruption. Long-term projects are the exception but even then adequate blocks of time should be allocated to allow students to "get into it" and make satisfying progress.

- Teach students to manage their time and to recognize plateau points in their work—natural breaking points at which a pause would be productive rather than disruptive.

- Make time for reflecting on what was accomplished—individually and as a group.

Simply put, physical growth—of the body or of the brain—require time. Time to explore, time to reflect, time to act, time to evaluate, time to try again and again until we get it right, until we master the concept or skill to be learned. And, clearly, the amount of time needed varies wildly from brain to brain depending on the amount of prior knowledge relevant to the current task, the brain's processing preferences, personal likes and passions, and so forth.

To understand the power of this brain-compatible element, it might be helpful to apply it to our own lives first. For example, how many of us would sit down to complete our income taxes on a short weekend, knowing that the task will take at least three to four days of uninterrupted work to figure it out and then get it computed? Or, how many of us are eager to take a two-hour task out of our in-basket when we don't have a two-hour time block and we know that, with interruptions, it will end up taking us six hours? How many of us jump into learning a new software program at work because we don't have the needed chunk of time? Answer: a very rare few.

Similarly, how many of our students refuse to engage in a learning task when they feel certain that they won't have enough time to complete it successfully? In too many classrooms the clock is the commander. Ten minutes for recess, 40 minutes for language arts, 20 minutes for P.E., 35 minutes for music. What percentage of misbehavior and acting out has its roots in the frustration that comes from knowing time is inadequate and failure a certainty? Just a guess, more than half.

Adequate time is a critical element for successful learning and performance. We must begin to value learning more highly than bureaucracy's demand for lock step schedules.

Immediate Feedback

Immediate feedback is a necessary element in the learning environment—both for pattern seeking and for program building (see Chapter 1). In all learning environments except the school, it is present in abundance. Consider, for example, when children first begin to talk. Each time they say something incorrectly, we immediately give them the correct word, usage, and pronunciation. Imagine letting all their mistakes pile up during the week and correcting them on Friday!

Or, think back to the time you learned to drive a car. Feedback was instantaneous and continuous. If you returned home with no dents and no tickets, your parents knew you had a fairly successful time! Similarly, when learning to play a game or sport or beginning a hobby, feedback is built in, immediate, and continuous. In such cases, the learning materials or the conditions themselves provided the immediate feedback, or your fellow adventurer interpreted your progress toward mastery. This is a far cry from the classroom setting where students must press for information with the often asked questions: "Is this right, teacher?" "Teacher, is this the way it's supposed to be?"

Frank Smith, in *Insult to Intelligence: The Bureaucratic Invasion of Our Classrooms*,[40] states that learning does not require coercion or irrelevant reward. Learning is its own reward. Feedback that tells us we have succeeded at a learning task produces a burst of neurotransmitters, producing a "chemical high" that is readily observable in the spark in a child's eye as the " aha" registers.

The more immediate, intrinsic, and unambiguous the feedback, the faster and more accurate the learning. For example, learning to ride a bike. If you don't get the balance right, you hit the ground. Ambiguous? Not! In contrast, taking an essay test that will be graded and returned next week (and that is fast as essay exams go!) or doing all the odd number problems for math homework and getting a response from the teacher hours or days after the task is done violates all the important rules for learning. By then, the brain either learned it wrong or didn't learn it at all.

Few worksheets or dittos provide feedback that is self-correcting or intrinsic. As a consequence, children feel rudderless, confused, powerless, dependent on someone else, and either anxious or bored. Hardly the characteristics of a bodybrain-compatible learning environment. Without immediate feedback, learning is seriously impeded and students are left to tug at their teacher's shirt sleeve to ask, "Teacher, teacher, is this right?"

USING *IMMEDIATE FEEDBACK* TO ENHANCE DEVELOPMENT OF INTELLIGENCE

Curriculum Development

- Re-evaluate the starting point of your curriculum content. Shift the point of view of your curriculum content from disciplines to a need to understand the real world: locations, events, settings. "Disciplines" are an artifact of Western culture's way of talking about the world, a classic example of the parts not adding up to the whole. Start with the whole—the real world and *being there* experiences that offer intrinsic feedback rather than external (teacher or expert) feedback. Focus on doing, on applying concepts and skills in productive ways.

- Design action-oriented inquiries whose tasks provide natural, real-world feedback as the students progress carry out the inquiry.

- Teach students how to use/adapt the 3Cs of assessment and other self-assessment tools. The 3Cs are: correct, complete, and comprehensive (see Chapter 17).

USING *IMMEDIATE FEEDBACK* TO ENHANCE DEVELOPMENT OF INTELLIGENCE

Instructional Strategies

- Teach students to identify what they will need before they begin a learning task—what LIFESKILLS, prerequisite skills and knowledge, and how to tell if they are being successful at coming to an accurate understanding of and ways to apply concepts and skills. Model/Teach them to use self-talk to help them when they feel confused, bogged down, or discouraged.

- Help sensitize students to the feedback built into the real world; help them learn to direct self-talk toward analyzing their own work and developing confidence in their own ability to provide feedback for themselves.

- Increase the number of "teachers" by organizing students into Learning Clubs; empower them to provide feedback. Also, eliminate tracking (students are equally unable to help each other), create multi-age classrooms (at least three grade levels is ideal), and arrange for cross-age tutoring.

- Limit your direct instruction to 16 minutes or less; during inquiry work, circulate among the students to give them immediate feedback individually and as a group.

- Allow sufficient time for students to be thoughtful about what they're doing and the progress they're making.

- Teach them to use simple, self-constructed or teacher-made rubrics by which they can assess their progress. Often just asking a self-assessment question helps guide learning.

 # Mastery

One of the greatest frustrations for teachers is "I taught them but they didn't learn." What happened?

In the ITI model, mastery means mastery at navigating through life, a higher goal than getting a high score on a multiple choice or true/false test. Mastery by only 20 percent of a class or fewer—the underlying assumption of the bell curve—is an unacceptable outcome for the billions we spend on education. Furthermore, brain research makes it quite clear that without meaning, there is nothing for the brain to remember except confusion and perhaps distaste for the topic.

A Dash of Common Sense

To assess mastery/competence in the ITI classroom, we recommend asking two commonsense questions:

"What do you want students to understand?" and

"What do you want them to do with it?"

These two questions parallel the two-step definition of learning used in the ITI model.

The Caines, in their book *Making Connections: Teaching and the Human Brain*, suggest four relevant and useful indicators to guide your evaluation:[41]

- The ability to use the language of the discipline or subject in complex situations and in social interaction

- The ability to perform appropriately in unanticipated situations

- The ability to solve real problems using the skills and concepts

- The ability to show, explain, or teach the idea or skill to another person who has a real need to know

These guidelines are imminently genuine and authentic; they also require both *being there* experiences and real-world practice using concepts and skills before the assessment process begins. For a discussion of learning to the level of mastery as a two-step process, see Chapters 4 and 5.

USING *MASTERY* TO ENHANCE DEVELOPMENT OF INTELLIGENCE

Curriculum Development

- Make sure what you're asking students to understand and be able to do is genuinely useful in the real world. Eliminate factoids* and always provide examples of uses for concepts and skills beyond the school walls.

- Base your curriculum in real-life locations. Use the real-world standards of mastery inherent in the roles of those who work/use the location. What concepts and skills from your curriculum must these people understand and be able to use? To what levels?

Instructional Strategies

- Help students tune in to the real-world standards that apply to what you are teaching. Eliminate any double standards—this is good enough for school but would get you fired on the job.

- Encourage students to question. "What is this good for?" "So what?" "Why is this important for me to know and be able to do?" Be prepared to answer such questions.

---

* When developing curriculum, there is no bigger enemy than factoids. They are interest killers and hard to record in long-term memory. For example, Columbus sailed in 1492, e.e. cummins used no capital letters and minimal punctuation when he wrote poetry.

Absence of Threat/Nurturing Reflective Thinking

In simple terms, fear limits exploration. Threat—real or perceived— significantly restricts, if not eliminates, students' ability to fully engage in the learning process. To explore the new and different and to be open to new ideas requires confidence that one is in a safe environment, one in which mistakes and difficulty in understanding/doing something are considered just part of learning, not an opportunity for sarcasm and put-downs.

Building intelligence—the capability to solve problems and produce products—requires exuberant and curiosity-driven exploration, full focus on the learning at hand, maximum activation of the senses and bodybrain partnership. For this, absence of threat is an absolute must, a prerequisite for reaching the mental state of reflective thinking.

For a fuller discussion of the role of emotion as a gatekeeper to learning and performance, see Chapter 2.

USING *ABSENCE OF THREAT/ NURTURING REFLECTIVE THINKING* TO ENHANCE DEVELOPMENT OF INTELLIGENCE

Curriculum Development

- Know your students. Make sure that your curriculum is age-appropriate and thus understandable to them. Nothing tears down students' sense of confidence faster than knowing that they don't understand what is going on.

- Develop, and begin with, inquiries that help students bring forward any prior experiences related to the key point.

Instructional Strategies

- Help students make connections between what they are now studying and their lives now—at school, at home, wherever they go. If you can't find a connection, don't waste your students' and your time teaching it. The world is full of urgent things for students to learn—for their safety, their health, their well-being, not to mention their future capacity to succeed at work and family life and be a contributing member of society.

- Provide a good mix of collaborative time and intrapersonal time, stimulation and time to be reflective.

- Provide immediate feedback in order to keep self-doubt and frustration at a minimum.

Notes

1 Gardner, Howard. *Frames of Mind: Theory of Multiple Intelligences*. (New York: Basic Books, Inc., 1985), p. x and *Intelligence Reframed*. (New York: Basic Books, Inc., 1999), p. 44.

2 As you read Chapters 9 and 10 about how to develop curriculum in the ITI model , you will notice that we do not utilize the naturalist intelligence. There are several reasons. First, Gardner states that the naturalist intelligence develops on its own in most children. We believe that well constructed being there experiences, along with teaching the scientific thinking processes, provide ample practice in observing, classifying, and using features of the environment. Second, the naturalist intelligence does not appear to be localized in a particular part of the brain, by Gardner's own admission. More importantly, however, the pattern-identification process inherent in the naturalist intelligence described by Gardner is, we believe, a description of how the brain generally functions. See Chapter 4.

3 Reuven Feurstein is an eminent cognitive psychologist, known for his groundbreaking research in cognitive mediation and practice. He has established the principle that "all children can learn" while working with culturally deprived, retarded, and autistic children. Professor Feurstein developed a classroom curriculum designed to build the cognitive functions of students diagnosed by others as incapable of learning. His program, Instrumental Enrichment, provides students with the concepts, skills, strategies, operations and techniques necessary to become independent thinkers.

4 Marian Diamond, author of several books on the brain, has been a Professor of Anatomy at Berkeley for over thirty years and was director of the University's Lawrence Hall of Science from 1990 to 1996. She is a pioneer brain researcher who has conducted numerous lines of research into the effect of the environment and hormones on the forebrain. She also has investigated structural changes in the cerebral cortex induced by an enriched environment and structural changes in the cerebral cortex as influenced by sex steroid hormones.

5 Hart, Leslie A., *Human Brain and Human Learning* (Covington, WA: Books for Educators, Inc., 1999), p. 87.

6 John Bruner, in his article, "A Bridge Too Far" (*Educational Researcher*, August, 1997) has challenged that a jump from brain research to classroom applications is too far a leap, that we don't have grounds for doing so, that we should, instead, be basing educational practice on the work of cognitive psychologists (he being one). While his cautionary tale is important—education is infamous for its leap to unfounded fads—there are brain research findings that have been confirmed and reconfirmed over the past twenty years. The concepts resonate with our intuitions and experiences, personal and professional. Furthermore, the curriculum development and instructional strategies recommended to translate them into action are not "new." They are proven strategies from the fields of psychology, sociology, and education (p.18).

7 Ratey, John J., *A User's Guide to the Brain: Perception, Attention, and the Four Theaters of the Brain*. (New York: Pantheon Books, 2001), p. 18.

8 Ratey, p. 20.

9 Marian Diamond provides an observation about the impact of boredom on young and adolescent rats: "A boring environment had a more powerful thinning effect on the cortex than an exciting environment had on cortex thickening. Young rats are obviously very susceptible to losing mental ground when not challenged, and that shrinkage shows up after just four days. In rodent "teenagers," at least, the shrinkage can begin to be reversed again after four days of enrichment." Given the number of parallels between the affects of enrichment and boredom on the brains of rats and humans that have proven true, this is

quite a disturbing observation. Among many things, it should cause us to reexamine the school calendar. It would appear that the traditional agrarian calendar with three months of summer vacation works strongly against those who most depend upon the public schools for learning. See *Magic Trees of the Mind: How to Nurture Your Child's Intelligence, Creativity, and Healthy Emotions from Birth Through Adolescence.* (New York: A Dutton Book, 1998).

10 "Use it or lose it" is more than a catchy phrase or metaphor. It applies to the brain "directly and literally." See *The Executive Brain: Frontal Lobes and the Civilized Mind*, Elkhonon Goldberg (Oxford: University Press, 2001), p. 209.

11 For a powerful, electrifying image of how dendrites grow and connect in the brain, see ABC News Prime Time, "Your Child's Brain" with Diane Sawyer (January 25, 1995).

12 William Calvin, author of *How Brains Think: Evolving Intelligence, Then and Now,* talks about competing choruses, each singing its own message or answer and trying to get others neurons to agree. The chorus best able to recruit neighboring neurons into singing its song determines which competing message wins out. An example of this is when we "can't make up our mind." Choice A or B, is it a cheetah or a leopard? (Conversations with William H. Calvin, January, 1997, Covington, Washington.)

13 Marion Diamond and Janet Hopson, *Magic Trees of the Mind: How to Nurture Your Child's Intelligence, Creativity, and Healthy Emotions from Birth Through Adolescence* (New York: Penguin, 1998), p. 26.

14 Ibid.

15 Jane Healy, *Endangered Minds: Why Children Don't Think — and What We Can Do About It* (New York: Simon & Schuster, 1990).

16 Diamond and Hopson, Ibid.

17 The second method of organization is pruning, the result of a chemical wash of neurons that are not connected. The synapses that carry the most messages get stronger and survive, while weaker, synaptic connections are cut out. Experience determines which connections will be strengthened and which will be pruned: connections that have been activated most frequently get preserved. Between about age ten and puberty, the brain will ruthlessly destroy its weakest connections, preserving only those that experience has shown to be useful. See Gopnik, A., A. Meltzoff, and Patricia Kuhl. *The Scientist in the Crib: Minds, Brains, and How Children Learn.* (New York: William Morrow and Company, 1999), pp. 186-187. See also Ratey, pp. 24-26. Also see pp. 19-26 for an electrifying description of how the fetal brain forms, connects, organizes, prunes, and operates.

18 Elkhonon Goldberg, *The Executive Brain: Frontal Lobes and the Civilized Mind*, (Oxford: University Press, 2001), p. 209.

19 Goldberg, p. 64.

20 Goldberg, p. 65.

21 Ratey, John J., *A User's Guide to the Brain: Perception, Attention, and the Four Theaters of the Brain.* (New York: Pantheon Books, 2001), p. 21.

22 Pert, Candace, *Molecules of Emotion: Why You Feel the Way You Feel.* (New York: Scribner, 1997), p. 179.

23 Our first introduction to the existence of at least 19 senses came from Bob Samples, *Open Mind, Whole Mind.* See also Robert Rivlin and Karen Gravelle, *Deciphering Your Senses* (New York: Simon and Schuster, 1984), Chapter 1.
There is an interesting history here. Robert Rivlin and Karen Gravelle in their book, *Deciphering Your Senses,* present the scientific evidence underpinning the 19 senses and give an historical perspective explaining why the mistaken notion of the five senses has persisted for so many centuries despite scientific evidence to the contrary. ". . . according to the Medieval

philosopher Cornelius Agrippa, arguing Plato's philosophy, 'Divinity is annexed to the mind, the mind to the intellect, the intellect to the intention, the intention to the imagination, the imagination to the senses, and the senses at last to things. For this is the bond and continuity of nature."

"There was, in fact, a divine relationship between the senses and the world they sensed. And, like many things in God's divine plan for the universe, the senses were seen to occur in fives—a prime number with considerable symbolic significance. How convenient, then, to think of the body as having five senses, corresponding roughly to the sensory organs (eyes, ears, nose, tongue, and skin). That the skin could feel both temperature and touch, to say nothing of pain, was somehow conveniently overlooked in order to align the essential unity of the human body with a metaphysical plan of the universe; to say we had eight or eighteen senses simply wouldn't do." p. 15

24 The power of the 19 senses is easily verified by our own experiences. Simply ask yourself to remember your most vivid memory from childhood. Analyze the scene in your mind's eye. You will discover input from most, if not all, of the 19 senses.

25 One can't overstress the importance of full sensory input through "being there" experiences in building the necessary neural wiring for understanding the concepts involved. Once understanding through sensory input and prior experience is brought together, secondhand input allows the learner to extend and expand learning.

26 Candace Pert's pioneering research (discovery of the opiate receptor, 1972) on how the chemicals inside our bodies form a dynamic information network, linking mind and body, is revolutionary. By establishing the biomolecular basis for our emotions Pert has come to the brilliant conclusion that it is our emotions and their biological components that establish the crucial link between mind and body. This does not repudiate modern medicine's gains; rather her findings complement

existing techniques by offering a new, scientific understanding of the power of our minds and our feelings to affect our health, well-being, and learning.

27 *USA Today*, May 13, 1992, p. 9.

28 Hart, Leslie A., *Human Brain and Human Learning* (Covington, WA: Books for Educators, Inc., 1999), p. 18.

29 A good example of the weakness of this approach is illustrated by the video, *A Private Universe.* Interviewers ask Harvard University graduates in their caps and gowns the answer to this question: "Explain the reasons for the seasons." Over 80 percent of the randomly selected students and faculty—despite their middle school and university science classes—give the "stove is hot" theory, i.e., in the summer the earth is much closer to the sun and is therefore hotter. In fact, the earth's orbit is nearly round; distance from the sun is not a factor. This despite the amount of formal teaching received—varying from none to classes in advanced planetary motion—yet another example of the power of the being there experience over secondhand information! The toddler's experience with hot stoves prevails.

Therefore, meaningfulness for elementary students must begin with firsthand, being there, here and now experiences. They provide the mental scaffolding for the words which represent the concepts and definitions of things they have experienced. The number of "experiences" must continuously increase so that students will have a basis for relating and applying new information.

30 Patty Harrington, associate of Susan Kovalik & Associates, Inc., trained teachers in the Slovak Republic through translators in the late 1990s. While doing a TRIBES training there, she did a process that called for participants to reflect on their feelings. Did they fee pensive, melancholy, sad, blue, or lonely. To her surprise, the translator used the same Slovak word each time. The Slovak language had only one word for all of those shades of meaning.

31 Healy, Jane. *Endangered Minds: Why Children Don't Think — And What We Can Do About It* (New York: Simon & Schuster, 1990), pp. 50-51.

32 Healy, p. 23 (a study of "typical" fifth graders by Dr. Bernice Cullinan, New York University. Ninety percent read four minutes or less per day. Cullinan concludes that "our society is becoming increasingly alliterate." She defines "alliterate" as a person who knows how to read but who doesn't choose to read. Such an alliterate "is not much better off than an illiterate, a person who cannot read at all.")

33 Healy, p. 72.

34 Healy, Jane. *Failure to Connect: How Computers Affect Our Children's Minds — And What We Can Do About It* (New York: Simon & Schuster, 1998), p. 110.

35 Susan J. Kovalik & Karen Olsen, *Kid's Eye View of Science* (Covington, WA: Books For Educators, Inc., 1994).

36 Healy, Jane. *Endangered Minds: Why Children Don't Think — and What We Can Do About It* (New York: Simon & Schuster, 1990), p. 69.

37 Ratey, John J., *A User's Guide to the Brain: Perception, Attention, and the Four Theaters of the Brain.* (New York: Pantheon Books, 2001), p. 37.

38 Ratey, pp. 150, 148.

39 Ratey, p. 148.

40 Smith, Frank. *Insult to Intelligence: The Bureaucratic Invasion of Our Classrooms* (New York: Arbor House, 1986), p. 29-30.

41 Caine, Renata and Geoffrey. *Making Connections: Teaching and Human Brain* (California: Addison-Wesley, 1994), p. 103.

Chapter 2: The Bodybrain Partnership — Emotion and Movement

There are two aspects of the bodybrain partnership that are critical to the classroom:

- Emotion—the gatekeeper to learning and performance. In the words of Dr. Robert Sylwester, "Emotion drives attention which drives learning, memory, problem solving, and just about everything else."[1] The role of the limbic system, highly interconnected with all parts of the brain and the core of emotion, has been studied for more than 50 years. A second biological system of emotion was discovered in the 1990s. This system operates as an inseparable bodybrain partnership.

- Movement to enhance learning—in many respects the mobility of the body grows the brain[2] and the motion centers in the brain are responsible for sequencing thought.[3] This area of brain research is changing our perception of brain development and processing. At one level it is absolutely astonishing; at another, it resonates with our intuition. The implications here for classroom life are enormous.

Emotions As Gatekeeper to Learning and Performance

Given the Western world's love affair with science and technology, with their underpinnings of rational, logical thought, investigating the biological basis of emotion has been slow in coming. But once begun, brain research in this area has exploded, especially in the last 15 years of the 20th

ITI Learning Principles

- Intelligence as a function of experience
- Bodybrain partnership—
  —Emotion as gatekeeper to learning and performance and
  —Movement to enhance learning
- Multiple intelligences
- Learning as a two-step process
- Impact of personality

century and early 21st century. Today we must talk in terms of a bodybrain partnership, an inseparable partnership running parallel, complementary information systems. One system is a combination of electrical and chemical, one wholly chemical.

Historical Perspectives About the Biology of Emotion and Learning

One of the earliest attempts to analyze the role of emotion in brain function emerged from Dr. Paul MacLean's attempt to describe the basic functions of the various structures of the brain. Working out of the National Institutes of Mental Health, Bethesda, Maryland in the early 1950s, MacLean was the first to make clear that emotions significantly affect brain functions and thus learning, memory, and behavior.

MacLean viewed the brain as three brains in one, each with specific responsibilities essential for human survival and growth, each constantly assessing the needs of the situation at hand to determine the most appropriate response. Coining the term "triune brain," Dr. MacLean described it as consisting of the brain stem, limbic system, and cerebral cortex.

Although the triune brain theory is a vast oversimplification of how the brain functions, MacLean's conceptualization is still often used when simplification is needed. However, much has been updated and the picture vastly enlarged. The assumption in MacLean's work was that we mostly operate from our cerebral cortex, known for its logic and rational thinking, home of academic learning. When emotional issues strike us, we occasionally "downshift" into the limbic system, the emotional area of the brain. Now we know that emotions are a function of the entire bodybrain partnership and are with us all the time. Emotions, in fact, filter incoming sensory input, modulating what the cerebral cortex attends to, processes, and stores in long-term memory. Emotions truly are the gatekeeper to learning and performance. But I'm getting ahead of myself here.

MacLean's triune brain theory is briefly described here to provide readers an historical perspective and to help place the triune brain theory within a useful context until it is retired altogether.

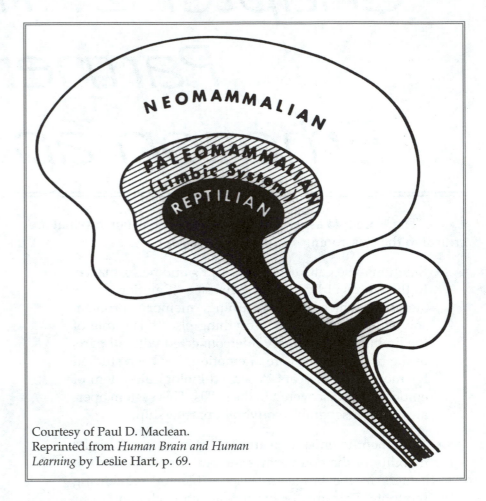

Courtesy of Paul D. Maclean.
Reprinted from *Human Brain and Human Learning* by Leslie Hart, p. 69.

The Triune Brain Theory

MacLean gave us a very useful simplification of overall brain structure, based on a great deal of knowledge available at the time about how animal brains have actually developed over the last 250 million years or so.[4] He suggested that we think of the present human brain as composed of three brains, of very different ages.

The Brain Stem. The oldest part of the brain, over 200 million years old, is often referred to as the reptilian brain. The existence of our species attests to the success of this part of the brain. It is thought to control genetic/instinctual behaviors such as hierarchies of dominance-submission, sexual courtship, defending territory, hunting, bonding, nesting, greeting, flocking, and playing.[5] The oldest brain also includes the cerebellum, or "little brain," a specialized structure that composes 10% of the brain but comprises 50% of its neurons. In the mid-1900s, the cerebellum was known to be involved in movement; more recent research suggests that the cerebellum also plays important roles in a wide range of brain functions including memory, spatial perception, language, attention, emotion, nonverbal cues, and decision-making.[6]

The Limbic System. The second brain, the **old mammalian or limbic system**, is many tens of millions of years newer and a far more sensitive and sophisticated brain than the brain stem. The limbic system is common to all mammals which flourished after most reptiles of the dinosaur age perished and became extinct about 60 million years ago.

The limbic system is composed of several interconnected structures, ranging from the size of an olive to a walnut, that emerge out of the cerebral cortex, including the amygdala, hippocampus, thalamus, hypothalamus, and cingulate gyrus. The limbic system is our brain's principal regulator of emotions. It also receives sensory data coming from the 19 senses, sending it along a fast track through the amygdala if the data suggest possible threat or arousal of intense emotion or along a slow track through the hippocampus for analysis and "thinking about" in the cerebral cortex[7] Thus, the limbic system can be thought of as our mental gatekeeper. Its roles include:

- Converting information that the brain receives into appropriate modes for processing, constantly checking information relayed to the brain by the senses and comparing it to past experience

- Directing information to the appropriate memory storage areas of the brain. (This function is needed because memories are not stored in one specific place, but rather are distributed throughout the brain in the areas functionally associated with the nature of the memory to be stored. Words, numbers, and visual images, for example, are stored in areas associated with the language center, the calculation center, and the visual cortex, respectively.)

- Transferring information from short-term to long-term memory[8]

The limbic system also regulates eating, drinking, sleeping, waking, body temperature, chemical balances such as blood sugar, heart rate, blood pressure, hormones, sex, and emotions. It is also the focus of pleasure, punishment, hunger, thirst, aggression, and rage.[9] The limbic system is a most busy place!

Despite the more recent development and larger size of the cerebral cortex (80 percent of brain mass), the limbic system has more connections going to the cerebral cortex than the cortex has going to the limbic system. According to Richard Cytowic in *The Man Who Tasted Shapes*, "While the cortex contains our model of reality and analyzes what exists outside ourselves, it is the limbic brain that determines the salience of that information. Because of this, it is an emotional evaluation, not a reasoned one, that ultimately informs our behavior . . . *it is emotion, much more than reason, that makes us human.*"[10]

The New Mammalian Brain or Cerebral Cortex. The cerebral cortex has been with us for only a few million years. In evolutionary terms, a very new item indeed. It is enormously more subtle and resourceful than the old mammalian, and many times as large as the other two brains combined. It is a multi-modal, multi-path system that, per minute, can process thousands of bits of information picked up through the 19 senses and forwarded via the limbic system. Given the volume of such information, it understandably is the slowest of the three levels of the brain. The cerebral cortex can reason, solve problems, analyze, create, synthesize, and handle a multitude of complicated tasks. This is the home of academic learning. This is the part of our brain which handles language, symbols, images for learning Shakespeare, exploring the complexities of science, studying ancient history, writing an essay, or contemplating the issues and problems of the future.

Evolution Versus Cogent Design. The triune brain was thus seen as resulting from nature's parsimony. According to evolution theory, old structures are rarely cast off. Rather, they are modified, improved, or added to (as seal legs became flippers or the delicate bones of our inner ear were remodeled from ancient gill structures). Thus, the reptilian brain was retained even as something better evolved and the newer brain was placed more or less on top of and around the older one. When a still better kind of brain evolved, it again took form over and around the older two.

MacLean's work, although now known to be an oversimplification, was paradigm-breaking at the time. For a society long-steeped in a belief in logical, sequential, linear thinking processes as the bedrock not only of "hard" science but for a total societal worldview, suggesting that emotion played an important role in the operation of the cerebral cortex was a bit of a surprise. But MacLean's work was just the beginning, a first step toward research into the effect of emotion on learning and performance.

In summary, the structures of the limbic system constitute an emotional switching station in the brain making learning and performance an emotionally driven function. As summarized by Dr.

Robert Sylwester, "Emotions drive attention which drives learning, memory, problem-solving and just about everything else."[11]

But there's more to the story. The groundbreaking work now being done on the chemical origins and operations of emotions by Dr. Candace Pert and others in the past 20 years suggests that there is a chemical information system used by the brain that parallels the electrical-chemical synaptic gap system. These chemicals, according to Pert are the "molecules of emotion."[12] Collectively referred to as "information substances," they are, as Paul Harvey would say, the rest of the story begun in Chapter 1. In effect, we learn through the cooperative interaction of multiple systems of the brain and body working together as an inseparable unit.

Information Substances: The Rest of the Story

Just as Paul Harvey's rest of the story adds a stunning twist that makes us view the earlier part of the story differently, so it is with brain research. For 100 years, scientists have understood the basic electrical-chemical building blocks of learning in the brain: nerve cells (neurons) grow dendrites (structures that receive information from other neurons) and axons (structures that send information to other neurons). Electrical impulses travel down the axon, turn into chemical messengers that jump (actually float across) the tiny gap (synapse) to the dendrites of the next neuron. Although there were many mysteries yet to be understood, such as how this all results in learning and memories, the basic explanation still holds true. During the 1950s, structures in the brain that process emotion were discovered; over the next 30 years, it became clear that emotion has a powerful impact on learning. Dr. Robert Sylwester's summary is no exaggeration: Emotion drives our attention, what we attend to determines what we perceive and thus drives learning, memory, problem-solving, behavior, and on and on.[13]

The neurotransmitters in the brain responsible for the synaptic leap, discussed at some length in Chapter 1, are but one category of "information substances" found throughout the body and brain that carry out the process we call learning. Likewise, the limbic system is only one source of "emotional messages" in the bodybrain partnership. The term "information substances" was coined initially by Francis Schmitt, elder statesman of neuroscience from the Massachusetts Institute of Technology, to describe a variety of transmitters, peptides, hormones, factors, and protein ligands that make up a second system. In this system, chemical information substances travel the extracellular fluids circulating throughout the body to reach their specific receptors, receptors on cells located not just in the brain but throughout the body.[14]

This second system parallels the conventional model of neuronal circuitry with its dendrites, axons, and synaptic leaps. Some neuroscientists now speculate that less than two percent of neuronal communication actually occurs at the synapse.[15] Less than two percent! Most of the information received by a neuron is taken in by the receptors at the cell's surface. And no wonder. The number of receptors on a neuron is staggering; current estimates are tens of thousands to a million plus per neuron.[16] That's a lot of potential for conversation! It would appear that the ability to perceive understandable patterns and learn from them is so important to survival that it cannot be posited only in one place or with one method of communication—not just one part of the neuron (at the synaptic gap) nor just in the brain. The entire body is involved.[17]

So just what are these "information substances" and what is their role in learning? These molecules, or ligands, are the basic units of a language used by cells throughout the organism to communicate across systems such as the endocrine, neurological, gastrointestinal, and even the immune system. As they travel, they inform, regulate, and synchronize.[18] Peptides are the largest category of information substances; one kind or another is produced in every cell in the body, not just by cells in the brain. Furthermore, every peptide now known to be produced within the body has receptors in the brain, thus qualifying each peptide to be considered a "neuropeptide." This means that the body talks to the brain, giving it information that alters its messages back to the body and vice versa.

According to Dr. John Ratey, "We are learning that emotions are the rules of multiple brain and body systems that are distributed over the whole person. We cannot separate emotion from cognition or cognition from the body."[19]

The Molecules of Emotion: The effect of such "conversations" on the organism is to change physical activity cell by cell and as a total organism, "*including behavior and even mood—the closest word to emotion in the lexicon of hard science.*"[20] Examples of outward manifestation of such inner "conversations" include a "gut feeling" about something; a first impression of someone as untrustworthy; a physical restlessness that something is wrong before you can put your finger on it; a spark in the eye that says, "I get it even though I can't yet explain it"; a passion for one's hobby; deep love for the beauty of nature; the contentment of a quiet hour spent with a special friend. As was foreseen by the now virtually abandoned triune brain theory,[21] core limbic brain structures such as the amygdala, hippocampus, and hypothalamus—which were long believed to be involved in emotional behavior—contain a whopping percent of the various neuropeptide receptors studied to date, perhaps as high as 85 to 95 percent.[22] Now add to that the startling finding that several of the key emotion molecules such as endorphins can be found in single-cell animals as well as on up the evolutionary trail. Peptides, it appears, have been carrying information since before there were brains, leading researchers such as Antonio Damasio to assert that "emotion is the highest part of our mindbody survival kit."[23] One of their key roles is to tell the brain what's worth attending to and the "attitude" with which one attends. Again, as so nicely summarized by Dr. Robert Sylwester, "Emotion drives attention and attention drives learning and memory, problem solving, and just about everything else."

Emotion As Filter. Another important piece of this new view of learning as a bodybrain partnership is the discovery that there are other locations in the body where high concentrations of almost every neuropeptide receptor exist. One example is the dorsal horn (the back side of the spinal cord) which is the first synapse with the nervous system where all somatosensory information is processed. In fact, in virtually all locations where information from the five senses—sight, sound, taste, smell, and touch—enter the nervous system, there are high concentrations of neuropeptide receptors. Such regions, called nodal points or hot spots, seem to be designed so that they can be accessed and modulated by almost all neuropeptides as they go about their job of processing information, prioritizing it, and biasing it to cause unique neurophysiological changes. Thus, peptides filter the input of our experiences, significantly altering our perception of reality and the input selected and allowed in during any learning situation.[24] According to Dr. Candace Pert, author of *Molecules of Emotion: Why You Feel the Way You Feel,* "Emotions and bodily sensations are thus intricately intertwined, in a bidirectional network in which each can alter the other. Usually this process takes place at an unconscious level but it can also surface into consciousness under certain conditions or be brought into consciousness by intention."[25]

Implications: In summary, this wholly chemical system of learning, that parallels the electrical-chemical system of neurons, dendrites, axons, and synapses as described in Chapter 1, expands our definition of learning in multiple ways. We now know that:

1) The body and brain form an inseparable learning partnership. Each sends messages out to the other which alters the messages that are sent back. Most sensory input (if not all) is filtered through/modulated by our emotions which direct our attention. What we attend to then drives learning, problem solving, and memory. Conversely, if we do not attend, learning and memory cannot occur.

2) Therefore, the environment of the body is critical—the physical surroundings and the quality of interrelationships of those in it (student to student and student-adult). Consequently, implementation of the ITI model begins with ensuring that the classroom and school-wide environment enhance rather than impede students' abilities to focus on the learning at hand and creating a sense of community characterized by absence of threat (real and perceived), by inclusion, influence, and affection.[26] See Part B, Chapters 8-10.

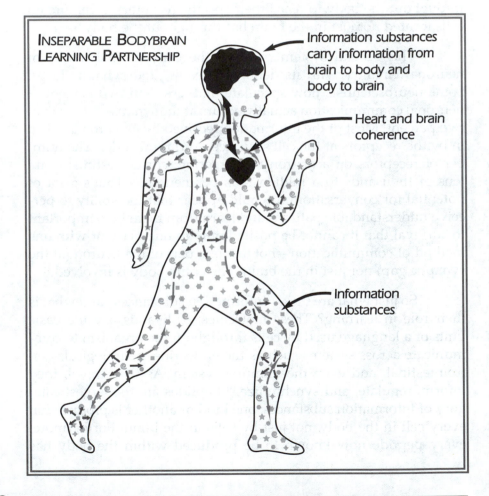

INSEPARABLE BODYBRAIN LEARNING PARTNERSHIP

Information substances carry information from brain to body and body to brain

Heart and brain coherence

Information substances

Movement to Enhance Learning

The Western world's view of the brain is that it is rational, logical, ruler of all; the body in this scheme has been primarily viewed as merely the vehicle that carried the brain from one cerebral task to another. And, if it was good looking and athletic to boot, so much the better! Now, however, it is clear that there is no hierarchy, no separation between the body and the brain. What the Greeks knew 2,000 years ago is being confirmed by today's high tech brain research—if you want the best performance from your brain, tune the body and brain together.

During the 1980s and 1990s, the popular press has extolled and sold the virtues of physical fitness as a means increasing mental sharpness and reducing stress, to overall health and well-being. But the story now emerging from brain research is amazing. As Carla Hannaford is fond saying, "The body grows the brain."[27] Indeed, animals that don't move, don't have a brain. And those like the sea squirt that move early in its life cycle, later reabsorb their brain when they permanently affix themselves to a stationary object.[28]

What Brain Research Is Telling Us

The brain research into the relationship between movement and cognition is nothing less than startling. The major findings that we believe are key for classroom teachers are:

- Movement is fundamental to the very existence of a brain. Only an organism that moves from place to place requires a brain.[29]

- The entire front half of the brain—the newest in evolutionary terms—is devoted to organizing action, both physical and mental.[30] "Higher" brain functions have evolved from movement and still depend on it.

- Movement is crucial to every brain function including planning and executing plans, memory, emotion, language, and learning.[31]

- The ability to mimic, one of young human's most powerful avenues for learning, is movement based.

Movement Is Fundamental. Only an organism that moves from place to place even requires a brain.[32] This is not a casual link! The brain and body are an inseparable partnership. As Dr. John Ratey points out, "What the brain communicates to the body depends largely on what messages the body is sending to the brain. Together they collaborate for the good of the whole organism."[33] In classroom life, this means that the body and brain are always talking and working together. When one partner is shut down, told to sit still and not move, the functioning of the other partner is deeply affected.

As we think about the traditions of the educational system we inherited, we can't help but marvel at how far off the mark some of its features are. Children sitting quietly in rows, not moving, not talking. What a recipe for failure to learn!

This suggests that the pendulum swings in school reform over the past century may have failed not because they were inherently flawed but because throughout those reforms the bodybrain partnership remained divided and thus ineffective at learning.

Half of the Entire Brain Is Devoted to Organizing Action. This is another powerful message for teachers. Half the brain! And the newest, most powerful parts of the brain at that. The frontal cortex learns, routinizes, and processes motor and mental functions in parallel. Movement, then, becomes inextricably tied to cognition.[34]

This feature of the physiology of the brain underscores the importance of defining learning as a two-step process: understanding and then *using* what is understood. It turns out that the brain *expects* to use what it understands.

Movement Is Crucial to Every Brain Function. Although our Olympic-level athletes have discovered the impressive power of the brain to improve the performance of its partner, the brain, we in the U.S. are slow to acknowledge reciprocal power of the body on the brain. According to Ratey, "our physical movements can directly influence our ability to learn, think, and remember. Evidence is mounting that each person's capacity to master new and remember old information is improved by biological changes in the brain brought on by new activity."[35]

What does this all mean for the classroom teacher? Nothing short of a revolutionary shift in our view of our students as learners. What this means is that the bodybrain partnership perceives, processes, and stores in long-term memory concepts and skills in terms of their usability and usefulness. Not useable (who cares?), not useful (relevant now), then, not worth learning. We must reframe what we teach and why we teach it. Learning not for the sake of learning but for the sake of using what we learn—for our own lives and as contributing citizens.

Ideally, the resources spent on textbooks, workbooks, blackline masters, and copy paper and machines should be redirected to *being there* experiences. Knowing how concepts and skills are *used* in the real world greatly enhance building long-term memories.

Mimicry. Startling research is emerging that suggests the presence of "mirror neurons," a subset of movement-related neurons in premotor cortex area F5[36] that buzz away when we watch someone do something that interests us. Whether these neurons merely assist us to understand or to mirror gestures or actions is still uncertain. Some researchers such as Ramachandran believe that mirror neurons play a bigger role than is generally appreciated. Ramachandran believes that not only are they the missing link between gesture and language but they help explain human learning, ingenuity, and culture in general. "Language, imitative learning, and mind reading, seemingly unrelated human developments, may all be shown to be linked through these intriguing nerve cells."[37]

Translating Brain Research into Action Using the Nine Bodybrain-Compatible Elements

The ITI model presents nine ways to translate brain research into action in the classroom and school. Each of the nine is described here. They are discussed in the order of their power to translate this area of brain research—the bodybrain partnership—into practical strategies in the classroom.

Absence of Threat/Nurturing Reflective Thinking

Bodybrain-Compatible Elements

- Absence of Threat/Nurturing Reflective Thinking
- Movement
- Collaboration
- Meaningful Content
- Choices
- Enriched Environment
- Adequate Time
- Immediate Feedback
- Mastery

Given the primacy of emotions to drive attention and thus memory, problem-solving, and virtually every other aspect of learning and performance, the number one job of a teacher is creating and maintaining an environment free from threat. Once this is in place, that environment must also actively nurture reflective thinking. These two qualities form the heart and soul of bodybrain-compatibility and are at the very heart of the ITI model. They are also the beginning point of implementation and the ongoing touchstone of ITI. Once created, they cannot be ignored but must receive consistent, on-going, **daily** attention from teacher and students.

Creating Absence of Threat

When creating absence of threat, it is important to consider two truisms:

- Like beauty, what constitutes threat—even perceived threat—are in the eye of the beholder. What is threatening to one person may not be considered threatening to another. However, that does not minimize the sense of perceived threat held by that person. Its affect on the functions of the bodybrain partnership are profound.

- Absence of threat does not mean absence of consequences. Misbehavior and failure to complete work have consequences in the real world and so should they in the classroom. What matters is fairness, consequences appropriate to the nature of the infraction, and emotional consistency of those who apply the consequences.

For some traditionalists, a little bit of threat is often considered a good thing,—"keeps 'um on their toes"and "shows them who's in charge." But, as Dr. John Ratey points out, the excess mental noise that goes on in the brain as a result of dealing with threat and stresses "can make it difficult to perceive what's going on, overloading other circuits of attention, memory, learning, cognition, emotional stability, or any other brain function." In effect, the system goes into information overload, which is precisely what can happen when highly anxious people take tests. "They will look at a test question and literally not see certain words, which causes them to misinterpret it and give the wrong answer. They may even miss seeing entire questions on the page. Their brains are so busy

dealing with the noise that the visual channels in the brain aren't open to perceive accurately. *Our brains are not infinite.* They run out of space, run out of gas, as it were. If the brain is busy trying to filter uncomfortable and frustrating noise, worries, or other concerns, there is less 'brain stuff' available for perceiving.[38] There are many aspects of our traditional curriculum and instructional that are threatening to students.

Curriculum and Threat. Curricular aspects that have a strong bodybrain–antagonistic effect include:

- Boring when too hard or too easy

- Difficult to understand if no perceivable relevance to their life; humiliating when they can't get it; source of acting out

- Frustrating because content is not understandable—the material is not age appropriate and/or is composed of factoids

Absence of Threat

Absence of threat does not mean absence of challenge or lack of consequences for misbehavior or bad choices. It does mean lack of real and perceived threat to physical and emotional safety

Instructional Strategies and Threat. Instructional strategies that have a strong bodybrain antagonistic effect include:

- Low standards for cleanliness, maintenance, and decor—lower than for most other public and private settings

- Lack of community building

- Lack of personal relationship between teacher and students

- Poor leadership—students uncertain about what's happening and why or what will happen next

- Restricting body movement in the classroom, limited to recess, lunch, and PE

- Adherence to rigid time lines, inadequate time to complete tasks

- Threat of bad grades (potential negative consequences from teacher, parent, and fellow students)

An environment with absence of threat is fundamental to learning and a prerequisite for reflective thinking.

USING *ABSENCE OF THREAT* TO ENHANCE THE BODYBRAIN PARTNERSHIP

Instructional Strategies

- Use the Lifelong Guidelines and LIFESKILLS full-time (see Chapters 7, 9, and 10).

- Ensure full membership in a community—the class family—plus being in relationship with the teacher.

- Use daily agendas and written procedures (see Chapters 7 and 8).

- Provide active, purposeful body movement in the classroom every hour to re-focus (release energy or re-energize as needed) the brain and body using activities that are an extension of what is being studied.

- Eliminate all pull-out programs except for short-term, urgent interventions.

USING *ABSENCE OF THREAT* TO ENHANCE THE BODYBRAIN PARTNERSHIP

Curriculum Development

- Teach students the personal and social skills they need to succeed with their peers and teachers.

- Eliminate fear of failure by ensuring that content is age appropriate, and thus understandable, and that inquiries are doable given current skill levels and option to choose inquiries based on intelligence(s) of strength.

- Base curriculum in being there locations that are kid-grabbers, ones that require that they do something and actively participate in. Study trips that are "look and listen" experiences don't readily engage the emotions.

- State curriculum as concepts; include how the concept is/can be used in the students' world.

- Allow students to make choices—among inquiries (how they learn required curriculum), about social/political action projects, yearlong projects, and other study tasks as appropriate.

Nurturing Reflective Thinking

The ability—and the inclination—to think reflectively is an invaluable habit of mind. It lowers stress and improves learning and decision making. In learning situations, reflective thinking allows students to move from "This is interesting but what's it good for; how can I use it in the future?" Without such automatic questioning, learning will be on the surface in the short run and will probably fail to trigger the brain's decision to store it in long-term memory.

While reflective thinking may seem a vague or elusive term, each of us can recall times when we were so immersed in something that we lost track of time and external distractions stayed at bay. Mihaly Csikszentmihalyi (pronounced CHICK-sent-me-high-ee) provides a wonderful description of the state of mind that is home to reflective thinking, a state he calls "flow experience."[39] This state of mind is attained in exceptional moments when we find ourself totally and completely immersed in a place where our heart, mind, and will are simultaneously interacting and to the point that outside distractions are not able to penetrate. This metaphor of "flow" is one that we have experienced, and can reflect upon as some of the best times of our lives. It is also a state of mind ideal for learning because engagement is extremely high and learning seems effortless.

Reflective Thinking As an Act of Discipline. Reflective thinking doesn't just happen automatically. It is an act of discipline. We must first slow down,[40] clear away distractions, focus our thoughts

> # Reflective Thinking
>
> *The ability—and the inclination—to think reflectively is an invaluable habit of mind. It lowers stress and improves learning and decision making.*

on what we're learning and doing and why, and use self-talk to guide our thinking when puzzled or stuck.

Second, to be reflective is a choice, a decision that can be made only by the learner. No teacher can hammer thoughtfulness into a student; it must come from within. The Greek/Latin base for the word educate means "to draw forth." As part of drawing forth, we need to set up conditions that nurture reflective thinking. Most importantly, we must model it and then provide ample opportunities for students to develop and practice it.

Impact of the Physical Environment. Humans beings are, as alertness to ensure survival demands, extremely sensitive to their environment. Children are even more so than adults. The ongoing impact of the physical environment of the classroom is extremely powerful. If you doubt this, think of your favorite environment, the one that relaxes you yet you remain alert and aware, fully enjoying your time there. Be that Yosemite Falls or your favorite five-star hotel, you know what an impact it has on your emotions and mental processing. In contrast, think of the environment that has the opposite effect on you—perhaps the teachers' lounge at your school with its machines and their fumes, messy coffee station, and old, uncomfortable furniture. Or, maybe it's the drab, dirty, crowded vehicle licensing office with its long lines and no place to sit while you wait; and, when your turn comes up you feel pressed to complete your tasks and so you hurry through, only half engaged in the tasks at hand. Or, maybe it's parts of your own aging school . . . the cafeteria/gym with stained ceiling tiles, unremitting, high-decibel noises (no sound dampener). Wherever this is, it's a place you dread going to and a cloud of gloom settles over you every time you even think about having to go there.

If any of this rings a bell with you, you already know that one's physical environment strongly affects one's ability to slip into a reflective state of mind and stay there. So it should come as no surprise that your first steps—even before school begins—is to address the physical environment of your classroom. At a minimum, it should be:

- Healthful—clean, well lighted, pleasant smelling, and free from harmful chemicals and allergens

- Aesthetically pleasing—calming colors and music, living plants, well organized, and comfortable furniture

- Uncluttered yet reflects what is being learned

An environment that meets these benchmarks eliminates competing sensory input to the learning at hand from within and from outside of the body thus making it easier for students to focus on what they're learning and to reflect on how and when and why they can use the concepts and skills they are studying. Without this reflec-

tive time, school is a blur and seems largely unrelated to their life. This is especially true in departmentalized settings.

USING *REFLECTIVE THINKING* TO ENHANCE THE BODYBRAIN PARTNERSHIP

Curriculum Development

- Teach students how to redirect themselves when things get in the way of their learning, for example, when any of the four psychological needs identified by William Glasser are not in place (belonging, fun, power, and freedom).[41]

- Teach students simple techniques, such as Freeze Frame, for bringing themselves to a reflective state of mind (see *Freeze Frame* by Doc Childre).

- Teach students how to direct their own learning—a foundational building block for becoming lifelong learners—by allowing them to exercise self-direction when appropriate. For example, choice of inquiries and helping develop inquiries, selecting their role to play in social/political action projects, and conducting a year-long research project on a topic of their own choosing.

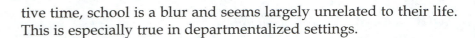

USING *REFLECTIVE THINKING* TO ENHANCE THE BODYBRAIN PARTNERSHIP

Instructional Strategies

- Ensure that the physical environment is healthful, aesthetically pleasing, and uncluttered (see Chapter 7).

- Offer rich input from *being there*, immersion, and hands on of real things so students can construct meaning rather than have to rely on attempts to memorize as a coping strategy.

- Provide adequate time for group and independent exploration.

- Be readily available to refocus, reenergize, and redirect students; during student work time, keep circulating through the classroom taking advantage of the teachable moment and building a personal relationship with each student.

- Balance time for collaborative learning balanced with personal time for applying skills and knowledge to individual interests, exploring related ideas, and reflect on what one is learning and how it could be used now and in the future (vocations and hobbies).

- Institute a mastery-based instruction with a pass/ not-yet-passed accountability system coupled with in-class and cross-age tutoring as needed until each student achieves mastery of the concepts of the curriculum.

Movement

With a nod to classical education, primarily the Greek tradition of training body and mind in a mutually supportive partnership, American education has long required physical education. Unfortunately, in practice P.E. is primarily training in sports, particularly competitive team sports such as football, baseball, basketball, with purported mental and character carry over bonuses.

Given what we know today, competitive sports should be extracurricular and P.E. should be renamed "movement to enhance learning" and become the province of the classroom teacher. In other words, we should teach students how to enhance their ability to learn through movement of their body.

Why? Memory of knowledge and skills also records the emotional state of the learner at the time the learning took place. If the emotion was negative and unpleasant, we prefer to suppress the content as well as the emotion. Statements such as, "I hate reading" or "I hate math" are really someone's way of saying, "Every time I think of reading or math, I feel bad. I remember the frustration and humiliation, feeling stupid and feeling like an outcast."

How many of us know people who know how to read but choose not to? They choose not to because there are so many negative memories. This suggests that teachers battle not only for the minds of their students (getting knowledge and skills into long-term memory) but also for their hearts (wanting to use what they have learned and doing so of their own volition).

Why do we bring this up under a discussion about the importance of movement and emotion? Because movement is the quickest and most reliable way to add fun to the moment. Movement resets our emotional state. It provides opportunities for wiggly students to let off steam, tired students to get reenergized. When movement is planned as an extension or application of the

concepts or skills being learned, additional parts of the brain wake up and content gets encoded in additional areas of the brain.

For the teacher searching for the key to his/her students' minds and hearts, eureka! You have found it.

Remember, movement in this context means using the bodybrain partnership fully and joyously to learn the concepts and skills of the curriculum—science, social studies, art, language arts, science, and technology. Movement for sports, the traditional view of P.E., is not included in this discussion.

USING *MOVEMENT* TO ENHANCE THE BODYBRAIN PARTNERSHIP

Curriculum Development

- Use movement as an extension or application of content rather than as a separate activity.

- Invite students to help you plan movement sequences that will help the class master concepts and skills.

- Teach students the skills for reading and using body language effectively. For example, miming, role playing, acting, public speaking, and dancing.

- The curriculum addresses movement both as a content itself (e.g., teaching students of the importance of movement in learning and positive emotional states) and as a means of enhancing academic learning (e.g., using the body to explore through the 19 senses and using the body to role play, react, and so forth).

USING *MOVEMENT* TO ENHANCE THE BODYBRAIN PARTNERSHIP

Instructional Strategies

- Use movement every hour. Whenever possible, make it an extension of the concepts or skills being studied. However, movement to reset emotions and prepare the bodybrain for a change of pace is also worthwhile.

- Add music and singing to your movement sequences. Melody, rhythm, rhyme, and words add fun and increase retention.

- Include these movement sequences during celebrations of learning,[42] parent nights, and cross-age tutoring.

- List the movement activities you currently use. Identify which contribute to learning curriculum content and which are "sponge activities." Add to your list as needed.

Collaboration

Almost all learning occurs in a social context. From birth we are genetically wired to learn through imitating others—from following our mother's instructions as an infant to play with others, be it a playground game of Red Rover, organized sports, or a community BBQ. We are social animals; collaborating isn't something we do, it is who we are and the context in which we live. Over the millennium, collaboration has often meant the difference between life and death. The John Wayne mythology of the Old West—of individualism writ large—runs counter to what really goes on in rural living— then and now. Collaboration, with few exceptions, has always increased the likelihood of success. However, like most social skills, collaborating—with family, friends, and in the workplace—must be learned, through modeling and practice. Done poorly, it is a lifelong source of emotional upset. Done well, it is the key to satisfaction and success throughout one's life.

Building Collaboration

The three stages of building a learning club are:

- *inclusion*
- *influence*
- *affection*

The end result is a sense of community and increased academic achievement.

Jeanne Gibbs

The jury has weighed in on this instructional strategy. Its power to improve the learning environment and increase academic learning is indisputable.[43] In short, learning how and when to collaborate is essential to our emotional health, capacity to learn,

USING *COLLABORATION* TO ENHANCE THE BODYBRAIN PARTNERSHIP

Curriculum Development

- Have students analyze historical events and literature for where collaboration, or lack of, was key in changing the course of national/world events and human lives.

- Make sure that the curriculum content of collaborative work is specifically designed for collaboration, not just putting students together to answer questions at the back of the chapter. An appropriate task for collaborative work is one that the brightest student can't do alone; every member of the group is needed to be successful. Otherwise, collaborative work negatively reinforces low social status for middle and lower achieving students and the brightest students end up doing all the work.

- Have students review the content of the Lifelong Guidelines/LIFESKILLS they will most need to be successful at their task and make decisions about how they will apply it to their work.

- At every being there location, have students focus on the most important Lifelong Guidelines/LIFESKILLS needed to be an informed participant at that location and those needed to be an employee there.

- Whenever feasible, require content-related movement during collaborative work.

USING *COLLABORATION* TO ENHANCE THE BODYBRAIN PARTNERSHIP

Instructional Strategies

- Keep in mind that collaboration has but two critical goals: increasing achievement and equalizing social status in the classroom (raising status of all to that of equal peer among peers).[44]

- Insist that students consistently use the Lifelong Guidelines/LIFESKILLS; no exceptions. As the adult in charge, you must ensure that the classroom environment is free from threat at all times.

- To equalize social status in groups, rotate the role of group leader frequently and equally (If you think that a lower achieving student will have difficulty with the content of a task which will then impede his/her leadership role, work with the student in advance so that he/she can carry out the leadership role successfully and thus grow in social status.

- Post processing: After they are finished with each collaborative task, have students analyze how well they utilized the Lifelong Guidelines/LIFESKILLS, how they felt about the process, how they could have improved both process and product, and, very importantly, what they learned about their personal and social skills for working together. How will they put that knowledge into action during the next collaborative work session.

- Convene class meetings at least once a day.

- Read student-written acknowledgments from the Acknowledgments Box at least once a day.

and our performance levels throughout life. In the classroom, skills and knowledge that help students keep their emotional state geared to learning are precursors to the rest of the curriculum.

The instructional strategies to implement collaboration, usually referred to as cooperative learning, are well known and proven. (Our favorite source is *TRIBES: A New Way of Thinking and Being Together* by Jeanne Gibbs.) In addition to these, the ITI model recommends numerous curriculum development and instructional strategies to ensure that students' collaborative work is consistent with what we now know about emotions as gatekeeper to learning and performance.

 # Meaningful Content

"You can lead a horse to water but you can't make him drink" is an old rural proverb that is equally true in the city and especially true in the classroom. Horses drink water only when they're thirsty. Students drink in what they find meaningful to them. Meaningfulness starts with an emotional reaction and continues with the "ah ha" experience that makes the eyes dance.

Renata and Geoffrey Caine describe the role of emotion and passion in learning in their description of what they call "natural thinking knowledge, " a combination of "felt meaning" and "deep meaning." "Felt meaning," is that "aha" response that occurs when something we've been trying to learn suddenly clicks into place and we "get it." It begins as "an unarticulated general sense of relationship and culminates in the 'aha' experience that accompanies insight."[45] According to the Caines, "such insight is much more important in education than is memorization."[46]

The second concept is "deep meaning," defined by the Caines as ". . . whatever drives us and governs our sense of purpose."[47] It includes all the instincts embedded in our reptilian brains, our needs for social relationships and an emotionally rich life, and our intellectual and spiritual needs.[48] These drives are sources of individual meaning, what people live for, and they are meaningful and drive our inner engines whether they are articulated or not and even whether or not we are conscious of them.[49] The important thing for us here is that ". . . people access passion when deep meanings are engaged." Deep meanings, therefore, ". . . provide a sense of direction because they govern what people look for and what they are willing to do, whether in sports, computing, music, finance, or writing poetry, or teaching. And, in part, deep meanings are a source of the energy that people are capable of bringing to bear on a task or activity."[50]

According to the Caines, when information, felt meaning and deep meaning come together, the result is "natural knowledge," knowledge so much a part of us that we refer to it as "second nature."[51] For example, "I love cars. I can't walk through a parking lot without diagnosing motors from the sounds they make. Fixing problems is second nature to me." With natural knowledge, "the learner has acquired a felt meaning for the subject or concept or procedure so that new information and procedures fit together. In addition, there is a sufficient connection with the learner's interests or deep meanings so that the information and procedures are personally relevant."[52]

Clearly, "natural knowledge" is arrived at by young children—outside of school and without the benefit of worksheets. What draws them on is the emotion of belonging to various "clubs"[53] (family, neighborhood play group, scouts club, school learning club, etc.) and through the exuberance of their natural search for meaning to their "why" questions begun as two year-olds.[54] Emotion and meaningfulness go hand in hand. You can't have a decision of meaningfulness without an emotional hook—something that grabs attention and elicits a strong desire to know more.

USING *MEANINGFUL CONTENT* TO ENHANCE THE BODYBRAIN PARTNERSHIP

Curriculum Development

- When selecting *being there* locations, look for ones that:
  - —are innately appealing to your students and will generate high levels of emotion

  - —students will consider useful to know about (from their perspective, of course)

  - —offer a high level of interaction and participation ("doing" raises emotional responses).

- Restate your curriculum as concepts rather than as lists of factoids (dates, definitions, etc.). Because concepts are generalizable to other situations, you will be more likely to intersect with students' existing areas of felt meaning and deep meaning.

- Develop inquiries allowing children to follow their natural curiosity—their whys and wherefores—when applying the skill and knowledge you want them to master.

- Allow students to participate in curriculum development so they can build in ways of using knowledge and skills that most interest them; invite them to write inquiries and then you select those you think are the best use of students' time.

USING *MEANINGFUL CONTENT* TO ENHANCE THE BODYBRAIN PARTNERSHIP

Instructional Strategies

- Build in "doing"—a natural blend of body and brain working in partnership which always produces more neurotransmitters that excite learning than sitting at one's desk.

- Utilize the power of membership in the learning club and classroom to expand and deepen what students find meaningful.

- Bring resource people to the classroom that students can respect and admire—the experts, the everyday heroes.

- Be passionate about what you teach! Show your love of learning, model the excitement and joy of being a lifelong learner.

 *Choices*

As every parent quickly learns, offering a two-year old a choice of A or B—do what I've asked or go to time out—significantly defuses a potential power struggle and improves the child's attitude toward the task chosen. The same is true in the classroom. Giving students a choice of inquiry A or inquiry B—often makes the difference between sloppy work performed with indifference or a project given one's personal best. Yet despite our experience and common sense, in schools we too often succumb to the law of bureaucracies: mind-numbing insistence on assembly-line sameness. We must leave behind the foolish insistence that the same input (textbook and lectures) will produce the same learning outcomes, that same equals equity and fairness, that misbehavior of a few should result in all receiving the same punishment regardless of circumstances. In our opinion, public education's worst, and most deadly, enemy is bureaucracy.

Offering choices is a frontal assault against the bureaucratic mentality of sameness and control and a huge emotional boost for the bodybrain partnership. Offering students choice strengthens their commitment to learn because:

- Having choices allows students to design their own path between too hard (leading to failure) and too easy (leading to boredom). It also allows them to alternate between intelligences of strength and those they are working on.

- The higher the level of interest, the higher the level of motivation and commitment to learn, and thus the higher the level of neurotransmitters generated to assist the learning process

- The power to choose gives students a measure of power and control over their own learning, perquisites for emotional stability[55] and becoming a lifelong learner.

- Having choices increases the likelihood of students' success in learning skills and knowledge and wiring them into long-term memory.

In many ways, having choice makes learning easier. As Frank Smith points out, thinking is made easy and effective when two fundamental requirements are met: 1) we understand what we are thinking about; and 2) the brain itself is in charge, in control of its own affairs, going about its own business.[56] "Thinking," he points out, "becomes difficult and inefficient when the brain loses

USING *CHOICES* TO ENHANCE THE BODYBRAIN PARTNERSHIP

Curriculum Development

- Develop inquiries which offer real choice rather than more of the same; this is particularly important for the practice and mastery of skills (reading, writing, speaking, and mathematics). Do so by building on the multiple intelligences and using real-life situations. Also make sure there are inquiries for learning club work and for individual exploration as well as for whole class assignment.

- Develop a sufficient number of inquiries to allow for real choice. Build up students' capacity to handle at least one out of four as quickly as you can. Being assigned one's choice of three out of 12 rather than three out of four is real choice.

- Invite students, from third grade and up, to develop their own inquiries from which you as teacher select the best. Learning to pose your own questions is more important to lifelong learning than being able to answer someone else's questions. Encourage students to apply the concepts and knowledge of your curriculum to areas of their personal interest.

control, when what we try to think about is contrived . . . it throws the brain out of gear. Something that in less forced circumstances might be thought about with ease becomes an obstacle, a blurred focus of contrary purposes, aggravated often by frustration and irritation." "The most difficult kind of thinking is that which is imposed on us by someone else. . ."[57]

 *Enriched Environment*

Given the choice of spending a day in a five-star hotel or in an old, ramshackle, filthy, chaotic, house on the corner of the busiest street in the city, which would you choose? Or, a day at Disney World/Epcot or at the nearby strip mall? In which environments would you smile the most, in which would time seem to pass quickly and without your notice? Clearly, the environments that were planned for you with your best interests in mind. Not only that, but the creators of such environments used the very best scientific research available at the time about the impact of color, interior design.

USING *CHOICES* TO ENHANCE THE BODYBRAIN PARTNERSHIP

Instructional Strategies

- Begin offering choices on a small scale. Start with a choice of two and set a time limit for the decision, after which you will make the choice for them.

- Shift your role from "sage on the stage" to "guide on the side" as quickly as you can. Nothing interrupts the deep state of reflective thinking called "flow" more completely than someone cutting across your thoughts; nothing kills exploration faster than someone giving the answer or obvious clues. In the ITI model, more teacher time and energy is spent developing, organizing, and orchestrating learning than "teaching" through direct instruction, controlling students, events, and adhering to a rigid schedule.

- Provide choice—between activities that you deem equally effective to help students learn the agreed upon curriculum for your school—whenever possible. Be open to thoughtful proposals from students; always ask them how their proposal will ensure that they learn concepts X and skill Y (those in the key points) that is part of your curriculum. Help them monitor their progress. Learning to "know when you know" and "know when you don't know" is essential to becoming a successful lifelong learner.

USING *ENRICHED ENVIRONMENT* TO ENHANCE THE BODYBRAIN PARTNERSHIP

Curriculum Development

- Plan for role models/experts.

- Create an immersion wall(s) that best simulates the real thing.

- Add hands-on-of-the-real-thing items, models, posters, videos, computer software, books, and so forth that directly support your key points and inquiries.

USING *ENRICHED ENVIRONMENT* TO ENHANCE THE BODYBRAIN PARTNERSHIP

Instructional Strategies

- Revisit the *being there* location, each time digging for greater understanding of how the conceptual and significant knowledge key points of your curriculum are used in real life.

- Request that your guest speakers/experts bring as many hands on and immersion items as possible. Work with them in advance to create scenarios for role playing, problem solving, and groupwork assignments. Emphasize *how to use* the knowledge and skills in as realistic a setting as possible.

Adequate Time

Lack of time is our society's number one cause of anxiety and stress. It starts early when infants must awake according to the family schedule instead of their own internal time clock. In school, our rigid schedules ensure that most children will fail to finish the initial task or, if speedy, run out of time on the second task. Or, and equally nightmarish for children, is too much time with nothing engaging to do and thus boredom sets in. The "baby bear" experience of time being "just right" is exceedingly rare. Few children learn good time-management skills because time is not under their control nor are most of the elements important to the task.

The more important completion of a task is to us, the greater the stress, anxiety, and frustration—all elements that add

up to perceived threat. Consequently, many students unconsciously withdraw their commitment to completion with high standards as a way of protecting themselves against high levels of emotional upheaval. In effect, our rigid schedules train students to not care, to be surface thinkers and mediocre performers. In most secondary systems, the departmentalized learning environments of junior and senior high fit such trained behavior perfectly and continue to further shape attitudes and behaviors that run counter to becoming effective lifelong learners.

USING *ADEQUATE TIME* TO ENHANCE THE BODYBRAIN PARTNERSHIP

Curriculum Development

- When writing inquiries, keep in mind the time frames in which you will have students use them, e.g., all morning or all afternoon, for an hour before the schoolwide assembly, the 30 minutes before the bus arrives for your being there experience, and so forth. If the inquiry requires more time than the schedule permits, even after using maximum flexibility, think through natural breaking points in advance.

- Teach students useful ways to organize their work and related materials. Help them find a balance between efficiently organized for tasks and their personality preferences, e.g., judging versus perceiving.[58] An optimum balance here will do much to reducing threat and enhancing reflective thinking now and for the rest of their lives.

- Embrace "less is more." Make it your number one goal for the year. Teach conceptually rather than "covering" all the chapters of a textbook.

USING *ADEQUATE TIME* TO ENHANCE THE BODYBRAIN PARTNERSHIP

Instructional Strategies

- Develop, with student input, written procedures for what to do when they finish their assignment early. Include "looking back" questions—questions that help them evaluate whether the information has reached their long-term memory, introspections about how they might use such information in the future, and other questions that help students real-ize that their learning is for them, not for the teacher or the grade point or other external audiences or purposes.

- Teach students time management skills. Include time management as a pre-, mid-, and post-process-ing question for collaborative work. Give students genuine control over relevant elements of their work so that they can genuinely practice effective time management.

- Model good time management practices and "talk out loud" as you think your way out of time crunch dilemmas and your stress reactions to them.

 ## *Immediate Feedback*

Immediate feedback that tells us if we're on track or not is one of the greatest sources of motivation. Lingering on with a task that we suspect we're doing "all wrong" and therefore will have to do over again and, worse, makes us feel stupid in the process, is a recipe for giving up, not caring, not wanting to try again.

Another motivation killer is having to rely on external sources for our feedback, especially a control figure such as one's classroom teacher. The older students get, the more they, like we adults, begin to resent being dependent on someone else and pow-erless.

In just these two examples, it is clear that inadequate feed-back produces highly charged negative emotions. It is critical that teachers master this late phase in the learning process; otherwise, all earlier efforts are in vain. In contrast, feedback that tells us we have succeeded at a learning task produces a burst of neurotrans-mitters, producing a "chemical high" that is readily observable in the spark in a child's eye as the "Aha" registers. As Frank Smith points out in *Insult to Intelligence: The Bureaucratic Invasion of Our Classrooms,* learning does not require coercion or irrelevant reward. Learning—driven by immediate feedback—is its own reward.

USING *IMMEDIATE FEEDBACK* TO ENHANCE THE BODYBRAIN PARTNERSHIP

Curriculum Development

- When developing an inquiry, make it clear and specific enough that students can judge for themselves whether they've completed it correctly, completely, and comprehensively. Use real world standards of performance whenever possible.

- Base the inquiries on real world settings and situations. The less abstract the assignment, the more likely students are to have a sense of what high standards are.

Instructional Strategies

- Select materials from the real world that have feedback built in naturally.

- Utilize peer review and feedback systems.

- Help students develop their own rubrics for judging their work.

Mastery

The emotional side of mastery is the foundation of positive self-concept, of seeing ourselves as a competent person, capable of handling whatever life puts in front of us. Such positive, learning-enhancing emotions are the life blood of the lifelong learner and, in the short run, they make the classroom sizzle with excitement and love of learning. The bodybrain partnership lives here—using what we understand, putting to use what we know and can do in ways **we** value.

Just as successful implementation of a mental program is its own reward, accompanied by feelings of accomplishment and increased satisfaction, having to abort a mental program that doesn't work is emotionally unsettling because it leaves us unsure of what to do next and decreases our sense of self confidence.[59] In other words, the brain has its own built in means of evaluating whether we've achieved mastery. The brain knows the difference between scoring 100% on a quiz versus being capable of performing something needed and valued in the real world.

USING *MASTERY* TO CREATE ABSENCE OF THREAT AND ENHANCE REFLECTIVE THINKING

Curriculum Development

- When developing an inquiry, make it clear and specific enough that students can judge for themselves whether they've completed it correctly, completely, and comprehensively. Use real world standards of performance whenever possible.

- Base the inquiries on real world settings and situations. The less abstract the assignment, the more likely students are to have a sense of what high standards are.

- Encourage students to write their own inquiries applying what they understand to problems and situations important to them. Make sure they state what actions would convince them they have mastered the knowledge or skill in the inquiry.

Instructional Strategies

- Select materials from the real world that have feedback built in naturally.

- Utilize peer review and feedback systems.

- Help students develop their own rubrics for judging their work. Whenever possible, reinforce their efforts to assess themselves in realistic ways.

Notes

1   Robert Sylwester has synthesized a good deal of research into a very useful and memorable phrase: "Emotion drives attention, attention drives learning/memory/problem-solving/just about everything else." Quoted in an unpublished paper entitled "The Role of the Arts in Brain Development and Maintenance." See also *A Celebration of Neurons: An Educator's Guide to the Human Brain.* (Alexandria, VA: ASCD, 1995), especially Chapter 4.

2   Conversations with Carla Hannaford, Summer Institutes sponsored by Susan Kovalik & Associates, summer, 1999. See also *Smart Moves: Why Learning Is Not All in Your Head* (Alexander, North Carolina: Great Ocean, 1995).

3   John J. Ratey, *User's Guide to the Brain: Perception, Attention, and the Four Theaters of the Brain* (New York: Pantheon Books, 2001).

4   MacLean's triune brain concept has been presented by him in a number of articles, some not readily accessible. See "The Imitative-Creative Interplay of Our Three Mentalities," in Harold Harris, editor. *Astride The Two Cultures* (New York: Random House, 1975), and "A Mind of Three Minds: Educating the Triune Brain" in *Education and the Brain, 77th Yearbook* of the National Society for the Study of Education (Chicago: University of Chicago Press, 1978). Hart refers to his concepts freely, based on his writing and conversations with him.

5   Richard Cytowic, *The Man Who Tasted Shapes*, pp. 159-161.

6   Robert Rivlin and Karen Gravelle, *Deciphering Your Senses* (New York: Simon and Schuster, 1984), Chapter 1.

7   Leslie A. Hart, *Human Brain and Human Learning* (Washington, Books for Educators, Inc., 1983), pp. 33-45.

8   Ned Hermann, *The Creative Brain* (North Carolina: Brain Books, 1990), p. 33. See also *A General Theory of Love* by Thomas Lewis (New York: Random House, 2000), pp. 51-54.

9 Hermann, p. 33.

10 Richard Cytowic, pp. 159-161.

11 Sylwester, see footnote 1.

12 Candace Pert, *Molecules of Emotion: Why We Feel the Way We Feel* (New York: Scribner, 1997), Chapters 1 and 7.

13 Sylwester, see footnote 1.

14 Pert, p. 139.

15 Pert, Ibid.

16 Conversations with Dr. Candace Pert at "Best of the Best Invitational" sponsored by Susan Kovalik & Associates, Tukwila, Washington, May, 1998.

17 An amazing but still mysterious discovery is the presence of cells through the digestive track—from mouth to anus—that are identical to neurons in the brain. Dr. Candace Pert and other scientists wonder aloud if these cells may be the source of our "gut feelings."

18 Pert, pp. 26-27.

19 Ratey, p. 223

20 Pert, p. 38.

21 Joseph LeDoux, "The Emotional Brain," presentation at Emotional Intelligence, Education, and the Brain: A Symposium, Chicago, IL, December 5, 1997. See also *The Emotional Brain: The Mysterious Underpinnings of Emotional Life* (New York: Simon and Schuster, 1996).
Given the typical time lag between findings within the brain research community and education, it will likely be some years into the 21st century before reference to the triune brain is abandoned and new ways of talking about, and implementing, the power of emotion in the bodybrain partnership are developed and put into widespread use.

22 Pert, p. 133.

23 Antonio Damasio, "Thinking about Emotion," presentation at "Emotional Intelligence, Education, and the Brain: A Symposium," Chicago, IL, December 5, 1997. See also *Descartes' Error: Emotion, Reason, and the Human Brain*, (New York: G. P. Putnam Sons, 1994).

24 Pert, pp. 141-142. Somasensory refers to any bodily sensations or feelings, whether it is the touch of another's hand on our skin or sensations arising from the movement of our own organs as they carry on our bodily processes.

25 Pert, p.142.

26 Pert, p. 33.

27 Carla Hannaford, presentation at the Susan Kovalik and Associates' "Summer Institute, 2000."

28 Ratey, p. 156.

29 Ratey, Ibid.

30 Ratey, p. 150, p. 148.

31 Ratey, p. 148.

32 Ratey, p. 156.

33 Ratey, p. 159.

34 Ratey, p. 158.

35 Ratey, Ibid.

36 William Calvin, "The Mind's Big Bang and Mirroring," unpublished manuscript, 2000, University of Washington, Seattle, WA.

37 Alison Motluk, writing in *New Scientist Magazine*, January 27, 2001. For further reading, see "Mirror Neurons and Imitation Learning As the Driving Force Behind 'the Great Leap Forward' in Human Evolution" by V. S. Ramachandran at www.edge.org/documents/archives/edge69.html; "Mirror Neurons and the

Simulation Theory of Mind-Reading" by Vittorio Gallese and Alvin Goldman in *Trends in Cognitive Sciences, Vol. 2*, 1998, p. 493; and "Language Within Our Grasp" by Giacomo Rizzolatti and Michael Arbib in *Trends in Neurosciences, Vol. 21*, 1998, p. 188.

38 Ratey, pp. 61-62.

39 Mihaly Csikszentmihalyi provides a useful definition for assessing engagement for learning. He identifies several necessary ingredients: See *Flow: The Psychology of Optimal Experience* (New York: Harper Row, 1990), pp. 74-75.

40 Part of "slowing down" is allowing the brain and heart to come into coherence. See *The HeartMath Solution* by Doc Childre and Howard Martin with Donna Beech (San Francisco: HarperSan Francisco, 2000). This fascinating book opens new windows on the relationship between brain and heart, a connection not considered important by neuroscience until very recently.

41 See the discussion about "processing the process" in *TRIBES: A New Way of Learning and Being Together* by Jeanne Gibbs (Windsor, CA: CenterSource Systems, LLC, 2001), p. 114.

42 For a description of Celebrations of Learning, an important instructional strategy in the ITI model, see pp. 21.6-21.9.

43 There are innumerable collections of data about the power of collaboration. A user-friendly source is *TRIBES: A New Way of Learning Together* by Jeanne Gibbs for classroom-oriented summaries of research from sociology, psychology, anthropology, as well as educational psychology. The book does a beautiful job of blending research and practical applications.

44 Cohen, Elizabeth, *Designing Groupwork: Strategies for the Heterogeneous Classroom, Second Edition.* (New York: Teachers College Press, 1994.) Chapter 3. This book offers an extremely straightforward, clear discussion of the social and psychological benefits of groupwork done well. Consider it a must for inclusion in your school's professional library.

45 Geoffrey and Renata Caine, *Making Connections: Teaching and the Human Brain* (Virginia: ASCD, 1991), p. 95.

46 Caines, p. 95.

47 Caines, p. 97.

48 Caines, Ibid.

49 Caines, p. 97.

50 Caines, Ibid.

51 Caines, p. 99

52 Caines, Ibid.

53 See discussion about Learning Clubs. Frank Smith, *Insult to Intelligence: The Bureaucratic Invasion of Our Classrooms* (New York: Teachers College Press, 1990).

54 Why questions for inquiries and *Scientist in the Crib*

55 William Glasser, *Control Theory*

56 Smith, p. 27.

57 Smith, Ibid.

58 Keirsey, David, *Please Understand Me II: Temperament Character Intelligence* (Del Mar, CA: Prometheus Nemesis Book Company, 1998).

59 Hart, pp. 160-161.

Chapter 3: The Multiple Intelligences

As any parent with two or more children knows, children's brains are different — in how they process experiences and information, in their talents and challenges, in their likes and dislikes, and more. If even the same gene pool can and does produce enormous variations, imagine the range of differences in a classroom of 30 students. However hard some schools may seek homogeneity for their teachers by sorting students according to age, IQ number, achievement levels, and so forth, teachers face a group of students whose brains are more different than alike. For handling such dizzying differences among learners, Howard Gardner's theory of multiple intelligences is, in our opinion, the most useful area of brain research. Gardner's work not only sheds light on how and why students approach learning differently but also points toward very practical strategies for dealing with such differences in ways that enhance the classroom learning environment for all — the teacher as well as each student.

Gardner's Theory of Multiple Intelligences

Until quite recently, intelligence was typically thought of as a general characteristic, that is, an I.Q. of 140 indicated an all-around smart person. Intelligence was a general capacity which every human possessed to a greater or lesser extent, one that was set at birth by genetics. Not true!

The new view, based in current brain research, tells a markedly different story. Although genes still play a role, experiences from conception to death also shape intelligence. Furthermore, our definition of intelligence is changing. In 1983 Howard Gardner, in his book *Frames of Mind: The Theory of Multiple Intelligences*, suggested that we each have seven intelligences. By intelligence he means "an ability to solve problems and/or create products."[1] What a wonderful definition of intelligence! A practical way to look at human potential and behavior across cultures.

ITI Learning Principles

- *Intelligence as a function of experience*
- *Bodybrain partnership—emotion as gatekeeper to learning and performance and movement to enhance learning*
- *Multiple intelligences*
- *Learning as a two-step process*
- *Impact of personality*

Gardner theorized that each of these intelligences is relatively independent of the others, with its own timetable for development, peak growth, and the like. On the other hand, ". . . only the blend of intelligences in an individual makes possible the solving of problems and the creation of products of significance."[2] And, very importantly, an individual's intellectual gifts in one area cannot be inferred from his/her capacities in another.[3] For example, high mathematical ability doesn't necessarily mean the student will also be reading above grade level.

Intelligence

"Intelligence is a problem-solving and/or product-producing capability."

Howard Gardner

Each of the seven intelligences Gardner discussed in his first book operates from a different part of the brain. This helps point the way to the whats and how-tos of curriculum designed to move us toward the elusive "maximum development" of each student. Our mission? To create 21st century Renaissance citizens. In contrast, most of today's curriculum addresses only two of the multiple intelligences—logical-mathematical and linguistic—yet all seven are needed to succeed in life.

To grasp the power of Gardner's theory of multiple intelligences, one must make a distinction between how students take in information (the visual, auditory, tactile, and kinesthetic modalities) versus how students process information inside their brains in order to first make meaning of the input and then use it to act upon the world. Remember that these intelligences are sets of problem-solving skills, not merely gateways through which information passes to reach the brain. Do not equate modalities with these intelligences.[4]

According to Gardner, intelligence ". . . entails a set of problem-solving skills, enabling the individual to resolve genuine problems or difficulties that he or she encounters and, when appropriate, to create an effective product; it also entails the potential for finding or creating problems, thereby laying the groundwork for the acquisition of new knowledge."[5]

Since his initial work in the early 1980s, Gardner has added an eighth intelligence, naturalist, and discusses a basis for two others—existential and spiritual. The following brief descriptions of the original seven intelligences plus naturalist will provide curriculum designers and classroom teachers alike with beginning outlines for restructuring curriculum for the classroom.

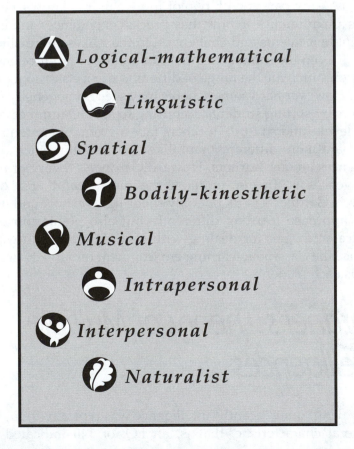

Logical-mathematical

Linguistic

Spatial

Bodily-kinesthetic

Musical

Intrapersonal

Interpersonal

Naturalist

Logical-Mathematical Intelligence—left hemisphere, front and back of both sides of the brain

This problem-solving and/or product-producing capability is the home of science and math. The core function of this intelligence is the interaction with the world of objects—ordering and reordering them, assessing their quantity, comprehending numerical symbols, appreciating the meaning of signs referring to numerical operations, and understanding the underlying quantities and operations themselves.[6]

Children high in logical-mathematical intelligence:

• Compute arithmetic problems quickly in their head

• Enjoy using computers

• Ask questions such as, "Where does the universe end?" "What happens after we die?" and "When did time begin?"

• Play chess, checkers, or other strategy games, and win

• Reason things out logically and clearly

• Revise experiments to test out things they don't understand

• Spend time working on logic puzzles such as Rubik's Cube[7]

This intelligence appears early and the most productive work is done by age forty if not by age thirty. The basis for all logical-mathematical forms of intelligence springs from the handling of objects; later these processes become internalized ("done in one's head"). One proceeds from objects to statements, from actions to the relations among actions, from the realm of the sensorimotor to the realm of pure abstraction—ultimately to the heights of logic and science.

The classical description of the development of this intelligence, the home of science and math, is that by Piaget; his work remains an accurate description of the logical-mathematical intelligence, but his work does not describe development of the other intelligences.

Linguistic Intelligence—predominantly left hemisphere—temporal and frontal lobes

Linguistic competence is the most widely and most democratically shared across the human species. As Gardner says, "one could not hope to proceed with any efficacy in the world without considerable command of phonology, syntax, semantics, and pragmatics."[8]

The core operations of language, used with special clarity, include sensitivity to the following: the meaning of words; the order among words, such as using the rules of grammar, and on carefully selected occasions, choosing to violate them; the sound, rhythm, inflection, and meter of words; and the different functions of language— its potential to excite, convince, stimulate, convey information, or simply to please.

The major uses of linguistic intelligence:

- Rhetoric—the ability to use language to convince others of a course of action

- Mnemonics—a tool to help one remember information

- Explanation—the ability to use oral and written language to teach and learn

- Metalinguistic analysis— the use of language to reflect upon language, to explain its own activities[9]

Without question, high linguistic intelligence is over 80 percent of the formula for success in traditional schooling. Without it, schooling is painful and frustrating to students and the failure rate is obscenely high despite their competence in the other intelligences. Current brain research makes clear that there are many ways of knowing, of taking in information about the world. The most powerful of these is not through reading or lecture, but rather, through full sensory input from the real world.

Children strong in linguistic intelligence:

- Like to write

- Spin tall tales or tell jokes and stories

- Have a good memory for names, places, dates, or trivia

- Enjoy reading books in their spare time

- Appreciate nonsense rhymes and tongue twisters; typically spell words accurately and easily

- Enjoy crossword puzzles or games such as Scrabble or anagrams[10]

Spatial Intelligence—predominantly right hemisphere

The core operations of this intelligence depend on the ability to image. It also involves the capacity to perceive the visual world accurately, perform transformations and modifications upon one's initial perceptions, and recreate aspects of one's visual experience, even in the absence of relevant physical stimuli. This intelligence should be arrayed against and considered equal in importance to linguistic intelligence. Loosely put, *the mind's link to language is through pictures, not sound.* This intelligence is as critical as linguistic intelligence because the two are the principal sources of information storage and solving problems.[11]

Spatial intelligence is a collection of related skills. The images produced in the brain are helpful aids to thinking; some researchers have gone even further, considering visual and spatial imagery a primary source of thought.[12]

For many of the world's famous scientists, their most fundamental insights were derived from spatial models rather than from mathematical lines of reasoning. Einstein once commented: "The words of the language, as they are written and spoken, do not play any role in my mechanisms of thought. The psychical entities which seem to serve as elements in thought are certain signs and more or less clear images which can be voluntarily reproduced or combined. . . . The above mentioned elements are, in my case, of visual and some muscular type."[13] Examples of imaging as a primary source of thought are Darwin and the "tree of life," Freud and the unconscious as submerged like an iceberg, and John Dalton's view of the atom as a tiny solar system.

It is important to note that spatial intelligence should not be equated with the visual sensory modality. Even people who are blind from birth can develop spatial intelligence without direct access to the visual world.

A keenly developed spatial intelligence is not only an invaluable asset in our daily lives but is also essential for understanding the application of what is learned in school.[14] This is particularly true in areas where the elements are abstract and unseen (microscopic in size or invisible physical science areas such as the forces of gravity, electricity/magnets, etc.).

Children strong in spatial intelligence:

- Visualize while reading

- Spend free time engaged in art activities

- Report clear visual images when thinking about something

- Easily read maps, charts, and diagrams

- Draw accurate representations of people or things

- Like it when you show movies, slides, or photographs

- Enjoy doing jigsaw puzzles or mazes

- Daydream a lot[15]

Bodily-Kinesthetic Intelligence—tendency for left hemisphere dominance in right-handed people, right hemisphere dominance in left-handed people

Characteristic of this intelligence is the ability to use one's body in highly differentiated and skilled ways for expressive as well as goal-directed purposes, such as the mime, actor, athlete, and tradesman. This intelligence also brings the capacity to work skillfully with objects, both those that involve the fine motor movements of one's bodily motions, and the capacity to handle objects skillfully.[16]

Not only is the body an instrument for acting on knowledge, to a degree greater than previously understood, the body is also an active partner in learning (see Chapter 2).

Children strong in bodily-kinesthetic intelligence:

• Use body language to communicate thoughts and emotions

• Do well in sports and recreational hobbies requiring physical skill and effort

• Move, twitch, tap, or fidget while sitting in a chair

• Engage in physical activities such as swimming, biking, hiking, or skateboarding

• Need to touch people when they talk to them

• Enjoy scary amusement rides

• Demonstrate skill in a craft like woodworking, sewing, or carving

• Cleverly mimic other people's gestures, mannerisms, or behaviors[17]

• Easily remembers information when given movement cuing systems. For example, the algorithm for long division could be expressed as: first you divide (clap-clap), multiply (tap crossed hands twice), subtract (outward slicing movement of both hands twice), and then bring it down (two hands pulling imaginary pipe down as if chinning yourself). (See *I Can Divide And Conquer* video and companion book by Martha Kaufeldt, available through Books For Educators. See back of this book.)

Involving the rest of the body in any learning event increases the neural activity of the brain and increases the flow of adrenaline which aids transfer from short-term memory to long-term memory.

Musical Intelligence—right hemisphere

This intelligence is the most separate from the other intelligences and is the earliest to appear. For individuals high in this intelligence, composing and performing at age five, as Mozart did, is not unusual. This intelligence makes itself known as early as age three. Core functions include pitch, melody, rhythm, timber (tone), and pattern.

Students who are unusually high in musical intelligence and relatively low in linguistic intelligence will use their musical intelligence skills to "translate" language into rhythmic patterns. An example of this type of student is the one whose body begins to jive and tap the instant the teacher begins to speak, stopping the second the teacher stops talking, restarting with the next burst of speech—all in rhythm with the teacher's words. Content in rhyme can be readily absorbed by these students while the same information in an uninspiring lecture or in the stilted prose of a science textbook can be completely indigestible. Monotone speakers have particularly deadening effects on highly musical students.[18]

Musically gifted children:

- Play a musical instrument and/or sing

- Remember melodies of songs

- Tell you when a musical note is off-key

- Say they need to have music on in order to study

- Collect records or tapes

- Sing songs to themselves

- Keep time rhythmically to music; hum and drum[19]

Intrapersonal and Interpersonal Intelligences

Both of these intelligences are far more diverse and culturally dependent than the previous six.

Extreme circumstances such as times of war, subjugation, famine, disaster in general, recession/depression, life or death situations, and death itself greatly affect the expression of these intelligences. All of these circumstances make demands for action that are unpracticed by most people. They are one-time or seldom experienced happenings. Yet the cultural beliefs and premises held by society demand that we respond to these events and express ourself in certain ways, depending upon locale, age, status in the community, etc. In short, these are problem-solving situations requiring problem-solving intelligences. Although not so dramatic, daily living demands the same kinds of problem-solving from us.

Intrapersonal Intelligence involves the examination and knowledge of one's own feelings, the "sense of self"—the balance struck by every individual and every culture between the prompting of inner feelings and the pressures of others.

The core capacity of intrapersonal intelligences is access to one's own feeling life—the range of our emotions; our capacity to instantly discriminate among these feelings and, eventually, to label them, to draw upon them as a means of understanding and guiding our behavior.[20]

At its advanced level, intrapersonal knowledge allows one to detect and to symbolize complex and highly differentiated sets of feelings, e.g., the novelist who can write introspectively about feelings, the patient or therapist who comes to attain a deep knowledge of his own inner world of feelings, the wise elder who draws upon his/her own wealth of inner experiences in order to advise members of the community.

Children strong in intrapersonal intelligence:

• Display a sense of independence or a strong will

• React with strong opinions when controversial topics are being discussed

• Seem to live in their own private, inner world

• Like to be alone to pursue some personal interest, hobby, or project

• Seem to have a deep sense of self-confidence

• March to the beat of a different drummer in their style of dress, their behavior, or their general attitude

• Motivate themselves to do well on independent study projects[21]

Interpersonal Intelligence involves looking outward toward the behavior, feelings, and motivations of others.

The core capacity of interpersonal intelligence is the ability to notice and make distinctions among other individuals and, in particular, among their moods, temperaments, motivations, and intentions.[22]

In an advanced form, interpersonal knowledge permits a skilled adult to read the intentions and desires of many other individuals— even when those have been hidden. This intelligence also permits us to act upon such knowledge, such as when influencing a group of disparate individuals to behave along desired lines; it's what we call leadership. We see highly developed forms of interpersonal intelligence in political and religious leaders (a Mahatma Gandhi or a John Fitzgerald Kennedy), in skilled parents and teachers, and in individuals enrolled in the helping professions, be they therapists, counselors, or concerned friends.

Interpersonally gifted children:

• Have a lot of friends

• Socialize a great deal at school or around the neighborhood

• Read people's intentions and motives

• Get involved in after-school group activities

• Serve as the "family mediator" when disputes arise

• Enjoy playing group games with other children

• Have a lot of empathy for others[23]

Naturalist Intelligence—allows people to distinguish among, classify, and use features of the environment.[21]

Howard Gardner suggests that this intelligence develops on its own in most children, " . . . particularly those who have a chance to spend time out of doors—in both rural and urban/suburban settings. The real trick is to maintain it, in the face of different pressures in school."[25] The naturalist pays attention to flora and fauna, noticing critical distinctions. Charles Darwin exemplifies the keen observation, curiosity, and awareness of patterns essential for strength in this intelligence. In a farming or hunting culture, persons strong in the naturalist intelligence are highly valued to ensure the group's continued success.

Placed in a culturally diverse environment, the naturalist picks up on characteristic patterns of speech, movement, dress, and the like with the result that he can both recognize group members and choose to conform and fit into the setting. People who move easily from mainstream to minority cultural environments are strong in naturalist intelligence.

Children who are talented naturalists:

• Ask many questions about their environment

• Delight in large collections of natural objects, e.g., insect collection

• Enjoy scouting or similar activity allowing them to pursue an interest at their own pace

• Stay intensely involved in an activity, not wanting to stop

• Are sensitive to patterns in the environment such as at the lake, in the woods, on the street, and in the classroom

• See structure and order where others see only noise or random elements[26]

Do the activities within each category strike a familiar chord? They should. Each of us is born with all of these intelligences but we tend to develop those valued by our culture (home, school, church, community). It is the goal of the ITI classroom to make sure that all intelligences are developed and used on a daily basis.

A Message to Teachers

The multiple intelligences identify important ways for students to solve problems and produce products, each of which operates from a different part of the brain. If students are having difficulty learning a concept or skill, provide inquiries which call on the intelligence(s) of their strength. Later, when their understanding is solid and they're practicing how to use concepts or skills in order to wire them into long-term memory, teachers should provide inquiries which call on other intelligences. This wide input and processing not only helps cement long-term memory but strengthens students' problem-solving and product-producing capabilities in all areas of intelligence.

Translating Brain Research into Action Using the Nine Bodybrain-Compatible Elements

The multiple intelligences are a major curriculum development tool in the ITI model. They are key when developing inquiries because they help the teacher build in choices and meaningfulness for students. (See Chapter 18.) They also serve as a check list for the teacher when creating an enriched environment.

Choices

Choice based on variety just for the sake of variety is a one-way ticket to hard work for teachers and an investment with minimal return for students. Choice must be purposeful—specifically planned ways to provide input and/or apply concepts and skills that will enable each student to achieve at high levels.

Bodybrain-Compatible Elements

- Choices
- Meaningful Content
- Enriched Environment
- Adequate Time
- Absence of Threat/Nurturing Reflective Thinking
- Collaboration
- Immediate Feedback
- Mastery
- Movement

USING *CHOICES* TO ENHANCE DEVELOPMENT OF THE MULTIPLE INTELLIGENCES

Curriculum Development

- Teach the theory of multiple intelligences to your students. Help them distinguish between the intelligences as ways of thinking and processing information versus subject content areas of the same name. For example, writing lyrics for a song is not necessarily using one's musical intelligence; it's likely just another linguistic activity. But figuring out how to use musical elements as a study skill, for example to go from Ds to As in college, is a way of using music to solve problems and produce products.[27] Also, doing arithmetic, carrying out the mechanics of a long division problem, is not the same as thinking mathematically to solve a problem in your environment. *The intelligences are a way of thinking, not a subject.*

- For every key point, develop at least 5-12 inquiries for each of the following intelligences: spatial, musical, and bodily-kinesthetic as well as logical/mathematical and linguistic. Then check that interpersonal and intrapersonal intelligence are addressed among the above five. Also check that inquiries address all levels of Bloom's taxonomy (see Chapter 17) and personality preferences (see Chapter 6).

- Encourage students to write inquiries for themselves and for the class. Select those you think will provide the best application and practice of concepts and skills for students.

USING *CHOICES* TO ENHANCE DEVELOPMENT OF THE MULTIPLE INTELLIGENCES

Instructional Strategies

- Have students identify their strongest intelligences and those they would like to strengthen. Have them set goals and strategies for developing their intelligences on a weekly basis.

- Prepare resource people to talk about how they use the multiple intelligence most critical to their area of work. Prep them for such questions from students as: "When did you first know you had this capability?" "How did you build it when you were a student?" "What other occupations could you have chosen using this intelligence?"
  Explore these same issues with people at your *being there* locations.

- Teach students to observe how fellow Learning Club members use their intelligences. After every collaborative task, have students analyze and process what they have learned from each other about using the intelligence(s) needed to successfully complete their work.

- Model respecting different ways of learning, solving problems, and producing products.

- When planning direct instruction and its immediate follow up, build in all seven multiple intelligences.

- Make the multiple intelligences a daily focus of your teaching. It is probably your most powerful means to empower students as learners now and throughout their lives.

Meaningful Content

Have you ever sat in a class and thought to yourself, "Why am I struggling so? This stuff can't be this hard. What's going on here?" If so, you were probably responding to a learning environment that didn't allow you to use your intelligence(s) of strength thus crippling your ability to learn. The moral of the story here is that much of meaningfulness is a function of how we go about learning rather than any innate quality of the concept or skill to be learned. For example, high interpersonal-intelligence people will happily absorb all kinds of concepts and skills if allowed to process them interpersonally. The same content approached intrapersonally may hold little interest and meaning to them. Likewise, study of the physics of sound waves may hold little interest to someone high in musical intelligence but low in logical/mathematical intelligence until he/she is allowed to apply the concepts to sound waves of various orchestral instruments from tuba to piccolo, bass viola to violin, piano to guitar.

Frank Smith, in *Insult to Intelligence: The Bureaucratic Invasion of Our Classrooms*, makes the point that when meaning is reached, "learning" occurs automatically and simultaneously.[28] The learner is always asking, What does this situation/information mean to me? How can I use it? How does it affect me now and in my future? "Making sense of the everyday world in relation to ourselves, our needs (physical, emotional, mental), and motivations (interests and need for fun in our lives) is our greatest concern and motivator."[29] According to Hart, "How much is learned by rote is a direct function of time and effort. But when the learning is meaningful we learn much faster and without effort."[30]

USING *MEANINGFUL CONTENT* TO ENHANCE DEVELOPMENT OF THE MULTIPLE INTELLIGENCES

Curriculum Development

- Help students discover and track their own intelligences.
- Know your students. Create curriculum that builds on their strengths when attempting to understand something new and learning how to apply it.
  During practice to cement such learning into long-term memory, encourage students to stretch using intelligences that aren't as well developed.
- When creating inquiries for individual use, develop some for intelligences that vary widely in complexity, knowing that students will select some that invite use of those intelligences that are most developed and will also select some that invite use of their least developed intelligences.

USING *MEANINGFUL CONTENT* TO ENHANCE DEVELOPMENT OF THE MULTIPLE INTELLIGENCES

Instructional Strategies

- Ask students what it would take to make the concept or skill to be learned meaningful to them. Know that each student's brain is different and that they will therefore process differently. Commit yourself to providing the kinds of input that they need to arrive at your levels of expectation.

- During direct instruction, provide input for all the intelligences; this increases students' understanding of the concept/skill and the perception of relevance.

- Provide opportunities for students to reflect on how well they're developing all of their intelligences.

- When students are reading literature, studying famous people, or attending a career day, have students analyze the intelligences most critical to that person and/or task.

Enriched Environment

The brain can't learn new things or make connections among previously learned concepts and skills without new input—a problem to be solved or a product to be made that forces us to "reshuffle the deck" of new sensory input. Thus, the elements we select to make learning come alive for students are crucial. In addition to taking into account the six kinds of input—with special emphasis on *being there* locations, *immersion*, and *hands on of the real thing*—we also need to take into account if and how that input will encourage and challenge the multiple intelligences. (For a discussion of levels of input, see Chapter 1.)

There are many examples of apparent fit that, once examined closely, don't accomplish the desired result. For example, a study trip to a grocery store would, on the surface, seem to address bodily-kinesthetic intelligence. But if the visit is a look-see-listen event, the body is walking and standing but not necessarily involved in solving problems or producing products. Similarly, a presentation by a visiting artist may challenge spatial intelligence or the visit may only be a linguistic experience on the topic of art.

Keep in mind that Gardner's theory of multiple intelligences is about how the brain solves problems and makes products. An enriched environment, therefore, must provide the substance for such thoughts and projects. Thus, the input must invite—even demand—action. An enriched environment is a purposeful environment that walks the tight rope between enough to activate the multiple intelligences and too much that results in clutter.

USING *ENRICHED ENVIRONMENT* TO ENHANCE DEVELOPMENT OF THE MULTIPLE INTELLIGENCES

Curriculum Development

- Check the power of every item you bring into your classroom to encourage solving a problem or producing products relating to your curriculum. Eye appeal is nice, interesting is nice, but the important questions are: "Does it invite problem solving? Will it play an integral role in producing a product?" If not, don't bring it into the classroom; your space is too limited. If yes, keep it and use it to build your curriculum, especially to design engaging inquiries.

Instructional Strategies

- Select *being there* locations that call upon and/or illustrate all the intelligences.

- Replicate/Simulate in your classroom the important elements of the *being there* location. If your replication/simulation is a mirror of the location, all the intelligences will be included automatically because real life is integrated and rich in its problems to be solved.

- Analyze hands-on-of-the-real-thing items; make sure their use (as a group) addresses all of the intelligences.

- Realize that what you find acceptable or endearing may have very opposite effects on some students due to their different strengths. Base your classroom decor and music on carefully researched principles of interior design and musicality, not on personal preferences.

Adequate Time

Solving problems and producing products are a far cry from rote memorizing; they require thinking and reflecting, searching for and understanding connections among prior and current learnings—all of which takes time.

Each of us can recall a time when we were deeply immersed in something and then were interrupted. Not only do we immediately feel irritated—a sense of loss—but when we can again return to the task, the enjoyment is gone. Worse, it takes some time before we are able to figure out where we were in our thinking/process. Inadequate time causes tremendous stress and kills motivation for all of us.

For teachers, inadequate time is lethal. Many a worthwhile and widely-supported school improvement effort has died a premature death because of inadequate time to plan together, study together, prepare together, and implement together. In fact, without time, "together does not and cannot happen."

For students strong in logical-mathematical intelligence, inadequate time to complete a project or come to a logical breaking point is intolerable.

When learning—especially when learning the skills and attitudes for becoming a lifelong learner and developing intelligences that are not our strengths—it is important to remember that the race is not to the swift but to the thorough. Working with the multiple intelligences is not just a means to an end but a worthy goal in its own right because of the long-term benefits.

USING *ADEQUATE TIME* TO ENHANCE DEVELOPMENT OF THE MULTIPLE INTELLIGENCES

Curriculum Development

- Always remember, developing an intelligence is not about getting the right answer but about practice; new ways of thinking to solve problems and produce products takes time—lots of time and lots of practice. Always have more inquiries on hand than you think you'll need.

- Help students understand the importance of developing all of their intelligences so that they will challenge themselves to do so.

- Assign practice in applying concepts or skills to real–world situations through homework. Use class time the next day to process what students learned about their intelligences. What they learn about themselves as a learner is far more useful over a lifetime than memorizing any one concept.

- Encourage students who need more practice to use spare time during the school day and at home to complete inquiries. Invite them to develop their own inquiries to practice with.

USING *ADEQUATE TIME* TO ENHANCE DEVELOPMENT OF THE MULTIPLE INTELLIGENCES

Instructional Strategies

- Be flexible; reduce or eliminate "regular schedules" with their specified time blocks.

- Let students' interests and excitement lead them. Learning to learn, learning how to steer one's own learning takes time.

- Provide adequate wait time; let students mull and stew and benefit from self-talk or dialogue with learning club members before you accept an answer to your question. Make answering a question an adventure in reflective thinking rather than a competition to be first.

- If students are to work at developing all their intelligences, create an environment that encourages students to slow down so they can talk their way through their work, shifting from strengths to weaknesses and weaknesses to strengths, comfort level to extreme challenge and back again. Allow students to tell you if they need more time and then alter the schedule accordingly.

- Plan direct instruction that uses all the intelligence. Alternate short periods of direct instruction with inquiries that invite the use of several different intelligences.

Absence of Threat/Nurturing Reflective Thinking

In Chapter 1 we made the case that absence of threat is a prerequisite for but not the same as reflective thinking. Reflective thinking assumes absence of threat but requires that we are allowed to think and solve problems and produce products thinking the way we think best, that is, using the intelligences of strength. It also requires, however, that we have multiple ways to tackle a problem in life, so that we can have many avenues to pursue, not just one tried-and-true approach.

Absence of Threat. Stress in all its forms, including threat (real or perceived), almost always makes us retreat to more familiar territory, coping strategies, and habits of mind. For example, when under stress, we tend to revert to old eating habits and styles of interacting with others. In the classroom, this translates into reverting to our problem-solving/product-producing strengths. If linguistic intelligence is not our strength and we are confronted with a paper-pencil test situation we believe we will fail, we are likely to revert to our strong intelligence. If that is interpersonal, we are likely to begin talking with our neighbor; if bodily-kinesthetic, moving about. Neither strategy assists in successful test taking.

Traveling the multiple intelligences is a balancing act between using our familiar strengths when content and situations are challenging versus learning to stretch ourselves to build problem-solving/product-producing strategies and approaches that are not our strengths. The most effective learners and performers are those who can, and are willing to, dance between the two. Again, our goal in public education ought to be the creation of Renaissance people, Leonard da Vincis of the 21st century.

Reflective Thinking. According to Einstein, "Imagination is more important than knowledge." His greatest insights came when he was in a dreamlike state, another kind of reflective thinking.

This is an important awareness. Nose to the grindstone, never taking time to look up or rethink what one is doing is a recipe for pain and inefficiency. Advances in thinking come from seeing with new eyes, an aha! preceded by a quiet moment of introspection and/or undirected, free-flowing thought.

The key here is to use your classroom leadership to create frequent times for students to work quietly on their own, developing their intrapersonal intelligence and helping them learn to use it to guide their problem solving and product producing efforts.

USING *ABSENCE OF THREAT AND NURTURING REFLECTIVE THINKING* TO ENHANCE DEVELOPMENT OF THE MULTIPLE INTELLIGENCES

Curriculum Development

- Teach students the theory of multiple intelligences. Have them assess their strengths and areas yet to be developed. Develop key points and inquiries just as you would for science or social studies.

- Make sure that the inquiries for each key point include all of the multiple intelligences. (For a discussion of each of the kinds of key points and inquiries—key curriculum structures in the ITI model—see Chapters 14 and 15.)

- When selecting inquiries for whole class use, select first those that use the greatest sensory input and manipulation of the information or skill, e.g., inquiries designed for bodily-kinesthetic and interpersonal intelligences and that are application-based. Select last those that are linguistic, especially those based on the knowledge and comprehension levels of Bloom's Taxonomy (see Chapter 17).

- Invite students to write inquiries that they consider a stretch for themselves, inquiries that require them to use an intelligence they want/need to develop.

USING *ABSENCE OF THREAT AND NURTURING REFLECTIVE THINKING* TO ENHANCE DEVELOPMENT OF THE MULTIPLE INTELLIGENCES

Instructional Strategies

- Create classroom procedures for instituting daily time periods for intrapersonal time. They are an important part of classroom leadership. For more information about procedures, see Chapter 8.

- Provide time for and model using intrapersonal time; orchestrate conditions that encourage reflective thinking.

- Invite students to reflect on their progress in developing one or two intelligences they don't normally use.

- Use processing questions after cooperative learning to ensure that students see the value of multiple intelligences, e.g., "Which intelligences did we use/could have used to complete this task?"

- During intrapersonal time, invite and encourage students to choose the inquiry they will work on or write their own.

- Involve students in writing inquiries they believe will best help them stay engaged and learn best.

Collaboration

When it comes to teaching students how to develop and use all of the multiple intelligences, collaboration is your most powerful tool. Why? Because a Learning Club composed of students with different intelligence strengths provides ongoing modeling of how each intelligence operates and contributes to a more effective result. And since imitation is a core learning strategy of all children, daily modeling of an intelligence by someone they like and respect is very powerful indeed. Understanding how the different intelligences work is a first step toward appreciating intellectual differences rather than being intimidated by them or feeling superior about them.

Likewise, collaboration among staff produces better products when differences are acknowledged and consciously used to achieve a better result.

USING *COLLABORATION* TO ENHANCE DEVELOPMENT OF THE MULTIPLE INTELLIGENCES

Curriculum Development

- Make sure that the content of each inquiry assigned for collaborative work requires several intelligences, not just linguistic, so that no one student by him/herself can do it. This ensures that each student must contribute and thus each intelligence is demonstrated to be important to successfully completing the task.

- Ensure a balance of inquiries using interpersonal and intrapersonal intelligences.

- Consider the match between the intelligences required by an inquiry and the intelligence strengths of the students assigned to be the leader of the group for that task. Develop additional inquiries if needed so that student leaders can be successful as leaders as well as learners.

USING *COLLABORATION* TO ENHANCE DEVELOPMENT OF THE MULTIPLE INTELLIGENCES

Instructional Strategies

- When establishing the membership of your collaborative groups, called Learning Clubs in the ITI model, use problem-solving/product-producing strengths as a major criteria. In your groups of five,[31] do your best to have strengths in at least four intelligences represented.

- Whenever students work on a group inquiry, have them analyze what intelligences they will most need to complete the assigned inquiry. This will alert students not strong in that intelligence to tune into that mode of solving problems or producing products. Similarly, during post-processing, have students analyze how they used/didn't use the multiple intelligences as they worked together. (Post-processing is an important strategy for maximizing learning in group settings—both of subject content and ability to work together as a group.)

- Have students analyze what intelligence the frequent group roles require, e.g., recorder, leader, materials gatherer. Encourage them to observe how specific roles and intelligences make the group successful.

Immediate Feedback

Each intelligence has its own built-in ways of thinking, e.g., shifting immediately to mindmapping information or creating a mathematical formula to show relationships, reading the directions first or "playing with it" first to figure it out. To learn new ways of thinking, immediate feedback is essential. The issue here is not about getting the right answer but about actually thinking differently. After-the-fact feedback is therefore useless. What is needed is "in-flight" assessments and adjustments. External feedback from teachers and fellow Learning Club members is therefore invaluable.

However, since external feedback is not always available, in the long run students must learn to expand their capacity for self-talk, a key factor in intrapersonal intelligence. Self-talk can provide a running dialogue for students. It can ask pertinent questions to guide the next attempt at solving the problem or get around a production problem to complete a project.

For example, co-author Karen Olsen has learned to rely on self-talk a great deal when writing a book. When writer's block appears, the self-talk begins. "Now, why am I stuck on this? Is it the content I'm hung up on or how to express it? Are my examples only linguistic or have I provided pictures of how it would look in the classroom (spatial input) and ways students could act on this idea (bodily-kinesthetic)?" And the internal dialogue continues. Are some of my questions hard to answer? You bet! Musical intelligence is my low suit still and interpersonal isn't my first preference but the beat goes on. Problem solving even for a linguistic task such as writing a book is greatly enhanced by use of all of the intelligences.

Lifelong learners and effective performers learn to use intrapersonal intelligence to redirect use of all the other intelligences.

USING *IMMEDIATE FEEDBACK* TO ENHANCE DEVELOPMENT OF THE MULTIPLE INTELLIGENCES

Curriculum Development

- Include in group inquiries a post-processing question that invites students to reflect on:

  — Which of the multiple intelligences, and what combinations of them, they used to complete their inquiry

  — How did they use these intelligences (give examples)

  — How well they used those intelligences

  — What they learned about the strengths of the group and how well the group modeled each intelligence

  — What each member learned about his/her ability to use each of the intelligences.

- Consider student misbehavior an indicator of curricular weaknesses. Analyze the intelligence students are using to create their product called misbehavior. They may be telling you that they need more inquiries using this intelligence.

USING *IMMEDIATE FEEDBACK* TO ENHANCE DEVELOPMENT OF THE MULTIPLE INTELLIGENCES

Instructional Strategies

- After post-processing, invite students to record their thoughts in their journals. Have them create a section of their journals called "Me and My Shadow" or "Are You Listening?" and record how they used self-talk to increase their power as a learner.

- Use student misbehavior as an indicator of limited range of instructional strategies, especially during direct instruction. Analyze the intelligence students are using to create their product called misbehavior. They are telling you that you need to utilize that intelligence during instructional time—direct instruction for the class as well as during one-on-one explanations.

- Find someone to provide immediate feedback to you about how well you provide immediate feedback to your students (and other issues you may choose).

 *Mastery*

In the ITI model, the focus of mastery is one's ability to apply concepts and skills in real-life settings in accordance with real world standards and expectations. Rote memory therefore is a small piece of success in the ITI model—a means to an end but not valued as an end in itself. It is the ability to use what is understood, not just repeat it back, that is valued.

Clearly, the ability to use what is understood requires facility in handling a wide range of circumstances and tools. The best way to acquire this flexibility and expertise is to develop the capacity to solve problems and produce products in each of the multiple intelligences. Until then, allow students to demonstrate what they understand using their strengths rather than their weaknesses and to practice what they know in various ways until the new information becomes stored in long-term memory.

USING *MASTERY* TO ENHANCE DEVELOPMENT OF THE MULTIPLE INTELLIGENCES

Curriculum Development

- When developing ways to determine student mastery—tests, rubrics for self-assessment and group feedback, and so forth—avoid only paper-pencil tools. Require ability to use concepts and skills in real world ways; instead of multiple choice answers to a single question, offer students their choice of assessment options based on spatial, bodily-kinesthetic, musical, and logical-mathematical intelligences which require students to "do" something, not just talk.

USING *MASTERY* TO ENHANCE DEVELOPMENT OF THE MULTIPLE INTELLIGENCES

Instructional Strategies

* Help students develop a sense of "knowing when they know" and "knowing when they don't know." If a little knowledge is a dangerous thing, a person with a little knowledge who perceives it to be a lot is a detriment to himself and to others. For example, the on-line investors who lose their retirement nest egg because they failed to recognize what they didn't know about investing. Or, the meetings we have sat through with people who hogged the agenda yet had no grasp of the extent of their ignorance on the topic (but nonetheless were adamant in their opinions). This is a nightmare in a democratic society when citizens gather together to solve a problem!

* Provide time for students to reflect in their journals about how they can tell if they know enough about a topic to make decisions responsibly and when they need to gather more information.

* Provide models of quality products so students can see what mastery looks like.

* Model for students how to use the different intelligences to assess a product or a problem-solving process.

* Involve students in designing portfolios that demonstrate mastery.

Movement

The multiple intelligences are rarely used in isolation—one at a time. Almost any real-world task requires a rich mixture of intelligences. *Being there* experiences are especially effective in making us to move about and use a combination of intelligences. In such active learning situations, movement and bodily-kinesthetic intelligence meld together. Thus, if you plan explorations of *being there* locations, you will automatically engage both movement and bodily-kinesthetic intelligence. Our only word of advice is this: Assign authentic action. Avoid the contrived.

USING *MOVEMENT* TO ENHANCE DEVELOPMENT OF THE MULTIPLE INTELLIGENCES

Curriculum Development

* Remember that bodily-kinesthetic intelligence is a problem-solving and product-producing capability. Inquiries should offer important problems to be solved and worthwhile products to be produced. Anything less is a waste of time and insulting to students. Always ask yourself, "If I were the age of my students, would I find this task worthy of my time? Would the task help me understand that concept or skill or learn to apply it? Would the task help me remember the concept or skill 10 years from now?

* Think movement, think action, think doing something worthwhile while practicing how to use key points.

USING *MOVEMENT* TO ENHANCE DEVELOPMENT OF THE MULTIPLE INTELLIGENCES

Instructional Strategies

- Because the motor areas of the brain sequence thinking, the more students *do* things with what they know, the more solid the learning. Add movement to every possible aspect of your instructional processes—from direct instruction to independent study and everything in between.

- Develop an active cross-age tutoring or buddy program that invites your students to demonstrate what they know to younger students. The tutor/buddy rule: Demonstrate, don't tell.

Notes

1   Recently Gardner has considered evidence for three additional intelligences: naturalist, spiritual, and existential. See Chapters 4 and 5, *Intelligence Reframed: Multiple Intelligences for the 21st Century* by Howard Gardner (New York: Basic Books), 1999. The naturalist intelligence is considered the strongest candidate so far. However, as you read through this chapter and Chapters 9 and 10 about how to develop curriculum in the ITI model, you will notice that we do not utilize the naturalist intelligence. There are several reasons: Gardner himself states that the naturalist intelligence develops on its own in most children. We believe that well-constructed *being there* experiences, along with teaching the scientific thinking processes, will provide ample practice in observing, classifying, and using features of the environment. Also, it is our contention that Gardner's comment that the "pattern-recognizing talents of artists, poets, social scientists, and natural scientists are all built on the fundamental perceptual skills of naturalist intelligence"* is incorrect. In our opinion, "pattern-recognition" as described in Chapter 4 is a general function of the entire brain, not just that of the naturalist intelligence. This is consistent with the fact that Gardner does not assign the function of naturalist intelligence to a particular region of the brain as he does the first seven intelligences.

Howard Gardner's definition of intelligence is an extremely useful alternative to the standard I.Q. number. See *Frames of Mind: The Theory of Multiple Intelligences*. (New York: Basic Books, Inc., 1985), p. x.

2   Gardner, p. x.

3   Gardner, p. xiii.

4   According to Gardner, "Intelligences are not equivalent to sensory systems." (Gardner, p. 68). The theory of multiple intelligences

expands and replaces our previous understandings of sensory input, such as the modalities. Such frames of reference were based upon observing *from the outside,* variations in student learning behavior and then, based on such observations, making assumptions about how students learn.

In contrast, current research into how the human brain learns—the focus of this book—is based on high-tech observations *of the inside.* These observations about what the brain is actually doing as it thinks and learns then allow us to determine what educational practices will assist the brain to do its job most naturally and thus most powerfully.

This difference is critical because although you may find considerable overlap in recommended instructional strategies for modalities and multiple intelligences, implementation of each of those instructional strategies must differ in subtle but powerful ways because the whys and whats behind what you are trying to achieve are different. In simple terms, modalities focus on instructional approaches and materials that provide input through different pathways to the brain—kinesthetic, taste, and smell as well as visual and auditory. In contrast, multiple intelligences focus on how the brain processes information once it gets to the brain—how it uses what it learns to solve problems and/or produce products. The difference is between the route through which input arrives versus ways of processing and thinking about what comes in.

5 Gardner, pp. 60-61.

6 Gardner, Chapter 7.

7 Thomas Armstrong, *In Their Own Way* (New York: Tarcher Press, 1987).

8 Gardner, Chapter 5.

9 Gardner, Ibid.

10 Armstrong, p. 20.

11 Gardner, p. 177.

12 Armstrong, p. 18.

13 Gardner, p. 190.

14 For a teacher-friendly tool for strengthening spatial intelligence, the best resource we have found is *Visualizing and Verbalizing for Improved Language Comprehension: A Teacher's Manual* by Nanci Bell (California: Academy of Reading, 1987).

15 Armstrong, p. 21.

16 Gardner, Chapter 9.

17 Armstrong, p. 23.

18 Gardner, Chapter 6.

19 Armstrong, p. 22.

20 Gardner, Chapter 10.

21 Armstrong, p. 24.

22 Gardner, Chapter 10.

23 Armstrong, pp. 23-24.

24 For reasons discussed in footnote 1, we do not use the naturalist intelligence in our curriculum work for the ITI model.

25 E.F. Shores, "Howard Gardner on the Eighth Intelligence: Seeing the Natural World," *Dimensions of Early Childhood,* Summer, 1995, pp. 5-7.

26 Shores, Ibid.

27 Co-author Karen Olsen interviewed a young man who had given up on college—frustration and low grades. After touring with a band for several years, he returned to college. Determined to succeed, and armed with information about Gardner's multiple intelligences, he began to figure out ways to use his considerable musical talent as study aids. For classes

with a lot of details and definitions, he would first choose a letter or word representing each element and then compose a short melody using those letters/words. Before long, he was composing and singing his way to high grades—consistently As and B+s.

28 Frank Smith, *Insult to Intelligence: The Bureaucratic Invasion of Our Classrooms*. (New Hampshire: Heinemann, 1986), p. 62.

29 Susan Kovalik, *Integrated Thematic Instruction: The Model*. (Washington: Susan Kovalik and Associates, 1992), p. 14.

30 Hart, p. 67.

31 Learning Clubs with four to five members are an ideal size. However, if students have never worked collaboratively before, you will likely need to start with groups of two and work up to five. This could take days or months depending on the personal and social skills of your students. The Lifelong Guidelines and LIFESKILLS are a crucial tool for teaching students how to work together. For useful ideas to teach collaboration, see *TRIBES: A New Way of Learning and Being Together* by Jeanne Gibbs.

Chapter 4: Pattern Seeking— Step One of Learning

A New Definition of Learning

Recent brain research is revolutionizing teaching by revealing how we learn. Leslie Hart, a pioneer in synthesizing and applying brain research to education, defines learning as a two-step process.[1]

::: Learning is a Two-Step Process

- Detecting and understanding patterns—a process through which our brain creates meaning

- Developing meaningful mental programs to use what is understood and to store it in long-term memory— the capacity to use what is understood first with assistance and then almost automatically

---

Hart's definition of learning is much more stringent than is what is currently used. In his view, students must not only be able to detect and understand patterns but also to use use them, first with guidance in familiar settings and then in varying situations on one's own until the ability to use the knowledge or skill is readily at hand, almost automatic.

This definition of learning carries us far beyond that assumed by makers of standardized tests. The typical multiple choice and true/false questions can be answered based on a faint ring of familiarity of one answer over another. "Choice B rings a bell. . . ." "Hmm, that statement doesn't sound familiar, so it must be false. . . ." The test takers don't even have to understand the content.

ITI Learning Principles

- Intelligence as a function of experience

- Bodybrain partnership —emotion as gatekeeper to learning and performance—movement and cognition

- Multiple intelligences

- *Learning as a two-step process*
  — *pattern seeking/meaning making*
  — *program building/wiring for long-term memory*

- Impact of personality

And step two of learning—being able to use what is understood and then to apply it until it becomes stored in long-term memory—isn't even considered by test makers.

Does it shock you that we spend billions of dollars on standardized testing based on ever-increasing state and federal standards but don't care whether learning can be be applied or will last beyond the exam? We hope so. We hope it will motivate you and your school to sit down and seriously apply brain research in all your program improvement efforts. A beginning point in your deliberations is to adopt a definition of learning that all can work toward. Hart's two-step definition is the most useful and useable we have found.

This new definition of learning underlies the curriculum process in the ITI model so it merits thorough discussion. We share Hart's explanation.

The Most Notable Characteristic of the Human Brain

The most notable characteristic of the human brain is its phenomenal penchant for seeking and detecting patterns. In his book, *Human Brain and Human Learning*, Leslie A. Hart stipulates that no part of the human brain is naturally logical while it is learning,"[2] i.e., making meaning. (This is distinguished from its ability to use information already learned in a "logical" or sequential way if the situation so requires.) Instead, the brain learns by sifting through massive amounts of input that is arriving simultaneously from all the senses, processing thousands of bits of information per minute. Obviously, such information is processed in a multi-path, multi-modal way with the brain attending to changes in the pattern of incoming data.

The simultaneity of its processing makes patterns obvious while processing along one avenue at a time, however speedily, would produce no "aha", no sense of an overall picture whatsoever. Imagine if the brain processed only one set of information at a time, e.g., first vision, then hearing, then bodily-kinesthetic, etc. Like the three blind men, recognizing an elephant would, at best, be an extremely time consuming and laborious task.

Pattern seeking progresses along a continuum: detection, identification, and understanding.

What Is a Pattern?

Hart defines a pattern as:

"An entity, such as an object, action, procedure, situation, relationship or **system**, which may be recognized by substantial consistency in the **clues** it presents to a brain, which is a pattern-detecting apparatus. The more powerful a brain, the more complex, finer, and subtle patterns it can detect. Except for certain **species wisdom** patterns, each human must learn to recognize the patterns of all matters dealt with, storing the **learning** in the brain. Pattern recognition tells what is being dealt with, permitting selection of the most appropriate program in brain storage to deal with it. The brain tolerates much variation in patterns (we recognize the letter *a* in many shapes, sizes, colors, etc.) because it operates on the basis of **probability**, not on digital or logic principles. Recognition of **patterns** accounts largely for what is called insight, and facilitates transfer of learning to new situations or needs, which may be called creativity."[3]

> # A Truism
> "Let me suggest that there is no concept, no fact in education more directly important than this: The brain is, by nature's design, an amazingly subtle and sensitive pattern-detecting apparatus."
>
> Leslie A. Hart

Examples of patterns include:

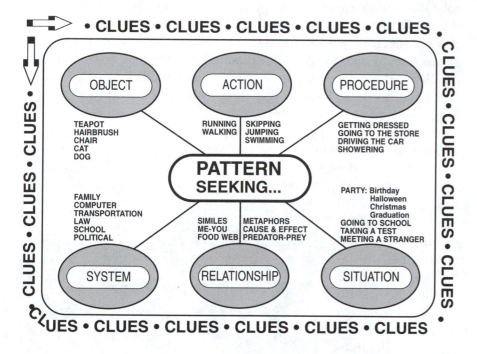

As the brain attempts to make sense out of the chaos which surrounds each of us, it constantly searches for patterns that can impose meaning on the input received. Its ""aha"" arise from detection of a recognizable (from the learner's perspective) pattern or patterns. This pattern detection propensity is seen in the operation of each of the senses. The ear registers every sound wave within its perceivable frequency but it attends only to those that provide a meaningful pattern. Sounds of traffic or workshop chatter are ignored and only the presenter's voice is tuned in or noted as a pattern to attend to. Similarly, the eye recognizes a chair; be it a three-legged milking stool, a church pew, or the more common no-frills chair at the kitchen table; it does so by looking for the pattern or **collection of attributes** necessary for something to be a chair when one wants to sit down.

From the time we are born until we die, the brain takes in these patterns as they present themselves, sorting and categorizing in an attempt to make sense out of our complex world. Learning takes place when the brain sorts out patterns using past experiences to make sense out of new input the brain receives.

According to Hart, the first step in learning is ". . . the extraction, from confusion, of meaningful patterns." In real-life settings, information comes at the learner in a way that can best be described as rich, random, and even chaotic.[4] Over the millenniums, the brain has perfected learning within such an environment.

This pattern-detecting aspect of the brain can be clearly seen in the brain's mastery of one of its biggest accomplishments: learning the mother language. Watch mothers just home from the hospital with their newborns (or even listen to them talk to their child in utero!). Mothers know how to teach language. They do not "dumb down" their language to the infant to single syllable communications. Instead, mothers discuss the everyday happenings of life and share their hopes and dreams for their little one—"When you grow up, you'll go to Stanford and become an astronaut. You'd like that very much, I think. Very, very exciting occupation." "Oops, in thirty minutes your father comes home from work; we'd better get dinner started. Let's see, mother's milk for you and hmmm . . . oh, oh, I forgot to buy flour to fix the main course tonight. I'll have to change the menu." Why do they do this? Because every noun and verb in the English dictionary (and in our

> *"The brain detects, constructs, and elaborates patterns as a basic, built-in, natural function. It does not have to be taught or motivated to do so, any more than the heart needs to be instructed or coaxed to pump blood. In fact, efforts to teach or motivate the pattern detection, however well meant, may have inhibiting and negative effects."*
>
> Leslie A. Hart

curriculum) is a pattern. Each has attributes that distinguish one word from another. The more experience with the attributes, the finer the patterns so that choosing among words such as pensive and melancholy is not a random choice but a decisive match with someone's emotions at the moment.

Such a barrage of sounds coming at the child in real-life fashion would at first seem a hopeless environment in which to master language. But an environment similar to the one previously mentioned — rich, random, even chaotic — gives large amounts of input to the child, and thus provides his or her mind with the opportunity to search for patterns. As educators, we have been carefully and logically taught that such an environment would make the task of learning a language impossible. Consequently, we teach English as a second language logically and carefully, "This is a pen. What is this? This is a _____." Unfortunately, the human brain does not learn well from such logical, tidy, greatly restricted input because it is so antagonistic to the learning methods the brain has perfected over the ages.

In short, the mind is genetically designed to learn from the natural complexities of the natural world. To the extent that schools oversimplify, or make logical, or restrict the world's natural complexity is the extent to which schools inhibit the natural workings of the mind and restrict a student's ability to learn. In contrast, input from the real world engages all of the senses. Logical, sequential curricula are highly brain-antagonistic. Comments Hart, "Perhaps there is no idea about human learning harder to accept for people familiar with classroom schools than this: that the ideal of neat, orderly, closely-planned, sequentially logical teaching will, in practice with young students, guarantee severe learning failure for most."[5] A common mistake of the public schools is stripping down the input to a small amount of content, all analyzed and dissected into small bits, so that the "right" answer seems inescapable. This does not work. Patterns are the building blocks of meaning, the heart of curriculum development.

Stripping a learning situation of its real-life richness also robs the child's mind of the possibility of perceiving pattern and thus making sense of what is in front of him/her. Ironically, we do this consistently with students who need special help. If they are slow, conventional wisdom has dictated that the task be broken into smaller and smaller pieces. We've now achieved pieces that are so small and so "easy" — only one item to focus on — that there is no longer any pattern to perceive. Consequently, Chapter 1 students with their finely-chopped, oversimplified diet say "I don't get it" which confirms to us that they are "slow." However, most Chapter 1 students are adept learners from real–world input. They come to us having learned their mother tongue and a wide range of skills for coping with life. Consider the immigrant child who is the translator for the entire family, the ghetto child with street savvy, the migrant child with flexibility and resourcefulness to figure out each new setting from town to town.

The amazing flexibility of the brain in its pattern seeking is apparent in its ability to recognize

> ## Learning: *Step One*
>
> *Pattern-matching is inherently pleasing because that is what our minds are designed (or programmed) for. . . . Quite apart from anything the teacher does. . . the student, being human, is a pattern-finder and a pattern-maker. Possibly the greatest obstacle to our making use of this not very startling principle is our ingrained notion that education is the acquisition and mastery of new material. What we "teach" and they do not "learn" is the "material."*
>
> —David B. Bronson[6]

the pattern of the letter *a*; we recognize it amid an amazing range of fonts, sizes, shapes, positions. This speed and flexibility can occur because the brain naturally works on a probabilistic basis. The brain does not add up, for example, all the parts of a cat until all parts are perceived and accounted for: four legs, a tail, fur, meows, purrs, etc.

Rather, the mind "jumps to the conclusion" that the pattern "cat" applies when only one or a few characteristics have been noted. While this jumping to conclusions sometimes gets us in trouble, it is crucial to rapid completion of myriad actions minute by minute. The rapid reader, for example, does not see every letter before deciding what the word is. Context clues or the mere outline of the word are used, in probabilistic fashion, to jump to conclusions.

In the example of our infant learning its mother tongue, language pours around the child for hours and hours a day. The more input, the more readily the child learns. The first patterns perceived are those that are most meaningful—the child's name and then the name of mom and dad. Patterns are at first quite gross, i.e., "Dadda" means any man in trousers. As the snickers erupt, the child's mind is alerted to a problem with the pattern and, over time, with continued rich input and immediate feedback, the patterns become more and more refined until, finally, the educated adult ends up with a vocabulary of 10,000-plus words with subtle shades of meaning and the ability to use them with considerable precision.

The entire structure of language is based on pattern. Plurals mostly end in *s* except for mice, moose, fish, etc. Past tense ends with *ed*. Words ending in *ing* are a real thrill for most children. When they first grasp the *ing* pattern, everything is jumping, leaping, hitting, running, etc., for several days until another pattern of language gets discovered. Every noun and verb in our language reflects a pattern.

Pattern-seeking is the brain's way of striving to extract meaning from the thousands of bits of input pouring into the brain each minute through the 19 senses. And, very importantly, what is one learner's pattern is another learner's hodgepodge. This is to say, we cannot predict what any one particular child will perceive as a pattern because so much depends upon prior knowledge, the existing neural networking of the brain used to process the input, and the context in which the learning takes place.

However, if the input is rich and varied, all learners can arrive at an understanding of the pattern to be learned.

Origins of the First Fundamental*

Over 80 years ago, for example, Aldous Huxley remarked:

What emerges most strikingly from recent scientific developments is that perception is not a passive reception of material from the outside world; it is an active process of selection and imposing of patterns.[7]

The findings Huxley referred to were well known in fields more scientifically oriented than education then and that are thoroughly established now. Brain researchers of the 1990s accept this as a given.[8] We do not have to look far for confirmation—our own daily experience tells us most convincingly that the brain has this ability and has it to an astounding degree.

Examples from Personal Experience

Imagine that you are attending a sporting event. People by the thousands stream by as you find your seats. The merest glance tells you they are all strangers. But now you see two figures that immediately seem familiar and in a moment you have identified them as former neighbors, Francine and Peter. Somehow, your brain has picked them out of this vast crowd; somehow it has separated them from all the other people you know so that you can identify them and greet them warmly by name. There is no question that our human brain can do this—usually effortlessly. (If we simply look at what we all can do, we begin to glimpse the enormous powers of the brain.)

The feat is even more impressive because you haven't seen these friends for three years, didn't expect to run into them here. Both are wearing clothes you have never seen them in. Francine has a new hair style, Peter wears sunglasses that partly hide his features.

---

* From here through page 4.10 are excerpts from *Human Brain and Human Learning* by Leslie A. Hart. (Covington, Washington: Books for Educators, 1999). Used by written permission of the publisher.

Yet, you recognized them as familiar while they were still 50 feet away.

Clearly, the recognition does not stem from any logical process. You did not check Francine's height in inches or Peter's weight in kilos. You put no measure to their middle finger bones, Bertillon fashion,[9] nor did you use a color-comparison guide to determine the shade of skin and hair. While Peter has a distinctive walking movement and Francine an animated manner, trying to measure or describe these exactly would be an impossible task. Let us grasp firmly the clear fact that your brain does not work that way but that it did quickly and accurately accomplish recognition and identification by some other means.

Nor was this an isolated, unusual phenomenon. If I were to display a teakettle, a paint brush, a handsaw, a necklace, a bunch of carrots, a pencil sharpener, a violin, a telephone, a sweater, a microscope, a toothbrush, a slice of Swiss cheese . . . you would recognize and name each in the same effortless way. You were plainly not born knowing these objects, so this recognition has been learned at some time between birth and the present.

We are so used to looking at something and immediately knowing what it is that we come to think of the process as automatic. Comparisons of eye and camera may also mislead us. A camera can't recognize anything; our brain can, using not only vision but also hearing, smell, touch, and other aspects of our senses.

When we are exposed to something quite unfamiliar, we simply do not see it in any meaningful way. To look inside some complex machine, for example, we may see only a confusion of forms. In a museum, observing some fossilized remains of various ancient animals, we may see only vague shapes, in contrast to what the curator sees. I often dramatize this in workshops by showing a newspaper in Arabic or Chinese. The participants see only squiggles that a moment later they are hopelessly unable to reproduce—although a person knowing the language would see headlines and news, information at a glance.

If we place a teakettle before a month-old infant, the baby will regard it with momentary interest but plainly have no notion of what it is. As adults we can see a vessel, a handle, and a spout; the baby can see none of this arrangement, only edges, shapes, and surfaces.

Even if the teakettle were made of unfamiliar materials or shaped like an elephant, we would recognize it as a teakettle. Any familiar item, from a paint brush to a necklace, would be identifiable. Moderate differences do not bother us a bit.

Examples from Classroom Life

Consider, for instance, the 20 different forms of the letter *a* that appear below. Despite the range of shapes they cover, we have no difficulty seeing any one as *a*. We could, of course, carry

A A A A A a a A a a a

A a A AAA a A A A

this recognition much further, to letters of many larger sizes, in different colors, formed of lights or dots, put into three-dimensional materials, tilted, laid on the floor, or seen on the side of a moving vehicle. Even holding just to typefaces available for printing, there are literally thousands of alphabets; handwritten, drawn, or printed forms add thousands more. There is no letter *a*, only a pattern we conventionally call *a*.

In the same sense, teakettle, paintbrush, carrots, violin, and the rest are patterns. Our knowledge of the pattern is what enables us to say what object is what. But we are by no means limited to hard, visual patterns. We can detect and learn patterns far more subtle or complex. In time, adults normally become quite familiar with such patterns as cat, city park, affection, boss, fraction, racial bigotry, jealousy, or adventurousness.

Just how the brain detects and recognizes patterns cannot be easily or quickly explained. Yet, it is an astoundingly powerful, subtle, living computer with billions of neurons at its command. We do know in a general way that *the brain detects characteristics or features and also relationships among these features.*

The lower-case letter *a*, for example, may consist of a hook facing left which may take a variety of forms,

connected to a more or less round enclosure form.

The relationship between these shapes has a key role. If the hook were 20 centimeters tall and the enclosure only a millimeter high, one might have much difficulty seeing it as an *a*. On the other hand, there is a different pattern for small *a* that lacks the

hook altogether that we can readily learn to accept as an alternate. It is illogical to have two forms but, as we have seen, logic is the least of the human brain's concerns.

Key Factors in Pattern Seeking

When looking at the brain as a seeker of patterns, consider five key factors: Use of clues and cues, use of multiple sensory input and prior experience, sensitivity to negative clues, categorizing down through patterns within patterns, and using probability.

Use of Clues and Cues

Our brain's ability to detect and identify patterns is impressive for its flexibility. We can be certain about our identification of something without needing to perceive most or even many of its features and relationships. With experience, in fact, we normally become extremely expert in using *clues* (sometimes the term *cues* is used in the same sense) to make very rapid judgments. We would not be able to read at all if we had to study all the features of letters. The capable reader goes much further and uses clues for whole words and even phrases.[10]

Use of Multiple Sensory Input and Prior Experience

In practice our pattern-detecting ability depends on clues from vision, hearing, touch, or other senses, on behavior and relationships, and/or on the situation. In short, *the ability to detect and recognize patterns depends heavily on our experience, on what we bring to the act of pattern detection and recognition.* The more that experience tells us what we are likely to be looking at, or dealing with, the less detailed, feature-type information we need to jump to a probably correct conclusion.

Sensitivity to Negative Clues

One reason we can rely on little information is the sensitivity of the brain to *negative* clues. When clues do not fit together rapidly within a pattern, or when one or more are jarringly strange or contradictory, our pattern-detecting apparatus quickly senses something wrong. Suppose that I am going to the house of people I have visited a couple of times before, on a dark suburban street where house numbers are hard to find. As I walk toward what seems to be the house, I come to a flagstone walk. It "doesn't feel right," prompting me to retreat and try the house next door. Or, perhaps another day I identify an all-black bird as a Brewer's blackbird. When I see a flash of color on the wing, I must revise my identification to "red-winged blackbird."

Patterns Within Patterns: Categorizing Down

In the example of recognizing friends Francine and Peter, only a yes/no kind of decision was involved—they were or were not those individuals. But more common is the detection and recognition of patterns *within* patterns, which leads to finer and finer discriminations, a process called *categorizing down*, a most important aspect of learning. For example, we can detect the pattern "animal," then categorize it down to "dog," and then to "Afghan hound." Or, observing a number of people at a gathering, we may categorize further by noting that the people are festively dressed, a "party," and then on seeing a cake with candles, conclude it's a "birthday party."

But we must note that a person from a country where birthday cakes are not a custom would not be prepared to interpret that clue the way we so easily do. Again, what the observer brings to the recognition act—in terms of prior relevant experience and previously acquired knowledge—plays a critical part. (It is startling to observe that in conventional teaching this absolutely fundamental principle is largely ignored.)

In small children, the process of enlarging pattern detection and extending and refining categorizing-down chains is often clearly observable. A girl just starting to talk may say "Daddy!" while pointing to any man who comes into sight—we gather she is using *daddy* in the sense of *man*. A little later, guided by such feedback as "No, that is not Daddy—Daddy is at his office," the child may point to any man who comes into the home, whether young cousin or elderly grandfather, as *daddy*. With further feedback, categories gradually get straightened out and *daddy* is used to mean only one

person. It may take much longer for the child to become clear on the fact that her friend also has a daddy (and some years to grasp the relationship). It may take still more time to be able to categorize surely from people to males, to relatives and friends, neighbors, policeman, mailman, Mr. Jackson (who lives next door), as well as boys, girls, and many other subtle relationships.[11]

It seems apparent that the brain must have some kind of organizational process that enables humans to rapidly categorize down patterns as they are detected, so that they can be identified quickly.

Matching. The principle of *matching* is well understood. In simplest terms, one receives an input from outside the brain—for example, visual input that comes from a door. Inside the brain, stored, is a pattern, *door*.[12] If the current input and the stored pattern pretty well match, recognition occurs. Looking in the night sky, one may see any one of several patterns that match up with stored patterns for *moon*. Hearing some sound waves that compose a certain pattern, we recognize it as the word *scarecrow*, since it fairly well fits our stored pattern for scarecrow. The matches do not have to be precise—another principle, *probability*, applies. This permits us to recognize "scarecrow" whether spoken by a child in a thin, high voice or by a man or woman in other pitches, and despite various pronunciations. *The brain searches for a probable match.* (If this were not so, we would all have a terrible time trying to read English, with its frequently weird spellings!)

Parallel Processing. But to operate effectively, the brain cannot afford to search sequentially through tens of thousands of stored patterns to find the match. It seems likely that patterns are grouped in categories within hierarchies, or layers, much as mail is addressed (reading from the bottom up and right to left):

The country (USA).

The state (Connecticut).

The city or town (Bethel).

The street (Maple Avenue).

The house number (628).

The person in that house (Mr. or Mrs.)

This method, we know, quite efficiently makes a match between the letter and one out of more than 250 million inhabitants. If the address (the input) is a little wrong, the letter may still be delivered but if the error is large, no match can be made, no delivery can occur.

Experimental studies suggest that the brain does not usually need as many as six steps to categorize down. (That investigation is beyond the scope of this book.) Nor is the brain limited to one linear chain of categorizing down (such as that illustrated above in addressing a letter). It can employ many such chains simultaneously, as we have noted. This "parallel processing" enormously speeds recognition. It's like having 1,000 clerks sorting the mail rather than just one.

Using Probability . . . Jumping to Conclusions

A variety of studies indicate that the brain naturally works on a *probabilistic* basis. The brain skillfully jumps to conclusions! It isn't an adding machine that must reach a correct total. For example, seeing a creature that has four legs, a tail, fur, and barks at a friend's home, we jump to the conclusion that the pattern "dog" applies. Why not "cat"? Because we pick up negative clues: Cats don't bark and ordinarily don't come aggressively to the door when a stranger enters. Why isn't it a monkey? Because the relationship of limbs is different. The situation also gives clues; we expect to find a dog in a home. If we visited a zoo, however, and found this same animal exhibited in a cage, we would assume it was not a dog but some similar creature. Our experience tells us that dogs are not displayed this way.

The Brain—A Master at Extracting Meaning from Confusion

This is the process of learning that Frank Smith and others aptly call "making sense of the world."[13] The ability that even infants have to gradually sort out an extremely complex, changing world is nothing short of astounding. And it's natural. But even more surprising still is that we learn *from input presented in a completely random, fortuitous fashion*—unplanned, accidental, unorder-ed, uncontrolled, the polar opposite of didactic classroom teaching.

Consider, for example, the sorting-out problem a child has to grasp for such patterns as *dessert, pie, and cake.* Since a great variety of dishes may constitute dessert, the child must extract the idea that meals have a sequence (program) and dessert is the last course. He or she must also learn that *dessert* does *not* mean a particular dish, or even a tight group or class of dishes. *Pie* presents few problems to an adult with years of experience to draw on but, to a toddler, an open pumpkin pie, a crusted blueberry pie, and a lemon pie heaped with meringue topping present little in common. Or does pie mean *round*, the most obvious feature? Unfortunately many desserts are round, particularly cakes—which vary from pie-like cheesecake, to coffee cake, to layered birthday cake elaborately iced and decorated.

While adults and older siblings may provide gentle, casual, and almost incidental corrective feedback when the child calls a pie a cake or doesn't regard a fruit dish as dessert and cries in frustration, it would be most unusual for anything resembling teaching or instruction to deal with dessert, pie, and cake as subjects. Yet in a few years, from this confused, random exposure and experience, the child has extracted the patterns, gradually coming to see which features and relationships have significance in which settings, and which can be ignored. Frequently, however, the child extracts a pattern that sooner or later has to be revised in the light of new information. For example, everything if let go falls—until someone presents a gas-filled balloon. Children often find the need to revise something disturbing. The world keeps proving more complicated, with more exceptions, than they had previously thought. Adults have a similar problem; in time, they may become less flexible, cling to old ideas, refuse to revise, and even try to avoid the input that forces the contradiction. "Nonsense . . . that's crazy . . . I won't listen . . . don't bother me!"

Even more amazing is the obvious ability of preschool children to extract rules about language from the quite random speech they hear about them and engage in. We hear such expressions as *sheeps* and *deers,* plurals plainly not picked up from adults or older children. The added *s* makes unmistakably clear that the small child has extracted a general rule for plurals—end with the *s* sound—and is applying it even to what will later be learned as special exceptions. In the same way, most youngsters will use such constructions as "Tommy hitted me," or "I falled down," showing that they have extracted the pattern of past tense and the use of the *ed* sound, again even where there are common exceptions. Yet it would be absurd to expect a three- or four-year-old to explain *plural or past tense.*[14]

These familiar experiences and others like them are so prevalent that we cannot reasonably doubt that all of us, at whatever age, *do extract patterns from the quite random, confused mass of input we are exposed to in the course of normal living. Nor can it be easily denied that the great bulk of practical knowledge we have and use to get along in the world is acquired in this way.*

A Word About Rote Memory. The great bulk of general learning occurs through extracting meaningful patterns from confusion. The only other important method is via rote memory. But while "pure" rote learning—straight memorization—appears to suffice, as in the case of learning the alphabet in sequence, even rote learning is greatly helped by detecting the patterns involved where patterns clearly exist, as in the multiplication tables. Or consider the marching band,

very much a rote activity. If the patterns in the music and in the maneuvers are understood, learning can be far faster and surer.

In Summary

In embracing a new definition of learning, it is important that we recognize a new view of the brain:

- The brain is by nature a magnificent pattern-detecting apparatus, even in the early years.

- Pattern detection and identification involve both features and relationships, processes that are greatly speeded up by the use of clues and a categorizing down procedure. (i.e., round ears or barks . . . not a house cat).

- Negative clues play an essential role.

- The brain uses clues in a probabilistic fashion, not by digital "adding up" of clues.

- Pattern recognition depends heavily on the experience one *brings* to a situation.

- Children must often revise the patterns they have extracted, to accommodate new experience.

Translating Brain Research into Action Using the Nine Bodybrain-Compatible Elements

Pattern seeking is the bodybrain partnership's way of making meaning of our world. The early phase of this process is detecting the existence of a pattern and then, through more experience with the concept or skill, coming to understand that pattern by exploring it and its uses to make sure that we understand it correctly and fully. The nine bodybrain-compatible elements will help you help your students to perceive and understand patterns in the curriculum and in their lives.

Although memorization does have a role in learning, it should have a minor one. As Frank Smith and Leslie Hart both affirm, *understanding takes care of learning.* **Things that are understood and used are readily retained in long-term memory.** Memorization is generally used as a teaching/learning tool only when there is no discernible meaning to the learner such as the order of the alphabet or when fast, automatic repetition is needed as with the multiplication tables.

Bodybrain-Compatible Elements

- Meaningful Content
- Movement
- Enriched Environment
- Adequate Time
- Immediate Feedback
- Mastery
- Absence of Threat/ Nurturing Reflective Thinking
- Choices
- Collaboration

The most critical job for a teacher is making learning meaningful for students. That being the case, teachers must go about curriculum development and choosing instructional strategies with a primary goal in mind: enhancing students' capacity to perceive and understand patterns.

The bodybrain-compatible elements in this chapter are discussed in the following order: meaningful content, movement, enriched environment, adequate time, immediate feedback, mastery, absence of threat/nurturing reflective thinking, choices, and collaboration.

Meaningful Content

Meaningfulness, like beauty, is in the eye of the beholder. But there are several things that teachers can do to increase the likelihood that students will perceive something as meaningful.

State Key Points As Concepts, Not Factoids

First, state what is to be learned as concepts (or significant knowledge directly linked to and necessary to support the concepts) rather than as factoids. Factoids have few attributes that give a sense of pattern. For example, "In 1492, Columbus sailed the ocean blue." Although catchy and cute, there is little for the brain to work on in terms of meaningfulness. This is a statement that only rote learning could lock into long-term memory.[15]

On the other hand, a concept is a rich collection of attributes that can provide a sense of pattern. For example: "Interactions among animals and plants to meet the need for food within a habitat are called a 'food chain' or 'food web'."

Rote memory is not needed here. In this conceptual statement, virtually every noun and verb is a pattern, each of which, with the possible exception of "habitat," is a pattern already familiar to students. Prior experience that can be pulled forward to help the students learn new content is a powerful ally. Furthermore, this concept allows students to place the information in a context they care about, e.g, their family and/or classroom pet(s), their favorite zoo animal, a local endangered animal, and so forth. (For a discussion of key points, see Chapter 14.)

Place Inquiries in Real-World Contexts

Second, for concepts or skills with which students have little or no prior experience, place the concept or skill to be learned in a real-world context. Develop inquiries that ask students to use the concept or skill in real-life situations. This heightens the sense of usefulness, an important trigger for the brain in transferring information to long-term memory.

For example: "A system is a collection of things and processes (and often people) that interact to perform some function. To study a system, one must define its boundaries." In this conceptual key point, every noun and verb is a pattern with which students are familiar. But, when put together in the above sentence, students may initially have no idea what is meant. However, when the concept is illustrated using first a bicycle and then one's school (transportation system, food system, classroom system and so on), the pattern becomes memorably clear and readily transferrable.

Similarly, few high school sophomores are innately interested in geometry but there are many who would be interested to learn how it applies to taking the best angle to run down and tackle a ball carrier, reading a map, driving a car, plotting the correct angle for a pool shot, and so forth.

Be Realistic

Third, when under the pressure of ever higher expectations, be realistic. Don't assume that because a concept is assigned to

your grade level, it can be made understandable to students at your grade level. Some patterns require simultaneous attention to numerous variables before the intended pattern can emerge. Many such ideas must be considered age-inappropriate.[16] For example, the chemical processes of photosynthesis for sixth graders, tectonic plate movement as a cause of earthquakes for third graders. For more information about age-appropriateness, see *Thinking and Learning: Matching: Matching Developmental Stages with Curriculum and Instruction* by Lawrence F. Lowery.

Input Is Essential for Pattern Development

In Hart's view of learning, *input* is a key factor. "Input is critically important in any kind of learning situation, whoever the learner and whatever is to be learned. The process of learning is the extraction, from confusion, of meaningful patterns. Input is *the raw material* of that confusion, what is perceived through the senses by the individual that bears on that particular pattern in any way."[17]

By way of example, Hart recounts how a suburban teenager might go about learning the concept of *city*:[18]

"Think of a 13-year-old suburban male who as yet has no clear concept of what is meant by city, although his teachers, his texts, and other sources have often presented that term. It easily can seem incredible to adults that children or adults less experienced in some specific area do not grasp a pattern that is already so familiar to those who already understand it. Once we have done the pattern extraction—a gradual process—and melded the concept into our collection of patterns, it seems so obvious that we have trouble putting ourselves into the brain of someone who has not acquired that pattern!

But how could this 13-year-old come to understand the main connotations of city? If he is told in school that a city is a place where many people live close together, he may fail to see why his suburb (or at least those denser parts of it) is not a city. If he has contact with commuters, he may assume that city means Boston or St. Louis or Los Angeles, or whatever city his community is near. If he visits that city occasionally, he may be impressed by traffic, noise, many stores, busy sidewalks, bridges, tall buildings, apartments, or development houses—yet a visit to another city may present quite different features, such as zoo, museum, or historic places. A trip to a downtown part of a nearby suburb may impress him as being to a city, since he experiences crowded sidewalks, many stores, movie houses, considerable dirt, and apparent crowding—yet if he refers to this place, technically a village, as city he may be corrected or receive some negative feedback, such as being tolerantly laughed at.

It seems simple enough to tell him what city means. But it isn't simple, when we get down to trying it. A dictionary may say something like "a closely settled place of significant size," or "a chartered, incorporated municipality," but such definitions simply introduce new questions. With little effort, the boy can learn by rote a "right answer" to give in school but that hardly amounts to pattern extraction. It may function more as a cover-up answer to conceal uncertainty or lack of insight. The distress of teachers who by accident discover that students able to give "correct" answers actually don't understand the topic at all has long been familiar. Most adults, too, experience chastening moments when by some circumstance they discover that conventional right answers are like thin ice over a deep lake of ignorance or misconception. From personal and professional experience, educators have long been aware that "telling" methods can prove extremely ineffective in instruction.[19] Despite much evidence to the contrary, they are heavily used in conventional teaching."

The bottom line here according to Hart is that "words fail to convey much meaning except as the hearer already has experience and extracted patterns that give meaning to the words. Consider two statements. A stock broker: "If you sell a security to establish a loss, you just wait 30 days to buy it back or it will be viewed as a wash sale but the waiting period doesn't apply to gains." Or, a musician, "Since the B-flat clarinet is a transposing instrument, the note you play from the written music will actually sound a fulltone lower." These are perfectly understandable statements if we bring prior experience to bear.

We must accept that words convey only limited meaning and that if our students lack relevant prior experience, we must rely on input from the real setting. Hearing speech intelligibly demands bringing information to the situation.[20] Even in social conversation, a comment or question off the subject usually produces a "Huh?" response until the new topic is settled on.

As Hart says, "While input via telling or lecture may be the most common and usually the easiest to provide in the classroom, it can prove ludicrously ineffective, even in supposedly simple situations."[21] The best environment for detecting and understanding patterns is to see them in their real-world context.

The power of real-world examples can't be overestimated. For example, the idea of 3/4 becomes clear only when it is recognized and used in multiple contexts such as the following:

Mathematical Patterns

3/4 inches	.75
75%	3/4 cup
750ml	9 inches
75/100	750,000
three-fourths	

USING *MEANINGFUL CONTENT* TO ENHANCE PATTERN SEEKING

Curriculum Development

- Because meaningfulness is in the eyes of the beholder, expect that your students' perceptions of what is meaningful will likely differ from yours. Thus, don't expect to start where you want students to end up. In other words, if a concept is substantive, don't begin teaching it in the form you want them to remember it, e.g., E=mc2. If you do, you will force students into memorization as a coping strategy rather than allowing them to construct their own understandings. Therefore, make sure that your curriculum has starting points that can reasonably bridge students' prior experience/ knowledge to current sensory input to understanding the concept or skill. For example, include in the statement of the key point examples of settings or uses that students can recognize from their daily experiences. Include common objects as examples such as a multi-speed bicycle to evoke students' prior knowledge about chains (only as strong as its weakest link, potential to connect to multiple gears large and small) as a precursor to learning about the food chain.

- Teach students to become aware of how they know what they know. Help them become conscious of how their brain seeks patterns in an attempt to create meaning. Also help them avoid "jumping to conclusions" based on a couple of clues that may be true but not key by become sensitive to negative clues. Create activities such as playing a modified version of the old TV game show, "I Can Name That Tune in . . . Notes." Instead of notes, use the attributes of a concept or skill.

USING *MEANINGFUL CONTENT* TO ENHANCE PATTERN SEEKING

Instructional Strategies

- Ensure massive amounts of sensory input through all 19 senses. Schedule frequent *being there* field studies—early in students' study of the concepts/skills described in the key points, at the end, and in between.

- Make the classroom a complete immersion experience for the *being there* location your curriculum is based on.

- Invite guest speakers that will present their experiences using *hands on of the real thing*. Insist that students include examples of their concepts/skills from their experiences.

- Deliberately use collaboration as a way of increasing input and use of concepts and skills.

- Have at least 100 resources related to the current topic of study available in the room—real things, models, diagrams, blueprints, sketches, and art objects, as well as books, magazines, multimedia, and the Internet.

- Use analytical tools that help students key in on important attributes of a concept or skill. For example, T-charts that compare what something is and what it is not, Venn-circles that compare similarities and differences between two items, and organizers that help students identify prior related experience (KWL charts that identify what we now think we know, want to know, and, afterwards, what we learned). For young children, dot-to-dot puzzles are useful to help them reveal visual attributes of things such as a frog or butterfly. (For more information on these organizers, see Chapter 17, especially page 17.5.)

 # Movement

Seeing firsthand how concepts and skills are used in real-world settings provides the richest possible environment for learning, especially when learning something new. Why? Because things in use have movement and motion to them. Who, what, why, and how are all attention-getting patterns. When the who becomes "I," patterns become richer, more engaging.

Furthermore, as discussed in Chapter 2, movement activates different areas of the brain and body, thus increasing the likelihood of retrieval later on. Many believe that some forms of memory, especially those associated with high emotional states, are stored in the body; others that movements of the body awaken memories that were being used when the memory was wired into long-term memory. In either case, the lesson for classroom teachers is that we *must* make the process of learning about concepts and skills mirror the ways those concepts and skills are used in real-world settings.

USING *MOVEMENT* TO ENHANCE PATTERN SEEKING

Curriculum Development

- Before you begin to write key points and inquiries, go experience how the concepts and skills are *used* in the real world. Practice them and the movements inherent in them until you have mastered them. Then, look around for other settings these same skills are used in, particularly settings/locations that students experience, e.g., a mall, home, school, neighborhood. Your curriculum should require the *use* of concepts and skills.

USING *MOVEMENT* TO ENHANCE PATTERN SEEKING

Curriculum Development (continued)

- Make your curriculum an experience in doing, not just reading about or hearing about.
  - Include in the statement of the key point examples of settings or uses that students can recognize from their daily experiences.
  - State your key points conceptually; eliminate factoids.
  - Develop inquiries that require application of concepts and skills to students' prior experiences and to other real-life situations so that students can readily understand what the concept/ skill is, why it's important, and how and when to use it.
- Develop, and involve students in developing, movements to mimic or act out the key attributes of the patterns within the concept or skill you are teaching. Include these in your direct instruction and in inquiries.
- When writing inquiries, first develop those that address bodily-kinesthetic intelligence and Bloom's taxonomy levels of application and analysis.
- When writing inquiries for linguistic intelligence, add movement through music, dance, rhythm (such as rap), and bodily-kinesthetic mnemonics.
- When developing immersion experiences, include role playing of the actions of people working and conducting commerce at your *being there* locations. Go for richness; focus on the most important attributes of the patterns of the concepts/skills in the key point.

USING *MOVEMENT* TO ENHANCE PATTERN SEEKING

Instructional Strategies

- In direct instruction, always address the questions of a journalist—who, what, when, where, how, and why in the real world—for the concept or skill you are teaching. Emphasize the how and why—the movement of how used and why.

- When selecting inquiries to follow up on direct instruction, lead with bodily-kinesthetic inquiries and those spatial and musical inquiries that call for movement. As with young children, the first step in understanding and using what we learn is often through mimicking.

- Because the movement centers of the brain are also responsible for sequencing thought, encourage students to create and use movements that mimic the sequence, steps, or actions of the concept/skill when in use. For example, reenactments of events or processes (a famous historical event such as the Boston Tea Party or the blood/oxygen flow through heart and lungs), miming (the travails of the Westward Movement), bodily movements that mimic shapes or actions (letters of the alphabet or a butterfly emerging from its cocoon), and hand jives (to represent the steps in computing a long division problem).

Enriched Environment

The pattern-seeking penchant of the brain is in diametric opposition to the assumptions underlying our traditional curriculum—its structure and content. Several erroneous assumptions are:

- Small, isolated pieces automatically add up to large pictures of real life

- The small, isolated pieces provide focus for the brain, making them easier to learn, especially for slow or limited ability students

- Study of "subjects" explains the world to students

> ## *Sensory Input*
>
> *In reality, nothing could be more unfair than giving two very different brains—and no two brains are alike—the same input and expecting the outcome to be the same. It's not only unfair, it's cruel.*

When these small pieces are presented through the sparse sensory input of lecture and textbooks/worksheets, pattern-seeking is paralyzed for lack of input and learning grinds to a halt.

Consequently, conceptual curriculum in an enriched environment is not a luxury, it is a necessity. Pattern seeking is only possible when there is sufficient sensory input for the learner's brain to sift for patterns. And, very importantly, prior experience, existing mental wiring, and temperament guarantee that what one student sees as a pattern will remain invisible or a tangle of confusion to another. Thus, "Different Strokes for Different Folks" is more than that title of a TV sitcom. In the realm of the brain, it is utter truth. An enriched environment—*being there experiences, immersion, and hands on of the real thing*—provides something for everyone, ensuring that every student can succeed in understanding the concept or skill at hand. **When input for a concept or skill is rich and varied, all learners can arrive at an understanding of the pattern to be learned.**

USING *ENRICHED ENVIRONMENT* TO ENHANCE PATTERN SEEKING

Curriculum Development

- Knowing there is a fine line between an enriched environment and a cluttered environment, make sure you have finished writing your key points and inquiries before you begin to gather resources to create an enriched environment. Once you know exactly what you want your students to understand and how you will have them use what they understand, be selective. Remove input about other topics from the room. Then, for each key point and inquiry, plan your input in descending order: first being there, then immersion, then hands on of the real thing, and so on. If possible, eliminate hands on of representational items in favor of the above three kinds of input. Include secondhand and symbolic input last; plan to use them during the latter stages of Step One of Learning—Pattern-Seeking.

USING *ENRICHED ENVIRONMENT* TO ENHANCE PATTERN SEEKING

Instructional Strategies

- Select materials that provide contrasting points of view so that the attributes of issues become clear through their comparison with each other, such as that of the polluter and of the family whose child developed cancer, land use through the eyes of the cattleman and the farmer.

- Include resource people. Work with them in advance so they understand what students have done prior to their coming and what new input would be most valuable.

- Use student-generated role playing and skits as formats for students to demonstrate the attributes of a concept/skill they are learning to use. Follow up these presentations with a discussion of what attributes of the concept/skill were demonstrated. Add any new ones to KWL chart and correct any misconceptions.

Adequate Time

Just as every brain is different, so is each student's approach to detecting patterns and making meaning. So, too, is the amount of time needed.

Factors that directly affect the amount of time students need to detect patterns and construct their own meaning are:

- Prior experience
- Whether the concept/skill is studied in its real-life context
- The kind and amount of input involves an intelligence of strength (see discussion of the multiple intelligences in Chapter 3)
- The wiring of the learner's brain

Regardless of why a student may need more time, the critical point is that we must provide it. To close the grade book on a student because he/she didn't master something in the allotted time is discrimination of the worst kind. The implicit message is that if you aren't like everyone else, you will be cut off and abandoned. In such an environment the focus is not on mastery but on the lock-step demands of bureaucracy.

In the ITI classroom, the "grade book" is held open until the end of the year. Demonstration of mastery the last day of school is as good as mastery the first day the key point is studied.

But we're getting ahead of ourselves here. Step One of Learning is pattern-seeking, constructing meaning, *understanding* the concept or skill described in the key point.

USING *ADEQUATE TIME* TO ENHANCE PATTERN SEEKING

Curriculum Development

- Review the curriculum you have planned for your monthly components and weekly topics. Do you have more than students can come to understand and learn to apply, not just get 80% on a pop quiz? If so, start cutting back. Be realistic! Resist the political pressures to "cover" what looks good (for more information about monthly components and weekly topics, see Chapter 17).

- To help you cut back, use the principle of "selective abandonment." Put at the end of your curriculum those things you believe are least important for students to understand and be able to apply. Chief among these are factoids that won't affect their lives five or ten years from now. Then, if you run out of time—and who doesn't!—you will have given students the gift of what will most serve them later in life.

- Create time by stating your curriculum as conceptually as possible and using examples of how that concept is used in contexts that students experience in their daily life. For example, science is everywhere around us and is directly experienceable; the fundamental concepts in social studies have their parallel wherever people congregate. (However, concepts in social studies are not as hands on as science; also, for young children, because they've grown up with something doesn't mean it's any easier to see than water is for a fish.)

USING *ADEQUATE TIME* TO ENHANCE PATTERN SEEKING

Instructional Strategies

- Just as there is a silent period before vocalization when learning another language, so there is a quiet period when students are learning a new concept or skill. Don't rush through such silences or periods of delayed responses. Allow students time intrapersonally to observe and sift through what they already know and how this new concept/skill relates to what they already understand and can do (the patterns and the interrelationships among the patterns); allow them time to explore the patterns involved and to arrive at their own understandings—about how things work, what makes things tick, why they might be important to them. Allow time for personal exploration through sketching or diagramming/graphing/mindmapping the patterns they see and how they interrelate with other patterns. Allow interpersonal time to try out what they understand, to correct and/or add to what they understand with nonjudgmental, supportive peers. Only then ask for personal performances that will be "graded" or critiqued by an audience. New understandings are not layered into the brain as separate things; they are integrated into prior understandings or patterns.

- Take time to plan for and effectively teach a concept or skill the first time. Effective first teaching is a huge time saver but you must invest time up front.

USING *ADEQUATE TIME* TO ENHANCE PATTERN SEEKING

Instructional Strategies (continued)

- Deep understanding comes from identifying attributes of things and their uses and coming to understanding interrelationships among them. Such mental work requires rewiring and new wiring—physiological tasks of the brain that require time and processing of new input. This requires time.

- Revisit the *being there* location at least once or twice between the initial and culminating visits. Assign inquiries to be completed, including adding to their KWL chart and answering questions such as "How to you know that _____?" and "Where else would you find this occurring and why?"

Immediate Feedback

Leslie Hart points out that the most difficult thing for a brain to do is unlearn something. We're all familiar with this one. Is it *maintanence* or *maintainence* or *maintenance?* And every time we have to spell the word, all three choices pop up with competing intensity? Why? Because each time they simultaneously come to mind as options, the wiring of the three is equally reinforced. Or, how about the < and > signs. Is the number off the pointed end the smaller? Or does it depend on the order in which you say them? Or, hang, it, I don't know! And you have trouble learning it because the confusion is wired in just as strongly as the right answer each time you try to recall which of the options is the correct one.

The number one purpose of immediate feedback is to prevent this kind of mental sputtering. Give feedback to students before they begin to practice something incorrectly or incompletely. Immediate feedback helps ensure that students come to a full and accurate understanding of a skill or concept—that they discover the critical attributes and understand how they fit together. This is especially important when students begin to integrate new experiences with prior learnings. For example, the videotape *A Private Universe*[22] provides an astounding example of how childhood experiences with heat (the closer you get, the hotter it becomes) override lecture and textbook. As the interviews with graduating Harvard students illustrate, even course work in advanced planetary motion can fail to dispel the assumption put together in childhood—that summers are hot because the earth gets closer to the sun.

The recent emphasis on effective first teaching and ensuring that students learn something correctly and thoroughly the first time is right on track.

USING *IMMEDIATE FEEDBACK* TO ENHANCE PATTERN SEEKING

Curriculum Development Guidelines

- Build checking for accuracy of understanding and performance—by learning club, partners, and self—into inquiries.

- Develop inquiries that require students to develop and use their own internal voice as they go through the two steps in learning—asking questions, checking their understanding, insisting upon looking for ways a concept or skill can be used in the real world, and so forth.

- Include in inquiries the criteria to be used in assessing performance or where such criteria exist.

- If students' understanding or performance is inaccurate, incomplete, or not yet wired into long-term memory, provide additional inquiries applying the same concept or skill until mastery occurs. Invite students who have reached an accurate and complete understanding of the concept or skill to write additional inquiries that might help create an "aha" for classmates. Have students review each other's inquiries using the 3Cs of assessment as they are developing them and immediately upon their completion.

- Use the language of pattern-seeking and program-building in inquiries so that students may assess their understanding and performance along the continuum of learning as a two-step process—pattern seeking to make meaning and program building to use what they understand.

USING *IMMEDIATE FEEDBACK* TO ENHANCE PATTERN SEEKING

Instructional Strategies

- Develop a repertoire of ways you can provide students with immediate feedback and use them often
  - Brief "talk with your neighbor" breaks during presentations to reflect on a question or check for understanding about something just presented
  - "Walk abouts" during collaborative work time to observe/listen to students as they work and to ask questions
  - Journal writing assignments asking students to reflect on what they've just learned and how they might use it in their lives now and in the future
  - Self-check procedures of many kinds, such as rubrics, answer sheets, self-developed criteria
  - Creating tasks to be completed while visiting resource person is still available to give feedback.

- Develop a repertoire of ways classmates can provide each other with immediate feedback and use them often
  - Use of rubrics by learning club members and study partners to check each other's work immediately (thereby eliminating overnight grading by teachers)
  - "Think-pair-share" and similar strategies from cooperative learning approaches[23]
  - Peer review and assessment.

- Develop opportunities for immediate feedback outside the classroom and do so often
  - Developing legitimate audiences who hold real-world expectations for work by students
  - Inquiries during *being there* study trips that require students to compare notes and check for accuracy.

Mastery

Given the ITI definition of learning as a two-step process — pattern-seeking for understanding and program-building for using what we understand — mastery must also be examined in these two steps because the ability to use what is understood begins with and builds upon how correct, complete, and comprehensive that understanding is.

When we become expert in a field, we know when we don't know something. When new to a field, a little bit of knowledge seems like great stuff and we often launch off with false certainty that we can do something. This is the source of the expression, "Taking off half cocked" or "Hell bent for leather" or "He's going fast to nowhere" and so forth. We've all been there. We thought we understood what to do and how to do it but once we got into it, disaster struck! We were humbled into an awareness that we knew only a fraction of what we needed to know.

Mastery, a Habit of Mind

Checking for mastery of understanding, the equivalent of looking before leaping, is an important habit of mind for students to develop. And it comes with two corner stones: a notable lack of arrogance that we know all that needs to be known and the self-confidence that we are capable of learning what we need to know.

Teachers nurture these two qualities by providing body-brain-compatible learning experiences. Arrogance about surface knowledge is counteracted by providing curriculum that explores concepts in depth and demands high levels of skill performance. Confidence in ability to learn blossoms in an atmosphere of success at learning — an environment that has high but appropriate expectations, that grades on mastered/not yet mastered, that provides plenty of learning support from both teacher and peers, and that holds the grade book open for mastery any time during the school year.

High But Appropriate Expectations

The clamor for higher expectations is a double-edged sword. Without question, the contribution of K-12 schooling to students' pool of knowledge and skills is unexcusably low. Yet the raising of the bar often results in state standards written by politicians, not educators. The results would be laughable if not so detrimental to students. For example, state curriculum standards from a southeastern state expects third graders to grasp an introduction to atomic fusion. Another led second graders to ponder the Preamble of the Constitution of the United States.

We cannot expect mastery of understanding of things that students' brains are incapable of processing due to the stage of their development—development that unfolds with age. Understandable curriculum—as compared to memorizable curriculum—is a must if we are to expect mastery. (For a discussion of age-appropriateness, see Appendix D.)

USING *MASTERY* TO ENHANCE PATTERN SEEKING

Curriculum Development Guidelines

- Make sure that the curriculum you present to students is in fact "getable" or understandable by children their age. If not, mastery is not possible. (If in doubt, see *Thinking and Learning: Matching Developmental Stages with Curriculum and Instruction* by Larry Lowery.)

- Embed the curriculum in *being there* experiences, preferably at real-life locations where people work and conduct commerce or where mother nature is at her most undisturbed. Make these experiences action-oriented rather than look and hear events. Seeing concepts and skills used by real people in real life settings makes recognition of patterns and their attributes much easier for students. It also increases motivation to learn and master.

- Include observation skills in your curriculum and teach students the verbal skills to report to themselves and others what they are witnessing. For example, see the discussion about using structure words to help students wire their brains for more effective language processing and comprehension in *Visualizing and Verbalizing for Improved Language Comprehension* by Nanci Bell. Better observation leads to more accurate and complete identification of the attributes of a thing, action, concept, or skill and thus a more comprehensive and in-depth degree of understanding.

USING *MASTERY* TO ENHANCE PATTERN SEEKING

Instructional Strategies

- Front load initial instruction with a wide variety of sensory input—*being there*, immersion, and hands on of the real thing. Stop frequently to provide students opportunities to experience and share observations; check frequently for accuracy and completeness of understanding.

- Have students use visual organizers for notetaking, such as KWL (*w*hat students know before you start, what they *w*ant to know, and later what they have *l*earned), mindmaps to show multiple relationships, Venn diagrams to compare attributes, and so forth, rather than the standard outline format. Have students compare their notes within their learning club, checking for accuracy and completeness, and resolving any differences in pattern-seeking before you move on. If more than one group has the same difference in understanding, bring the issue to the whole class. Tease out what previous learnings are interfering with correct understanding of the current concept or skill and then re-teach by giving correct information about both prior and current concepts/skills. Then, recheck for understanding. Ask students, grades three and up, to write inquiries that would help them understand the differences between prior and current concepts. Select the best ones and allow students to choose which one or two they will complete.

Absence of Threat/Nurturing Reflective Thinking

The complaint du jour of 21st century living seems to be "I'm too busy to think." We're too busy to do anything but react. For fight-flight circumstances, this is workable. But not for academic learning.

Our classroom environments must not only be safe, they must also show students how to slow themselves down enough to be reflective. Why? Because pattern recognition depends heavily upon bringing together prior experiences with current input. To do so, students must be able to take time to put together several possible lines of inquiry rather than blurting out a guess. This requires uninterrupted time for sustained reflection.

USING *REFLECTIVE THINKING* TO ENHANCE PATTERN SEEKING

Curriculum Development

- Teach students the elements of Mihaly Csikszentmihalyi[24] "flow" experience as applied to optimal learning. Help students recognize how to adjust their state of mind and/or learning environment so that they are in the best possible frame of mind for learning and remembering.

- Allow students to propose alternative ways of approaching a concept or skill that "makes more sense to them" and choice of additional situations for applying what they are learning.

USING *REFLECTIVE THINKING* TO ENHANCE PATTERN SEEKING

Instructional Strategies

- During whole-class instruction

  - Eliminate distractions

  - Provide a peaceful yet businesslike atmosphere with background music, non-vocal with 60 beats per minutes

  - Provide wait time

  - Allow students to volunteer an answer rather than worry about being called on

  - Provide reflective time before journal writing

- During collaborative work

  - Build in time for students to jot down their own thoughts before joining a brainstorming or discussion session

  - Teach group leaders to insist on wait time when questions are posed to the group

- Provide a range of individual performance formats such as individual study projects, inquiries for personal choice, and journal writing.

- Invite students to learn to nurture the environmental elements that produce a their own "flow" experience.

 *Choices*

Unless our goal is blind uniformity of both process and outcome, there is no justifiable reason for insisting on only one way of doing something. For example, we teach and accept only one algorithm (a mathematical term for pattern) for multiplication when there are more than 16 that do the job just as well. And likewise for long division, addition, and on and on.

As each brain is wired differently due to genetics, environment, and prior experiences, we should allow students to choose the patterns for solving a problem that work best for them while still producing accurate answers and useful products. Demanding that a brain operate in a specific way is the quickest way to frustration and a major disruption to reflective thinking.

USING *CHOICES* TO ENHANCE PATTERN SEEKING

Curriculum Guidelines

- Teach students that there are usually multiple ways to go about solving problems. Provide several examples and then let them devise others. Once you determine that the child has a pattern that they prefer—and that unfailingly produces correct answers—stop teaching other ways/patterns, even if they are the traditional ones.[25] Accept their method/pattern if it consistently gives them correct answers. As the saying goes, "If it ain't broke, don't fix it." Examples include many areas of mathematics such as multiplication, division, multiplication, addition, percentages plus decoding, spelling.

USING *CHOICES* TO ENHANCE PATTERN SEEKING

Instructional Strategies

- The world outside of school doesn't offer simplistic options such as true or false, *a* or *b*. Encourage students to begin to develop their own alternatives. When only one option is presented and not well understood, students must resort to memorization. When several patterns are examined and are understood well enough to make a choice among them, students needn't resort to memorization.

- When teaching a concept or skill, always illustrate several ways it can be used and give several examples of what it is not. Such attributes assist pattern seeking and meaning making by clarifying the pattern and making it more specific. Also, the fuller their sense of the pattern, the more likely they are to recognize it in their prior experiences.

Collaboration

A close-knit collaborative group such as a Learning Club is an ideal medium for pattern seeking. If you have constructed your Learning Clubs to ensure a range of intelligences (see Chapter 3), personality preferences (see Chapter 6), and interests, then you have supplied your students with a veritable gold mine of patterns. Working closely with people representing such diversity in ways of thinking, organizing, carrying out tasks, and so forth opens a whole new vista on life—with new patterns come new possibilities. Collaboration is a powerful way to enrich the mental life of your students. It also encourages students to sharpen their strengths and learn the value of enhancing their undeveloped areas.

USING *COLLABORATION* TO ENHANCE PATTERN SEEKING

Curriculum Guidelines

- Teach students to look for patterns. Model it in your questioning strategies and when leading approaches to solving problems and producing products.

- Teach them the patterns in thinking and behavior in the multiple intelligences, personality preferences, and their own habits of mind.

Instructional Strategies

- Ask the Learning Clubs to "process the process" frequently (see *Tribes: A New Way of Learning and Being Together* by Jeanne Gibbs). Also ask such questions of the class as a whole; have students reflect, verbally and in their journals, on what they've learned.

- Incorporate the terms "patterns" and "attributes of a pattern" into your direct instruction and assessment questions. Help make students aware of the pattern-seeking operation of their brain.

Notes

1 With each succeeding book he wrote about how the brain learns, Leslie Hart continued synthesizing his conceptualization of the two fundamental brain concepts: pattern detection, addressed in this chapter, and program building, described in Chapter 6. His initial definition was simple and to the point:

> The process of learning is the extraction, from confusion, of meaningful patterns

and

> Learning is the acquisition of useful programs

The revised edition of his book takes yet another step forward, defining learning as a two-step process—step one involves input, step two involves output. Each step is in turn divided into two stages.

> Part one : **Input stage: Pattern detection** consists of first identifying or recognizing the pattern and, secondly, making meaning of the pattern including its relationship to other patterns.
>
> **and**
>
> Part two: **Output stage: Program building** consists of learning to apply what is learned, at first experimentally and consciously, and then, after practice and wiring it up into long-term memory, applying what is learned with the almost automatic ease and skill of the expert.

This conceptualization of learning is an extremely important contribution to the field of learning because it is comprehensive enough to cover the wide range of practicalities that teachers,

administrators, and parents face on a daily basis—from establishing curriculum to instruction to assessment.

For example, if we use Hart's two-step definition of learning when we examine current standardized testing instruments, we see that the ubiquitous multiple choice and true-false items call for no more than identification of a pattern (this choice *sounds* more familiar than that choice). *Understanding* the pattern is not necessary. Knowing how to use the information is well beyond the scope of the test and long-term memory of how to use it isn't even an issue.

This fuller, more comprehensive view of learning provides a set of lenses for examining all issues of curriculum, instruction, and assessment. It also provides a useful perspective when considering resource allocation and the success of improvement efforts.

See *Human Brain and Human Learning, Updated,* by Leslie A. Hart (Covington, Washington: Books for Educators, 1999).

2 Hart, p. 133.

3 Hart, p. 387.

4 Hart, p. 1407.

5 Hart, p. 142.

6 David B. Brown, "Towards a Communication Theory," *Teachers College Record,* May 1977, p. 453.

7 See *The Human Situation* (Lectures at Santa Barbara, 1959), Pierro Ferrucci, ed. (New York: Harper & Row), p. 173. Also compare George A. Kelley, *A Theory of Personality* (New York: W. W. Norton, 1963): "Man looks at his world through transparent patterns or templates which he creates and then attempts to fit over the realities of which the world is composed" (p. 17).

8 That the brain learns by detecting patterns among incoming sensory data has been amply confirmed by numerous brain researchers since the first edition of this book in 1983. See *The Growth of the Mind and the Endangered Origins of Intelligence* by Stanley I. Greenspan with Beryl Lieff Benderly (New York: Addison-Wesley

Publishing Company, 1997), p. 114 and *Molecules of Emotion: Why You Feel the Way You Feel* by Candace B. Pert (New York: Scribner, 1997), p. 147.

9 Alphonse Bertillon (1853-1914) devised an elaborate system for positively identifying individuals in spite of their variety. It was intended primarily for criminal justice purposes. Later, finger-printing proved far simpler but the system is still used by physical anthropologists.

10 John B. Carroll, speaking of the mature reader, suggests that it may be true, "astounding as it may seem, that reading is based upon a capability of instantly recognizing thousands or even tens of thousands of individual word patterns, almost as if words were Chinese characters not structured by an alphabetic principle." See *Theories of Learning and Instruction, 63d Yearbook of the National Society for the Study of Education* (Chicago: University of Chicago Press, 1964), p. 341. For actual use of Chinese, see "American Children with Reading Problems Can Easily Learn to Read English Represented by Chinese Characters," by Paul Rozin and others, in *Psycholinguistics and Reading*, Frank Smith, ed. (New York: Holt, Rinehart and Winston, 1973), Chapter 9.

11 Much can be learned about the process of learning by observing how young children build their vocabulary and the knowledge of the world that that vocabulary represents. In going about this prodigious feat, children make great use of categorizing down. If something is at first not understandable, children, if unguided, rarely resort to repeated attempts at memorization of the original input or memorization of a definition. Instead, they move on, gulping in massive amounts of new input until they hit upon a kind of input that finally provides a recognizable pattern, triggering the "aha" response.

12 Just because the brain has stored a pattern for "door" does not mean that it has stored all of the attributes of the pattern called door in a single location. A truly startling quality of the brain is that it can access bits of information stored in different locations and array it to make sense, and do so with astonishing speed.

13 See Frank Smith, *Comprehension and Learning* (New York: Holt, Rinehart and Winston, 1975), p. 1. The "make sense" concept has been widely discussed by many brain researchers. Harry J. Jerison, for example, suggests that reality is "a creation of the brain, a model of a possible world that makes sense of the mass of information that reaches us through our various sensory (including motor feedback) systems." See *The Human Brain* (Englewood Cliffs, N. J.: Prentice Hall, 1977), p. 54.

14 This stage of language acquisition is familiar to many parents, teachers, and others who have contact with children. It has been discussed by many psycholinguists. See, for example, James Britton in *The Teaching of English, 76th Yearbook of the National Society for the Study of Education* (Chicago: University of Chicago Press, 1977), p. 11.

15 Rote memory should be kept to a minimum; instead, focus on reaching an understanding via pattern seeking/meaning making. However, when rote memorization is necessary, use CUE—an acronym from the ITI model representing three methods which help ensure that students will remember. *C* stands for creative, such as use of skits or role playing or writing lyrics to a familiar tune. *U* stands for useful, such as having students make a connection to how a concept or skill is used in their lives. *E* stands for emotional, making an unforgettable emotional impact on students through the fun and adventure of a study trip, the sadness when animals die in oil spills, or the joy and deep satisfaction of making a contribution to others.

16 For a description of what makes concepts or skills age-appropriate, see *Thinking and Learning: Matching Developmental Stages with Curriculum and Instruction* by Lawrence F. Lowery, University of California, Berkeley, professor, Graduate School of Education and member of the board of directors for the Lawrence Hall of Science. Dr. Lowry also served as principal investigator for the FOSS project (Full Option Science Systems) developed under the auspices of the National Science Foundation and for the Equals Project (math for girls).

17 Hart, p. 223.

18 Hart, p. 141+142.

19 The Kovalik ITI Model expresses this concept by contrasting the typical input of the traditional classroom life (*second hand* and *symbolic*) and the input needed for fully brain-compatible learning (primarily *being there* and *immersion* when used as follow up to *being there*). The difference in the amount of sensory input, and thus learning, is enormous. Sensory input from *being there* and *immersion* experiences are especially important when learning something new.

20 Scientists investigating speech and listening to language have produced an impressive body of knowledge, much of it long established. Yet, apparently, it is all but unknown to most educators, who commonly refer to "auditory" and "listening" skills and similar ideas far off the mark. For an excellent discussion, see George A. Miller, *Language and Speech* (San Francisco: W. H. Freeman and Co., 1981), especially Chapter 6.

21 Hart, p. 134.

22 *A Private Universe* is a fascinating video illustrating the power of concepts generated by full sensory input as a child to override adult learning limited to lecture and reading. Harvard graduates are interviewed in their caps and gowns. The question "What makes for the seasons?" is answered the same by liberal arts students and those with science backgrounds, even including a course in advanced planetary motion—the earth gets closer to the sun in the summer (thus hotter) and farther away in the winter (and thus colder).

23 See *Cooperative Learning* by Spencer Kagan (San Clemente, CA: Kagan, 1994).

24 See *Flow: The Psychology of Optimal Experience* by Mihaly Csikszentmilhalyi (New York: Harper, 1990).

25 The authors believe that our reading and math reforms have failed over the years because we have persisted in finding one way to teach all students instead of finding a best way for individual students. For example, children that learn to read at age four and who can read and spell years ahead of their grade level, have discovered their own patterns for decoding and spelling. It is a disservice to inflict the standard phonics lessons on them. Doing so usually slows down their reading speed and often also diminishes their enjoyment of reading without providing any benefits. The more unconscious their system of pattern seeking, the more space they have in their conscious mental processing to deal with comprehension. On the other hand, students who haven't detected patterns for decoding that work do need the standard phonics lessons. Pattern identification and understanding is as unique as each child's brain. And, it is far more powerful than our brief lessons can ever be. So, observe your students' pattern-seeking processes and outcome carefully. Complement them rather than force them.

Chapter 5: Program Building-
Step Two of Learning

Our behavior, and that of our fellow human beings, has long been one of life's greater mysteries. Behavior—its building blocks and why specific building blocks are chosen at any one moment in time—must be understood if we are to create schools that foster real learning.

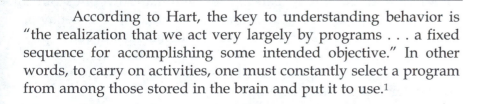

LEARNING IS A TWO-STEP PROCESS

- Detecting and understanding patterns—a process through which our brain creates meaning

- Developing meaningful mental programs to use what is understood and to store it in long-term memory—the capacity to use what is understood first with assistance and then almost automatically

According to Hart, the key to understanding behavior is "the realization that we act very largely by programs . . . a fixed sequence for accomplishing some intended objective." In other words, to carry on activities, one must constantly select a program from among those stored in the brain and put it to use.[1]

Hart defines a *program* as:

"A sequence of steps or actions, intended to achieve some GOAL, which once built is stored in the brain and 'run off' repeatedly whenever need to achieve the same goal is perceived by the person. A program may be short, for example giving a nod to indicate 'yes,' or long, as in playing a piece on the piano which requires thousands of steps. A long program usually involves a series of shorter subprograms, and many parallel variations that permit choice to meet conditions of use. Many such programs are needed, for instance to open different kinds of doors by pushing, pulling, turning, thumbing a button or lever, and on. Language requires

ITI Learning Principles

- Intelligence as a function of experience

- Bodybrain partnership —emotion as gatekeeper to learning and performance—movement and cognition

- Multiple intelligences

- **Learning as a two-step process**
  — pattern seeking/meaning making
  — **program building**

- Impact of personality

many thousands of programs, to utter each word, type it, write it in longhand, print it, and so forth. Frequently used programs acquire an 'automatic' quality: they can be used, once selected, without thinking, as when one puts on a shirt. Typically, a program is CONSCIOUSLY selected, then run off at a subconscious level. In general, humans operate by selecting and implementing programs one after another throughout waking hours."[2]

To understand the power of Hart's statements, consider some everyday examples. Simple ones are such things as a procedure for putting on one's shoes. There are the "right-foot-first" people and the "good heavens, no—the left first" folks. Same with putting on a coat. For high good humor, watch someone in a restaurant offering to help another with their coat. Of course the assistant offers the coat in the manner that he or she would put it on—from the left, high up near the shoulder while the recipient turns to receive the coat low from the right and the awkwardness ensues.

Or, how about the shower? Your favored hand grabs the soap and that soap knows just what to do. Zip! You're done with the shower. But, if for some temporary reason that hand can't get wet, the soap no longer remembers what to do. The result is much fumbling about, a shower that takes much longer, and the feeling of not being quite as clean and refreshed as usual. You can almost hear your mother's voice asking, "Did you wash behind your ears?"

For another example, think how many of us have driven miles with absolutely no recall of the journey. A little scary! Or, after being reassigned to a new school, we find ourselves one morning in the parking lot of our former school. How did that happen!

The basic cycle in using programs is:

1 Evaluate the situation or need (detect and identify the pattern or patterns).

2 In response to the incoming patterns, select the most appropriate program from those stored.

3 Implement the program.

For example:

Situation:	You're invited to a party
Step 1. Evaluate:	Is it a birthday, graduation, holiday, costume, or office party? (Each demands certain consideration, appropriate dress, gift, contribution to the potluck, etc.) Ah, it's a birthday party.
Step 2. Select:	Because it's a birthday party you prepare to RSVP, buy a present, wear party clothes, and eat a skimpy breakfast and lunch because you know there will be cake and ice cream.
Step 3. Implement:	You execute your plans and have a great time.

As in the previous example, the first step in the learning process is detecting pattern. Once a situation has been analyzed, and if action is required, the brain scans its repertoire of stored programs, selecting the one that is most appropriate or calling forth two or more and using them in fresh combinations. Towards a positive end, such capacity to "use old programs in fresh combinations" underlies what we call creativity.[3]

Used negatively, this evaluate—select—implement process is seen in the case of the student who repeatedly misbehaves. Wanting to attract the teacher's attention, this student reaches into his/her mental bag of programs and, as unconsciously as the driver arriving at the wrong parking lot, automatically pulls out a behavior that will attract attention. Unfortunately, the behavior also makes the teacher furious. In such students' mental bag of programs, there are too many of the "wrong" behaviors/programs and too few of the "right" ones, i.e., ones that get the attention of the teacher but without the anger.

Equally somber is the child-grown-adult who has no program for using multiplication for real-world applications such as computing mortgage payments or figuring the real cost of an item he/she let ride on the VISA charge card. Unpleasant consequences flow from lack of appropriate mental programs.

Successful implementation of a mental program is its own reward, accompanied by feelings of accomplishment and increased satisfaction. Aborting a mental program that doesn't work is emotionally unsettling because it leaves us unsure of what to do next and decreases our sense of self confidence.[4] When orchestrating your curriculum, provide the time and experiences that allow youngsters to master new information and add it to prior knowledge in a meaningful way, thereby creating new mental programs.

Hart, in fact, defines learning as "the acquisition of useful programs." "Learning," such as getting an A on a paper/pencil test, which does not result in acquisition of a mental program is not learning from Hart's perspective because it doesn't stick. Hart points out that information that does not become part of a program is usually unretrievable. For example, recall your sophomore college days and the traditional western civilization class. The characteristics of this stunning experience: yearlong, 99.9 percent lecture, and an enormously fat textbook. For the mid-term and final exams, you used the ubiquitous blue book. Weeks later when the blue book was graded and returned, you glanced inside. To your total shock, there were paragraphs of stuff you didn't even recognize—never heard of before! A classic example of information that never became part of a program and, thus, is unretrievable and often unrecognizable, even a bare three weeks later. In other words, most information that we use is embedded in programs; the corollary is: information that is not used is also not retrievable and, if truth be told, was probably never "learned" in the first place. Thus, "covering information" is a colossal waste of time for both students and teachers.

The implications for the classroom of the 21st century are obvious—students must master concepts and skills with depth of understanding and use what they understand. We in turn need to present less content and give students time to "use" the information again and again in varying settings until the information is recallable in a usable form, i.e., a behavior, a program.

It should be noted that programs and subskills are not identical and have little in common. A program, while it can be enormously complex, such as driving a car, is a sequence for accomplishing some end—a goal, objective, or outcome—an end with meaning to the learner. Subskills, such as the blend *ch* or the short *i* are not a sequence for accomplishing some end; they are experienced as isolated, fragmented pieces. In contrast, the program to be attained is the act of reading—an insight young students can easily miss.

To reinforce the difference between pattern-seeking (making meaning of input) and program building (using what is learned), consider diapering a baby. Everyone recognizes the patterns diaper and baby; But, as Diane Keaton makes clear in the movie, *Baby Boomers*, not everyone can diaper a moving baby. The same is true with returning a rental car. Everyone knows what the words *car*, *return*, *rental*, and *airport* mean. But not everyone has a mental program of the steps for *returning a rental car to an airport*.

> *Joe Bag-of-Donuts off the street corner would probably agree that if schools were doing their job, students would be able to remember what they were taught years later. And, if not, we're wasting tax payers' money and students' time. Recent brain research now tells us how to do that. Building programs is the key; practicing how to use information to wire the brain for long-term memory is critical.*

Because this discussion of building programs and wiring knowledge and skills into long-term memory is so critical to what we as teachers do in the classroom, we are providing here part of Hart's description of program building from his book *Human Brain and Human Learning*.

SECOND FUNDAMENTAL OF LEARNING: WE LIVE BY PROGRAMS*

Extraction of patterns—identifying and making meaning of them—constitutes the first of two steps in learning. But plainly enough, we do not live by sitting in an armchair and detecting patterns. We live by doing, by action. Thus, the second step in learning is the development of mental programs to use what we know, i.e., the patterns we have come to understand. Step two in learning is defined as "the acquisition of useful programs.

THE MYSTERY OF BEHAVIOR

For thousands of years, back to the dim origins of humans, behavior has seemed largely a mystery. What people did seemed utterly haphazard, unpredictable, and unexplainable.

Teachers have long struggled with the behavior of their charges, often to the degree that class management threatens to push instruction into a secondary function. Even corporate personnel specialists confess to being frequently surprised and baffled by the behavior of workers, for all the "motivation" that pay and prospects of advancement would seem to offer. More than half of marriages in the United States go astray; the inability of spouses to understand each other, even after years of intimacy, stands out. At any gathering of parents, the difficulties of comprehending the strange worlds children inhabit take a prominent place in the discussions.

However, in the last four decades and more, researchers studying the brain and several other disciplines have made progress on many fronts. When their findings are brought together and unified, our understanding of human behavior can take a great leap. This opens

---

* The follow discussion about the second fundamental of learning, pages 5.4-5.9, is excerpted from *Human Brain and Human Learning* by Leslie A. Hart. Used with permission of the publisher.

the door to revolutionary advances in education and gives us the chance to catch up, at least somewhat, with the discoveries resulting from the dazzling and often upsetting advances in technology.

THE BASIS OF BEHAVIOR: PROGRAMS

"The key to understanding human behavior is the realization that we act very largely by programs. The word *programs* need not alarm us with visions of robots. It means simply a fixed sequence for accomplishing some *intended objective.* In other words, we act to carry out some purpose, some personal, individual, and usually self-selected purpose—the exact opposite of robot behavior.

Suppose, for example, that I wish to telephone my dentist. I pick up the phone, push the buttons in a certain order, and put the receiver to my ear to wait for the call to go through. I have executed a program for making a phone call. Should I call him again tomorrow, I will go through just about the same procedure.

Should I wish to phone a local store, I may have to use an additional program to find the number. I get the phone book, look up the listing, then dial—a variation of the program I used to call my dentist.

If now I want to visit the store, I must implement a longer program. I go to my car, take out my keys, find the right one, unlock the door, open it, get in, put the key in the ignition switch, fasten the seat belt, turn the switch and start the engine, release the parking brake, put the car in gear, press the accelerator pedal—just to start on my trip. To get there in my accustomed way I go through a series of dozens of steps, including the right choices of turns at street intersections. Yet I can "reel off" this program with the greatest of ease, hardly giving any attention to what comes next, much as I can put a cassette in a player and have the tape reel off a musical or other program.

Clearly, one of the reasons for our huge brain is that as humans we need and use a great number of programs to carry on our complex activities—thousands of times as many as the most intelligent of other animals. Exactly how that is achieved remains unknown, although the progress of researchers in the neurosciences suggests that we may have a good start toward understanding the neuronal, chemical, and molecular mechanisms involved within another few years.[6]

The Source of Programs

Present knowledge makes clear that programs can be acquired in two distinct ways: *transmitted with the genes* or *learned after birth.* As a general rule, the more brainpower an animal has, the more it learns after birth. The more neocortex or new brain it possesses, the greater the relative reliance on after-birth learning. We see once more why the laboratory rat and other small experimental animals can shed so little light on human learning: Their programs are largely species wisdom, transmitted genetically, while humans use the splendid new brain to do most learning after birth, over many years.

No aspect of being human appears more dominant than this incessant accumulation of programs. The process, of course, is most rapid in the earlier years then gradually tapers off. But since we live in a world that changes constantly, we are under far greater pressure than our forebears to continue to learn, to continue acquiring new programs. The man of 75 who is given a video tape recorder to honor that birthday must master some new programs to operate his new machine. A few centuries ago the programs acquired by age 25 would pretty well see one through a full life; today much of what is learned by age 25 will become obsolete. Failure to keep on learning can prove restrictive, costly, or embarrassing.

How Programs Work

To carry on activities, one must constantly *select* a program from those that are stored in the brain and *implement* it—put it into use.[7] Even to walk across the room, one must use an extremely complex program involving many of the body's 600-plus muscles and the shifting of weight from one side to the other as the feet alternate in moving forward. The program has to be repeated every two paces, with continual fine adjustments to change direction or to pick up and carry articles. To walk, one program is used; to go up stairs, another; to go down stairs, a third. To take a stroll outside one may have to use programs for going uphill, downhill, crossing rough ground, jumping over

a puddle, or running a few steps to avoid traffic. *Each time, the program in use has to be switched off and another selected and switched on.* The brain does this so smoothly that we ordinarily are not aware of the switches being thrown, but this is the main key to our present insight into behavior.

If I am getting dressed in the morning and open a drawer full of shirts, I must make a conscious selection of which I will wear. After I have made that choice, opening up the shirt, putting it on, and buttoning it up "runs off" as a kind of automatic program to which I don't have to give any conscious attention unless something goes wrong— I find a button missing—and interferes.

Which shirt will I select? It depends on a perception of the *pattern* I will be dealing with. If I am going to a business meeting, I select a dress shirt; if I plan to make some repairs, I choose a work shirt; if I plan to exercise, I choose another type of shirt. Even more subtle patterns may influence me: I may want a conservative dress shirt for the meeting or a brighter one if the meeting will become a celebration with old friends. Though the decision may be trivial, I cannot act until some decision is made. (Following fixed habits or rituals, where possible, avoids decisions and so may seem more "comfortable.")

In much the same way, we select the most appropriate program from those stored in the brain to deal with what is happening at the time. For example, seeing stairs ahead, I select a going-up-stairs program. Having accidentally jostled somebody, I choose an offering-apology program. Facing an arithmetical problem, I tap my division program. Meeting a neighbor, I select a greeting program, complete with smile, nod, and suitable words.

THE PROGRAM IMPLEMENTATION CYCLE

In each of the above examples, a basic cycle is plainly in use. One must:

1. *Evaluate* the situation or need (detect and identify the pattern or patterns being dealt with).

2. *Select* the most appropriate program from those stored.

3. *Implement* the program selected.

Human behavior looked at in these terms may hardly seem simple but such a perspective provides more penetrating insight.

Key Observations

For educators, viewing behavior as a function of the program implementation cycle significantly expands our ability to observe and analyze student behavior during the learning process. Key observations include:

1. Unless the learner can reasonably and accurately evaluate the need or problem at hand (that is, detect and identify the patterns involved), the cycle goes astray at the outset. The student simply does not know what to do.

   A familiar example is a student trying to cope with an arithmetic problem couched in words. Unable to detect the pertinent pattern, the student flounders, wondering whether to add, or divide, or give up entirely. Another example is spelling of longer words. Lacking any sense of the structure or pattern of the word, the student tries to simply remember the order of the letters—perhaps producing some weird versions.

2. People can access and use only those programs they already possess. However much one may be coerced or urged, or motivated or rewarded, there is no way to perform the program *unless it has already been stored.* He or she does not know how to do it. No program, no ability to perform the needed action.

   There is no way to force a person to ride a bicycle, or play Chopin on the piano, or write a scientific paper, if those programs have not previously been acquired. That many other people can do these things has no bearing. Yet in almost any classroom, at any level, this principle is ignored. On the playground, one may hear a child being called "clumsy" or "poorly coordinated" when the real difficulty is that the child has not yet learned certain programs. In homes, parents

scold children; in businesses, bosses scold employees—all in the same futile way for the same futile reason. *If the program has not been acquired, the solution is to acquire it,* not in criticizing, labeling, or giving a poor mark, practices that prove devastating to learners.

3. A student cannot implement a program unless given the chance to do so.

   A test question might ask, "How can you verify the correct spelling of a word?" The answer intended is, "Look it up in a dictionary." A student who gives that answer, we must note, is not using that program. Rather, he or she is *using a program for answering a question on a test.* So commonly are tests used in instruction that this all-important difference may be overlooked; students may pass tests yet often be unable to carry out the programs themselves—a complaint loudly uttered today. Similarly, if students are always *directed* to use certain programs, there is no way to know whether they can detect the pattern, have a program to select, and can implement it. Rather, they are implementing programs *for following directions.* Such "learning" may prove fictitious.

As I indicated earlier, a program always has a goal, an objective—it is an activity to achieve some intended outcome. What happens if the program selected and implemented does not work?

WHEN PROGRAMS DON'T WORK

During the program implementation cycle, the brain asks, "What *pattern* am I dealing with; what *program* should I choose to deal with it?" The most appropriate program is then implemented. Usually it will work. If it aborts, the brain must recycle—pattern detection, program selection, implementation. Let's say that I have taken out my keys to open the car door. I insert the key but it won't turn—the program *aborts.* I must now go through the three-step cycle again: reevaluate the situation, select another program that seems appropriate, and implement that. Perhaps I have the wrong key, in which case I recycle to find the right one and try again. Perhaps the lock has jammed, so I recycle to the unusual program of going around to the opposite door.

Aborting Programs Is Disturbing

Aborting a program *always causes some degree of emotional shift* because the failure of a program to work is in general disturbing and *threatening,* especially when no workable alternative program can be found. The degree to which programs usually work when implemented to achieve the intended goal serves as a direct, continuous measure of how well one has "made sense of the world," how competent we generally are. Programs *should* work. When they do, confidence in oneself increases; when too often they don't, confidence diminishes.[9]

Impact on Self-Confidence. Teachers have long sensed that self-image and the belief that one can successfully learn is important to self-concept and, in turn, to learning. Brain research now concurs. An individual's confidence rises or falls when programs do or do not work. We can see, too, that children whose parents or teachers have over-directed their activities and over-stressed second-person estimates of achievement, may mistrust their own ability to evaluate situations and select appropriate programs.[10]

This program view of behavior, I submit, is consistent both with present scientific understandings of the brain, and with what we can clearly see—once we know where to look—in the normal functioning of children, other adults, and ourselves. True, we cannot see into another person's brain to observe what pattern-detecting abilities and programs have been established there. However, we can see with new insights what happens when that person is allowed to use what he or she considers the most appropriate program—or when the individual has none to apply, or can't identify the pertinent pattern to begin with.

ACQUISITION OF USEFUL PROGRAMS

The word *useful* in "acquisition of useful programs" deserves attention. Primarily, it means useful to the individual who will possess the program—in that person's view, rather than in someone else's view or to satisfy some supposed social or other standard. While it is true that one can be coerced into acquiring a program and may use it under duress, such programs are likely to become unused as soon as the duress ceases, if good mental health prevails. If use of the forced program does continue, it usually will signify either superstitious ritual, with anxiety that something dreadful will occur if it is not used, or the inappropriate behavior that goes under the common name of neurosis. *Inherently, the use of a freely learned program satisfies; that of a coerced program brings back the old fears under which it was built.* We see this in mild form when people do arithmetic with obvious pain and reluctance and, in more serious degree, when individuals who have been forced to learn a musical instrument well cannot bear to play before an audience in later life.

Transfer of Learning

In a far wider sense, *useful* conveys the possibilities of *transfer* of learning, which can greatly increase the speed of new learning. For example, a program for roller skating can readily transfer to ice skating; one for using a typewriter keyboard can easily be extended to using a computer keyboard which then can serve as a mental anchor for learning new information about the computer. *The ability to transfer some of these behavioral building blocks, adapting and adjusting them to new needs, explains why some individuals can master a new task far more rapidly than others* who lack the programs to transfer, or who in some cases may not yet have recognized the similarity of pattern involved which leads to and permits transfer.

Source of Creativity

The capacity to use old programs in fresh combinations seems to underlie what we call creativity. Greater sensitivity to pattern similarities facilitates the transfer. While I would doubt that sensitivity can be directly taught, it seems probable that it can be facilitated.

THE POWER OF PROGRAMS

The implications for education of the program concept of behavior—*evaluate, select, implement* program cycle—are stupendous, bringing not only fresh insights into human behavior but also generating some major guidelines for improving learning achievement.

To summarize:

1. We live by programs, switching on one after another, selecting from those that have been acquired and stored in the brain.

2. As humans, we are far more dependent on programs acquired by the tens of thousands after birth, in contrast to animals that rely more on programs genetically transmitted.

3. A program is a fixed sequence for accomplishing some end—a goal, objective, or outcome. Our human nature makes the working of a program pleasurable; the concept of some after-the-event "reward" is neither necessary or valid. However, feedback is essential to establish that the program did work more or less as intended.

4. We can use only those programs that have already been built and stored. What programs another person has, or many people have, has no bearing. If a person does not possess a program, efforts to force its use are absurd.

5. We routinely use a three-step cycle: evaluate the situation (involving pattern detection and recognition), select the program that seems most appropriate from our store, and implement it.

6. The abortion of a program—upon its failure to work—calls for recycling. When a high proportion of self-selected programs work well, confidence rises; when too many programs are aborted, confidence is reduced and the learner may become far less able to self-select programs.

7. Although laboriously built, fully acquired programs have an automatic quality that can easily lead one to forget that other individuals may not have acquired these programs.

8. Learning can be defined as the acquisition of useful programs.

9. Learning progress can be properly evaluated only by observing *undirected* behavior.[11] Questioning and testing dealing primarily with *information* can reveal little. It shows only poorly what individuals can *do*.

10. Effective transfer of learning depends on using established programs in new applications and combinations. (Skill in putting together new combinations may equal "creativity.") The learner who can adapt established programs to new tasks, by seeing similarities of patterns involved, learns much more rapidly than one who cannot.

11. In general, if we regard human learning and behavior in terms of continually asking "What program is being used?", sharp new insights can be gained, and many confusions avoided.

When extracting patterns and building programs, specific information may be helpful to the task or even required. But, this does not imply that there is necessarily any great virtue in "stuffing the head with facts."

It can be handy to carry in memory certain information that will be frequently used. For example, we may store the phone numbers of a dozen people we often contact so we don't have to look them up each time. If patterns are involved, such information is much more easily remembered as when one knows that Tim, Linda, and Vance all work in the same office, and can be reached though its main number, at hours when that office will be open.

In our real world today, there exists vastly more information than can be memorized and it tends to change or obsolete rapidly, so that trusting memory can be treacherous.

A better strategy than trying to collect facts is to possess programs for finding various information—knowing what reference books are available and how to use them, or where to obtain help. But until specific information is linked to need for pattern or program, it serves little purpose. When such needs exist, learners typically "gobble up" information at an astonishing rate because they see it has immediate and meaningful application.

Translating Brain Research into Action Using the Nine Bodybrain-Compatible Elements

Of the five principles of learning gleaned from recent brain research, the redefinition of learning is the most revolutionary. As mentioned earlier, our billion dollar a year testing industry stops far short of measuring learning by this new definition. So, too, do all the traditional tools teachers have inherited, with the possible exception of rote memorization. That schools teach until students can use what they learn in practical, real-world ways—and remember what they've learned years later—is a wholly new expectation. It is long overdue but nevertheless a bit unnerving.

Where to start? Right here, with lots of commonsense.

First, what do we want students to understand? Look at this from a parent's point of view. Ask them. Survey your own life's lessons. What do you wish you had understood much earlier in life before the lessons got so expensive? Better interpersonal skills, a better understanding of interest and financing, auto

Bodybrain-Compatible Elements

- *Movement*
- *Meaningful Content*
- *Immediate Feedback*
- *Mastery*
- *Adequate Time*
- *Enriched Environment*
- *Choices*
- *Collaboration*
- *Absence of Threat/ Nurturing Reflective Thinking*

mechanics for drivers, savings from conserving (electricity, water, recycling garbage, and so forth), gourmet cooking on a budget, how to create and stick to a budget, investment strategies, tips on child rearing. Probably these and much, much more.

Also, look at what's worth knowing from your students' point of view. Every generation faces its unique challenges as well as those that plague us all. What are those special challenges facing your students? What knowledge and skills would help them most?

The answers to these questions will help you focus your curriculum on what's important to know and be able to do.

The question that will help you revamp your instructional strategies is "What do we want them to do with what they understand?" Whatever that is, students must begin to do it. That doing will transform your classroom.

Movement

Because it is the movement centers of the brain that sequence thinking, it is essential that movement—doing—be part of learning from beginning to end, from the conception of curriculum content to instruction to assessing outcomes. Said more strongly, restriction of movement and all forms of passivity restrict learning. So, whether such active learning is a personal preference or not, we owe it to our students to make learning in our classroom the active, joyful process that it naturally is.

USING *MOVEMENT* TO ENHANCE PROGRAM BUILDING

Curriculum Development

- Make sure your inquiries clearly state what students are to **do** with what they understand—in practical, real-world ways.

- Design inquiries that ask students to act out the sequence of steps or processes inherent in the key point.

- Always include inquiries that require use of bodily-kinesthetic intelligence for solving problems and producing products.

- Provide the real-world tools and materials needed to produce the product called for in the inquiry.

USING *MOVEMENT* TO ENHANCE PROGRAM BUILDING

Instructional Strategies

- During direct instruction, checking for understanding, and groupwork, include as many forms of the dramatic arts as you can; for example, role playing, miming, simulations, planned and impromptu skits, impersonations (of people and machines), and so forth.

- Assign moment activities not just for the sake of movement but to activate the bodily-kinesthetic intelligence.

Meaningful Content

Just as beauty is in the eyes of the beholder, so too is meaningfulness in the eyes of the learner. The brain is ruthless in its judgments about what is worth sending to long-term memory versus what will simply fade away from short-term memory. Its most important criterion is whether something is meaningful to the learner, something that is useful, that will be called upon again.

USING *MEANINGFUL CONTENT* TO ENHANCE PROGRAM BUILDING

Curriculum Development

- Ensure that your *being there* locations allow for doing not just looking and that those responsible for hosting the visit are prepared for students do research— ask questions, compare answers, delve into behind-the-scenes information (clarify the boundaries ahead of time), and so forth.

- Make sure your inquiries ask students to apply the key point to situations that are part of students' current world as well as future situations.

- Ask students to write inquiries for your key points that apply the concept or skill to their lives. Select those that best relate to students' current experiences and assign them to students for homework which they can share with parents and siblings, groupwork which will give them more perspective, and for individual work which will provide reflection time.

Instructional Strategies

- Provide adequate time for students to reflect on what they're learning—how it applies to their lives now and in the future, to their community and the world.

- Require journal writing every day; include at least one assignment that asks students to reflect on what they've learned today and two ways they can apply it during the coming week.

- Involve students in self-assessment processes.

Immediate Feedback

Creating programs, especially accurate ones, is impossible without feedback. Assembling sensory input into understandable pieces then wholes, training the muscles to use what is understood—at every step along the way our learning is a set of approximations under refinement.

The best feedback is that built into the learning situation and materials—inherent, immediate, consistent. For example, learning to ride a bike, play a saxophone, use a hand lens or microscope, match yesterday's colors for painting in oils or water color, and so on. In each case, learners knows immediately if they have successfully performed the action. No one needs to tell them.

The most hazardous kind of feedback for learners to rely on is teacher feedback. Why? Because it is external not internal, and therefore can't be replicated by the learner, and because it is rarely immediate due to the demands on the teacher by other learners. Grading papers overnight, even by the end of the day, does little to help a learner develop accurate programs. To be useful, feedback must come at the time the learner is engaged in using the knowledge or skill. This axiom is urgent when learner and new material meet.

This discussion brings up some interesting observations about homework. From a brain research point of view, it is clearly a mistake to assign a page of division problems if students have not yet mastered division because it is likely that they will get as much practice doing division wrong as they will doing it right. This only serves to deepen the confusion and makes reteaching more difficult the next day. On the other hand, if students have already mastered division, why should we burden them with a page of busywork? In our opinion, homework should consist primarily of students applying concepts and skills to real-life situations around the home and neighborhood through meaningful projects.

Because some learners need more feedback and thus more time to learn a particular concept or skill, homework assignments are a way to vary the time and number of practices.

USING *IMMEDIATE FEEDBACK* TO ENHANCE PROGRAM BUILDING

Curriculum Development

- For every inquiry you develop for students, think through what means and level of feedback students will receive in the process. Will the situation and materials provide the needed feedback? If not, can Learning Clubs do an adequate job or are all the members at ground zero relative to the concept or skill to be learned? How available are you as teacher? Can you shift your role to guide on the side so that you can freely roam and provide sufficient feedback to all?

- If adequate feedback can't come from the learning situation and materials of the inquiry, make sure the forms of feedback vary, as they do in real life. Among the choices, include inquiries that:

  - Require students to develop rubrics for self assessment and to practice the 3Cs of assessment.

  - Require Learning Club members to provide feedback to each other. Have students assess both the quality of the feedback received and what they learned in the process of analyzing and providing the feedback.

- Develop long-term projects such as the Yearlong Research Project, social/political action projects, service projects, Kids Vote America, and so forth.

USING *IMMEDIATE FEEDBACK* TO ENHANCE PROGRAM BUILDING

Instructional Strategies

- Ask students frequently, on a scale of 1-10, how well they think they will remember what they are learning 10 years from now. If less than 9.5, ask them what it would take for them to wire the knowledge/skill into their long-term memory. Follow up on those suggestions by having them write their own inquiries and then follow up on those inquiries. Assign those you approve of to be done as homework or in-class assignments. Your goal here is for students to learn to become responsible for their learning outcomes. If you've chosen your content well, they will willingly take up this responsibility.

- Commit yourself to effective first teaching goals and strategies. Intend to make your first lesson so effective that additional teaching or, heaven forbid, re-teaching/remedial teaching is unnecessary. Guided practice allows you to ensure that early learning is correct and sufficient to override previously-held misconceptions.

- Develop a deep repertoire of feedback strategies, such as three before me, peer response, self-assessment with rubrics and the 3Cs, target talk, coaching by knowledgeable peers and experts, teaching a younger buddy (through the act of teaching, they discover what is not well understood), and so forth.

Mastery

Mastery and an accurate program wired into long-term memory are one and the same thing. They are the outer and inner manifestations of each other.

To reach mastery, see the recommendations for curriculum development and instructional strategies for the other eight body-brain-compatible elements.

Adequate Time

Those who liken the brain to a computer fail to appreciate the true biological nature of the brain. While it may take nanoseconds to switch from 0 to 1 and back again, the gist of learning in computers, learning in the brain requires physiological growth of neurons, dendrites, axons, and time for mylination to occur. Such growth takes time.[12] Wish as we may, wish as we might, there are no short cuts except going at it as if we understood how the brain works. That would call for teaching it well once, guiding practice of application in varying circumstances (not just rote memorization), and having students use it—without birdwalking—until the physiological process is completed and learning has been hard-wired into long-term memory. Teaching the concept and skill of division in a single, uninterrupted day is a perfect example of adequate time in action. Please see the video, *Divide and Conquer: A Concept in a Day*, by Martha Kaufeldt. Division Day has been replicated in schools and districts across the country over the past 15 years; the results are always the same. Mastery for all students that day and a program wired into long-term memory that doesn't slip away over time.

USING *ADEQUATE TIME* TO ENHANCE PROGRAM BUILDING

Curriculum Development

- Use your *being there* locations to naturally integrate content and skills. Thus, a one-hour writing assignment about their favorite ecosystem equals two hours of learning because language arts and science are both used simultaneously. This helps free time for practicing basic skills, such as writing, math, speaking, and so forth, without ever losing focus on the study of ecosystems. Similarly, if the focus were on math, you could explore the math possibilities at your current *being there* plus revisit earlier sites while maintaining focus on math.

- Develop, and have your students (from grade three and up) help you develop, lots of inquiries—more than you think you'll need. For substantive concepts, that means a dozen or more. For significant knowledge key points, perhaps five to eight inquiries. There is no magical number of inquiries that are needed. The richness of the sensory input, extent of prior related experience, degree of personal interest, all affect the speed and depth of learning.

USING *ADEQUATE TIME* TO ENHANCE PROGRAM BUILDING

Instructional Strategies

- Eliminate pull-out programs. Invest your resources in more effective instructional strategies and improved curriculum in each classroom.

- Eliminate rigid schedules; use time flexibly. Make the schedule from day to day fit the learning. On some days, science is the focus all day with skills hitchhiking along as a means to practice a concept or significant knowledge.

- Take advantage of teachable moments.

- Teach students to assess their progress toward building a program. Have them assess where they are almost hourly:

Step One: Recognizes the pattern

Understands the pattern

Step Two: Can apply/use what they understand with assistance

Can apply/use what they understand without assistance and almost automatically

Enriched Environment

With the goal of developing programs in mind, any discussion of enriched environment will have to bury the "rich for the sake of richness" idea. Planning for an enriched environment is a calculated process, not an artistic fling. Every item you allow through the doors must relate directly to the concepts and skills being studied for the month. Further, most of the items should allow learners to handle and do something with them as they practice applying what they understand.

USING *ENRICHED ENVIRONMENT* TO ENHANCE PROGRAM BUILDING

Curriculum Development

- Give each item that you bring in the acid test: Is it needed for an inquiry or for direct instruction? If not, don't bring it. There is a huge difference between interesting things and related things. Stick with those things that are conceptually related and significant to acquiring an understanding of the concept.

Instructional Strategies

- Plan your immersion environment to not just look good but to be user friendly.

- When experts visit the classroom, ask them to bring items that students can handle and do something with. Look-and-admire items are nifty but from the bodybrain learning partnership's point of view, nowhere near as powerful.

- Invite students to contribute to the immersion environment. Their items can be kept in a guest corner, available for only a couple of days.

Choices

Because every brain is different—in wiring, in prior experiences, in interests—every student goes about using what they understand differently. For example, remedial readers use reading skills much more fully if they get to choose the content—car magazines or fashion magazines, spy novels or *Ranger Rick*, sports magazines or *National Geographic*. This is true for all learners. If we can see ourselves in the action, we are more able to learn and remember something.

USING *CHOICES* TO ENHANCE PROGRAM BUILDING

Curriculum Development

- When developing inquiries, make sure that there are some for each intelligence so that students can choose their level of difficulty. If the content is unfamiliar, allow them to begin with their intelligence of strength. As they become more adept at using the knowledge or skill of the key point, encourage them to use inquiries calling for intelligences that are less developed.

- Encourage students to develop inquiries that would allow them to apply the key point in an arena of personal interest.

Instructional Strategies

- Encourage students to expand their interests, to develop hobbies, and to explore careers. Use those interests as examples for concepts and skills you are teaching.

Collaboration

The number one cause of passivity in the classroom is being stuck in the role of listener. As listener, there is no chance to check one's thoughts for understanding, to explore possibilities, or to try out how to use something. Collaboration pulls the learner out of passivity and thrusts him/her into using what is learned through conversation, joint problem solving, through carrying out a project. In effect, collaboration multiplies the number of teachers in the room, increases the amount of practice applying key points, and increases the level of challenge.

USING *COLLABORATION* TO ENHANCE PROGRAM BUILDING

Curriculum Development

- Design inquiries that can't be done by any one member of the Learning Club working alone. Increasing the challenge and making real the need for each member to participate forces students to dig deeper and seek connections and relationships that would otherwise remain hidden.

Instructional Strategies

- Don't fly by the seat of your pants when framing collaborative tasks. The potential of collaboration to cement learning into long-term memory is too great to be handled casually. Be purposeful and on target. See *Designing Groupwork* by Elizabeth Cohen.

Absence of Threat/ Nurturing Reflective Thinking

Although absence of threat is listed last, it should be understood from reading previous chapters of this book that it must be teachers' first consideration and that, for this discussion of program building, it is accepted here as a given. Academic learning is all but impossible without an atmosphere of no threat. But absence of threat is only the beginning of the emotional continuum. In-depth learning begins to occur when the learning environment nurtures reflective thinking.

USING *REFLECTIVE THINKING* TO ENHANCE PATTERN SEEKING

Curriculum Development

- Create inquiries requiring students to practice what they understand on their own—through homework, individual projects, and the Yearlong Research Project. Require them to personalize/adapt an inquiry to an area of special interest to them.

Instructional Strategies

- Create a daily journal entry assignment: How does/could this concept or skill apply to your personal life?

Notes

1   To grasp the significance of Hart's conceptualization and definition of learning as a two-part process, consider for a moment what is required of a student taking a typical standardized test with its multiple choice and true-false items. With both kinds of test items, the right answer is present. The student has only to detect the answer (pattern) that is most familiar (a process usually accompanied by a small niggling in the back of the brain that says, "Hey, we've heard of that one before!" "Familiar" doesn't represent understanding of the concept inherent in the test question; ability to apply in a real-life setting is clearly light years away. Thus, in essence, the multi-billion dollar testing juggernaut assesses only the first half of the first stage of learning. To push this realization further, consider the Friday quiz, also typically weighted heavily toward multiple choice and true-false items. Sometimes 80% is accepted as indication of mastery; sometimes it is considered sufficient to just record the letter grades, A-F, and then the whole class moves on to the next topic.

If America is disappointed in the student outcomes of its public schools, it must examine what definition of "learning" is serving as the basis for the design and implementation of its curriculum and instructional practices. If Hart's two-part definition of learning were adopted, outcomes would—and do—soar because it forces profound and radical change at the very core of the business of teaching-learning. See *Human Brain and Human Learning* by Leslie A. Hart (Covington, WA: Books for Educators, 1999), p. 166.

2   Hart, pp. 156-157.

3   Hart, pp. 166-167.

4   Hart, p. 167.

5   Hart, p. 161.

6   Recent research suggests that memory storage is not restricted to the brain only but is a bodybrain function (see Chapter 5). However, until researchers can provide a clear, detailed picture of how this functions, we will continue to refer to the brain as the location for storing programs.

7   Dr. Jose M. R. Delgad has stated this as: "To act is to choose one motor pattern from among the many available possibilities and inhibitions are continually acting to suppress inappropriate or socially unacceptable activities." See "Intracerebral Mechanisms and Future Education," *New York State Education*, February 1968, p. 17.

8   James Doran, director of Algonquin Reading Camp, Rhinelander, Wisconsin, has demonstrated to me a simple, quick technique for giving students a sense of pattern that produces startling gains in their competency in spelling. His brain-compatible methods also produce large, rapid gains in reading.

For truly surprising gains in reading, see *The Auditory Discrimination in Depth (ADD)* and the *Visualizing and Verbalizing for Improved Comprehension* programs by Lindamood-Bell. For information, contact the Lindamood-Bell Reading Processes Center, San Luis Obispo, California 1/800-233-8756.

9   Self-esteem or self-concept programs have long had a questionable base, primarily a "touchy-feely" approach aimed at "feeling good about yourself" as a result of others telling you that you are a "good person" (sometimes in the face of evidence to the contrary). Current brain research tells a different story about the brain producing and receiving its own opiate-like molecules as a response to mental programs that work, to a sense of competence in handling the world. See *Molecules of Emotion: Why You Feel the Way You Feel* by Candace B. Pert, Ph.D. (New York: Scribner, 1997); *The Growth of the Mind and the Endangered Origins of Intelligence* by Stanley I. Greenspan, M.D., with Beryl Lieff Benderly (New York: Addison-Wesley Publishing Company, 1997), p. 104; and "The Neurobiology of Self-Esteem and

Aggression" by Robert Sylwester (*Educational Leadership*, February, 1997, Volume 54, No. 5), pp. 75-78.

10 Parents might well ask if this over-emphasis on valuing of performance by a second person might not also contribute to the extraordinary power of peer groups and peer pressure during the teen years (and beyond). See Alfie Kohn, *Punished by Rewards: The Trouble with Gold Stars, Incentive Plans, A's, Praise, and Other Bribes* (Boston: Houghton Mifflin, 1993) and *Beyond Discipline: From Compliance to Community* (Alexandria, Virginia: ASCD, 1996).

11 Teachers "driving" a conventional class and initiating most activity have little chance to observe what students do on their own. In good "open," Montessori, or similar settings, teachers can readily become observers because they have time and can be more detached. Students feel relaxed, absorbed in their work rather than on guard against criticism or a bad mark.

12 We speak here of academic learning. Some kinds of life-and-death experiences cause the brain to grow dendrites instantly, ready to assess the situation and respond during the incident. Academic learning, however, must travel a slower learning route.

Chapter 6: Impact of Personality

What Makes Us Tick?

Personality preferences or temperaments strongly impact the learning process, affecting how learners take in information, how they organize during learning and when applying learning, what they value when making decisions, and their orientation to others. We are born with these preferences or temperaments. The place we call home—where we feel most comfortable on each of these four areas of behavior—remains relatively unchanged throughout life.

However, preferences are just that—preferences. They are preferred ways of behaving but one is not "stuck" at any one place along a scale. Rather, the point here—and the usefulness of this notion—is that anyone can slide along the scales if and when he/she so chooses.

Intelligence

"Each person is a unique bundle of relatively stable 'personality traits' overlaid by more temporary emotional states and colored by ever-shifting moods and feelings."

William Poole,
The Heart of Healing, 1993

All it takes is the desire to do so, practice to acquire the skills needed to operate from another point along the continuums, and then willingness to be a bit uncomfortable as we leave "home."

For more information, see *Please Understand Me: Character and Temperament Types* by David Keirsey and Marilyn Bates[1] whose work is based upon that of Carl Jung and the team of Meyers and Briggs. It is an extraordinarily readable, practical book. Give yourself the gift of reading it, of reading about the self inside, hidden beneath the classroom roles of teacher and student. See also www.keirsey.com. Because the construct of personality preferences is used widely in the corporate world, there are numerous magazines and newsletters available as well.

ITI Learning Principles

- Intelligence as a function of experience

- Bodybrain partnership —emotion as gatekeeper to learning and performance—movement and cognition

- Multiple intelligences

- Learning as a two-step process

- **Impact of personality**

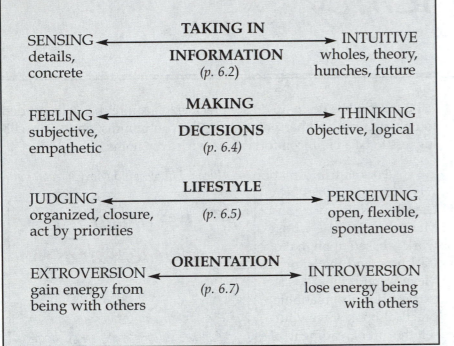

Personality Preferences

The four behavior continuums of the Jung—Myers/Briggs—Keirsey/Bates exploration of personality preferences are:

TAKING IN INFORMATION *(p. 6.2)*

SENSING
details,
concrete
←————————→
INTUITIVE
wholes, theory,
hunches, future

MAKING DECISIONS *(p. 6.4)*

FEELING
subjective,
empathetic
←————————→
THINKING
objective, logical

LIFESTYLE *(p. 6.5)*

JUDGING
organized, closure,
act by priorities
←————————→
PERCEIVING
open, flexible,
spontaneous

ORIENTATION *(p. 6.7)*

EXTROVERSION
gain energy from
being with others
←————————→
INTROVERSION
lose energy being
with others

Give students, grades three and up, the Keirsey-Bates temperament survey the first week of school. Explain the behaviors typical of the ends of each continuum or scale plus:

- Where they are on the scales

- Where the members of their Learning Club are on the scales

- That they can learn to "slide" along the scales when success in communicating with another is important to them

Taking In Information[1]

Knowing how we and our students take in information is critical both to teaching content and guiding behavior. Differences in this area are at the root of most friction, exasperation and, occasionally, the complete inability to get along with people—family, friends, co-workers, students. Never mind differences in values or interests; if the information received isn't what the speaker intended communication and relationships quickly roll downhill. How we take in information can definitely alter the incoming message, especially if our way differs considerably from that of the speaker.

It is important to note here that this concept describes the internal "wiring" of the mind—*how it works* when it acquires sensory input and munches it about to make meaning of it, to relate it to prior learnings, to make it meaningful, to apply it. This is different from the issue of how one acquires information or brings it in from outside. ***At issue here is what the brain does with what it gathers and the form it prefers it in as it does so***. For example, input in small pieces versus whole chunks or concrete details as perceived through the physical senses versus pondering over theory, hunches, and what ifs.

TAKE IN

SENSING————————————————**INTUITIVE**

details, concrete   **INFORMATION**   wholes, theory,
hunches, future

Sensing

Those who prefer to learn via details and concrete input, called sensors, learn by dealing with what can be seen, heard, touched, or otherwise directly experienced. Figuratively, they're from Missouri, the "show me" state. They learn by gathering details, collecting them one after the other, and fitting them together until they snap into place, into a pattern that makes sense. This is much like putting together a puzzle without knowing what the framework or picture is ahead of time. Most of us are this kind of learner—75 percent of the population.[2]

Sensors on the very end of the continuum need assistance in seeing and applying the big picture—the parts in relationship to the whole and to each other. They often have difficulty dealing with two or more competing but not fully compatible ideas. Ambiguity is unsettling to them. Sensors learn best by being allowed to interact with the real world, not textbooks which are an abstraction of the real world and so fragmented that the pieces never add up. The real world helps them see how the pieces fit together.

Intuiting

In contrast, intuitors are sometimes referred to as the "big W" people—*whole notion*. They prefer to begin with the "big picture"—a framework or theory to give meaning to the pieces. Intuitors want to know the theory or the why behind a thing before they get into the details about it; they work well going from theory to application. They are "what if" people, preferring to deal with the possible rather than the details of the actual; they deal in hunches, the future, and things from the realm of abstraction. Often they are very impatient with details and consider the typical school curriculum quite boring.

It is important to note, however, that the end result for both sensors and intuitors is the same—a full understanding of the concept and the particulars. Only the route and, at times, the speed in reaching the destination differ. One kind of learner is not smarter than another. Just different.

Bloom's Taxonomy and How Students Take in Information.

While it is true that Bloom's taxonomy is not truly hierarchical (higher representing "better" thinking), the different levels do require different mixes of "pieces and wholes" thinking—taking in and processing input like a sensor or like an intuitor. Again, one is not better than the other because both are needed in real world problem-solving. However, it is essential that curriculum be developed to give each student ample practice in every level or mix in order to enhance their problem-solving/product-producing capabilities as adults. (For a discussion of how to use Bloom's taxonomy in curriculum development, see Chapter 18.)

The chart below illustrates the approximate nature of "pieces to wholes" mental processing required by curriculum developed at each level of Bloom's Taxonomy: K=knowledge, C=comprehension, AP=application, AN=analysis, E=evaluation, S=synthesis.[3]

TAKE IN

SENSING————————————————————————INTUITIVE

INFORMATION

K	C		AP		AN		E	S

For example, intuitive learners prefer working on inquiries that require them to apply, analyze, evaluate, and synthesize information. They typically find inquiries written for knowledge and comprehension quite boring. Sensors, on the other hand, are often frustrated with inquiries written at the evaluation and synthesis levels. Our job as teachers is to help students spread their wings to become proficient learners from all kinds of input in all kinds of settings.

Implications for Sensors. The implications here for curriculum in a bodybrain-compatible classroom are critically important when designing instructional settings and processes for students to experience. When comparing and organizing, the sensor generally tends to work with smaller pieces. At first glance, our traditional curriculum would seem ideal for these students—small pieces for learners who prefer pieces. Unfortunately, the pieces of the curriculum, e.g., 847 skills for reading, are so small that they don't "add" up, they don't make sense.

When information is presented via second-hand sources, which it typically is, perceiving meaning is even harder. Worse yet for the sensor is information presented via symbolic sources; learning becomes nigh on impossible for most sensors. It is therefore not surprising to find that, of those students who drop out of school before completing the 8th grade, 99.6 percent of them are sensors.[4] A truly shocking statistic! The typical curriculum does not help the sensor develop a sense of how the pieces of the curriculum and their world come together. It fails to give sensors a big picture of what's going on and why it's important—crucial triggers that tell the brain to store something in long-term memory.

SENSORS

Curriculum Development and instructional strategies

- Develop key points that are conceptual rather than factoids.

- Always teach concepts and skills in the context of real-life uses familiar to students. Focus on why and how lines of inquiry. Check for understanding of the big picture as you go.

- Revisit your *being there* location numerous times, going more in-depth and more big-picture each time. Focus on how people use the concepts and skills of your curriculum in order to be intelligent users/participants at that location.

- Lead with inquiries based on the middle levels of Bloom's Taxonomy—application. Then progress to the upper levels—analysis, evaluation, and synthesis. Finish program-building practice with comprehension and knowledge—the form of most tests.

INTUITORS

Curriculum Development and instructional strategies

- Develop key points that are conceptual rather than factoid.

- Always teach concepts and skills in the context of real-life uses familiar to students. Focus on how the theory is applied and the details of how it is done.

- Early in your direct instruction, explain the theory behind what is being studied so that the details make sense and have a post office box in the brain.

- Lead with inquiries based on the middle levels of Bloom's Taxonomy—application. Then progress to the upper levels—analysis, evaluation, and synthesis. Finish program-building practice with comprehension and knowledge—the form of most standardized tests.

Implications for Intuitors. Since most of the curriculum and instructional tools of the traditional classroom are fragmented and piecemeal, intuitors are frustrated and bored much of the time. Extreme intuitors, like the extreme sensor, often act out their frustration. These are the curriculum-induced behavior problem students in our schools. These are the under achievers, students we know could and should be doing much better than they are.[5]

Decision Making[6]

Effective decision-making is a bedrock skill for lifelong learning. Among many important decisions is the recurring "Do I want to learn this, or not?" "Will mastering this concept/skill move me toward my goals?" "What are my goals as a learner?" "What do I want to specialize in when I grow up?" "What's my answer to peer pressure to use drugs?" And on and on.

The decision-making scale described by Keirsey and Bates examines what people value as they perceive and weigh the facts, events, circumstances, and their own thoughts and feelings in order to make a decision. Because decision making is a skill so fundamental to success in life, we must give our students the gift of learning about themselves and others.

DECISION

FEELING————————————————————————**THINKING**

subjective, empathetic   **MAKING**   objective, logical

Feeling

Those at the feeling end of the scale strongly value *how the decision will affect others,* more so than the logic or principle(s) of the factors involved. As a consequence, their decisions tend to be subjective and empathetic. For example, if a "feeling" police officer stopped a car for rolling through a stop sign en route to the hospital delivery room, he would likely conclude that, under the circumstances, allowing the nervous young father to get the soon-to-be mother in labor to the hospital as quickly as possible was more important than applying the usual consequences for the stop sign infraction. He might even decide to escort them to the hospital.

Thinking

The "thinking" decision-makers *value the objective, logical elements.* If the principle is "x" then the choice of "y" is obvious, inescapable and not to be distorted by extraneous circumstances or the reactions of the people involved. Thus, a "thinking" police officer observing the same stop sign infraction would likely conclude that labor pains do not necessarily signal imminent birth and that the safety of others as well as the mother-to-be and child is of paramount importance. The nervous husband should receive a ticket *and* be monitored for several blocks to ensure that he doesn't speed or run another stop sign.

Life in a Bureaucracy. It is not difficult to imagine the reactions of feelers and thinkers making decisions together in our public school bureaucracy which tends to zigzag between extremes and non-action. For example, zero tolerance drug/weapon policies violate the feelers sense of justice when a bystander is swept up in a dragnet because he/she is a friend of one of the offenders and thus was in the wrong place at the wrong time.

On the other hand, thinkers are driven to distraction when the system turns a blind eye to instances of bad behavior because of political pressure, lethargy of individual staff not wanting to bother applying the consequences, or the issues don't show up on the system's radar screen even though it bugs students. Some inconsistencies in decision making are part of human behavior and teacher judgment about individual differences. However, when students participate in pull-out programs and must deal with multiple teachers, all of whom decide procedures and behavior differently, students become frustrated. The solution lies not in having more rules but in opening up the dialogue about the importance of decisions and how each of us weigh the alternatives.

FEELERS

Curriculum Development and instructional strategies

- Because the willingness to learn is the learner's choice/ decision, remember to provide inspirational pep talks when engaging students in new lines of inquiry. Focus on feelings.

- Guide student reflection on how they felt about working together and how successful they were in sliding along the scale to increase the potential for group success. Ask "How did you feel about _____?" kinds of questions. Use "processing the process"[7] following collaborative work to focus their attention on what they value when they make decisions.

- When disciplining the feeling student, always point out how his/her actions made the other person feel.

- When studying literature or history or conducting a class meeting, make sure that you point out the emotional issues and themes, the angst of the situation.

Life in a Learning Club. Collaborative work can really strain relationships if students aren't aware of personality preferences. For example, thinkers often object to procedures not being followed properly, "A rule is a rule." Feelers often react to the nature and circumstances of an issue and the perceived fairness, regardless of the rules. Needless to say, groupwork goes much more smoothly for students and teacher if students are taught this information about decision-making early in the year as part of group development and LIFESKILLS.

THINKERS

Curriculum Development and instructional strategies

- Because the willingness to learn is the learner's choice/ decision, remember to provide convincing arguments and "what if" explorations when engaging students in new lines of inquiry.

- Guide student reflection on how personality preferences helped or hindered group work and how successful they were in sliding along the scale in order to accomplish the task. Ask "What/how well did you think about _____?" kinds of questions. Use "processing the process"[7] following collaborative work to focus their attention on what they value when they make decisions.

- When disciplining the thinking student, always point out the consequences of his/her actions. Ask "What if" questions such as "What if you were Jack and someone did that to you?" "What if Jack had fallen a little harder and broken his arm?" "What would it take for you to control your temper a little bit more?"

- When studying literature or history or conducting a class meeting, make sure that you point out the "what if" questions. For example, what if others had joined in the same behavior, would the society/class/family collapse?

Lifestyle[8]

Lifestyle refers to how people like to organize their lives—not lifestyle as in living high on the hog. On one end of the scale are people who live life by judging—not in the sense of good or bad but rather by decree or judgment, e.g., in Camelot, by decree of the king, it only snows between certain hours during certain months of the year. Camelot is a very orderly, predictable world.

On the other end of the scale are the spontaneous folk who attend to what's happening right now, not five minutes ago, not in response to agreed upon priorities (unless that's what's going on now). These people are open, flexible, and tolerate ambiguity.

LIFESTYLE

JUDGING————————————————————PERCEIVING

organized, closure, priorities   open, flexible, spontaneous

In any group setting, it is essential to value the qualities on the other end of the lifestyle scale (and anywhere along it). A healthy tension between demand for organization and attention to the events and demands of the moment almost always produces a better result, a better mouse trap, greater learning for students, and better curriculum and instructional programs by teachers.

Judging

The judging person likes a great deal of organization and closure, avoids surprises and ambiguity, and prefers clear priorities. These are the makers (and doers!) of to-do lists, people who set and work toward priorities, and who are adamant about closure and nailing down loose ends. The judging person is the one to announce in a loud voice during a meeting, "Well, what's the decision here? We've wasted 25 minutes and no decision has been made! For heaven's sake, let's stop the jawing and make a decision before more time is wasted!" Ambiguity is intolerable, closure (even if the decision is a bad one) is highly valued. Also, judgers do not like surprises in their world. They plan carefully to make things run smoothly and predictably.

Perceiving

Perceivers, on the other hand, literally "perceive" their environment *right now,* take in new information, perceive the essence of what's happening now—minute-by-minute and then respond to the "right now" situation. Forget the to-do lists and last week's priorities. The moment is now!

Perceivers are frequently described as open, flexible, spontaneous. And those are the nice words to describe them! Colleagues who are in supervisory or close teaming roles with the perceiver often use other, not-so-kind descriptors! For example, deadline for a perceiver means "It's almost time to start." A loose end, not a problem; it's never too late to rethink an issue or change one's course of action. Ambiguity? No worries. Handle things as they come up; just improvise a little. Got a fire to put out, a crisis to handle? Here is your person! Spontaneity is the hallmark of the perceiver.

Working Together. For the judger and perceiver to work together—as team teachers or as students in a cooperative learning group—is assuredly a strain. For example, imagine traveling together . . . the judging person is likely to insist upon arriving at the airport at least an hour in advance, pre-paid ticket with pre-assigned seating designation in hand. In contrast, the perceiver is likely to cut arrival time down to the very last minute—no ticket and, not unlikely, no reservation. He/She is the last passenger to enter the plane, giving a slight leap to clear the widening gap as the jetway is withdrawn.

In classroom settings, the perceiving student is an anomaly, a square peg which the highly routinized bureaucracy tries to jam into a round hole. Spontaneity? This is **the** schedule. Flexibility? You may choose the odd-numbered questions for homework or the even-numbered ones. Distracted by the real world outside the window? None of that. Get back to your work.

> ## Lifelong Traits
>
> *Although born with these personality preferences, we can learn to shift our behavior along the four temperament scales. This is a critical skill when operating in the real world where things are as they are, not as we'd like them.*

Although approximately 48% of the general population is an SP personality, a combination of sensing and perceiving, only two percent of teachers are SP types. This means that few SP children will ever have an SP teacher who understands and can appreciate their temperament type.

JUDGERS

Curriculum Development and instructional strategies

- Realize that being a judger is innate. Ambiguity and unmade decisions are genuinely unsettling and even upsetting. Judgers appreciate and expect directions to be clear and well thought through. Changing directions makes them uncomfortable.

- Be organized. Have an agenda every day and follow it. When you deviate, do so for a good reason and explain why and how you will handle the change, such as when undone tasks will get finished.

- Develop and use written procedures. When many parts of the day are predictable, judgers can then begin to handle small amounts of ambiguity and develop their tolerance for doing so over time.

- Develop inquiries that are clear and unambiguous about what is to be done and what the final product is to look like.

- Judgers often have their own schemes for organizing and may resist the teacher's method. When possible, invite students to come up with ways of organizing, tackling problem solving or producing a product. However, be watchful for the student that insists there is only one good way to do things. Help those students develop more flexibility, to operate based on the circumstances of the moment rather than a fixed view of the world.

PERCEIVERS

Curriculum Development and instructional strategies

- Realize that the rules and essence of bureaucracy create an especially difficult environment for perceivers. Just getting by from minute-to-minute is a strain. Provide moments of relief through humor, guiding birdwalks instead of just cutting them off, allowing for choices, and most of all, appreciating the differences instead of becoming annoyed by them.

- Realize that being a perceiver is not a temporary disability. It is a personality preference from birth onward and it is part of who that person is. The role of education is to expand students' options in life rather than punish them because who they are is frequently and, to a bureaucracy, often fundamentally irritating. Therefore, teach perceivers to use their perceiving tendencies to good advantage and to recognize when those tendencies are a disadvantage. Teach them when and how to slide along the scale when circumstances call for it.

- Ensure that choice is available and then help the perceiver to complete the chosen inquiries/tasks.

- Whenever possible, assign perceivers to jobs that have some unpredictability to them, that challenge their resourcefulness.

- Develop inquiries that ask them to challenge themselves, to follow their instincts.

Orientation to Self and Others

Extroversion and introversion are two commonly known qualities. Much of the folk wisdom about them is accurate enough to be useful. Not so well known, however, is the energy flow that occurs.

Extroversion

Extroverts gain energy from being with others. For example, when completely fatigued, extroverts go where there are people such as to a party—arriving early and going home late, returning refreshed and frisky. In the process, they literally absorb energy from others. Thus, many introverts, find it exhausting to be around a highly extroverted person.

Introversion

Introverts, on the other hand, lose energy when around other people. When tired, a party or any grouping of people is the last place introverts want to go. They instead prefer to go off to a quiet place alone and re-energize from the inside out. It is important to note, however, that just because introversion is the preferred orientation, it does not follow that the introvert cannot behave like an extrovert. Many introverts can socialize and dramatize along with the best of the extroverts. Many have jobs that require a high degree of extrovertive behavior. However, the energy cost to an introvert for such jobs is very high, the basis for "burn-out" for many.

EXTROVERTS

Curriculum Development and instructional strategies

- As teacher, master the ability to "gear up" and "gear down" your energy flow to match that of individual students and groups. Model it for students; teach them how to do it.

- Understand that extroverts "think out loud" and need talking time to learn. Develop a tolerance for "busy noise" when students are talking yet still on task.

- Make sure you build in group interaction time (even groups of two). Include inquiries that call for group work. Vary the nature of the activities to best fit extroverts at times and introverts at others. For example, a steady diet of cooperative learning assignments is as deadly for introverts as an unvarying lecture is for extroverts.

- Provide quiet time for extroverts to learn to appreciate their own company. Teach them to use their inner voice as a learning partner, to talk themselves through things on their own, especially when solving problems and producing products.

INTROVERTS

Curriculum Development and instructional strategies

- As teacher, master the ability to "gear up" and "gear down" your energy flow to match that of individual students and groups. Model it for students; teach them how to do it.

- Active learning requires huge mental energy which can easily be drained away from introverts by interactions with others. Classrooms that are "out of control" or that overuse cooperative learning or have lots of conflict (student-student and student-teacher) can become incapacitating for introverts, stealing the energy they need for learning. Use your classroom leadership to create an environment that doesn't rob energy from introverts. Include among the choices for students inquiries that call for individual work, work in teams of two rather than five, and so forth. Create quiet corners where introverted students can go during the day to reenergize themselves.

- Teach introverts how to participate in groupwork without becoming drained of energy and uncomfortable.

- Make sure you have a balance of introvert-extrovert activities. For introverts, reflection time and journal writing, SSR reading time, individual projects, and working in pairs rather than as a learning club. For extroverts, collaboration, collaboration, collaboration — with as many people as possible!

The Power of Personality

The power of personality upon school participation and achievement is enormous. First, we should stop expecting everyone to be like us; we need to begin to understand and appreciate our differences and learn how to make them an asset, rather than an irritant, in the daunting task of succeeding in life.[10]

Second, we must keep foremost in our minds that powerful learning (greatest depth, speed, ability to apply) occurs when learners are able to operate consistent with their mental wirings. Thus, we must recommit ourselves to the idea that schools must remold themselves to fit children rather than expecting children to change how they learn to try to fit with how schools teach. For example, although 38 percent of the general population are a combination of sensor and perceiver (SP), only 2 percent of teachers are that temperament type. On the other hand, 56 percent of teachers (compared to only 38 percent in the population at large) are sensor-judgers (SJ).[11] Thus, it is rare for SP students to ever have an SP teacher, someone who understands them. On the other hand, SJ students have many teachers whose temperament matches theirs; school is a relatively comfortable experience for them.

Most shocking of all, 75-90 percent of at-risk students are SP personalities. They are not "drop outs," they are "push outs." The system is simply too structured, too rigid, too boring, too oppressive.[12] While an SJ student has less than a 3.8 percent chance of becoming a drop out, an SP student has a 34.2 percent chance of dropping out. This means that an SP students is nine times as likely to become a casualty of the system—for no other reason than the temperament with which they were born.

> *We must recommit ourselves to the idea that schools must remold themselves to fit children rather than expecting children to change how they learn to try to fit with how schools teach.*

Notes

1 David Keirsey and Marilyn Bates. *Please Understand Me: Character and Temperament Type.* (California: Prometheus Nemesis Book Co., 1984) pp. 16-19.

2 Keirsey and Bates, p. 160.

3 Olsen, Karen D. *Making Bodybrain-Compatible Education a Reality: Coaching for the ITI Model.* (Covington, Washington: Books for Educations, 1999), Chapter 7.

4 Keirsey and Bates, p. 160.

5 It's not just students who "act out" when the curriculum is boring and/or the instructional strategies don't fit how they learn. Think of your colleagues during inservice trainings. Sensors are driven to distraction by theories (which they tend to call "ivory tower notions"). A successful inservice for them is one with a minimum of theory and a maximum of practicality—specifics and step-by-step how tos.
Intuitors, on the other hand, are often insulted by step-by-step how tos, especially those that are highly detailed and, to them, obvious once they understand the theory or general principles behind the details. They chafe at presentations that do not give them the theory or framework from which the details flow. It just "doesn't make sense"if they have no frame of reference from which to judge the value or usefulness of the specifics.
The lesson here is that we teach the way we learn but if we want all children to learn from us, we must teach as intuitor and sensor.

6 Keirsey, pp. 20-22.

7 Jeanne Gibbs. *TRIBES: A New Way of Learning and Being Together* (Windsor, CA: CenterSource Systems, LLC, 2001), p. 114.8 Keirsey, pp. 22-24.

9 Keirsey, pp. 14-16.

10 Keirsey, p. 97.

11 Keirsey, p. 160.

12 Olsen, Karen. Unpublished study based survey of more than a hundred district administrators in California assigned responsibility for reporting and improving their district's dropout rate, 1985.

Part B

Stages of Implementation: Stage 1

Because the ITI model is so all-encompassing—providing a single framework for viewing the entire range of curriculum development and instructional strategies needed to translate current brain research into the classroom—it is essential that teachers avoid trying to do it all the first year. Full implementation of the ITI model is a three-to-five year effort. The experience of thousands of ITI teachers can be distilled into several pieces of hard-won advice:

1) Start at the beginning.

2) Do first what brain research says needs to be done first. Don't jump ahead to the things you most like to do, such as integrating curriculum, when you're just starting Stage 1.

3) Do thoroughly and well those parts that you begin with before moving onward. Drips and drabs aren't sufficient to make for real change in outcomes. Make an agreement with yourself to move through any discomfort you might experience rather than to avoid it.

4) Consciously maintain practices from prior stages as you begin a new stage of implementation.

5) Be kind to yourself and enjoy the journey as you go!

As you proceed, know that the ITI model has many resources to support you. One of the most valuable is *ITI Classroom Stages of Implementation* by Karen D. Olsen and Susan Kovalik and its companion *ITI Schoolwide Stages of Implementation*. The rest of this book is organized around the stages of classroom implementation. Each goal or benchmark for curriculum and instructional strategies is accompanied by practical "how to" suggestions for achieving that goal.

Part B addresses Stage 1 of the *ITI Classroom Stages of Implementation*—where and how to begin. Chapter 7 describes what to do before students arrive; Chapter 8 addresses what to do the first day of school, and Chapter 9 discusses what needs to be accomplished before moving on to Stage 2. The criteria for assessing Step 1—making the environment bodybrain compatible—is applied 100% of the day.

Part C discusses Stage 2 of the *ITI Classroom Stages of Implementation*—entry level for making curriculum bodybrain-compatible—and what needs to be accomplished before moving on to further improving curriculum. The criteria for implementing Stage 2 is applied only for that portion of the day, week, or year for which the teacher has developed bodybrain-compatible curriculum using the ITI model.

Part D provides practical steps for working toward total curriculum integration as described in Stages 3-5.

ITI Classroom Stages of Implementation was distilled from the experiences of more than 500 teachers who implemented the ITI model over a 10-year period while improving science education in the Mid-California Science Improvement Program. The stages were designed to provide a road map for teachers and their coaches. Much hard-earned wisdom is packed into these descriptions of curriculum, instructional strategies, expectations, and indicators.

Guidelines

The stages described in *ITI Classroom Stages of Implementation* are:

- Stage 1: Entry level for making the learning environment bodybrain-compatible
- Stage 2: Entry level for making curriculum bodybrain-compatible
- Stages 3-5: Advanced levels of curriculum work to refine and expand integrated curriculum.

The stages of implementation are an invaluable guide. They help clarify pictures of end goals as well as next steps. They are also a useful tool to assess progress toward implementing a bodybrain-compatible learning environment individually and as a group.

Before School

CURRICULUM

- Become familiar with state and district standards and assessment practices.
- Visit potential *being there* locations that could provide real-world experiences with the concepts/skills of the standards.
- Establish/update your list of promising guest speakers and topics.
- Get a class list of your students with phone numbers and addresses. Send a postcard or letter to each student and welcome them to your class. Introduce yourself and tell them a little about what they will be learning.

INSTRUCTIONAL STRATEGIES

- The classroom is:
  - Healthful (free of toxins, clean, well-lighted, well-ventilated with air fresh, pleasant smelling, and of proper temperature, and safe)
  - Aesthetically pleasing (calming colors and music, living plants, and well laid out for multiple uses)
  - Uncluttered yet reflects what is being learned.
- Seating is arranged in clusters with easy access to work tools
- Teacher meets frequently with a professional or peer coach who supports his/her implementation of a bodybrain-compatible /teaching learning environment.

First Day of School and Thereafter

CURRICULUM

The bodybrain-compatible element of absence of threat and nurturing reflective thinking is taught as an important and ongoing part of the curriculum. Such curriculum contains:

- The Lifelong Guidelines, including the LIFESKILLS
- The role of emotions in learning
- The personal and social skills for collaboration
- How to utilize reflective thinking

INSTRUCTIONAL STRATEGIES

- The teacher's classroom leadership and management is based upon modeling the Lifelong Guidelines and LIFESKILLS. The atmosphere is participatory rather than dictatorial. "Discipline" is based upon helping students develop the personal and social skills and behaviors needed to successfully practice the Lifelong Guidelines rather than upon a system of externally imposed rewards and punishments.
- Written procedures and agendas provide consistency and security for students.
- The calmness of the teacher's voice contributes to a settled classroom environment.
- Collaborative learning is a frequently used instructional strategy.
- The teacher meets frequently with a professional or peer coach who supports his/her implementation of a bodybrain-compatible teaching/learning environment.

Accomplish Before Moving On

CURRICULUM

- The concept of multiple intelligences, defined as problem-solving and product producing capabilities, is taught early in the year and is a frequent, ongoing topic for post-lesson processing of collaborative work.

- Time frames for activities and areas of study are no longer rigid and students have adequate time to complete their work.

INSTRUCTIONAL STRATEGIES

- Limited choices are introduced through student selection of supplies, time allocations, materials and processes used for completing projects, and other developmentally-appropriate options.

- The teacher includes real-life experiences—being there, immersion, and hands-on experiences—to supplement classroom instruction; resource people are invited to the classroom.

- The teacher is developing a variety of instructional strategies to supplement direct instruction.

- The teacher meets frequently with a professional or peer coach who supports the implementation of a bodybrain-compatible learning environment for students.

Stage 1 of implementing ITI begins not with themes or integration but with the brain research relevant to creating a bodybrain-compatible environment in which learning can occur.

Implementors are advised to go slowly with curriculum development until significant strides toward maintaining a bodybrain-compatible learning environment is achieved. While a bodybrain-compatible learning environment cannot be fully realized until curriculum becomes bodybrain-compatible, curricular changes have little impact if the learning environment is not consistent with how the brain learns.

Stage 1, entry level into a bodybrain-compatible environment, is to be applied to the classroom 100% of the time. Note that this stage is broken into three parts in order to give teachers greater focus on where and how to begin.

Chapter 7: What to Do Before Students Arrive

Where and how to begin your program improvement efforts? Start with brain research firmly in mind. Your number one goal is to make your classroom a bodybrain-compatible environment. Once that is in place—for you as well as for your students—powerful learning will occur.

Much of the foundation work for Stage 1 occurs before the school year even begins. In architecture, function follows form or, said another way, form dictates function. Similarly, the behavior and attitudes our students bring to our classrooms are a reaction to the institutional, bureaucratic environment of our public schools. Students come to our classrooms with "school behaviors," a reaction to bureaucratic institutionalism. These school behaviors are typically far from the polite behaviors expected when they visit a friend's house and want to earn the right to come again. The moral of the story here is that if we want different behaviors, we must change the environment and thus students' perception of school.

Such changes seem simple enough: Make the environment non-institutional and more like home. Yet, like many simple things, this is easier said than done. Plan to make changes both in the physical environment and in relationships.

For the physical environment, make classrooms and common areas healthful, aesthetically pleasing, and uncluttered. In terms of relationships, begin by leading rather than managing the classroom. Plan ahead by creating written procedures and a daily agenda to provide consistency and security for students from the moment they step through the classroom door. For the first day, create a minimum of procedures to begin with; then, involve students in creating additional ones.

As you plan for students, remember to plan for your own needs. Set aside the necessary resources, especially time, to ensure that you have opportunities to meet frequently with a professional or peer coach who has mastered the ITI model in his/her own classroom and can support your implementation of a bodybrain-compatible learning environment.

This chapter provides practical advice for implementing the before-school aspects of Stage 1 of the *ITI Classroom Stages of Implementation*.

The Classroom Is Healthful

Negative "messages" from the environment often set off behaviors that impede student learning and frustrate teachers. For example, a dirty, ill-kempt classroom tells occupants that they aren't valued; if no one cares, why should students?

And, as life in the 21st century becomes more technology-based, our environment—indoor and outdoor—is becoming increasingly more chemical-laden. Forty years ago, healthful was defined as clean, an absence of dirt.

Today, the definition of healthful must include the invisible as well as the visible—the presence of toxic off-gassing. We must look at the dark side of noise-snuffing carpets, energy conservation measures dictating that heating/cooling systems restrict inflow of fresh air and windows be sealed shut, high-tech machines that spew gases (copiers and laser printers and more), art and science chemicals, the ubiquitous and potent cleaning compounds, and the effects of poor maintenance (allergens, toxic molds, and chemicals). We must take a new look at our classrooms and school campuses using a 21st century awareness of healthful. We must inform ourselves and take responsibility for acting upon our knowledge.

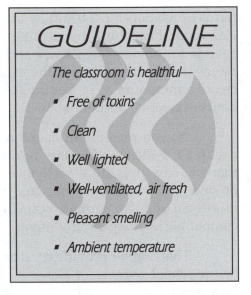

GUIDELINE

The classroom is healthful—

- Free of toxins
- Clean
- Well lighted
- Well-ventilated, air fresh
- Pleasant smelling
- Ambient temperature

Free of Toxins

A growing body of evidence makes it clear that unhealthy environments can and do cause serious learning and health problems for students and staff alike. Learning and behavior problems include: headaches, fatigue, weakness, exhaustion, listlessness; depression, easy crying; moodiness, anger, confusion; excessive talking, explosive speech, stuttering, slurred speech; inattentiveness, disruptive behavior, impulsiveness; nervousness, irritability, agitation; a short attention span, inability to concentrate; memory loss, learning problems; numbness and/or tingling of face, hands, arms; dizziness, clumsiness; restless legs, finger tapping, tremors, tics; excessive fatigue and tiredness, nightmares; hyperactivity, wild unrestrained behavior, and increased sensitivity to odors, light, sound, temperature, touch and pain.[1]

Medical problems resulting from major, long-term toxic exposure include measurable abnormalities in the blood, nervous and immune systems, and in the brain. These health effects can be permanent, including later reproductive problems, or can even cascade into "spreading syndrome," a condition in which previously tolerated chemicals become intolerable. In serious "sick building" situations, Norma Miller, editor of *The Healthy School Handbook: Conquering the Sick Building Syndrome and Other Environmental Hazards In and Around Your School*, suggests that 80

Self Check

For toxins:

- Decrease in hyperactivity, absenteeism, complaints of feeling ill, and trips to the nurse's office.

- Behavior at home and school is congruent.

- Overall sense of well-being for students and staff.

percent of those who become sick get better in six to twelve months; 15 percent do not improve; and 5 percent may become worse in spite of therapy, moving into spreading syndrome, their health forever compromised and their future in doubt.[2]

These are shocking statistics. Unfortunately, they are the rule rather than the exception. There is much to suggest that a significant portion of misbehavior, learning problems, and even the dramatic increases in special education enrollments and classifications, such as ADD, maybe a result of chemical poisoning. Creating and maintaining a healthful environment must become the number one priority of teachers, administrators, school boards, and parents.

A sage comment about education is, "If you think education is expensive, try ignorance." Likewise, if we think it is too expensive to face up to these environmental issues, we are not looking at the exponential increase in costs due to rising special education enrollments and lifelong damage to student and adult health.

At a research conference at Texas Woman's University to establish ecological guidelines for a healthful school building, 60 environmental specialists from 26 states and two other countries gathered to share concerns about construction and maintenance of healthful school buildings. The top ten major areas, listed in the order of their importance, are:[3]

1. Heating, cooling, and ventilation
2. Pest controls
3. Cleaning products
4. Chemicals
5. Fragrances
6. Site selection
7. Lighting
8. Remodeling the school building
9. Floors
10. Art supplies

The pervasiveness of toxins suggested by this list is truly hair-raising. And the symptoms of the chemicals involved reads like a Who's Who of reasons why students are sent to the principal's office. For a list of particularly toxic chemicals, their location, and symptoms, see page 7.4.

Pesticides. Pesticides are not harmless. They are intended to kill target organisms. Even in small quantities in larger animals, they can seriously poison. Many believe that the mushrooming numbers of children with learning problems is attributable to the increase in toxins in the environment. According to Norma Miller, "Classroom environments can be extremely volatile sites, constantly offgassing pesticides that have been applied repeatedly for years in the same routine fashion. The general application of pesticides fails to address those micro-environments where insects actually live. Instead, poisons are placed within the confines of the classroom, making it possibly the most toxic place a child will spend time in during his or her entire life."[4]

As Norma Miller points out, most school systems don't have a policy that specifically addresses issues surrounding pesticide use. She recommends that such a policy include:

- "Establishment of specific contractual amendments that will attract vendors capable of delivering services to contract specification. Policies that have allowed for low-bid acceptance as the norm should be modified. A stringent policy of bid acceptance that emphasizes value for dollars spent based on a 60% technical and 40% value standard will better serve both the contractor and the school system.

- Discontinuance of the practice of routine spraying.

- Reduction of pesticide use, targeting specific amounts (percentages) over a given period of time. Not many school systems are equipped to move from one approach to another overnight. It is important, therefore, that time constraints be imposed, and that appropriate scheduling be followed when the practice of routine spraying is discontinued.

Chemical	Where It Is Found	What It Does
Benzene	Adhesives, anthraquinone colors, art class, auto exhaust, cigarette smoke, degreaser/solvent, eggs, fossil fuel, fungicide, gasoline, glue, paint, paint stripper, plastics, room deodorizers, solvents, spot removing products, synthetic fibers, tobacco, smoke, VOCs*, water, wood finish	**Cause of cancer. Immunotoxic.** Anorexia, aplastic anemia, blurred vision, bone marrow and central nervous system depression, chromosomal abnormalities, dermatitis, disorientation, drowsiness, drunken behavior, euphoria, irritation of eyes and gastrointestinal and respiratory tracts, fatigue, headache, leukemia, leukopenia, light headedness, loss of appetite, multiple myeloma, pancytopenia, paralysis, polyneuritis, reproductive hazard
Toluene	Adhesives, carpets, classrooms, cleaners, composite wood products, room deodorizers, floor tile, fossil fuel, fuel additive, gasoline, furniture, glue, insulation, lacquer, liquid paper/white out, paint, paint thinner and stripper, petroleum products, polyethylene, polyurethane wood finish, printing materials, solvents, tobacco smoke, varnish, wallcoverings, water	**Cause of cancer. Narcotic.** Brain malfunction, central nervous system damage, depression, disorientation, irritation of eyes, lung, nose, and skin, fatigue, hoarseness, irritability, kidney, liver and spleen damage, loss of coordination, marrow suppression, reproductive hazard, and, with prolonged exposure, permanent neurological damage
Methylene chloride	Adhesives, classrooms, coffee, epoxy, furniture, glue, paint, paint remover, pharmaceuticals, phenolic thermosetting resins, wallcoverings	**Suspected carcinogen. Mutagen.** Bronchitis, central nervous system and heart damage, irritation of eyes, lung, and skin, metabolizes to carbon monoxide in blood, pulmonary edema or lung fluid
Trichloroethane	Art class, duplicating fluid, vinyl floortile, VOCs, degreaser/solvent, dry cleaning fluid, fumigants, insecticides, insulators, paint, solvent, water	**Cause of cancer.** Dizziness, headaches, possible liver damage

* VOC = volatile organic compounds

Taken from *The Healthy School Handbook: Conquering the Sick Building Syndrome and Other Environmental Hazards In and Around your School*, Norma L. Miller, Ed.D., Editor, page 9.

- Determining that staff members understand the pesticide regulations and the reasons for them. Staff members who apply pesticides either should be state-certified or should practice under the guidance of certified applicators. Anyone who violates pesticide regulations during the application of a pesticide, especially by applying a pesticide prohibited by the policies of the system or state, should face disciplinary action. Contractors who send in workers without proper documentation should be dismissed.

- Notification of all concerned when pesticide application is scheduled.

- Documentation of all chemically sensitive students, teachers, and other persons who are involved in the daily function of the building.

- Provision on request of full disclosure of the materials used by both the school system and its contractors.

- Establishment of standards for pesticide use. It should be determined which pesticide will have the least negative impact on human beings and which areas will be acceptable for the application of the pesticide."[5]

From *The Healthy School Handbook: Conquering the Sick Building Syndrome and Other Environmental Hazards In and Around Your School* by Norma L. Miller, Editor. Washington, DC: National Education Association, 1995, p. 228.

How to Locate and Eliminate Toxins

- Get educated. Two resources to begin with are: *The Healthy School Handbook: Conquering the Sick Building Syndrome and Other Environmental Hazards In and Around Your School* by Norma Miller and *Talking Dirty with the Queen of Clean* by Linda Cobb (New York: Simon & Schuster, 1998).

- Know your students' allergies before the first day of school and make sure that the materials, live animals, and *being there* locations will not trigger an allergic or asthma attack.

- Give colleagues and students the benefit of the doubt when they tell you they don't feel well at school but okay at home. Listen to their complaints and take action.

- Create a school committee composed of staff and parents to investigate complaints. Set policies and procedures to determine priorities for eliminating toxins. Budget resources each year to handle situations as they arise.

- Set and closely monitor school policies for chemical use for pests, weed treatments, and cleaning—which, how, when.

- Where possible, enlist the assistance of students to help identify and solve problems.

- Recognize that this is a community problem and the community deserves to know the extent of the problems their children face. Enlist the support of parents and community—time and talents as well as money donations.

Cumulative Affects. The dangers of one-time exposure are considerable enough but the real problem that educators must face is accumulated effects of multiple toxins. The figure below illustrates the total-body-load theory of human disease and ill-health. No single factor is the complete culprit but each factor adds a burden to the body's adaptive capacity; disease develops when the body's ability to adapt has been exceeded.

The Classroom Is Clean

Clean is clean. It is the clean you make your house when special guests are coming. It means absence of dirt. It means shiny windows, beautiful ceilings and walls with good paint and no water stains, gleaming floors/carpets unstained and free of dust, molds, and other allergens. It means desks without last year's fingerprints, art project mishaps, and gum. It means clean.

Somehow we've come to accept a second-rate standard for cleanliness in our schools. And, whether we like it or not, the degree of cleanliness signals clearly how much we value our guests and ourselves. If we want students to choose to be in our classrooms, we need to let them know by our deeds that they're welcome and valued. Nothing you do can mask a dirty environment or mute its messages to students, parents, and colleagues. A dirty environment clearly signals that there are no standards here, people have to be here, and are powerless to change their situation. These are all the wrong messages for a school to telegraph to its students.

If you think we're over-reacting here, guess again. Children love cleanliness and classy surroundings (think Disneyland standards). Standards of cleanliness, tidiness, "classiness," and professionalism do matter.

Making the Most of Resources. Although insufficient resources for proper maintenance and repairs is the rule rather than the exception, before you campaign for an increase in your maintenance budget, analyze what is happening/not happening now. It is always possible to make better use of what we have. The most frequent culprit is lack of agreed-upon policies and procedures—an overall plan of priorities. Or, the plan is written but unknown to most and followed by few.

Here are some questions to ask:

- Exactly what cleaning is done daily? What are the standards?

- How do day-to-day procedures build in time for non-daily, rotational needs such as washing windows, sanitizing desks, washing walls, cleaning carpets, and so forth?

- Who should be notified when things are not done according to the plan? When first reports aren't responded to, what is the follow-up process?

Often maintenance staffs are not under the direct supervision of the principal or, even worse, the staff's needs and priorities are theirs alone. They are said to run the school. If so, make some changes. Create a maintenance/repairs advisory committee composed of teachers, parents, community members (especially those who with good reputations for supervising high quality maintenance and repair services), the principal, and the maintenance staff. Put the cards on the table. Hammer out agreements and priorities. Politics must be made to bow to the health needs of children.

Recruit and Delegate. For the most part, teaching is a solitary act. But the issue of a healthful environment is too important to allow yourself and your students to be left hanging. If your school administration doesn't insist on clean and won't assign anyone to help you, recruit help from parents and students. Don't be bashful. They have as much vested interest in their classroom as you do.

Need tissues in the classroom but it's not in your school's budget? No soap in the bathroom? Ask for donations. Bathrooms superficially cleaned and a health hazard? Let parents press for higher standards. This is their school for their children.

Also, recruit students for tasks similar to those chores they would perform at home. If you want the maintenance staff to perform more of the major cleaning projects such as window washing, cleaning walls, sanitizing desks, etc., then make the students responsible for cleaning up their own daily messes . . . just as they are responsible for at home so that their parents can spend their time on real cleaning and repair tasks.

Getting Started. As we know from cleaning our own home—and keeping it clean—cleaning is difficult if our space is cluttered. To get your space really clean, you may first have to conquer clutter (see discussion on page 8.14). Before attempting to clean, remove clutter—all of it. If possible, move everything but the furniture out into the hall. Then, scrub, sanitize, paint. Scrutinize the carpet. If it's not cleanable to acceptable health (not just visual) standards, have it removed immediately; if cleanable, get it cleaned immediately using as chemical-free a process as possible.

Before you move anything back in, make sure that it is absolutely essential to what you are studying this year. If not, don't let it through the door. Keep visible only those things that will be used this month; store things needed for the rest of the year in cupboards that have doors (or solid colored curtains) and thus can be kept out of sight.

Items that will not be used this year should be removed from the classroom. Recycle (give them to teachers who can use it), give it away, throw it away, or store off-site. Then, clean the room and everything in it.

Don't stop until the room meets your standards for your own home . . . you know . . . if your future mother-in-law were coming to visit for the first time. Now that's clean!

Don't Overlook the Restrooms. Like it or not, the bathrooms your students regularly use are a big part of maintaining a healthful environment.

If your bathrooms are frequently trashed by students, perhaps students are expressing their discontent about the lack of cleanliness and the inadequate supplies (no toilet paper or soap or towels). If you want to turn things around, hold a bathroom celebration on the weekend. Invite parents and students to the party. Deep clean, paint, and decorate the bathroom. Make it look as much like yours at home (or what you'd like yours to look like!). Add a touch of wallpaper or special paint for color and class. Post relevant LIFESKILLS and procedures where necessary but don't make it look like a military camp. And add a sign telling users how to report a problem, e.g., "If you find something wrong in this bathroom, come to room X to report it. Thank you for helping us keep our bathroom clean."

Also take note of in-classroom sinks and drinking fountains. Not only should they be visually clean but they must be kept sanitary.

Hanging in There. To maintain this new standard of clean, talk with your custodian. Share your intentions and standards for your classroom. Ask what you can do to help him/her help you achieve and maintain your goals. Pride is a powerful motivator. Help both of you be proud of your classroom.

Tell your maintenance person what allergies you and your students have. Together select cleaning products for use in your classroom. Choose those that don't leave toxic fumes; naphtha, creosol, lye, formaldehyde in disinfectants and ammonia, ethanol, or chlorine bleach in scouring powders are particularly bad. For nontoxic alternatives, see *Talking Dirty with the Queen of Clean* by Linda Cobb. See also the discussion of pollutants and ventilation, pages 8.10-8.12.

Mastering the Art of Clean

- Make the most of your resources by ensuring there are daily procedures both for day-to-day cleaning and for larger jobs, parts of which need to be done each day to ensure they are completed as expected.

- Make sure that the daily procedures are performed as expected.

- Involve parents and the community in maintenance issues. It is their school and their children. Ask their advice, recruit their assistance, and delegate tasks.

- Involve students; help them become responsible for cleaning up their own daily messes so that maintenance staff can address larger cleaning issues.

- In your own classroom, raise the bar. Insist on standards of cleanliness at least as high as those you maintain at home.

- Before school starts, find out what allergies your students have. Plan materials and resources accordingly.

- Pay attention to the bathrooms.

- Schoolwide, create a maintenance/repairs advisory committee composed of teachers, parents, community members, the principal, and the school maintenance staff. Hammer out agreements about standards and priorities within current resources and determine if additional resources are needed, where, and why.

Self Check

The Classroom is Clean

Clean to meet the evaluative yardstick of our senses:

- Visual—no dust bunnies, streaks and smears, discoloration, dullness/lack of shine; nothing broken or ill-functioning; no clutter (no furniture, resources, materials not in current use)

- Smell—no odor, no allergens/antigens such as molds, bacteria, dust. Air filters are cleaned every two months or more often as needed; carpeting is deep-cleaned twice a year and removed when it can no longer be cleaned to standards. Air purifiers are installed in each classroom that needs one.

- Touch—no stickiness or roughness (from dried materials on surfaces or from scraps and cracks)

- Sanitation—absenteeism due to illness by school contagion less than 1 percent

The Classroom Is Well-Lighted

Lighting in schools has been examined from various points of view over the past 50 years. Sufficient light to easily read a book, see work on one's desk, and see the board have long been the accepted standards for classroom lighting. More recently, energy conservation issues have prevailed. Aesthetics is also a consideration. However, recent research goes beyond these typical issues and makes it clear that light—amount, intensity, and color spectrum—have a profound affect on people of all ages, not just children. For those new to the body of research about the effects of light on physical, emotional, and brain function, the findings are quite startling. The implications for teaching and learning are huge.

Effects of Lighting on Physical and Emotional Health.

John Ott, pioneer and giant in the study of the effects of light on humans believes that "humans are photosynthetic," that full-spectrum light acts as the ignition switch for all human biological functions: "The light-mediated process known as photosynthesis in plants is, in my opinion, the same thing as metabolism in humans."[6] According to Fritz Hollwich, M.D., "Light is a primal element of life. Artificial light may be an optic substitute but is by no means equivalent to nature's light in physiological terms."[7] Light from the sun synchronizes most body functions; its absence or imbalance can cause a reduction in our physiological, emotional, and intellectual functioning.[8]

Light not only permits us to see but, through its stimulation of the pineal and hypothalamus glands, also affects virtually every function of the body. The spectral properties of sunlight are fundamental to the:

- Endocrine system, biological clock, immune system, circulatory system, respiratory system, and sexual development
- Ability to control stress and fatigue
- Healthy functioning of the nervous system.[9]

Most of us spend the majority of our waking hours drenched in light whose spectral characteristics differ markedly from those of sunlight. Artificial sources of light fail badly to duplicate the full spectrum of natural sunlight which casts a broad, continuous rainbow of colors.[10]

Most indoor artificial light tends to be weak in strength and density and distorted in terms of color.[11] One component of natural light, which we rarely receive indoors, is ultraviolet light. It is virtually absent from incandescent lighting, shielded in standard fluorescent tubes, and blocked by normal window pane glass and eyeglass lenses. According to Faber Birren in *Light, Color, and Environment,* UV stimulates blood circulation, lowers blood pressure, prevents rickets, increases protein metabolism, decreases fatigue, stimulates glandular activity, stimulates white blood cell activity, increases the release of endorphins, and enhances the production of vitamin D, thereby increasing the absorption of calcium and phosphorus.[12]

According to Richard J. Wurtman, M.D., 16 hours of artificial lighting provides less physical and emotional benefit than one hour of natural lighting.[13] Prolonged exposure to artificial lighting has been associated with:

- Irritability, eyestrain, headaches, fatigue
- Hyperactivity, allergies, frequent minor illnesses
- Inability to concentrate, vision problems
- Susceptibility to osteoporosis and rickets
- Increased incidence of dental cavities
- Changes in heart rate, blood pressure, electrical brain wave patterns, hormonal secretions, and body rhythms
- Depression/Seasonal Affective Disorder, alcoholism, suicide (the third leading cause of death for young adults), weight gain, anxiety, and insomnia.[14]

In short, natural sunlight is a key ingredient in maintaining our health and mental acuity for learning—*a vital nutrient.* Lack of sufficient light affects many children and adults so much that their behavior, learning, and performance are significantly impaired.[15]

Effects of Lighting on Brain Function and Achievement. Modern indoor life, with its radical changes in the amount, intensity, and color spectrum of our lighting, challenge our brain in many ways that make learning more difficult for all of us. The difficulties arise indirectly from physical symptoms described previously, and directly, due to actual changes in brain waves and disturbances in producing various neurotransmitters.

Studies show surprisingly strong effects of lighting on brain function. For example, lack of natural light from the sun results in:

- Increased incidence of anxiety and irritability, an inability to tolerate stress, difficulty in getting started in the morning, crying spells, and an overall decrease in activity levels, specifically in the fall semester[16]

- Overeating, oversleeping, and sluggishness[17]

- Increased absenteeism (more than double)[18]

- Lower achievement scores[19]

Given the billions of dollars spent on public education each year, it makes no sense to "stack the cards against educational success by ignoring issues of polluted light."[20]

⁛ Using Light to Improve Learning & Performance

- Conduct a thorough analysis of the light in your classroom and other areas where students spend a lot of time. Check for:
  - Amount of lighting for near and far work (the old-fashioned measurement of whether a student can see his/her work at desk and board)
  - Intensity (high enough to prevent eye strain but without glare)
  - Color spectrum (the color spectrum matches natural sunlight).

- Remove the omnipresent, blue-spectrum fluorescent tubes; substitute full-spectrum tubes that mimic natural sunshine. Replace or repair lights that hum.

- Add incandescent lighting to special reading areas and the teacher's desk.

- Install/Repair window treatments that block the glare of direct sun but allow sunlight in (shades that mount at the bottom of the window and pull up are often more useable than those that hang from the top).

- During design and renovation of schools, insist on windows in every classroom and all offices, full spectrum fluorescent lights, and separate switches for each bank of lighting.

- Consider visual needs and sensitivities of students when drawing up student seating assignments.

- Keep exposure to computer screens, videos, and TV to a minimum.[21]

Well-Ventilated

The two most essential fuels for the brain are glucose and oxygen. Proper diet supplies the first. Fresh air provides the second. Without fresh air—oxygen—learning is impossible. Fresh air means an absence of neurotoxins and biological allergens/antigens such as molds, bacteria, viruses, dust mites, dust, pollens, and so forth.

The importance of fresh air to a healthful environment can't be overemphasized. Most of the pollutants discussed earlier off-gas into the air and thus become a ventilation/fresh air problem. For example, all of the issues in the top 10 most serious indoor sources of pollution identified in the Texas Woman's University study (see page 8.3) except lighting impinge on air quality—adequate oxygen and absence of toxins. Thus, the adequacy of a school's ventilation system should be the first system analyzed and have first call on resources.

The authors have yet to see a large building whose HVAC (heating, ventilation, and air conditioning) system really works, i.e., provides a pleasant environment (good air quality and appropriate temperature) for everyone year around.

Before the advent of so many chemicals, the biggest challenges to air quality were the products of human bodies—carbon dioxide, moisture, odors. Now, like cleanliness, we need to recognize a 21st century definition of well-ventilated: complete absence of toxins and full presence of fresh oxygen, pleasant smelling (the absence of odor), and a constant, appropriate temperature.

For an excellent discussion of current challenges for ventilation and toxin removal, see *The Healthy School Handbook: Conquering the Sick Building Syndrome and Other Environmental Hazards* by Doris Rapp, often cited in this chapter, and her videotape, *Environment-ally Sick Schools—What You WANT and NEED to Know: A Guide for Parents and Teachers.*

Providing oxygen—fresh air with no neurotoxins and allergens—to the brain is the most important contribution to learning that educators and taxpayers can make. The formula is a simple one: "No oxygen, no learning."

Improving Ventilation and Providing Fresh Air

- Listen to those who complain about poor air and not feeling well. They are your "canaries"—your indicators of air quality.

- Check the intake and outflow points of your system(s) to make sure that outflow from the ventilation system and any other outflow points do not feed dirty air into the "fresh air" intake.

- If you have windows that open, open them (monitor when the outside might be unsafe). Your goal is to have fresh air at head height. Make a point of asking yourself, "How's the air in here right now?" Ask this question at least once every hour. Does it smell of body odor, is the air stale, do students look alert yet calm?

- Insist on the maximum percentage of fresh air exchange allowed by law in your state. Reducing fresh air intake to conserve energy is absurd—far less expensive than lost learning due to inattention caused by low oxygen levels to the brain and or the presence of neurotoxins and allergens. If the allowed exchange rate is inadequate, lobby your legislature for exemptions for those schools that can prove a need for more fresh air intake. If your school is located in an area of high outdoor pollution, widen your political action focus.

Improving Ventilation and Providing Fresh Air *continued*

- Thoroughly clean the system, including duct work, each year before school starts. Replace the air filters at least every two months. Add purifying systems to areas of high concentrations of chemicals or classrooms whose students or teacher are particularly sensitive to poor ventilation.

- Given the rate of introduction of new chemicals into the environment, analyze the chemical composition of every item that comes onto the campus, from construction materials to cleaning agents, computers to book print, white board markers to science and art supplies, particularly items brought on to the campus in large quantities.

- Eliminate artificial fertilizers, pesticides, or herbicides from playgrounds and athletic fields because these chemicals are tracked in and can build up in high concentrations.

- When designing or remodeling a single story building, compare the long-range costs (purchase, maintenance, and repair) of a heat pump HVAC unit for each classroom versus the large, centralized unit. Individual units over time are often more cost-effective, not to mention pleasant ,because each classroom can have the temperature the occupants want, contaminants from elsewhere in the building spread less readily, and each room has access to fresh, high-oxygen outside air.

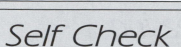

Self Check

Well Ventilated

- All exhaust vents are properly separated from in-take vents.

- Filters fit and are free from dirt, molds, and bacteria. Duct work is also clean and free from contaminants.

- Air purifying machines have been installed in each classroom where needed.

- Water leaks are fixed immediately; pockets of mold and bacteria have been eliminated; all drain traps contain water to decrease sewer gas.

- Buses run their engines only when in motion.

- An Integrated Pest Control System has replaced all routine pesticide/insecticide treatments.

Pleasant Smelling

The most pleasant smelling environment is one that has no particular smell, just a sense of air that is fresh and well-oxygenated. That means absence of smell from cleaning chemicals, body odor, mold from air conditioners and other sources, stale air, dust, old books with mites, and so forth.

Use of potpourri and air fresheners on a regular basis is not desirable because some of your students may be allergic to them. On an occasional basis, to heighten an immersion or hands on experience, adding an odor can be very useful, provided, of course, no student has a allergic reaction to the fragrance used.

When adding a smell to the classroom, use natural rather than artificial sources.

Ambient Temperature

A steady, reliable temperature of 68 degrees in the winter and 76 degrees in the summer helps students stay focused on learning. Yet few centralized systems can deliver. Our recommendation is careful monitoring of windows that open and, whenever possible, a separate HVAC unit for each classroom.

Safe

That our public schools provide a safe environment is assumed, at least a minimal level of care. But the truth is that delayed maintenance and repairs often present real safety hazards. Examples include, an electrical supply inadequate to the demands of the classroom, broken or missing plates for electric plugs and switches, furniture that is ill-fitting, unsteady, chipped, cracked, splintery. Other hazards include tears in the carpet, loose throw rugs, coats and boots on the floor due to lack of hangers, and so forth. The list goes on.

Unfortunately, timely maintenance is a common budget-cutting target. School board members and administrators need your support and input as they address competing priorities.

▦ Safety First

- Take a fresh look at your classroom. As you come through the door, crouch down to the height of your students. Slowly survey the room. What safety hazards do you see?

- Run your hand over and around the edges of the furniture. Fix any rough or sharp edges and surfaces.

- Written procedures for handling toxic chemicals are in place and known to staff.

- Written procedures for handling each classroom pet are posted and used by students.

Aesthetically Pleasing

Aesthetics is defined as the study or theory of beauty and of the psychological responses to it. It is the branch of philosophy dealing with art, its creative sources, its forms, and its effects. While this is more inclusive than necessary for our purposes here, the sense of rigor implied is important to the classroom. That is to say, the scientific research behind the physiological, mental, and emotional impact of color and other elements of design, versus interior design based on personal preference or tradition, is critical. By basing classroom design on research findings, we can create classrooms that nurture reflective thinking for the highest possible percentage of our students.

For a workaday definition of aesthetics, we will focus on two areas: art and design. Art is usually thought of in terms of line, shape or form, value, texture, and color. Design is often thought of in terms of space, color, composition, different materials and techniques, and purpose or use.

Our ultimate criteria of acceptability and excellence in these areas is not how chic or groovy or cool a classroom may look but rather how well it nurtures reflective thinking. Questions to ask under each category of art and design include the following:

Purpose in Design. To what extent do the elements allow you to implement the bodybrain-compatible elements to best advantage? For example, does the form of the room allow such functions as Learning Clubs, community circle, and other group projects? For intrapersonal space and time, an "Australia" or time-alone space? For movement, immersion and hands on of the real thing, and ready access to needed resources, materials, and tools? Does it provide an attractive entry that provides transition into the room?

Space. Is there a sense of spaciousness yet a location for every purpose and a place for everything and everything in its place without clutter and crowding? Does the layout allow for flow and freedom to move about? Has all unnecessary furniture been removed? Is the teacher's desk in an inconspicuous place?

Color. There is plenty of hard data about the physiological, emotional, and mental effects of color. To ignore it when designing and remodeling schools and even a single classroom is to squander public resources. There is great power in color. We need to learn to harness it as a way to enhance learning. For example, intense reds, yellows, and oranges overstimulate students, making it difficult for them to focus on learning; the incidence of discipline problems is high. Other colors, especially the cool colors, greens and blues, are soothing and calming, inviting reflection and introspection.

As color emits its effects on students every minute of every day, it should be considered one of our strongest instructional allies. Accordingly, color should be selected with great care.[22]

Historically, elementary schools have used either institutional colors such as drab greens and grays or the ubiquitous white, or they have used bright, vivid colors such as red, orange, and yellow. Recent color research would have us avoid both extremes. Recommended colors for classrooms that enhance intellectual work include the following:[23]

- For preschool and elementary grades, light salmon, soft warm yellow, pale yellow-orange, coral, and peach. For example, such combinations as light salmon walls and forest green floors

- For upper grade and secondary classrooms, beige, pale or light green, and blue-green; where students face one direction, side and back walls in beige, sandstone, or light tan with front wall in medium tones of gold, terra-cotta, green, or blue

- For libraries, pale or light green (creates a passive effect that enhances concentration)

If we want to nurture reflective thinking, we should choose the colors that most enhance it.

Like any well-decorated five-star hotel, color schemes should consist of a basic color and not more than two or three accent colors on the walls. Multiple patterns, such as bears around one bulletin board and crayons or geometric patterns around another, are a violation of every good design principle. If you wouldn't do something in your own living room, re-think it for the classroom. Somehow we've developed some strange traditions for color and interior decoration for school classrooms.

The design principles of understated and simple elegance are as important for the classroom as they are for the board room of a multinational corporation.

Color and light go together. Color should not allow glare and should maximize the visual appeal of the classroom.

Texture. Because classrooms must be so utilitarian, they often consist of one smooth artificial surface after another. Very boring to the eye. Plants, a fabric-covered couch or wooden rocker, desk lamps with fabric window shades, and a handwoven rug or ceramic floor tile all help add texture and eye appeal to the classroom. Conversely, limit the number of doorless/curtainless shelves; their "stuff," be it book spines or piles of papers, provides the kind of texture that amounts to clutter.

Line. What lines catch the eye? Rows of desks/tables that make the room appear long and skinny? Chaotic lines from haphazard arrangement of chairs, bookcases, etc.? Consider a three-to-four-inch wide solid accent color strip around the room about three to four feet from the ceiling. This draws the ceiling down, making the room more kid-sized and gives the eye a line to follow to view the room from one end to the other.

Value. Could a visitor entering your room identify what you and your students value in the learning process? What you are currently studying? What is your focus?

Cluttered Classroom Illustration
by Sue Pearson, *associate*, Susan Kovalik and Associates

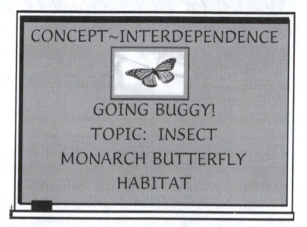

CONCEPT~INTERDEPENDENCE

GOING BUGGY!
TOPIC: INSECT
MONARCH BUTTERFLY
HABITAT

LIFESKILL
OF THE WEEK
CARING

Focused Classroom Illustration
by Sue Pearson, *associate*, Susan Kovalik and Associates

Uncluttered, Yet Reflects What Is Being Learned

Somewhere along the line, we have confused an enriched environment with a cluttered environment. If we don't have things hanging from the ceiling, floor to ceiling word walls, student work from the last month(s), bulletin boards in multicolors, and more, then too many of us feel we don't have an enriched environment.

Our goal is an uncluttered but rich environment. The walls set the itinerary for the month and where that fits within the year-long theme. Print and non-print material support the content being learned. An uncluttered, well designed room significantly improves student and teacher performance and enjoyment. It's well worth the effort. (See classroom designs on pages 7.16 and 7.17. and the video *One Day Makeover for Your ITI Classroom* with Dottie Brown.)

Seating Is Arranged in Clusters with Easy Access to Work Tools

Of all the images of school that bespeak a mindless bureaucracy at work, the academy award must go to rows of desks bolted to the floor in rigid rows. No talking, do your own work, keep your eyes to yourself, and the like.

In the bodybrain-compatible classroom, students need flexibility in seating to fit the nature of their work. If possible, trade your desks for tables and chairs.

The size of the clusters—two to five students—will depend upon the collaborative skill of your students. If you think your students will have difficulty handling participation in a group of five, begin with two and work upward.

Teacher Meets Frequently with a Professional or Peer Coach

Support is critical to your success. Make sure you get assistance through both formal and informal venues.

Finding a Coach

Insist on frequent, at least once a month, support from a coach who has implemented the ITI model at Stage 3 or higher. While peer coaching (two peers at nearly the same level of implementation) can and does work, the process is agonizingly slow. The blind leading the blind, both strangers to the landscape, is too costly in terms of time, effort, and lost opportunities.

In addition to your coach, find a colleague who is committed to implementing the ITI model and who is willing to share deeply about professional issues and growth. The combination of a coach and a partner is very powerful. Ask the coach to work with the two of you as a team. Triads are also a good size for coaching.

Implementing As Team Member or Solo

Analyze where your peers are. What knowledge of and commitment to bodybrain-compatible education do they share? Whether you are to implement solo or as a member of a team is critical to your planning.

As any parent knows, consistency is critical when it comes to behavior guidelines. So it is with the Lifelong Guidelines and LIFESKILLS of Stage One. Schoolwide implementation as a team effort is clearly the best way to go, the more so with older students. But students will respond to consistent use of the Lifelong Guidelines and LIFESKILLS in their classroom. The solo approach does work for students but, as with most tasks, working alone is harder.

ITI schools that use the Lifelong Guidelines and LIFESKILLS begin implementing them in a variety of ways. Some just dive right in! The staff agrees that these behaviors will help expedite the learning process by providing absence of threat for the students and nurturing reflective thinking. The school wants such social and behavioral guidelines, they want them now, and they also want them schoolwide.

Other sites reach schoolwide consensus more slowly, first initiating schoolwide discussions and then providing ITI training (e.g., the Lifelong Guidelines and LIFESKILLS Power Pack provided by Susan Kovalik & Associates) and opportunities for the staff to practice and learn strategies.

In other schools, teams of teachers begin using Lifelong Guidelines and LIFESKILLS in their classrooms, using the resources of the team for support and maintaining an ongoing dialogue with other colleagues about the progress of their students.

Implementation moves more quickly and is more rewarding if others at your school have adopted the Lifelong Guidelines and LIFESKILLS as their model for interacting with students. But never overlook the power of one—a single teacher leading the way.

Whatever your situation, you can start now. Start in your own classroom and let the Lifelong Guidelines and LIFESKILLS grow from there. They have a way of taking on a life of their own as students, parents, and other staff embrace their use.

The Advantages of Implementing Schoolwide

There are many advantages from implementing the Lifelong Guidelines and LIFESKILLS on a schoolwide basis. First, there is a common focus or belief system that has been chosen as the necessary building block for developing school community.

Second, continuity is apparent from class to class; everyone is hearing, understanding, and using the same terms and practicing the same actions. Third, change comes more rapidly because the Lifelong Guidelines and LIFESKILLS are used consistently and throughout the day. Last, the "spill-over" factor is high: The students will take the desired behaviors into other areas of their lives outside school—at home and in group situations such as neighborhood play, sports, scouts, and so forth. With everyone involved at the same time, there is an opportunity to build common understandings and buy-in very quickly.

Team Implementation

Implementation by a small group (grade level or team) is somewhat harder because there may not be universal support or even an understanding of the importance of using the Lifelong Guidelines and LIFESKILLS as community-building strategies by those outside the team. In addition, lack of consistency—between the classroom and other locations within the school—makes the process slower. Mixed messages always interfere with the learning process, especially for students having behavior problems.

Solo Implementation

If you are doing this alone, you will have to work hard to create an alternative culture on campus, one which your students will see as viable and valuable. The process of implementation at the classroom level is, however, the same whether implementing solo, as a team, or schoolwide. In general: Start the first day of school, work intensively during the first four to five weeks, and reinforce daily thereafter.

Notes

1 Miller, Norma, editor. *The Healthy School Handbook: Conquering the Sick Building Syndrome and Other Environmental Hazards In and Around your School.* Washington, DC: NEA Professional Library, 1995. p. 5

2 Miller, p. 23.

3 Miller, p. 64

4 Miller, p. 244.

5 Miller, pp. 247-248.

6 John Ott, photobiologist and trailblazing researcher as quoted in Miller, p. 203.

7 Miller, p. 195. See also *The Influence of Ocular Light Perception on Metabolism in Man and Animals* by Fritz Hollwich, M.D.

8 Miller, p. 196.

9 Miller, Ibid.

10 There are numerous books and articles that catalog the detrimental effects on health and brain wiring on children who spend too much time in front of computer and TV/video screens. See also Miller, Chapter 10, especially pages 195-206.

11 Miller, p. 197.

12 Faber Birren as quoted in Miller, p. 208.

13 Richard J. Wurtman quote in Miller, p. 197.

14 Miller, p. 196.
   Seasonal Affective Disorder (SAD) is a common companion, if not the source, of childhood and adult depression. It is believed that winter's feeble light rays, some 70% weaker in intensity and duration than summer sunlight, are responsible for the deep depression experienced by 5% of the population and for the less serious *winter blahs* familiar to some 30-40% of the population. This is significant because the pineal gland, "the light meter and conductor that orchestrates our body clocks plays a vital role in virtually every aspect of human function, regulating reproduction, growth, body temperature, blood pressure, motor activity, sleep, tumor growth, mood immune function, and even longevity. And, interestingly, the *activity of the pineal gland is governed by environmental light.*"
   Dr. Thomas A. Wehr of National Institute for Mental Health believes that SAD has "a tremendous impact on children's ability to function in school. They start out the school year fairly strong, thinking they will enjoy it. In November, it starts to fall apart. They sleep 12 hours a day. They're not creative. They've lost the spark. Those with winter depression are slowed down." Miller, pp. 212-213.

15 "Energy- and money-saving concerns have created classroom lighting conditions that foster the 'sunlight starvation syndrome.' The light distribution in our schools tends to be so deficient in most parts of the natural spectrum that we may just be fighting an uphill battle, attempting to teach students in 'the twilight zone.' It's time to acknowledge that light is a *cooperating teacher* in every classroom." Miller, pp. 196-197.

16 Miller, p. 213.

17 Ubell as quoted by Miller, p. 213.

18 Wohlfart as quoted by Miller, 209.

19 There are dozens of studies detailing increased achievement when the typical fluorescent tubes are replaced by full spectrum tubes or natural sunlight. See Chapter 10, *The Healthy School Handbook* by Norma L. Miller.

20 Miller, p. 213.

21 Jane M. Healy, Ph.D., *Failure to Connect: How Computers Affect Our Children's Minds.* (New York, Touchstone, 1998).

22 We highly recommend *Color and Light in Man-Made Environments* by Frank H. and Rudolf H. Mahnke (New York: John Wiley & Sons, 1993).

23 The Mahnkes are deeply committed to color and design based on hard-science rather than on personal preferences and individualistic style because color has decided and specific physiological effects on humans that are universal rather than culture-dependent.

Chapter 8: What to Do the First Day of School & Beyond

First Day of School and Beyond

ITI Classroom Stages of Implementation

Stage 1

Entry level for making the learning environment bodybrain compatible

CURRICULUM

- The bodybrain-compatible element of absence of threat and nurturing reflective thinking is taught as an important and on-going part of the curriculum. Such curriculum contains:
    - The Lifelong Guidelines, including the LIFESKILLS
    - The role of emotions in learning
    - Personal and social skills for collaboration
    - How to utilize reflective thinking.

INSTRUCTIONAL STRATEGIES

- The teacher's classroom leadership and management are based upon modeling the Lifelong Guidelines and LIFESKILLS. The atmosphere is participatory rather than dictatorial. "Discipline" is based upon helping students develop the personal and social skills and behaviors needed to successfully practice the Lifelong Guidelines rather than upon a system of externally imposed rewards and punishments.
- Written procedures and agendas provide consistency and security for students.
- The calmness of the teacher's voice contributes to a settled classroom environment.
- Collaborative learning is a frequently used learning strategy.
- The teacher meets frequently with a professional or peer coach who supports his/her implementation of a bodybrain-compatible learning environment for students.

Making the Most of Anticipation

The big day has arrived. You are ready and the students are full of anticipation. For sheer exuberance and excitement, nothing beats the first day of school. Kindergarteners have been talking about school for months. Their mothers are full of anticipation and dread simultaneously. First graders "can't wait." Who is my teacher? What kind of person is she/he? Will my teacher like me? Will I like her? Will my classmates like me? Will I like them? Even upper grade students have geared up their curiosity about what will it be like this year. "Will any of my friends be in my class with me?" "What will my teacher be like?" "Will school be fun?" The excitement is contagious.

THE FIRST DAY OF SCHOOL

Instructional Strategies

- The teacher's classroom leadership and management are based upon modeling the Lifelong Guidelines and LIFESKILLS. The atmosphere is participatory rather than dictatorial. "Discipline" is based upon helping students develop the personal and social skills and behaviors needed to successfully practice the Lifelong Guidelines rather than upon a system of externally imposed rewards and punishments.

- Written procedures and agendas provide consistency and security for students.

- The calmness of the teacher's voice contributes to a settled classroom environment.

Leadership Versus Managing the Classroom

For teachers, this is your most powerful moment. As any self-improvement, Dale-Carnegie kind of course will tell you, first impressions are powerful and lasting. And, as any substitute knows, we have 60 seconds in which to establish who we are and what we're about, that our classroom isn't about typical school with worksheets and boredom, anxiety and dread.

The first day of school is a social event of importance, treat it that way. Model what your parents taught you about being a host/hostess. Follow the same procedures you would if you were inviting yet-to-be-met guests to your home.

Few people like to be managed; we'd rather be led by a leader who possesses both vision and common sense and who, above all, keeps our best interests at heart—collectively and individually. The ITI approach to the issue of classroom management and discipline is to be proactive—to lead rather than control, to inspire rather than manipulate. Thus, the leadership you display on the first day must be your finest in the classroom for the entire year. Even before the first day of school, there are several leadership steps that will make your first moments together go smoothly.

The Invitation. First, send a written invitation to your students— a real note through the U.S. mail.[1] Welcome them, tell them how pleased you are that they will be coming to your classroom, that you look forward to spending the year with them. Tell them something about yourself and what you have planned for them. Give the date for your classroom's Back to School Night; ask that they invite their family.

The Greeting. Greet your students as you would greet guests coming to your house. Greet them at the door. Shake each one's hand. Exchange a word of welcome with them. Tell each one you're glad he/she came and that you're looking forward to the year. Let your work in preparing the room for them tell them that they are important to you. Point out the posted procedures[2] for arriving to class and help each student understand and follow them. As students pass by, give each a piece of puzzle that they will use to find their fellow Learning Club members.[3] Plan to greet students at the door each and every day.

Settling In. As you would at a sit-down dinner, invite them to find their name tag, where to put their personal belongings, what they can do to settle in and feel comfortable.[4] Preparation says that you care, you value their coming.

Introductions — Inclusion Activity. Once students have settled in to their assigned seating, give them an inclusion activity to do with fellow members of their Learning Club to help them get to know each other.[5] At the dinner table, this is the equivalent of the host or hostess introducing each guest by providing a key piece of information about them and directing the conversation along those lines until comfort levels have been established and conversation takes on a life of its own.

Written Procedures

Written procedures are a multi-purpose instructional strategy. They are a systematic and unambiguous way to teach students the personal and social skills they need to be successful as a learner and team player in your classroom and beyond. They are also a primary tool for extending your classroom leadership during times when students are working independently or in groups. Having said all this, it is clear that a lot is riding on written procedures. We beseech you to handle them with care. Think them through carefully and be 100 percent consistent in having students adhere to them. And remember, procedures are not "rules". They are guides for success.

Before the first day of school, you should have the written procedures described here ready to go. Others can be developed later with the participation of students. For the first day, be prepared with written procedures for the following:

- Morning entering the classroom
- Leaving at the end of the day
- Leaving and re-entering during the day for regular events, such as recess and special subjects, and for special events, such as schoolwide assemblies
- Lunch room procedures
- Learning Club
- Community Circle
- Quiet time

Daily Agenda

Once students have settled in and met the members of their Learning Club, introduce the daily agenda.[6] Like written procedures, the daily agenda is a key element in your classroom leadership. Posted for all to see through the day, it continues to put forth your intentions for the day—what students will do and the key pieces that you will do. It is also an important means of teaching time management skills to students. As each task is completed, check it off your classroom agenda and have each student learn to check it off the agenda they copy down each morning upon entering the classroom.

Keep in mind that the agenda is not a time schedule. The only times written on it are for special events for which students can't be late, such as the bus for a study trip, class photo appointment, and so forth. The agenda is a mindmap of the important tasks of the day from the students' point of view. It is not the same outline as for lesson planning.

Completion of a daily agenda is occasion for a mini-celebration and the LIFESKILL of Pride.

Be sure to include on your first agenda the date for your classroom's Back to School Night.[7]

Calm Voice

A voice of calm is the voice of someone who picks his/her words carefully. Repetition of directions and expectations soon begins to reflect impatience. Daily agendas and written procedures do much to allow teachers to speak calmly because there is no need to repeat directions or scold when students don't comply with the teacher's expectations. Save your voice and your students' willingness to listen for the important things.

Self Check

Instructional Strategies

- Students applied the Lifelong Guideline/LIFESKILL focused on during the day. They worked cooperatively using the identified personal and social skills.

- Students displayed an emotional tone appropriate for the learning tasks.

- The teacher feels the day went well and feels as if he/she has a "good class" this year. He/she is looking forward to the days and weeks to come.

The First Day of School

Although we adults might think of curriculum as the stuff of state standards and textbooks, for students, curriculum is what we ask them to do and how we ask them to do it. Where we might think curriculum hasn't begun until the textbooks have been passed out, students see curriculum in the way the bus driver treats them, how (or if) and principal greets them at the door of the school, and what the teacher says from the moment students see him/her.

THE FIRST DAY OF SCHOOL

Curriculum Development

- The bodybrain-compatible element of Absence of Threat and Nurturing Reflective Thinking is taught as an important and ongoing part of the curriculum. Such curriculum includes:

  — The role of emotions in learning and performing

  — The Lifelong Guidelines, including LIFESKILLS

  — The personal and social skills for collaboration

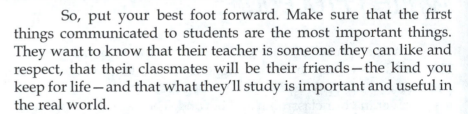

So, put your best foot forward. Make sure that the first things communicated to students are the most important things. They want to know that their teacher is someone they can like and respect, that their classmates will be their friends—the kind you keep for life—and that what they'll study is important and useful in the real world.

Our advice is to keep the textbooks and other traditional materials on the shelf during the first week of school. Focus full time on the curriculum content described in the box above.

Teaching Students About Absence of Threat and Nurturing Reflective Thinking

Because the purpose of your being together is learning, tell your students that you want them to understand how their brain works. Make models,[8] introduce the role of emotion in learning and performing. Start the first day of school and teach an aspect of how our brains work each day for the first month; after that, use every teachable moment to reinforce what they've learned and to help them learn to apply it in practical ways.

How much you choose to teach students about how their brain learns depends on their age. It is our experience that students K-6 can grasp the concepts; it is the vocabulary that may need adjusting. And yet, don't underestimate them! Just as kindergarteners love the sound of big words, such as the names of dinosaurs, they can pick up on many of the brain terms, cerebral cortex, molecules of emotion, limbic system, frontal lobes, and so forth.

The Role of Emotions in Learning and Performing. The content about the pivotal role of emotions in learning and performing is presented in Chapter 2; for examples of key points and inquiries for first and fourth grades, see Chapters 13, 14 and 15.

In truth, we *cannot control* our emotions. They are our body-brain's way of letting us know what's going on inside. But we **_can_** **_control our_ _responses_ _to our emotions._** This is a critical distinction for students to understand and a critical choice to make every time an emotion comes up. Because we feel something doesn't mean we have to act on it. For example, everyone gets angry, even furious, from time to time but we can choose to **not act** on that anger. Likewise, everyone feels jealous from time to time but we don't have to attack or undermine the person we envy. Model having control over your responses and include it as a topic during class meetings and other appropriate forums.

Also discuss with students how their emotions filter their perceptions of what's going on around them. For example, the person with a negative outlook on life tends to see all the things that are wrong or not good enough while the person with a positive view sees what's good.

The Lifelong Guidelines and LIFESKILLS

Teaching **and using on a daily basis** the Lifelong Guidelines and LIFESKILLS is the heart of Stage 1 of implementation and is the ongoing foundation for all later stages of implementation. They provide a set of standards for behavior by students, staff, and parents. They set the expectations and tone for all interactions that occur every school day—adult-adult, student-adult, and student-student. Chapters 9 and 10 explain the Lifelong Guidelines and LIFESKILLS and how to teach them. We also highly recommend *Tools for Citizenship and Life: Using the ITI Lifelong Guidelines and LIFESKILLS in Your Classroom* by Sue Pearson. With a separate chapter for each of the Guidelines and LIFESKILLS, it describes why and how to practice the guideline/skill, what it looks like in the real world, what it looks like in school, more than 400 inquiries (whole group and small group/individual), signs of success, suggested literature (by grade spans: primary, intermediate, and middle/high school), and sample family letters.

The Lifelong Guidelines and LIFESKILLS form the fabric of your classroom. They are always front and center, always a topic of the teachable moment when student behavior is particularly conducive to learning and citizenship as well as when it goes awry.

For the first day of school, introduce students to target talk and the Appreciations Box.[9]

Personal and Social Skills for Collaboration

The personal and social skills for collaboration are the skills that make our lives work. They are the basis for making and keeping friends, getting along with co-workers, and most importantly, maintaining a loving and healthy nuclear and extended family. Knowing this, don't lose patience and give up on what might at first seem like a waste of time. The difference in the quality and depth of learning that occurs once a sense of community or class family has been achieved is phenomenal—believable only when you've experienced it. Be patient. Keep at it.

The most important personal and social skills for collaboration are included in the Lifelong Guidelines and LIFESKILLS. Select those that your students most need to practice and begin the first day.

Learning Clubs. Our favorite resource for teaching students the skills needed for powerful collaboration is *TRIBES: A New Way of Learning and Being Together* by Jeanne Gibbs.

Community Circle. Community Circle is a structure for the entire class to meet together to solve problems or share appreciations. See the procedures for community circle on page 8.6.

Self Check

Curriculum Development

- Explained the purpose of the daily agenda; checked off agenda items as they were completed. Students also checked off items on their copy of the agenda.

- Students followed all written procedures, some with reminders and redirection. Students helped develop another set of written procedures, e.g., for lunchroom or library.

- Used at least two inclusion activities.

Meeting with a Coach

As discussed in Chapter 7, pages 7.18-7.19, coaching on a regular basis is critically important. If you don't already have a coach assigned to you by the end of the first day of school, don't hesitate. Ask for one. Schedule yourself to meet for an hour or two

every two weeks if at all possible. Again, small amounts of time frequently is more productive than all day twice a year. Also find a peer coach to work with you and join you when the you meet with your professional coach.

Schedule and Lesson Plan for the First Day of School

As any parent, and author, knows, it's risky to offer advice because it unerringly finds its way to that person's stubborn streak, however small and well hidden it might be. So, with apologies in advance, we offer some great ideas from a gifted teacher and associate of Susan Kovalik & Associates, Sue Pearson. Pick and choose as you like but our best advice is to make a trusting leap and try Sue's recommendations. Do everything. By Christmas, you'll find yourself weeks ahead of where you usually are.

The first daily schedule and lesson plan is for primary grades, the second for intermediate grades.

THE FIRST DAY OF SCHOOL

Curriculum Development

- The bodybrain-compatible element of Absence of Threat and Nurturing Reflective Thinking is taught as an important and on-going part of the curriculum. Such curriculum includes:

  — The role of emotions in learning and performing

  — The Lifelong Guidelines, including LIFESKILLS

  — The personal and social skills for collaboration

Primary Grades—Schedule for the First Day of School

8:30	ARRIVAL
8:45	STANDARD TASKS
9:00	INTRODUCTIONS/INCLUSION
9:15	DAILY AGENDA
9:30	MOVEMENT/SNACK/LAVATORY
9:45	KEY POINTS & INQUIRIES ABOUT COMMUNITY
11:00	MOVEMENT/MUSIC
11:15	DIRECT INSTRUCTION/INQUIRIES
11:50	LUNCH ROOM PROCEDURES
12:00	LUNCH
12:30	STORY/REST TIME
1:15	DIRECT INSTRUCTION/INQUIRIES
1:45	MOVEMENT
2:00	NURTURING REFLECTIVE THINKING
2:15	REVIEW COMMUNITY, BRAIN MODEL, BRAIN SONG
2:30	LEARNING CLUB CLOSURE
2:45	LEAVING PROCEDURES/DISMISSAL

Primary Grades—Lesson Plan for the First Day of School

➤ Note to Teacher: Your goal is quality of experience, not quantity of information; be sure to provide adequate time for each inclusion activity and key point. These key points need extensive development using literature, discussion, reflection, journaling, and real-life experiences.

8:30 ARRIVAL: Await students at the classroom door; welcome them with a handshake, "high five," or a hug. Give each student a "puzzle piece" (see Puzzle Inclusion Activity at the end of this lesson plan). Make sure each student reads and follows the "Morning Procedures."

8:45 STANDARD SCHOOL TASKS: Allow time for opening ceremonies (pledge of allegiance, songs, and so forth) and for standard school procedures such as taking attendance and lunch count, collecting notes, and performing any other tasks required by your school district.

9:00 INTRODUCTIONS: Introduce yourself. Share some hobbies, interests, and family information. Introduce "sharing ball" procedures. Then, using the sharing ball procedures with-

---

➤ This symbol indicates a note to the teacher.

in each Learning Club, have each student introduce him/herself to members of the Learning Club by saying, "My name is _____ and I like to _____."

▶ Note to Teacher: Walk around the room offering support for the shyer students and to ensure that no one student in a group monopolizes the time. Allow students a few minutes to exchange information.

Sharing Ball Procedure

1. One person holds the ball & shares.

2. Share name & interests in about 2 minutes.

3. Others use active listening.

4. Pass the ball to another.

9:15 DAILY AGENDA: Tell the students that an agenda—the plan for the day—will be posted every morning on the board (overhead, flannel board, white board) and that it is their responsibility to copy it in their spiral notebook.

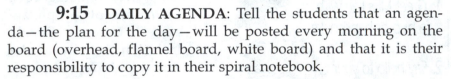
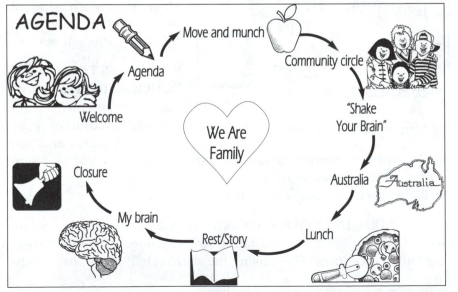

AGENDA

We Are Family

Welcome → Agenda → Move and munch → Community circle → "Shake Your Brain" → Australia → Lunch → Rest/Story → My brain → Closure

Snack Time Procedure

1. Clear off desk or Table.

2. Get your snack.

3. Join your group.

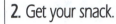
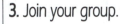

4. Eat quietly.

5. Clean up when done.

Explain each part of the agenda, why it will be used every day, and how it will benefit both students and teacher. Invite students to predict the written words by observing the accompanying graphics. Allow them sufficient time to copy the agenda, words, and graphics. As the day unfolds, check off each item on the agenda as it is completed. Have the students do the same on their own agendas. Explain that the agenda is a time management and organizational tool and that it will be used every day. Any items not completed will be assigned as homework or done the next day.

9:30 MOVEMENT/SNACK/QUIET TIME/RESTROOM
▶ You may wish to introduce the following movement activities from *Brain Gym* by Paul E. and Gail E. Dennison: Lazy 8s, Thinking Cap, and Hook-ups. Also see the book and video, *How to Make Learning a Moving Experience* by Jean Bladyes.

For snack, use the "3 before sugar rule" to judge the

Quiet Time Procedure

1. Find your personal space. Stay there during quiet time.

2. Listen to music. No talking.

3. Read a book, write, or draw.

Restroom Procedure

1. Quietly signal the teacher.

2. One at a time.

3. Wash hands.

4. Come right back.

snacks. Permit students to bring only those items whose top three ingredients are not sugar or another form of sweetener.

Play quiet, instrumental music, approximately 60–beats per minute.

Ask students to use only their 12–inch voice while talking with each other.

9:45 KEY POINTS & INQUIRIES ABOUT COMMUNITY

Conceptual Key Point—

The special spirit of community doesn't just happen in a classroom because everyone shows up, sits in groups, and does cooperative learning activities. Building community is a deliberate process that all members of the classroom—students and teacher—must take responsibility for nurturing throughout the school year. Creating community is a three-step process: inclusion, influence, and affection.* Our beginning point for creating community is using the Lifelong Guidelines and LIFESKILLS:

- TRUSTWORTHINESS
- TRUTHFULNESS
- ACTIVE LISTENING
- NO PUT-DOWNS
- PERSONAL BEST/LIFESKILLS

Inquiry for Direct Instruction—

Think about your best friend; recall three things that you like best about him/her. Share those qualities with the class. Discuss with your Learning Club what your best friend has taught you about the Lifelong Guidelines. Share with your Learning Club which Lifelong Guideline you most appreciate your best friend using when you're together.

---

* See *TRIBES: A New Way of Learning and Being Together* by Jeanne Gibbs.

➤ Record student responses on the board and group their responses as best you can. Then have students compare the list they generated to the Lifelong Guidelines.

Inquiry for Whole Class Discussion—

Identify the three most common qualities your Learning Club values in best friends. Have the recorder for your Learning Club read these to the rest of the class.

Skill Key Point—

Present the procedures for the community circle. They should replicate some of these examples:

COMMUNITY CIRCLE Procedures
1. Come to the circle area when your Learning Club is called.
2. Find a place on the rug (circle, line, etc.) to sit. Sit where you can see everyone and everyone can see you.
3. Sit comfortably in your own personal space.
4. Remember to use the Lifelong Guidelines throughout Community Circle time.
5. When you hear the chimes, it is time to use active listening.

➤ These procedures could be sung to the tune of "Supercalifragilisticexpialidocious." Introduce the chimes as a reminder to "actively listen." Ask the students to name the tool and parts (chimes, mallet) and to observe how the hammer is used to gently strike the metal rods. Ask them to identify the number of tones the chimes can make (one per metal rod/cylinder). Instruct them to show active listening (you/me, ears, eyes, heart, and undivided attention) when they hear the chimes. From here on, use the chimes as one of the strategies to call for active listening from the students.

Lead the students in the TRIBES activity, "Community Circle" (see pp. 219-220, *Tribes: A New Way of Learning and Being Together*).

Conceptual Key Point—

In a community, people come together to create a safe place to live and work. In order for our class community to be safe for everyone, there are certain guidelines that community members must be willing to follow. When problems occur, people talk together to solve them in peaceful and fair ways.

➤Topics for Whole Class Discussion—

- What guidelines would make our community a safe place to learn? Hint: Think about what we learned about our best friends.

- Discuss their guidelines and the Lifelong Guidelines as acceptable behaviors for our classroom community. Get agreement to use the Lifelong Guidelines.

- Recite Lifelong Guideline Pledge:

  "I am Trustworthy, Truthful, and an Active Listener, too.
  I will do my Personal Best and give No Put-Downs to you!"

Significant Knowledge Key Point—

Our brains will help us learn many new things this year. When our brains feel safe and are protected from danger, they learn and remember more information. We, as a community, can all help each other's brains by practicing certain safety rules and learning ways to solve our problems. In our classroom, we will all work hard to build a community based on using the Lifelong Guidelines and the LIFESKILLS. The Lifelong Guidelines are the behaviors we will use with each other so that we can be successful in school and life.

➤Tips for Direct Instruction About the Lifelong Guidelines-

- Lead a general discussion on each Lifelong Guideline. Record what students think each guideline means on a classroom wall where everyone can see and refer to them.

- Teach a sign for "Active Listening" that can be used immediately, such as "Give me 5" or silently-held hand in the air with fingers spread apart to represent the five elements of active listening—you, eyes, ears, heart, and undivided attention.

- Provide examples of working together, such as "Community Jobs." Introduce these community jobs; use real-world terms when possible, e.g., horticulturist (plant care-taker), messenger (delivers materials to the office, personal trainer (in charge of recess equipment). Brainstorm the performance standards for each of these jobs. Choose volunteers to demonstrate/pantomime the task being done incorrectly and then correctly. Invite the students to describe one more job that they feel is needed in the classroom

Inquiries for Choice — For Learning Clubs or Individuals

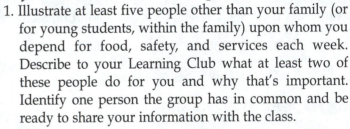

1. Illustrate at least five people other than your family (or for young students, within the family) upon whom you depend for food, safety, and services each week. Describe to your Learning Club what at least two of these people do for you and why that's important. Identify one person the group has in common and be ready to share your information with the class.

2. Identify at least five community services that you and your family depend on to stay healthy and safe. Record your finding on the T-chart under the following headings: HEALTH, SAFETY, CONVENIENCE, FUN.

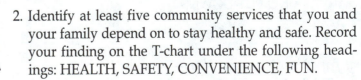

3. Write a story or draw a picture that shares a time when you cooperated with another person and it helped both of you. Share your product and explain what happened as a result of your cooperation.

4. Brainstorm with your Learning Club two or more ways you will work to build a community using the Lifelong Guidelines of Trustworthiness, Truthfulness, Active

Listening, No Put-Downs, and Personal Best. Prepare your ideas for class sharing time.

5. In your journal, write about a time or draw a picture of a time you used one of the Lifelong Guidelines. Explain your choice to a partner.

11:00 MOVEMENT/MUSIC

➤Teach one of the brain songs (e.g., "Shake Your Brain" by Red Grammer on the CD *Teaching Peace* or one of those listed at the end of this lesson plan). Allow the students to create movements that demonstrate the meaning of the lyrics. Practice the song twice. Afterwards, provide reflection time asking questions such as: How did this song make you feel? Which motions will be the easiest for you to remember? What changes do you notice in your feelings? Does anyone know another brain song that the class could sing later in the week?

11:15 DIRECT INSTRUCTION

Significant Knowledge Key Point—

Our brains will help us learn many new things this year. When we feel safe and are protected from danger, our brain learns and remembers more. As a community, we can all help each other feel safe by following certain agreements. Agreements to use the Lifelong Guidelines and the LIFESKILLS will help us get to know and respect one another so that we can be better learners.

➤Direct Instruction with these Materials: A copy of *Franklin Goes to School* by Paulette Bourgeois or *Chrysanthemum* by Kevin Henkes plus a chart tablet and colored markers (blue, green, red, black).

Anticipatory Set: Ask questions such as: Did anyone feel a little nervous about coming to school today? What made you feel nervous ? How did your body let you know it was nervous? What did you do to try to feel less worried? Were any of you excited? What feelings did you have? Share a personal story of your own

first day at school. Explain that you have a story where the main character shares some of their same feelings.

Direct Instruction: Read aloud the book you chose. Ask the students to do a "thumbs up" when they have the same feelings that Franklin (or the character in your book) does. Use a "thumbs down" when they have different feelings. Obviously, there will be some story parts when there will be "thumbs up" and "thumbs down" simultaneously depending on each student's individual experiences and personal feelings. Ask questions that focus on feelings, For example, how did you feel on your first day of kindergarten? How did your family help you prepare for school? Do you still feel nervous or excited when school is starting? Why do you suppose you feel that way?

➤Acknowledge that each of us can and do have different reactions to things and that our reactions change over time. By asking questions such as these, you also provide an opening for you to share your own childhood recollections of school as well as an opportunity to share your excitement as the teacher of this class! Participate in the discuss as well as supervise it. Let your students know who you are.

Inquiry —

Compare your feelings about the first day of school with Franklin from the story *Franklin Goes to School*. Tell your partner how your feelings and Franklin's are alike. Share how your feelings were different than Franklin's. Listen to your partner's feelings. Explain your feelings about school to your classmates when the teacher invites you to share.

Skill Key Point: Using a T-chart —

There are many kinds of T-charts. The common element is that they have two or more columns which allow us to compare or contrast information about a topic. Two T-charts we will use often are the KWL and LSF (see pages 21.4).

T-Chart of My Feelings Before School

LOOKS LIKE	SOUNDS LIKE	FEELS LIKE
smiling	"I can't wait to go!"	happy
crying	"I'm scared!"	nervous
laughing	"It will be fun."	good
unhappy face	"I don't want to go!"	scared

Review some of the answers offered by the students. Emphasize the variety of feelings that were shared. Suggest that the class revisit the chart in one week for another check on feelings and any changes that may occur.

11:50 LUNCH PROCEDURE

12:00 LUNCH/RECESS

Go To Lunch Procedure

1. Clean work area.

2. Get your coat & lunch.

3. Line up at the door and stand quietly.

4. Proceed to cafeteria.

12:30 REST TIME/ STORY TIME

Rest Time Procedure

1. Find your quiet space and stay there during rest time.

2. May listen to music. No talking.

3. If you don't feel sleepy, take a toy with you and play quietly.

Younger students may require a short rest time after lunch for the first few days until they are back into the routine of school. This is an excellent time to play some quiet, classical music with 40-60 beats per minute which helps to regulate the heartbeat after strenuous activity.

12:45 DIRECT INSTRUCTION

Significant Knowledge Key Point (continued)—

 Our brains will help us learn many new things this year. When we feel safe and are protected from danger, our brains learn and remember more. As a kind of community, we can all help each other feel safe by following certain agreements. By agreeing to use the Lifelong Guidelines and the LIFESKILLS, we will get to know and respect one another so that we can be better learners.

Story: *Alexander and the Terrible, Horrible, No-Good, Very Bad Day* by Judith Viorst

Predictable story: Invite students to repeat chorus whenever it appears: "It was a terrible, horrible, no-good, very bad day."

Judith Viorst's story centers on a young boy, Alexander, for whom everything is going wrong. His response? "I'm going to Australia!" Use Alexander's experiences as an introduction for your class's own personal "Australia," a small corner of the room where the students can visit to relax, refocus and reflect. Lead the students to this special area.

The following items are suggested for Australia

- Some type of chair (rocking, Adirondack, stuffed, bean bag, large pillows)

- Procedures for visiting Australia

- Small table covered with cloth

- Lamp

- Timer-Executive oil drip (about 10 minutes) or some other quiet timer

- Headset with classical music tapes in basket ~ optional

- Stress relief "squeeze ball"

- Small class photo or inspirational quotation in a frame. Invite students to visit "Australia," a "safe" place for the brain to reflect and the heart to heal. A comfortable place in the classroom with a rocking chair, Adirondack lawn chair, bean bag, pillows, or cushions. Teaching strategy: Tell each student to write his/her name on a small piece of paper. Pull names out, one at a time, for visits to Australia on this first day, thereby preventing a rush to Australia.

Demonstrate the use of any special items (e.g., timer, headset). Write procedures for using Australia with the students. Choose two or more students to demonstrate the procedures.

Inquiry —

 Draw a picture of a "safe place" you go to when you are feeling sad, mad, angry, or stressed. Share this special place with your teacher. Add it to the "My Special Place" book. ("My Special Place

 Book" can be as simple as a binder with plastic sleeves. Slip each drawing into one of the sleeves and add a title page)

"Australia" Procedure

1. Wait your turn. One person at a time.

2. Start the timer (only 10 minutes).

3. Put items back in their place.

4. Return to your seat when time is up.

1:15 MOVEMENT

The activities from *Brain Gym* can be repeated with simple aerobics added.

1:45 DISCOVERY INQUIRIES

Conceptual Key Point —

 Learning is the result of a partnership between our brain and our body. Our brain talks to our body and our body talks to our brain. The number one topic of conversation is our emotions. How we feel affects how we learn.

Significant Knowledge Key Point —

 The heart and brain tend to match each other. If your heart is racing, you brain is also in high gear. If your heart slows, your brain calms down.

Inquiry —

 Have students discuss with a partner:

— What emotions are you feeling now?

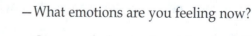 — Can you feel your heart beating? How many times per minute is it beating? (Have students county for 15 seconds and then multiply by four.)

— How fast is your brain working?

—How can you calm yourself (after getting excited or running around) to get ready for learning?

—Share your findings with your Learning Club.

▶Today is but an introduction to these ideas. Continue studying about the impact on emotions for fifteen minutes a day over the next two weeks, and into the school year.

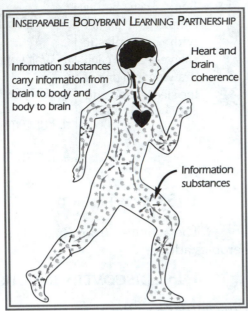

INSEPARABLE BODYBRAIN LEARNING PARTNERSHIP

Information substances carry information from brain to body and body to brain

Heart and brain coherence

Information substances

2:00 REFLECTIVE THINKING: Quiet Time with Music

▶Many students need time alone to think while their brains begin to integrate new information. Build this into each day. Suggest that your students reflect on their experiences today.

Inquiry—

Take time to calm your heart and brain. When your heart and brain are both calm, think about your day. Discuss the following questions with your Learning Club, then have your recorder share two of the most memorable things with the class.

• What have you learned today that you want to share with your family?

• What would you like to remember forever?

2:15 REVIEW KEY POINTS OF THE DAY

Guide a review of "What makes a community?" and "How brains work best when people feel safe and why." Sing the song "Shake Your Brain." Invite two or more students to model the movement/motions for the rest of the class.

2:30 Learning Club CLOSURE

Review the sign(s) for "Active Listening." Teach the students to use the "Sharing Ball" (a standard item in each Learning Club basket of materials). Start with one student in each group (wearing the most red, blue, green, etc.) who will share. Question: What one word describes how you feel right now? Proceed around the group until each student has shared (right to pass is always an option).

2:45 LEAVING PROCEDURES

▶Introduce "end-of-the-day procedures" for the students to complete before leaving the classroom.

2:55 DISMISSAL

▶Be present at the door to share a "good-bye" handshake, hug, or "high five" with each student as he/she leaves.

End of Day Procedure

1. Clean your area.

2. Help others straighten up.

3. Put items in your pack.

4. Say goodbye to others.

5. Share 1 thing you learned.

TEACHER'S OVERVIEW OF THE FIRST DAY OF SCHOOL for INTERMEDIATE GRADES

8:30 ARRIVAL

8:45 STANDARD SCHOOL TASKS

9:00 INTRODUCTIONS

9:15 DAILY AGENDA

9:30 INCLUSION ACTIVITY

10:00 DISCOVERY INQUIRIES

10:20 REFLECTIVE THINKING

10:30 MOVEMENT/SNACK/RESTROOM

10:45 CONCEPTUAL KEY POINT

11:00 WHOLE CLASS INQUIRY

11:15 MOVEMENT/MUSIC

11:30 COMMUNITY CIRCLE

12:00 LUNCH PROCEDURES/LUNCH

12:45 REVIEW MORNING

1:00 KEY POINT/INQUIRY

1:45 RECESS

2:00 KEY POINT/INQUIRY

2:45 SIGNIFICANT KNOWLEDGE KEY POINT

3:15 PLEDGE/LEARNING CLUB CLOSURE

3:30 DISMISSAL

Intermediate Grades—Lesson Plan for the First Day of School

▶Note to Teacher: Your goal is quality of experience, not quantity of information; be sure to provide adequate time for each inclusion activity and key point. These key points need extensive development using literature, discussion, reflection, journaling, and real-life experiences.

8:30 ARRIVAL: Await students at the classroom door; welcome them with a handshake, "high five," or a hug. Give each student a "puzzle piece" (see My Piece of the Puzzle directions that follow). Make sure each student reads and follows the "Morning Procedures." Tell them to look for procedures every morning.

8:45 STANDARD SCHOOL TASKS: Allow time for opening ceremonies (pledge of allegiance, songs, and so forth) and for standard school procedures such as taking attendance and lunch count, collecting notes, and performing any other tasks required by your school district.

9:00 INTRODUCTIONS: Introduce yourself to the students. Share some hobbies, interests, and family information. Introduce "sharing ball" procedures. Then, have the students use

Morning Procedures

1. *Be Friendly.* Greet Mr. Smith with a handshake or hug.

2. *Be responsible.* Hang coat/sweater on the hook by your name.

3. *Be organized.* Remove school materials from from your pack.

4. Place pack by your coat and take school materials with you.

5. Sit where you see your name.

6. *Be caring.* Greet 3 or more students with a big "Hello!"

7. *Be ready.* Copy the agenda.

Notes

the sharing ball procedures to introduce themselves to members of their Learning Club by saying, "My name is _____ and I like to _____."

▶ Note to Teacher: Walk around the room offering support for the shyer students and to ensure that no one student in a group monopolizes the time. Allow students a few minutes to exchange information.

9:15 DAILY AGENDA: Tell the students that an agenda—the plan for the day—will be posted every morning on the board (overhead, flannel board, white board) and that it is their responsibility to copy it in their spiral notebook.

Sharing Ball Procedure:

1. Take the ball from the basket.

2. Follow directions for who goes first. Only one at a time.

3. Pass the ball by handing to the next person.

4. Actively listen to the person holding the ball.

5. Last person to share returns the ball to the basket.

sufficient time to copy the agenda, words, and graphics. As the day unfolds, check off each item on the agenda as it is completed. Have the students do the same on their own agendas. Explain that the agenda is a time management and organizational tool and that it will be used every day. Any items not completed will be assigned as homework or done the next day.

9:30 INCLUSION ACTIVITY: "My Piece of the Puzzle"

▶ Check to ensure that every student received a puzzle piece as they entered the room. Then, post the "My Piece of the Puzzle" Inquiry so all can easily see it.

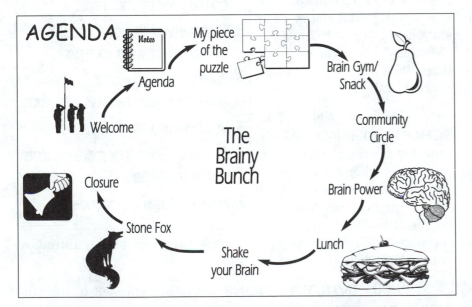

Explain each part of the agenda, why it will be used every day, and how it will benefit both students and teacher. Allow students

 **"My Piece of the Puzzle" Inquiry**

1. When the music starts, stand up, push in your chair, take your puzzle piece, and walk around the room.

2. Find puzzle pieces that fit with yours. When you find a match, stay with that person. Continue to find students with other pieces that fit with yours.

3. When you have all the pieces that fit together to make a rectangle, send a messenger to the teacher for a piece of oaktag.

4. Working together, paste all the pieces on the oaktag to make a completed jigsaw puzzle.

5. Choose a name for your Learning Club and print it with a dark marker at the top of your poster.

6. Hang the poster on our "Getting to Know You" bulletin board.

➤ *Directions for preparing "My Piece of the Puzzle"—*

For each group, gather up one piece of 9"x 12" construction paper and one piece of 12"x 18" oaktag (the light color is different from the color of the construction paper), and one black marker.

1. Right before school begins, use your class list and divide the students into groups or what ITI calls "Learning Clubs."

2. Determine how many students will sit together and where the location of the groups will be. (For example, five students in a group: Group 1 near the door, Group 2 by the teacher's desk, Group 3 next to the classroom library, Group 4 by the windows, and Group 5 near the overhead).

3. Using one piece of construction paper start with the first group. Divide the paper into puzzle pieces, one for each student in the group. Using the marker, write one student's name on each piece. Make the patterns of the cut unique for each group.

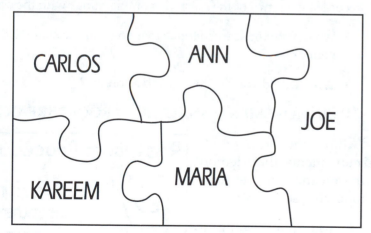

4. Repeat this pattern for each individual group until done.

5. Cut out the pieces.

6. Be ready to hand each student his/her own piece upon entering the classroom.

➤ Give the students parameters for selecting a name for their Learning Club, such as a name that represents powerful learners or the power of the brain.

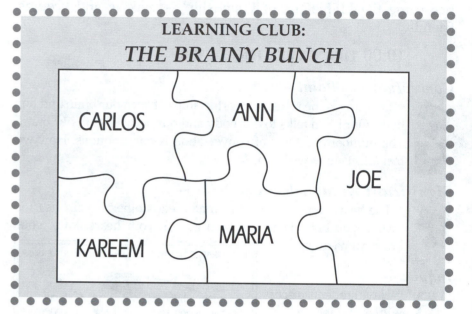

Inquiry—

 After completing the puzzle, each Learning Club conducts a "Spotlight" interview of each of its members. Each student is asked two questions by each member of the group to learn more about their hobbies, interests, and family.

Process the Process Inquiry—

 As a Learning Club, "process the process" for this set of inclusion activities. Ask questions such as: What did you like best about this activity and why? What was the most difficult part for you? The easiest part? What would you do differently next time in order to learn more about each other?

➤Tell the students that change in the membership of the Learning Clubs will change each month by using inclusion activities that are fun. For example, a variety of codes, word searches, several clues on index cards to lead the students to find the other members of a new Learning Club. Tell them that the purpose is to give them opportunities to get to know each other well and to practice using the LIFESKILL of Friendship — making and keeping friends.

10:00 DISCOVERY INQUIRIES

Conceptual Key Point —

Learning is the result of a partnership between our brain and our body. Our brain talks to our body and our body talks to our brain. The number one topic of conversation is our emotions. How we feel affects how we learn.

Significant Knowledge Key Point —

The heart and brain tend to match each other. If your heart is racing, you brain is also in high gear. If your heart slows, your brain calms down.

Inquiry —

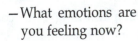

Have students discuss with a partner:

—What emotions are you feeling now?

—Can you feel your heart beating? How many times per minute is it beating? (Have students count for 15 seconds and then multiply by four.)

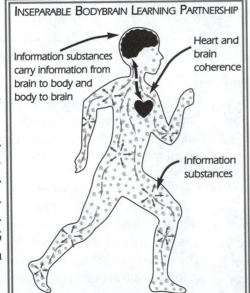

INSEPARABLE BODYBRAIN LEARNING PARTNERSHIP

Information substances carry information from brain to body and body to brain

Heart and brain coherence

Information substances

—How fast is your brain working?

—How can you calm yourself (after getting excited or running around) to get ready for learning?

—Share your findings with your Learning Club.

➤Today is but an introduction to these ideas. Continue studying about the impact on emotions for fifteen minutes a day over the next two weeks and revisit it throughout the school year.

10:20 REFLECTIVE THINKING: Quiet Time with Music

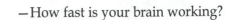

➤Many students need time alone to think while their brains begin to integrate new information. Build this into each day. Suggest that your students reflect on their experiences today.

Inquiry —

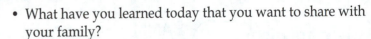

Take time to calm your heart and brain. When your heart and brain are both calm, think about your day. Discuss the following questions with your Learning Club, then have your recorder share two of the most memorable things with the class.

• What have you learned today that you want to share with your family?

• What would you like to remember forever?

10:30 MOVEMENT/ SNACK/RESTROOM BREAK

Allow the students to create movements that demonstrate the meaning of the lyrics to the following songs.

➤You may want to introduce the following movement activities from *Brain Gym* by Paul E. and Gail E. Dennison:

Restroom Procedure

1. Quietly signal the teacher.

2. Wash hands.

3. Come right back.

Lazy 8s, Thinking Cap, and Hook-ups. Also see the book and video, *How to Make Learning a Moving Experience* by Jean Bladyes. Preview the video so you will have an appropriate activity to show to the students.

Snack time/quiet music playing/students talking with Learning Club members.

Snack Time Procedure

1. Clear off desk or table.

2. Get your snack.

3. Join your group.

4. Eat quietly.

5. Clean up when done.

10:45 CONCEPTUAL KEY POINT

Conceptual Key Point: Community

The special spirit of community doesn't just happen in a classroom because everyone shows up, sits in groups, and does cooperative learning activities. Building community is a deliberate process that all members of the classroom—students and teacher—must take responsibility to nurture throughout the school year. As described by Jeanne Gibbs in *TRIBES: A New Way of Learning and Being Together*, creating community is a three-step process: inclusion, influence, and affection. Our beginning point for creating community is using the Lifelong Guidelines and LIFESKILLS.

> TRUSTWORTHINESS
>
> TRUTHFULNESS
>
> ACTIVE LISTENING
>
> NO PUT-DOWNS
>
> PERSONAL BEST/LIFESKILLS

Whole Class Inquiry —

Think back over your school experiences. Choose the year you feel you were an enthusiastic, successful learner. Using pencil or

fine point markers, create a mindmap sharing five or more reasons you feel that class supported your needs as a learner. Share the results with your fellow Learning Club members during Round Robin (sharing information in a clockwise way in the group).

➤ See *Cooperative Learning* by Spencer Kagan. Bring your mind-map to Community Circle later in the morning.

11:15 MOVEMENT/MUSIC

This is an opportunity to move around the room, either in a structured (exercises) or non-structured way (become familiar with the classroom and where materials are located). This is a good time to introduce the Lifelong Guidelines songs with the video *Spread Your Wings* by Jeff Pedersen.

11:30 KEY POINT/COMMUNITY CIRCLE/T-CHART

➤ Introduce the chimes as an "active listening" tool. Teach the other signals that you plan on using when students need to be active listeners, such as "Give me 5." (Silently hold hand in the air with fingers spread apart to represent the five elements of the Chinese Tang symbol— you/me, eyes, ears, heart, and undivided attention.) Also see *Spread Your Wings: The Lifelong Guidelines* by Jeff Pedersen, CD and video which has a song for each of the Lifelong Guidelines. Creating new lyrics for common melodies is also a fun activity.

You

Eyes

Undivided Attention

Heart

Ear

Significant Knowledge Key Point—

While living in a community provides benefits to all, it is essential, if the community is to survive and thrive, for the members to value inclusion, practice cooperation, increase problem-solving skills, and develop collaborative strategies with one another.

▶ Discuss the concept of community: Lead the students through a discussion of community that leads to a general definition of the term. Draw on the students' personal experiences, real-life stories, literature, and other topics to draw out prior understandings.

- Invite the students to share information from their mindmaps regarding characteristics of classrooms in which they were successful learners.

- Write the attributes on a chart tablet either in list or mindmap form. Use this information as a lead-in to adopting the Lifelong Guidelines (and LIFESKILLS) as acceptable behaviors for everyone (adults included) to use in the classroom. Using the Lifelong Guidelines will build community and promote successful learning.

- Introduce each of the Lifelong Guidelines and assess the students' understandings of these concepts by having them record their ideas on a chart.

- Decide as a group which Lifelong Guideline to first focus on. (Hint: No Put-Downs is especially important in the intermediate grades.)

▶ This is a good time to show video clips of TV shows that use put-downs continuously.

Community Circle Inquiry

Lead the students in the TRIBES activity, "Community Circle," pp. 219-220.

COMMUNITY CIRCLE Procedures

1. Come to the circle area when your Learning Club is called.

2. Find a place on the rug (circle, line, etc.) to sit. Sit where you can see everyone and everyone can see you.

3. Identify and sit comfortably in your own personal space.

4. Remember to use the Lifelong Guidelines throughout Community Circle time.

5. When you hear the chimes, it is time to use active listening.

▶ MATERIALS: The individual handouts of Lifelong Guidelines and LIFESKILLS, plus chart paper, and markers.

Lifelong Guidelines—

Create a T–Chart using the Lifelong Guideline the students have selected as their starting point. Use a large chart tablet so you can collect information for all of the Lifelong Guidelines/ LIFESKILLS in one place. Ideas can be added throughout the school year. Following is an example of how such a chart might look:

T-Chart with Put-Downs

LOOKS LIKE	SOUNDS LIKE	FEELS LIKE
arms crossed	You can't play with us!	left out
laughing at clothing	Where'd you get that old thing?	humiliation
laughing at answer	"You sure are stupid!	hurt
no one noticing	"Who's she/he?	isolation

▶ For the second day of school, plan on doing a second version of this chart so that it looks like the following chart.

T-Chart with NO Put-Downs

LOOKS LIKE	SOUNDS LIKE	FEELS LIKE
Students greeting each other	Hi! How are you today? Want to play at recess?	welcome
High fives!	Great job! You mastered the 7 times tables.	capable
Someone waving	"Maria, come join us."	belonging

Additional ideas can be put on the chart as students notice them in literature, common experiences, newspaper articles, biographies, and real-life adventures.

12:00 LUNCH PROCEDURES/LUNCH

12:45 REVIEW MORNING

Circle up by birth day and share with two other persons and share what they learned from this morning. Check the agenda and cross off the items that have been accomplished. Discuss why the procedures will help the students.

1:45 RECESS

2:00 KEY POINT/INQUIRY

Go To Lunch Procedure

1. Clean up your work area.

2. Get your coat & lunch.

3. Line up at the door and stand quietly.

4. Proceed to cafeteria.

Significant Knowledge Key Point (continued) —

While living in a community provides benefits to all, it is essential for the members to value inclusion, practice cooperation, increase problem-solving skills, and develop collaborative strategies with one another, if the community is to survive and thrive.

▶ MATERIALS: One copy (or class set) of *Stone Fox* by John Reynolds Gardiner. This story:

- Is written at a third/fourth grade reading levelbut revered by students in grades 2-8 (regardless of students' reading level)

- Includes each Lifelong Guideline and LIFESKILL (great for beginning of the year introductions)

- Grabs the emotions (read this story before you use it with the students; it is emotionally compelling)

- Develops the concepts of community/survival

- Focuses on problem-solving skills

- Centers on a non-traditional family (grandpa and grandson)

- Is only ten chapters long (short enough to complete in one or two weeks)

While this book is a favorite, there are many others (*Charlotte's Web, My Side of the Mountain, Where the Red Fern Grows*, or a personal choice) that provide a basis for developing the concept of community, Lifelong Guidelines, and LIFESKILLS through literature.

▶ *Pre-reading strategies:*

- Locate your state in relation to Wyoming on a U.S. map. Determine if any students have visited Wyoming.

- Determine what kind of pets, if any, the students have at home. Lead a discussion of the kinds of "jobs" dogs do.

- Discuss the Husky as a canine breed—where and why the breed was developed.

- Have students write in their journals their predictions for why the book is titled *Stone Fox* and what they think the story plot might be.

- Review strategies for decoding new words.

▶*Reading:* Chapters 1 and 2 can be read aloud by the teacher, individually by each student, with a partner, or in the Learning Club

Inquiry —

Develop a mindmap that focuses on Lifelong Guideline/ LIFESKILLS used by the three human characters in the first two chapters of *Stone Fox*. Name the three main characters. Identify one or more Lifelong Guidelines and or LIFESKILLS each character uses. Write that word on a line; include the page number where this example can be found. Defend your choices with your Learning Club during inquiry share time. For example:

- Little Willy and Grandpa used the LIFESKILL of a Sense of Humor

- Stone Fox? Doc Smith?

2:45   KEY POINT

Significant Knowledge Key Point —

Classrooms are one kind of community. In order for a community to expand and flourish, the members must decide on a set of agreements that will facilitate teamwork, encouragement, and cooperation. Agreements to use the Lifelong Guidelines and LIFESKILLS will allow us to know and respect one another so we can each learn effectively.

▶Guide your discussion with the following ideas:

- Ask students to review the information from their mindmaps and the T-chart created in the morning.

- Present the LIFESKILL of Cooperation as a goal for Learning Club projects/inquiries. Brainstorm attributes the LIFESKILL of Cooperation. Ask the students to locate the word in class dictionaries to be sure of the definition.

- Invite the students to reflect on an activity/ situation/inquiry when they have been part of a collaborative group. Provide time for a "popcorn" share (strategy where group members may "pop" out their answers in any order providing they still follow the Lifelong Guideline of Active Listening.

- Practice writing "Popcorn Procedures" together (students and teacher).

3:15   PLEDGE/LEARNING CLUB CLOSURE

Inquiry

With your Learning Club members, create a Lifelong Guidelines Pledge. Use rhyme or free verse, including the names of the Lifelong Guidelines and the word "community." Motions/ Signing may also be included. Share this pledge tomorrow during Community Circle.*

End-of-Day Procedure

1. Organize the items in your area.

2. Help others straighten up the Learning Club materials.

3. Put important items in your pack.

4. Say goodbye to others.

5. Share one thing you learned with the teacher on the way out the door.

(*During the next Community Circle, students can vote for the pledge they feel best expresses the principles of the classroom community. Or the best parts of each pledge can be combined to make a totally unique verse. From that day on, recite the class pledge after the Pledge of Allegiance.)

3:30 DISMISSAL

Notes

1 The invitation should be a personal note. It needn't be lengthy or detailed. The important message is that you're inviting them to share a wonderful year with you.

2 For examples of procedures, see Chapter 20, pages 20.11-20.12.

3 For a description of this inclusion process, see page 8.16.

4 If you live in a northern climate requiring lots of heavy clothing or if your classroom has nowhere to hang coats and carry bags, your procedures will need to be quite detailed.

5 For a description of inclusion processes, see page Sharing Ball (pp. 8.8, 8.16), Community Circle (8.9, 8.20), and My Piece of the Puzzle (8.16).

6 For examples of daily agendas, see Chapter 20, page 20.5.

7 We strongly recommend you hold Back to School Night for your classroom during the first or second week of school—even if the rest of the school holds one later.

8 Although the triune brain theory has largely been abandoned for a larger view of how emotion affects learning, there is still value in teaching students (adjusted for the age of your students, of course) about their brain and its functions, for example, brain stem and cerebellum, limbic system, and cerebra cortex.

9 For more information about the Acknowledgements Box, see Chapter 2.

10 One of our favorite resources for mindmapping is *Mapping Inner Space* by Nancy Margulies.

Chapter 9: The Lifelong Guidelines and LIFESKILLS

The Lifelong Guidelines and LIFESKILLS

The Lifelong Guidelines are a result of asking the question: "What qualities do you want in a lifelong partner?" Conversely, these Lifelong Guidelines also ask you to consider what qualities you should possess to make someone want to spend a lifetime with you. Also, what qualities would you hope a stranger on the street would have? A neighbor? However you ask the question, under whatever the circumstances or length of time of interaction, these five qualities come out high on the list. They form the foundation for positive, valued relationships and make learning joyous and powerful. They are also the keystone to good classroom leadership and, more than instructional strategy, help eliminate threat and enhance reflective thinking. The Lifelong Guidelines must become internalized. They shape the culture of the classroom.

An invaluable tool for teaching the Lifelong Guidelines and LIFESKILLS is *Tools for Citizenship and Life: Using the ITI LIfelong Guidelines and LIFESKILLS in Your Classroom* by Sue Pearson. With a separate chapter for each of the Guidelines and LIFESKILLS, it describes why and how to practice the guideline/skill, what it

looks like in the real world, what it looks like in school, more than 500 inquiries (whole group and small group/individual), signs of success, suggested literature (by grade spans: primary, intermediate, and middle/high school), and sample family letters.

For a discussion of the Lifelong Guidelines, see the following excerpt from *Tools for Citizenship & Life: Using the ITI Lifelong Guidelines and LIFESKILLS in Your Classroom*, pages 10.2-10.16.

Lifelong Guidelines

TRUSTWORTHINESS: To act in a manner that makes one worthy of trust and confidence

TRUTHFULNESS: To act with personal responsibility and mental accountability

ACTIVE LISTENING: To listen attentively and with the intention of understanding

NO PUT-DOWNS: To never use words, actions, and/or body language that degrade, humiliate, or dishonor others

PERSONAL BEST: To do one's best given the circumstances and available resources

---

TRUSTWORTHINESS:

To act in a manner that makes one worthy of trust and confidence

What Is Trustworthiness?

If we were artists commissioned to paint a masterpiece representing the Lifelong Guideline of Trustworthiness, we would choose for our model a mother rocking her infant child, the baby's eyes intently studying her mother's face, a tiny hand reaching up to touch her mother's cheek. The purest form of trust in life is child to mother. The parent provides food when the child is hungry, warmth when cold, and comfort when hurt. This relationship between mother and baby is a child's first experience with trustworthiness.

Yet we know there are other pictures in which food is late or lacking, comfort is in short supply, and warmth is missing. What do such babies begin to learn about trustworthiness? They learn that "people in my world are not reliable." Such early experiences with family and caretakers impair a child's ability to have confidence in other people.

Trustworthiness: An Umbrella in Stormy Weather. Trustworthiness, identified by specific attributes such as reliability and dependability, is vital because it is an umbrella under which we protect ourselves from stormy weather. Each one of us needs at least one such umbrella for protection—if not a trustworthy friend, at least a parent or close family member with whom we can talk and know that our words will go no further. We need to trust that those close to us will adhere to the Lifelong Guidelines and LIFESKILLS. Likewise, we need to be the umbrella of protection for other people by providing confidentiality, steadiness, and support during those occasional drizzles, steady rains, and torrential downpours that life presents.

Trustworthiness Is a Double-Sided Coin. But trustworthiness is more than an umbrella in stormy weather for us as we seek out those who are trustworthy, safe, and comfortable to be with. Trustworthiness is a double-sided coin, a two-way street. It isn't just what we receive; we in turn must be trustworthy for others. Students must be taught that they can't expect the gift of trustworthiness from others if they are not trustworthy in return.

The Lifelong Guideline of Trustworthiness requires that parents and teachers teach both sides of Trustworthiness—how to give it and how to receive it. To do so, we must teach children the sign posts for recognizing this characteristic in others. Who is really deserving of their trust so others don't take advantage? How do they extend their trust so that relationships of all levels can deepen and enrich their lives?

Why Practice Trustworthiness?

The Lifelong Guideline of Trustworthiness forms the basis of relationships—effective working partnerships, close friendships, healthy family bonds, and the long-lasting intimate relationship of husband and wife. Simply put, if people can't trust us, they don't want to be around us—it's too risky. The lower the level of trustworthiness, the more distant people remain. And, because few pursuits in life are solitary, most goals require the participation of others. If we are to succeed in our goals, we must become a trustworthy person.

For Staff. The higher the stakes become, the more crucial trustworthiness becomes. Designing seal rings for the space shuttle booster rocket, problem-solving safety design issues on the Boeing aircraft assembly line, doing customer service in a small business whose owner has just invested his entire life savings into his business are examples of everyday work environments in which our trustworthiness and ability to work as a team can have life-and-death or life-changing impact.

Can your colleagues feel secure that you are dependable (the job gets done), consistent (high quality of work), and reliable (follows directions and meets deadlines)? Does our level of trustworthiness evoke a degree of credibility? Does our supervisor feel confident and secure when assigning tasks to us, working on projects with us, or discussing confidential information with us?

As trust-building skills improve, we are more likely to be included in upper-level planning and decision making. Such involvement is a key element in satisfaction in the workplace.

For Students. Close relationships of any kind, including teacher-student and student-student, cannot exist without trustworthiness. It is the cornerstone of respect and liking. One can love someone without liking and respecting them—a common burden of children abused by their parents. Trustworthiness is also the source of one's sense of security, safety, and confidence.

A key ingredient in the Lifelong Guideline of Trustworthiness is emotional consistency—that the student knows the teacher cares about him/her and that the teacher's emotional and physical behaviors are consistent with that love, that no matter what happens, the student knows he/she will be fairly treated.

When students feel safe and secure in the classroom, learning becomes paramount because the bodybrain can focus on learning. The atmosphere in the classroom, instead of tense and fraught with suspicion, is calm and steady. The teacher can be relied on to keep her word when students share problems. Consistency is the standard for student actions, both in application and outcome.

For Families. When a teacher is known to be trustworthy, relationships with students' families will flourish. A teacher who consistently and fairly applies rules and consequences wins respect from both students and adults. Family members recognize that we are working with them, not against them, in the education of their child. Generally, the more we know and understand about a child's circumstances, the greater the possibility that the teacher can provide emotional support, which in turn will promote academic learning. The parent-teacher relationship exudes confidentiality, whether relating to family or school concerns; this raises the level

of trustworthiness for all involved, leading to additional exchanges of pertinent information.

Note: The only time a teacher must divulge confidential information from a student is when some form of abuse is apparent. Many states have laws requiring that this information be disclosed, and indeed, the penalties are severe if this type of action is not reported. A student sharing this type of information is crying out for help and trusting that we will provide guidance, backing, and support.

How Do You Practice Trustworthiness?

We practice being trustworthy by not abusing others' trust; we don't share confidences, ignore deadlines, spread rumors, talk behind backs, lie, cheat, steal, or exhibit any of the other behaviors that would abuse trust.

The beginnings of trustworthiness lie deep within our childhood experiences. As infants, was food consistently there when we felt the pains of hunger? Were we changed when wet and uncomfortable, rocked when ill, comforted when frightened? If the answers to these questions are yes, then we felt trust in our caretaker. On the other hand, were we left to wonder if food would come or if someone would take care of us when we were ill or frightened? Did our caretakers keep their word? Did they model good judgment and integrity? Clearly, the development of trust and trustworthiness in the classroom comes more quickly for some students than for others. Whatever it takes, however, it is our job as educators to develop future citizens who are trustworthy and who are capable of trusting in those who have earned their trust.

Making Wise Choices. Trustworthiness is the result of making wise choices over time—some wise, others not so wise. The ability to do so, however, isn't automatic. It takes practice, in the midst of which we make mistakes—lots of them! For instance, when sent to deliver a message, does the student attend to the task at hand or slowly meander through the hallways disrupting other learners by waving in classroom windows? Do you remember some of these situations from your own childhood experiences? One friend shares a secret with another, who promises not to tell. The two are part of a trust-building pact. Did the secret get told as soon as another warm body was in sight or remain private? Remember going to a friend's house and promising to return home by dinner time? Were you at your place at the dinner table or nowhere to be seen? Remember finding money around the house or at school? Did you search for the owner or pocket the cash? These are all examples of early trust-building opportunities.

At school, does a trip to the bathroom take a few minutes or is it necessary to dispatch an escort to accompany the unreliable student back to class? Can the child be trusted to complete her own work and not to copy someone else's work? Will the child tell the truth even though negative consequences may result? Does the student return forms and homework on time, turn in "found" objects and money, work hard to eliminate put-downs from his vocabulary, and do his personal best consistently?

As adults, every action we take, every deed we accomplish, every word we utter, creates the person others see us to be. People either believe us or they don't. Building trust is a definitive example of actions speaking louder than words because all of the good intentions and promises in the world will not be able to compensate for jobs not done, deadlines ignored, secrets revealed, and promises broken. Therefore, tell the truth, work to your personal best, keep your word, exceed expectations—be a person viewed as reliable, dependable, and believable.

Building a Reputation Takes Time. A reputation of trustworthiness is slowly earned since it is based on a collection of positive experiences among people over time. Consistency, reliability, and honest actions all typify a person who is worthy of our trust. The same is true for each of us. Our actions and reactions will be watched for awhile, before we are known to be trustworthy.

Adults must recognize that trustworthiness develops in stages. Expectations of trustworthiness for five-year olds should be more basic than expectations for fifteen-year olds. Students must understand that each time trust is broken, it takes longer to be restored; sometimes trust can be irrevocably broken.

TRUTHFULNESS:

To be honest about things and feelings with oneself and others

What Is Truthfulness?

Truthfulness has many aspects; its complexity unfolds as students mature. It is a difficult Lifelong Guideline to practice. Its attributes are complex and often dependent upon circumstances. The definition of truthfulness that follows is the result of brainstorming by a class of teachers and administrators at U.C. Davis, California.

"To be truthful means being honest about things and feelings . . . being honest with ourselves and with others. Being truthful is not always easy because truth is not absolute (black and white) and two seemingly contradictory statements could both be the truth depending upon the perspectives of the observers (for example, the blind men discovering the elephant). It takes courage to be truthful because others may disagree.

"Being truthful requires good judgment about:

- What to say (possible risk to our source of information)

- When to say it (in private or before others)

- To whom to say it (to the person responsible for the problem/situation or as a complaint to anyone who will listen)

- How to say it (with sensitivity and tact or intended to hurt)

* Karen D. Olsen, instructor, extension course in brain-compatible learning at the University of California, Davis, 1993.

"Truthfulness is a critical building block for human relationships and therefore has significant consequences for each of us, both short-term and long-term."*

Preserving the Truth. Preserving the truth depends on each one of us refusing to exaggerate, change, or vary the facts we are sharing. This requires careful observation and clear thinking as we perceive and analyze a situation; it also requires precise communication when sharing about it.

Whether it's the policeman asking, "What happened here? Which driver caused the accident and how?" or the parent asking, "How did this happen? Who started this?" the situation calls for the truth. How well did we observe the incident? Do we stick to the facts or make inferences that may or may not be true? Are we committed to telling the truth despite consequences?

Why Practice Truthfulness?

Most people will believe what they hear unless the information is proven to be inaccurate. After that, the informant's word is not as good as it used to be; people then listen with a sense of disbelief or the feeling that they should check another source. Recall the story from Aesop's Fables about the boy who cried wolf. The boy lied so many times about the wolf being after the sheep that when the wolf really did attack, none of the villagers responded to his cries for help. If we aren't truthful at all times, people—especially family and friends—will be suspicious when we share stories; they'll want proof or verification from other sources. The greater the number of lies and careless statements that pass through our lips, the more corroboration our listeners will need.

It is important, sometimes even a matter of life or death, that people believe us. Nothing is as precious as our reputation that we say what we mean and mean what we say. Truthfulness is the bedrock of trustworthiness.

_____
* See *The Leadership Challenge* by James M. Kouzes and Barry Z. Posner, Jossey-Bass, Inc., San Francisco, CA, pp. 21-22.

Effective Relationships Rely on Truthfulness . Based on a survey of more than 15,000 people, 88 percent chose honesty as the key trait of effective leadership.* Honest people have credibility; credible leaders gain the trust and confidence of their followers. They keep their promises and follow through on their commitments. In contrast, people who consistently lie are shunned, have few friends, and have fewer options for well-paying employment.

In personal relationships, if we can't be trusted to tell the truth with even insignificant information, how can anyone believe that our important ideas are true? By always telling the truth, friends, family, and co-workers will believe what we say. We become respected and valued members of our families and communities.

When the Lifelong Guidelines of Truthfulness and Trustworthiness are present, a sense of community develops. Then, all members are less likely to be dishonest because each is genuinely cherished for who he/she is. When we belong, we have something to lose if we break the norms of our group. When we belong, there is no need to create some persona bigger and better than in real life.

Benefits to Telling the Truth. According to Dr. Abraham Kryger, D.M.D., M.D., there are real benefits to telling the truth. Among them are: greater success/personal expertise, an increased sense of grounding/confidence, less anxiety/worry/guilt, increased ability to deal with crises/breakdowns, improved problem-solving abilities, improved interpersonal relationships, greater emotional health/control of one's emotions, increased ability to influence others, better sleep, better health, increased ability to think well/reason soundly, less need to control, good humor, and greater self-expression and self-satisfaction.** Do those sound like qualities you'd like

_____
* *Benefits of Telling the Truth* by Dr. Abraham Kryger, D.M.D., M.D., http:www.wellnessmd.com/tellingtruth.html. See also Bill Moyer, *The Truth About Lies,* videotape, 1987.*

** The lie detector test is based on physiological evidence of the body's reaction to lying—more rapid pulse and rise in blood pressure. Also see *The Orman Health Letter* published monthly by TRO Productions, Inc., Baltimore, M.D., and http://www.wellnessmd.com/tellingtruth.html

in your life? Truth—and its dark twin, lies—drive world events, nudge the fall of civilizations, and sculpt our lives like no other character trait.

Consequences of Not Telling the Truth. There are also consequences that result from not telling the truth. Some of these consequences according to Dr. Kryger are: more frequent failures/frustrations in life, being distrusted by others, lack of self-esteem/self-confidence, dysfunctional interpersonal relationships, inability to self-correct, and stress of many kinds. Almost all types of human stress can be traced to not telling the truth at one level or another.*

How Do You Practice Truthfulness?

Always tell the truth! It was Mark Twain who said, "If you tell the truth, you don't have to remember anything."* It is easier to remember what really happened, what words were really spoken than to try to recall a made-up story or a distorted version. You also practice the Lifelong Guideline of Truthfulness by telling the entire truth immediately rather than telling the story a little bit at a time until finally the whole truth emerges. Credibility is easy to destroy with just some simple untruths told in a moment to either create a better impression, deny involvement, or refuse to acknowledge that an incident has occurred. As a teacher, you're on stage; be honest with your class. Remember, what you do is more important than what you say you do!

Recognize That There are Barriers to Telling the Truth. When teaching students about the Lifelong Guideline of Truthfulness, we must admit to ourselves and to them that there are formidable barriers to telling the truth in our society. Perhaps the biggest is refusing to accept that it is possible to tell the truth. A widespread but false belief held by many is that it isn't humanly possible to tell the truth. That is just a handy excuse that absolves us of the need to question our lack of truthfulness.

A second powerful barrier is fear of consequences of telling the truth. For example, fear of the boss firing us, of someone close

* Mark Twain, *Notebook*, 1984.

to us losing respect for us, or of people retaliating for our having challenged their belief system or not knowing how to disagree with a friend whose "truth" are far different from our own.*

Practice, Practice. Have students share stories and repeat information as accurately as possible. Teach them to write terms and facts on paper so they can refer to them if needed. Show them the importance of being willing to recheck any data that seem to lack credibility by going back to the source of the information. Teach students many problem-solving strategies; when logical, natural choices are available, a student is less likely to lie. Avoid setting a trap for a student as when you already know the answer but ask the question anyway. All you accomplish is "catching" him/her in a falsehood. Why not "catch" someone when telling the truth and thus reinforce the desired, rather than the negative, behavior.

Seek Work Places and Friendships That Value Truthfulness. Telling the truth isn't always easy. Often, telling parents, friends, the boss, and co-workers the truth brings unpleasant consequences. However, telling a lie under these circumstances almost always has far-reaching consequences, often of greater severity than if we simply spoke the truth up front and accepted the consequences, as unpleasant as they might be. Once we're caught lying, people lose faith and confidence in us. In work relationships and with friends, this is devastating.*

One final caution. Sometimes people in power will ask for our "honest" opinion about plans, choices, and situations. If the level of trust in that business or organization is high, we feel comfortable in sharing our thoughts. If it's low, our risk is much greater, particularly if our true beliefs are not what the person in power wants to hear. Rather than be part of a lie that will have unwanted consequences for us and others, we should look for work settings where truthfulness is truly valued. During interviews, ask questions that will reveal the level of truthfulness in that culture. By gathering as much information as possible before accepting a position, we can make more informed decisions.

* *Benefits of Telling the Truth* by Dr. Abraham Kryger, D.M.D., MD http//www.wellnessmd.com/tellingtruth.html. See also Bill Moyer, *The Truth About Lies*, videotape, 1987.

ACTIVE LISTENING:

To listen with the intention of understanding what the speaker means to communicate

What Is Active Listening?

Hearing is an inactive, involuntary process that occurs when the ears pick up sound waves being transmitted by some kind of vibration and forward them to the brain. Listening, however, is an active, voluntary process which includes recognizing, understanding, and correctly interpreting messages received. Listening requires participation, patience, energy, and the intention to "get it"—not just what the speaker said but what he/she intended to communicate.

To actively listen, the brain must be physiologically active. Not only must it perceive the sounds correctly but it must also compare words to emotional nuances for consistency, then convert words into images that can be analyzed, compared, and stored for future reference. This is an extremely active process requiring neural wiring that, unfortunately, one out of four students haven't developed by the time they start school.* However, such wiring can easily be developed in the classroom. For more information, contact Lindamood-Bell Learning Processes Center, San Luis Obispo, California, 800/233-1819.

Most people listen passively. That means the sound acts on them—enters their ears—but they don't actively and consciously participate in the process; they don't exert effort in order to listen and attend to what they are hearing. An example is listening to a music tape or book tape while driving or a CD while cleaning the house. In contrast, active listening is more complex than passive listening because it demands that we listen with our eyes, ears, heart, and undivided attention as illustrated in the TANG, a Chinese character for "to listen."* An active listener not only hears but also pays close attention, focusing on the words, ideas, and emotions of the speaker.

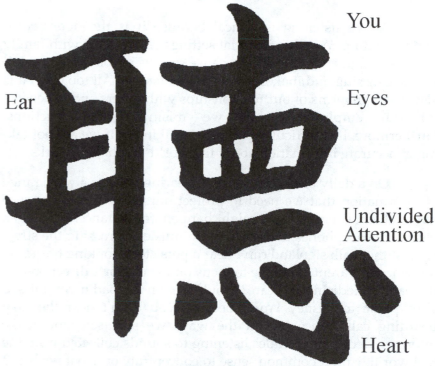

You

Ear

Eyes

Undivided Attention

Heart

The active listener is more than a receiver. In many ways, he assists the speaker to deliver his message by providing encouragement, such as attentive body posture, full eye contact, positive body signals, and multi-tiered acknowledgements, such as "Mmm; uhuh; yes; I understand; I agree; yes, interesting; I heard something about that yesterday . . . tell me more." The listener is saying to the

---

* Not surprisingly, the more hours spent in front of a television, the less time spent developing language. See *Visualizing and Verbalizing for Improved Language Comprehension* by Nanci Bell, p. 21.

* For a wonderful discussion of the meaning of the Chinese symbol for "to listen," see *TRIBES: A New Way of Learning and Being Together* by Jeanne Gibbs, 1999, pp. 93-94 . The book also provides many ready-to-go activities for students to practice the Lifelong Guideline of Active Listening. See also *ITI: The Model* by Susan Kovalik, 1997, 1994 edition, pp. 26-27.

speaker, "I understand. Your ideas and message are important to me and to others in the room. I will listen while you communicate with me and then I will ask questions if I disagree or don't understand. Above all, I respect your opinions and your right to speak."

Why Practice Active Listening?

Active listening is critical because it is the doorway to understanding. Whether in social settings, at work, or with family and friends, not "getting it" can cause serious problems. At best, it is embarrassing and makes us feel like outsiders. All too often it is also costly in terms of our relationships with others and expensive for our employers when we misinterpret instructions. Furthermore, it is difficult to be successful in life if we are not taking in accurate information about the world and how it works.

On a daily basis, our sense of hearing collects a wide range of information that we need to protect ourselves and to enhance our problem solving. What might happen, for instance, if a jogger, wearing head phones and listening to music, is crossing the street against the walk sign and can't hear a persistent honking horn? Or, if a worried parent is unable to focus on the doctor's directions for the baby's medicine and care? Wouldn't you feel sad if you missed your plane to Disney World because you didn't hear the final boarding call? Since one of the ways we stay safe and make informed decisions includes listening to sounds collected from the real world, isn't it common sense to concentrate on what we hear?

Unlike reading, we can't regulate the pace of someone else's speech, replaying it again to check an unfamiliar word. Thus, we may miss important information reported to us and respond in a peculiar way. To immediately understand what we hear, it's crucial that we perfect the skill of listening well. We can only talk intelligently about a topic when we can grasp what is said to us. To be able to listen well gives us confidence when communicating with others. Listening in the real world is an everyday skill.

Spotlight on Brain Research. Most educators don't realize that active listening—turning words into mental images that can be processed and stored in short- and long-term memory—requires neural wiring that over 25 percent of the population does not have or has not developed sufficiently to succeed in school. Nanci Bell, author of *Visualizing and Verbalizing for Improved Language Comprehension*, describes typical symptoms of oral language processing difficulty, any one of which would increase difficulty and frustration in learning as well as in social settings. Unfortunately, most people who have difficulty with language processing display more than one of these symptoms. It is a sobering list:*

1. *Individuals may frequently not understand jokes.* Language humor depends on imagery, whereas sight humor (pie in face) does not and is more easily understood. Almost everyone gets sight gags but not everyone gets language-based humor.

2. *Individuals may not understand concepts of cause and effect.* To process cause and effect relationships you must be able to process a gestalt from which to judge an effect.

3. *Individuals may not respond to explanations given in language.* If a student's performance needs correcting, a "talking to" may be only partially understood or not understood at all because the student is connecting to only a part of the oral explanation.

4. *Individuals may ask and re-ask questions that have already been answered.* The individual hears the answer but is unable to process and connect to the given information and will therefore ask the same question again, only phrased differently. Such individuals are often not aware that they are asking the same question over and over, only with modified language.

5. *Individuals may not grasp the main idea or inferences from television shows or movies, although they may get a few details.* The individual may seem to miss concepts or nuances from

---

* See page xxi, *Visualizing and Verbalizing for Improved Language Comprehension* by Nanci Bell, Gander Publishing, Inc., Palo Alto, CA, 1991.

movies they've seen. In discussions with them, they don't interpret the movie or story sequence well.

6. *Individuals may lose attention quickly in conversation or lectures.* Students who are unable to connect to the gestalt of language will find that in a few minutes, often less, they are "lost" and may drift away mentally and/or physically.

7. *Individuals may have weakness in auditory memory and in following directions.* These symptoms may be severe and labeled as aphasia* . . . [or] be subtle weaknesses that cause others to suspect lack of intelligence or lack of motivation. In fact, individuals with these symptoms will frequently doubt their intelligence.

Ms. Bell also points to a link between listening difficulties and oral language expression:

"The oral language comprehension weakness is often accompanied by an oral language expression weakness. Individuals experience difficulty organizing their verbalizing and expressing themselves easily and fluently or they are verbal but scattered, relating information out of sequence. For example, a student on academic probation, with severely impaired auditory and reading comprehension, frequently interjected irrelevant comments in conversation. His comments were disjointed both unto themselves and to the topic. Consequently, he was often viewed as mentally disabled."**

Every teacher can list students who have exhibited these frustrating symptoms. There is more to being an active listener than most people realize.

---

* Aphasia is the loss of a previously held ability to speak or understand spoken or written language due to disease or injury of the brain.
** See page xxi, *Visualizing and Verbalizing for Improved Language Comprehension* by Nanci Bell, Gander Publishing, Inc., Palo Alto, CA, 1991.

How Do You Practice Active Listening?

If these listening difficulties sound familiar, you owe it to yourself and your students to read Nanci Bell's book. Use it as a teacher's manual with your entire class every day for 30 minutes for at least six weeks. You'll be astounded at the transformation in academic capability of individual students and the class as a whole.

Once the necessary neural wiring is in place, more traditional classroom strategies for teaching students to pay closer attention, try harder, focus more, and so forth, can be used with greater success.

Proficient listening requires the neural wiring to process language plus the social skills our society has come to expect of listeners. There are many ways for students to practice these social-based listening techniques.

Using the Chinese Symbol for Listening. The Chinese symbol which depicts "to listen" as an act involving ears, eyes, heart, and undivided attention is a good place to start. It offers a handy visual and expands the meaning of the verb "to listen." In addition, teach children that the intention to "get" what the speaker intends to communicate is a critical element. Listening with intention helps the listener "hear" with an open mind and rid him/herself of any prejudicial notions that would corrupt the speaker's message. Many poor listeners get so involved in the speaker's style of delivery they miss the message. Listening with ears, eyes, heart, undivided attention, and with the intention to receive the intended message are keys to active listening.

Social Expectations

In Western culture, certain behaviors are expected of a good listener, including "attending skills" and "follow-up skills." Attending skills include not interrupting the speaker, listening for what he/she intends to say rather than what we want or think he/she will say, holding eye contact, using open body language, and offering some encouraging responses ("Wow!" "Then what happened?" "Really?" "I understand") and actions (nodding, smiling).

Personal Behaviors. To form a more accurate impression of a speaker's intended message, we must pay constant, careful attention. When we lose our concentration, we also lose much of the information. There are a number of ways to help ourselves focus on listening and collecting information.

- Limit distractions. Change places to promote concentration.

- Look at the speaker. Observe body language (open versus closed), listen to the tone of voice (pitch, quality, and timbre), and note facial expressions as clues to emotions. In many instances, the medium is the message—most of the message is communicated non-verbally.*

- Focus your attention on the meaning of words used; use signals (head nodding, smiles) to indicate you understand.

- Create pictures in your mind of what you're hearing.

- Visualize how this information fits with what you already know and what it means to you. Expect to act upon what you are hearing.*

---

* "The Importance of Effective Communication," Northeastern University, College of Business Administration, October, 1999. http://www.cba.neu.edu/ ~ewertheim/ inter/commun.htm

NO PUT-DOWNS:

To not use words, actions, and/or body language to degrade, humiliate, or dishonor others

What Are Put-Downs?

Put-downs are words and body language that imply, "I am better than you. I have more money than you, I am smarter than you, or I have more options than you." The objective is to elevate the speaker's social standing and power. By creating a laugh at someone else's expense, the speaker gains power in the situation by controlling the behavior of others and undermining relationships among those in the audience and with the targeted person. Put-downs are also a way of avoiding the real issues of the moment. They often mask unconscious feelings of jealousy, anger, fear, or inadequacy. Whether from one person or a group, the goal of put-downs is always the same—humiliation, power, control, and increased social status.

The body language of put-downs—actions and body movements, such as rolling the eyes, tapping the forehead, caricaturing, and so forth—are honed to an art form in sitcoms and other popular media in our society. They are every bit as powerful as words.

Sometimes put-downs affect us more deeply than usual. For example, when they're spoken by people we like and trust or by people we want to like us, the results are devastating. We feel betrayed. If the people whose opinion we so value express something negative about us, then it must really be so. Also, if the comments are aimed at a sensitive area (e.g., physical changes during puberty, being overweight or underweight, being an immigrant with beginning English skills, and so forth), students often feel shame about something over which they have little or no control. Similarly, when we receive put-downs in front of our peers, the humiliation and shame deepen as we lose face.

Why Practice No Put-Downs?

Put-downs among adults produce a lack of trust which is extremely detrimental to an educational agency, especially when it trickles down to influence students' attitudes and behaviors. If a staff is to pursue efforts to improve the school program, put-downs must be eliminated. To be open to learning is to be vulnerable. We're open to snickers when we make mistakes or admit we can't answer a question. Every student should be able to approach new opportunities and learning experiences without dreading verbal abuse.

When we refuse to allow put-downs in the classroom, we're teaching respect for all people, ideas, and situations. We're building a positive emotional climate in our classroom so that our students feel comfortable enough to risk an answer, offer a thought, and try some new skill without worrying about mocking remarks or gestures. This is particularly important for students in the middle position of sibling birth order whose skills and knowledge can't match the older sibling but who don't have the safety of "being the baby." Prohibiting the use of disparaging remarks is akin to constructing an invisible shield that protects and nurtures.

How Do You Practice It?

To change a negative habit to a more positive one, we first must recognize the negative behavior that needs to change. Thus, we must first teach students to recognize put-downs and become sensitive to their effects despite their pervasiveness in our mass media and society. Many students look on the word plays of put-downs as a form of humor, overlooking that it's at the expense of others.

Next, we must create an action plan to eliminate put-downs and encourage respect for others.

Recognizing the Need to Change. Select a video clip ripe with put-downs. Have your students identify and count the put-downs he/she hears and sees. Discuss with your students how they would feel if they were on the receiving end of these put-downs. Next, focus on comments heard in the classroom and school common areas. Ask your students to observe the participants. Who is handing out the put-downs? Who is the brunt of the put-downs? Who has power and social position and who doesn't? Refer to Glasser's needs list: belonging, power, fun, and freedom.* Which of these fundamental human needs is the speaker missing? If put-downs occur in your classroom, what's missing from your classroom environment? Look for patterns that demand change and then, with your students' help, create an action plan.

The Importance of Modeling. Creating an environment free of put-downs requires constant modeling by all adults. The entire school staff (administrators, teachers, aides, custodial workers, cafeteria staff, and parent volunteers) need to understand their role as role models for students. A "Do as I say but not as I do" atmosphere doesn't work. Post the Lifelong Guidelines/LIFESKILLS around the school for all to see and follow. Initiate discussions about the harmful effects of put-downs. If a put-down is heard, deal with it immediately using a calm, rational manner before the situation escalates.

Taking Responsibility for Eliminating Put-Downs. Everyone plays a part in eliminating put-downs. To begin cleansing your classroom of put-downs, eliminate the put-down banter that is passed off as humor. Recall a comment that had dual interpretations and then the speaker quickly said, "Just kidding!"—but you never knew the intent for sure. As the saying goes, "Many a true word is said in jest." Second, agree on a "cancel" signal. Whenever someone says a put-down, other family members simply say, "Cancel." The hurt is canceled, the "power play" is canceled.

Practicing the Lifelong Guideline of No Put-Downs requires a concerted effort from all members of the school community. Otherwise, the realization of a caring, risk-taking, nurturing, fellowship of learners has little chance to succeed.

* See *Choice Theory: A New Psychology of Personal Freedom* by William Glasser MD, HarperPerennial, New York, 1998, pp. 31-41.

PERSONAL BEST

One's best possible performance given the time and resources available

What Is Personal Best?

For those using the ITI model, the Lifelong Guideline of Personal Best is defined by the 18 LIFESKILLS defined here. To pursue one's personal best means working to develop and strengthen each LIFESKILL.

Quality work is never an accident; it is always the result of combining clear goals, high standards, knowledge and skills, and genuine effort. It represents the wisest choice among many options matched with commitment, perseverance, and wise use of time, talents, and resources. There is no one way to achieve a sense of fulfillment but doing one's personal best on a consistent basis is the best road we know of to reach that end.

The Lifelong Guideline of Personal Best is not about treats, rewards, or bonuses; it's about a deep sense of personal satisfaction for a job well done, mastering a skill, or making a contribution.

Personal Best Is Not a Fixed Standard. Personal Best is not about perfectionism. Personal best is the result of our consistent pursuit of a moving target within an ever-changing terrain. Our performance in the same activity looks different over time. As our competence grows, our performance improves. As the tools, time, and resources available to us improve, our performance improves.

For example, while supporting your family (emotionally, financially, and physically), you might take up jogging. You try hard to improve your running technique but you struggle to com-

---

* *Nicomachean Ethics* by Aristotle, 350 BC., translated by W.D. Ross. *The Internet Classics Archives/Works by Aristotle,* http://classics.mit.edu/Browse/browse-Aristotle.html

plete the course. You're doing your personal best in both areas—family life and jogging—but your jogging skill and capabilities in no way compare to those of a professional athlete who devotes full focus and time to his/her athletic pursuits. Personal best is using the utmost effort possible and striving for a heightened stage of excellence. This may or may not translate into being Number 1, the winner, the hero; in the real world, such status is rare. But all of us can achieve our personal best.

The Lifelong Guideline of Personal Best is one's best possible performance at the time, under the circumstances of the moment, and using the tools, time, knowledge/skill, and resources available at the moment. This, of course, takes into account the LIFESKILL of Resourcefulness!

Personal Best Is a Mindset. What drives you to do your personal best? The most important element is a clear vision of your goals and personal performance standards and love of what you are doing. When such vision and love are united, you want to do your best! The secret about goals is to make them personal—to focus on your performance, not on the status or glamour of the project, job, or assignment. Athletes strive to surpass their previous personal accomplishments. This provides a vision that pushes them to constantly improve. Then, love the process of working toward your goals, celebrating each step toward your vision.

Doing one's personal best is a way of life, not an isolated incident.

Why Practice Personal Best?

Aristotle wrote, "We are what we repeatedly do. Excellence, then, is not an act, but a habit."* The Lifelong Guideline of Personal Best is transferable from one sector of life to another—in family and social life, in one's job, in religious experiences, and in recreational activities. You can't work on excellence in one area and not have it show up in other areas. But the converse is also true: Refusing to do

 **LIFESKILLS**

CARING: To feel and show concern for others

COMMON SENSE: To use good judgment

COOPERATION: To work together toward a common goal or purpose

COURAGE: To act according to one's beliefs despite fear of adverse consequences

CURIOSITY: A desire to investigate and seek understanding of one's world

EFFORT: To do your best

FLEXIBILITY: To be willing to alter plans when necessary

FRIENDSHIP: To make and keep a friend through mutual trust and caring

INITIATIVE: To do something, of one's own free will, because it needs to be done

INTEGRITY: To act according to a sense of what's right and wrong

ORGANIZATION: To plan, arrange, and implement in an orderly way; to keep things orderly and ready to use

PATIENCE: To wait calmly for someone or something

PERSEVERANCE: To keep at it

PRIDE: Satisfaction from doing one's personal best

PROBLEM SOLVING: To create solutions to difficult situations and everyday problems

RESOURCEFULNESS: To respond to challenges and opportunities in innovative and creative ways

RESPONSIBILITY: To respond when appropriate; to be accountable for one's actions

SENSE OF HUMOR: To laugh and be playful without harming others

your personal best in one area will show up as laziness or avoidance in other areas.

Some people start out by thinking, "Doing my personal best is too difficult! I'll have to work really hard." But think of the opposite — do you really want to work toward personal worst or mediocrity? You may have to expend the same amount of effort to achieve less. Does that make sense? Self-respect — and the respect of others — depends heavily upon performing consistently at our personal best.

How Do You Practice It?

As we're sure the Army has discovered, the slogan "Be all that you can be!" is far more easily said than done. Not that it is a mystery. But to achieve our personal best requires a broad range of personal and social skills that need to be learned early and practiced daily until they become dependable habits of mind rather than now-and-then skills we pull up when we get in a pinch.

The Lifelong Guideline of Personal Best is defined by 18 LIFESKILLS as shown on the previous page. To the surprise of many, children seem to have an intuitive grasp of the LIFESKILLS. The word and concept of "perseverance," for example, is no hurdle at all for kindergarteners. And they seem delighted to be let in on the secret of how to succeed at things — when they want something, they know how to go about getting it. What a wonderful gift so early in life. One might say that the road to success in life is paved with 23 yellow bricks: the 18 LIFESKILLS and five Lifelong Guidelines.

In addition to keeping our feet on the yellow brick road, we must also:

- Identify a vision, set personal goals.

- Continuously self-evaluate in order to improve as needed (attitude, performance, or goal-setting) and to revise or completely redesign our plans as needed.

- Welcome suggestions from others with a different perspective and who may have unique experiences to share.

- Understand that we will make mistakes but that we can turn them into life lessons; accept the realization that we have discovered a way ***not*** to do something, a necessary fine-tuning of our thinking. Thomas Edison discovered over 2,000 ways not to make the light bulb before he found a way that worked.* We should expect to refine our methods, thinking, and techniques—any variation that might improve us or our product. Feel pride in our heart when all of these LIFESKILL efforts combine as one and provide us with the experience of doing our personal best.

Does this sound like a recipe for adults only? Not true. Even five year olds can set a vision of what they would like to be when they grow up although it may and often does change weekly. At five, many of the skills being learned have feedback built into the learning event; they don't have to ask, "Teacher, is this right?" They are able to judge for themselves. As for welcoming suggestions from others, they are used to getting plenty of advice from grown ups! And when it comes from learning from mistakes, young children do it with much more grace than adults do.

Can children younger than five learn these aspects of doing the Lifelong Guideline of Personal Best? In their own age-appropriate ways, absolutely! It may in fact be more difficult for high school students and adults to learn the Lifelong Guideline of Personal Best because there is a lot of unlearning of old attitudes and habits of mind that must first be shed.

Reminder

Pages 9.2-9.14 are excerpted from *Tools for Citizenship & Life: Using the ITI Lifelong Guidelines & LIFESKILLS in Your Classroom* by Sue Pearson. The book also provides a separate chapter for each LIFESKILL that discusses what the LIFESKILL is, why it is important, and how to practice it. Most importantly, the book contains 500 inquiries, activities ready-to-go for teaching and student practice of each Lifelong Guideline and LIFESKILL. It also recommends literature books whose characters illustrate the Lifelong Guidelines and LIFESKILLS—successes and possible life consequences if they are not used. We strongly recommend this book to you. It will make your first day of school and succeeding weeks much, much easier.

---

* *A 2nd Helping of Chicken Soup for the Soul: 101 More Stories to Open the Heart and Rekindle the Spirit* by Jack Canfield and Mark Victor, Health Communications, Inc., Deerfield Beach, Florida, 1995, p. 253. See also *Thomas Alva Edison Home Page,* http://www.thomasedison.com.

Chapter 10: Getting Started with the Lifelong Guidelines and LIFESKILLS

There are innumerable ways to begin using the Lifelong Guidelines and LIFESKILLS. This chapter contains the advice from those who have gone before you as described in *Tools for Citizenship and Life: Using the ITI Lifelong Guidelines and LIFESKILLS in Your Classroom.*

To get off to a good start, plan thoroughly before you begin; set and keep to an organized schedule when you do start and be willing to suspend any sense of disbelief in the power that the Lifelong Guidelines and LIFESKILLS can have in your life and in that of your students. Your most rewarding and satisfying years of teaching are just around the corner!

Consider the following planning steps:

- Take time to reflect; do a self-evaluation.

- Start with the Lifelong Guidelines; begin the first day of school.

- Create a schedule for the first four to five weeks; know what you want to do each day.

- Use real-world happenings to capture the "teachable moment."

Take Time to Reflect

Before you begin, take time to assess your own personal understanding of the Lifelong Guidelines and LIFESKILLS. Which ones are strengths for you? Are some "just okay?" Are some not as strong as they need to be? Remember, these behavior guidelines are something you must live and model, not just "teach" about.

The Importance of Self-Evaluation

Evaluate yourself in relation to each of the Lifelong Guidelines and the LIFESKILLS. Where are your strengths? Which skills need work? If you're like co-author Karen Olsen, some of the Lifelong Guidelines and LIFESKILLS will make you squirm. Organization? Karen had to jump up from the computer and start organizing and cleaning her house. You can't just talk about the Lifelong Guidelines and LIFESKILLS, you have to do them! (See the discussion about modeling in Chapter 20.)

Bring It Home

The classroom is your living room and students need to feel welcome. As you reflect on your own use of the Lifelong Guidelines and LIFESKILLS as a teacher, it often helps to picture how you would want your own children, nieces and nephews, or grandchildren treated; then, commit yourself to treating other people's children that same way. The quality and nature of the connections between the teacher and his/her students, and among students, are the basis for all else in the classroom, especially academic learning. You need to model the behaviors you would show to honored guests visiting your home and business—behaviors that exemplify truthfulness, trustworthiness, active listening, no put-downs, and personal best.

Start with the Lifelong Guidelines the First Day of School

What usually works best is to introduce all five Lifelong Guidelines at once as a collection of behaviors to enhance learning and being together for everyone. Then, go back and teach each Lifelong Guideline in-depth using the instructional strategies described in Chapters 3 and 4 and, of course, keeping C.U.E.* (*C*reative, *U*seful, and catching their *E*motions) in mind.

However, before the first day of school, make sure you have created an environment that supports the Lifelong Guidelines and LIFESKILLS in your classroom and that you communicate to parents what you are doing.

---

* C.U.E. is an acronym in the ITI model to remind teachers of the power of emotions as gatekeeper to learning and performance.

Enhancing the Physical Environment

The physical environment speaks a continuous message to students. So, design it with care. Choose a focal point in the classroom/school to display the Lifelong Guidelines for immediate reference. The back of the room, for instance, is not a handy place. Until everyone is totally familiar and comfortable with the Lifelong Guidelines, daily visual reminders will help in recognizing and identifying expectations. With the terms and definitions posted, it's easier to remember to use target talk (see chapter 20) as a reinforcement strategy. Some teachers also prepare copies of the Lifelong Guidelines (and later, the LIFESKILLS) for every student to place in his/her binder or notebook. Providing copies for parents helps to provide a basis for common vocabulary between the home and school and allows for reinforcement and connections outside of the school day.

Parent/Family Involvement

Parents want to know what is happening in the classroom. The Lifelong Guidelines and LIFESKILLS provide an excellent opportunity to share and make real-life connections with your students' families. Whether you're part of a schoolwide effort or working alone in your classroom, it's important to keep family members informed of the behaviors that are expected in class.

A newsletter is one vehicle for building understanding of the Guidelines. First, send a general introduction to all the Lifelong Guidelines and LIFESKILLS (see the sample letters at the end of this chapter). In future issues, offer more information about the specific activities students will be doing.

For parents who want to reinforce the Lifelong Guidelines and LIFESKILLS at home, we recommend the parent version of *Tools for Citizenship and Life: Using the Lifelong Guidelines and*

LIFESKILLS in Your Classroom called *Character Begins at Home: Using the ITI Lifelong Guidelines and LIFESKILLS in Your Home* by Sue Pearson and Karen D. Olsen. These two books work as companions to nurture the home-school partnership.

Create a Schedule

Good teaching is not an accident. You must have a month-long plan that tells you what to do from day to day. The following plans are recommended by numerous ITI practitioners and associates of Susan Kovalik & Associates. Adopt or adapt to fit the needs of your students.

Plan #1: One a Week

The "one a week" plan is a popular one with ITI teachers. Its strength is that it allows you to focus in depth on one Lifelong Guideline (and later on, one LIFESKILL) at a time. This is particularly important with younger students.

- Week One — Trustworthiness

- Week Two — Truthfulness

- Week Three — Active Listening

- Week Four — No Put-Downs

- Week Five — Personal Best

The following outline offers suggestions for teaching and providing practice for the Lifelong Guideline each day during each of the five weeks. For example, for the first week focusing on the Lifelong Guideline of Trustworthiness:

- Monday — definition of the Lifelong Guidelines of Trustworthiness illustrated through literature and song

- Tuesday — video segment showing both use and non-use of Trustworthiness plus discussion and role playing

- Wednesday — song, T-chart, and literature illustrating Trustworthiness

- Thursday — role playing and literature illustrating Trustworthiness

- Friday — song, role playing, and journal writing illustrating Trustworthiness

For the second week focusing on the Lifelong Guideline of Truthfulness, you could use the same combination of teaching strategies as shown above or change them as you see fit. Likewise, for the third, fourth, and fifth weeks focus on the remaining Lifelong Guidelines of Active Listening, No Put-Downs, and Personal Best. Follow the suggestions or feel free to change them according to your intuition.

For descriptions of each of the above teaching strategies, such as how to use literature, songs, role-playing, and so forth, see Chapters 20 and 21.

Plan #2: One a Day and Repeat

The "one a day and repeat" plan is also workable. Designed by Joy Raboli, its strength is that it allows students to see where they are going by the end of the first week. This is useful for older students from upper elementary through high school. You decide based on your own students' needs, learning patterns, and temperament.

Under this plan, set aside a small portion of each day to develop a deeper understanding of the Lifelong Guidelines. The time of day isn't important, although most teachers prefer to have a set schedule so they are sure to teach them each day. This plan focuses on a particular Lifelong Guideline each day of the week and repeats the week throughout the month.

- Monday — Trustworthiness
- Tuesday — Truthfulness
- Wednesday — Active Listening
- Thursday — No Put-Downs
- Friday — Personal Best

For example, a schedule for Plan #2 might look like this:

LIFELONG GUIDELINES
TRUSTWORTHINESS   TRUTHFULNESS
ACTIVE LISTENING   NO PUT-DOWNS
PERSONAL BEST

		Mon	Tue	Wed	Thu	Fri
		DAY ONE **TRUSTWORTHINESS**	**DAY TWO** **TRUTHFULNESS**	**DAY THREE** **ACTIVE LISTENING**	**DAY FOUR** **NO PUT-DOWNS**	**DAY FIVE** **PERSONAL BEST**
WEEK	ONE	**TRUSTWORTHINESS** Define~Story~Discuss	**TRUTHFULNESS** Define~Story~Discuss	**ACTIVE LISTENING** Define~Story~Discuss	**NO PUT-DOWNS** Define~Story~Discuss	**PERSONAL BEST** Define~Story~Discuss
	TWO	**TRUSTWORTHINESS** Video~Tally~Graph	**TRUTHFULNESS** Video~Tally~Graph	**ACTIVE LISTENING** Video~Tally~Graph	**NO PUT-DOWNS** Video~Tally~Graph	**PERSONAL BEST** Video~Tally~Graph
	THREE	**TRUSTWORTHINESS** T-chart~Role Play~Real Life	**TRUTHFULNESS** T-chart~Role Play~Real Life	**ACTIVE LISTENING** T-chart~Role Play~Real Life	**NO PUT-DOWNS** T-chart~Role Play~Real Life	**PERSONAL BEST** T-chart~Role Play~Real Life
	FOUR	**TRUSTWORTHINESS** Creative Writing~Journal	**TRUTHFULNESS** Creative Writing~Journal	**ACTIVE LISTENING** Creative Writing~Journal	**NO PUT-DOWNS** Creative Writing~Journal	**PERSONAL BEST** Creative Writing~Journal
		The Bears on Hemlock Mountain, The Velveteen Rabbit, The Secret Garden	*Berenstein Bears Tell the Truth, Sam, Bangs and Moonshine, Pinocchio*	*3 Little Pigs-Wolf's Point of View, Charlotte's Web, Horton Hears a Who*	*Ugly Duckling, Ira Sleeps Over, Crow Boy, Whipping Boy, Charlie Brown books*	*Amazing Grace, Stone Fox, The Giving Tree, The Three Little Pigs, Brave Irene*

Plan #3: Your Choice

A few teachers have asked why they even have to have a plan for introducing and teaching the Lifelong Guidelines and LIFESKILLS. They have felt that it should just be taught naturally, whenever the circumstances are appropriate. We, too, believe in teaching them in the most natural way possible during the "teachable moment." But, we also know that current curricular demands have a way of pushing the best of intentions aside. The result, all too often, is that focus is lost and so are the lessons to be learned.

Are these the only lessons that teach about the Lifelong Guidelines? No. There are many more. Our purpose is to offer some beginning points. Go back to your own roots and experiences for "hooks" that will help you make the Lifelong Guidelines and LIFESKILLS memorable and part of the fabric of classroom life.

When to Teach the LIFESKILLS

Remember that the LIFESKILLS are not separate from the Lifelong Guidelines; they define the Lifelong Guideline of Personal Best. Begin teaching the LIFESKILLS only when you are ready to teach the Lifelong Guideline of Personal Best.

To teach the LIFESKILLS, use the same approaches that worked well for you when teaching the Lifelong Guidelines:

- Create and maintain a schedule for at least two weeks ahead; know what you want to do each day.
- Use real-world happenings and capture the "teachable moment."
- Make your "lessons" memorable.

Remember that developing habits of mind and heart take time. Master the instructional strategies described in Chapters 12 and 13 so they are readily available for daily use. Above all, have fun with your students. Learning values and appropriate behaviors may be serious business but it need not be joyless! Enjoy watching your students (and yourself!) grow.

Use Real-World Happenings to Capture the "Teachable Moment"

The real power in teaching the Lifelong Guidelines and LIFESKILLS comes from making them part of daily living. This means using real-world happenings to capture the teachable moment rather than depending on an occasional, carefully prepared or canned lesson.

For a discussion of daily teaching strategies that will allow you to capture the "teachable moment," see Chapter 20, especially target talk.

The "curriculum content" of the teachable moment lies right at your finger tips—your own experiences with school as a child and your students' current and past experiences with school. For older students, include current events from community, nation, and world.

Teacher's Childhood Experiences at School

Since students love hearing stories of their teacher's experiences, begin by telling about your own learning experiences in school. When did you feel safe enough in school to take a risk? What things happened that kept you from being the best student you could be? What mistakes do you still regret? What were your most embarrassing moments? Use your LIFESKILL of Sense of

Humor. Avoid becoming preachy. Let children know that our lives are a work in progress and that the Lifelong Guidelines and LIFESKILLS are lifelong pursuits.

For more extended or formal lessons, invite students to share examples of situations when they have felt safe and comfortable enough for learning to take place. Ask for examples of behaviors that prohibit or limit learning for them. Provide time for small groups to create a mindmap or other visual organizer detailing conditions that promote learning for everyone. Then present the Lifelong Guidelines (or later, the LIFESKILLS) and suggest that the learning clubs organize their responses to match up with a Lifelong Guideline/LIFESKILL. For example, if one learning club's mindmap has, "It helps us when people listen to our ideas," this would support the Lifelong Guideline of Active Listening. Another group may have, "When people speak respectfully to us, we can concentrate on learning," and might decide that this links to the Lifelong Guideline of No Put-Downs. After all of the positive learning behaviors have been categorized, agree that these guidelines will be part of classroom life.

Students' Experiences at School

From a student perspective, a school day is full of experiences—good and bad. Use these events and interactions at school as the context for discussing the Lifelong Guidelines and LIFESKILLS. During community circle or class meetings, invite the students to share some of the problems they have experienced during school, past and present, that kept them from concentrating on learning, e.g., fights on the playground, name calling, use of put-downs, a bully who frightened them, and friends telling lies.

Current Events

For older students, a discussion of current issues in the news can lead into the Lifelong Guidelines and LIFESKILLS. Pose pertinent questions to promote analysis of what Lifelong Guidelines or LIFESKILLS helped the people to solve the problem or accomplish what they did. And what Lifelong Guidelines and LIFESKILLS didn't the people use that landed them in the predicament described in the news articles. What characteristics in people do the students admire?

Teach Students Strategies for Coping and Cleaning Things Up

Living the Lifelong Guidelines and LIFESKILLS requires two key strategies: coping when others don't follow the Lifelong Guidelines and LIFESKILLS and cleaning things up when we don't follow them. Here are some strategies for coping:*

- Ignore it.
- Walk away or do hook-ups.
- Go to another game or activity.
- Talk it out.
- Use an "I" message. I feel . . . when you. . . .
- Go back and try again.
- Apologize if needed.
- Tell him/her/them to stop.
- Take a stop to cool off.

* Created by Sue Pearson, associate, Susan Kovalik & Associates

- Count from 1 to 25 to cool off.

- Take 10 deep breaths.

- Problem-solve with a friend or with my learning club.

- Add to class meeting agenda.

- Draw a picture to show what happened.

- Write in my journal.

- Do a "freeze frame" (see *Heart Math Solutions).*

    Here are some strategies for cleaning things up:

- Make sure you understand how you made the person feel when you didn't follow the Lifelong Guidelines and LIFESKILLS

- Apologize with more than a simple "I'm sorry." Be specific. Restate the harm that you did, such as hurt their feelings, humiliated them in front of others, bruised their arm. Ask for their forgiveness.

- Ask them what you can do to make it up to them. If it's within reason, appropriate to the damage inflicted, do it without delay and do it sincerely.

- Learn from your mistakes. Ask yourself why you did what you did. Was it to feel important? To avoid looking less than perfect? To avoid consequences for earlier misbehavior? Remember, whittling away at others *never* makes us feel better about ourselves. Figure out how to meet your own needs. That is your responsibility and one no one else can do for you.

Instructional Strategies

To make the Lifelong Guidelines and LIFESKILLS come alive, you will need numerous instructional strategies in your bag of tricks. See Chapters 20 and 21.

Communicating with Parents/ Families

Whichever schedule for incorporating the Lifelong Guidelines and LIFESKILLS you adopt/adapt, be sure you communicate to families what you are doing, how, when, and why. The following letters can help open a teacher-parent dialogue about first the Lifelong Guidelines and then later the LIFESKILLS.

It Starts with Staff

Implementing the Lifelong Guidelines and LIFESKILLS must begin with the adults on campus—all staff, not just teachers and classroom aides. This means bus drivers, coaches, cafeteria personnel, maintenance staff, parent volunteers, and visitors. Everyone. To get each one on the same page, generate a T-chart just as you would with students. The T-charts on the next page were generated by teachers and administrators at a Summer Institute training. The differences between what is and what would no longer be are drastic. The Lifelong Guidelines and LIFESKILLS are something everyone does. "Do what I say, not what I do" has never worked and never will.

LIFELONG GUIDELINE—
Truthfulness

Looks Like:	Sounds Like:	Feels Like:
eye contact	ownership by using "I" statements	safe, non-threatening
active listening	open communication	respectful
cohesiveness, okay to disagree	verbal reinforcement, compliments	opinion is valued
calmness	constructive feedback	validating, supportive

Behaviors Should No Longer Look, Sound, or Feel Like:
▪power trips ▪dishonesty ▪deceit ▪gossip ▪politics ▪cliques ▪labeling others

LIFELONG GUIDELINE—
Trustworthiness

Looks Like:	Sounds Like:	Feels Like:
communal resources	addressing issues directly	equality
whole staff collaboration, professional mutual respect	sharing useful information	team effort productive
laughter	sharing ideas/curriculum	safety, family
living up to responsibilities; keeping one's word	adequate time to discuss differences	support is dependable

Behaviors Should No Longer Look, Sound, or Feel Like:
▪rumors ▪favoritism ▪missing materials ▪frequent absences ▪terrified new teachers ▪competition ▪power struggles ▪put downs of children ▪fear of failure ▪betrayal ▪empty promises ▪gossip

LIFELONG GUIDELINE—
Active Listening

Looks Like:	Sounds Like:	Feels Like:
eye contact	respectful silence awareness on speaker	non-judgmental
open body language	collegial, refreshing, connection	energized
nodding, smile	respond with respect, calm voices	respectful, trusting
focused attention	one voice at a time	positive atmosphere

Behaviors Should No Longer Look, Sound, or Feel Like:
▪misunderstood ▪rude interruptions ▪feelings of inequality ▪excluded ▪isolation ▪anger ▪frustration

LIFELONG GUIDELINE—
No Put Downs

Looks Like:	Sounds Like:	Feels Like:
energized gatherings	authentic conversations	supportive/understanding of peers
cooperation	no blaming someone else	loyalty to those not present
collaboration	appreciating input	willing to risk
a well functioning community	willing to hear other perspectives	safe teaching and learning environment

Behaviors Should No Longer Look, Sound, or Feel Like:
▪sarcasm ▪personal attacks ▪insults ▪demeaning ▪inferiority ▪disgust ▪prejudice

LIFELONG GUIDELINE—
Personal Best

Looks Like:	*Sounds Like:*	*Feels Like:*
professional appearance	open communication willingness to share	relaxed
self-confidence	comments of appreciation	positive, warmth
organized	open to others perspective	team pride
walk the LIFESKILL talk	talk the LIFESKILLS talk	contagious atmosphere of excellence

Behaviors Should No Longer Look, Sound, or Feel Like:
▪negative and lack of willingness to improve ▪blaming others for problems ▪sloppy
▪refusal ▪apathy

Date _____

Dear Family,

Who doesn't want to have a sense of community whether it be in the neighborhood, an organization, a church, or workplace? Community is that sense of belonging one feels when many hearts and minds come together to work toward a common goal and live by a common set of behavioral standards.

In our classroom, we will follow the Lifelong Guidelines of:

- TRUSTWORTHINESS   • ACTIVE LISTENING   • PERSONAL
- TRUTHFULNESS   • NO PUT-DOWNS   BEST

These five Lifelong Guidelines provide consistent parameters and expectations of conduct in our mini-community—what behaviors to expect from ourselves and others. They are the social outcomes we set for the community. They also ensure that all students are in an environment that encourages exploring, discovering, and learning.

These behaviors contribute to a sense of workability in life, not only in our classroom now, but also as an adult.

Sometime during the sixth century B.C., Lao-Tzu (a name meaning "old sage") wrote:

"The journey of a thousand miles begins with a single step."

As we venture into learning and living each guideline, I invite you to join us on our journey and provide an important supportive role in the development of our classroom community. We will keep you up-to-date with our progress through letters, newsletters and projects.

Sincerely,

Your child's teacher

Date _____

Dear Family,

Our class has been working hard to learn to live by the Lifelong Guidelines in our classroom community. Our efforts will continue throughout the year as we attach new meanings and deeper understandings of their application. At this time, we are ready to progress from group standards and expectations, the Lifelong Guidelines, to those that are more individual, the LIFESKILLS.

The fifth Lifelong Guideline, "PERSONAL BEST," is defined by 18 LIFESKILLS:

CARING	FLEXIBILITY	PERSEVERANCE
COMMON SENSE	FRIENDSHIP	PRIDE
COOPERATION	INITIATIVE	PROBLEM SOLVING
COURAGE	INTEGRITY	RESOURCEFULNESS
CURIOSITY	ORGANIZATION	RESPONSIBILITY
EFFORT	PATIENCE	SENSE OF HUMOR

The Lifelong Guidelines and LIFESKILLS will be introduced in our community one at a time. This will assure that all students arrive at common understandings of the meanings of each and how to practice them.

Margaret Mead, a famous anthropologist, provides an inspiring quote to spark our journey:

"Never doubt that a small group of thoughtful,
committed people can change the world.
Indeed, it is the only thing that ever has."

Once again, we invite you to learn with us as we venture forth in creating our classroom community.

Sincerely,

Your child's teacher

Chapter 11: What to Accomplish Before Moving to Stage 2

Although the ITI model is best known for its curriculum development processes and structures, those curriculum development efforts have little power until the learning environment becomes bodybrain-compatible. The most common misstep in implementing the ITI model is starting Stage 2 too early. By too early we mean before the teacher has mastered the instructional strategies described in Stage 1. Mastery, in this case, means the ability to recognize immediately the need for such strategies and the ability to use them without hesitation, even automatically. This is critical because if a teacher must still refer to his/her notes about how to do target talk, agendas, procedures, collaborative learning, Lifelong Guidelines/LIFESKILLS, *being there* experiences and so on, he/she cannot fully concentrate on the content at hand or "read" students to determine if are they getting it or not (and if not, why not).

However, this is not to say that students must have fully mastered the Lifelong Guidelines or LIFESKILLS and that the classroom is a pool of calm waters. It may take your students some time to alter their previous behaviors, particularly upper grade students. Introducing truly engaging curriculum makes students more willing to acquire the personal and social skills that create powerful learning.

But, pace yourself. Don't move to Stage 2 too soon but don't wait for perfect student behavior before you begin to provide bodybrain-compatible curriculum. Begin small, such as an integrated half day built around a *being there* experience on campus or in the neighborhood. Then, build slowly, such as an integrated topic unfolding over two consecutive afternoons, full day, or two days.

The important thing is to learn from your successes and mistakes. Take the time to be thoughtful when assessing what's just happened and jotting down notes about what to do differently next time. Be sure you give yourself sufficient time to plan so that your implementation is your best effort at implementing well-conceived curriculum rather than an impromptu plunge with so many serendipitous events that, even if successful, can't be replicated.

Gathering Your Tools

Just as a cake is only as good as its ingredients, classroom curriculum is only as good as the curriculum and standards teachers have to work from. If you're lucky, your district's curriculum and state standards consist of relatively few, good conceptual statements rather than a laundry list of factoids. Why? Because the more conceptual the curriculum, the easier it is to integrate across content areas. For example, a fifth grade science concept, "All structures and systems, living and non-living, are made up of smaller parts and/or processes," can be used to frame study of governmental systems, economics, the family car or the community mass transit system, a well-written essay or even paragraph, composition of a painting, study of the human body, design and selection of plays for a football game, and the list goes on endlessly.

In contrast, a science statement such as "Plants consist of roots, stem, and leaves" is almost impossible to use as a means of integrating other content areas. Factoids are lifeless for students and dead end streets for teachers.

Catch a Concept

Before you begin implementing Stage 2, experiment with concepts—how to extract them from your district and state standards, how to use *being there* experiences to make them come alive and integrate across subject content lines in a natural rather than contrived way.

Mining for Gold. However exasperating your state and district standards and mandates may be to you, they are better than no starting point at all. And with a little work, they can be very useful.

First, identify the concepts in the curriculum. For inspiration joggers, see *Science Continuum of Concepts for Grades K-6* by Karen D. Olsen et al. Using the concepts identified in this book as

organizers, see how the elements from your district's curriculum and state standards cluster around them. Using a large sheet of paper, mindmap the content with key words. Start with the most overarching concepts such as the one about structures and systems. just mentioned on the left side of this page. What science ideas from the standards relate to this concept. When looking at non-living systems, what concepts or significant knowledge from social studies can be clustered around it? For example,

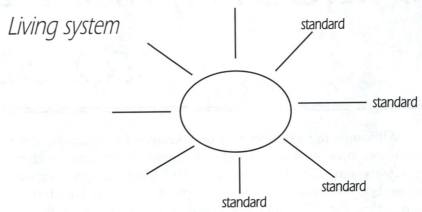

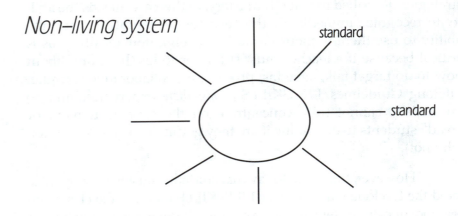

Color coding is helpful. For example: yellow for concepts, blue for significant knowledge, and green for skills.

Less Is More—Setting Priorities. As you sort through your standards, you no doubt will discover that there is too much curriculum to teach in a way that students can complete both steps of the learning process: pattern seeking (understanding) and program building (using what they understand).

Given that there is too much to "cover," make sure that what gets left undone is the content, usually factoids, that is least important for students to know 10 years from now. We call this process "selective abandonment." Teach the most important content first.

Thus, for your first adventures into developing bodybrain-compatible curriculum at the end of Stage 1, select those concepts that you feel are most important and are most interesting to you.

Work Smarter, Not Harder

While developing curriculum that is both bodybrain-compatible and addresses state standards and local mandates may seem overwhelming, start your journey by standing on the shoulders of those who have gone before you. There are many resources available.

An Internet Discussion Forum. The SKA list, an Internet discussion forum hosted by Susan Kovalik & Associates and actively participated in by those implementing the ITI model, can answer many specific questions you have. Use this resource to gather ideas and get your questions answered. The forum is available at no cost. (See www.kovalik.com for subscribing directions and information.)

Transitioning from Traditional Teaching Tools to ITI Tools. Developing curriculum—key points and inquiries—is only part of your learning curve as you prepare to enter Stage 2 of *ITI Classroom Stages of Implementation*. Teaching from key points and inquiries is considerably different from teaching from textbooks and workbooks/worksheets. For your first steps into this transition, we recommend you select ready-made, tried and true key points and inquiries. Then, your full focus can be on your instructional strategies rather than on also having to confront problems in curriculum content.

There are several good sources for mini-curriculum consisting of integrated, conceptual curriculum for an afternoon, day, or week. Sources include:

- Colleagues now implementing ITI at Stage 3

- Curriculum from the Model Teaching Week training provided by Susan Kovalik & Associates that launched you into the ITI model

- The SKA listserve previously described

- The *Curiosity Shop Kits* series produced by Susan Kovalik and Associates and available through Books for Educators.

The *Curiosity Shop Kits* were designed to give teachers experience teaching from key points and inquiries rather than from textbooks and workbooks/worksheets and to provide models for writing key points and inquiries. The kits consist of a children's book about the subject plus key points and inquiries. They provide curriculum for one to two weeks if pursued full-time and in depth or more than a month if used for afternoons only.

The kits include:

- *Touching Art* (Grades 1-4) by Patty Harrington

- *Amazing Insects* (Grades 1-5) by Pattie Mills

- *Young Detectives* (Grades 2-5) by Patty Harrington

- *Amazing Fish* (Grades 3-6) by Nicole McNeil-Miller

- *Super Nifty Origami Crafts* (Grades 3-8) by Judy Eacker

- *A Drop of Water* (Grades 4-8) by Ann Ross

- *The Train: A Magnificent Machine* (Grades 4-8) by Sr. Patt Walsh

- *A Horse Is a Horse, Of Course* (Grades 4-8) by Dean Tannewitz
- *I've Got a Secret* (Grades 4-8) by Ann Ross

Timing Is Everything

Like so many things in life, the timing of your initial efforts to implement bodybrain-compatible learning is critical. We have one simple, but powerful, recommendation. As you near the end of Stage 1 and are looking ahead to Stage 2, prepare and implement small amounts of integrated curriculum frequently rather than engage in one or two charges of the light brigade.

Be kind to yourself. You're a learner as well as the teacher. Plan and prepare thoroughly for small time frames such as one afternoon or a special day. Milk each experience for as much wisdom as you can squeeze from it. Then do another that is slightly longer. Then another.

By the time you complete Stage 1, you should have at least half a dozen mini-curriculum episodes under your belt and, in the process, developed a system for pulling conceptual statements from your state standards and local mandates, developed a knack for using *being there* experiences as a means for integrating all content areas in a natural way, and become comfortable with teaching based on key points and inquiries.

You're now ready to begin implementing Stage 2.

Stages of Implementation: Stage 2

Part C, Chapters 13 through 16, describes how to implement Stage 2 of *ITI Classroom Stages of Implementation*. The beginning steps in making curriculum bodybrain-compatible assume that significant progress has been made implementing Stage 1, making the learning environment bodybrain-compatible.

Whereas Stage 1 applied to the classroom 100% of the time, Stage 2 is applied only to that portion of the day, week, or year for which teachers have developed bodybrain-compatible curriculum using the ITI model. The time frames and content that teachers may select to begin implementation of their bodybrain-compatible curriculum vary widely. Typically teachers begin where they feel they will be the most successful and expand from there. Whatever the starting point, however modest or bold, these descriptors at this stage apply only during the time when a teacher is implementing his/her bodybrain-compatible curriculum.

The descriptors for curriculum and instructional strategies for Stage 2 are outlined on the following page.

ITI Classroom Stages of Implementation **Stage**

Entry Level into Integrating Curriculum

Entry level for making curriculum bodybrain compatible

2

CURRICULUM

- Teacher provides for real-life experiences by basing the integrated curriculum upon a physical location, event, or situation that students can and do frequently experience through *being there*. Science is either the core for or a prominent part of curriculum integration.

- Teacher has identified the concepts and skills that will be taught to the levels of mastery and application. Key points focus on critical concepts rather than on isolated facts.

- Inquiries for each key point provide students with choices and multiple opportunities for real world application; they also allow multiple ways of problem-solving and producing products. Some inquiries are designed specifically to provide realistic opportunities for students to practice citizenship, e.g., social/political action activities and collaborative grouping practices.

- The curriculum includes most of the elements that appear as a natural part or extension of the being-there focus, e.g., science, math, technology, history/social studies, fine arts, as well as mathematics, reading, writing, and oral expression. Integration of content is natural, not contrived.

- Content is age-appropriate.

INSTRUCTIONAL STRATEGIES

- Immersion and hands-on-of-the-real-thing are the primary input used to supplement and extend *being there* experiences.

- Instructional strategies are varied and provide the most effective methods for the particular content at hand. For example, direct instruction and ITI discovery processes, collaboration and personal study time, mindmapping organizing materials, and cross-age/multi-age interaction.

- Resources to support the theme are multiple, varied, and rich. Resource people and experts are regular visitors to the classroom. Visits to off-campus learning sites are frequent and serve as the organizers for the curriculum being studied.

- Choices are regularly provided through inquiries and other means.

- Adequate time is allowed to let students complete their work.

- There are sufficient inquiries for students to complete to ensure mastery and development of mental programs for using the knowledge and skills of the key points.

- Collaboration is effectively used and enhances learning for academic and social growth.

Chapter 12: My Reality—How and Where to Start Integrating

Where to Start

It shouldn't take a swami to remind us to start where we are yet somehow we seem to commit ourselves to doing things that are far away from where we currently are or from what we most need to be doing. For example, we launch into cooperative learning before we have control of the classroom, institute daily timed tests in math before we've mastered teaching the skills whose perform-ance is to be timed, embrace whole language literature approaches to reading before we have a handle on how to teach reading, or start integrating curriculum before the district/school adopts a more concept-based curriculum.

Perhaps this is all part of our fast-paced, competitive world, but it has killed many an improvement effort. To take on imple-menting brain research in the classroom, we must be far more intro-spective and careful. We must to slow down, take a deep breath, and assess our situation thoroughly and honestly. To help us make such an assessment, we should enlist the help of those who are truly expert at what we're considering. The early stages of any change effort are always the most dangerous because we must make fundamental decisions that set our course of action, often

irrevocably, and must do so at a time when we know the least. Too often we don't know enough to know that we don't know. So, choose an expert coach early on and work closely and frequently with him/her.

Realities to Consider

Before starting Stage 2, there are numerous personal and political realities to consider. First the politics of education general-ly, then the issues of your school, and, lastly, your personal/pro-fessional issues.

The Politics of Education

Our bureaucratic system is fiercely resistant to changes in its curriculum. James Beane, highly regarded expert in curriculum for middle school reform, laments the "absent presence" of a key question to guide the 40-year-old middle school movement—"What's worth learning?" He attributes such unwillingness to engage in this question to the fear that explicitly asking the question might cause a rift in the reform movement.[1] Failure to ask this question makes school reform efforts ineffective in the long run.

At risk of causing some discomfort for yourself and others, you must entertain this question at your school and in your classroom: What's worth learning? Although how we live and work has changed a great deal in the past 100 years, the content of our curriculum has changed only minimally. We need to ask anew, "What's worth learning?"—from the students' point of view, from the needs of future citizens, and from our own perspective.

Is character education needed in our turbulent times? If your answer is yes, maintain a strong focus on the Lifelong Guidelines and LIFESKILLS. Is greater understanding of science and technology as it impacts our daily life and the health of the planet important to our decision making at the polls? If yes, then emphasize science in your theme and during *being there* study outings. Is greater expertise in computer technology important, then find out how best to teach students to utilize computer and Internet technologies and what is age-appropriate for each age level.

Although the curriculum standards developed by many states are better than ever before, curriculum for the demands of living in the 21st century is still a future goal in most states. And even with the best of standards, there is usually a large gap between the standards and the curriculum tools available to teachers in their classrooms. That is to say that a shotgun wedding of thoughtful, conceptually stated standards with textbooks and worksheets is, from a classroom point of view, little better than having no standards at all.

Ask common sense questions and search for common sense answers. Bringing our traditional curriculum into the 21st century won't happen in a day but you must begin today to do so.

Never underestimate the power of curriculum as both enemy and ally—enemy because it is to difficult to change, ally because conceptual, engaging curriculum is so powerful in improving student learning.

Also, never confuse where you are with where you want to be. If your district's curriculum is still quite traditional, if you're still required to use textbooks as the course of study, then plan numerous small chunks of integrated curriculum based in the areas of the curriculum that are the easiest to make more conceptual. Successful sets of half days for a week are a better learning experience for both students and teachers than a month-long extravaganza that careens around the corner, leaving you frustrated and at a loss for how to fix it when things go awry.

Start small, start slow, start as part of a team. And do it often. Small amounts of time used effectively are always a better recipe for success than large chunks of time during which we realize that we didn't know enough to plan sufficiently.

Curriculum Issues at Your School

Where is your school in its task of developing/adopting conceptual, age-appropriate curriculum? If the job hasn't been done at the district level yet, is the climate favorable to allow your school to proceed?

If you are starting out on the ITI journey alone, will the principal and district curriculum director approve your work to make curriculum bodybrain-compatible for your classroom? Have you communicated with your parents about your plans?

When you communicate with others about your intentions, be sure you show them an example. Here is a factoid, here is what it could look like to become more conceptual, and here are the state standards that would be addressed by it. Also explain the connection between conceptual curriculum and brain research. Conceptual curriculum is rich in patterns to aid understanding and memory.

Where Are You?

Teaching from a physical location requires a teacher to be much more knowledgeable about subject areas than is needed to teach from a textbook. Are you willing to become a learner, and model it? Are you willing to say to students, "I don't know but together we can find out."?

What are your current content strengths? What are your strengths teaching the basic skills? For many of us, we consider our content strengths less than we'd like because we've had to focus so on teaching the basic skills. However, a hard-earned lesson from the thousands of teachers who have gone before you is this: Do **not** base your theme in the basic skills. Base your theme in the content areas. First choice is science, a distant second is history/social studies? Why? Because science is everywhere, giving you the widest possible choice of *being there* locations to choose from and is the most directly experienceable through all 19 senses. It also offers the most natural extensions into the other subject areas, especially social studies and art.

Why not base themes in the basic skills? Because the basic skills should be taught as a means to an end, not the end itself. For at least 90 percent of us, we compute and measure and diagram to better understand something, not just for the sake of computing, measuring, or diagramming. Similarly, we read and write not just for the fun of decoding and crafting a well-turned sentence but because we want to understand others and make ourselves understood. Basic skills also provide few conceptual hooks into other content areas.

How to Proceed

How to proceed often depends on a lot of elements and conditions over which we have no control. If we can't influence decision making over barriers in our way, accept them, adjust your plans according, and get approval and support to operate as forerunner or pioneer.

Start Small, Implement Frequently. Again, our advice, start small with small time frames and implement them frequently. Your goal is to master the art and science of making curriculum body-brain-compatible—Stage 2 of the *ITI Classroom Stages of Implementation*—in one year. Quality is more important than quantity; three short, successful integration episodes are more important than one long one that is less than successful. Ending your first year of curriculum work with a full week of integration that really works is a significant milestone.

Curriculum's Biggest Pitfall. Perhaps the biggest mistake new ITI planners make is to combine curriculum development and lesson planning. Handling two tasks at once may seem to be an efficient use of time but it isn't. It's a killer. It takes far more time and both jobs are made infinitely more difficult by combining them.

For example, you have a great activity, one students have always loved, and you want to make a key point for it. Looking for a concept to justify that activity takes you far afield of your original focus. You begin to replan the theme to make it "fit."

Or, you're planning in your head how you're going to teach the concept of habitats but you can't decide if a particular inquiry should be used as part of your direct instruction or as a Discovery Process or as a Learning Club activity. There are benefits in all three directions but until you decide how the rest of the lesson will go, you can't make up your mind. So now your curriculum development work stalls out.

Add to this dilemma working with a partner, who is probably having the same conversation in her head, and you have a very frustrating day ahead of you.

So, please believe us and repeat these words to yourself: ***Complete*** your curriculum development process of writing key points and inquiries ***before*** you begin to lesson plan. If lesson planning reveals a gap in your curriculum, fill it, then get back to lesson planning. *Never, ever, ever combine lesson planning and curriculum development.*

Notes

1 James A. Beane, *A Middle School Curriculum: From Rhetoric to Reality* (Ohio: West-Camp Press, Inc., 1990), p. 2

Chapter 13: Developing Curriculum Based on a Physical Location

In our opinion, the two most convincing areas of brain research are: 1) the importance of emotion in learning and 2) the need—the absolute requirement—for full sensory input to the brain through all 19 senses. For teachers, this means that first the content we expect students to learn must be meaningful to them and then that the amount of sensory input from the traditional tools of textbooks, worksheets, lectures, and an occasional video or internet scan is wholly and indisputably insufficient. Gasp!

While the chasm between what is and what should be in our public schools may seem unsurmountable, the solution is easier than one might imagine: **Anchor your curriculum and instruction in *being there* locations**. Don't teach from a book, teach from the real world—a backyard, a mall, a park in the neighborhood, a grocery store. Real places where real people go to get their needs met—as shopper, as business person, as someone looking for a place to play, relax, or be entertained.

Teaching from the real world rather than from a book solves both dilemmas posed by brain research: High interest and engagement spark positive emotions for learning and real-world locations provide full sensory input and meaningfulness.

Some readers may complain that their district doesn't allow money for field trips. We're not talking about *field trips* or end-of-the year *travel rewards*. We are talking about **study** trips designed in accordance with brain research findings about how the human brain learns. Is there a difference? You bet! Is it doable? Affordable? Yes, if we choose locations very near the school that we and our students can revisit frequently by walking or by taking a short ride on public transportation.

Are we talking about throwing away textbooks? No. But we are suggesting that textbooks be used as one of many resources, not as *the* curriculum and paramount teaching strategy.

Are we talking about ignoring state standards? Absolutely not. Standards adopted by the district tell us what we as teachers are expected to teach our students. And we owe our students a curriculum with no gaps and no repetitions. District-adopted curriculum standards are essential.

Your entry into Stage 2 of the *ITI Classroom Stage of Implementation* is your entry into making curriculum bodybrain-compatible.

Stage 2

Integrating Curriculum Based on Real-Life

Entry level for making curriculum bodybrain compatible

CURRICULUM

- Teacher provides for real-life experiences by basing the integrated curriculum upon a physical location, event, or situation that students can and do frequently experience through "being there." Science is either the core for or a prominent part of curriculum integration because an understanding of science and technology is so key to the role of citizen in the 21st century.

- The curriculum includes most of the elements that appear as a natural part or extension of the *being there* focus, e.g., science, math, technology, history/social studies, fine arts, as well as mathematics, reading, writing, and oral expression. Integration of content is natural, not contrived.

INSTRUCTIONAL STRATEGIES

- Immersion and hands-on-of-the-real-thing are the primary input used to supplement and extend *being there* experiences.

- Instructional strategies are varied and provide the most effective methods for the particular content at hand. For example, direct instruction and ITI discovery processes, collaboration and personal study time, mindmapping, organizing materials, and cross-age/multi-age interaction.

- Resources to support the theme are multiple, varied, and rich. Resource people and experts are regular visitors to the classroom.

A **reminder**: Start small . . . an integrated half day, then day, then two days, and finally a week. Small chunks of integrated curriculum that are well-planned, well-implemented, and occur frequently are more productive than a few large, overwhelming chunks. Quality is far more important than quantity, especially during your first year implementing Stage 2 of the *ITI Classroom States of Implementation*.

Anchoring and Integrating Curriculum in Real-Life Locations

Anchoring curriculum content and assessment in the real world, and letting real life integrate it naturally, reverses traditional curriculum planning during which one begins with the prescribed content of traditional disciplines, fragmented by scheduling and departmentalization, and then searches for ways to make it come alive for students. Thus, the beginning point and the heart of the matter is selecting *being there* locations which are completely engaging to students and that are rich examples of the concepts and skills identified in the state standards/district curriculum.

Choosing a physical location as the anchor for curriculum is critical to the ITI model for several reasons:

- The best way to ensure that students quickly grasp an accurate and comprehensive understanding of the concepts and skills of the curriculum is to allow them to experience the concepts in their real-world contexts.

- Once students understand concepts in one location, the concepts can be generalized to other locations and used to make predictions about events past and future.

- Each of us must understand how our community works in order to become an informed citizen.

Curriculum Development

- Teacher provides for real-life experiences by basing the integrated curriculum upon a physical location, event, or situation that students can and do frequently experience through "being there." Science is either the core for or a prominent part of curriculum integration.

Advice About Selecting Physical Locations

Selecting physical locations upon which to build your curriculum is the most critical curricular decision you will make for the year. Like any builder, you will need to choose carefully as the nature of the foundation you select will determine the stability and strength of the building. The bigger and more solid the foundation, the bigger the building can become. The more empowering your curriculum can be.

Be assured that the basic skills, because they are just that—basic and universally needed—can be taught using any location in which they can be applied. For example, almost any mixture of natural and man-made settings will demonstrate the science concepts from your state standards. As for history/social studies, just add people to your location and you will have a window through which to view human nature past, present, or future. For math, use the numbers built into your physical location—how far, how long, how tall, how wide, the volume of, how many years since, cost per square foot, and so forth. All other areas of curriculum can be similarly accessed.

Before selecting a physical location, do your homework. Think through the following steps.

Step 1: Analyze the Potential of the Site to Teach What Your Students Need to Learn

When scouting locations, analyze their potential for serving as the basis for curriculum using the following criteria. Ideal locations:

- Invite authentic use of the concepts and skills outlined in your state/district curriculum standards

- Provide maximum sensory input (using as many of the 19 senses as possible)

- Capture student interest and enthusiasm and lead them to eagerly ask questions on the first visit and each revisit

- Have significant carry-over potential, i.e, if students come to understand this setting well (science and technological aspects as well as historical and social science concepts), they will be able to unlock doors in many other settings

- Be a prototype for learning *how* to learn about the real world

- Be readily accessible so the class can visit it regularly, allowing for in-depth exploration. Transportation costs are zero (can walk) to minimal (public transportation) and travel time still allows for adequate time for learning

Remember that you are not developing curriculum for separate subjects which must have a designated amount of seat time per day. Let the locations integrate the content naturally. Then, if halfway through the year or semester you feel a subject area has been receiving insufficient attention, concentrate on it during the study of your last *being there* experience. Remember, let the world integrate your curriculum naturally.

Step 2: Visit the Site

First, go to each location with new eyes. Pretend you've never been there before. Get curious! Look everything over from a fresh perspective. Look behind the scenes. Imagine what others see—those who work there, those who come there to shop, visit, enjoy. What do these folks need to know to perform their roles well? What does the visitor need to know to get the biggest bang for his/her buck, to make the wisest decisions, to avoid being taken advantage of, or to enjoy it most fully? And, here's an interesting challenge, how would the location and its operations be different if people fully understood the content and skills you plan to teach your students?

Consider the common grocery store. Been there a million times? Yes, of course. But have you ever been behind the scenes and looked at it from the business perspective? Would you be amazed to discover that the typical profit margin for grocery stores is two to three cents on the dollar? Ever wonder how many items change price, when, how often? The possibilities for study are unlimited. Profit/loss, employer/employee relationships, the demographics of the clientele/distributor, legal restrictions, health inspections, competition, energy costs, OSHA requirements.

Second, interview people—those who create the environment (employees and owners) and those who come here (clients/customers and sightseers). Skip past the knowledge and comprehension questions—dive right into Bloom's Taxonomy levels of application, analysis, evaluation, and synthesis—that's where the fun and engagement are! Ask them why they choose to work or shop here. What about this place makes you proud to be here?

Third, if your focus is human nature (history/social studies, fine arts) and you teach intermediate grade students, consider applying Marion Brady's conceptual framework to each location. What does it tell you that didn't meet the eye until the framework caused you to see new relationships and thus to ask new questions and seek new connections?[1] For example, Brady's conceptual framework applied to a grocery store might look like the following:

At a grocery store for example, what *patterns of action* seem particularly intriguing?

- Distributing wealth—Given that net profit is only two to three cents on the dollar, where does all the rest of the income go? A lot of wealth is being distributed here. Where does it go? What are salaries for management, full-time, and part-time?

- Controlling behavior—How does the store control behavior of employees through management and theft reduction procedures and of customers through advertising and marketing ploys?

- Boundary control—Given that some grocery chains such as Safeway hold virtual vertical monopolies in many areas (dairy farm to the shelf), where are the boundaries for big corporations? How do lack of boundaries of one monolithic chain affect other grocery stores, food suppliers, and consumers?

How about *cultural premises*?

- The "good life"—How does the perception of the "good life" affect buying patterns?

- What trends in pricing or foods or over-the-counter drugs are there? What triggers such trends? What is their effect?

And what can *demographic data* tell us?

- What are the age and gender of the shoppers? What does this information suggest about the neighborhood served by the store and possible gender-stereotyping issues?

- What are the cost factors of prepared foods vs. preparation-intensive foods purchased? What questions does this raise about the age and gender of shoppers and their homemaking capacities/capabilities? What does this say about corporations' judgments about how some corporations judge the homemaking capacities/capabilities of America's families?

How about the *physical environment*? As a man–made environment, what messages does it give, inadvertently and by design, to customers?

- What symbols are used? Why?

- What attitudes and values do the clothing of customers and workers reflect? Are they consistent with what people say they are?

- What kind of climate did the store architects and decorators create? Why?

- What other countries provide food for this store? What economic impact does this have on our farmers and producers?

And, finally, in terms of pattern-detection, what are the *systemic relationships* between these issues of patterns of action, cultural premises, demographics, and environment? What new ideas emerge when these issues or elements are looked at together? For example, What perceptions of the "good life" (cultural premise) does the grocery store market to (distribution of wealth) and how widespread is the population (demographics) that holds those pictures of the "good life"? What symbols and architect/decor elements (physical environment) does the store use to convey its marketing? How does the store attempt to control shoppers' behaviors?

After such analysis of a location's natural curriculum potential, go back to your curriculum work started in Chapters 11 and 12. Make sure you are on target with your state/district curriculum standards. Match them to each location so that integration is as natural as possible.

Step 3: Hit the Library and Internet

Solid curriculum can't be developed from information off the top of one's head and our typical curriculum tools are limited: state standards/district curriculum offer an outline and textbooks provide but summary, superficial information. Expect to become a learner. Open yourself up to the joy of discovery; don't expect to have all the answers. The era when what you knew by age 25 would carry you through a lifetime is long gone. Learning how to learn and learning to embrace the necessity for learning with enjoyment are the demands of our time.

Pursue the concepts which you believe will most allow students to unlock meaning in other settings. Ask yourself what could be generalized, what could be used to predict events or happenings in other locations. In effect, from the students' points of view, "Where's the beef?" What are the most empowering concepts and skills you can them?

Keep in mind that the availability of resources is an important consideration when selecting a location. You should expect to have at least 100 resources in your room—books, magazines, print of all kinds written at a range of readability levels, plus multimedia options which capitalize on today's powerful technology.

STEP 4. Revisit Your Curriculum

Is it as conceptual as you can make it? (See discussion in Chapter 11.) Have you prioritized the content so students will have time to understand and learn to apply the most important concepts, significant knowledge, and skills?

Are your curriculum choices solid, acceptable to your supervisors, and explained thoroughly to the parents? If so, you are ready to begin developing key points and inquiries.

Self Check

Curriculum

Once all the sites and the curriculum for them have been chosen for the year using steps 1-4, ask yourself the following questions:

- Are science and technology at the core of your focus? Given we live in the Age of Technology and that it is the side effects of technology—not the arts, not history/social studies or physical education—that are polluting our air and water and scouring the landscape, citizens must understand the forces at work and be prepared to make well-informed decisions about such issues.

- Do I have too much? Will I end up "covering" content but leaving students without a chance to wire it into long-term memory? If the answer is yes, and it too often is, then make sure that you have included the most important concepts and skills early on. Reschedule the rest to the end of the year. If time allows, address it. If not, don't feel guilty. The authors have never seen a course of study or curriculum guide that could be taught to mastery in one year. Most contain enough content for two to three years. We call this process of rescheduling content "selective abandonment." Simply put, if we can't do it all, we must establish priorities. Make sure that what gets left behind is what's least important for your students.

- Have you allowed the physical locations to call forth your content in a natural way? If the fit at a location seems a little contrived, would it integrate more naturally into another site?

Examples of Curriculum Based on a Physical Location

Because a picture is worth a thousand words, what follows are examples of curriculum based on a physical location that would last approximately 3-4 days if implemented all day each day or for a week if implemented on half days. We recommend such small chunks during the first months of Stage 2 of the *ITI Classroom Stages of Implementation* because they provide teachers a chance to plan thoroughly, implement well, and learn from what occurred before beginning another chunk.

Notice that these curricula are, in their structure, a mini version of a yearlong theme. There is an overarching concept for the theme which functions like a yearlong theme and an organizing concept/theme for each day much like that for a monthly component. Melding things together into meaningful, memorable wholes is the goal of integrating curriculum.

However small your start, it can be an experiment in the whole concept of integration.

Location: Carolina Bays

developed by Dottie Brown, South Carolina
appropriate for upper elementary

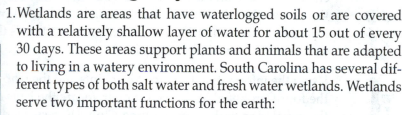 Conceptual Key Point:

As our population grows, people need more space in which to live. As humans develop land, we destroy or change habitats of plants and animals that naturally live there. Every area has unique species that depend on native habitats. Destroying habitats may destroy these species and upset the balance of nature. When given the choice to develop or preserve these native habitats, humans must consider the worth of the natural habitat in relation to the survival of the human species.

Day 1

Significant Knowledge Key Points:

1. Wetlands are areas that have waterlogged soils or are covered with a relatively shallow layer of water for about 15 out of every 30 days. These areas support plants and animals that are adapted to living in a watery environment. South Carolina has several different types of both salt water and fresh water wetlands. Wetlands serve two important functions for the earth:

   • Wetlands are like sponges that absorb water and help prevent flooding in areas beyond them.

   • Wetlands act as filters, cleaning pollutants and poisons from the water

2. The Carolina Bays are a unique wetland habitat found mostly in North and South Carolina. They are egg-shaped, surrounded by a white sand ridge and tall pine trees. Carolina Bays provide the homes for more than 30 endangered species, including rare salamanders, the red-cockaded woodpecker and the Venus flytrap.

Other plants and animals that make their home in the Carolina Bays include black bears, otters, bobcats, raccoons, deer, barred owls, red shouldered hawks, copperheads, water moccasins, and wild turkeys. In some cases the bays are the only place where these animals or plants can be found.

Inquiries:

1. *Simulate* a wetland habitat. Following the directions on the wetlands lab sheet, *demonstrate* the functions of a wetland, observe, and record the results. Based on your observations *make* two inferences for each simulation.

2. Either with a partner or by yourself, *choose* two inhabitants of the Carolina Bays. *Research* your choices and *write* a two-paragraph description of each. Be sure your description explains why the Carolina Bays are necessary for the survival of these plants or animals. *Construct* a two- or three-dimensional representation of each of your choices to place on the immersion wall. Make it as realistic as possible, based on your research and what we learned on our study trip. Be sure your construction is the same size as the real plant or animal.

3. Using the information from the key points and the map of the four Carolina Bays in your binder, *locate* the bays on the aerial map with your Learning Club. *Discuss* the distinguishing features that mark them as Carolina Bays and the similarities and differences you find in each bay. Be prepared to *share* your discussion.

Application of Language Art Skills:

Main Idea and Supporting Details

- After reading the article, "Red-Cockaded Woodpecker," to yourself or a partner, create a display that illustrates and explains the main idea of the article and the important details that support the main idea.

Application of Math Skills:

Problem Solving[2]

1. A recent study by the Department of Natural Resources shows that there are 2,651 Carolina Bays in South Carolina that are two acres or larger. From that total, it is estimated 97% have been altered in some manner.

   Question: How many bays are left in South Carolina that have been untouched or unaltered by man?

   Question: What are the ultimate consequences of the bays disappearing?

2. The red-cockaded woodpecker, found in the Carolina Bays makes its home in the mature long leaf pines (80-120 years old) and loblolly pines (70-100 years old) that are found in the bays. Every family group of red-cockaded woodpeckers needs an average of 200 acres of habitat space to meet its needs.

   Question: If a logging company harvests the largest pine trees in a five square mile area, how many red-cockaded woodpecker families could be displaced or destroyed?

   Question: There are an average of seven birds in each family. How many red-cockaded woodpeckers are in the five square mile area?

Self Check

Curriculum

- The location immediately engages students' attention and enthusiasm and sustains willingness to learn during over time. Students are eager to gather resources to study the knowledge and skills of the state standards/district curriculum.

- The location provides a powerful illustration of how the knowledge and skills are used.

Day 2

Significant Knowledge Key Point:

The Carolina Bays are a unique wetland habitat found mostly in North and South Carolina. They are egg-shaped, surrounded by a white sand ridge and tall pine trees. Carolina Bays provide the homes for more than 30 endangered species, including rare salamanders, the red-cockaded woodpecker and the Venus flytrap. Other plants and animals that make their home in the Carolina Bays include black bears, otters, bobcats, raccoons, deer, barred owls, red shouldered hawks, copperheads, water moccasins, and wild turkeys. In some cases the bays are the only place where these animals or plants can be found.

Inquiries:

1. STUDY TRIP: *Record* observations of the Carolina Bays in your wetland journal. Be sure you include all the animals you see and evidence of those you didn't see. Include plants that are pointed out by our guide. *Record* written or sketched descriptions of specific areas from which we take soil samples.

2. STUDY TRIP: Within the space marked off, *measure* and *Record* the DBH (diameter at breast height) of each pine tree. (See math skill key point and lesson) *Discuss* your results with your Learning Club to determine if the area you surveyed would be suitable for a group of red-cockaded woodpeckers. Be prepared to *share* your results and inferences with the class.

Skill Key Point:

Circumference and Diameter

• A diameter is a line segment that passes through the center of a circle and has both end points on the circle. Circumference is the distance around a circle.

Inquiries:

1. Create a tape for measuring DBH. Measure and draw a one inch line and draw a circle around it. Using a string, mark the circumference and transfer it to your tape. Do the same for a two-, three-, and four-inch line.

2. Study and discuss with your Learning Club the pattern from the previous activity. Try to discover a formula for finding circumference if you have the diameter. Be prepared to share with the whole class.

3. Using the formula for circumference, find the circumference for diameters from five inches to twenty inches. Mark them on your DBH tape.

Day 3

Significant Knowledge Key Point:

Carnivorous plants live in wetland areas where the soil is poor in nutrients such as nitrogen. These plants have adapted by developing special features, such as parts that capture and digest insects and small animals to get the nutrients the soil does not provide.

Inquiries:

1. *Observe* the Venus flytrap on your desk. Using the tweezers, place an insect in its leaves and observe what happens. *Record* your observations and *draw* a diagram of the Venus fly trap in your wetland journal. *Discuss* with your Learning Club the possible functions of all the parts that you see and make inferences about how the plant lives and uses the parts to meet its needs for survival.

2. *Read* about the Venus flytrap and share with your Learning Club what you understand. *Compare* the infor-

mation about the Venus flytrap with the inferences you made in your journal and *record* any new or different information. Now that you understand the functions of each part of the plant, *label* the parts of your diagram and *explain* to one other person how they work. *Record* your explanations in your wetland journal with your diagram.

3. Choose another carnivorous plant that we brought back as a specimen from our study trip. *Observe* how this plant catches and digests insects. *Record* and *sketch* your observations (or use the quick take camera and import the picture from the computer) in your wetland journal.

4. *Compare* two of the wetland habitats we visited in a Venn diagram. Be sure to include data from our study trip, especially where it concerns the specific population densities of carnivorous plants.

5. *Compare* two carnivorous plants we found on our study trip in a Venn diagram. Be sure you include in your comparison the specific habitat locations in which they were found.

6. Choose a carnivorous plant that interests you. *Research* the plant and choose one of the following ways to *describe* what you know about how the plant meets its needs.

Inquiries for CHOICES:

1. Dramatize, in a two-minute skit, the plant you have chosen as it reacts with its environment. Be sure your performance shows clearly that the plant you are dramatizing is carnivorous and illustrates special adaptations the plant has developed.

2. Compose and sing a song that tells about the plant you have chosen and describes how it meets its needs.

3. Draw and label the plant you have chosen, explaining the unique qualities that cause it to be carnivorous.

4. Create and design, to scale, a carnivorous garden on graph paper that you can later plant using the carnivorous plants gathered from our study trip. Be sure the soil in the location chosen for the garden matches the soil samples tested after the study trip. Be sure the dimensions in the actual garden correspond to the scale drawing in your plan.

Application of Math Skills:

Area, Averaging

Using the data from the quadrant densities collected by each Learning Club on our study trip, compute the following:

• With your Learning Club, figure the area of the Venus fly trap patch. Be prepared to share your answer and your procedure for finding the area.

• With your Learning Club, project the number of Venus fly traps growing in the area. Be prepared to share your answer and your procedure with the class.

Application of Language Arts Skills:

Writing–Friendly Letter

• Identify the components of a friendly letter in today's "Morning Message."

• Compose a friendly letter to the guide on our study trip. In the body of the letter, thank him for taking the time to go with us, include two new things you learned, and your favorite part of the visit. Peer edit for the five parts of the friendly letter, correct capitalization, punctuation, and spelling.

Responding to Literature

- Read pp. 4-11 of *Lured In* to yourself, with a partner, or with me.

- "Milling to Music" — Walk around in time with the music thinking about what you just read. Each time the music stops, share with the person you are facing something you read that answers the question being asked.

Sequence of Events (Jigsaw and Ensemble[3])

- Read the section in *Lured In* that is assigned to your jigsaw group. Develop an "Ensemble" presentation that describes the sequence of events for the capture and digestion of insects by the carnivorous plant your group read about. Present your "Ensemble" to the whole class. Be sure each event is clearly described and in the correct sequence.

Day 4

Significant Knowledge Key Points:

1. Every human use of land affects wildlife habitat positively or negatively. What humans do with land is a reflection of human priorities and lifestyles. When people do not understand the valuable functions of wetlands, they can be seen as swampy wasteland. Each year many wetlands are lost to draining, filling, pollution and development. Carolina Bays have been lost to golf courses, housing developments, farms, highways, and more.

2. Humans have the ability to create energy or bring in energy that allows a habitat to exceed its natural limits or remove energy sources that are necessary for a system to stay in balance. Understanding the impact that development has on a natural system is necessary to preserve the health and balance of the surrounding natural area. Several government agencies as well as environmental groups have worked to make the public aware of the effect development has on the bays. In some cases there are restrictions and fines for altering Carolina Bays if it impacts the natural system without providing a way to preserve or balance it.

Inquiries:

1. *Brainstorm and research* all the possible land uses you can come up with for the Carolina Bays wetlands. For each use, make a list of positive factors and a list of negative factors. Create a display and present your results to the whole class.

2. ROLE PLAY — *Simulate* a town meeting where your group represents one of the following:

- A local special interest group representative, you must convince the town council members to allow you to develop the area you want to use. You must be able to tell the council members and community how you are going to use the land, what the negative effects to the natural wildlife might be, what the negative effects of the land use for the local community might be, and how this particular use of the land will benefit the community. Be sure to have a persuasive speaker, some neat and creative visual aids, and anything else that you think might help your cause.

- Town council members—You must understand the value and functions of the local wetlands. You will need to decide if the benefits of the proposed land uses for the community are more important than the value of the natural environment.

- Local environmental group—You must know the value and functions of the local wetlands. It is your role to speak out for the natural wildlife in the area.

- Community members—You must be able to listen to the discussion and decide what you think is best for your community. Generate reasons and be able to defend them.

3. *Choose* one of the land use interest groups from the brainstorming discussion—it should be a different one if you represented one in the town meeting. *Create* a proposal for land development for your interest group that would ensure some balance or compromise with the natural habitat. How will you convince the community that you are aware of the value of the environment you are impacting and responsible for doing what creates the least negative effects possible.

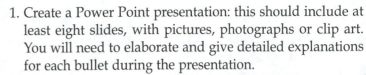

Inquiries for CHOICES:

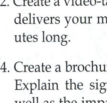

1. Create a Power Point presentation: this should include at least eight slides, with pictures, photographs or clip art. You will need to elaborate and give detailed explanations for each bullet during the presentation.

2. Prepare and delivery an oral presentation with visual aids: this should be at least three minutes long, should be given without being read, visual aids could be posters or overhead transparencies.

2. Create a video-taped commercial with music or songs that delivers your message. This should be at least three minutes long.

4. Create a brochure describing a Carolina Bay to the public. Explain the significance and importance of the bays as well as the impact of development. Be sure to include the graph you made of the bays in Horry County along with any other statistics you learned that are important.

5. Develop and film a public service commercial which explains to the general public the significance and importance of our Carolina Bays. Be sure to include the graph you made of the bays in Horry County along with any other statistics you learned that are important.

Skill Key Point:

Graphing

- A graph presents data in a visual way that makes it easier to understand it and see relationships in the data. To make a graph information must be collected and displayed in a way that shows the relationships between the elements being investigated and the numbers associated with each.

Inquiries:

- Using the map showing distribution of Carolina Bays in South Carolina, find the total number of bays in each quadrant and **graph** the results.

- **Create** a graph in Microsoft Excel to use in your brochure or commercial showing only the counties in quadrant #1.

Application of Language Arts Skills:

Cause and Effect

- After reading *The Lorax*, find and discuss with your Learning Club at least five cause and effect sequences. Illustrate them on a poster and share with the whole group.

- Create a clone book of *The Lorax* using one of the Carolina Bays we visited. Substitute the plants and animals of The Lorax with real ones we've studied this week.

Day 5

Significant Knowledge Key Point:

1. When making decisions about land use, responsible developers consider:

- The value of the land to be developed in terms of its functions and inhabitants that may be destroyed or misplaced.

- The maximum amount of housing and businesses the area can accommodate and still allow for the natural system to exist either around or nearby the development.

- The production of waste and contaminants and a plan for elimination that has the least adverse effects on the natural surrounding system.

- A plan for preserving natural wildlife that may be destroyed or misplaced

Inquiries:

1. **Design** a community on or near a wetland habitat that has the least negative effects on the natural environment. Be sure your plan shows you have considered the important factors in the key point.

Inquiries for CHOICES:

1. Present your design in a Power Point presentation that has at least eight slides. Be sure you have included all the criteria for responsible development in your presentation.

2. Present your design on a poster. Be sure you have included enough details and your explanations are elaborate enough to show your audience you have considered all the criteria in the key point.

3. Present a three-dimensional construction or model of your development. Explain thoroughly how your model preserves or balances the natural habitat you have altered.

4. Considering the information about the red-cockaded woodpeckers discussed during our first day of studying the Carolina Bays, **design** a community with the least adverse effects on the wetland environment. Be sure your development plan includes dimensions and plans for preserving the woodpeckers' habitat.

5. Using information from research done by your Learning Club, **compose** a math word problem. Exchange problems with another Learning Club. **Discuss** methods for solving the problem your Learning Club got and solve it.

Application of Language Arts Skills:

Graphing

1. Using the map showing distribution of Carolina Bays in South Carolina, find the total number of bays in each quadrant and graph the results.

2. Create a graph in Microsoft Excel showing only the counties in quadrant #1 to use in your brochure or commercial.

A Friendly Letter

- The parts of a friendly letter can be easily remembered if our bodies are used as a mnemonic:

    —Your head = the head of a letter

    —A handshake = the greeting

    —Your body = the letter's body or text

    —Close your feet and hands together = the closing

    —Imitate a seal clapping = your signature (or seal)

1. *Identify* the components of a friendly letter in today's "Morning Message."

2. *Teach* the parts of a friendly letter to a younger buddy by making analogies with body parts. Help him/her write a letter to someone they need to send a message to.

3. *Compose* a friendly letter to our guide on the study trip. In the body of the letter, thank him for taking the time to go with us, include two new things you learned, and your favorite part of the visit. Peer edit for the five parts of the friendly letter, correct capitalization, punctuation, and spelling.

Similes and Metaphors

1. After listening to the story *Wet*, discuss with your Learning Club what similes and metaphors you heard and which things were being compared. *Discuss* how they made the images in the story more vivid than they would have been without the comparisons.

2. *Write* a paragraph describing the Carolina Bay we visited. Use at least one simile and one metaphor to make your paragraph more descriptive.

Inferences/Drawing Conclusions

1. After reading the article, "Scientists Seek to Save Mysterious Depressions," *discuss* with your Learning Club the possible causes of the depressions that make the Carolina Bays. *Draw* a conclusion based on your reading and discussion of the article as to how you think the Carolina Bays were formed. *Write* a paragraph in your wetland journal explaining your conclusion. Support your ideas with information from the text.

2. After reading the article *"Red-Cockaded Woodpecker,"* *explain* the importance of 100 year old trees for these birds to the other members of your Learning Club. After discussing the article, *write* your explanation in your wetland journal.

Inference/Cause and Effect

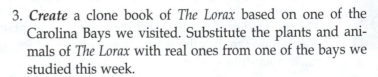

1. After reading the article *"Red-Cockaded Woodpecker,"* *discuss* with your Learning Club what might happen to the red-cockaded woodpecker if all the long leaf and loblolly pines were cut down and new ones were planted. After your discussion, *record* your inference in your wetland journal

2. After reading *The Lorax*, *find* and *discuss* with your Learning Club at least five cause and effect sequences. *Illustrate* them on a poster and *share* with the whole group.

3. *Create* a clone book of *The Lorax* based on one of the Carolina Bays we visited. Substitute the plants and animals of *The Lorax* with real ones from one of the bays we studied this week.

Location: Construction Site & Power Plant

developed by Dottie Brown, South Carolina
appropriate for upper elementary

The construction site or power plant you visit could be a local utility district, a hydro-electric dam, or other power conversion site, for example at major structures such as a lumbermill or industrial/commercial building.

Model Teaching Week
Developed by Dottie Brown

Theme: The Whole World in Our Hands
Component: Pay Now or Pay Later
Topic: Using Electricity Wisely

DAY 1	DAY 2	DAY 3	DAY 4	DAY 5
"Lightning to Lightbulbs"	"Charge it up"	"Let it Flow"	"We're Wired Up!"	"Switched On"

Conceptual Key Point:

In our complex world we use increasingly more and complicated sources of power and machines to help meet our daily needs. Many tools and machines that help us do our work are powered with electricity. Electricity powers machines that help make our homes light at night, keep us warm in the winter or cool in the summer, keep our food cold so that it won't spoil, as well as many other uses. Electrical energy occurs naturally or can be generated and controlled by man.

Day 1

Significant Knowledge Key Point:

Lightning is a huge electrical spark caused when wind causes water droplets in clouds to rub against and collide with ice crystals. Because of this friction (rubbing together), particles in the clouds become charged. Negative charges in the clouds are attracted to positive charges on the ground. We can tell how far away an electrical storm is by measuring the difference in time between the flash of lightning we see and the sound of the thunder. Knowing when to expect a storm or how far away it is allows humans to move to a safe place or make other decisions about our activity that could be affected by the storm.

Inquiries:

1. In your Learning Club, **brainstorm** all the uses for electricity that help us in our everyday lives. Share the results with the rest of the class. **Make** a chart with all the ideas.

2. In your Learning Club, **create** a room plan for your house, keeping in mind that some rooms need to be larger than others depending on their function. Be sure to remember where the outside windows are and what electrical appliances you might put in each room. **Measure** the length of each wall in your house.

3. With your Learning Club, **draw** and **cut** out electrical appliances for each room of your Learning Club's house. **Place** them in appropriate places in your house on the immersion board. **Label** each one with a word-processed label.

4. (Whole group) **Simulate** a storm by **creating** a flash of light and then the sound of thunder. **Count** the seconds between the lightning and thunder. **Use** the formula to determine how far away the lightning (storm) is. **Record** your observations and data in your science journal.

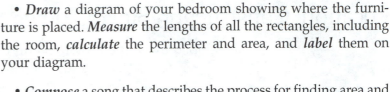

5. By yourself or with a partner *sequence* the events in the creation of lightning. *Draw* each step in your step book and *write* a sentence to explain it.

6. After *listening* to the story, *Thunder Cake*, *pair-share* with a partner one experience you have had with a storm and the LIFESKILLS you needed. *Tell* one new thing you have learned about lightning.

7. *Listen* to the story, *Teach Us, Amelia Bedelia*. *Pair-share* with your partner how the multi-meaning words in the story confused Amelia Bedelia. With your partner, *look* up the five electricity words in the dictionary and *discuss* the different possible meanings they could have. *Find* each word in the Discovering Electricity book. *Read* the sentences that use each electricity word. *Write* a new sentence using the electricity word in the same context as the book. *Tell* your partner the LIFESKILLS you used to work together.

8. *Mill* to music. Take turns with your partner *using* the multi-meaning words in a sentence. If you are second, the word must be used differently than the meaning in the first sentence.

Skill Key Point:

Perimeter and Area

Perimeter is found by measuring the length of each side of a figure and adding all the measurements together.

Area is the amount of space within a figure. The area of a square or a rectangle is found by multiplying the length by the width.

Inquiries of CHOICES:

• By yourself or with a partner *measure* the lengths of the sides and *calculate* the area and perimeter of three rectangular shapes in the classroom and *record* them in your journal.

• *Draw* a diagram of your bedroom showing where the furniture is placed. *Measure* the lengths of all the rectangles, including the room, *calculate* the perimeter and area, and *label* them on your diagram.

• *Compose* a song that describes the process for finding area and perimeter. Include the correct *calculation* of at least one figure in lyrics.

• *Create* a memory movement for remembering how to calculate area and perimeter. *Perform* it by yourself or with others for the class, using it to calculate at least one figure. With your Learning Club, use the measurements you made of the walls of your house to *calculate* the area and perimeter of each room. *Record* the results in your journal to use later.

Day 2

Significant Knowledge Key Points:

1. Static electricity occurs when negative particles are transferred from one object to another through friction. Objects that gain extra negative particles have a negative charge. Objects that lose negative particles become positively charged. Most objects have the same amounts of negative and positive particles and have no charge. Like objects repel one another and unlike charges attract one another. Observing static electricity allows us to see how electricity is created and released in nature.

2. After studying the properties of static electricity, many early scientists began to imagine ways man could use electricity as an energy source. As they learned more about electricity and its ability to travel in a current, many inventors began to use electricity to create ways to make our lives easier.

Inquiries:

1. (Learning Clubs) *Test* the charges in a comb and some confetti. Following the directions on your lab sheet, *observe* what happens in each situation. *Record* your observations from the first and the second tests in your science journal. *Discuss* your observations and inferences with your Learning Club and *write* your conclusions in your journal.

2. (Learning Clubs) *Demonstrate* the reactions of two balloons in the static electricity tests on your lab sheet. Predict the outcome before each test and write it in your journal. *Record* your observations. Discuss the outcomes with your Learning Club and write your inferences and conclusions in your journal.

3. (Whole group) *Observe* the interactions between a charged balloon and running water. *Discuss* your observation with a partner.

Inquiries of CHOICES:

Individual or with a partner

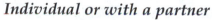
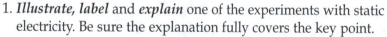

1. *Illustrate, label* and *explain* one of the experiments with static electricity. Be sure the explanation fully covers the key point.

2. Compose and sing a song describing static electricity.

3. Role-play or demonstrate the actions and reactions of two electrically-charged objects.

4. Circulate through a "gallery walk." Read each inventor or invention card with a partner. Choose an invention or inventor that you would like to know more about. Use the graphic organizer to organize the topics of your research paper.

5. Research the invention or inventor you have chosen for your paper. Be sure that your notes reflect the paragraph topics in

your graphic organizer and the electricity key points for the week. Use the research graphic organizer to record your research notes. Be sure your notes paraphrase your sources and are in your own words.

6. Read the *Kids Discover* magazine about Thomas Edison by yourself or with a partner. Locate as many electricity words as you can find from the semantic word map. Share the words you found with a partner. Choose five inventions mentioned in any of the articles in the magazine and summarize what the articles explained about them.

Inquiries for CHOICES:

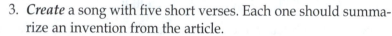
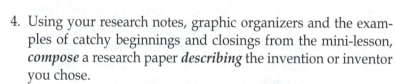

1. *Create* a summary poster that illustrates and briefly describes five of the inventions.

2. *Create* an invention book that summarizes five of the inventions featured in the articles. Illustrate the inventions.

3. *Create* a song with five short verses. Each one should summarize an invention from the article.

4. Using your research notes, graphic organizers and the examples of catchy beginnings and closings from the mini-lesson, *compose* a research paper *describing* the invention or inventor you chose.

Skill Key Point:

Events in a story are often linked together because one event has caused another event to happen. This relationship is called cause/effect. Words in the text that can be clues to a cause/effect relationship are: because, so, therefore, thus.

Inquiries:

1. (Community Circle) *Start* a "cause/effect chain." First person *states* a situation, and the next person in the circle *tells* the effect it has.

2. *Read* the excerpt from *Dear Mr. Henshaw* with a partner. *Mark* each cause-and-effect statement you find with a post-it note. *Choose* three cause-and-effect situations from the story and *write* them in the light bulb wheel.

3. *Share* (using pair-share format) one cause-and-effect statement that you wrote with your partner. *Share* one cause and effect statement with the whole group.

Day 3

Significant Knowledge Key Point:

All objects are classified according to how well they conduct electricity. Conductors readily carry an electric current. Semi-conductors conduct an electric current to a lesser degree. Insulators do not usually conduct electricity at all. Knowing which matter conducts electricity or insulates helps us to use electricity safely by sending a current through matter that conducts while protecting ourselves from it with matter that insulates. The amount of electrical current flowing through a conductor is measured in Amperes (amps).

Inquiries:

1. *Predict* with your Learning Club, which items at your table will conduct electricity and which ones won't. *Discuss* the reasons for your predictions. *Write* your predictions and your reasoning in your journal.

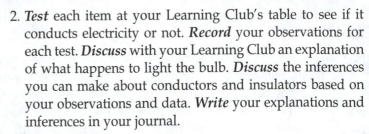

2. *Test* each item at your Learning Club's table to see if it conducts electricity or not. *Record* your observations for each test. *Discuss* with your Learning Club an explanation of what happens to light the bulb. *Discuss* the inferences you can make about conductors and insulators based on your observations and data. *Write* your explanations and inferences in your journal.

3. *Draw* a diagram of the apparatus used to test for conductivity. *Label* all of the parts and write a brief explanation of how it works.

4. *Problem solve* with your Learning Club using the information in your journal. *Calculate* how many outlets you will need for each room in your house to carry the correct number of amps to run the electrical appliances you placed in them.

5. By yourself *write* a paragraph describing your problem solving process to find the number of outlets needed in your house.

Inquiries for CHOICES:

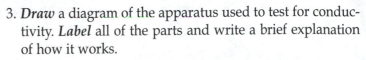

Use the appliance chart in your journal to *calculate* the total number of amps of electrical current that your house's conductors could carry. *Explain* your problem-solving process to the class.

- *Decide* which appliance would most likely be used in your house each morning, afternoon and evening. *Create* a visual to share with the rest of the class that displays electrical use in your house from greatest to least according to time of day.

- *Estimate* the number of amps that could flow through your bedroom (or another room in your house) if all the appliances were turned on at once. Use the appliance chart in your journal. *Explain* your problem-solving process to the class.

Day 4

Significant Knowledge Key Point:

1. In order for an electrical current to flow, it must have an uninterrupted conducting path. This is called an electric circuit.

There are two kinds of electric circuits. A series circuit has only one electrical path, and any break in the path will interrupt the flow of electricity. A parallel circuit has multiple paths. A break in one path will not interrupt the flow of electricity in the other paths. Knowing the properties, advantages and disadvantages of each kind of circuit can help us to understand why an appliance may or may not work, make decisions about energy conservation and create more complex electrical environments.

Inquiries:

1. **Build** a series or parallel circuit that will light each room in your Learning Club's "house". **Discuss** your plan for wiring your house with each other before you begin. **Explain** to each other how the materials will be used and how the electricity will flow through the house.

2. **Draw** a diagram of the wiring in your house. **Label** the electrical parts. **Describe** the circuit. **Tell** if it is a series or parallel circuit and **explain** why.

3. **Create** a flow chart that describes what you know about the flow of electricity through a circuit to make something work. **Read** the article, "Relay Race," about telegraphs and discuss the sequence of events in the story as well as the sequence of events that enables a message to travel from the sender in one end of the country to the receiver in the other end of the country. **Describe and illustrate** the sequence in a step book.

4. By yourself or with a partner, use the measurements for your Learning Club's house to **calculate** the length of wire you will need to complete the circuit of electricity in your house. **Share** your results with the rest of your Learning Club. **Compare** your results with the others in your Learning Club and **decide** together the total length of wire you will need.

Day 5

Inquiries for Assessment:

1. **Design** and **create** an invention that uses electricity to meet a need that could help make life easier in some way or solve an everyday problem. **Draw** a diagram of your invention and how it should work. **Write** a brief explanation of how the invention is helpful and how it should work. If your invention does not work as you planned it after you build it, write an explanation of why you think it did not work. Be sure to use all of our key points for the week in your invention and your explanations.

2. **Edit** your research paper first by yourself, then with a partner. Use the rubric on the following page to be sure you have included or corrected everything. Rewrite it in its final form. Read it to a partner. Be ready to **present** it to the class.

RUBRIC FOR INVENTIONS

	Invention Design	Invention Construction	Explanation Of Invention
Excellent (3)	Design is well thought out, meets a need or solves a problem, reflects key points for the week	Construction reflects the design, is well assembled, demonstrates significant knowledge of key points	Explanation is clearly written, demonstrates clear knowledge of how the invention works or should work, shows extensive knowledge of key points
Satisfactory (2)	Design shows thought and effort, attempts to meet a need or solve a problem, reflects at least one key point	Construction reflects the design, care and effort are evident in the assembly, knowledge of key points is evident	Explanation is fairly clear, shows some idea of how the invention should work, shows knowledge of key points
Needs Some More Work (1)	Design is not well thought out, the need for the invention is unclear, key points are not reflected in the design	Construction does not reflect the design, invention is not well constructed, little or no evidence of understanding of key points	Explanation is unclear, unable to determine how the invention should work, little knowledge of key points
Not Acceptable (0)	Little or no design for invention, no apparent reason for invention, no evidence of key points	No construction, no evidence of knowledge of key points	Little or no explanation, no evidence of knowledge of key points

Classroom tools created by
Dottie Brown

Date: Observer:

Measurement and Data Collection				
SPECIES	HABITAT	AREA	DENSITY	MOISTURE CONDITIONS

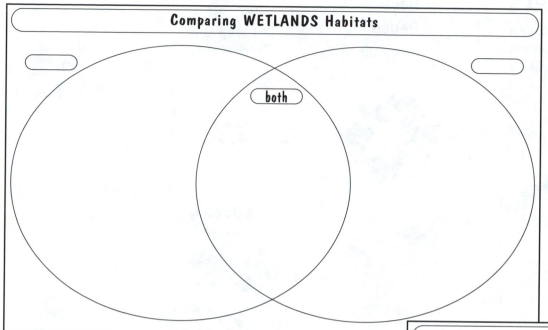

Comparing WETLANDS Habitats

both

Classroom tools created by
Dottie Brown

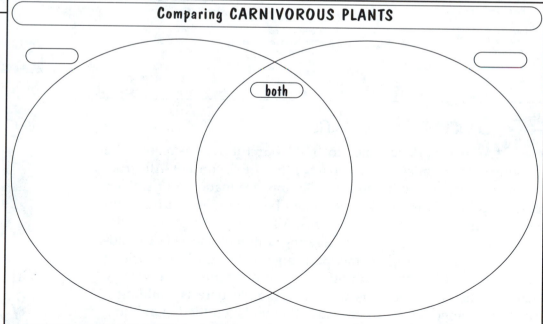

Comparing CARNIVOROUS PLANTS

both

Yearlong Theme: Building Our Future

developed by Linda L. Jordan
adapted from Pattie Mills, Joy Raboli, and Sue Pearson
appropriate for upper elementary

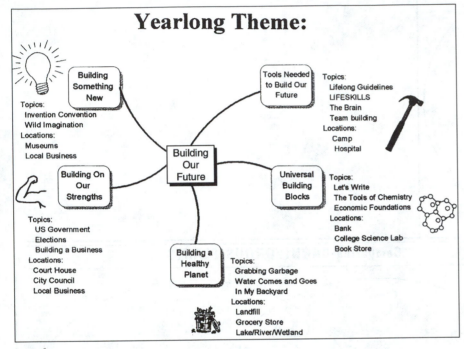

Yearlong Theme:

Building Something New
Topics:
Invention Convention
Wild Imagination
Locations:
Museums
Local Business

Building On Our Strengths
Topics:
US Government
Elections
Building a Business
Locations:
Court House
City Council
Local Business

Building Our Future

Tools Needed to Build Our Future
Topics:
Lifelong Guidelines
LIFESKILLS
The Brain
Team building
Locations:
Camp
Hospital

Universal Building Blocks
Topics:
Let's Write
The Tools of Chemistry
Economic Foundations
Locations:
Bank
College Science Lab
Book Store

Building a Healthy Planet
Topics:
Grabbing Garbage
Water Comes and Goes
In My Backyard
Locations:
Landfill
Grocery Store
Lake/River/Wetland

Conceptual Key Point:

As we work together to build our future, we realize the varying systems integrating as part of the whole concept. All structures and systems, living and non0living, are made up of smaller parts and/or processes. We as human beings can either maintain or upset the balance of these systems. All these systems work independently, yet interdependent creating different aspects of building. Thus, our yearlong theme: Building our Future. The yearlong theme is divided into subtopics or components with weekly themes. The component used as an example here is Building a Healthy Planet, and our weekly theme is entitled: Grabbing Garbage.

Reduce
Reuse
Recycle
Refuse

Building a Healthy Planet

GRABBING GARBAGE

Who me?

Where does it go?

Day 1

Significant Knowledge Key Points:

1. Waste disposal is considered one of the biggest environmental and social issues of your time. When we throw something away, it ends up somewhere. All methods of getting rid of something creates pollution problems.

2. Every man, woman, and child in the United States produces an average of four pounds of garbage a day that needs to be disposed of somewhere.

Inquiries:

1. Create a "Grabbing Garbage" journal in which you record all the trash that you personally dispose of each day this

week at home and at school.

2. Collect the garbage from our classroom. Analyze and categorize it, wearing plastic gloves when you do the sorting. Discuss with your learning club what you discover as you sort the garbage and what you have learned after having categorized your trash. Record your findings in your journal.

3. Weigh the amount of trash you collected. Write the weight on the weight chart in the room. Predict if your classroom trash will be more or less than the average four pounds per person.

Day 2

Significant Knowledge Key Points:

1. Most of our garbage is dumped and buried in landfills, many of which are quickly filling up resulting in issues about what to do with our waste. Some landfills may become toxic because of improperly disposed of materials which may lead to unhealthy situations.

Inquiries:

1. Design and construct a landfill with a partner. Choose any materials in the classroom. Be prepared to tell about and show the following to the class:

• Three or more labeled parts of your landfill.

• Life of the landfill (number of years it can be used) and how you determined that.

• How your landfill is environmentally safe.

2. Use a t-chart or Venn diagram to compare a landfill with a dump. Discuss your findings with a partner, your learning club or your teacher.

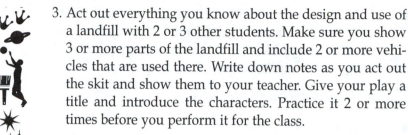

3. Act out everything you know about the design and use of a landfill with 2 or 3 other students. Make sure you show 3 or more parts of the landfill and include 2 or more vehicles that are used there. Write down notes as you act out the skit and show them to your teacher. Give your play a title and introduce the characters. Practice it 2 or more times before you perform it for the class.

4. Create a pamphlet that encourages others to use a landfill properly and not dispose of unhealthy materials. Choose one of the following ways to create your pamphlet:

• On a tri-fold paper by hand

• On the computer

Distribute the pamphlet to the adults in the building or to your parents.

Skill Key Point:

1. The main idea of a story is a key idea that the author wants you to remember after you have read it.

Inquiries:

1. Select a book from our class library with a partner. Pick one paragraph to read together. After reading the paragraph state the main idea. Be prepared to share it with the class.

2. Listen to The Lorax by Dr. Seuss. Draw a picture or write a sentence showing the main idea of the story. Share it with a partner, your learning club or the teacher.

3. Read one of the following books together as a learning club. The Berenstein Bears Don't Pollute by Stan and Jan Berenstein, Garbage, by Kids Discover, The Magic School Bus Meets the Rot Squad, by Joanna Cole. After reading

the book write the main idea and share it with the teacher. Create and present a skit that demonstrates the main idea of the story. Make sure you check for understanding by asking the audience the following questions:

- What is the main idea?

- How do you know?

Processing the Process

The following are sample questions for students and teachers to process the quality of a learning experience immediately afterward.

Processing Time for Students:
Questions to ask the students:

1. What was the most fascinating thing you learned and why?

2. What lifelong guideline and LIFESKILLs should a person who understands the value of disposing garbage properly have and why?

3. What is one thing you will share with others? Why did you choose that one thing?

Processing Time for Teacher:
1. Did the anticipatory set excite of hook the students' interest in learning about the importance of proper waste disposal? What evidence did I see?

2. What evidence did I see that demonstrated understanding of proper waste disposal?

3. What inquiries were the most popular choices by the students? Why? Were some not chosen? Why?

4. Did this topic lead to interest in further exploration? Give some examples you observed.

5. What specific things would I change if I did this again?

Student Assessment—Factual and Emotional:
1. Students will explain and demonstrate how what they learned about garbage fits into the big picture of systems.

2. Students will explain and/or demonstrate how a landfill is constructed and used.

3/ Students will reflect on their feelings about the waste crisis before and after studying it.

4. All inquiries will be assessed using the 3Cs: correct, complete, and comprehensive.

Day 3

Significant Knowledge Key Point:

1. By being a responsible citizen and consumer we can help solve our waste crisis. We can have less trash going into the landfill by using the four R's- refuse (say no), reduce (use less), reuse (use again) and recycle (bring back new.)

Inquiries:

1. Search through the trash you have collected and put it in one of the following categories: refuse, reduce, reuse, and recycle. Create a mind map showing what you found and share it with a partner or your learning club.

2. Dissect a package of gum with your learning club. Be prepared to explain the following to the class:

- Type of gum

- Total pieces of wrapper in the package

- Types of materials used in the packaging

- Your opinion -- is this product good for the environment?

3. Create and present a song, rap, rhythmic poem or chant to help you recall and to teach others the 4 R's. Give your creation a title; practice it 2 or more times. Perform it for the class.

4. Choose one or more pieces of trash from your collection. Invent a new product. Tell the following about your product to the class:

- It's name.

- It's purpose or use.

- Materials you reused.

Day 4

Conceptual Key Point:

1. Waste disposal is considered one of the biggest environmental and social issues of your time. When we throw something away, it ends up somewhere. All methods of getting rid of something create pollution problems.

Inquiries:

1. Create an advertisement to encourage others to use the 4 R's. Choose 1 of the following ways to do your advertisement: write and draw about it on a poster, tell about it by recording on an audio cassette tape for a radio show, or act it out for a television newscast. Practice presenting your choice 2 or more times before sharing it with your learning club or the class.

2. Create a manual or guide that instructs others on the proper methods to dispose of garbage. Include the follow-

ing in your manual/guide:

* Title page, which includes the title and the author's name

* Three or more illustrations

- Five or more pages of information

Share the manual/guide with your local newspaper.

3. Create a written plan for your school or home that encourages others to dispose of waste in a healthy, safe way. Share your plan with the principal or your parents.

Skill Key Point:

1. A friendly letter is a personally written message. The letter format itself contains certain standard elements, which include the date, greeting, body, closing, and a signature.

Inquiries:

1. Write a letter to thank the people on our being there trip for allowing us to visit and for their time and knowledge. Include all the standard elements of a friendly letter.

2. Write a letter to the teacher to tell your thoughts and feelings about the week and how you are going to encourage people in your family and community to make better decisions about discarding garbage. Include all the standard elements of a friendly letter.

Reflections on Refining Your Curriculum

In the brain-compatible classroom, curriculum development begins with the real world, as naturally integrated, and focuses on revealing what is important to know and be able to do at a particular location, such as a forest, a hospital, an estuary, a mall. Mastery of the basic skills of reading, writing, 'rithmetic, and concepts from curriculum content areas is more readily achieved by all students, and at much higher levels, than when pursuing the traditional curricular road starting with the disciplines and limiting sensory input to classroom settings.

Compare your school district's curriculum to the state standards. What concepts and skills do you need to add? Which should you put aside? If you cut your standards into strips that can be easily grouped and regrouped, you will probably discover that the two are more alike than not. Also, by clumping content and skills, you will be able to make your key points more conceptual, plus organize them according to their relevance to each *being there* location.

Based on your research, make final selection of those concepts, significant knowledge, and skills that you will include in your curriculum during study of this site.

Notes

1 Brady, Marion. *What's Worth Teaching? Selecting, Organizing, and Integrating Knowledge*. (Kent, Washington: Books for Educators, 1989), pp. 35-78. According to Brady, "What should be important is not that every learner assimilate a specific amount of history, chemistry, mathematics, or literature- the precise components of which are always arbitrary- but that the learner have an opportunity to experience history, chemistry, mathematics, and literature. The learning skills and the acquisition of knowledge will follow from the development of interest in a subject. Forcing anyone to learn skills when there is no interest in or familiarity with the subject usually results in permanent failure and antipathy."

2 These examples of inquiries also include the data to be analyzed. Usually, inquiries state just the action to be taken.

3 Ensemble is a creative strategy for linking movement, sound, narration, and action to specific learning goals. For more information, contact its developer, Dr. David Dynak, through www.theatre.utah.edu/faculty/dynak.html.

Chapter 14: Developing and Using Key Points

Once you have selected your physical locations for *being there* experiences and have made some basic decisions about the content of your curriculum, you are ready to develop key points— statements of the essential core of knowledge and skills all students are to learn and be able to apply in real-world settings.

Developing and Using Key Points

ITI Classroom Stages of Implementation **Stage 2**

Entry level for making curriculum bodybrain compatible

CURRICULUM	INSTRUCTIONAL STRATEGIES
• Teacher has identified the concepts and skills that will be taught to the levels of mastery and application. Key points focus on critical concepts rather than on isolated facts. • Content is age-appropriate.	• Key points are taught using a variety of instructional strategies including *being there* visitations, demonstrations by visiting experts, the discovery process, peer teaching (in Learning Clubs and cross age tutors), as well as direct instruction.

The Purpose of Key Points

As discussed earlier, learning is a two step process:

1) Making meaning through recognizing and understanding incoming data (pattern-seeking) and

2) Using what is understood (building mental programs)

Thus, our goal when developing curriculum should also be twofold:

- To enhance pattern detection using *key points*
  (and also eventually through the yearlong theme as described in Chapter 17)

- To promote development of mental programs using *inquiries*

In this chapter, we will introduce you to key points—a proven method in ITI to help students identify and come to understand the patterns within the concepts and skills of your curriculum. Chapter 15 will discuss how to help students learn to use what they understand by doing activities called inquiries.

Key Point Defined

A key point is a clear, concise statement of a concept, related significant knowledge, or a skill that you want students to know and be able to use. It is a pattern—a collection of attributes—that when taken together add up to a specific thing, an action, or a quality. For example, sharp pointed ears, a long tail, and a meow sound is a cat. Two metal objects pulling toward each other suggests one is a magnet. Or, here comes Calvin home from school and Hobbes has been stalking through the house on his way to the living room door . . . Whooosh! An over-exuberant tiger knocks Calvin flat. Detecting and understanding such patterns is the brain's way of making meaning of our world.

Factoids Defined

Factoids are statements of fact that offer little potential for detecting patterns because they represent such a small dot of life and thus offer few attributes for students to grab on to. Factoids rarely make it past short-term memory processing. A week after the test, all is forgotten. Unfortunately, most textbooks consist primarily of factoids and thus are difficult to learn from. Their content is watered down, written in short, simple sentences for low readability, and summarized so briefly as to be cryptic and seemingly unrelated to real life or student experiences. Most curriculum—state standards as well as district level—has traditionally been over-weighted with factoids. For example, weekly vocabulary-building lists in English classes which do not relate to other concurrent areas of study, definitions in science for which students have no prior or current experience, and strings of historical dates for which students have little context.

Before you begin to write key points, you must analyze the standards/curriculum you are required to teach and organize them under umbrella concepts (see Chapter 8). Restate or "bump up" the factoid statements to statements of significant knowledge and then group them under the concepts. When the concepts are taught through *being there* experiences and understood in their real-world contexts, your standards will be easily learned and remembered. As Frank Smith says, "Understanding takes care of learning."[1] If students can understand the umbrella concepts, the details are easily assimilated into long-term memory.

Structuring Knowledge

For all the criticism of textbooks and black line master worksheets, homespun curriculum is no better if it is more of the same and doesn't fit how the brain learns. Good curriculum enhances students' capacity to extract meaningful patterns and develop useful mental programs. Good curriculum helps students build larger, more abstract conceptualizations and generalizations about the world. This is the stuff that empowers.

DEVELOPING KEY POINTS

Curriculum Development

- Teacher has identified the concepts and skills that will be taught to the levels of mastery and application. Key points focus on critical concepts rather than on isolated facts.

Thoughtful attention to the structure of knowledge is as necessary for developing good curriculum as it is for good lesson planning and effective selection of instructional approaches and strategies.

The ITI model uses three kinds of key points:

- **Conceptual** key points which provide an umbrella for significant knowledge key points
- **Significant knowledge** key points related directly to a conceptual key point, providing information necessary to understand the concept
- **Skill** key points—a basic skill needed to unlock meaning about the conceptual and/or significant knowledge key points

Why three kinds of key points? Sounds a bit busy? Early in the development of the ITI model, there was just one kind of key point. We learned two lessons. First, when content is truly integrated, even students didn't recognize they were learning math or how to write a paragraph. Designating skill points as such helps teachers communicate to supervisors, peers, and parents that skills are being taught, which ones, and when. Second, we learned that teacher's key points tended to mirror the district/school's curriculum. Until the recent turn of the century state standards movement, traditional curriculum consisted primarily of factoids. Working with conceptual and significant knowledge key points tends to sustain ongoing attention to making key points more conceptual with more potential for pattern seeking.

Concept Versus Significant Knowledge?

Waste no time worrying over whether a key point is truly conceptual versus just significant knowledge. The gray line between is a moving target. The important issue is to push yourself to be as conceptual as possible and to avoid factoids.

Conceptual Key Points. As a general rule, a statement is conceptual if it can be generalized and transferred to other locations. *If* students understand, through studying the animals in their classroom and in the creek behind the school, that the physical characteristics of animals determine what they can do and how they do it in order to meet their needs, *then* they can quickly make accurate assumptions about what seashore animals can do and how the first time they see them. They will know what to observe closely and don't have to "start from scratch" figuring out each animal. In brain research terms, students have a mental pattern against which to test new learnings—a pattern or template that works to unlock meaning wherever they go.

Significant Knowledge. A piece of knowledge is significant only if we can use it. Does it help us understand a bigger picture? Does it give us concrete examples of a concept in action? Does it bring us the Aha! we've been searching for? This kind of knowledge is more memorable and more likely to be wired into long-term memory.

In contrast, however, if the content is just "stuff," factoids needed to answer a question on a test, the brain will find it difficult to learn and almost impossible to transfer to long-term memory without lots of rote memorization.

Ghosts of the Past

Structuring curriculum to make it truly brain-compatible would be a relatively straight-forward task were it not for our traditions as an educational system and our own habits of mind developed through personal experiences in schools as both student and teacher. The stumbling blocks to overcome when developing key points include:

- Pressures (and habit) to "cover" content vs. teaching students to the level of understanding and application

- Factoid or surface-level information which isn't relevant to the learner's world and is little more than an introduction to vocabulary and terms

- Content that sounds important but is not age-appropriate

- "Telling" about instead of creating opportunities for students to experience it through *being there* and immersion environments in which students discover and apply what they are learning

- Personal traditions we've developed over the years that linger in lesson plans and file drawers of accumulated resource materials

Relationship Among ITI Key Points & Inquiries:

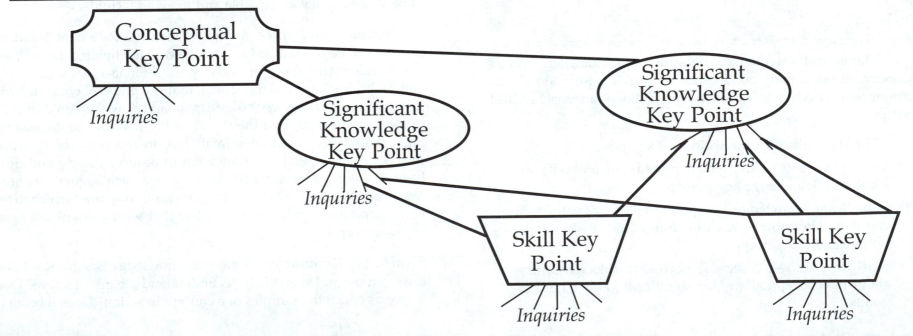

How to Enhance Pattern Seeking

As mentioned earlier, and repeated here for emphasis, developing curriculum is a pattern-enhancing task, particularly when writing key points. We must learn to think about content as patterns—the knowing of which allows students to generalize, transfer, and predict when confronted with new situations. As we saw in Chapter 4 in the discussion of the brain as pattern-seeker, at a simple level, every noun and verb is a pattern to the brain and a beginning place to look at curriculum. Combine these nouns and verbs into a conceptual statement and you have a large and rich collection of patterns. Further, knowing that the whole is bigger than the sum of the parts (the concept is bigger than the words that describe it), knowing what each word means is only the beginning. Grasping the big idea requires some bumping up. From a student perspective, the more conceptual the key point, the more interesting and engaging the study. The larger the pattern, the more powerful the learning in terms of its potential for transferring to new locations and situations and serving as a basis for predicting what will be present and how things will operate.

Developing Key Points: Some Examples

Using a location as the basis for developing key points is far easier than trying to write them from a written standards or a course of study while sitting around a conference table. At a *being there* location, focus on what's going on—what people are *doing* and what they need to know to function effectively.

Chapter 13 illustrates key points for three locations: Carolina Bays, a construction site, and a city park. Please re-read these examples with this chapter in mind.

For further examples of the process of developing key points, let's role play visiting a veterinarian's office as a source for curriculum development.

Role Playing: Visit to a Veterinarian's Office. Suppose you had chosen as one of your locations a veterinarian's office with hospital facilities. It's only a 10-minute walk from the school campus. As you sit waiting to chat with the veterinarian as part of your research about the location, you notice that about half of the animals look seriously in need of a vet but the others look fine. Nothing wrong that you can see. What gives here? After some pondering, it suddenly becomes clear. Some of the animals are here for emergency treatment of injuries and illnesses, and others for preventative care.

This waiting room provides fertile ground for a curriculum developer. Remembering that one should start with a concept, a pattern that will empower students to generalize to other situations and allow them to predict what might happen in related situations, you mentally search for just the right big idea. Two possibilities pop to mind: From both the pet owner and vet's point of view, prevention is a solid concept to anchor curriculum. Or, if you're looking at your district's science curriculum, you might also want to incorporate a couple of the science concepts relating to parasites and diseases.

As you sit in the waiting room, a rack of brochures catches your eye, one in particular by Heartgard, "To Protect Your Dog . . . Ask for the Heartworm Preventative That Has a Heart." Great reading! Yet in this small brochure are the makings of some powerful key points. Minus the information about the product, what you see about worms is shown on pages 14.6-14.7.

From the information in this pamphlet, you identify the following key points.

Conceptual Key Point. Remember, a good conceptual key point is one that can be generalized to many settings.

- Because internal parasites have evolved such a wide array of methods of reproduction and acquiring access to a host, all animals, including humans, are host to internal parasites. For example, worm infestations in dogs can occur in a variety of ways: via infected mosquitoes, via eggs in feces, via the mother before birth, via mother's milk, and via larvae penetrating the skin.

- The best treatment for parasites is prevention.

Significant Knowledge Key Points. Facts abound in this pamphlet; the challenge is recognizing which are significant—really important for students to know in order to build a conceptual understanding of internal parasites sufficient to become a competent pet owner. We chose:

- Worm infestations can occur in puppies very early, through the mother before birth and immediately afterward through the mother's milk.

- Because of mosquitoes' extended flight range (15 miles) and their tendency to seek protected areas when the weather begins to turn cold (such as your home or doghouse), heartworms are found in all 50 states. Thus, house dogs can become infected as well as dogs that are kept mostly or even entirely outdoors.

- Treatments to kill worms can sometimes lead to death because the remains of the heartworms drift into the lungs and cause potentially fatal blood clots.

Where heartworm disease comes from...

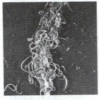

Mosquitoes transmit heartworm disease.

Mosquitoes transmit heartworm disease by biting an infected dog, then passing the infection on to other dogs they bite. Developing heartworms migrate to the dog's heart, where they can grow up to 14 inches in length as they mature. If not removed, they can cause permanent heart and lung damage and even death. But you may not see any signs before it's too late. And once diagnosed, the treatment for heartworm disease can be dangerous and costly.

How it spreads....

Heartworm infections are common along the Atlantic and Gulf coasts and the Mississippi River Valley and its tributaries, and now have been reported in every state

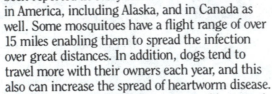

Heartworms can grow up to 14 inches in length.

in America, including Alaska, and in Canada as well. Some mosquitoes have a flight range of over 15 miles enabling them to spread the infection over great distances. In addition, dogs tend to travel more with their owners each year, and this also can increase the spread of heartworm disease.

When the weather begins to turn cold, mosquitoes often try to find protected areas such as inside your home or doghouse. So even dogs kept mainly indoors can become infected. They are also at risk when taken for walks or released in the yard.

The American Heartworm Society has documented an increase in cases of heartworm disease.

Heartworms aren't the only threat to your dog

Roundworms (Ascarids) and Hookworms: There are two important species of ascarids and hookworms that commonly infect all dogs. These intestinal parasites can cause poor growth—and even death. Dogs of all ages are at risk, but puppies are particularly vulnerable. Your veterinarian can diagnose these infections in your dog by examining a fecal sample to determine if eggs are present.

Puppies are often born with roundworms (Ascarids)...

Roundworms (ascarids)
Toxocara canis

Many puppies are born with roundworms, which they contract from their mothers before birth. These worms can also be passed in egg form through a dog's feces. Roundworms live and grow in a dog's intestines, and can

reach lengths of up to 7 inches. Dogs suffering from a heavy roundworm infection appear potbellied, have a dull coat, and may experience vomiting and diarrhea. Lung damage, pneumonia, and liver damage may also occur.

Roundworm (ascarids)
Toxascaris leonina

Hookworm can be fatal...

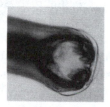

Hookworm
Ancylostoma caninum

Hookworms are also common in puppies. If left untreated, heavy infections can cause a puppy's death within weeks.

Hookworms can be passed through the mother's milk, or in egg form via the feces. Infection can also occur as the result of larvae penetrating the skin (causing a local rash), after which they migrate via the bloodstream to the intestines. Hookworms can cause diarrhea, severe anemia, and weakness. Dogs may also lose weight due to the bloodsucking of hookworms.

Hookworm
Uncinaria stenocephala

Taken from "To protect your dog . . . Ask for heartworm preventive that has a heart." Heartgard [30]

- The presence of internal parasites is often hard to detect until serious damage to the host, even death, has occurred. Regular tests as recommended by a veterinarian help determine if parasites are present.

Skill Key Points. We usually think of skill key points as those necessary for academic success. However, in the real world, skill key points also include the skills needed to use what we understand. The following skill key points include the need for math skills as well as for pet ownership:

- Most medication dosages are measured using the metric system in milliliters (ml) or cubic centiliters (cc) rather

than ounces. Precise measurement is important. The measurements on the syringe may differ from the directions on the medicine bottle so one must be able to convert measurements. For example, one cc is the same as one ml. One fluid ounce equals 30 milliliters; five milliliters is about one teaspoon.

- Medications are often given to dogs orally with a food morsel by holding the dog's mouth open, inserting the food far back in the mouth, and then holding the dog's mouth closed until it swallows.

- Shots are usually delivered in the loose skin at the top of the neck/shoulders by first pulling up the loose skin and inserting the needle sideways so as to avoid hitting the spine or muscle.

These inquiries about internal parasites are examples of "chunky" or lengthy key points. "Chunky-style" key points are needed when the individual sentences would be factoids by themselves but take on a larger meaning when grouped together. Clearly, not all key points are lengthy; some can be easily and concisely expressed in a single, short sentence: "E=mc2." Or, "Soil is not just 'dirt'; it is made from broken rocks, decaying plants, decaying animals, and animal waste (fertilizer)."

Rule of thumb: Let the content dictate how best to represent a key point and keep in mind the age of your students.

Helpful Hints for Developing Key Points

Our number one recommendation is that you find a partner to work with. Two heads and multiple hands make for a lighter load. And a second perspective is invaluable when you get stuck. Also, join the listserve hosted by Susan Kovalik & Associates (see www.kovalik.com for instruction to subscribe).

Other recommendations include brainstorming, interviewing people at your *being there* location, putting yourself in your students' shoes, remembering who the curriculum is for, and avoiding discouragement.

Start with a Brainstorming Session

Brainstorming is useful in two ways. First, it helps us to uncover what we know (and don't know) about an area; this gives us an inkling of how much onsite and library research we need.

Second, brainstorming helps us test the depth of our understanding. A long list of factoid information with few conceptual statements alerts us to the need to explore the "whys" behind the areas of study and to search for real-world applications for students. Before we can expect to teach students, we must ourselves have answered the question "Why is this information or skill important? How can I use this information in my life today and in the foreseeable future?"

Get together with an ITI buddy—someone who understands your search for more conceptual rather than fact-oriented key points, preferably someone at your grade level. Use him/her as a sounding board. "What is essential?" is the most important question you can ask yourself; the quality of its answer will determine the power of your key points.

Interview from a Workplace Perspective

When you interview people at your *being there* locations, make sure you include a cross section of perspectives. Key questions are: What skills, knowledge, and attitudes/values allow you to be successful at this job? What are the top five in priority order? What are the prerequisites for getting the job. What skills, knowledge, and attitudes/values would help you do a better job and/or be more satisfied with your work?

Since the focus of the ITI curriculum is on understanding and then using that understanding, the focus of many of your key points will come from your interviews of people at the location (those that provide the services/products/entertainment and those who use them). What concepts, knowledge, and skills are needed?

Put Yourself in Your Students' Shoes

When visiting your physical location to determine what is most significant to know, step out of your shoes as a teacher and look at the location afresh. Picture it from your students' perspectives. What is their prior knowledge, what kind of patterns would they perceive, how would they go about figuring it out?

As we know from the power of mirroring[2], it is crucial that students "see" themselves in the people they watch. If students were to ask themselves the driving questions of their childhood—the whys and wherefores—would their answers make them want to fully engage in this location? The perennial why and wherefore questions of childhood are:

- "What are you doing?"

- "Why are you doing this? Is your 'why' important to me, too?"

- "May I join you? I want to join your 'club'."

• "What do members of this club do and know and how do they go about it?"[3]

How would your students answer these questions? If your curriculum planning can build upon the brain's natural exploration of these questions, it will allow students to use their brains as they work naturally and thus most powerfully. To extend this, allow students to help you build additional curriculum after the initial visit to the site.

Use Multiple Resources

When implementing the ITI model, it is essential for teachers to provide a variety of resources for the students to use during each monthly component. Although the Internet seems to have eclipsed more traditional sources of information, your resources should also include the traditional library print materials.

When you visit the librarian at the public library, don't be shy. Provide him/her with a copy of your key points about two or three weeks before the start of your next component. Be sure to specify the range of reading levels in your classroom (make sure you stretch the top level). Tell the librarian if your students require material in a language other than English. You will likely receive anywhere from 40 to 80 books and other materials in your classroom for each monthly component.

A librarian can also provide other types of curriculum resources for teachers. One of the most valuable resources available from the public library is contact information for the local, state, and federal governmental agencies. For example, state and federal senators and representatives, local, state, and national groups concerned with the environment and conservation of natural resources, chancellors of foreign embassies with diplomatic relations with the United States, etc. Many librarians now assist with Internet research as well. Needless to say, the professional dedication of the librarian and his/her expertise make it easier for teachers to implement the ITI model.

To become lifelong learners, students must learn how to seek out the information and determine its useability for their purposes. Have students write letters seeking information that is closer to the source—more authentic and less pre-digested. Writing to a real audience also strengthens student communication skills and reinforces the point that there are unlimited resources available for the asking. As they write their letters:

• Insist that they send professional quality letters ("perfect" in form, spelling, etc.); teach students to proofread each other's letters.

• Have students compose letters on a computer whenever possible.

• When appropriate, include a cover letter written by you explaining the ITI model and the purpose of having students involved in the letter–writing process.

An enriched classroom where students have access to a comprehensive range of resource materials, will have more than 100 books, magazines, and other material gathered from multiple sources for each month's study. Also, don't overlook students as a resource. Ask each of them to bring relevant resources; again, it's an important skill for lifelong learning. It's not unusual for students to become so proficient in identifying resources that they will bring in three to six hundred books, magazines, and other materials for the last monthly component.

The Internet. For classrooms with at least one computer, the Internet can bring the world to your classroom. While surfing is easy and fun, students need to develop their critical analysis skills to determine the veracity of information. In the past, this job was performed by the publisher; after all, their reputation depended upon such issues. But the Internet, for all its blessings as a research tool, is a "buyer beware" resource.

Teaching students how to evaluate information gleaned from the Internet is an absolute must. Ask your librarian for the most useful research tool to evaluate the validity of your sources.

Don't Forget Who the Curriculum Is For

Keep your students clearly in mind. This curriculum is for the those sitting before you today. And remember, the lower the level of achievement of your students, the greater your challenge.

Be playful. Go back to your own childhood memories. What things interested you the most then? What would you as a youngster find interesting today at the *being there* locations you have chosen? And remember, you don't have to know the answer to be interested! Let the questions roll!

Don't Get Discouraged

You're breaking new ground here so don't be surprised if you experience some of the frustrations of a pioneer. Be prepared to let go of old habits of mind and old beliefs about curriculum. Be flexible—the thinking processes needed to identify effective key points are neither linear nor sequential. Feel free to jump from one step to another, forward, backward, and sideways. Don't plan to fully complete one step, never to return, before moving on to the next.

Self Check

Developing Key Points

The key points:

- Clearly and concisely describe what is essential for students to understand and be able to do with what they understand
- Represent the most important concepts, knowledge, and skill key points for students to understand and be able to apply
  - From the *being there* location
  - From the state/district curriculum standards
  - For future citizenship

Self Check

Developing Key Points (continued)

- Are conceptual versus factoid
  - Are transferrable to other locations and situations
  - Their patterns help students understand a bigger picture
  - Students can generalize from them to understand new things and processes in new surroundings

- Are age-appropriate

- Significant knowledge key points directly relate to a conceptual point. That is, they are:
  - What is most important to know in order to understand the conceptual key point
  - Sufficient to create a full understanding of the conceptual key point

- Are specific enough to guide both teacher and students in their planning and working

- Say something important enough to warrant 11-16 minutes of direct instruction or an hour or more of the discovery process (see Appendix B); are significant enough to warrant the time spent on them by both teacher and student

- Apply to the real world and to the students' world (now and in the future)

- Define what will be assessed and are specific enough to serve as the basis for authentic assessment

Age-Appropriate Content

The current state standards movement is both a blessing and a curse. The blessing is that it has produced better curriculum outlines nationwide than ever before. The curse is that the mix of high expectations and high profile politics has too often resulted in curriculum that sounds impressive, such as the study of nuclear fission at third grade, but that is outrageously kid-unfriendly. Some of these mistakes are just tradition carried forward; some are new.

Because such content is beyond what students of that age can understand, students must resort to memorization, an onerous task that rarely delivers the information into long-term memory. Such an exercise can rob students of their joy in learning and their confidence in themselves as a learner.

Curriculum Development

- Content is age-appropriate.

While it is unquestionably true that the brain grows best when it is challenged and that high standards for children's learning are important, it is also true that curriculum needs to be considered in terms of age-appropriate challenge.

The notion that the human brain unfolds in predictable developmental stages goes back to Maria Montessori ninety years ago and to Jean Piaget seventy years ago. While the details of their work have been debated endlessly, recent brain research has confirmed most of their basic premises. The application of their work to today's curriculum and textbooks reveals that a large percentage of the concepts identified for elementary students is, in fact, beyond

what students can understand at those ages; they may be able to memorize and parrot them back but that does not indicate a real understanding. This is particularly true in science. For example, the solar system as a subject for second or third graders is wildly age-inappropriate. The concepts are highly abstract and not experienceable—the ground on which we stand is spinning at hundreds of miles an hour and the distances between planets are computed in millions of miles or even light years, a measurement that challenges most adults.

David Elkind, after lengthy studies of the effects of stress upon children, preschool through high school, suggests that pressure on students to learn things that their minds cannot comprehend may in fact be harmful to the brain, causing it to organize itself to do memorization instead of seeking understanding. Recent research supports his views.[4]

Yes, dinosaurs are fascinating, but how do you connect a happening of 250 million years ago to today? Dinosaurs have been dead and gone for 65 million years. In contrast, today's disappearing species deserve our full attention. To quote Dr. Larry Lowery, professor of science education and staff member at the Lawrence Hall of Science, UC Berkeley, "Do not confuse enthusiasm with understanding." Because students are enthusiastic about something does not mean that they understand it or that it has relevance or value in terms of helping them understand their world. This is not to say you can't have an extracurricular Dinosaur Club for those who are interested or that it wouldn't be a fascinating subject for the students to develop at home with their parents and siblings. And, if there were a shortage of curriculum, perhaps. As it is, time is precious and we have too little of it.

Something that is age-appropriate for students means that they can and do make meaning of what they are studying, can apply it in their real, away-from-school-worlds, and can explain it to someone who has a real need to know. For the young child, this usually results because of *being there* experiences, not from lecture or secondhand presentation of abstract concepts.

For more information about age-appropriate content, see Appendix D.

Self Check

Age–Appropriate Content

- Students can and do grasp the meaning of the concept after sensory input from *being there* and immersion experiences. They don't need to rely on being *told* what the concept is and memorizing the answer; they understand it.

- Students show they understand a concept by restating it in their own words and by being able to use what they understand in differing situations (not a repeat of the same situation used in the lesson).

Using Key Points

Keep in mind that key points have a dual audience. For the teacher they are a guide for short- and long-term planning and the basis for built-in assessment (daily, weekly, monthly, end-of-the-year). For the students, they spell out in advance what is to be mastered and are a guide to daily tasks and long-term adventure. Key points constitute the centripetal force that pulls meaning from the real world into the shared space of learner and teacher.

USING KEY POINTS

Curriculum Development

- Key points are taught using a variety of instructional strategies including *being there* visitations, demonstrations by visiting experts, the Discovery Process, peer teaching (in Learning Clubs and cross age tutors), as well as direct instruction and the other strategies discussed in Chapters 19-21.

Key points are the gist of lesson planning—they provide the what and why for direct instruction and for exploratory and collaborative activities. They are also the content focus for teacher assessment and student evaluation.

When the teacher believes that the Discovery Process[5] is the most powerful instructional approach, key points focus the teacher's material gathering and planning efforts, guide lesson design, and help frame clear questions for the students to pursue.

When the teacher thinks that direct instruction is the most appropriate instructional format, key points provide goal and content. Information is presented in ways that are *c*reative, *u*seful, and have an *e*motional bridge (CUE). The essence of direct instruction is that it's what you want the student to understand (key points) and be able to do (inquiries). The presentation should be rich enough to start the brain's detection of the pattern contained in the key point. Real-life artifacts and situations, guest speakers, 3-D models, real charts/maps/illustrations, poetry, rhyme, and other creative tools. For a discussion of the instructional strategies considered key to the ITI model, see Part E, Chapters 20-22.

Once the key points are determined, the next step in developing curriculum is creating inquiries—activities using firsthand sources through which students can build the mental programs to use what they understand about the key points.

Self Check

Using Key Points

- The key points are written and shared with students so that they know clearly what they are expected to learn.

- The key points guide all lesson planning and selection of instructional strategies.

- Key points are taught using a variety of instructional strategies specifically selected for each key point. *Being there* and immersion input is the focus of the instructional strategies.

- Students know exactly what they are expected to understand and be able to apply. Middle and upper grade students monitor their own progress.

NOTES

1   For a book chock full of common sense and level-headed criticism of our educational system, read Frank Smith's *The Bureaucratic Invasion of Our Classrooms.*

2   See Alison Motluk, writing in *New Scientist Magazine,* January 27, 2001. For further reading, see "Mirror Neurons and Imitation Learning As the Driving Force Behind 'the Great Leap Forward' in Human Evolution" by V. S. Ramachandran at www.edge.org/documents/archives/edge69.html; "Mirror Neurons and the Simulation Theory of Mind-Reading" by Vittorio Gallese and Alvin Goldman in *Trends in Cognitive Sciences, Vol. 2,* 1998, p. 493; and "Language Within Our Grasp" by Giacomo Rizzolatti and Michael Arbib in *Trends in Neurosciences, Vol. 21,* 1998, p. 188.

3   "Childhood whys and wherefores" is a phrased coined by the authors to focus attention on the natural workings of a child's mind when confronted with the real world.

4   See work of Jane Healy and Marion Diamond listed in the bibliography.

5   For a description of the ITI Discovery Process, see Appendix B.

Chapter 15: Developing and Using Inquiries

Inquiries: Where the Action Is

Close your eyes for a moment. Picture yourself as a child in your third or fourth grade classroom. What do you see? If your classroom was a traditional one, your picture probably includes lots of seat time, reading alone, doing worksheets, and filling up pages in your workbooks.

Brain research has made it very clear that the human brain is not a passive receptacle. It demands that we act on the world, eliciting high sensory input for the bodybrain learning partnership to munch on. In short, it demands action. John Dewey's maxim from 60 years ago is true: "We learn by doing."

In the ITI classroom, action is planned for and carried out through inquiries. They frame how students will go about deepening their understanding of the concepts and skills identified in the key points and practicing their use until a mental program is developed and wired into long-term memory.

Inquiries are at the heart of your curriculum-building efforts. They are the point at which words become realities, the talked about becomes one's own experience, where "talking about science" becomes "doing science," where reading about historical figures becomes experiencing their problems and dilemmas.

Inquiries make learning active and memorable (see Chapters 4 and 5 for discussion of the importance of pattern-seeking and program-building to the learning process).

When you close your eyes and picture an ITI classroom, you will see inquiries used in many ways: an assignment during direct instruction to check for understanding, a task for collaborative work, a project for independent study, a homework assignment, a "test" item for authentic assessment, and more. No doubt about it: Inquiries are where the action is and where memories are formed.

Inquiries are also a key way of ensuring meaningful choice and development of all the multiple intelligences.

> ## Inquiries
>
> Inquiries are a key curriculum development structure in the ITI model. They are activities that enable students to understand and apply the concept, significant knowledge, or skill of a key point. The primary purpose of inquiries is to enable students to develop mental programs for applying, in real–world situations, the key point. They make learning active and memorable.

ITI Classroom Stages of Implementation

Developing Inquiries

Stage 2

Entry level for making curriculum bodybrain compatible

CURRICULUM

- There are inquiries for each key point. Each inquiry provides students with choices and multiple opportunities for real-world applications and allow multiple ways of solving problems and producing products. Some inquiries are designed specifically to provide realistic opportunities for students to practice citizenship, e.g., social/political action activities, community service, and special classroom and schoolwide events.

INSTRUCTIONAL STRATEGIES

- Choices are regularly provided through inquiries and other means.

- Adequate time is allowed to let students complete their work and to develop multiple intelligences.

- Collaboration is effectively used and enhances learning for academic and social growth.

- The teacher gives assistance and coaching to individuals and groups as they work.

DEVELOPING INQUIRIES

Curriculum Development

- There are inquiries for each key point.

- The set of inquiries for each key point provides students with choices and multiple opportunities for real-world application and allow multiple ways of solving problems and producing products.

- Some inquiries are designed specifically to provide realistic opportunities for students to practice citizenship, e.g., social/political action activities, community service, and collaborative group practices.

Inquiries Defined

Inquiries are a key curriculum development structure in the ITI model. They are activities that enable students to understand and apply the concept, skill, or significant knowledge of a key point. The primary purpose of inquiries is to enable students to develop mental programs for applying the key point in real–world situations. They make learning active and memorable. They also force us to judge the mettle and worth of our curriculum.

The ultimate test of the worth of any curriculum is this:

What to you want students to understand

AND

what do you want them to do with what they understand?

If your answer is so that they can pass the state standards test, look deeper. We owe it to our students to prepare them for their most important role—informed, active citizenship.

If we can't come up with a real-world use of a key point, then one of two things is true: The information or skill is in fact not key and teaching it would be a waste of student and teacher time *or* our own knowledge base is insufficient. In either case, expect the writing of inquiries to dredge up some surprises and some questions that may not be comfortable to answer. What you will discover, and what thousands of ITI teachers before you have discovered, is that much of our traditional curriculum is brain antagonistic. If our intent is to implement the best of what we know about recent brain research, we must make our curriculum bodybrain-compatible. For most states, the state standards developed during the late 1990s are a step in the right direction.

A test of curriculum: How can students apply the following concepts? How can the knowledge empower students? How can they use them in real-world situations? If you cannot answer these questions,you cannot write powerful inquiries. For example, the following are typical concepts from state standards. While they may seem abstract and distant from students' lives as they are stated, inquiries, such as those on the next page, can bring them home and make them real.

- When warmer things are put with cooler ones, the warm ones lose heat and the cool ones gain heat until they are all the same temperature. A warmer object can warm a cooler one by contact or at a distance.

- There are three ways in which heat can go into or out of something. Conduction is the transfer of heat from one thing to another by direct touching, such as a frying pan sitting on top of an electric stove or the heating element in an electric water heater .
Convection is the transfer of heat through moving air currents such as in the circulating air in forced air furnaces or cold air entering the house through cracks around poorly insulated windows and doors.
Radiation is the transfer of energy through light such as the heat generated by an electric light bulb, a computer, or warmth from the sun.

- We can affect these heat transfer processes by using insulation, materials that are poor conductors of heat.[1]

Very real applications for the concepts on the previous page include the following):

▪ Analyze your home (house or apartment) identifying all the ways the family attempts to stabilize temperature by adding heat via conduction, convection, radiation, and insulating against heat loss. Analyze incidental/accidental ways by which heat is added and lost. Determine how effective/adequate the attempts to insulate are. List three ways insulation could be made more effective; estimate savings over a 10-year period and 30-year period.

1. Record your information on a chart or poster. Share your findings with an adult family member and record their response. Share what you have learned about the heat loss and gain to your Learning Club.

2. Compare your home to a friend's home. Determine which home is easier to keep stabilized and which is more economical. Record in your journal at least three reasons to explain your conclusion.

Would you be interested in this issue if we told you that you could save from $40,000 to $70,000 over a lifetime plus keep the coastal intertie system from brown-out or going down altogether? And be more comfortable in your home? Such applications satisfy us that we have some concepts worth learning, that we're on the right track. So, now we can develop inquiries that will help students understand and apply these concepts in real-life, in memorable ways.

How to Write Inquiries

Inquiries are not activities for the sake of keeping students busy; they are carefully crafted learning experiences that give students an opportunity to discover, understand, apply, and extend the content of the key points. Inquiries put action into the students' day; they demand we go for real life, the *being there*, the tangible product.

Tools for writing inquiries include:

• The ABC Guidelines

• The Inquiry Builder Chart which combines the multiple intelligences and Bloom's Taxonomy of Cognitive Objectives

The "ABC" Guidelines

Once you know precisely what you want students to understand and to be able to do with what they understand, the following "ABC" guidelines and the verbs from Bloom's Taxonomy of Cognitive Objectives[2] (see the Inquiry Builder on page 15.8) will help make writing inquiries surprisingly straight-forward.

The "ABC" guidelines are:

• <u>A</u>lways start with the action in mind—what are students to do in order to practice applying what they understand to real-world situations. What actions do you need to see them perform to be convinced that they have developed a mental program for using the content of the key points? Starting the sentence with an action verb helps focus on the action to be taken; it makes the inquiry an imperative statement, a directive for action. For example, "Analyze your home identifying all the ways the family attempts to stabilize temperature . . . ."

• <u>B</u>e specific with your directions so that students can see the outcome or finished product in their mind's eye—what the inquiry is asking them to do. Have you stated exactly what you expect them to do? Are there choices within the inquiries that entice every student in your class to become excited about learning and to be challenged? Is it feasible considering the resources and time available? (Don't underestimate. Few things frustrate as much as an exciting task with no time to do it.) Be clear about the end product of the inquiry.

State what's to be done and the specifications for the final product so that students can be successful the first time. If the instructions are clear, you will be spared each student coming to ask for clarification. Avoid words such as "all" or "as many as you can" or "some." The differences in perceptions trouble students as well as teachers. Inquiries should be written so that students can see the outcome or finished product.

- *C*onnect to the key point. Will doing this inquiry help students understand and be able to apply the concept or skill in the key point?

Using Bloom's Taxonomy of Cognitive Objectives

As a reminder, the levels of Bloom's Taxonomy are:

Knowledge— The student recalls or recognizes information.

Comprehension— The student changes information into a different symbolic form.

Application— The student solves a problem using the knowledge and appropriate generalizations.

Analysis— The student separates information into component parts.

Evaluation— The student makes qualitative and quantitative judgments according to set standards.

Synthesis— The student solves a problem by putting information together which requires original, creative thinking.

Bloom's Taxonomy Is Not a Hierarchy of Difficulty. Contrary to popular opinion, Bloom's Taxonomy does not represent a hierarchy of levels of difficulty, knowledge being the easiest and evaluation and synthesis the hardest. For example, students who are not strong in linguistic intelligence find knowledge the most difficult because everything is about words. Conversely, application and analysis, usually considered harder are often easier because application takes the content into real situations that can be experienced directly without relying on words. Bloom's Taxonomy as used in the ITI model is a categorizing of kinds of actions that can illustrate understanding and mastery of concepts, significant knowledge, and skills.

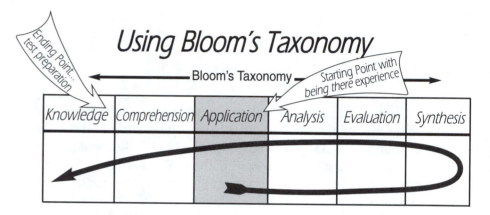

Bloom's Taxonomy and Personality. It is often said that at least 80% of the assignments given students in traditional schools are at Bloom's knowledge and comprehension levels—paper-pencil test and worksheet kinds of responses, all heavily linguistic. Although there is strong political pressure on test results and "teaching to the test," it is educationally unwise to start where we want to end up. Starting with and focusing on details makes pattern detection harder and leaves little opportunity to apply what one is learning and thus getting it transferred to long-term memory.

As explained in Chapter 6, emphasizing knowledge and comprehension levels leaves out glimpses of the whole and of context. This makes learning harder for sensors who have trouble seeing how things come together (75% of the population) and frustrates intuitors who prefer to work from a big picture (25% of the population). (See "Taking in Information," pp. 6.5-6.5)

Our best advice is to start in the middle of Bloom's Taxonomy (with application and analysis) and then move to evaluation and synthesis. Assign students inquiries at the comprehension and knowledge levels last, as preparation for test-taking.[3]

Using the Multiple Intelligences. The verbs associated with the levels of Bloom's Taxonomy are shown in the Inquiry Builder on page 15.8. They are listed on the left from top to bottom. Note that intra- and interpersonal intelligences are omitted because each affects the social context of the inquiry rather than its content. The naturalist intelligence is also omitted for reasons explained on page 3.22.

How to Use the Inquiry Builder

Think of the Inquiry Builder as your personal genie. When you know what you want students to learn—you have a written key point in your hand—and you know how the knowledge or skill of the key point is used in the real world, then summon your personal genie. Request that the genie zero in on the action verbs for the application and analysis levels of Bloom's Taxonomy—the first and second columns of the Inquiry Builder chart. Pick a verb that matches the action of using the concept or skill of the key point. Start the inquiry with that word and you're off and running. For examples of curriculum developed using the Inquiry Builder, see pages 15.7 and 15.9.

Plan on developing at least five to twelve inquiries for each conceptual and significant knowledge key point and at least three to eight for each skill key point. Strive for a balance of Bloom's levels and the multiple intelligences. A balance will ensure the widest possible choice for students. This gives students many, and varied, opportunities to expand their repertoire of successful problem-solving and product-producing approaches.[4] An empowering curriculum assists learners to expand their range and power of problem-solving and product-producing capabilities. The goal of the ITI classroom is to create 21st century Renaissance minds.

Shaping Inquiries to Audience and Purpose

When writing each inquiry, it is helpful to think ahead. How and in what context will the inquiry be used? For example, will this inquiry serve as the whole class activity that follows your direct instruction to provide a reality check or will it be your lead discovery process question that will replace a direct instruction presentation? Will it be an assignment for collaboration or for independent work? Would it work best for partners or triads? Or, is this inquiry the best real-world application of knowledge and skill and therefore the inquiry that should become your assessment tool for determining mastery? Coding each inquiry to indicate its intended purpose is a useful practice throughout Stage 2 of the *ITI Classroom Stages of Implementation*. The codes prove very useful when lesson planning and especially vital during those midstream course redirections. Once you have built a mental program for taking into account the multiple intelligences and Bloom's Taxonomy when developing inquiries, coding will not be necessary. Until then, however, it is a useful tool for ensuring that your inquiries are varied, interesting, and effective.

Audience: Keying each inquiry to the seven intelligences helps planning which inquiries would be most useful. We recommend you lead with bodily-kinesthetic inquiries and end with linguistic.

> LM — logical-mathematical
> L — linguistic
> S — spatial
> BK — bodily-kinesthetic
> M — musical
> IA — intrapersonal
> IE — interpersonal

Purpose: The following codes indicate intended use with student:

> C — whole class inquiries
> G — small group (at least two students)
> I — individual or independent
> A — assessment of mastery

Does this sound like an incredible amount of work? Initially, yes. But you'll soon find that once you've developed a mental program for writing inquiries, it becomes almost automatic, like making soup from your favorite recipe. *Once you have mastered writing inquiries, this coding can be discontinued.* Early on, however, it is extremely useful and well worth the effort.

Students As Curriculum Developers

Don't overlook your students as a resource. Once they understand a key point, they can design innumerable ways to practice applying it. Teach them the ABC rules of writing inquiries. You will find that they can develop inquiries with imagination, great creativity, and surprising challenge. Their inquiries are often even better than those of their teacher. Choose from among their inquiries those that complement yours. In so doing you will increase student's abilities as lifelong learners and lighten your load.

Developing inquiries is also a good thinking exercise for students because one can't pose a good question or frame a worthwhile learning task without a good understanding of the key point and its application in the real world. So, once a week, assign students, from third grade and up, an inquiry that says: "Develop an inquiry for today's key point that asks for its most creative yet practical application in real life."

Examples of Inquiries

These inquiries follow being there experiences at a local power plant and/or a construction site.

Whole Class Inquiries

- *Analyze* with your Learning Club the items at your table. *Predict* which will conduct electricity and which ones won't.

Discuss the reasons for your predictions. *Report* your predictions and your reasoning in your journal.

- *Experiment with/Test* each item at your Learning Club's table to see if it conducts electricity or not. *Report* your observations for each test. *Discuss* with your learning club an explanation of what happens to light the bulb. *Discuss the inferences* you can make about conductors and insulators based on your observations and data. *Write* your explanations and inferences in your journal.

- *Draw* a diagram of the apparatus used to test for conductivity. *Label* all of the parts and *write* a brief explanation of how it works.

- With your Learning Club and using the information in your journal, *determine* how many outlets you will need for each room in your house to carry the correct number of amps to run the electrical appliances you placed in them.

- By yourself *write* a paragraph describing your problem solving to find the number of outlets needed in your house.

Inquiries for Small Group or Individual Choice

- Use the appliance chart in your journal to *calculate* the total number of amps of electrical current that your house's conductors could carry. *Explain* your problem solving process to the class.

- *Decide* which appliance would most likely be used in your house each morning, afternoon and evening. *Create* a visual to share with the rest of the class that *displays* electrical use in your house from greatest to least according to time of day.

- *Estimate* the number of amps that could flow through your bedroom (or another room in your house) if all the appliances were turned on at once. *Use* the appliance chart in

Inquiry Builder

Starting Point with being there experience

Ending Point... test preparation

— Bloom's Taxonomy (adapted) —

		Application	Analysis	Evaluation	Synthesis	Comprehension	Knowledge
MULTIPLE INTELLIGENCES	*Logical/ Mathematical*	▪apply ▪solve ▪convert ▪expand ▪schedule ▪sequence ▪organize	▪question ▪solve ▪inventory ▪compare ▪distinguish ▪differentiate	▪estimate ▪measure ▪choose ▪predict ▪judge ▪select ▪assess ▪value ▪rate ▪review	▪design ▪infer ▪classify ▪hypothesize ▪prepare ▪formulate ▪propose	▪describe ▪calculate ▪identify ▪explain ▪retell ▪recognize ▪sequence ▪organize	▪label ▪name
	Linguistic	▪apply ▪teach ▪translate ▪interview ▪communicate	▪analyze ▪debate ▪criticize ▪discuss ▪question ▪investigate ▪interpret	▪critique ▪interpret ▪discuss ▪rate ▪relate ▪probe ▪judge ▪justify	▪compose ▪rewrite ▪propose ▪infer ▪adapt ▪debate ▪impersonate ▪produce	▪review ▪describe ▪discuss ▪express ▪report ▪explain ▪restate	▪name ▪tell ▪label ▪recall ▪define ▪record ▪narrate ▪list ▪memorize
	Spatial	▪diagram ▪exhibit ▪translate ▪teach ▪illustrate ▪make ▪apply ▪chart ▪summarize ▪graph	▪disassemble ▪differentiate ▪diagram ▪distinguish	▪predict ▪estimate ▪measure ▪judge	▪formulate ▪plan ▪propose ▪arrange ▪design ▪organize ▪restructure	▪locate ▪sort ▪identify ▪compare ▪describe ▪illustrate ▪recognize ▪relate parts	▪interpret ▪adapt ▪draw ▪match ▪sketch
	Musical	▪perform (solo or group) ▪harmonize ▪practice ▪rhythm ▪synchronize ▪teach ▪(characterize) ▪(express) ▪(select)	▪analyze ▪compare ▪interpret	▪interpret ▪critique ▪defend ▪(characterize)	▪create a variation ▪express ▪improvise ▪convey emotion ▪symbolize ▪compose ▪tell a story ▪transpose	▪rehearse ▪practice ▪(express)	▪memorize ▪imitate ▪recite
	Bodily/ Kinesthetic	▪apply ▪rhythm ▪dramatize ▪mime ▪operate ▪(teach) ▪(demonstrate) ▪(practice)	▪interpret ▪disassemble ▪experiment ▪diagram ▪(inventory)	▪rehearse ▪(measure) ▪(debate)	▪convey emotion ▪tell a story ▪(invent) ▪(assemble) ▪(design) ▪(construct) ▪(arrange) ▪(prepare) ▪(classify)	▪perform ▪(locate)	▪imitate ▪play

( ) = could have this quality if so designed.

your journal. *Explain* your problem solving process to the class.

Inquiries for Individual Students

1. *Design* and *build* a series or parallel circuit that will light each room in your Learning Club's "house." *Discuss* your plan for wiring your house with each other before you begin. *Propose* to each other how the materials will be used and how the electricity will flow through the house.

2. *Diagram* the wiring in your house. *Label* the electrical parts. *Describe* the circuit. *Determine* if it is a series or parallel circuit and *explain* why.

3. *Create* a flow chart that describes what you know about the flow of electricity through a circuit to make something work. *Read* the article, "Relay Race," about telegraphs and discuss the sequence of events in the story as well as the sequence of events that enables a message to travel from the sender in one end of the country to the receiver in the other end of the country. *Illustrate* and *describe* the sequence in a step book.

4. By yourself or with a partner, use the measurements for your Learning Club's house to *calculate* the length of wire you will need to complete the circuit of electricity in your house. *Share* your results with the rest of your Learning Club. *Compare* your results with the others in your Learning Club and together *determine* the total length of wire you will need.

Inquiries for Assessment

1. *Design* and *build* a model for an invention that uses electricity to meet a need that could help make life easier in some way or solve an everyday problem. *Diagram* your invention and how it should work. *Write* a brief explanation of how the invention is helpful and how it should work. If your invention does not work as you planned it after you build it, *analyze* why you think it did not work and record your analysis in your journal. Be sure to use all of our key points for the week in your invention and your explanations.

2. Edit your research paper first by yourself, then with a partner. Use the rubric to be sure you have included or corrected everything. Rewrite it in its final form. Read it to a partner. Be ready to present it to the class.

For more examples of inquiries, see the ITI curriculum in Chapter 13.

How to Use Inquiries

Inquiries serve many purposes. For the teacher, they are an extension of the discussion of "what's worth knowing" and a key building block in lesson design as the framework to be performed individually, in small group, or as an entire class. They give structure and focus to what students will do to reach understanding of the patterns in the key points and to develop programs for applying the key points. They can also serve as an assessment instrument.

For the students, inquiries outline the game plan, allowing them to work with a sense of self-directedness and without dependence on the teacher. They provide significant choices for students while keeping them aimed at what's most important to learn and be able to do. Lastly, they provide the foundation for authentic assessment, not only reflective of the real world but in the real world. Students get a sense of standards in real world.

Self Check

Developing inquiries

- The inquiries:
  - Are clearly related to the key point(s) — not just activities for the sake of activities
  - Apply/expand the key points and show real-world connections, especially those relevant to the learner
  - Structure student work in ways that encourage students to take action and in the process ask questions and seek their own answers
  - Provide genuine choice for students
  - Are worthy of the time to be spent

- Help students learn to learn like experts:
  - See "larger" patterns and more complex chunks, e.g. the difference between a good chess player and a grand master
  - Have a grasp of context — analysis of the context as well as the characteristics
  - Store information differently than novices, e.g., novices tend to memorize new information; an expert can read or hear something once and remember it, immediately incorporating it into what they already know.[5]

- There are inquiries for each key point. Each inquiry is designed to help students deepen their understanding of a particular concept, knowledge, or skill as they practice using what they understand in real-world situations. Most of the inquiries are based in the being there location and/or classroom immersion experiences.

- There are sufficient inquiries (5-12) for students to complete for each key point to ensure mastery and development of a program wiring the concept, knowledge, or skill into long-term memory.

Self Check

Developing inquiries (continued)

- The inquiries require each student to expand his/her problem-solving and product-producing capabilities. Students themselves have noticed that they have more ways to approach problem solving and that they are more adept at creating products.

- The inquiries require each student to expand his/her problem-solving and product-producing capabilities. Students themselves have noticed that they have more ways to approach problem solving and that they are more adept at creating products.

- There are inquiries that can be assigned for a wide variety of instructional purposes and strategies, e.g., during direct instruction as a means of checking for understanding, for collaborative groupwork, for independent study projects, for homework assignments, etc.

Notes

1 See the *Science Continuum of Concepts, K-6* by Karen D. Olsen.

2 Although Bloom's Taxonomy of Cognitive Objectives was originally developed as a tool for improving the rigor of college testing, the dozens of action verbs associated with each "level" are useful mind joggers that help us vary the actions requested, thereby avoiding boredom.

3 See Frank Smith's *Bureaucratic Invasion of the Classroom.*

4 For a discussion of developing students' multiple intelligences, see Chapter 3.

5 See *Making Connections: Teaching and Learning and the Human Brain* by Renata and Geoffrey Caine, p. 156.

Chapter 16: Assessing Competence Vs. Grading

The goal of the ITI model—and the innate drive of the human mind—is mastery. Mastery, not in the sense of "mastery learning" of each of 834 discrete skills of reading, but rather mastery as in competence: capacity, sufficiency; possession of required skill, knowledge, qualification; sufficient means for a modest livelihood. Not only has the student mastered a skill or a concept but he/she knows when and how to apply it in the real world in similar but varying circumstances. It has been incorporated into a mental program for storage in long-term memory (see Leslie Hart's discussion of programs, Chapter 5). Such mastery and competence is at the heart of positive self-concept; it gives a sense of empowerment and ability to direct one's life; it is the brain's innate search for meaning.

In contrast, assessing students' progress traditionally means sorting and grading and creating bell curves. Such reduction to comparative numbers via true-false and multiple choice formats is affordable but tests only the first stage of learning—pattern detection (see Chapter 4). Whether students can use what they understand in meaningful, real-world situations that would enhance their futures is considered too costly and messy to assess. These simple and simplistic formats compare one student with another rather than plumb the depth of student knowledge. Pitting students against each other causes stress for students and redirecting them from intrinsic rewards to external rewards. In too many instances, it also creates either low self-esteem or a sense of false assurance.

From a teacher perspective, the demands of standardized testing distort our views of what's valuable for students to know by forcing us to test what's easy to assess rather than what's important to know and be able to do as future citizens.[1]

There is yet another, more crucial reason why traditional evaluation and grading is brain-antagonistic; it totally ignores how learning takes place. As Leslie Hart, pioneer in applying brain research to education, states: "Learning is the acquisition of useful programs."[2] In contrast, selecting A, B, C, or D on a multiple choice exam or choosing between true/false options based on a tiny niggling that we've heard of one of the choices before, doesn't indicate understanding nor is it enough to create a mental program for long-term memory. And, as Hart points out, information that does not become embedded in a mental program is information that is irretrievable.[3]

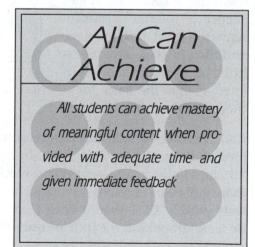

All Can Achieve

All students can achieve mastery of meaningful content when provided with adequate time and given immediate feedback

Before we go on, check with your own experience. Do you recall your college days, cramming all night for your essay exam in your sophomore World Civilizations class? Mountains of data with little or no application to real life. By the time the Blue Book essays were returned, there was stuff in yours that you had never heard of before! Even the handwriting looked strange. Surely, you said to yourself, this must be someone else's! But, sadly, it was yours . . . what a waste of time, money, and effort.

Even in more active forms of classroom assessment, doing something once or twice does not a program make. Thus, even an "A" on a true/false or multiple choice test can mean little in terms of long-term memory. And grades of less than an "A" usually mean that the learner, at the time, still harbored uncertainty or misunderstandings. Such tentative feelings indicate that an accurate mental program had not been put in place and thus he/she remembers little or nothing six weeks later. This is the basis for teachers' common complaint: "I taught them but they didn't learn."

> ## What's Important
>
> In the ITI model, assessment is based on two questions:
>
> - What do you want students to understand?
>
> - What do you want them to do with what they understand?

In life outside of the classroom, the difference between mastery and the bell curve is stark. In the real world, a "C" or even a "B" is wholly insufficient. Who would want to fly in an airplane that had been serviced by a mechanic who had just passed skill tests with a "C-"? Would you? Certainly not! How about just a little leak left behind by your plumber? Is that OK with you? No!

In such situations what really matters is mastery. It is a cruel lie to tell students that a "B" or "C" is OK. The simple but painful truth is that a grade of "B" or "C" represents failure to achieve mastery. To come close to mastery but not succeed is, in the long run, no better than an "F" or never having taken the class at all.

All of this may sound unduly harsh, even spiteful. But if we are honest with ourselves, the evidence of students failing to become competent is all around us.

New Perspectives About Assessment

Two trends offer some hope: application of current brain research (the major topic of this book) and authentic assessment, often referred to as performance-based assessment. Both require massive changes in curriculum content and structure, in the means of assessing student learning, and in attitudes—of teachers, students, and the system.

Brain research and the ITI model ask two simple but powerful questions about assessing our students' learning:

> **What do we want students to understand?**
> (As defined in the key points)
>
> **What do we want them to do with what they understand?** (As described in the inquiries)

Similarly, two valuable ideas from the authentic assessment movement are:

- Use real-life settings and real-world levels of expectation[4]

- Assess what's worth assessing rather than what's easy to assess

Renata and Geoffrey Caine, two authors committed to helping educators apply brain research, propose using at least four relevant indicators for determining mastery:[5]

⠿ Real—World Tests of Mastery

• The ability to use the language of the discipline or subject in complex situations and in social interaction

• The ability to perform appropriately in unanticipated situations

• The ability to solve real problems using the skills and concepts

• The ability to show, explain, or teach the idea or skill to another person who has a real need to know

---

These approaches to assessing mastery focus on competence in real life rather than performances on artificial tasks found only in school. Unfortunately, all too often, there is no change in the curriculum against which student outcomes are assessed. Authentic assessment of unauthentic curriculum results in more work for staff but little change for students. Likewise, creating brain-compatible assessment processes to assess brain-antagonistic curriculum is a waste of time and energy and money.

This chapter discusses several tools for evaluating student learning that are bodybrain-compatible and satisfy district requirements for accountability.

USING THE TOOLS AT HAND

In an ITI classroom, there is no need to invent or buy tests or assessment instruments beyond what the teacher has already created when implementing the ITI model. To answer the ITI assessment questions—what do you want students to understand and what do you want them to do with it—requires no special tools or instruments. They are already built in.

Your Curriculum

Authentic assessment of unauthentic curriculum is simply not possible. Thus, your first step must be to ensure that the curriculum you ask students to master and yourself to assess is, in fact, authentic. In ITI that means that the curriculum must be conceptually stated rather than a collection of factoids, be based in the real world, and be age-appropriate.

The Role of Key Points in Assessment. Key points state clearly what's worth learning and, therefore, what's worth assessing (see Chapter 14). They provide the base for instructional planning, they serve as an official communique to parents and peers about curriculum content and expectations, and they can record what is being taught and learned in your classroom. By giving key points to students up front (except when conducting a discovery process), you put students in the driver's seat, able to take the initiative and self-direct their learning. Key points are the perfect focus for assessment tools and procedures.

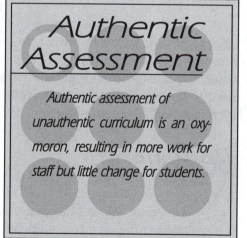

Authentic Assessment

Authentic assessment of unauthentic curriculum is an oxymoron, resulting in more work for staff but little change for students.

Your first assessment task, therefore, occurs early in curriculum planning—how you translate your district/school's curriculum and state standards into key points. Are they conceptual? Are they based in the real world? Are they meaningful enough to be transferred into long-term memory? If yes, developing key points and inquiries that lead to meaningful assessment is a much easier task.

The Role of Inquiries in Assessment. Inquiries require the kinds of observable actions from students that allow a teacher—and parents and the student—to determine whether the student has accurate understanding of a key point (concept or skill), can use it in real-world contexts, and has wired this capability into long-term memory. Mastery has occurred when students can apply the concept/skill in ways described by the Caines on the previous page. Such a level of mastery ensures that the concept/skill has been wired into long-term memory, precisely the point of schooling.

Rubrics

Rubrics are another useful assessment tool because they specifically describe the attributes of a successful product. There are many excellent sources of commonly needed rubrics available through state and national curriculum organizations. They are also relatively easy to construct. Involve your students in the process to increase skills for self-assessment.

Be Patient

Learning doesn't happen overnight. Recall Leslie Hart's definition of learning as a two-step process: the extraction from confusion of meaningful patterns and then the development of mental programs for using what is understood. These physiological changes in the brain take time. Jumping to assessment before both steps are complete is an utter waste of time and is even cruel.

Thus, before you start formal assessment, use your best judgment to determine if formal assessment is warranted or still premature. To decide if students are ready for assessment, look over each completed inquiry. Here are possible questions to ask:

- How many inquiries has the student successfully completed?

- Do these inquiries represent all the multiple intelligences or just his/her favorite?

- Do these inquiries call for real-world performances assessed with real-world expectations and standards?

- Have these inquiries provided the student with enough practice to ensure that the knowledge/skills are wired into long-term memory?

Inquiries

Inquiries are ready-made performance-based assessment tools. All that one needs to add to the inquiries are criteria to guide professional judgement regarding how well students have learned.

The chart on the following page will help you determine how fully and deeply the student has applied and practiced the concept or skill. Assign each inquiry a number and then organize the completed ones. For example, write the number of each completed inquiry in a box that best characterizes the nature of the inquiry by kinds of intelligence used or level of Bloom's Taxonomy. Has the linguistically strong student stayed in his/her safe harbor of linguistic tasks? Or, did the student have little choice in selecting such inquiries because you as teacher developed too few inquiries, most of which called on linguistic intelligence? Or, did the student complete inquiries at only one or two levels of Bloom's Taxonomy, typically knowledge and comprehension?

Ensuring Mastery

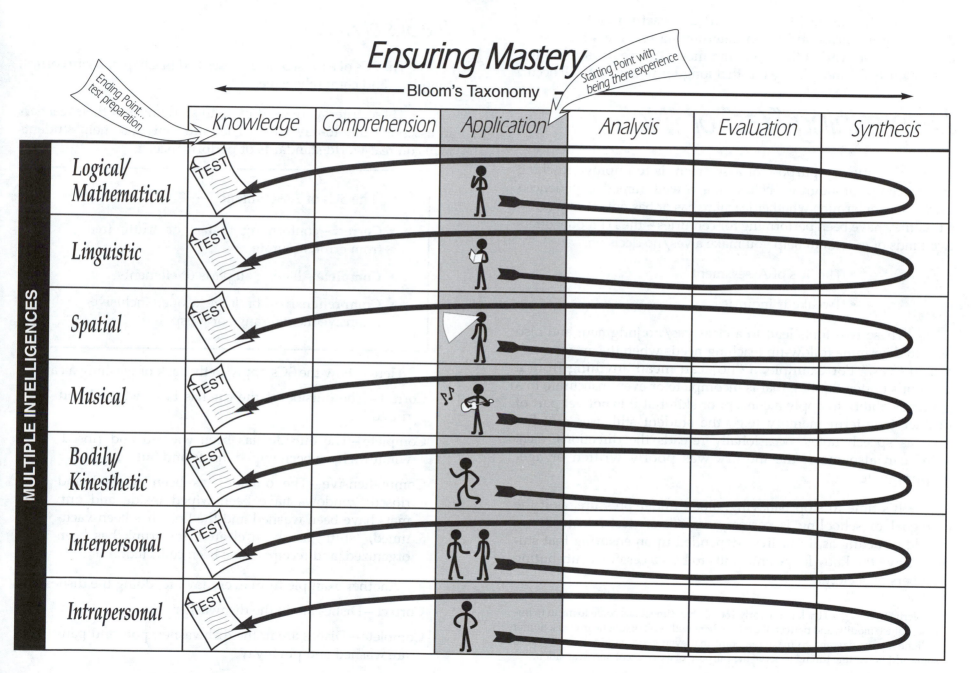

The "Ensuring Mastery" chart is a useful tool both when developing inquiries and when determining readiness for assessment. The more varied the input and more diverse the application and practice, the more likely it is that long-term memory will occur.

Determining "Yes" or "No"

The primary purpose of assessment is to improve teaching and learning. Although we believe that a well-trained, experienced teacher can determine whether learning has or has not taken place—a task they have been performing for centuries—the ITI model offers two kinds of criteria to help you make a yes/no decision:

- The 3Cs of Assessment

- Tweaked* Inquiries

These two tools lead to a clear yes/no judgment and also help to determine follow-up teaching needs when the answer isn't a firm "yes." For example, a "no" can mean anything from a student's understanding that is incomplete or even inaccurate to a student's ability to apply a concept or skill but it is not yet part of his/her long-term memory (e.g., the student still uses crutches such as speech notes, occasionally rereads the directions, etc.). "No" can also mean the inquiry was poorly written or age-inappropriate.

It's time to stop behaving, albeit under pressure, as if the end goal of schooling is correct answers on tests. Instead, we should be acting as if our lives depended upon ensuring that students have the knowledge and skills to be successful, contributing members of society.

---

* The verb "tweak" goes back to the early 1600s. Over time it has come to mean to fine tune, adjust, modify, and perfect. We offer it here with a bit of tongue in cheek humor to lighten your day and to make the point that even good inquiries usually need some additional fine tuning to serve the purpose of assessment and evaluation.

The 3Cs of Assessment

The 3Cs of assessment, as described in Chapter 5, are correct, complete, and comprehensive.

These criteria are used by both students and their teachers in assessing day-to-day work. They are tools that help students focus on real-world standards of performance.

> ### The 3Cs of Assessment
>
> - **Correct**—conforming to fact or truth; free from error; accurate
>
> - **Complete**—having all parts or elements
>
> - **Comprehensive**—of large scope; inclusive; extensive mental range or grasp

Here is how the 3Cs apply to the task of washing a car:

Correct—The outside of the car has been washed and rinsed.

Complete—The outside has been washed and rinsed; windows have been wiped inside and out.

Comprehensive—The outside has been washed and rinsed; windows have been wiped inside and out; mats have been washed and the floor has been vacuumed; "stuff" has been cleared, the trunk has been organized, and receipts have been collected.

Another example from everyday life, doing the dishes:

Correct—Dishes are in the dishwasher

Complete—Dishes are in the dishwasher; pots and pans are washed and put away

Comprehensive—Dishes are in the dishwasher; pots and pans have been washed and put away; the stove and counter area has been wiped, the table cleaned and place mats shaken; the sink is scrubbed; floor is swept and the garbage taken out

For a classroom example, consider the assignment to define "egg":

Correct—Female cell of reproduction

Complete—Female cell of reproduction in all species, large and small, delicate and robust; can vary in size and color

Comprehensive—Female cell of reproduction across all species, large and small, delicate and robust; can vary in size and color; can develop inside and outside of the body. Can have different size, shape, and strength of shell, i.e., from very hard, ostrich, to very delicate, frog; can be fertilized in a petri dish; can be harvested and frozen for future use

It's estimated that 80% of parent wrangling with their children over "unfinished" work and 80% of poor work in the classroom is due to lack of understanding or misunderstanding between adult and child about the criteria for judging performance. A discussion with a child about what the 3Cs would look like when applied to a particular task will greatly increase the quality of the performance and the satisfaction of all involved.

The 3Cs can be used to judge mastery for any activity when it is clearly defined.

The Tweaked Inquiry

Inquiries are ready-made performance-based assessment tools. While not all inquiries need to carry the burden of formal assessment, all require observable action of students.

For classroom purposes, assessment should help improve the teaching-learning process. For that, applying the 3Cs to students' performance on an inquiry plus drawing on teacher experience analyzing student projects are usually adequate to determine mastery.

However, for more formal assessment purposes and when communicating with parents and colleagues, inquiries may need to be tweaked to make judgment less subjective and more objective, i.e., three people assessing the same performance would agree. To build in objectivity, ensure that all the needed assessment elements are clearly there—**who** will know and be able to apply **what**, **how well**, **how** measured, and **when**. Thus, the goal of tweaking is to make the yes/no (mastered or not mastered) assessment determinations less of a subjective leap and more obviously based on criteria understandable to students and parents. Add/Strengthen any missing elements that would help guide your professional judgment regarding how well students have learned, i.e., whether their patterns are correct and a mental program has been built. Procedures and examples for tweaking follow.

The Elements of Successful Assessment

Successful assessment is relatively straightforward. It must answer the basic question: **Who** will do **what**, **how well**, as measured by **what**, and **when**?

Elements of a measurable test item:

- **Who**—all students (not just the "good" students)

- **What** students should do/know and be able to apply (the concept or skill described in the key point)

- **How**—as described in the inquiry

- **How well**—framed by the inquiries with rubrics and inquiries judged according to the "3 Cs" of mastery

- **When**—as described in the inquiry (e.g., within the next 10 minutes, by the end of the day, by tomorrow morning, by the end of the week or month. When is often understood and may not need to be stated.)

⣿ How to Tweak an Inquiry

- First, select two or three inquiries which you feel would be the best real-world application of the content or skill you want to assess. Make sure that reading ability or a particular intelligence is not a fundamental prerequisite to succeeding.

- Analyze these inquiries to determine the intelligence(s) which the performance requires (see discussion of seven intelligences in Chapter 3).

- Avoid inquiries whose prerequisite skills might interfere with accurate assessment of the content or skills being examined. For example, inability to write short essay might preclude the student from expressing their mastery of a concept or skill.

- Take time to craft the inquiries; build in real-world contexts and situations. Inquiries which reflect only linguistic or logical/mathematical intelligences or inquiries that are busywork with no real-world application (or for other reasons are just not brain-compatible) are useless as assessment tools. (For discussion of inquiries, and particularly writing inquiries using the seven intelligences, see Chapter 19.)

Together, key points and inquiries provide the basic assessment tools. How to handle the remaining two elements, who and when, is quite clear in a brain-compatible learning environment. All students can achieve mastery of meaningful content when provided with adequate time and given immediate feedback (either by the learning materials/situation itself or by the teacher).

Examples of Tweaking

Here are some examples of key points and inquiries and how to tweak them to make yes/no decisions about mastery more objective and clear cut for you, students, and parents. It isn't difficult.

Example from Typical Fifth Grade Curriculum:

Conceptual Key Point: A system is a collection of parts and processes that interact to perform some function. Many things can be looked at as a system or as part of a system. To study a system, one must define its boundaries and parts.[6]

Inquiries:

1) In your Learning Club, analyze a bicycle. Experiment with drawing boundaries which would define a system within the bicycle. Draw the boundary of at least five different systems; record your findings and explain why you chose the boundary you did for each system. Share your findings with at least one other Learning Club.

2) Select one of the systems identified in Inquiry #1 above. Analyze the structures and describe the parts and processes that interact to perform some function. Identify the function performed. Record your findings in your science notebook. Share your findings with other members of your Learning Club.

3) Based on what your Learning Club now knows about parts and processes of structures and systems, complete a KWL

(now **k**now, **w**ant to learn, **l**earned during study) chart for your Learning Club. Contribute your group's ideas to the creation of a KWL chart for the class.

First, step: Analyze these three inquiries. Which one is the best real-world application of the content or skill you want to assess? We would choose the first one.

Second step: Ask yourself if the action required by the inquiry is a real-world test of understanding and being able to apply the conceptual key point. Answer: Mostly yes but the action required needs tweaking. For example, the "what" is incomplete. Add "Describe the parts and processes of the system you chose and the functions these parts and processes create."

Would this inquiry as written tell you if each member of the Learning Club understood and could apply it? Answer: Probably not. Tweak it by making it an individual task.

Does this inquiry provide a time frame for completion? No.

So, once tweaked, the inquiry would look like this:

"Working alone, analyze a bicycle. Sketch the bicycle. Experiment with drawing boundaries which would define a system within the bicycle. Draw the boundary of at least five different systems. Describe in your science journal why you chose each boundary.

Then, select one of five systems and diagram its parts and processes. Describe on the diagram the functions that those parts and processes perform together. Add this diagram to your science journal.

Complete your work by the end of the day. Before submitting your journal to the teacher to review, look over your work. Analyze it using the 3Cs of Assessment. If improvements need to be made, ask your teacher for extra time."

As tweaked, this inquiry now allows you to answer the question who will do what, how will they do it, how well must they do it, and when or in the time allowed:

- **Who**—a particular student working alone

- **What** the learner will do/know and be able to apply— how to define boundaries of a system

- **How**—by analyzing and identifying five systems of a bicycle and describing the parts and processes of one of those systems and the function the parts and processes create

- **How well**—framed by the inquiries and judged according to the "3Cs" of mastery

- **When**—by the end of the day plus additional time as discussed with the teacher

You now have an assessment tool that would allow you to say quite objectively, "Yes, the student understands and can apply this concept."

Final question: Has the student truly mastered this concept, that is, is it part of his/her long-term memory? Understanding and applying are the beginning steps. But, in your professional judgment, has the student developed a mental program for long-term memory? If in doubt, ask the student to select his/her favorite toy (must have moving parts). Have him/her do the same inquiry but substitute this toy for the bicycle. Still in doubt, you select a toy or machine and have him/her do the same inquiry again. To repeat Leslie Hart: "Learning is the acquisition of useful programs." Programs are anchored in long-term memory.

TRANSITIONING TO MASTERY

For older students who have mastered the system, substituting procedures to assess mastery/competence for grading based on seat time and quizzes is not a minor event. For many students, particularly the higher achieving, the major motivation is how many points are needed to get a desirable grade or how many pages, exactly, does the essay have to be? A class with only two grades, mastery or no credit can come as a real shock. Have to think? Do one's personal best when mediocre will pull the desired grade? Students may resist the changes.

So, be prepared. Think through concrete steps for transitioning students. Here are some tried and true methods. But remember, these are transition steps* on the way to full bodybrain-compatibility. Don't get stuck on them. Your ultimate goal is an assessment system with only two possibilities—mastery (a grade of A if you have to use letter grades) or no credit (an incomplete). Using assessment tools based on the key points of curriculum and measured by hand-crafted inquiries keeps teachers and students focused on mastery every day. Again, the goal is to acquire useful mental programs.

Introduce the 3Cs

After ensuring that your key points and inquiries are well crafted, introduce the 3Cs. Begin using the criterion "correct" first. Any assignment that does not meet this criterion is returned to the student, repeatedly if necessary, until the work is correct.

After a week or so, and with some forewarning, add the criteria of complete and comprehensive—but only after you have taught the notion to students with multiple, clear examples.

---

* Ann Ross, associate, Susan Kovalik & Associates, was the first ITI teacher to develop a comprehensive system for weaning students off the external rewards/punishments of grades and into a more internally-driven appreciation for learning and mastery. Thank you, Ann, for your ideas.

During this transition to inquiries demanding real-life application and real-life standards of workmanship, you may feel that adapting your old "points for grades" system is needed. If so, don't forget that it is a transition stage. Truly brain-compatible assessment is much further down the road.

A Point System for Transitioning to Personal Best

If your students are firmly attached to a point system, shift what you give points for. Award points for completing inquiries written to Bloom's taxonomy with performance judged using the 3Cs. For example:

Knowledge	1 point
Comprehension	2 points
Application	5 points
Analysis	6 points
Evaluation	8 points
Synthesis	9 points

Students will soon realize that taking a short cut, doing the more time-consuming but more interesting inquiries gives them more points. Furthermore, using the 3Cs to judge performance rather than looking for the "right answer" moves them toward ownership of their work and taking more responsibility for their own learning.

Remember, however, giving points is a transitional ploy only. Leave it behind as quickly as you can. (For a stunning discussion of the problems created by external rewards, see *Punished by Rewards: the Trouble with Gold Stars, Incentive Plans, A's, Praise, and Other Bribes* by Alfie Kohn.[7])

Becoming Responsible for One's Own Learning

Becoming a lifelong learner requires taking responsibility for one's learning—seeking it and keeping at it until mastery is achieved. A first step is giving students the game card—a chart which lists every key point for each component. An abbreviated version of the key points listed on the bulletin board or illustrated in your curriculum mindmap is fine. This should be a permanent part of each student's notebook and a key part of his/her assessment portfolio.

Students should be responsible for selecting and conducting demonstrations of their mastery. This helps students develop an appreciation for what it means to know something in depth as contrasted with realizing that their knowledge is superficial.

Again, assessment in the ITI model is based on mastery. Feedback is given on a mastered/passed or not-yet-mastered/no-credit-yet basis, **not** on a pass/fail basis. Timelines should be flexible. Mastering a key point the last day of school should count as much as mastering it in the first week. Mastery is mastery.

Assessment in Group Settings

Another transitional issue to face is that of individual vs. group, competition vs. collaboration. Some students may initially resist the idea of receiving the same number of points each member of the group received. High-achieving students will complain that their grades will be pulled down, that other students will "cheat" or copy from their work. High-achieving students may in fact hog the task and low achieving students may be intimidated and withdraw from participation. Until a sense of community is reached and such differences melt away, base assessment primarily on individual inquiries.

Again, this is a transitional approach only. For help in developing curriculum appropriate for groupwork and for equalizing social status, see *Designing Groupwork* by Elizabeth Cohen.

Death of the "Right" Answer

Yet another transition, for students and teacher, is a shift away from the teacher as the authority to the individual learner as the person responsible for figuring things out. In real life, there is no 40 hour-a-week person who follows us about shouldering the responsibility for ensuring that the information we encounter is trustworthy or pointing out that we really didn't get it when our boss explained a new procedure. A hallmark of the lifelong learner is determining what information is reliable and whether or not we truly understand it.

Accordingly, you will want students to develop their own resources for making such determinations. One useful classroom rule which handles the spontaneous, short-term questions, is "Three Before Me"; students may not ask the teacher a question until they have first asked three other students.

To handle the need for immediate feedback without you providing the right answer, have Learning Club members assess each other's inquiry using the 3Cs of assessment. Each member initials the inquiry and returns it to the student who requested feedback. Only after reworking the inquiry and making all necessary corrections does the work go to the teacher for feedback. It is easy for the teacher to quickly look at the student's binder and determine if the inquiry satisfies the 3Cs. If not, a note is written next to the inquiry asking the student to rethink or redo it. Students can redo the inquiry or select a different one. Again this is their choice. But the message is clear: What matters in real life is mastery, competence.

Initially, frustration for older students may be high. They may wallow in disbelief or even anger. Teachers need to be patient and maintain their high expectations. By midway through the year, almost all students will have accepted the process as the way things are done in this classroom. Although some students may take longer to adjust, refuse to lower your expectations; eventually all of the students will come to understand the importance of mastery in your classroom and especially for their lives.

As shifts in these attitudes begin to occur and alternatives to traditional assessment gain credence, the door will open to yet more bodybrain-compatible assessment practices, e.g., no points for inquiries completed, only a check-off on key points mastered.

Eventually, the internal student motivator becomes the satisfaction of mastery itself and the confidence of knowing one is a competent problem-solver which is a necessary ingredient for a contributing member of society.

This shift to internal motivation is greatly aided by implementation of the LIFESKILLS, especially Personal Best (see Chapters 9 and 10). Again, the goal of the ITI classroom is mastery with all students receiving an "A."

The Mechanics of Keeping Track

The mechanics of tracking progress toward mastery can take on a life of its own. The end result is almost always a far less bodybrain-compatible atmosphere than we had intended and we begin to have that cheerless feeling of being embedded in mindless requirements.

To help counteract the bureaucratic tug of the system, keep in mind the nine elements of bodybrain-compatibility. For example, adequate time demands that there is no reason a teacher should close the grade book on students just because one grading period has ended and another begun. Our goal should be mastery, whenever it occurs. Continue working with those individuals even while moving on with the class to the next component. Again, the expectation of the teacher and the clear message to students is MASTERY!

If students are involved in keeping track of their progress toward mastery of the key points and in daily work on inquiries, they can stay focused on their work; the teacher needn't nag. Even better, if the curriculum for your next component is based in the real world, students will see additional examples of the key points they are still working on.

Keeping Track of What's Important

The mechanics of using key points as the main assessment tools in the classroom are surprisingly easy. The teacher simply converts his/her grade book into a record of each student's mastery of key points. Key points are listed across the top, students' names along the left. A simple check can suffice or a teacher may choose to record the date and the number of the inquiry used as the assessment tool. The discussions that will ensue around what it means to "know that you know" and "know that you don't know" will be invaluable for students as they begin to piece together what it means to become a lifelong learner and responsible citizen.

Keep a chart showing each student's progress toward mastering each key point. A simple chart will suffice—students' names from top to bottom of page on the left and number of the key point from left to right along the top. Indicate the date each key point is mastered. Note: mastery is mastery; either the key point is mastered or is not yet mastered. No grade is given, only a date when mastered. Such a chart shows at a glance which key points a student needs help with. This can be done through cooperative learning groups or one-to-one contact with the teacher. This process is repeated until every student masters all key points for a component. Students really become interested in how they are progressing and want to master every key point. If the component ends with any student still having key points to master, the teacher should continue to provide support for individual students through using Learning Club partners, cross-age tutors, and other resources until mastery has been achieved. The expectation is for mastery by all students.

Use spiral notebooks. Have students use a spiral notebook in which they keep a record of every key point, the mindmap (their notes) of direct instruction, the inquiries they have completed, and the research they conduct. This helps students gather all the things they need under one cover. Unlike three-ring binders, contents don't get lost.

Note: Be sure student buy the spiral notebooks that come three-hole punched so they can be stored in a notebook binder. It helps students organize their papers or assignments. It provides an easier way for teachers to keep track of student inquiries for checking purposes. If work is generated on a separate sheet of paper, it can be stapled onto a page in the spiral notebook.

A Most Important Reminder

Consistent with the multiple intelligences, students should be allowed to demonstrate mastery in a variety of ways rather than being limited only to linguistic processes such as reading and checking a box, writing, or oral presentations. We must stay focused on whether the student understands the key points, can apply them in real-life settings, and has created programs for the skills or concepts connected with them. The means of expressing mastery through an inquiry should not be a simultaneous test of linguistic ability. Therefore, be sure to select inquiries that require solving problems/producing products from all of the multiple intelligences.

Guidelines for Assessment

- Only assess what's important to know and **be able to do**. Be authentic.

- Help students learn to assess their own mastery using the 3Cs and self–made and other rubrics.

- Focus assessment on what students can **do** with what they understand **and** whether it has become wired into long–term memory.

Notes

1 The traditional curriculum of our public schools is bodybrain-antagonistic in numerous ways:

- It consists primarily of factoids rather than concepts

- Its tools (textbooks and workbooks/sheets) are heavily dependent on linguistic intelligence

- It was codified over a 100 years ago before we had brain research to inform us

- The times and how we live have changed significantly; so should our content

2 See *Human Brain and Human Learning* by Leslie Hart, a brilliant and user-friendly examination of brain research applied to school settings.

3 Hart's insistence that learning be defined as a mental program for using what we understand is a revolutionary idea, especially in the world of assessment and evaluation. See Chapter 5.

4 Fred Newman, one of the primary leaders of the authentic assessment movement, states, "The idea of authentic achievement requires students to engage in disciplined inquiry to produce knowledge that has value in their lives beyond simply proving their competence in school."

5 Renata and Geoffrey Caine, *Making Connections: Teaching and Learning and the Human Brain*, p. 156.

6 This conceptual key point was taken from *Science Continuum of Science Concepts, K-6* by Karen D. Olsen (Covington, WA: Center for the Future of Public Education, 1995), p. 40.

7 Alfie Kohn, *Punished by Rewards: the Trouble with Gold Stars, Incentive Plans, A's, Praise, and Other Bribes.*

Stages of Implementation:

Stages 3-5

Implementing Stages 3-5

Implementing Stages 3-5 of the *ITI Classroom Stages of Implementation* requires that the bodybrain-compatible learning environment created in Stage 1 has been well established and is consistently nurtured and maintained *all day* and that the tools for developing bodybrain-compatible curriculum from Stage 2 are consistently and effectively used *during the time targeted for implementing ITI curriculum.* The amount of time that ITI curriculum is implemented increases through the stages.

In addition, Stage 3 builds on a yearlong theme and emphasizes social-political action projects as training for citizenship. ITI curriculum is to be implemented at least 25% of the time. Stage 3 is also the first time that a basic skill area is expected to be taught as well as practiced through the high interest area of the ITI theme. Using the curriculum of the theme to practice and teach the basic skills increases through the stages until full integration is achieved. (Note that Stage 5 expects up to 90% of the day to be organized by the yearlong theme. It is likely that there will be content areas that a district/school will insist be taught in a specified way that cannot be integrated into the theme. This is political reality; accept it as is. Implementing a truly bodybrain-compatible learning environment for 90% of the day is an enormous gift to your students and an extraordinary achievement by you as a top-flight master teacher.)

Stage 4 adds the richness of a microsociety for citizenship training and for increasing performance. ITI curriculum is to be implemented at least 50% of the time.

Stage 5 emphasizes schoolwide implementation, creating multi-age classrooms (preferably a three-year span) and/or using looping patterns by which students stay with the same teacher two to three years, and fully integrated use of technology. ITI curriculum is implemented at least 90% of the time.

Creating a Yearlong Theme & Practicing Citizenship

CURRICULUM

- A yearlong theme, prominently displayed on the wall for both students and teacher, serves as the framework for content development. On average, more than 25 percent of instruction during the school year is based upon body-brain- compatible curriculum developed for this theme.

- Curriculum content, as expressed in the key points, enhances pattern-seeking, making it easier for students to perceive and understand the most important ideas and concepts in the curriculum. Inquiries are designed to help students make connections to the real world, to practice using the concepts and skills of the key points, and to develop mental programs and store them for long-term memory. Inquiries that provide experiences in citizenship, such as social/political action activities and collaborative grouping practices, occur weekly.

- Most of the time, the curriculum includes almost all of the elements that appear as a natural part or extension of the *being there* focus, e.g., science, math, technology, history/social studies, and fine arts, as well as mathematics, reading, writing, and oral expression, including second language acquisition.

- The content of the theme is consistently used as a high interest area for applying the skills/knowledge currently being taught in at least one basic skill area (e.g., math, reading, writing).

- Curriculum for collaborative assignments is specifically designed for group work.

INSTRUCTIONAL STRATEGIES

- Immersion and hands-on-of-the-real-thing are the primary input used to supplement and extend *being there* experiences.

- All instructional time during the theme and for a growing portion of time during the remainder of the day is based upon the progression of

Being there ➤	*concept* ➤	*language* ➤	*application to the real world*

rather than the traditional progression of

Language ➤	*concept* ➤	*application*

- Collaboration is used daily whenever it will enhance pattern seeking and program building.

- Time is allocated in accordance with the nature of the tasks and student and teacher need for adequate time; such time allocations are made in recognition of the need to develop programs for using knowledge and skills in real-world contexts.

- Peers and cross-age tutors substantially increase teaching and practice time for students in areas of individual need.

Citizenship through a Microsociety for Integrating Basic Skills

CURRICULUM

- Curriculum is based predominantly on visitable locations that provide *being there* experiences and connections with the real world.

- The yearlong theme includes a compelling rationale statement for the conceptual idea and provides an unforgettable pattern-shaper for students. On average, more than two-thirds of instructional time during the school year is based upon bodybrain-compatible curriculum developed for this yearlong theme.

- The context of the theme is used daily as meaningful content for teaching at least two areas of basic skills (e.g., math, reading, writing, oral expression, second and primary language acquisition) and is used for applying all the basic skills.

- The development and practice of citizenship continues to be a central focus of curriculum.

INSTRUCTIONAL STRATEGIES

- Learning experiences are predominantly based on real life, immersion, and hands-on-of-the-real-thing; the teacher regularly utilizes on-site explorations and discovery processes to make learning real for students.

- All instructional time during the theme and for a growing portion of time during the remainder of the day is based upon the progression of

| *Being there* ➤ *concept* ➤ *language* ➤ *application to the real world* |

rather than the traditional progression of

| *Language* ➤ *concept* ➤ *application* |

- Basic skills taught within the theme are taught as a means to an end, not as an end in themselves. Thus, while the teacher utilizes specific techniques for teaching the basic skills on a daily basis, student's primary focus is on the meaningful content which the basic skills help unlock.

- The teacher takes advantage of the power of "incidental learning" (as defined by Frank Smith) to build mental programs applying the basic skills.

- Choices, to allow for individual students' ways of learning, interests, and needs, are consistently provided.

- Students use technology as a natural extension of their senses to explore and learn.

Schoolwide Implementation

CURRICULUM

- The yearlong theme serves as the framework for content development and implementation for all basic skills and content 90% of the day/year. Key points and inquiries effectively enhance pattern seeking and program building.

- The curriculum of the district, provides each teacher with pattern-enhancing tools for curriculum planning.

- Bodybrain-compatible curriculum is implemented school-wide, providing consistency for students as they move through the school.

INSTRUCTIONAL STRATEGIES

- All instructional strategies identified in Stages 1 through 4 are in place 90% of the year.

- Students have the same teacher for two or more consecutive years (due either to multi-aging or the teacher moving with the students).

- The teacher utilizes the power of incidental learning during both planned instructional strategies and unplanned teachable moments.

- Technology in the classroom allows teachers and students full access to databases and communication systems throughout the country and the world. *Being there* experiences near the school are used as a starting point from which to examine similar, age-appropriate situations around the world.

Chapter 17: Creating a Yearlong Theme

Creating a Yearlong Theme

CURRICULUM

- A yearlong theme, prominently displayed on the wall for both students and teacher, serves as the framework for content development. On average, more than 25 percent of instruction during the school year is based upon bodybrain-compatible curriculum developed for this theme.

- Most of the time, the curriculum includes almost all of the elements that appear as a natural part or extension of the *being there* location, e.g., science, math, technology, history/social studies, and fine arts, as well as mathematics, reading, writing, and oral expression, including second language acquisition.

- The content of the theme is consistently used as a high interest area for applying the skills and knowledge of at least one basic skill area (e.g., math, reading, writing).

INSTRUCTIONAL STRATEGIES

- All instructional time during the theme and for a growing portion of time during the remainder of the day is based upon the progression of:

Being there ➤ *concept* ➤ *language* ➤ *application to the real world*

  rather than the traditional progression of:

Language ➤ *concept* ➤ *application*

Do you have trouble remembering 10 unrelated items such as train, sweater, lottery ticket, hip hop lipstick, water filter, lamb shank, bit, gasket, key, and web? How about a trip to the grocery store? Have trouble remembering the 10 items needed to restock the pantry? Do you cruise every isle hoping for that little jolt of recognition that this is an item you intended to get? Yes?

But what if the 10 unrelated items were Christmas presents for the family? For example, five-year-old nephew Sam has a passion for electric trains; 17-year-old daughter Sally is wild about alpaca sweaters; Aunt Sandy religiously buys lottery tickets every Wednesday and Saturday; 13-year old Wendy, your babysitter, loves hip-hop anything; 12-year-old son Jon is going on an extended camping trip and needs a safe water filter; you found a farmer who will sell Uncle Frank half a lamb so the lamb shank is just a starter and a bit of a joke; daughter Jan's horse isn't performing well and needs a new bit; nephew James is desperate to learn how to work on cars so you are wrapping up, with a needed manifold gasket, the name of the man you hired for 10 hours to teach him; 16-year-old niece Kathy wants a diary with lock and key for privacy; and sister Elizabeth is looking for a spider web to replicate in stained glass so you find the perfect book on spiders. Now, if these were members of your family, couldn't you find this list of 10 now related items much easier to remember? And if the items were for a Thanksgiving dinner instead of miscellaneous household replacement items, wouldn't you find the task considerably easier? Absolutely!

Why? Because in both cases, there was an organizing idea—Christmas presents and Thanksgiving dinner—that gave meaning to the otherwise unrelated items. Suddenly they're understandable and memorable.

In similar fashion, the yearlong theme gives meaning to otherwise unrelated curriculum content, making learning faster, easier to put into use, and more readily retrievable. What we're talking about here is the power of a pattern to give meaning to incoming information. See the sample themes on page 17.8.

Creating a Yearlong Theme

The purpose of the yearlong theme is a serious one. Primarily, its role is to enhance the brain's search for patterns and meaning by creating a giant pattern, a large mental web. When recognized as a pattern by the learner, this web serves as the mental organizer for the year, the glue, for everything studied under it. It provides an "address" in the brain for processing and retaining the knowledge and skills of the entire year. (See Chapter 4 for a discussion of the brain as pattern-seeker, a key brain research concept underpinning the ITI model.)

> ## CREATING A YEARLONG THEME
> ### *Curriculum Development*
>
> * A yearlong theme, prominently displayed on the wall for both students and teacher, serves as the framework for content development. On average, more than 25 percent of instruction during the school year is based upon body-brain-compatible curriculum developed for this theme.

The Framework for the Yearlong Theme

The yearlong theme is a simple structure. In mindmap form it looks like the graphic on the next page.

When implementing ITI curriculum daily, even if for only an hour or so a day in the early stages of implementing, the components are usually about a month in length; the topics are usually for a week. However, as curriculum often takes on a life of its own, be prepared to follow the teachable moments. Feel free to extend or shorten any topic as best serves students and your responsibilities for curriculum content.

Also, if you have chosen to initiate implementing your ITI curriculum in concentrated bursts, such as half days for a week, your components might represent a week and topics just a day (rather than a month for components and a week for topics). The themes shown in Chapter 13 are curriculum designed for half days for a week.

You choose the time frames; the theme structure will work with time spans long or short, full days or parts of days. What's important here is that there is an obvious pattern or conceptual relationship between the theme and each of its components and, in turn, from components to topics.

Remember, curriculum development is a pattern-enhancing task. Think in patterns, speak in patterns—connections, relationships, even nouns and verbs.

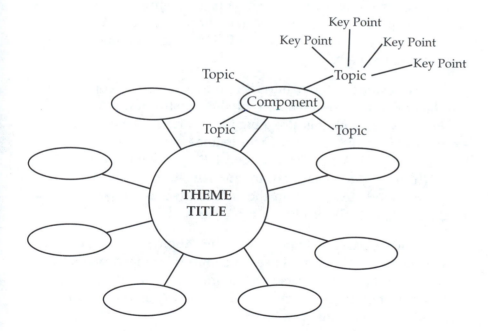

Parts of an ITI Theme

THEME: The universally recognized big idea/concept that you believe is critical for students to understand and be able to apply. It is conceptually powerful enough to hold and organize a wealth of concepts, ideas, thoughts, significant knowledge, and skills.

THEME TITLE: A kid-grabbing title that conveys the essence of the theme's concept It names the concept of your theme in a jazzy way.

PATTERN SHAPER: A pattern instantly familiar to students that connects the monthly components together.

COMPONENT: A concept that best represents what is to be studied at the *being there* location. It is also a part of or an extension of the concept of the theme. Components also relate to each other; the pattern shaper makes the flow from one component to the other predictable and understandable.

TOPIC: An area of study that teaches the concept of the component. It is an aspect of the component's *being there* experience.

KEY POINTS: Essential concepts, knowledge, and skills that all students are to learn. Key points are based in the physical location selected for the component and in your state/district curriculum standards.

INQUIRIES: Opportunities to practice using in real-world situations the concepts, knowledge, and skills identified in the the key points; such practice leads to mastery and long-term memory.

RATIONALE: Statement of why you believe the concept for the theme (with its components and topics) is worthy of a year's study by your students.

Friendly Advice About Yearlong Themes

Those who have gone before you have learned several important lessons about yearlong themes:

- The organizing idea must be a concept that students are familiar with from the beginning—one they understand or intuitively grasp. If you have to teach the idea to them to start with, it will not serve as a powerful organizer. Students must have had large amounts of sensory input about the concept from prior experience and thus already have an address in the brain to which further learning can be anchored.

- Students must hold positive emotions about the concept and an accurate understanding of it.

- Be patient. If you're like most ITI teachers, things don't seem to "click" into place until after the eighth or ninth revision. As you work on your theme, and go through multiple revisions, you will find that it becomes easier with practice. Eventually enhancing pattern seeking becomes a way of thinking about curriculum.

Note that Christmas presents and the contents of a Thanksgiving dinner meet all the above requirements. It is thus not surprising that they would make help the brain learn and remember. **However,** please note that holidays and teddy bears are *not* concepts found in state curriculum standards. The year theme must be a powerful, central concept from your state/district curriculum standards named by a kid-grabbing title. Your goal is kid-friendly but powerful themes. For example, "What Makes It Tick?" is a kid-grabbing title for a serious investigation of technology in our everyday lives; "Home Is Where the Heart Is" represents the concepts of habitat and interdependence; and "We, the People" is a launching pad for in-depth study of the U.S. Constitution and how it frames our personal and social lives.

The Ties That Bind. The theme and its sub parts should "stick together" because they are extensions of the most important concepts or patterns to be studied. Such a theme empowers students because they can see at a glance, for example, how the weekly topics grow out of/support the monthly component and how each of the monthly components grows out of/supports the concept of the theme.

Some ties are very tight and draw the whole year into a singular focus. An example is the "We, the People" theme whose monthly components are the goals of our government expressed in the preamble of our constitution.

For some concepts, however, the ties or patterns that bind the monthly components to the theme are more subtle. Yes, there's a relationship but it isn't obvious or strong enough to tie things together for students. When that happens, the pattern shapers "pattern shapers" shown on the next page are invaluable. Patterns shapers help the brain see how each monthly component grows out of the yearlong theme concept **AND** how each component flows from one to the next.

For example, the pattern shaper for "We, the People" is #6, familiar patterns—the preamble of the constitution outlining the goals of government. It is also a big idea, pattern shaper #17. Other examples of familiar patterns include lines from a famous poem or song ("See the USA from Your Chevrolet") or the life cycle of a butterfly (from egg, to caterpillar, to chrysalis, to beautiful butterfly), or Robin Hood stealing from the rich to give to the poor, and so forth. Think metaphorically.

The pattern shaper for the theme, "We all Life Downstream," is #10, varied uses. A common primary grade theme uses pattern shaper #7—backyard to universe—literally from one's home, to school, to the neighborhood park, to. . . . (For young students, the universe that can be experienced directly through their 19 senses is usually quite close by.)

The possibilities are endless.

Pattern Shapers

1. Location from which a perspective is taken—e.g, Golden Gate Bridge, Colorado River, International Space Station

2. Person, animal, or thing from which a perspective is taken—e.g., ecologist, pioneer, lumbermill owner, logger, spotted owl, old-growth forest

3. Habitats

4. Systems—e.g., transportation, communication, law, school

5. Chronology or sequences of events (start from *here and now*)

6. Familiar patterns—e.g., life cycles, cause and effect, movie and song titles, song lyrics, famous poems, vegetables

7. Backyard to universe—e.g., neighborhood, city, nation

8. Structures—e.g., bridges, houses, coliseums, airports

9. Famous, exciting explorations

10. Varied uses—e.g., recreation, trade, transportation

11. Seriation—e.g., small to large, rough to smooth

12. Famous people or groups of people

13. Happening (large or small) or major event

14. Geography/region

15. Comparisons, e.g., now/then, predator/prey

16. Wondering or question

17. A big idea/concept—change, interdependence

18. Other . . .

Again, curriculum is a pattern-enhancing activity. The patterns you use to bind your theme together into a memorable whole is an extremely important decision.

Cautionary Tales. Having discussed what a good theme is, it is helpful to provide some cautionary advice.

- Avoid cool and "cutsie." An organizer that is cute or cool may be unrelated to what you want students to learn and students are quite adept at detecting things that are contrived. Also, the cool or cutsie theme may have meanings attached to it that distort the concepts to be learned, thus leading to misinterpretation. Instead, go for power. Build on concepts inherent to the concept of the theme/theme title.

- A hard-earned lesson is this: Don't confuse enthusiasm with understanding or the potential for long-term learning. Yes, students are enthralled with dinosaurs and teddy bears and holidays but does their study empower students' lives 10 years from now as much as study of technology or interdependence or the impact of our constitution? Absolutely not.

- Avoid fragmentation and departmentalization. Each of the components should be a supporting idea or sub-concept of the theme concept, not a start-from-scratch idea. In other words, the concept of the theme should be a big enough idea that coming to understand and apply it will require an entire year.

Where to Start

Creating a yearlong theme is not a logical or sequential thinking task, nor is it a process of simply sequencing a set number of given pieces. Some people first choose their locations. Some start with a theme idea from their state/district standards and then go in search of locations that best teach those concepts and skills. The truth of it is that the four stages of developing ITI curriculum—selecting a physical location, identifying key points, developing inquiries, and creating a yearlong theme—are usually carried out concurrently. The decisions about one stage affect the others.

There are, however, four prerequisites. You must:

- Have scouted your school's environment for powerful teaching locations and identified the best alternatives

- Have reached general agreements with yourself and fellow teachers regarding what your students are to learn (see Chapters 13, 14, 15)

- Have decided whether your goal is integrated or inter-disciplinary curriculum

- Know who you will be working with in terms of both colleagues and students

Thinking It Through

Here are some tips for testing the power of your theme.

Evaluating the Concept for Your Theme

What we choose to teach to application and mastery—and what we choose not to teach or only "cover"—are high stakes decisions with major implications for students and their futures. How many of us are successful in our fields because a teacher cajoled us into learning to the level of mastery rather than just to get a grade? How many of us live a life of deep satisfaction because of interests unveiled by a teacher that became hobbies or led to our ability to contribute to society in meaningful ways?

Concepts for a Theme. What's worth teaching is an enormous question that should not be taken lightly or made hurriedly in response to the pressures of politics or tradition. What's worthy of students' attention? What's critical to their ability and willingness to participate as an informed citizen? Some concepts to ponder as idea starters include:

art	adaptation	balance	beauty
cause/effect	celebrations	citizenship	communication
conflict	change	courage	curiosity
culture	cycles	dependence	democracy
development	discovery	diversity	duty
ecology	economics	exploration	family
form	foundation	freedom	function
global	habitat	happiness	identity
interdependence	institution	independence	judgment
justice	labor	legacies	liberty
logic	love	matter	music
nature	necessity	opinion	philosophy
poetry	power	perspective	principle
progress	quality	relationship	stewardship
survival	symbolism	time	truth
tyranny	universal	war/peace	wisdom

Theme Title. The theme title is also an organizational tool, a hook into students' imaginations and their prior experiences. A kid-grabbing theme title is a notion which students—through ample experience or intuition—already understand and find motivating. It is an appealing twist representing the concept of your theme. It provides an address in the brain to receive and process new learning, to bring together new and old to ensure retention in long-term memory. The kid-grabbing theme is a cognitive structure that greatly facilitates the pattern-seeking and program-building functions of the brain.

Examples of theme titles that grab student interest include:

Science	Social Studies
What Makes It Tick?	Quest for Power
You Can't Fool Mother Nature	It's All in Your Head
Home Sweet Home	We Are the People
Circles of Life	The World in Our Hands
On the Move	Wisdom Seekers
A House Is a House for Me	Whose Life Is It Anyway?
A River Runs Through It	Making a Difference in the World
Home Is Where the Heart Is	See the USA in Your Chevrolet
Where Did You Go H2O?	Surviving the Journey
Patterns in Nature	Incredible Journeys
Where the Sidewalk Ends	Profiles in Courage
Color Me a Rainbow	What Goes Around, Comes Around

Whatever you choose, be sure you settle on something that fires your enthusiasm as well as that of the students.

Rationale. The rationale is your answer to the question "What's worth learning?" should be recorded as part of your theme. Make a bold statement about why the theme merits a year of study and how it will benefit your students. Place it prominently on the theme mindmap so your purpose is clear to all.

Examples of rationale statements include:

- "We, the People" — Democracy can not be sustained if its people do not understand, support, and exercise the responsibilities as well as the rights of democracy on a daily basis.

- "Circles of Life" — Learning about the circles of life will allow us to discover more about ourselves and help us determine which circles affect us and which ones we can affect.

- "Searching for Balance" — Adolescents are often searching to find balance within themselves; not quite children, not quite adults. They also need to understand how to "balance" who they are with their place in a world that is trying to find balance to survive.

Evaluating Monthly Components and Weekly Topics

The *being there* locations drive selection of the monthly components and their weekly topics. Ask yourself: What's it all about? Why did I select this location? What is urgent for my students to understand about this location? What does this location illustrate about other locations and their issues that students will face? You are looking for patterns or hooks that students can carry with them for the rest of their lives.

Look at the location and its human issues afresh. Leave the old subject area boundaries behind. What is important to know about this now, in the year 2005, 2013, and beyond?

Remember, curriculum development is a pattern-enhancing task. Think in patterns, speak in patterns. See the world anew through patterns. What one pattern may reveal another pattern may leave hidden. What one pattern may link to naturally, may never come under consideration with another pattern.

Test your monthly components and weekly topics for the year against your childhood memories. What grabbed your fancy when you were the age of the students you are now preparing to teach? What title would have grabbed your attention and fired your enthusiasm while at the same time staying true to your organizing concept? Whatever this is, it becomes the title of your theme.

Am I on the Right Track?

Curriculum is both highly personal and intellectually challenging. You will know you are on the right track when you can say yes to the following self check items.

Self Check

Creating a Yearlong Theme

- You're excited about about your theme and so are your students.

- It has substance that relates to the real world. It facilitates pattern identification and recognition of interrelationships among ideas, theories, events, situations, and objects.

- The concept underlying the theme and related content is meaningful from the students' point of view. It helps students more effectively process, store, and retrieve what is learned, to be able to anticipate what comes next, and to generalize to other situations.

- The content is age-appropriate.

- It is worthy of your time creating it and your students' time studying it. The rationale behind the theme is compelling for you and for students.

- Materials are readily available and the physical locations can be visited frequently.

- The yearlong theme serves as an organizer for the teacher when building curriculum and gathering materials throughout the year.

- For both teacher and students, it establishes the itinerary for the year.

Examples of Yearlong Themes

Although there may be a perfect storm or a perfect 10, there is no such thing as a perfect theme. Your goal isn't perfection but power to engage, not the pinnacle of your life's work but an expression of your willingness to go the extra mile so that all students can succeed.

"We, the People" uses the preamble of the U.S. Constitution to outline issues to be addressed through a yearlong theme based in history/social studies. This is an example of pattern shaper #6, a familiar pattern.

Theme: Goals of democracy
Pattern shaper: Familiar pattern
Rationale: Democracy can not be sustained if its people do not understand, support, and exercise the responsibilities as well as the rights of democracy on a daily basis.

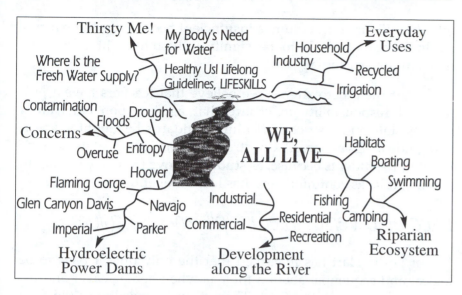

Thirsty Me!

My Body's Need for Water

Where Is the Fresh Water Supply?

Healthy Us! Lifelong Guidelines, LIFESKILLS

Household Industry

Everyday Uses

Recycled

Irrigation

Contamination

Drought

Concerns

Floods

Overuse

Entropy

Hoover

Flaming Gorge

Glen Canyon Davis

Navajo

Imperial

Parker

Hydroelectric Power Dams

Industrial

Commercial

Residential

Recreation

Development along the River

WE, ALL LIVE

Habitats

Boating

Swimming

Fishing

Camping

Riparian Ecosystem

"We All Live Downstream" also uses pattern shaper #6. The location is the Colorado River. The theme is cause and effect, and the pattern shaper is "various uses." The rationale is that water is necessary to sustain life and its use and misuse directly affect our quality of life.

"Home Is Where the Heart Is" uses form and function as the concept, kinds of homes as the pattern shaper, and the rationale that all living things have a basic need for shelter that can come in various forms and have various uses. This is a great example of a yearlong theme for younger elementary students.

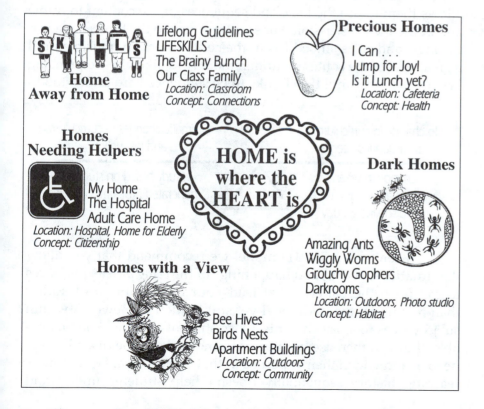

Home Away from Home

Lifelong Guidelines
LIFESKILLS
The Brainy Bunch
Our Class Family
Location: Classroom
Concept: Connections

Precious Homes

I Can . . .
Jump for Joy!
Is it Lunch yet?
Location: Cafeteria
Concept: Health

Homes Needing Helpers

My Home
The Hospital
Adult Care Home
Location: Hospital, Home for Elderly
Concept: Citizenship

HOME is where the HEART is

Dark Homes

Amazing Ants
Wiggly Worms
Grouchy Gophers
Darkrooms
Location: Outdoors, Photo studio
Concept: Habitat

Homes with a View

Bee Hives
Birds Nests
Apartment Buildings
Location: Outdoors
Concept: Community

Big City Treasures

- Industrious Industry
- Capital Connection
- Tourism Talk
- Big City Lights (energy, electricity, light)
Location: Downtown Detroit

Treasures Within

- Lifelong Guidelines
- LIFESKILLS
- How we Learn
Location: Classroom

Treasures of Our Heritage

MICHIGAN'S TREASURES

- The Three Fires
- Voyagers
- Culture Clash
- Our place in the Universe
Location: History Museum

Treasures of our Water

- Treasures of the Creek
- Riding the River
- Great Lakes & Great Ships
- Nature's Balance (ecosystems)
Location: Detroit River, Blakely Creek

Digging for Treasures

- Sifting through the Soil
- Iron Country
- More Underground Treasures
- Simple Machines– Complex Work
Location: Schoolyard

Treasures of our Land

- Pondering Plants
- Fertile Fields
- Grazing through the Grass
- Green Gold
Location: Farm/Forest

"Michigan's Treasures" is based on the concept of interdependence and exploration is the pattern shaper. The rationale is that the natural and other types of resources in Michigan have helped its people to survive and prosper over time and reinforces individual responsibility to care for Michigan's resources.

Using a Location to Integrate Content in Your Theme

The current models of integrating curriculum are largely academic and abstract. They range from keeping curriculum and instruction as it is but altering the calendar so related topics can be studied at the same time to, at the other extreme, completely altering curriculum and instruction and integrating curriculum around selected ideas or problems generated by students. The ITI model is in the middle of such a continuum.

USING A LOCATION TO INTEGRATE CONTENT IN YOUR THEME

Curriculum Development

- Most of the time, the curriculum includes almost all of the elements that appear as a natural part or extension of the *being there* location, e.g., science, math, technology, history/social studies, and fine arts, as well as mathematics, reading, writing, and oral expression, including second language acquisition.

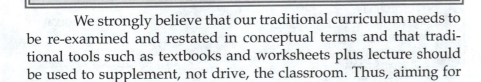

We strongly believe that our traditional curriculum needs to be re-examined and restated in conceptual terms and that traditional tools such as textbooks and worksheets plus lecture should be used to supplement, not drive, the classroom. Thus, aiming for interdisciplinary curriculum is insufficient because traditional curriculum content needs to be significantly rethought and made much more conceptual.

At the other extreme, we believe that teachers have a professional responsibility to ensure that agreed-upon curriculum such as state and district curriculum standards be taught at specified grade levels as agreed. Constructivist curriculum at its extreme is unfair to students because, as students move from one teacher to another, it lacks continuity and has lots of repetition and gaps.

Integrated Versus Interdisciplinary Curriculum

Leslie Hart has remarked that the only time it pays to be logical and sequential about a topic is when both speaker and listener are experts in the field. Their deep knowledge of the field allows them to use the logic and sequences of the content to frame and guide their discussion. For someone new to the topic, however, the logic and rules embedded in the content remain invisible until a great deal of the content is understood. And, likewise, sequencing has no meaning until the chunks to be sequenced are understood.

No change in curriculum or instructional strategies	Dramatic changes in curriculum and instruction
Change in when things are taught for interdisciplinary study	Study based on student-generated problems or issues

Therefore, in the ITI model we recommend that you allow the situations, events, and happenings of the *being there* experiences to call forth the patterns that lead your curriculum work rather than relying on the traditional yet still hidden frameworks within subject areas to assist students. Once students become knowledgeable, they can then use traditional frameworks in the disciplines to deepen and widen their expertise in that subject area. For example, teaching history sequentially doesn't help students understand conceptual issues in history. Exploring why wars erupt requires studying the early effects of several wars concurrently. If we are to learn from history, we need to group common events together to get the lesson. Once students understand the lessons of history—once the patterns make sense—the details from the sequence of history are more readily learned and are far more likely to be remembered. Note here that this discussion does not ask that you take sides and vote for either conceptual or sequential, black or white. The point here is that starting where we want to end up—students understanding the unfolding history of mankind—is not necessarily the best way to begin teaching students. We need to start where our students are, write curriculum in ways that enhance their ability to detect and understand pattern, teach those patterns through

---

Self Check

Using Location to Integrate your Theme

- Students are unaware of the seams between the subjects. For example, while visiting the grocery store, where products come from (geography), the traits department heads look for when employing (character education), math skills (computing profit margin), the technology behind how pricing is kept current with changing market conditions (computers and radio frequencies), methods for reducing shoplifting and restrictions on those methods (history/social studies), and more are seen as a singular, coherent picture.

- The most important concepts and skills of the state standards are taught through the location and taught to mastery.

- Students readily apply concepts and skills when solving a real-world problem; they are able to bring multiple disciplines to bear as needed.

---

real-world experiences, give them practice in applying/using what they understand, and then help them extend their learning into the varied forms of evidence of mastery that we require.

Why is this important? It is the difference between truly integrated curriculum versus interdisciplinary curriculum. The authors argue that *integrated curriculum based in being there experiences is far easier to learn, to use, and to store in long-term memory.* Once acquiring this base, students are prepared to excel at traditional approaches to the various disciplines and, more importantly, at any mix of such concepts and skills in new locations and situations.

This choice, although it may sound academic, is important. If you choose to develop interdisciplinary curriculum, you will be closely tied to textbooks and workbooks. If you choose integrating curriculum, you will be more free to use *being there* experiences as a way of organizing concepts and skills from your state/district curriculum standards into meaningful chunks for students.

Constructivism at the Extreme Versus Integration

The core values of constructivism align well with brain research. Making meaning is a completely individual task and each learner goes about it differently (see discussion of pattern-seeking and program building in Chapters 4 and 5). Yet, taken to its extreme, it ignores the political realities of state standards and professional responsibilities to students and parents.

The middle, and we believe wholly defensible ground for constructionist thinking, is that one begins with required concepts from the state standards and then works flexibly with students to make those concepts come alive.

The ITI model adds a twist to that: With concepts from the state standards in mind, find physical locations that best illustrate and teach those concepts. Then, allow the real-life goings on to integrate curriculum naturally as well as allow students to help develop inquiries and further pursue ideas of greatest interest to them.

Teaching Basic Skills Through Being There Experiences

Teaching basic skills is serious business. Failure is a high-stakes issue for students, a life-long limitation on employment potential and personal growth. Therefore, making changes in how we teach the basic skills should be done carefully and systematically. First think through how the theme content can be used to apply basic skills. Once successful with that step, then use the theme content to teach the skills. If you leap into both phases—application and teaching—before you're ready, students will pay the price.

INTEGRATING BASIC SKILLS

Curriculum Development

- The content of the theme is consistently used as a high interest area for applying the skills and knowledge of at least one basic skill area (e.g., math, reading, writing).

In Stage 2 of the *ITI Classroom Stages of Implementation,* envisions using the theme experience to practice those basic skills that naturally extended from the *being there* location. At this stage of your journey, the transition to integrating the basic skills should include full use of the *being there* experience as a place to systematically practice at least one area of the basic skills, i.e., math, writing, reading, oral language. By Stage 4, the theme experience should be the basis for *applying* all the basic skills and for *teaching* at least two basic skill areas.

Self Check

Integrating Basic Skills

- There is a written plan for shifting the application of at least one area of basic skills to the *being there* theme experience. Needed inservice has been planned and carried out.

- Each classroom teacher carefully monitors students' progress in developing mental programs for using the basic skills.

- Students love their theme work time and related homework assignments. They look forward to it and are aware that they are learning practical, lifelong skills.

Chapter 18: Citizenship Through Social/Political Action and a Microsociety

Preparing students to become participating citizens in our democratic society is a core value of the ITI model. It can and should be done in small and big ways on a daily basis. Two of the most effective ways are involving students in social/political action projects and in living and learning in a dynamic microsociety.

Social/Political Action Projects

Social and political action projects are key not only for citizenship training but also because they require that students apply concepts, knowledge, and skills in real-world ways. Using what they know increases the breadth and depth of their learning and the likelihood that such learning will become wired into long-term memory.

Social/political action is a call to action, moving from knowing about to doing something that matters. It grows organically out of students' experiences studying the theme. It's what students find important and compelling. It might take the form of lobbying the city council for a stoplight at the school, pressing the EPA or local governmental entity to complete a toxic clean up, urging other students not to eat tuna that doesn't carry the dolphin-friendly symbol, picketing the superintendent's office to get the kindergarten toilets fixed and the restroom reopened, replanting mangrove forests, working in a soup kitchen, visiting the elderly, ensuring that homeless children get school supplies, launching an anti-drug campaign at school, and so forth. In the process of such projects, young citizens discover the levers of our democratic system, learn the personal skills to make their opinions heard and considered, and develop the courage and perseverance to press on until problems get resolved. They also develop a commitment to give back to society through service projects, governmental internships, voter responsibility, etc.

Social/political action projects are usually undertaken as an entire class although Learning Clubs could take on separate parts of a class project. There are no hard and fast rules here, just the intent to have students engage in something meaningful and experience the deep sense of satisfaction that comes from making a contribution to the world and helping make it a better place.

Resources to assist you and your students identify, plan, and carry out social/political action projects include: *The Kids Guide to Service Projects: Over 500 Service Ideas for Young People Who Want to Make a Difference*, and *The Kids Guide to Social Action: How to Solve the Social Problems You Choose–and Turn Creative Thinking into Positive Action* by Barbara A. Lewis, and *Enriching Curriculum Through Service Learning* edited by C.W. Kinsley and K. McPherson.

Self Check

Social/Political Action

- The call to action is genuine, a project chosen by students.

- The project is a natural outgrowth of the experiences of the theme.

- The project is a sincere contribution to improving the life of others.

- The work of the project will require a wide range of knowledge and skills, including basic skills as well as social and personal skills. The standards for this work are those of the real world. For example, a letter must be perfect in spelling and grammar, a speech must be informative and delivered with conviction and presence, the information presented must be accurate and fair, appointments must be scheduled and kept as agreed, and so forth.

- Social/political action projects are conducted at least two to three times a year.

A Microsociety

Against the backdrop of innumerable achievements of our technological era, we must rank as a major shortcoming our failure to involve children in our adult world. Most children have not a clue what their parents do for a living and thus are learning precious few of the skills necessary to build a successful life.

The reasons are many: It's unsafe for children to roam about the neighborhood as they could 50 years ago; more people are employees, not entrepreneurs or owners of mom-and-pop operations that involved the children from an early age onward; and many jobs have become fantastically specialized so that even if children did accompany their parents to work, they would be hard pressed to see the big picture of what's going on. And yet, the challenges facing future citizens continue to mushroom.

A powerful antidote to these conditions is a microsociety on campus. A microsociety not as an add-on, something done after school or on special days but as a fully integrated, daily ingredient in the vibrant life of the school.

Francie Summers, a truly gifted administrator in Las Vegas, Nevada, and her hard-working, capable staff have demonstrated the power of such a microsociety at two schools. Her current campus, Edith Gareheim Elementary, a K-5 school, is a great illustration of the power of a microsociety to not only induct the young into the roles of citizenship but also to dramatically increase academic performance.

A second fully-developed microsociety has been created at Sul Ross Elementary, Waco, Texas, by an equally talented staff with similar increases in academic performance.

Key features of these two microsociety models include:

- Using the Lifelong Guidelines and LIFESKILLS to shape the culture and define the way we treat others

- Replication of essential elements of community life such as daily mail delivery, a banking system (training provided by a bank), an inhouse monetary system capable of exchanging real dollars for "Gareheim Gold," a newspaper and TV station, stores open daily for such necessities as extra pencils and pens, special paper, snacks, a recycling service, and more

- Governmental services such as a court system that convenes weekly or more often if needed, a city council that legislates the rules of behavior for its citizens, local EPA, business license bureau, and so forth

- Class and individual businesses which operate every week, some daily. "Going to Town Day," which occurs three to four times a year, provides a sales outlet for all businesses and a breathless exchange of Gareheim Gold in a fast-paced, two-hour period. Prospective business owners must mull through an approvable business plan, buy a business license, arrange for advertising over the schoolwide intercom or student-run TV station and newspaper, and rent retail space

- Engagement in city projects of importance, such as the fifth grade developing an architectural plan to turn an empty lot across the street from the school into a city park (the plan was accepted by the local authorities and became a reality)

- Community participation through volunteerism, monetary donations, and business partnerships

- Parent participation

- Participation of younger siblings

The richer the microsociety, the more real it is to students. The more real it seems, the more fully they embrace participating in it. The microsociety creates a real need to know, making learning deeper and more comprehensive.

Self Check

A Microsociety

- The microsociety is seamlessly woven into the life of the school. Students participate in some aspect of the microsociety on a daily basis.

- Every student participates in his/her class business (recycling program, convenience store) or school-wide project (post office, newspaper, TV station, a bank). In addition, many students also run a business in partnership or as sole proprietor.

- Although students are aware that theirs is a microsociety of their own making, they value being a member and realize that they are learning invaluable business and citizenship skills.

- Students understand the importance of learning to use what they learn—from the Lifelong Guidelines to academic concepts and skills to everyday common sense.

- Staff uses the high-interest experiences of the microsociety as a proving ground for students to apply basic skills. For example, every business must calculate its expenses and percentage of profit/loss.

- The microsociety is student run; staff serve as guide on the side, not sage on the stage.

▦ Behaviors of Responsible Citizenship

- Participates in community dialog; informed voter

- Treats others with respect and courtesy

- Obeys the law; works through the system to change those laws he/she believes are unfair or wrong

- Practices conservation

- Maintains a positive work ethic; is developing the personal and social skills to be financially self-sufficient

- Takes responsibility for personal health

- Is committed to family and does his/her part to make the family a successful unit

- Is tolerant of religious, racial, ethnic, gender, and age differences

▦ The Power of a Microsociety

"Our Title I school serves children and families from poverty. ITI works for our students because it makes them feel worthy as individuals. It unleashes their natural curiosity in such a way that learning makes sense and the world around them is understandable. They know they can make positive changes in their world and be productive, responsible citizens. ITI is powerful and changes the lives of children and the adults who work with them."
—Terri Patterson, Principal , Sul Ross Elementary, Waco, Texas

"ITI has had a dramatic impact on students, staff, and the community during the eleven years I have served as principal at two microsociety schools. The students have acquired the knowledge to be successful in school and in life; staff have felt empowered as professionals and are excited about teaching. The communities have been exceedingly supportive because they have reaped the benefits as we 'grew responsible citizens'."
—Francie Summers, Principal, Edith Gareheim Elementary, Las Vegas, Nevada

Part E

Instructional Strategies

Creating and maintaining a bodybrain-compatible learning environment requires a range of instructional strategies. The next two chapters describe those particularly key to the ITI model. Chapter 20 outlines those instructional strategies needed on a daily basis—strategies that must become an automatic mental program for teachers, available at a moment's notice for the "teachable moment" as well as for one's written lesson plan. The instructional strategies addressed in Chapter 20 include:

- Modeling

- Target talk

- Agendas

- Discussion, including processing the process

- Literature

- Songs

- Movement

- Journal writing

- Written procedures

- Graphic organizers

- Clear criteria to clarify performance expectations

Chapter 21 describes strategies that may not be used on a daily basis but are nevertheless vital. They can lend power to your teaching when introducing and reteaching important concepts, skills, and/or behaviors. The instructional strategies addressed in Chapter 21 may be used as often as you wish. They include:

- Literature to introduce or reteach

- Video clips

- T-Charts

- Discussion

- Role playing

- Social/Political action

- Celebrations

Because the focal point of Stage 1 of the *ITI Classroom Stages of Implementation* is creating a bodybrain-compatible teaching/learning environment through use of the Lifelong Guidelines and LIFESKILLS, the content examples for the instructional strategies in both chapters 20 and 21 are those for teaching the Lifelong Guidelines and LIFESKILLS. The content for Chapters 23 and 24 is drawn from the two books describing how to implement the Lifelong Guidelines and LIFESKILLS: *Tools for Citizenship and Life: Using the ITI Lifelong Guidelines and LIFESKILLS in Your Classroom* by Sue Pearson and *Character Begins at Home: Family Tools for Teaching Character and Values* by Karen D. Olsen and Sue Pearson.

Chapter 22 discusses strategies for ensuring that the basic skills are effectively taught.

Chapter 19:
Integrating Basic Skills

Misconception About ITI

A major misconception about the ITI model is that it is fine for the content areas, such as science and social studies, but that it doesn't teach the basic skills—reading, writing, and arithmetic. This is not true. The ITI model does, however, recommend that these basic skills are best taught through the content, as a means to an end, not as an end in themselves.

Why? Because brain research is very clear: Meaningful content makes learning easier and more memorable. The subskills of reading, the definitions of parts of speech, and rules of thumb for writing an essay come across as dry rules unless given a meaningful context and engaging, stimulating, experienceable content. And rules seldom grab and sustain our attention like a nice, juicy, transferrable concept (transferrable to something we want to do in our own life), or learning to write a business letter so that we can lobby for governmental actions consistent with our firmly held beliefs, or going on an exciting field trip.

Teaching the Basic Skills Is Serious Business

As discussed in Chapter 17, teaching basic skills is serious business. And even though test scores across the nation strongly suggest that we need to change how we teach the 3Rs, experience suggests that bridges shouldn't be burned until we are on solid footing on the other side.[1] In other words, even the old ways of teach reading that weren't as effective as we would like are better than no way of teaching reading. Half a loaf—or in this case, half a year's growth in reading—is better than no loaf or no growth at all.

Are we arguing here for business as usual? Absolutely not. But we do argue for taking the high road when planning changes in how we teach the basic skills. Before you abandon the old, make sure that you have rigorous understanding of the new and enough training to achieve outcomes for students as least as great as what you had been using before. This is not a time for leap of faith. The futures of your students hang in the balance. A year or two of on-the-job training until we reach a reasonable standard of mastery is grossly unfair to our students; they have but one shot at first and second grade. They can't wait for us to pull things together; the river of life for them continues to move them onward.

Thus, our advice is to explore first how to use the high-interest *being there* and immersion experiences of the theme to *practice* using an area of basic skills. Then, when fully trained and prepared, begin to teach basic skills through the theme. Note that the *ITI Classroom Stages of Implementation* is organized this way (see Appendix A).

This chapter describes five ways to integrate the basic skills in the context of other subjects and real life:

- Full integration of all subjects and skills in the "Classroom of the 21st Century" (see pages 19.2-19.10)

- An integrated day to teach a basic skill—division—in a single day (see pages "A Concept-in-a-Day," 19.11-19.

- How to anchor math in real life (see "'Anchor' Math," pages 19.14-

- A list of 50+ real writing experiences that can be used to practice or teach writing skills (see pages 19.17-19.18)

- How to organize a yearlong research project (see page 19.18)

Classroom of the 21st Century*

Skills are taught in the Integrated Thematic Instruction classroom but they do not drive the curriculum. Content drives the curriculum and skills are taught as they relate to the content, as their usefulness becomes apparent. Before public education took hold in this country, many young boys were apprenticed to skilled laborers in a variety of fields. This is a perfect example of the power of relevant context for learning skills. As they learned a trade, boys learned all the skills associated with that trade, and there was never a doubt as to "Why?"

Skills only have meaning within the larger context of their usefulness. When they are useful, they are learned. Children do not learn to speak because adults want them to; children learn to speak because it is useful. This is true of adults as well; we know it from our own experience. I took five years of Spanish while attending public schools, but it wasn't until I moved to an ethnically diverse area that I needed to know Spanish. Suddenly it became useful; there was a reason to learn a second language. Reason and purpose accelerate learning.

Thus, skills are taught in the brain-compatible classroom, but only within the context of the content of the integrated theme. The difference is that skills do not drive the curriculum. Instead, they are placed within a meaningful framework. For example, learning the sound "a" in isolation has no meaning without the larger context of a word. The word "heel" only has meaning within the larger context of a sentence because the "heel" of a shoe is different from the "heel" who broke last night's date. Likewise,

---

* Pages 25.1-25.10 are taken directly from the ITI book, *Classroom of the 21st Century* by Robert Ellingsen. This book is a companion to a video of the same title. Both are published by Susan Kovalik & Associates (see order form at the back of this book). Together, they document Robert's classroom application of the ITI model as a framework for integrating all basic skills and content areas. Used with the written permission of the publisher.

learning how to compute the area of rectangles has no meaning without the context of a useful application such as "How many cans of this color paint do we need for this part of the room?" Without the context of the theme, the mastery of the skill becomes meaningless. The question invariably will be asked, "Why?" and "Because I told you so" is not a satisfactory answer.

So how does one make something like computing the area of rectangles useful within a theme? I teach the skill within a meaningful framework. Each year my class performs a Shakespearean play. As part of our preparation, the class designs and paints stage flats of scenery for our performance. Each of the five flats are 4' by 8' and the students need to construct scale drawings of their set design. Students find the area formula a useful tool as they construct their own three-dimensional, miniature sets. Frank Smith states that "learning is incidental."[2] Learning takes place within the course of everyday, real activities. It is within the context of this real activity—building a stage set—that students learn the geometric concept of area.

Reading

You learn by doing. A child does not learn to speak by learning about speaking; a child learns to speak by speaking. So, first and foremost, when teaching reading, let students read. And since usefulness is a prime motivator, what the students read must relate to the topic being explored in some meaningful way. Sara Zimet notes that conventional "reading texts emphasize skill, and reading is taught for the sake of the skill itself [whereas] we need to shift our emphasis from 'reading to learn to read' to 'reading about something meaningful while learning to read.' By emphasizing the process to the exclusion of meaningful ideas, we sacrifice the raison d'etre for learning to read."[3]

Children's fantasies and realities are so much more exciting than the boring words and scenes of most basal reading texts. For this reason my method has been to use children's novels to teach reading. As I plan my year theme, I brainstorm possibilities for the reading component. During the PATHFINDERS component of my theme, the novel I selected was *My Side of the Mountain*[4] by Jean George. It is the story of a boy who ventures into the wilderness and learns to survive without the trappings of modern life—a perfect fit with our study of Lewis and Clark and the other pathfinders of history.

All students should have equal access to rich, significant literature. Oftentimes educators separate their poor readers from their good readers. And where are these poor readers placed? Into a basal text that is even more simplistic and contrived than the one from which they were pulled, thereby compounding their difficulty in searching for meaning. **ALL students should have an enriched curriculum.**

All students of all abilities in my classroom read *My Side of the Mountain*, some with ease, some with difficulty, but all with fascination and enjoyment. Each day a selection is assigned. Students make the free choice of whether to read silently, with a partner, or orally in a group. The only requirement is that they meet with the teacher at least once a week for an oral reading check. When students are entrusted with the power to make their own choices, they tend to self-select the appropriate placement given their ability. My poorer readers chose to meet with me daily. But when they came to reading group, they were joined by other students making the choice to read orally, a heterogeneous group full of good reading models. Why do we put poor readers only with poor readers? Who will model correct reading behaviors for them?

Heterogeneous reading groups, in addition to being academically sound, have the extra benefit of building self-esteem. There is no "dumb group." It builds the sense that "we're all in this together" and encourages understanding and acceptance of individual differences.

Granted, there are students who can legitimately benefit from extra help. I do think moving to a more enriched curriculum will eliminate the need for some diagnostic/prescriptive services, but not all. What about those students? They do need extra help but that help should be **offered within the bounds of the curriculum and tied closely to the theme** of their classroom experience. And the single most meaningful place for a child is with the classroom teacher. Pull-out programs should be avoided at all cost. I propose, instead, a **pull-in program** where specialists work with students within a self-contained, safe, supportive classroom. Logistics can be a problem to overcome but we need to do what is best for kids, not what is most convenient for the bureaucracy.

Comprehension. The best way to learn to read is to read. But there is more to reading than correctly decoding words. The Spanish alphabet is phonetically regular and I have learned my sounds well. I can go into many classrooms, pick up a Spanish reader and pronounce word after word with only the slightest Anglo accent. But am I reading? Correctly calling words with no understanding is not reading, and phonics, while a helpful tool, is only that—a tool for correct decoding. Phonics does not concern itself with understanding. How is comprehension addressed in the ITI classroom? Not with worksheets.

I propose to involve students more actively in the comprehension process. Once more I find Bloom's Taxonomy to be an amazing aid in this respect—simple to use, but powerful. Daily, after reading period, the class comes together for a discussion of the day's selection. A copy of Bloom's Taxonomy is placed on the overhead and the class uses this to discuss the story. This copy is the only comprehension worksheet the students receive during the year. At first, the teacher may use it to ask questions, but, with practice, students become quite adept at generating the questions and at knowing the level at which they are being asked to think. This is metacognition at its best—knowing how to learn and knowing when you are doing it.

Once a week I obtain a written record of their work by having learning teams brainstorm questions, present them to the class, and choose a specified number to answer. Students then write the

questions and answers neatly, in complete sentences, and with correct spelling and capitalization—a much more active approach than that elicited by most commercially produced worksheets. How, you might ask, do students complete a neat and grammatically correct paper? First, they are held accountable for it. Expectations are everything. Second, in the absence of worksheets, students have many more opportunities for real writing; the worksheet doesn't do the writing for them. And finally, no one is left without support. Students have their cooperative learning team to assist them and the teacher, as part of the learning team, is constantly circling the room, encouraging and giving **immediate feedback.**

Reading Skills. Although teaching the skills of reading can sometimes be frustrating and tedious, we must accept that these skills are there to support reading. However, if a skill does not directly aid a student in decoding and comprehending of a passage, then its viability needs to be seriously questioned. Skills for the sake of skills—because it's in the workbook—is a grave mistake. For example, I have clear and painful memories of trying to teach students how to identify accent marks in words with a program that even went so far as to differentiate between primary and secondary accents. The irony, of course, is that the students could already read the words. Nevertheless, they failed in that all-important skill: the fine distinctions in stress. The question remains: "Was the skill useful?" And a further question continues to haunt us: "How many of these workbook skills, which consume such a large part of a student's learning time, are necessary to produce successful and lifelong readers?" Teaching skills is not teaching reading; reading teaches reading—the practice of extracting meaning from print. Skills can be a useful aid, but only within a larger context, and only when they are useful. They are not an end in themselves.

When skills are taught when they make the most sense—when they are needed to understand something—they are learned more easily and are more readily wired into long-term memory. For example, teaching students how to use an index when they begin their research projects and find using an index a helpful way to locate information; time lines are taught as students study historical events; and outlining is taught as students write research papers. Workbooks, which present skills in an arbitrary fashion, are both unnecessary and unproductive.

Parts of Speech. We all teach them. Apparently students never learn them--why else do we ALL teach them? My class is introduced to parts of speech during our GEOGRAPHY component. As students study our state, they find one location for each letter of the alphabet, plot it on a grid, compute miles and kilometers from our location, and use that location in an ABC book. This provides ample opportunity for work in a wide variety of skills: alphabetical order, map skills, and mathematical computations. Students then write their own ABC books, using a pattern established in the *Oregon ABC Book*: "Adrian Albright, the adorable actress, anticipates acclaim in Ashland's amphitheater."[5] Children identify proper nouns for people and places, adjectives to describe the nouns, verbs to state the action, and adverbs to describe the verbs. And all this is done within the context of their own writing, about locations they have studied in their home state. This is the teachable moment, that point in time when students are most in tune with the learning. Why? Because it is useful, it is creative, and it is emotional—there is a healthy dose of fun as students stretch their imaginations.

As I developed the skill component of the reading program, I found that the skills are repeated in a cycle. Of the thirty skills taught in the intermediate level of the Houghton-Mifflin reading series, twenty-one are taught at two grade levels, and an amazing seventeen are taught at all three grade levels. Why, then, must students be placed in ability groups, forever labeled, with no chance for reprieve, when all levels are working on the same skills?

In the ITI classroom, skills are introduced in the large group, students work on the skill only until they have mastered it, and students continue working on that skill until it is mastered. There is no low group, middle group, or high group. Instead there is a guide word group, a syllabification group, etc. Within these temporary, flexible groups are students with a wide range of achievement levels, all of whom need practice with the same skill. Once again, the "we're all in this together" attitude is developed.

Artificial demarcations convenient to the authorities are torn down and students work in heterogeneous settings.

Vocabulary. Vocabulary development is an ongoing process. In a meaningful classroom environment it happens continuously at an informal level, just as children originally learn the spoken language. "All children except the most severely deprived or handicapped acquire a vocabulary of over 10,000 words during the first four or five years of their lives. At the age of four they are adding to their vocabulary at the rate of twenty new words a day. By seven this rate may have increased to nearly thirty words. . . . By late adolescence the average vocabulary is at least 50,000 words."[6] How is this done? Not by worksheets, not by looking words up in the dictionary, not by formal instruction. It is done because the brain is the organ for learning; it will learn what is useful. The 50,000 words children pick up by adolescence are words they find to be useful.

The key to formal vocabulary instruction is to make it useful and meaningful to the student. The obvious method in an ITI classroom is to closely tie vocabulary instruction to the theme.

Current events are an integral part of the brain-compatible classroom because the brain-compatible classroom focuses on the real world. Knowledge of current events is essential for the politically active populace of a democracy. The brain-compatible classroom is the classroom that prepares students to take on this role as active citizens.

OREGON TODAY is the name given to the current events strand of our curriculum. Each morning one student is responsible for sharing an article related to the theme. That article then becomes part of our classroom collection folder where all articles are filed and classified. Once a week an article is chosen to be the class' reading selection for the day. Learning teams read, mindmap, and discuss the article. They are also responsible for choosing the one word that interests them most. Learning teams share their word with the class and the class then has five new vocabulary words, one word per learning team. These words are entered into the students' personal dictionaries and onto our Oregon Today vocabulary chart for continual reinforcement. Whenever a student finds that word in any other reading, a star is added to the chart. A very simple approach but, tied to the theme, it becomes meaningful. And the probability that the word is learned and stored increases.

Writing

A pattern is forming: children learn to speak by speaking and to read by reading. Little wonder, then, that children learn to write by writing. That is not to say that merely writing, with no skill instruction, will produce literate citizens. But we do know that heavy doses of skill instruction, separated from the meaningful context of real writing, do not work. The literate student must write every day. And that writing must have purpose and an audience.

The journal approach to daily writing is an exceptional example of real writing assignments. Students keep a notebook full of their own musing: dreams, concerns, and questions, a daily record of their lives. This is real writing in its truest sense because it is student-centered and student-directed. There are no contrived topics or arbitrary limits on length. Writing is useful because it becomes a vehicle by which children connect with the outside world, taking what is within and giving it form and substance.

I have had much success with this method, yet I know that not all teachers have. When I've compared notes with my colleagues for whom it hasn't worked, I find one noticeable difference: I write back to the author—not just a few sprinklings of "great" or "good point," but written feedback of significant length and meaning. If a child writes to me about his/her pets, I write about my pets. If a child writes about favorite foods, I write about mine. The journal becomes a dialogue between us; it establishes rapport. Finally, it provides a meaningful context within which to place skill instruction.

I recommend several different approaches to writing. Journals are but one component of the writing program, writing folders are another. Journals are daily jottings. The writing folder is for long-term story development and is worked on every day during

WRITERS' WORKSHOP, a time when students learn the writing process: pre-writing, rough draft, revision, editing, and publishing. Children use the skills developed during writers' workshop to develop their own creative writing. Works in progress are filed in the writing folder until that time the student determines the piece is ready for publication. Occasionally specific assignments are given if they fit the theme, but more often students are engaged in constructing stories from their own imaginations. Many states have ongoing summer institutes where teachers learn the writing process. The key is that the teacher also becomes a writer and models for the class his own ongoing work. My students assisted me in writing my story "Reggie at the Bat." The students, in a sense, become apprenticed to the teacher as author.

Teaching Writing Skills

The daily journal and the writing folder provide the structure for direct instruction of skills. They are the blueprint. Once they are in place, the skills, which are the building materials, can be used to construct literacy. But where would they be placed with no blueprint as a guide? Teaching skills such as capitalization and noun/verb agreement, apart from any meaningful writing, is like giving the carpenter the 2' x 4's and asking him/her to build a house without a plan. The product would be a haphazard, rickety construction, destined to come tumbling down and ill-fitting the needs of its inhabitants.

Once the framework of real writing is in place, skill instruction can proceed. A variety of methods can be used. Basal English series offer pages of practice, and there is nothing wrong with their occasional use as need dictates. But why go through the book cover to cover? Why let the textbook publisher dictate the curriculum when it is the classroom teacher who is the educational expert? It is the teacher who, having student writing in hand, can diagnose and prescribe skill instruction appropriate to the needs of each particular group of writers.

If, in their writing, students are writing conversations, and writing them incorrectly, then that is the teachable moment—the appropriate time to teach the correct use of quotation marks. If certain words are consistently misspelled, then they become a part of that student's spelling list. If letters are continually formed illegibly, then handwriting instruction is called for.

The theme itself may provide opportune times to address particular skills. During our Shakespeare unit, the class play is *A Midsummer Night's Dream.* This is the perfect opportunity to introduce apostrophes. The play's title becomes a meaningful "hook" on which to attach the skill instruction.

To ensure that skill instruction proceeds at a systematic pace I have a daily editing practice modeled after the DAILY ORAL LANGUAGE series (D.O.L.). Admittedly, the name is a bit misleading. A more accurate title might be DAILY WRITTEN LANGUAGE, as the editing task is with paper and pencil. The program's title stems from the fact that once the written editing assignment is complete, it is processed orally.

A short selection, full of errors, is placed on the board most mornings when students enter the classroom. They know from the posted daily agenda that their first task is to edit this selection. Once again, cooperation is encouraged. Later in the morning the class meets together and orally processes the passage, finally recopying a fully corrected final version. This happens over time until the majority of the class has mastered the skill and can independently write a perfect copy the first time. New writing skills are then introduced, taken from common errors occurring in journals and writing folders. Those students who still have not mastered the original skill continue to meet with me during Writers' Workshop.

Math

For five years I had avoided integrating mathematics. I was tied to the text, my own math anxiety holding me back. Finally, I had no choice if I wanted a fully integrated classroom—math was the only subject still on the outside. What I found, to my amazement, was that math is the simplest of all skill areas to integrate. All that is needed is statistics, real-life numbers to work with. How lucky! Statistics are everywhere!

Cobblestone magazine is a history magazine for young people. In September, 1980, the entire issue was devoted to Lewis and Clark. It became our "basal text" for the week, the base of study for all subjects, including math. It is a rich source of statistics about the Lewis and Clark expedition. Those below are only a small sampling of the statistics available, providing many opportunities for real world "story problems." But, given the full immersion of the students into reliving the Lewis and Clark expedition, they become more than mere "story problems"; they become real-life applications.

Available Statistics:

- Lewis and Clark started their journey up the Missouri River on May 14, 1804.

- The entire central basin of North America was purchased from the French for four cents an acre, or a total of $15,000,000.

- A Scotsman named Alexander Mackenzie had published an account of the same region in 1793.

- The Great Falls were a series of five large waterfalls that stretched over 15 miles on the Missouri River.

- From beginning to end, the walk over the Rocky Mountains took three-and-a-half months.

- On their return trip, Lewis and Clark separated for six weeks to explore different regions.

- Lewis and Clark returned to St. Louis on September 23, 1806.

Problems to Be Solved Based on the Available Statistics:

- How many years ago did Lewis and Clark begin exploring the Louisiana Purchase?

- How many acres of land did Thomas Jefferson purchase from France?

- Approximately how many miles were between each of the Great Falls of the Missouri River?

- Assuming that all months are thirty days long, how many days did it take Lewis and Clark to cross the Rocky Mountains?

- Using your previous answer, how many weeks did it take Lewis and Clark to cross the Rocky Mountains?

- How many days were Lewis and Clark separated during their trip?

- 30 days have September, April, June, and November. All the rest have 31, excepting February, which has 28. Knowing this, what was the total number of days of the Lewis and Clark expedition?

This last problem is the most difficult of all. Very few of my fourth graders answered it correctly at first. But I've never seen such excitement, motivation, and problem-solving strategies as when students attempt it.

Problems such as these form the core of THEME MATH, a term I use with students to distinguish it from other components of the math program. Theme math uses **real-world** problems closely tied to the content. Students attack these problems with more motivation than the artificial problems of basal series. The interest is built in; the students have some curiosity to find out more about whom and what they have been studying.

The amount of thinking involved is awesome when compared to a basal text. Students need to identify the problem, find the data necessary to solve the problem, identify the operation needed to solve the problem, and then finally compute the answer. What's more, the statistics are not conveniently listed for them as they are for you here. Students search for them within the context of the historical narrative.

Theme math is a prime motivator for students to learn mathematical skills. Suddenly there is a reason for memorizing those basic facts, to KNOW—**to really know** everything about the Lewis and Clark expedition. In addition, theme math is an excellent way to build conceptual understanding of the four operations (addition, subtraction, multiplication, and division). Students develop a sense of what addition looks like, how it "feels" and sounds compared to the other operations. *And all the while they are working in the realm of the real world, with real numbers*—**APPLICATION!**

It is essential that the teacher understand the purpose of theme math. It is to build *conceptual understanding*, not to drill on memorization of facts and computations. Students who have not memorized their multiplication facts are still capable of understanding the concept of multiplication. *Memorization of facts should not be a prerequisite to opportunities for applying concepts.* If anything, building the concepts should come first, giving the student the meaningful framework before the individual skill bits are put into place.

Math Skills. Mathematical computation is an essential life skill. Theme math does not replace that. But it does enhance computation by giving it meaning and purpose. Computation is still addressed. In fact, within this meaningful context of the theme, computation is learned much more readily.

DAILY ORAL MATH (D.O.M.) is one way to reinforce math skills. Similar to daily oral language (the daily drill in written language), it is a short and sweet math review. Alternating with D.O.L., it may consist of four problems reviewing the four operations, or it may be other math skills more closely aligned with the day's thematic activities. Skills such as a review of the formula for computing area during our Shakespearean set design, or using a scale of miles to compute distance during our GEOGRAPHY component can be reinforced during D.O.M. The daily agenda points out that this is one of the first tasks to be completed. Later in the day, student volunteers solve the problems for the class, modeling correct form and computation.

Day in the Life Of

So how does it all come together? How does the teacher orchestrate all the various elements of a brain-compatible classroom? The ITI model is truly unique in that it draws from a wide variety of excellent approaches and sources and synthesizes them into a coherent, seamless whole. Language experience is an excellent approach to teaching reading, but what about math? The university sponsored writing projects teach writing in a brain-compatible way, but what about social studies? Math Their Way is an experiential and hands-on approach to mathematics instruction, but what about science? The ITI approach seeks to break down these artificial walls between curricular areas, take the best from each, and infuse brain-compatible instruction into all subjects for a truly integrated whole. And it does so with a profound respect for the professional expertise of the classroom teacher.

Flexibility is the key word in planning a fully integrated day, week, month, or year. School schedules are arbitrary demarcations of time and **are highly brain-antagonistic.** Lessons should not be forced into the artificial constraints of a set time period; **the content should determine the schedule.** The self-contained classroom offers the greatest opportunity for fully integrating subject areas.

I hesitate to share specifics of a daily schedule because the model will find a unique implementation in every classroom. **The power of the model lies in its adaptability to individual teaching styles.** The graphic on this page is my plan for the week. A plan could take many forms. One a picture of a typical day in the life of a brain-compatible classroom starts a schedule for flexible frameworks to be altered as content dictates. My 9:00 A.M. starting time

and a 3:30 P.M. closing time made it possible for me to think of the instructional day as being divided into four blocks: two morning periods and two afternoon periods.

I recommend that you begin the day with the theme. It provides students with a focal point for the day's activities. In a classroom not yet fully integrated, this would mean beginning the day with the content area on which the theme is based, e.g., a classroom whose theme is "Entomology" would begin the day with science. The benefit of the fully integrated classroom is that all subjects relate to the theme and the day may begin with whatever subject area makes the most sense within the context of the day's topic. What the teacher organizes is a blend of common elements which maintain a sense of stability and comfort for students, intermixed with a daily flow of ever-changing events and topics — a miniature slice of real life. Here is an example:

SOCIAL STUDIES

KEY POINTS
Lewis and Clark

COBBLESTONE
History Magazine

ART

CLAY SCUPTURE
Pathfinders

WATERCOLOR
Birds of Oregon

MATH

LEWIS & CLARK
Story Problems

D.O.M.
Scale of Miles

LEWIS AND CLARK

JOURNALS

ORNITHOLOGY

BUSINESS LETTER
Wildlife Organization

BOTANY

WRITING

MY SIDE OF THE
MOUNTAIN

OREGON TODAY
L & C Sculpture

THE JOURNALS OF
LEWIS AND CLARK

SCIENCE

READING

Generally, I begin my day[7] with a language arts block. When students enter the classroom, they are greeted by me personally, a daily agenda detailing exactly what will occur that day, and background music playing softly to enhance thinking. The rule is quiet study as students begin their tasks: DAILY ORAL LANGUAGE and/or DAILY ORAL MATH to review skills, then on to silent and/or oral reading of the day's selection, followed by independent work with ongoing INQUIRY projects. At some point I bring the class together for stretching, aerobics, and relaxation—important techniques which help focus students' bodies and minds on the topic for the day. This is followed by a discussion of the day's reading based on Bloom's Taxonomy and a large group discussion and correction of the skills review. Finally, during OREGON TODAY, the current events article for the day is shared.

The second morning block is reserved for science and social studies. This is when students receive and work with the key points of instruction. Lecture, reading, discussion, films, experiments, and inquiries all receive equal emphasis as conceptual understanding of the major thematic components is built. Each day sees a different focus. Perhaps a lecture and reading on the key points early in the week, moving toward more interactive pursuits by the end of the week, with possible closure of the week, topic, or entire component by Friday.

The first afternoon block is reserved for mathematics. This is equally divided between THEME MATH for concept building and MATH GROUPS for computation practice. Oftentimes the week begins and ends with THEME MATH to provide a frame within which the rest of math instruction is placed.

The final afternoon block returns to language arts. A skill is introduced or reinforced with the large group. This is followed by a large group WRITERS' WORKSHOP where works in progress are shared and elements of good writing are discussed. Students then move on to independent writing time, engaging in real writing activities such as JOURNAL, letters, and creative writing of their own choice. During this independent time the teacher is free to confer with individuals and/or conduct SKILLSHOPS, the small, temporary, and flexible skill groups.

What about other subject areas such as art, music, and computers? They all find a place in the schedule as appropriate. Sketching and watercolor techniques are taught when the day's reading concerns that subject, e.g., Sam's sketching of his falcon. Students work with clay after reading and discussing a newspaper article about a local sculptor and his Lewis and Clark statues. Pioneer songs and instruments are used to prepare for the class' Oregon Trail adventure. Computers are used during the writing process as students edit and publish their work. Computers are also used when software exists that enhances understanding of the topic, such as the Oregon Trail or Pathfinders simulation games. Everything fits. It's just a new fit. In the traditional classroom, content is made to fit the schedule; in the ITI classroom, **the schedule is made to fit the content.**

A self-contained, heterogeneous classroom is a superior design for the ITI classroom. There are fewer interruptions to fragment the day, the sense of belonging is more fully developed, and students aren't segregated according to ability. Because the mathematical problems are selected mostly with an eye to their meaningfulness, assignments and group collaboration guidelines are set up to ensure that all students, of varying degrees of ability, experience success. Problems are solved within the learning team and calculators are allowed.

For a fuller inside look into Robert Ellingsen's approach to integrated thematic instruction using the ITI model, see his video and book of the same name: *Classroom of the 21st Century* by Robert Ellingsen. Available through Books for Educators. See the back of this book.

Orchestrating a Concept-in-a-Day: Long Division*

It is estimated that it takes two years and three months for students to learn long division. The division facts are introduced in the third grade, the algorithm is introduced in the fourth grade, and again in the fifth and sixth grades. From year to year, the same instructional pattern, even into the basic math courses in junior and senior high—the teacher does a problem on the board, the class does a number of "practice" problems at their desks, and then students are responsible for completing ten to twenty problems for homework.

While attending a week-long Susan Kovalik Model Teaching Program, Martha Kaufeldt was challenged to address this problem by orchestrating the learning environment and curriculum in such a way that it would be possible to INTRODUCE and have the students achieve MASTERY of the CONCEPT AND COMPUTATION OF LONG DIVISION **IN A SINGLE DAY!**

Martha's work pioneered the notion of teaching a major concept in a single day. Since her Long Division Day in 1986, thousands of students across the country have been able to master division in a single day using this approach.

Here is her story.

---

* The description of orchestrating a concept in a day, pages 25.10-25.13, is a summary of Martha Kaufeldt's experience as described in her book *I Can Divide and Conquer: A Concept in a Day!*, a teachers' handbook for implementing Division Day in their own classroom. The book is a companion to the videotape of the same name published by Susan Kovalik & Associates. See the order form at the back of this book.

For the first three months of school, my thirty-three fourth and fifth grade students worked on sharpening their accuracy in addition, subtraction, and multiplication. Division facts were memorized by rote. Seventeen other fifth and sixth grade students in our school were recommended by their teachers as students who had mastered the skills of multiplication but had failed to master division.

The day before Division Day all fifty students met. I led them verbally through some relaxation techniques and also asked them to see their own success in learning long division. They all took a pretest in division and were given encouraging words about what would happen the next day.

Overview of the Day's Activities

Theme for the day: I CAN DIVIDE AND CONQUER!

In planning the day, I knew I had to address several important areas: how to ensure positive performance, the format for each activity station, and methods of orchestrating learning.

Elements Used to Program Positive Performance

- Students saw their success
- Each student received a "goodie" box with pencil, slate, and name tag
- Students were divided into groups of five. Group building activities included adopting a famous mathematician who would serve as the group mascot for the day
- Incentives were given at every other station
- Mini-stickers were given to anyone who ASKED FOR HELP
- Direct instruction was limited to 11-16 minutes per hour

- Group work was provided at each station (45 minutes)
- Relaxation periods were provided throughout the day
- Lunch was provided by parents. Pizza was divided into different numbers of slices
- Each student earned an "I CAN DIVIDE AND CONQUER" badge and a certificate at the end of the day
- Warm, loving, enthusiastic adult leaders were always available

Format at Each Station

To simplify training of volunteers and to ensure students had the opportunity to think through each activity, the format for each station was the same: tell, show, solve, and check. Each process is written as a direction to the adult responsible for a station.

Tell

- Read problem aloud—(every student)
- Discuss what the problem is asking or describing. Have students restate in own words
- Point out (ask students to identify) DIVIDEND and DIVISOR
- Ask students to close eyes while you help them visualize the problem. Use a soothing voice while using lots of descriptive words. Ask students to see themselves in the picture, doing the sorting or dividing
- Draw students' attention to manipulatives they will be using, e.g., beads, beans, etc. Point out that they are substitutes for the real thing

Show

Have students work out the problem with the manipulatives. If possible, each student should have his/her own set of manipulatives. If not, work it out cooperatively. Have students:

- Repeat the problem two or more times if necessary until they can confidently show the problem
- Identify quotient and remainders, if any (have a special place for the "remainder" to be placed)

Solve

As each student solves a problem, have them:

- Demonstrate how a problem is written as a number sentence
- Identify terms
- Begin a step-by-step approach to the algorithm.—divide, multiply, subtract, bring down—and frequently relate their computation to what has been done with manipulatives
- Have students work out problem on graph paper for accuracy
- Ask each to turn to his/her partner and ask the partner to explain the problem in "MATH SPEAK"

Check

- Demonstrate how to check by multiplying and adding remainder
- If there is time, make variations of the problem and ask students to solve
- Write a comment in each student passport if you feel student has mastered that problem

- If the student needs more help, continue working, or ask the student to come back at free-choice time, or direct student to a roving helper

- Repeat center to next group. Give incentive rewards to students in second center

Methods of Orchestrating Learning

Because our Divide and Conquer Day was just that, a single day, I needed to vary the ways to help students learn. My strategies included:

- Using the Library Media Center with assistance from the Media Specialist

- Providing 26 different learning stations, each with concrete examples to illustrate concepts

- Providing choices at those stations students were allowed to choose among

- Adhering to two management standards for the day: No Put-Downs and Active Listening

- Providing a snack station (set up by parents, graham crackers and juice)

- Having students work through recesses and taking breaks as needed

- Organizing students into groups of five

- Recruiting and training at least 15 adults to help: parents, aides, student teachers, and community volunteers

- Soliciting addition money—mini-grants and parent donations

Maximizing Input to the Brain

Each segment of the day was designed to maximize input to the brain. Every activity and presentation provided visual, auditory, tactile, and kinesthetic sensory input. In addition, students were allowed to make selections that would maximize the kind of sensory input that would best assist them.

Visual

The problem to be solved was presented on the bulletin board and in the student handbook. Students used manipulatives to SEE the problem.

Auditory

Every station leader explained each problem. Students in turn explained the problem using Math Speak. A hand-jive was developed for the mathematical algorithm of division—first you divide, then multiple, subtract, and bring it (the remainder) down.

Tactile

Each of the 26 stations used different sets of manipulatives. Most were common classroom items as well as shells, buttons, small cars, and dominoes.

Kinesthetic

Kinesthetic activities included Division P.E., Division Drama, Division Art, Division Music, and a hand jive (a set of hand motions representing the algorithm of division—first you divide, then multiple, subtract, and bring it (the remainder) down.

Choices

Choices for students included art, music or drama stations, flexible environment breaks when needed, and more help on a one-to-one basis. Feeling that they were in control of their learning truly empowered students to feel that they "conquered division."

Outcomes

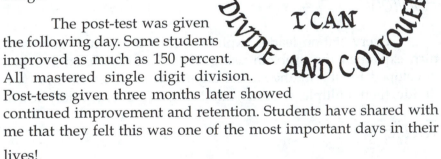

At the end of the *seven hour day* (yes, they came early and stayed late!), students received a certificate and a badge.

The post-test was given the following day. Some students improved as much as 150 percent. All mastered single digit division. Post-tests given three months later showed continued improvement and retention. Students have shared with me that they felt this was one of the most important days in their lives!

To see how brain research can be used to teach a single concept and how to apply it to mastery—and to long-term memory—see Martha's video and book of the same name: *I Can Divide and Conquer.* Available through Books for Educators. See the back of this book.

"Anchor" Math*

Not only did Leslie Hart coin the term "brain-compatible," he has also given us ways to "anchor" math to real-life experiences of children. His book, *Anchor Math: An Informal Book for All Who Teach Elementary Math and Want to Greatly Increase Student Achievement,*[7] is a treasure trove of wonderfully simple but instantly doable ways of making numbers and mathematics real to students.

Hart illustrates how to teach math in ways that create "mental programs." For a starting point, Hart says that it may be helpful, or at least intriguing, to think of math languages in three clusters.

Three Levels of Math Language

Practical Math

"Practical" math help us deal with the mostly concrete world of here and now, including all of our daily transactions, ordering, physical work, current data, etc. Examples: spent $144.75 for clothes, poured 12 cubic yards of concrete, produced 12,000 widgets, have 322 patients in the hospital.

Projective Math

"Projective" math helps us deal with what should, or could, or might happen. You plan out a trip, or work out estimates for a new business, or figure out how fast a rocket will likely be traveling within four minutes after launch, or how many cases of measles

---

* Pages 19.14-19.17 of this chapter are excerpted from *Anchor Math: An Informal Book for All Who Teach Elementary Math and Want to Greatly Increase Student Achievement* written by Leslie Hart and published by Books for Educators (see order form at the back of this book).

could occur within the next two years.

Investigative Math

"Investigative" math helps us dig out significant concepts by using mathematical techniques, e.g., trends and relationships, limits, and interactions. We might analyze election results to see the role played by racial concerns or gain some insight into an intricate chemical reaction. Included would be "game" math, essentially playing with numbers or mathematical elements for no immediate, "real" purpose.

Our purpose, or need, would determine which kind of math we do. Outside of classrooms, nobody does math without some purpose in mind. (That should make us think about some things we do in classrooms.)

THE CONCEPT OF "n-NESS"

Let us assume that a particular student is able to

– Name the digit . . . "five"

– Write the digit

– Count off objects to match the digit

It still may be true that the student does not have the sense of that number, a sense that we can call "five-ness." This sense of number constitutes one of the main foundational elements of grasping math and being able to do or interpret math with ease and confidence. Some people like to say that the student "feels" the number—which is all right if you like that expression.

Another way to put it is to say that the student has acquired a sense of "shape" for that number and a direct approach, not a "counting" approach.

For instance, if the student hears "five" and then counts one-two-three-four-five, that is a slow and cumbersome way, as compared with directly feeling "five-ness."

This sense of "n-ness" can readily be encouraged and developed by the teacher . . . and, as we shall see, it can be applied not only to the digits but to many numbers as they are "anchored." (The term "anchor" will be explained soon.)

Suppose we ask a 10-year-old student: "What is the difference between numbers 23 and 24?" One student may reply, "24 is one more than 23." That is correct but not the reply we are seeking.

Another student says, "Oh, they are very different! 23 is a stiff, awkward number while 24 is wonderful—it can be the hours in a day, or two dozen, or 4 x 6, or 3 x 8. . . . I can do all sorts of things with it." We can exult, "Ah, this student has really learned the "anchor" math way; this student feels the number." Numbers have shapes and characters and personalities, much as do people. Math becomes much more interesting and easier to do when "the numbers come alive!"

INTRODUCING "FLEXING"

We can use the problems of scanty three-ness to illustrate a simple technique for exploring numbers and patterns to which I'll attach the name "flexing." If you don't care for that term for this activity, use another or create your own. The idea is simple: *push the number, or pattern, or quantity around* in all the ways you can think of.

To flex 3, for example, you pose the question to students: how many ways can you arrange 3 markers? (The markers can be plastic chips, coins, beans, bottle caps or pebbles, or marks on paper or chalkboard. It's a good idea to vary the markers so that the patterns become attached to the number, not to the markers.)

On this page are some of the arrangements possible for 3. For higher numbers, the variations increase.

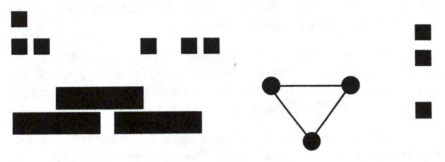

Flex . . . and find patterns.

Flexing has several purposes that enhance math learning. To begin with, of course, experience with three-ness can be greatly expanded. Of major general importance is encouraging students to *explore* on their own and as a member of a little team and at times and in ways hinted at or prompted by the teacher. Most of the time there should be no rules—anything goes. (For example, the counters can be stacked up; who said no?) At other times restraints can be imposed for the moment: the markers must be put in one dimension (or two or three), or must stay within a 2-inch square or other figure given (or must touch), and so on.

Such exploration contrasts with sitting meekly in place and doing only what one is told. Youngsters have a strong, genetic drive to *explore*—as we can plainly see by watching any normal toddler. Allowed to explore, learners find math far more interest-

ing, even absorbing. But we can go beyond that benefit, major as it is. In the conventional math schoolroom, numbers push children around. Many become a little gun-shy as they find the numbers given to them to deal with often overpower or intimidate them. In addition, they probably tremble before the "right answer," which must be obtained on penalty of some kind of disapproval or low mark. What a difference when we begin early on to show students that **they** can push numbers! And that, in many instances in math, there is no simple, right, carved-in-stone answer, or at least none that can be found without substantial investigation. When we set students free and "empower" them, they become almost different people. Further, they begin building understanding—from experience—of when a simple calculated answer will do and when it will not. That usually makes them much better at calculating when it is required because they acquire a feeling of confidence that lets their brains work at their best.

One more benefit may be discerned. Flexing gives room for a *creative* approach, as strict calculating does not. So, some students, who might otherwise be considered on the "dumb" side, suddenly show unexpected ability. This can help teachers abstain from judgments about students which are too quick and easy—and perhaps from making unneeded judgments at all.

Get into the act yourself. Can you suggest any flexes of 3 not shown here? Here's a sample of a hint: overlap.

Why do we all need to learn arithmetic? There's a good solid answer to that question: so that we can *measure*. That's what this math is for—measuring. We need to measure how much things cost, how much they weigh, how far away or big something is, how long a trip takes, how many watts a light bulb draws, where on the dial a favorite radio station will come in, our body temperature and much, much more.

To see Hart's vision of making math accessible to students, see *Anchor Math: An Informal Book for All Who Teach Elementary Math and Want to Greatly Increase Student Achievement.* Available through Books for Educators. See the back of this book.

Real Writing Experiences

Too many traditional writing assignments lack meaning and purpose—a topic of little interest to students and no real audience (except the teacher's and his/her grade book). Again, using brain research as home plate, no meaning, no engagement. The second most disliked assignment, following closely on the heels of fear of speaking before one's peers, is writing. And yet, the skill of expressing oneself in written form in a variety of circumstances is very important, allowing us to influence people and events.

How do we turn the tide? Often the writing experiences assigned to students are either creative writing or essays. In between these extremes are at least fifty real experiences that we may use in our lifetime.

Real-Life Writing Products

For writing to be meaningful and engaging, rather than contrived and boring, there must be a real purpose and a real audience. The list of writing products below illustrate the possibilities for meaningful writing assignments.

Letters to:
relative
friend
pen pal
editor of a paper
association
service club
congratulate

Letters of:
sympathy
recommendation

farewell
complaint
resignation
protest
regret
apology
independence
civil rights
peace

Speech:
sales pitch

sermon
state of the nation address
inauguration
judicial decision
nomination for office
political campaign

Newspaper article for:
front page story
editorial
advertisement
obituary
movie review
sports story
advice column

How-to manuals:
operate a specific piece of equipment (bicycle, skateboard, Nintendo, VCR)
survival (wilderness, on the subway, when visiting a foreign country)
airline safety instructions

Writing for an audience:
monologue
dialogue
poetry
eulogy
interview
(ten questions to ask a famous person)
recipe
menu
dictionary
encyclopedia entry

Writing for social/political action to:
president of the U.S.
federal or state legislative representative
governor
mayor
city council
school board

Special issues such as:
declaration of war
declaration of independence
civil rights
environmental protection

Advertisement for:
school lunch program
yearbook
magazine
newspaper
television
books or movies

Invitation to:
party (be specific)
dinner
weekend outing
conference (boy scout, girl scout, 4-H, etc.)
join an organization

The Personal Writing Binder

Encourage each student to have a writing binder with the student's own best examples of how to write, address, and respond to a variety of situations. In addition to the final product, all drafts preceding the final copy are included; these edited pages are good reminders of WHY something is done and the writing/editing skills he/she has developed.

This binder can be added to year by year so that a worthwhile reference will always be at your students' fingertips.

The Yearlong Research Project

Research is the ability to gather, analyze, organize, and eventually synthesize information about a topic. In the ITI classroom, we invite students of all ages to keep a yearlong collection binder filled with data about a topic of their choosing from within the yearlong theme. Their challenge: to become an expert on that topic.

By the end of the second week of school, all students select a topic for their yearlong research project. Two students may choose the same topic. What's important is that each student has content that fires their interest.

To help facilitate information gathering, ask parents to send their old magazines and newspapers to class. Provide at least 45 minutes a week for students to seek, read, and organize information. In addition, have at least 20 different addresses where students can write for information, such as those in the yellow pages of your phone book, the *Encyclopedia of Associations* at your public library, and so forth).

As they collect information, have the students:

- Highlight important points

- Create a mindmap of three new facts learned from each article

- Begin to organize the information into categories, such as letters sent and received, pictures (of projects, locations, people visited), audio or video interviews, and so forth. Eventually they will organize the information into a document with a table of contents, an index, a summation or executive summary of what was learned, and explanation of the most important content behind the summary.

- Share with a younger buddy every two weeks what they are learning

- By the end of the year, identify and invite to class their favorite resource person

- As a culminating activity, present the highlights of their research through a 10-minute multimedia presentation

The most important lessons from the yearlong research project are:

- Developing an awareness of what it means to truly know something about a topic, to become expert at it ("to know when you know and know when you don't know")

- Spawning a hobby or vocation and paving the way for lifelong interests

- Learning the necessary research skills to find, collect, organize, and synthesize information

Notes

1 During a mammoth school improvement effort in California during the mid and late 1970s called Early Childhood Education (ECE), the State Department of Education was pulled up short with a devastating discovery, one borne out by reform programs around the country. Whenever significant change is asked of teachers, the test scores of one-fourth of the teachers—or one-fourth of the schools—experience a drop in test scores for the first year or two before moving back upward and eventually surpassing the original benchmarks. This back sliding occurred primarily when teachers were ill-prepared to succeed with the new tools and methods but had been coaxed into leaving the old behind.

2 Smith, Frank, *Insult to Intelligence: The Bureaucratic Invasion of Our Classrooms*, New York: Arbor House, 1986.

3 Zimet, Sara Goodman, *What Children Read in School*, New York: Grune and Stratton, 1976.

4 George, Jean Craighead, *My Side of the Mountain*, New York: Penguin USA, 2000.

5 Torrence, Susan and Polansky, Leslie, *Oregon ABC Book*, T.P. Publications, 1983.

6 Smith, Frank, *Insult to Intelligence: The Bureaucratic Invasion of Our Classrooms*, New York: Arbor House, 1986.

7 This structure for organizing the day, illustrated on the next page, was developed by Robert Ellingsen, over a five-year period. It is offered here as a beginning point, not a model. Structure for the day should ensure that the basic skills are included on a daily basis but should also flow with the content and encourage full integration.

Chapter 20: Instructional Strategies Needed Every Day

When it comes to creating a bodybrain-compatible learning environment, a rich variety of instructional strategies is not a luxury, it is an absolute necessity. The strategies discussed in this chapter are critical and needed on a daily basis. They help you orchestrate your classroom proactively to avoid issues of classroom management often viewed in terms of discipline or "making" students behave better. As no one would want to follow a leader who had only one approach to getting a job done, few students become enthusiastic followers of a teacher whose sole method of teaching consists of lecture and worksheets. The focus should be on student learning and making your classroom a place that maximizes learning opportunities by acting on brain research findings.

Our best advice to you is to practice each of these strategies until you can implement each one at a moment's notice. Like any good mental program, they should become automatic and part of who you are as a teacher, not strategies that you prepare for and teach from cue sheets or other mental prods. All students want something worthwhile to do and learn that is fun in the process. The role of instructional strategies is just that.

Needed daily instructional strategies include:

- Modeling
- Target talk
- Daily agenda
- Discussion
- Direct instruction
- Literature
- Songs
- Movement
- Written procedures
- Graphic organizers
- Journal writing
- Clear performance criteria

Modeling

The single most powerful instructional strategy—regardless of what you are teaching—is modeling. As you already know, "Do what I do" is always more powerful than "Do what I say."

However, consistent modeling of the values and beliefs of a lifelong learner and a contributing citizen—core goals of the ITI model—are more easily said than done. Be prepared for some self-evaluation.

For example, when preparing to teach the Lifelong Guidelines and LIFESKILLS, reflect on your own conduct and be open to fine tuning any less than perfect manners, attitudes, and conduct. Muster the courage to make appropriate changes. Model for your students how to make changes in long-standing patterns of behavior. Remember, modeling isn't about being perfect, it's about showing others how to be the best human being possible—imperfect perhaps but always improving and always willing to make amends for mistakes.

To model is to commit oneself to making one's outer and inner life—words and actions—congruent and consistent.

Do As I Do

As teachers, we are one of the most powerful role models in the lives of our students. They study us carefully, whether they appear to or not. They watch to see if we are offering up only "token" lessons about being a learner or productive citizen or if we truly believe that such skills are important social and behavioral guidelines for *all* to follow—at home and elsewhere. Take time to visualize exactly the kind of person you want to be and what you want mirrored in your students' behaviors. Then, define and write

---

* Because target talk and modeling are the two most powerful ways to teach the Lifelong Guidelines and LIFESKILLS, both strategies must be fully mastered, i.e., must become second nature, automatic.

down strategies that will achieve these personal goals. Remember, you're on stage and actions always speak louder than words.

Learn to walk your talk. Also learn how to discuss with your students those times when you or they fall short. Again, modeling is not about being perfect but about continually improving.

Target Talk

The second most powerful strategy for teaching skills and behaviors such as the Lifelong Guidelines and LIFESKILLS is to acknowledge their use as they occur, taking advantage of the teachable moment—when the demonstration of, or need for, the appropriate behaviors or skills occurs naturally. Target talk* provides an opportunity for your students to understand what the behavior or skill looks like, sounds like, and feels like, and does not look, sound, or feel like, in varying situations. Such on-the-spot feedback helps build shared understandings of the Lifelong Guidelines and LIFESKILLS as a common language for talking about the behaviors that go with them. You'll be surprised how quickly your students, regardless of age, will make target talk comments about the behavior of others . . . and you. Be prepared!

The Goal of Target Talk

As Pat Belvel* points out, misbehavior is a teaching opportunity. It is a symptom that students do not know enough of the appropriate behaviors and/or know too many of the wrong behaviors. She developed "target talk" as a teaching tool to provide clear pictures of expected behaviors. As adapted for use in the ITI model, it is extremely effective for teaching students desirable behaviors and skills such as the Lifelong Guidelines and LIFESKILLS.

---

* Pat Belvel, TCI Consulting of San Jose, CA, specializes in trainings on classroom management and peer coaching.

Additional pictures of what a behavior or skill does and doesn't look like, sound like, and feel like are essential, especially when that behavior or skill is conceptually rich and its application to real life is complex. Mastering the Lifelong Guidelines and LIFESKILLS is a lifelong pursuit. For example, the attributes of truthfulness are not only complex but often subtle and frequently circumstance-dependent. Be patient.

Students need lots of opportunities for guided practice and heaps of patience—the ability to apply many of the nuances come with maturity. Learning to apply behaviors, attitudes, and/or skills, such as the Lifelong Guidelines and LIFESKILLS, is a lifetime endeavor, a work in progress. Have patience, knowing that social and self-awareness doesn't spring full blown but is developmental, unfolding over time. Continue the dialogue of target talk on a daily basis so that it becomes part of the fabric of classroom life.

How to Use Target Talk

Target talk is simple to use if you leave behind any habits of lavishing praise for behavior or overusing/misusing "I statements." For example, saying "I like the way [John] is using his time while he waits for . . . ," is a bondage statement that may control behavior for the moment but keeps the focus on pleasing the teacher rather than on students developing their own sense of what's right or wrong, appropriate or inappropriate. Target talk helps students develop responsibility for their behavior.

Target Talk in Three Steps. The three steps of target talk are short and to the point. For example:

- First, use the student's name. "Mike, . . ."

- Second, label the Lifelong Guideline/LIFESKILL that the student is using. "Mike, you were using the Lifelong Guideline of Active Listening. . ."

---

* Teachers should take care to ensure that no student is left out. Anonymous acknowledgements written by the teacher can ensure that all students receive an acknowledgement each week.

- Third, identify the action. "Mike, you were using the Lifelong Guideline of Active Listening when you faced the speaker, looked interested, and were able to tell in your own words what the speaker meant."

With these three steps, verbal feedback is quick and easy. The same steps should be used for short written acknowledgements—from the teacher and from other students. Written acknowledgements are important because they provide a long-lasting communication, a treasured note that can be referred to again and again. An easy device for capturing such written comments is the Acknowledgement Box.

Acknowledgement Box. Comments for the Acknowledgment Box can be written by both teacher* and students, signed or anonymous. They should be brief, nonjudgmental, and follow the three-step format described above: "I want to acknowledge Jack for using the Lifelong Guideline of No Put-Downs when he gave me useful feedback about grammar and spelling on my thank-you letter to the Governor." Whenever you have a spare moment during the day, such as when getting ready to move on to a new activity, simply pull three or four acknowledgements from the box and read them aloud to the class. Students are always eager to hear positive things others have to say about them.

Remember, the purpose of giving and receiving acknowledgements* is to encourage your students to reflect on their behavior and build their own internal dialogue about it. They will soon begin to feel the acknowledgement inside because they themselves said so, not the teacher, not another student; the student's own perspective then becomes the motivator and guide of behavior. This decreases the power of peer pressure now and later.

---

* Acknowledgements differ from compliments in subtle but powerful ways. Compliments arise from the speaker having applied his/her criteria for what's good or commendable. Acknowledgements are a way of applying generally accepted criteria, such as the Lifelong Guidelines and LIFESKILLS. The goal is to redirect students from relying on external standards to relying on internal ones.

Avoid Value Judgment. Target talk is best done without value judgment. As the Sergeant in the TV series *Dragnet* would say, "Just the facts, ma'am." The facts are: *who*, *what* Lifelong Guideline or LIFESKILL was demonstrated, and *how* it was used. Such clear statements provide immediate feedback about use of the desired behaviors. Students see the Lifelong Guidelines and LIFESKILLS in action and make their own judgments about how useful they are. This independent analysis is critical to building character traits, values, and attitudes—and their related behaviors—that will last a lifetime.

Using Target Talk to Correct Misbehavior

Target talk is a potent teaching tool to deal with misbehavior and it is easy to use. First ask "What happened here?" Then, "What Lifelong Guidelines and/or LIFESKILLS didn't you use?" Lastly, "What Lifelong Guidelines and/or LIFESKILLS could you have used to have prevented this situation?" Remember to remain neutral in tone. This is the teaching phase of correcting misbehavior. And always make sure students understand how their misbehavior made the other person feel. Strengthening students' awareness of how their behavior affects others is a critical step in helping them internalize the Lifelong Guidelines and LIFESKILLS.

The consequences phase—sometimes referred to as the punishment—should always be in proportion to the gravity of the act. For example, if serious physical or emotional harm occurred, the consequences should be grave. Likewise, don't overreact if the misbehavior was irritating but didn't cause injury or damage. Also, if the misbehavior occurs due to unclear expectations, such as lack of procedures that spell out the expected personal and social behaviors (see page 20.11-20.12), point the finger back to yourself. Such misbehavior is hardly the student's fault and it's a teaching opportunity.

Any consequences should also be related to the situation in which the misbehavior took place. For example, if serious misbehavior took place on the playground, the student should not be allowed to be on the playground with others for a specified period and/or under specified conditions. If the misbehavior was bad language or teasing another student in class, perhaps suspension of a classroom privilege would suffice. If the misbehavior was hitting and hurting someone, a class meeting is in order and serious consequences applied.

Before jumping to consequences, always discuss with the student the impact of his/her behavior on the other person(s). Make sure he/she understands and has some emotional feel for what that person suffered. And, always ask the misbehaving student how he/she could "clean it up" or make amends with the wounded party and what consequences/punishment would help him/her to remember not to do such things again. Often students are harder on themselves than adults would be.

If the student's recommended solution is sufficient, apply it. If the impact of the misbehavior is serious, such as hitting someone or damaging their property, additional consequences are appropriate.

If such conversations between you and a student fail to curb the behavior, add an audience—the injured student plus whoever else was present; if necessary, add all of the members of his/her Learning Club or even the entire class. However, do so only after you have created a sense of community in the classroom—a community in which that student is fully a member. In our experience, the only students that continue to misbehave are those who feel no connection to others and therefore feel they have nothing to lose by misbehaving. Students want to belong, they want to matter, they want to be loved and respected. When they are included, when they belong, they value what their peers think.

Note: If your school requires schoolwide adherence to a particular disciplinary program and process, make sure that you talk with your principal about how you intend to use the Lifelong Guidelines and LIFESKILLS. Get his/her approval to proceed as mutually agreed.

Agendas

Few meetings in the business world kick off without a written or clearly explained agenda. Nor should a classroom day begin without giving students a road map. Where are we going? How are we to get there? These are critical questions, especially if we want to teach students to become self-directed lifelong learners.

Agendas are not schedules as in 8:30–10:00 reading, 10:00–10:15 recess, 10:15–11:15 math. Typically there are no time frames indicated unless they are critical, such as for a schoolwide assembly or leaving on a study trip.

Agendas are a combination of major idea chunks, such as wetlands and watersheds; important events, such as a visiting classroom expert; and the major kinds of activities that students will be responsible for, such as SSR, inde-

pendent study, completing inquiries, and so forth. Whenever possible, use graphics instead of words. For early primary students who have not yet learned to read, the entire agenda must be pictorial.

Discussion

The more you and your students refer to and use the Lifelong Guidelines and LIFESKILLS, the more natural they will feel and the more spontaneous your responses and those of your students will become. Think through in advance ways to:

- Identify the Lifelong Guidelines/LIFESKILLS and their power to direct the course of our lives (e.g., "Do you think _____'s life would have turned out differently if he/she had used more of the LIFESKILL of _____? If so, how would it have been different?"

- Give succinct and memorable behaviors consistent with the Lifelong Guidelines/LIFESKILLS (e.g., discussing a local newspaper article: "The five-year old boy saved his family's lives because he was the only one who put his flashlight where he could remember it at a moment's notice. Without his LIFESKILL of Organization, he and his family couldn't have seen well enough to gather together and escape the fire."

- Avoid value judgments; allow students to make these judgments for themselves, thus internalizing the behaviors. For example, "Three students at the high school were just arrested for selling drugs. How will this affect the course of their lives? What do you think motivated them to do what they did? What Lifelong Guidelines/LIFESKILLS could they have used to make money over the next 15 years?" (the probable length of their prison term)

- Identify other ways people use the guidelines, both in and out of school. For example, "What Lifelong Guidelines and/or LIFESKILLS does your best friend have? Which do you admire/appreciate about him/her the most? How do his/her Lifelong Guidelines/LIFESKILLS make your life happier and better?"

Discussion should be part of your formal introduction to and ongoing teaching of each Lifelong Guideline and LIFESKILL. It can occur during your planned lesson, carry over to classroom conversation at the cafeteria, and pop up during the day as part of interactions to solve a problem or correct behavior.

Discussion is most powerful when it occurs immediately after an event or situation. For example, having two of your students sit in the principal's office awaiting discipline for fighting on the playground doesn't provide the immediate feedback they need for learning. Instead, stopping them at the moment and holding an impromptu discussion with those present would do just that. Discuss with them what Lifelong Guideline or LIFESKILL they did not use (that caused the problem) and what Lifelong Guidelines and LIFESKILLS they could have used to prevent the fighting. This, of course, should then be followed up with appropriate consequences plus having both parties clean up the problem—apology plus whatever else is appropriate to make amends.

An excellent resource for structuring discussions and other forms of groupwork is *TRIBES: A New Way of Learning and Being Together* by Jeanne Gibbs and *Cooperative Learning* by Spencer Kagan.

Processing the Process

A specific form of discussion is "processing the process"* a term coined by Jeanne Gibbs in *TRIBES: A New Way of Learning and Being Together.* It is a simple but powerful instructional strategy that asks students to analyze not what they just did but how they did it. In other words, how did the process of working together go? Did it help them or hinder them in getting the task done? What could they have done differently? Or, in the case of working with the Lifelong Guidelines and LIFESKILLS, how well did they use the LIFESKILLS of Organization and Effort? What would they do differently next time? What did they learn about working together or about themselves? Are they improving in their use of the

* See *Tribes: A New Way of Learning and Being Together* by Jeanne Gibbs, pp. 114-116

LIFESKILL of Initiative? And so on. The teacher, sometimes with input from students, asks questions appropriate to the moment.

This same idea is also very useful before an activity. For example, "What Lifelong Guidelines and/or LIFESKILLS will you need to do well at this task? If you used them, what would it look like, sound like, and feel like; what would it not look, sound, and feel like? What do you need to do and not do to successfully use those Lifelong Guidelines and/or LIFESKILLS?"

Direct Instruction

Lecture has its place but it is a limited one. It is the driest version of direct instruction which typically provides little sensory input beyond hearing and seeing the speaker. By direct instruction in the ITI model, we mean a presentation by the teacher that is limited to 11-16 minutes per hour and that is accompanied by full sensory input to as many of the 19 senses as possible when working an immersion environment.

Direct instruction should be looked at not as an end in itself—the way to teach—but rather as the catalyst to student work on inquiries. Direct instruction can lead the way or follow a discovery process. It is best done during the teachable moment when students are already fully engaged in their work and hungry for more answers.

There are many models and trainings for direct instruction. Choose one that works for you and is bodybrain-compatible for your students.

Literature

There is nothing better than a great story to pique students' interest and curiosity and, in the process, to teach a meaningful lesson. For your daily focus or story time with students, select a story rich with examples of what you want to teach, such as the Lifelong Guideline or LIFESKILL you are currently focusing on or that addresses an important incident/situation from the day. Which stories offer strong examples of Trustworthiness? Truthfulness? Active Listening? Integrity? Which teach the destructiveness of Put-Downs? Which support development of Personal Best or Resourcefulness? There are stories that immediately come to mind because they teach about all of the Lifelong Guidelines and many of the LIFESKILLS. For example, *Charlotte's Web* by E. B. White, *Stone Fox* by John Reynolds Gardiner, *Shiloh* by Phyllis Reynolds Naylor, *My Side of the Mountain* by Jean Craighead George, and *Red Fern* by Wilson Rawls. The strong characterizations created by the various authors grab youth (and often adults) emotionally.

At the end of the story (or chapter in the case of a longer story), discuss the use and/or non-use of the skill or behavior you want to teach. For example, invite your students to make connections between situations and actions of the characters and the Lifelong Guideline and LIFESKILL that you want to focus on. Provide time for them to locate and share situations in the book when the characters were using that Lifelong Guideline or LIFESKILL. Conversely, ask for examples when the characters were not using them or even deliberately ignoring them. Are students able to identify the consequences? It is always easier for students to see the consequences of the behavior of others than their own. Then, ask students to transfer both types of examples from the book into their own real-life experiences. You'll discover that such discussions strengthen relationships and help to keep the lines of communication open.

Recommended Literature

For recommended books for each Lifelong Guideline and LIFESKILL, see *Tools for Citizenship and Life: Using the ITI Lifelong Guidelines and LIFESKILLS in Your Classroom** by Sue Pearson. Following the lists of books for students are resources for teachers. The material ranges from philosophical to "how-to." Some are serious while others offer a lighter touch. Pick and choose according to your interests and needs.

Use your personal experiences and judgment to determine which stories are good choices for your own students, both in content and age appropriateness.

Pre-Reading Student Books Is Important

It is important that you read each story before you read it aloud to your students. First, you will want to determine if the story content and language are consistent with what you want your students to experience. Such previews allow you to sidestep objectionable language, skip parts that students might find upsetting, determine if the content and language are appropriate for your students, and to consider its fit with your students' life experiences.

By pre-reading you also familiarize yourself with the story and find comfortable discussion spots and those places in the plot that will most effectively highlight the importance of a certain skill or behavior you want to teach and connect to your students' experiences. It also allows you to add a bit of drama to your reading.

For a discussion about how to use literature to introduce or reteach a Lifelong Guideline or LIFESKILL, see Chapter 21.

---

* For additional titles and inquiries, see *Character Begins at Home: Family Tools for Teaching Character and Values* by Karen D. Olsen and Sue Pearson. Available from Books for Educators, Inc.—888/777-9827; e-mail: books4@oz.net; www.books4educ.com

Songs

Songs are a wonderful teaching device. They combine the power of memorable melody and the rhythm and rhyme of poetry and significantly increase the likelihood that what is learned will become stored in long-term memory. Best of all, singing is fun and something that all can do; musical talent and training are not required. Also, rather than giving your students a stern lecture about behavior, try breaking into a song. What a delight!

Available resources to help you launch your musical career include *Spread Your Wings: The Lifelong Guidelines* by Jeff Pedersen (available in video, CD, and audio cassette) and *LIFESKILLS* by Russ and Judy Eacker (CD or audio cassette plus songbook).* Or, log on to http://www.kovalik.com and follow four easy steps: Go to ITI Information, click on ITI Links, click on ITI Resources, then select Jean Spanko's ITI Songbook. Jean is a gifted ITI teacher who uses the ITI model with middle school students. The lyrics, written to favorite oldies, are delightful and singable. Students will pick up the melody and lyrics in a flash. Samples of Jean's work include "Pride, Great Pride" and "Resourcefulness."

Once you have started using songs as a teaching device, encourage students to develop lyrics to their favorite tunes. Students delight in writing such songs. Plus, it extends and deepens their ownership of each Lifelong Guideline and LIFESKILL. Also, writing lyrics is a painless invitation to writing and reading.

_____

* Available through Books for Educators.

Pride, Great Pride

(to the tune of *Ain't She Sweet?*)

Pride, great pride
Feel it way down deep inside.
When you just can't rest
Until you do your best,
Feel that PRIDE.

Mastery,
Just remember "CCC"
When it's correct, complete,
And comprehensive
How proud you'll be.

When you've got pride
You'll aim much higher.
That little spark
Becomes a fire.

Pride, great pride
Feel it way down deep inside.
When you just can't rest
Until you do your best,
Feel that pride!

© Jean Spanko

Resourcefulness

(to the tune of *This Old Man*)

When you face problems tough,
Resourcefulness will be enough
Look around for answers,
Change your point of view.
Great ideas will come to you.

Keep your mind focused well;
Stay away from folks that tell you
That "This won't work,
we tried it once before."
Show those people out the door.

If you fail, don't give in
Try your first ideas again.
The solution may be
Just a step away.
Be resourceful every day.

When you're stumped, you can ask
Trusted friends to share your task.
They can listen well
And dream along with you...
Give a different point of view.

Think in ways new and strange.
There's a world that you can change.
Be resourceful and you'll
See the answer clear.
All the world will stand and cheer.

© Jean Spanko

Used by written permission of Jean Spanko.

Movement

Few among us consider ourselves a movement specialist. We haven't mastered movement and exercise for ourselves much less our students. There are clear reasons in our minds why we chose not to become a P.E. specialist. Are we striking a familiar chord here? If so, rest assured that what we are talking about with movement here is a far cry from such discussions.

The motivation behind movement as a critical bodybrain-compatible element in the ITI model is not movement for the sake of movement or exercise because it's good for you but rather because movement is critical to the functioning of the brain and therefore to learning. And it's not just any movement, it is the kind of movement associated with using what is learned and also movement to reset students' emotional states to a level appropriate to the next activity. This can include the traditional "letting off steam" as well as focusing the brain for learning, reenergizing for a shift to a new topic of learning, or simply relaxing and taking a break.

Movement and Content

Your first goal in using movement is to integrate movement with the content being studied. Allow and encourage students to use their bodies to increase sensory input, practice ways to use what they understand, and to hard-wire learning into long-term memory. For example, make study trips truly exploratory not just look and see. Develop hand jives and whole-body movement routines as mnemonic devices. Develop role-playing plots and actions that illustrate the concepts and skills to be learned. Create dance routines based on the concepts or skills. Add movement to songs. And so on. Be creative. And, above all, have fun!

Once you get started, the ideas will flow. And don't be afraid to involve students. Invite them to write inquiries that have

them develop explorations, hand jives, role-playing scenarios, dance routines, songs, and so on.

To get you started, the following resources provide pictures that will stir your imagination:

- *Stage 2 of the ITI Stages of Implementation: Intelligence Is a Function of Experience* (video, 14 minutes)
- *ITI in the Urban Middle School* by Nicole McNeil-Miller (video, 15 minutes)
- *Thinking on Your Feet* by Jean Bladyes
- *Multiple Intelligences and the Second Language Learner* by Jo Gusman (video, 40 minutes)
- *Strategies for Teaching and Learning Professional Library: Strategies for Teaching Dance, Strategies for Teaching Music, Strategies for Teaching Visual Arts,* and *Strategies for Teaching Drama* (book series)

Movement and Emotion

Because emotion drives attention and all other aspects of learning, the emotional states of students are critical to your success as a teacher (and to your students' successes as learners). Thus, you must learn to teach students how to handle their emotional life so they can maximize their learning.

We all know there are times that we feel so keyed up we can't concentrate or so listless that we can't get going. It's the same for our students. There are times when we need to help them slow themselves down and times when we need to help them speed themselves up. Movement can do both.

When and how? Well, some of those times are givens and utterly predictable. Other times they occur serendipitously.

Planning for Movement

Because movement is so key to optimum functioning of the bodybrain learning partnership, it should be planned for as carefully as for the 3 Rs.

Predictable Moments. The predictable moments when movement is helpful include coming back to the classroom after recesses, lunch, and schoolwide events; changing activities, especially from a high-energy task to a low-energy one or vice versa; or in the middle of a long task such as test-taking or working on a challenging inquiry. Movement facilitates smooth transitions and a flow from one activity to the next.

For such predictable moments, develop movement activities that grow out of your content.

Unpredictable Moments. Although when the unpredictable moments occur may be a surprise, that they will occur is virtually guaranteed. So, develop a handful of movement routines that you can do at a moment's notice. For example, if you see glazed eyes that signal little learning is taking place, shift gears and energize with simple stretches, deep breathing, or Brain Gym movements. Such activities may have nothing to do with the content of the theme but they will get the job done.

Resources

Good resources for these activities include:

- *Emotion: Gatekeeper to Performance* with Dr. Candace Pert, Susan Kovalik, and Carla Hannaford (30-minute video)
- *How to Make Learning a Moving Experience* by Jean Blaydes (video and booklet)
- *Let's Get Moving: Movement in the Classroom* by Diane Berry (95-minute video and booklet)
- *Smart Moves: Why Learning Is Not All in Your Head* by Carla Hannaford
- *Brain Gym for Teachers*

Things to Avoid

Resist the urge to stifle movement, even irritating and distracting movement. Instead, redirect it. Highly bodily-kinesthetic students simply can't keep still and even if they could it would shut down their most powerful intelligence for learning. Redirect, redirect, redirect. For example, for those that can't keep their hands still or to themselves, give them a spongy, squishy ball to manipulate; the ground rule is that they can handle it any time they want or feel they need to so long as they don't bother other people with it.

For students who constantly pop up out of their seat and walk around, seat them in the back of the room and allow them to get up and move around whenever they feel they need to so long as they don't bother other people.

What you're dealing with in these instances is not short-term behavior problems but student need to develop lifelong strategies for handling themselves in appropriate ways—ways that enhance their ability to learn and to be considerate of the needs of other people.

Written Procedures

Perhaps the most common cause of misbehavior is lack of agreement among teacher and students about what behaviors are expected. The teacher expects "x" and that's news to the students! The result is unnecessary friction and lots of frustration for both teacher and students.

Written procedures are an important classroom leadership strategy in the ITI model. They help you plan ahead for frequent events (entering and leaving the room, what students should do when they've finished an assignment), for social interactions (greeting others politely and cheerfully, going to and coming from assemblies, birthday parties, classroom celebrations), and for tasks (doing homework, cleaning up after learning-club projects). By describing what social and personal behaviors are expected, these procedures allow students to be successful.

As you develop written procedures, think of answers to the following questions. What do students need to know and be able to do in order to do what's appropriate? How are they expected to behave? What are they expected to bring/have? Whenever feasible, involve students in developing such procedures.

By writing procedures on chart paper and posting them, students can refer to them whenever necessary. After their introduction and initial practice, some teachers create a Procedures Binder for each Learning Club. This allows quick referral and avoids clutter.

Procedures help prevent confusion and misbehavior and also eliminate the need to state expectations over and over again. As a bonus, guest teachers (substitute teachers) find such procedures extremely helpful as well.

Procedures should be:

- Clear
- Simple and easy to read
- Sequential
- Stated in the positive
- Illustrated

Good Morning!

1. Greet Mrs. Kay with a handshake
2. Hang up your coat, hat & pack
3. Put homework & notes in basket
4. Check tools
5. Greet learning club members
6. Work on Journal

Office Procedures

1. "Good morning."
2. "My name is _____. I am in _____'s class."
3. "I am here for _____."

Quiet Place

1. One person
2. Sh-h-h-h
3. Turn timer

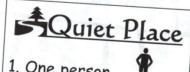

Group Work PROCEDURE

1. Cooperate
2. Soft voice
3. Take turns talking
4. See **3** before me
5. Share ideas
6. Do your personal best
7. Clean up

Morning Procedure

1. Greet your Learning Club members with a smile.
2. Copy the agenda.
3. Work on any unfinished inquiries.
4. Think about a LIFESKILL goal to work on today.

End of the Day Procedure

1. Organize your materials, Learning Club's basket, books, & folder.
2. Clean up your area.
3. Copy Homework Assignment. Check for understanding with a partner.
4. Say, "Good-bye," or, "See you tomorrow," to the teacher and your Learning Club members.

Intrapersonal Procedure

1. Work alone.
2. Work silently.
3. Quietly ask the teacher or a partner for help if you don't understand something.
4. Check your finished work for evidence that it is an example of "PERSONAL BEST."

Graphic Organizers

Graphic organizers are important learning tools because they can show the rich relationships that exist among concepts, ideas, and elements. Although this is very important for all students, it is especially critical for students high in spatial intelligence and those who have difficulty seeing the whole picture (see Chapter 6). No other instructional process can illustrate such relationships as clearly or efficiently.

Kinds of Graphic Organizers

There are various kinds of graphic organizers. All allow us to record information in ways that make the information more understandable. Some deal with precise comparisons and relationships such as the axis graph and bar charts; these work well when dealing with quantities. Others illustrate interrelationships of many facets of many items such as mindmapping and Venn circles; these work well when dealing with qualitative aspects such as the attributes of concepts.

Choose the form of graphic organizer that would best assist the reader to perceive and interpret the data that you most want him/her to analyze and understand. Useful, and easy to use, graphic organizers include:

- Bar and circle graphs assist the observer to compare quantities of numerous items.

- Axis graphs assist in observing for directions or trends in the quantitative interaction of two things. It also indicates how much of which of two ingredients must be increased or decreased in order to reach a desired goal.

- Venn circles assist the observer in comparing two entities for differences and similarities.

- Column charts simply separate out the data by designated characteristics (e.g., bookkeeping formats and decision-making formats such as P.M.I. or plus, minus, and interesting/neutral effect).

- Mindmaps are capable of presenting a large amount of data and, most importantly, showing the interrelationships among that data. Because it is a visual format, it gives the brain more clues for analyzing relationships and remembering the big idea and its relevant details.

Why Use Graphic Organizers

The strength of graphic organizers is that they enable us to see relationships which in turn pushes us to see a bigger picture. They also bring up questions that would never have occurred to us. The pursuit of answers to such questions happily leads us further into the concepts, into ways to apply them in similar and differing situations.

For more information, see *Visual Tools for Constructing Knowledge* by David Hyerle, ASCD.

Examples of Graphic Organizers

The graphic organizers on this page are examples of mindmaps for key points about owls—for primary grades and for intermediate. The mindmap on the next page is yet another example of how visuals can help a learner remember information. Adding color adds another dimension, especially for those high in spatial intelligence.

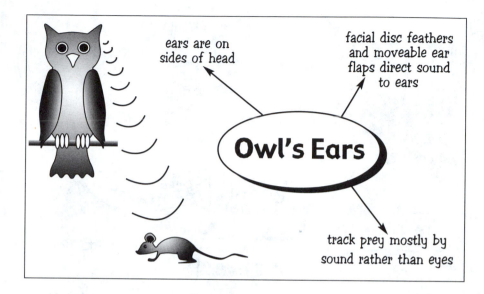

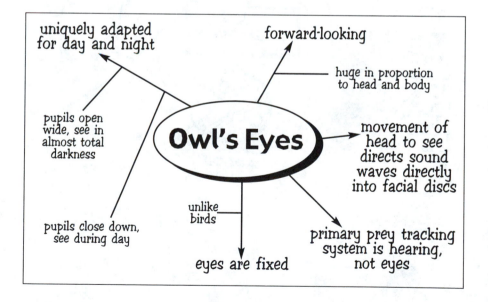

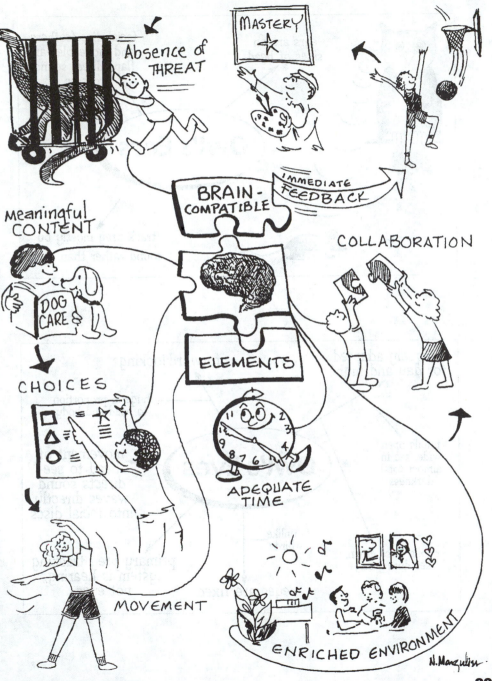

Journal Writing

Journal writing is an excellent device to help students process what they are learning or thinking about a topic. With no one looking over their shoulder or judging their words, they can reflect on what they truly think and feel. Since writing is thinking on paper, the very act of writing requires students to sort through their thoughts, reflect on their feelings, and organize their ideas.

Journal writing is a useful medium in many ways since it provides opportunities for students to reflect, respond, react, and reply to a wide variety of ideas, comments, and stories. It is a powerful instructional tool. Use it daily to offer for students chances to revisit, review, and renew previous beliefs and thoughts and to compare them to new ones. It is particularly useful in providing adequate time to reflect about their experiences relating to the Lifelong Guidelines and LIFESKILLS.

Note: A journal differs from a diary which primarily records what occurs from day to day. Periodically you may read and respond to student thoughts in a written dialog. Rule of thumb: Write as much back as the student writes to you. This encourages length and depth in their writing.

Although reading student writing can sometimes before overwhelming due to the sheer volume of it, keep in mind that "writing is the inking of our thinking"—it's as close as we can get to seeing what goes on the students' heads.

Clear Performance Criteria

It's difficult to do our personal best and meet other's expectations if the criteria for the task are not clear. Often, what is perceived as misbehavior is the result of not knowing what is expected, in behavior and/or performance. Written procedures describe expectations for personal and social behaviors but criteria for performing tasks or jobs are also needed. In the real world, such criteria are often called specifications. Call them what you wish but they are critical.

"Is It Done?" How to Avoid the Arguments

A common source of arguments is whether or not a task was done according to expectations of the person who assigned the job to be done—whether written or not. "I'm finished!" says the student. "No, you're not," says the teacher. The problem: Uncommunicated or misunderstood criteria for completing a task. Students shouldn't have to ask, "Teacher, is this right?" The criteria should be clear so that students can assess their own performance.

What kinds of assessment do you plan to use? Decide in advance so that you can communicate a clear picture to students before they begin. Your ultimate goal is criteria that meet real-world standards for excellence.

The 3Cs of Assessment. The ITI model applies the 3Cs of assessment to inquiries/activities/tasks:

- Is it complete? Is the job completed as stated in the directions or inquiry? Does it meet the specifications described in the inquiry? Does it reflect real-world standards for work performed in the workplace while remaining age-appropriate? Does it reflect pride in workmanship and personal best?

- Is it correct? Is the information/action accurate?

- Is it comprehensive? Has the student addressed the task as thoroughly as possible given his/her capabilities at this age? Did the student follow just the specific directions or did he/she handle closely related tasks that, if left undone, would adversely affect the outcome of the assigned job? For example, if asked to clean the sink in the classroom, did he/she also wipe up the toothpaste dripped on the nearby countertop?

Keep in mind that criteria should "grow" as the student's capabilities grow. What was Personal Best at age six might well be unacceptable at age nine.

For a full discussion of assessment, see Chapter 16.

Chapter 21: Strategies for Introducing and Reteaching Concepts and Skills

In addition to the instructional strategies that should be used daily, as described in Chapter 20, there are numerous strategies especially powerful when introducing or reteaching a concept or skill. They may be used as often as you wish but usually not every day. They include:

- Video clips
- Literature
- T-Charts
- Role playing
- The Discovery Process
- Social/Political action
- Celebrations

Video Clips

Good videos, like good literature, are a terrific teaching resource. But not the entire movie; students typically spend more time than they should watching movies and TV. Think video segments. Even movies that may seem objectionable in their entirety have short segments with powerful messages for students (and adults). Usually a 5-8 minute clip is sufficient. Whether it models the concept or skill you are trying to teach or demonstrates the lack of it, both are needed to help students develop a clear picture of what they are targeting. To really know what something is, we must also know what it isn't. This is particularly important when applying new behaviors or habits of mind such as the Lifelong Guidelines/LIFESKILLS to everyday life. For example, when is telling the truth being rude and uncaring? When does being trustworthy cross the line and leave one feeling taken for granted? When does doing your personal best become dangerous to your health?

Video clips are often a good lead-in to be followed by T-charts and discussion. Charlie Brown movies, for example, contain examples of put-downs that all ages can understand, from five-year olds to adults. After viewing a Charlie Brown video, ask your students to tally up the number of put-downs they recognize during a brief segment; then, through discussion, have them relate these put-downs to real-life situations and personal experiences. Students are often appalled by the number of nasty comments expressed in the guise of humor. The humor doesn't seem as funny anymore.

Associate Sue Pearson loves the video, *Harriet the Spy*, by Louise Fitzhugh. It's quirky storyline focuses on the Lifelong Guideline of Trustworthiness, or the lack of it. Seeing a clip from a video with "new eyes" is a beginning step in recognizing put-downs in classroom and home behaviors that we never noticed before.

To extend the video experiences, prepare follow-up topics to practice solving problems related to current issues such as name calling or disparaging remarks about physical attributes or family circumstances.

One last reminder: Make sure that the video clip you select is age-appropriate, i.e., understandable to students in your class.

Literature

Ways to use literature on a daily basis are discussed in Chapter 20. With a bit more planning and focus, literature can be effectively used to introduce a concept or skill and for re-teaching when needed.

There are innumerable ways to use literature to introduce or reteach. Here are but a few. Remember to think of changes you would make for your own students and your literary choices. The examples here are for teaching a Lifelong Guideline or LIFESKILL. (See *Tools for Citizenship and Life: Using the ITI Lifelong Guidelines and LIFESKILLS in Your Classroom.*)

- Character Web: Read a book that exemplifies one of the Lifelong Guidelines or LIFESKILLS. Write the name of one main character in the center of a piece of chart tablet paper. Draw a circle around the name. Add rays coming out from the circle, similar to a child's drawing of the sun. (For very young students, consider using a felt story board with images rather than words.) Have your students identify a Lifelong Guideline or LIFESKILL that this storybook character used to solve problems and reach his/her goals. Write the target word on the ray and the action below the ray. For example, based on *Charlotte's Web*, put the name Wilbur in the center circle. Add a ray; above it write Perseverance; under the ray write the descriptors of action from the text, e.g., "He thought and thought until he created a plan to help save his friend Charlotte, the spider." (See an example of such a character web on the next page.)

- Identify three Lifelong Guidelines or LIFESKILLS that were used to solve a problem in the story. Identify two Lifelong Guidelines or LIFESKILLS that were not used and thus contributed to problems.

- Read a traditional story such as *The Three Little Pigs*. Rewrite the ending as if the pigs had used the Lifelong Guideline of Personal Best to solve their problem with the wolf.

- After reading a biography or autobiography, label three or more Lifelong Guidelines or LIFESKILLS that the person used well. Link them to actions from the book. Next, invite members of your Learning Club to share their experiences in developing these same Lifelong Guidelines or LIFESKILLS. Using a Venn diagram, identify the behaviors associated with the selected LIFESKILLS that the book character and your learning-club members have in common and which behaviors are different. Again using a Venn diagram, compare two LIFESKILLS you use to do your personal best with those used by a character in the story.

- After completing several stories, play "Who Am I?" Choose a character from a previously read book. Share the Lifelong Guidelines/LIFESKILLS used along with one or two related actions to carry out the Lifelong Guidelines/LIFESKILLS. Invite other students who have read the book to guess who the character is.

- Compare three LIFESKILLS used by two well-known people. Select people from different time periods and settings such as Madame Curie and Rosa Parks. List three LIFESKILL strengths they have in common. List three weaknesses that each one has. Discuss whether or not the LIFESKILLS are unique to the time period/setting of the story.

- Find local newspaper articles describing problems that are occurring because people didn't use the Lifelong Guidelines/LIFESKILLS. Read the articles with your students and have them determine which Lifelong Guideline or LIFESKILL was or wasn't used. Ask students to share their thinking with other members of their learning club.

Hopefully these few ideas will have you thinking in many different directions. Perhaps you remember a favorite biography and think, "Of course, why didn't I ever mention perseverance when we read about Thomas Edison or Rosa Parks?" Or, perhaps you recall a link to humor using *Charlotte's Web*? How about the courage shown in *The True Story of Ruby Bridges*? Eventually, you'll wonder why you ever thought it would be hard to make connections. They'll be popping up everywhere!

Sample character web for *Charlotte's Web*:

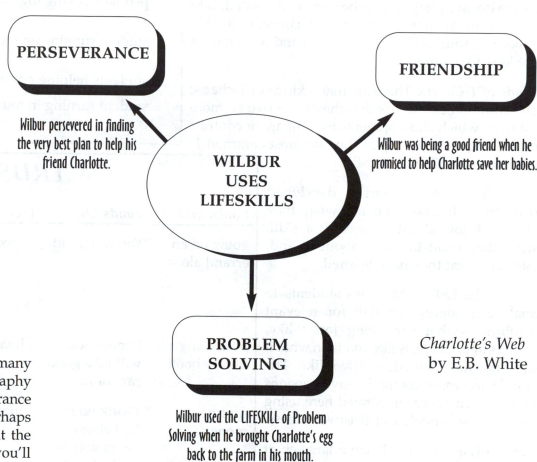

PERSEVERANCE

Wilbur persevered in finding the very best plan to help his friend Charlotte.

FRIENDSHIP

Wilbur was being a good friend when he promised to help Charlotte save her babies.

WILBUR USES LIFESKILLS

PROBLEM SOLVING

Wilbur used the LIFESKILL of Problem Solving when he brought Charlotte's egg back to the farm in his mouth.

Charlotte's Web
by E.B. White

T-Charts

An excellent way to introduce a concept or skill, including a Lifelong Guideline or LIFESKILL, and to do an in-depth refresher course if needed, is to brainstorm pictures of what that concept or skill looks like, sounds like, and feels like and what it does not look like, sound like, or feel like.

Kinds of T-Charts. There are many kinds of T-charts. The common element is that they have two or more columns which allow students to compare or contrast information about a topic. The two most common T-charts are the KWL and LSF.

The KWL T-chart is developed over time. It asks students what they already **know** about a concept or skill, what they **want to know** about it, and, later on, what they have **learned.**

The LSF T-chart asks students to analyze a concept or skill for relevant attributes—what something *l*ooks like, *s*ounds like, and *f*eels like and then what it does not look, sound, and feel like. The simple and more comprehensive versions of such T-charts are illustrated here using the Lifelong Guideline of Trustworthiness.

How to Use T-Charts. Using a large chart tablet, write the name of the concept or skill across the top of the page; select two or more attributes that will help students focus on key aspects of the concept or skill. Create and name these columns. By

TRUSTWORTHINESS

Looks Like	Sounds Like	Feels Like
students sharing ideas	"I've got a secret!"	safety
people working together	"Will you teach me how to do that?"	comfortable
student running an errand	"Please take this to Mrs. X down the street."	I'm trusted
students helping one another	"Would you help me?" "Yes."	friendliness
student turning in found object	"I found this. It belongs to someone else."	honesty

TRUSTWORTHINESS

Looks Like	Sounds Like	Feels Like	Doesn't Look Like	Doesn't Sound Like	Doesn't Feel Like
going on an errand alone	"You can do it!?"	special	someone supervising you	"I know you can't get there without getting into trouble."	sarcastic
borrowing a library book	"I know you will take good care of it."	honored	losing a library book	"I think somebody stole it!"	distrust
finding money	"Thank you for bringing the money to the lost and found."	trusted	pocketing found money	"Finders keepers! Losers weepers!"	suspicion
going to a friend's house	"Be home on time."	someone depends on me	sneaking out of the house	"I wouldn't do that. Trust me!"	lying

adding a comparison of what something is to what it isn't, students can more easily develop a broader and deeper understanding of what they are learning.

Then, ask students to think of personal experiences at school or situations from stories they have read that will fit into each category. Allow them sufficient time to think to fill in the spaces with minimal prompting. Let them use their own words (for younger students, draw simple pictures to illustrate the meaning). Once students can connect new learning to previous personal experiences, learning speeds up significantly. As for the Lifelong Guidelines and LIFESKILLS, students' intuitive understanding of them is often surprising.

Save the T-chart(s) and add to the columns daily throughout the first week of study and weekly thereafter as students identify more attributes. The more pictures students have for a concept or skill, the more adept they will become in applying them in real-world settings and the more likely the concept/skill will become wired into long-term memory.

Role Playing

Role playing is highly appealing to students; there is action to watch, dialogue to hear, and a story line to follow. The emotional impact makes it easier for students to see connections to real life. Therefore, consider role playing to illustrate concepts about which your students may hold misconceptions or may have difficulty learning.

Role playing can be formal—with time allowed to invent and rehearse an assigned scenario—or spontaneous. Both are powerful. Role playing is especially effective for teaching students alternative responses. For example, set up a simple situation: "Instead of ____ [hitting Jack], role play what Lifelong Guideline or LIFESKILL you could have used."

Conversely, if a story or incident worked out well, ask the question, "What if Kenny had not used the Lifelong Guideline or LIFESKILL of _____? Role play what would have happened then."

Be playful. Know that for many students, hearing about something is seldom as powerful as seeing it. And, because education is about giving students options in life, what better way than to have them experience those options now through role playing in the safe environment of your classroom.

Discovery Process

The ITI Discovery Process is designed to encourage curiosity and initiative—key LIFESKILLS for becoming a lifelong learner and a contributing citizen. It is an opportunity to present students with an object, specimen, or problem and let them discover both the questions and the answers. This process is exciting and allows Learning Clubs to orchestrate their own learning. It is used most effectively when the Lifelong Guidelines and the LIFESKILLS are in place.

The steps in the Discovery Process are:

1. Stimulating curiosity

2. Setting standards and expectations

3. Providing lead-up time

4. Orchestrating the exploration

5. Providing small group follow-up time

6. Capturing the teachable moment

7. Assessing student learning

8. Creating long-term memories through outreach

For a description of how to use each of these steps, see Appendix B.

Social and Political Action Projects

Social and political action projects—midway into study or as a culminating activity—put learning to the test. They require students to apply what they have learned to personal use in the real world. What we know from brain research is that locking knowledge and skill into long-term memory takes practice—multiple uses in varying situations. Test taking is usually performed from short-term memory. In contrast, social and political action projects immerse students in complex projects that extend over time, thus giving rich, engaging practice that ensures mastery and long-term memory storage of a wide range of skills and knowledge.

Young citizens of a democratic society should start learning the gears and levers of democracy as preschoolers. Several good resources to guide your students through planning and carrying-out social/political projects include: *The Kid's Guide to Service Projects: Over 500 Service Ideas for Young People Who Want to Make a Difference* and *The Kid's Guide to Social Action: How to Solve the Social Problems You Choose—and Turn Creative Thinking into Positive Action*, both by Barbara Lewis, and *Enriching Curriculum Through Service Learning*, edited by C.W. Kinsley and K. McPherson.

The projects don't have to last a lifetime. Two to four weeks is enough to make the learning memorable and have an opportunity to make a difference.

The Lifelong Guidelines/LIFESKILLS should be an integral part of any social/political action project. They describe the personal and social skills your students need to take action about a problem or societal issue, be it assisting at a home for the elderly (singing, helping with a Christmas party, writing letters, going out for fresh air and conversation), volunteering at a soup kitchen (cooking, serving, helping organize provisions), offering to help a neighbor just home from the hospital (taking care of his/her yard for a month, feeding pets, doing dishes, and so forth), taking on city hall or big corporations.

Connect projects to the study of a Lifelong Guideline or LIFESKILL. For example, when studying the LIFESKILL of Resourcefulness, have your students start a business (walking a neighbor's pet, mowing lawns, washing windows, teaching others how to use the Internet or make a web page, delivering newspapers). When studying the LIFESKILL of Initiative, look around the neighborhood. What political action is needed? A crosswalk light at a dangerous intersection, pollution to be cleaned up, an empty lot to be made safe, drug pushing outside the school to be cleaned up, low voter registration in the neighborhood?

Celebrations of Learning

How will you celebrate your accomplishments as a class family and as an individual? Pride—personal satisfaction in a job well done—is an important source of motivation to do one's personal best the next time. Celebrate the day by day triumphs. Learn to appreciate them as everyday miracles in the life of your students. Also schedule big celebrations as conclusions to lengthy projects. Let your love and joy in your students grow as they grow. Celebrate accomplishments, celebrate hard work, celebrate the love of learning.

Do note, however, that celebrating accomplishments is far different from receiving a reward. While rewards, such as ice cream treats, a trip to McDonald's, and so forth, work in the short run, they are extremely detrimental in the long run. Your goal is to instill in your child the desire to do what is needed because it needs to be done. For a hair-raising discussion of the dangers of rewards, see Alfie Kohn's book, *Punished by Rewards: The Trouble with Gold Stars, Incentive Plans, A's, Praise, and Other Bribes.* Surprisingly enough, external rewards work against us; they extinguish the behavior that is rewarded. The key to development of character, values, and attitudes implicit in the Lifelong Guidelines and LIFESKILLS and the skills and attitudes to become a lifelong learner is helping students internalize them rather than externally reward them.

Celebrations and Long-Term Memory

Celebrations of learning give our students a chance to share their knowledge in ways that solidify long-term memory. They are orchestrated revisits of key points that allow students to show off their newly acquired skills and expertise and, in the process, enhances mental program-building. As such, they are serious work as well as a celebration of learning.

Although included in this chapter about strategies for introducing and reteaching concepts and skills, the teaching is by students. Their audience is their parents and other students. Celebrations are an effective way to lead parents to a better understanding of the positive impact of the ITI model and to let them observe collaborative learning in action.

Celebrations require planning and creative orchestration but garner valuable support for your program. You might think about inviting grandparents, community members, and the guest speakers you've had. Also, don't forget about school custodians and administrators—our environmental and financial supporters! Everyone will be quickly caught up in the excitement of the students. By popular demand, students often ask for more than three celebrations per school year.

The Making of a Celebration

Celebrations can take a variety of forms, allowing you to highlight your curriculum in a way that best suits the nature of a particular monthly component. As you plan your three celebrations consider the following ideas developed by our associate, Lynette Baumann.*

---

* Lynette Baumann is a fourth grade teacher in Michigan and also teaches courses in elementary curriculum and multiple intelligences theory. Implementing the principles of ITI profoundly changed her view of teaching and has truly made "learning come to life" for her and her students.

1. *Performance Celebrations*

A play or other dramatization is an ideal way to close a segment of study. If the number of acting parts seems limited, think about allowing the lead roles to be played by more than one student, or switching players after each scene so experiences can be shared. Another suggestion is to form narrator teams. This keeps the audience attentive because of variety and added volume. An additional bonus derived from team narrations is that a student with reading difficulties can be supported by strong readers who model fluency and reinforce vocabulary.

Finally, don't miss the opportunity prior to a performance for students to introduce key vocabulary or background information. An overhead projector works particularly well for this.

2. *"Earn Your Diploma" or "Find the Hidden Treasure" Celebration*

Having worked diligently to complete some very detailed projects, designed information boards that display many of the key points from the theme, and mastered skills, students are now ready to share. However, if you are not sure parents and guests will understand the full depth of what students have accomplished, consider an "Earn Your Diploma" or "Treasure Hunt" night. Such a structure will insure that your guests are focused and actively involved in seeking information.

As a class, prepare a "quiz," or a "treasure hunt"—a list of activities or questions to which answers or discoveries will be found in the projects, experiments, or information boards the students have prepared. The students understand they will guide or lead their parents and guests toward finding the CORRECT information. No one should score less than 100 percent. Once completed, each student evaluates the activity and awards a "diploma," or gives "buried treasure" to each participant. This type of celebration not only keeps the parents well directed but the students, too. It also serves as an ideal reinforcement of concepts learned, especially if students have to become well versed in other students' projects. It is a good idea for students to rehearse this celebration by inviting another classroom to go through the process prior to the evening event with parents and guests.

3. Station Celebration

With station celebrations, small groups of students are responsible for teaching or demonstrating certain key points while guests rotate through the stations. This is an ideal way to exhibit the different aspects of the curriculum you have covered within your theme. For example, one group could demonstrate math skills while another shows social studies concepts or performs a science experiment. Another might demonstrate how to make a mindmap or read a short story. Regardless of the nature of the stations, audience participation is always a winner and it encourages the parents and guests to be attentive.

We combined this celebration with a short performance and, when we gathered together for our play, Rudyard Kipling's *How The Whale Got His Throat*, one student introduced some key vocabulary words we had learned and another showed the migratory paths of humpback whales while telling about the whale we had adopted.

As a finale, we invited the audience to sing "The Whale Song," a ballad we had rewritten so that the lyrics reinforced the whale we had studied. Once again, the overhead projector came in handy. When it was all over, we served whale cookies and "sea swill"—yellow lemonade with blue food coloring to make green lemonade. (How scientific!)

The children love being involved in brainstorming for the type of celebration that seems appropriate for the content and skills they have been learning. We have yet to find a community that doesn't change its attitude about what goes on in school once they have attended a celebration of learning.

Basic Ingredients for a Successful Celebration

- Schedule it in the evening when parents and guests can easily attend and you can spread out and use the media center and hallways.

- Begin planning for this event early, ideally at least a month in advance. This allows you adequate time to orchestrate a meaningful evening and to generate anticipation in both parents and students.

- Be sure all students have a significant role. This is their night to shine and your night to show the power of your ITI curriculum, instruction strategies, and the power of "brain-compatible" learning.

- Have a rehearsal. Invite another class in for a dry run. Be sure everyone knows what is expected of them (performers and audience).

- Prepare an easy-to-follow agenda. Let your guests know what is expected of them as well.

- Make invitations clear. Parents and other adults are welcome but, depending upon the nature of your celebration event, you may not want to include younger siblings. If so, state that clearly on the invitation and explain why. Make the starting time easy to remember and catchy—7:07 or 7:11 aren't likely to be forgotten.

- Have extra help available. Let someone else be in charge of taking pictures or pouring refreshments, especially if you have younger students.

- Invite the custodians. Make them your honored guests. They will love the special attention and be more likely to be helpful in the future, rather than complain about the extra work your enriched environment may create for them.

Celebrating the Success with the Lifelong Guidelines

Because internalizing and consistently using the Lifelong Guidelines and LIFESKILLS requires minute-by-minute awareness and, in many cases, considerable personal change, plan celebrations specifically for accomplishments with the Lifelong Guidelines and LIFESKILLS.

Examples of Celebrations include:

• Planned and scripted drama skits performed by students for special gatherings of other students (younger buddies and/or same age or older students). These skits replicate and/or demonstrate the results of students' favorite inquiries/projects about the topic of study just concluded

• A LIFESKILLS Fair for Parents, a special evening during which your students plan LIFESKILL "booths" — demonstrations of what his/her favorite LIFESKILLs mean and how to use them. Students can work as a learning club, in partners, or individually.

• A LIFESKILL Day planned for the entire class during which students, as members of a small group of 2-5 students, carry out their plans to practice that Lifelong Guideline or LIFESKILL for the entire day (or whatever time period is chosen). Projects can be carried out on campus (Caring and Friendship with younger buddies, reading to them, helping them learn to use the library), at a nearby public park (Effort and Cooperation, clean up projects, trail restoration), or at a museum or aquarium (Curiosity, a behind the scenes tour). The possibilities are endless. On return to class, have each group give a 3-5 minute presentation of how

the LIFESKILL of the day helped make that day special for them—more interesting, more fun, more friendship.

Taking time to acknowledge students' success in implementing the Lifelong Guidelines and LIFESKILLS helps foster an experience of that deep sense of personal satisfaction that comes from doing one's best, making a contribution to the group, doing the right thing because its the right thing to do. These celebration provide the initial external feedback that promotes an internal sense of pride—earned and deserved.

Appendices

A: ITI Classroom Stages of Implementation

B: The ITI Discovery Process

C: Communicating with Parents

D: Age-Appropriate Curriculum

Appendix A: ITI Classroom Stages of Implementation

This description of stages in implementing ITI in the classroom grew out of a need to assess the progress and results of implementing ITI over long-term, intensive, large-scale efforts, particularly those funded by the David and Lucile Packard Foundation to improve science education in grades K-6 and middle schools. The questions were obvious enough:

- To what degree are teachers implementing what we know from recent brain research about how humans learn? How would we know and what happens when they do?

- Are there common patterns in implementation stages, results for students, and responses from staff and parents that can be predicted? If so, support could be better designed at all stages of implementation.

- Do the outcomes vary when implementation is schoolwide vs. limited to a few individuals or teams?

Because the degree of change and restructuring inherent in the ITI model is so great, single-dimensional views of a classroom and school are not adequate. Many issues must be examined simultaneously with full understanding of the rich webbing of one aspect to another. Thus, curriculum and instruction cannot be examined profitably in an isolated sense. What is needed is a simultaneous view of the interaction of curriculum, instruction, and brain biology. And the assessment tools to do so must speak of practicalities as well as theory, tools that are cast in down-to-earth language reflecting a common, shared vocabulary. This description can be used to assess program implementation at the classroom level on an individual or team basis. To assess implementation on a schoolwide basis, see ITI Schoolwide Stages of Implementation.

The stages provide a blueprint for action from which to start. There are step-by-step descriptions of how to achieve full implementation of the ITI model, from its bodybrain-compatible roots to full integration of all basic skills and content areas. The stages are without time frames and deadlines—speed and quality of implementation are a function of levels of commitment reflected in district and school policies and resource allocation to support bodybrain-compatible education.

While the items in the "Expectations" column may seem unduly optimistic, they are the very real outcomes experienced in dozens of schools across the country where bodybrain-compatible learning through the ITI model is implemented schoolwide and at the level of quality described at each of the stages of implementation.

Significant improvement of America's public education system and quantum jumps in student outcomes are possible and very doable. The necessary tools are within our grasp.

Stage 1

Entry level for making the learning environment bodybrain compatible

■ CURRICULUM

Before School

- Become familiar with state and district standards and assessment practices. (C11)

- Visit potential *being there* locations that could provide real-world experiences with the concepts/skills of the standards.(C13)

- Establish/update your list of effective guest speakers and topics. (C13)

- Introduce yourself to your students. Get a class list of your students with phone numbers and addresses. Send a postcard or letter to each student and welcome them to your class. Tell them a little about what they will be learning. (C8)

First Day of School and Thereafter

- The bodybrain-compatible element of absence of threat and nurturing reflective thinking is taught as an important and ongoing part of the curriculum. Such curriculum contains:

  — The Lifelong Guidelines, including the LIFESKILLS

  — The role of emotions in learning

  — The personal and social skills for collaboration

  — How to utilize reflective thinking (C8)

- Citizenship is being developed and practiced through the using the Lifelong Guidelines and LIFESKILLS.

Accomplish Before Moving On

- The concept of multiple intelligences, defined as problem-solving and product producing capabilities, is taught early in the year and is a frequent, ongoing topic for post-lesson processing of collaborative work. (C3)

- Time frames for activities and areas of study are no longer rigid and students have adequate time to complete their work.

■ INSTRUCTIONAL STRATEGIES

Before School

- The classroom is:

  — Healthful (free of toxins, clean, well-lighted, well-ventilated with fresh air and proper temperature, pleasant smelling, and safe)

  — Aesthetically pleasing (calming colors and music, living plants, and well laid out for multiple uses)

  — Uncluttered yet reflects what is being learned. (C7)

- Seating is arranged in clusters with easy access to work tools. (C7)

- Teacher meets frequently with a professional or peer coach who supports his/her implementation of a bodybrain-compatible/teaching learning environment.

First Day of School and Thereafter

- The teacher's classroom leadership and management is based upon modeling the Lifelong Guidelines and LIFESKILLS. The atmosphere is participatory rather than dictatorial. "Discipline" is based upon helping students develop the personal and social skills and behaviors needed to successfully practice the Lifelong Guidelines rather than upon a system of externally imposed rewards and punishments. (C8)

- Written procedures and agendas provide consistency and security for students. (C20)

- The calmness of the teacher's voice contributes to a settled classroom environment. (C8)

- Collaborative learning is a frequently used instructional strategy.

- The teacher meets frequently with a professional or peer coach who supports his/her implementation of a bodybrain-compatible teaching/learning environment.

Accomplish Before Moving On

- Limited choices are introduced through student selection of supplies, time allocations, materials and processes used for completing projects, and other age-appropriate options. (C15, 3)

- The teacher includes real-life experiences — *being there*, immersion, and hands-on experiences — to supplement classroom instruction; resource people are invited to the classroom. (C1)

- The teacher is developing a variety of instructional strategies to supplement direct instruction. (C1)

- The teacher meets frequently with a professional or peer coach who supports the implementation of a bodybrain-compatible learning environment for students.

[C,#] = Refers to the chapter(s) that describes how to implement this aspect of a bodybrain-compatible classroom.

Entry level for making the learning environment bodybrain compatible

Stage 1

EXPECTATIONS

- Absence of threat has been established in the classroom. The culture of the classroom nurtures reflective thinking.

- Students are beginning to take responsibility for their own behavior through the use of the Lifelong Guidelines and LIFESKILLS.

- An atmosphere of mutual respect and genuine caring is obvious among and between students and adults. Students do not put each other down; their behaviors with each other support absence of threat and the nurturing of reflective thinking.

- Students demonstrate collaborative skills, e.g., active listening, taking turns, and respect for others' opinions.

- Students focus their attention on learning as soon as they enter the classroom.

- Lack of self-directedness and responsibility for learning has been replaced by a student focus on school as a safe and pleasant place to learn and grow; there is a growing sense of calm and openness.

- Parents understand the purpose and research behind bodybrain-compatible education and are supportive of the teacher's efforts.

- Parents notice evidence of use of the Lifelong Guidelines and LIFESKILLS at home.

- Teacher confidence and enjoyment in teaching increases.

INDICATORS

- Post-lesson processing about academic or collaborative experiences occurs daily.

- Classroom and schoolwide discipline problems have declined significantly.

- Differences in student engagement when real-life experiences are provided are obvious to teacher and parents.

- Teacher includes student input when selecting work for the student's portfolio folder.

Stage 1 of implementing ITI begins not with themes or integration but with the brain research relevant to creating a bodybrain-compatible environment in which learning can occur.

Implementors are advised to go slowly with curriculum development until significant strides toward maintaining a bodybrain-compatible learning environment are achieved. While a bodybrain-compatible learning environment cannot be fully realized until curriculum becomes bodybrain-compatible, curricular changes have little impact if the learning environment is not consistent with how the brain learns.

Stage 1, entry level into a bodybrain-compatible environment, is to be applied to the classroom 100 percent of the time. Note that this stage is broken into two parts in order to give teachers greater focus on where and how to begin.

Stage 2

Entry level for making curriculum bodybrain compatible

■ CURRICULUM

- Teacher provides for real-life experiences by basing the integrated curriculum upon a physical location, event, or situation that students can and do frequently experience through *being there.* Science is either the core for or a prominent part of curriculum integration. (C13)

- Teacher has identified the concepts and skills that will be taught to the levels of mastery and application. Key points focus on critical concepts rather than on isolated facts. (C14)

- Inquiries for each key point provide students with choices and multiple opportunities for real-world application; they also allow multiple ways of problem-solving and producing products. Some inquiries are designed specifically to provide realistic opportunities for students to practice citizenship, e.g., social/political action activities and collaborative grouping practices. (C3, 15, 18)

- The curriculum includes most of the elements that appear as a natural part or extension of the being-there focus, e.g., science, math, technology, history/social studies, fine arts, as well as mathematics, reading, writing, and oral expression. Integration of content is natural, not contrived. (C13)

- Content is age-appropriate. (C14)

■ INSTRUCTIONAL STRATEGIES

- Immersion and hands-on-of-the-real-thing are the primary input used to supplement and extend *being there* experiences. (C1, 15)

- Instructional strategies are varied and provide the most effective methods for the particular content at hand. For example, direct instruction and ITI discovery processes, collaboration and personal study time, mindmapping to organize materials, and cross-age/multi-age interaction. (C20, 21)

- Resources to support the theme are multiple, varied, and rich. Resource people and experts are regular visitors to the classroom. Visits to off-campus learning sites are frequent and serve as the organizers for the curriculum being studied. (C13)

- Choices are regularly provided through inquiries and other means. (C15)

- Adequate time is allowed to let students complete their work. (C15)

- There are sufficient inquiries for students to complete to ensure mastery and development of mental programs for using the knowledge and skills of the key points. (C15, 17)

- Collaboration is effectively used and enhances learning for academic and social growth. (C15)

[C,#] = Refers to the chapter(s) that describes how to implement this aspect of a bodybrain-compatible classroom.

EXPECTATIONS

- Students participate actively by initiating ideas, responding to the teacher's questions, staying on task with minimal guidance from the teacher, and so forth.
- Students see the connections between the classroom and real life.
- Mental fibrillation has been replaced by a sense of calm and purpose, relaxed alertness, and confidence in success in learning.
- School as a place to learn and exercise one's personal best is the accepted norm.
- Absentee rates are dropping, library checkout rates are increasing.
- Students engage in problem solving in a collaborative manner at least once a day.

INDICATORS

- Post-lesson processing about academic and social experiences is a part of each collaborative activity.
- On-going assessment of student progress is evaluated using selected inquiries to determine mastery of key points, e.g., projects, presentations, and some traditional tests.
- Both teacher and student select work for the student's portfolio folder.
- Assessment of mastery is based upon the 3Cs of Assessment and assessment inquiries.

The beginning steps in making curriculum bodybrain-compatible assume that significant progress has been made implementing Stage 1, making the learning environment bodybrain-compatible.

Whereas Stage 1 applied to the classroom 100 percent of the time, Stage 2 is applied only to that portion of the day, week, or year for which teachers have developed bodybrain-compatible curriculum using the ITI model. The time frames and content that teachers may select to begin implementation of their bodybrain-compatible curriculum vary widely. Typically teachers begin where they feel they will be most successful and stretch from there. Whatever the starting point, however modest or bold, these descriptors at this stage apply only during the time when a teacher is implementing his/her bodybrain-compatible curriculum.

Stage 3

Creating a Yearlong Theme & Practicing Citizenship

■ CURRICULUM

- A yearlong theme, prominently displayed on the wall for both students and teacher, serves as the framework for content development. On average, more than 25 percent of instruction during the school year is based upon bodybrain- compatible curriculum developed for this theme. (C147, 13-15)

- Curriculum content, as expressed in the key points, enhances pattern-seeking, making it easier for students to perceive and understand the most important ideas and concepts in the curriculum. Inquiries are designed to help students make connections to the real world, to practice using the concepts and skills of the key points, and to develop programs and store them in long-term memory. Inquiries that provide experiences in citizenship, such as social/political action activities and collaborative grouping practices, occur weekly. (C14, 15, 5)

- Most of the time, the curriculum includes almost all of the elements that appear as a natural part or extension of the *being there* focus, e.g., science, math, technology, history/social studies, and fine arts, as well as mathematics, reading, writing, and oral expression, including second language acquisition. (C13)

- The content of the theme is consistently used as a high interest area for applying the skills/knowledge currently being taught in at least one basic skill area (e.g., math, reading, writing).

- Curriculum for collaborative assignments is specifically designed for group work. (C14-15)

■ INSTRUCTIONAL STRATEGIES

- Immersion and hands-on-of-the-real-thing are the primary input used to supplement and extend *being there* experiences. (C1)

- All instructional time during the theme and for a growing portion of time during the remainder of the day is based upon the progression of

| *Being there* ➤ | *concept* ➤ | *language* ➤ | *application to the real world* |

rather than the traditional progression of

| *Language* ➤ | *concept* ➤ | *application* |

(C1)

- Collaboration is used daily whenever it will enhance pattern seeking and program building. (C1-6)

- Time is allocated in accordance with the nature of the tasks and student and teacher need for adequate time; such time allocations are made in recognition of the need to develop programs for using knowledge and skills in real-world contexts. (C1-6)

- Peers and cross-age tutors substantially increase teaching and practice time for students in areas of individual need.

[C,#] = Refers to the chapter(s) that describes how to implement this aspect of a bodybrain-compatible classroom.

Stage
3

■ EXPECTATIONS

- Students demonstrate the Lifelong Guidelines and LIFESKILLS throughout the day (in and out of the classroom); students are self-directed.
- Students as well as the teacher use the ITI 3 3Cs of Assessment as a means of assessing learning.
- Students exercise more shared leadership while doing collaborative activities and they actively seek connections to and applications in the real world.
- Student absentee rates drop to less than 3 percent; visits to the school nurse due to emotional, upset-based problems drop significantly. Library circulation rates increase by 50 percent.
- Parents report student levels of interest in school and learning are higher than ever before. Parents' support levels are higher than ever before; volunteerism has doubled.

■ INDICATORS

- Celebrations of learning and social/political action are key assessment tools for each component; they are designed to allow students to demonstrate mastery and application of the key points in the curriculum and to learn the skills and knowledge necessary for effective citizenship.
- Selections, for the portfolio folder, of work completed as part of the theme are made primarily by the student.
- Assessment of mastery is based upon a variety of relevant measures. For classroom use, curriculum and instructional planning are based primarily on the 3Cs of Assessment applied to assessment inquiries and other individual and group inquiries.

Stage 3 assumes that a bodybrain-compatible learning environment has been well established and is consistently nurtured and maintained throughout the day (Stage 1) and that the tools for developing bodybrain-compatible curriculum are consistently and effectively used during the time targeted for ITI curriculum (Stage 2). Stage 3 represents a refinement of implementing a bodybrain-compatible curriculum for students. Targeted time for ITI curriculum increases to approximately 25 percent of the year in Stage 3.

If either Stage 1 or 2 is not fully in place at this time, do not attempt to apply this stage regardless of the amount of teacher-developed curriculum being implemented. It is the quality, not the quantity, of ITI curriculum that is key. The power of the ITI model lies with its bodybrain-compatible underpinnings.

Stage 4

Citizenship Through a Microsociety & Integrating Basic Skills

⠿ CURRICULUM

- Curriculum is based predominantly on visitable locations that provide *being there* experiences and connections with the real world. (C13)

- The yearlong theme includes a compelling rationale statement for the conceptual idea and provides an unforgettable pattern-shaper for students. On average, more than two-thirds of instructional time during the school year is based upon bodybrain-compatible curriculum developed for this yearlong theme. (C17)

- The context of the theme is used daily as meaningful content for teaching at least two areas of basic skills (e.g., math, reading, writing, oral expression, second and primary language acquisition) and is used for applying all the basic skills. (C19)

- The development and practice of citizenship continues to be a central focus of curriculum. (C18)

⠿ INSTRUCTIONAL STRATEGIES

- Learning experiences are predominantly based on real life, immersion, and hands-on-of-the-real-thing; the teacher regularly utilizes on-site explorations and discovery processes to make learning real for students. (C1, 20, 21)

- All instructional time during the theme and for a growing portion of time during the remainder of the day is based upon the progression of

Being there ➤ *concept* ➤ *language* ➤ *application to the real world*

rather than the traditional progression of

Language ➤ *concept* ➤ *application*

(C1-6)

- Basic skills taught within the theme are taught as a means to an end, not as an end in themselves. Thus, while the teacher utilizes specific techniques for teaching the basic skills on a daily basis, student's primary focus is on the meaningful content which the basic skills help unlock. (C19)

- The teacher takes advantage of the power of "incidental learning" (as defined by Frank Smith) to build mental programs applying the basic skills. (C5)

- Choices, to allow for individual students' ways of learning, interests, and needs, are consistently provided. (C1-6)

- Students use technology as a natural extension of their senses to explore and learn.

[C,#] = Refers to the chapter(s) that describes how to implement this aspect of a bodybrain-compatible classroom.

Stage 4

EXPECTATIONS

- All students master the key points in all content and basic skill areas.
- Students demonstrate responsibility for their learning and act in a self-directed, self-initiating manner throughout the day; they have internalized the Lifelong Guidelines, including LIFESKILLS, and use them as the basis for interacting with others off campus as well as in the classroom and throughout the school campus.
- Students use what they learn in school to creatively solve real-life problems.
- Student absentee rates drop to less than 1.5 percent; visits to the school nurse are for serious physical illness, not for emotional upset.
- Library circulation rates are double those before the implementation of bodybrain-compatible/ ITI learning.
- All students who have experienced a bodybrain-compatible program implemented at Stage 3 or higher for at least three years perform at or above grade level; the average for the classroom is one grade level or more above national norms.

INDICATORS

- Except for district-required assessments, grading on the bell curve has been replaced with assessment of mastery and program-building demonstrated by culminating performances chosen by the teacher (using selected inquiries and the ITI 3 3Cs of Assessment).
- Students' yearlong research projects reflect high interest and understanding.
- Guest resource people acknowledge the high degree of student understanding.
- The class newspaper or magazine, published at least twice a year, reflects writing skills at least one year above grade level.
- Students, having learned to assess their own learning, participate in parent-teacher conferences, describing how selections of their work demonstrate their progress (academic, personal, and social); they set goals for learning during the next component of the yearlong theme.

Stage 4 assumes that a bodybrain-compatible learning environment has been established (Stage 1) and that the tools for developing bodybrain-compatible curriculum as described in Stages 2 and 3 are fully in place. Stage 4 represents a further refinement and extension of those tools and a consistent implementation of bodybrain-compatible curriculum for students for at least 50 percent of the time during the school year. If Stages 1, 2, and 3 are not fully in place, do not attempt to apply this stage regardless of the amount of time teacher-developed curriculum is being implemented. Again, the power of the ITI model lies with its bodybrain-compatible underpinnings.

Stage

5

⬡ CURRICULUM

Schoolwide Implementation

- The yearlong theme serves as the framework for content development and implementation for all basic skills and content 90% of the day/year. Key points and inquiries effectively enhance pattern seeking and program building.(C13, 14, 15, 17)

- The curriculum of the district, provides each teacher with pattern-enhancing tools for curriculum planning.(C12)

- Bodybrain-compatible curriculum is implemented schoolwide, providing consistency for students as they move through the school.

⬡ INSTRUCTIONAL STRATEGIES

- All instructional strategies identified in Stages 1 through 4 are in place 90% of the year. (C20-21)

- Students have the same teacher for two or more consecutive years due either to multi-aging or looping (the teacher moving with the students).

- The teacher utilizes the power of incidental learning during both planned instructional strategies and unplanned teachable moments.

- Technology in the classroom allows teachers and students full access to databases and communication systems throughout the country and the world. Being there experiences near the school are used as a starting point from which to examine similar, age-appropriate situations around the world.

[C,#] = Refers to the chapter(s) that describes how to implement this
aspect of a bodybrain-compatible classroom.

❖ EXPECTATIONS	❖ INDICATORS

* Self-responsibility for and self-initiated engagement in learning are valued schoolwide and clearly evident. Students display a love of learning and keen curiosity; they are mastering the skills and attitudes that make lifelong learning a reality.

* Students direct their own learning by assisting in the development of inquiries and the refinement of key points. They can identify and know how to pursue lifelong interests and career options; in focusing on these efforts, they can apply what they know to real world situations.

* Students have learned the personal and social skills for solving problems. They recognize the need for everyone's participation when making decisions that affect all. The classroom is a model of effective citizenship in action.

* Parent-teacher conferences have become student-parent-teacher conferences that, in the upper grades, are led by the student.

* Students initiate and engage in a wide range of community volunteer tasks, social and political action projects, and other means of contributing to society.

Like Stages 3 and 4, Stage 5 assumes that a bodybrain-compatible learning environment has been established (Stage 1) and is being maintained at a high level and that the tools for developing bodybrain-compatible curriculum, described in Stages 3 and 4, are in place and are highly refined as. Stage 5 represents an extension of those tools and a consistent implementation of bodybrain-compatible curriculum for students 90 percent of the time during the school year. If either Stage 1 or 2 is not fully in place and consistently nurtured and maintained or if Stages 3 and 4 are not in place, do not attempt to apply this stage. Again, the power of the ITI model lies in the quality of the implementation of its bodybrain-compatible underpinnings.

Appendix B:
The Discovery Process

Curiosity, the Great Motivator

When to use the Discovery Process? Whenever you are introducing a firsthand item—a specimen (owl pellets, worm farms, kiwi fruit), something unusual (starfish, oak galls, nests, etc.), something about which you want to pique student interest.

The Discovery Process takes full advantage of a child's natural curiosity. It is an opportunity to explore both the questions and answers, to explore connections between prior experiences and new, fact and fiction, to lead one's own learning.

In the ITI model, the Discovery Process is usually a Learning Club activity. In the spirit of two heads are better than one, working together usually uncovers the most patterns and the richest, most complex connections.

The steps in the Discovery Process are:

1. Stimulating curiosity

2. Setting standards and expectations

3. Providing lead-up time to prepare for the task

4. Acting as "guide on the side" during the exploration

5. Providing small group follow-up time

6. Capturing the teachable moment

7. Assessing student learning

8. Creating long-term memories through outreach

Step 1—Stimulating Curiosity

This is your chance to open the doors to wonder and awe for your students and a chance for them to experience being active, self-directed learners. This isn't direct instruction time, this is a time to ask questions, pose "what ifs," and drop amazing facts. Have fun! Get excited yourself! Tell your students that they are going to have a most amazing time.

Step 2—Setting Standards and Expectations

Setting standards and expectations for behavior and performance is critical. In addition to the everyday expectations to use the Lifelong Guidelines and LIFESKILLS, clearly establish those standards and expectations specific to the nature of the event.

In ten minutes or less:

- Identify the necessary procedures for working with a specimen (live or otherwise).

- Discuss use of exploratory tools, procedures, or other special equipment they will be using.

- Review what teamwork looks like and sounds like and does **not** look and sound like.

It's critical that the teacher is an enthusiastic leader. Yes, handle the snake, touch the shark, open the owl pellet, reach for the worms, and watch the live owl with fascination.

A KWL T-chart (see Chapter 24) is an effective tool to help students focus their thoughts. For the *K* column, have them list what they already know; in *W* column, list what they want to know. This discussion helps them set their expectations and begin to develop strategies for exploring. Afterwards, in the third column, have them list what they learned.

Step 3—Providing Lead-Up Time

Before beginning the Discovery Process, students need time to assimilate what they have heard, seen, and experienced during Steps 1 and 2. This needs to be done both individually and as a group. Provide time for students to discuss their mindmaps, share something from their personal experience, ask themselves, "Where does this fit into my knowledge/experience base?" and so forth. This is the time for communicating, a time during which students must actively and purposefully manipulate information in order to extract as much meaning from it as possible so that information is accurately stored in the brain.

The internal dialogue that occurs in answer to the question "How does this affect me?" is critical to activating the brain's attention mechanisms and its determination to store something in long-term memory.

During this settling in, getting comfortable period, students might be sketching a specimen, comparing pictures with the real thing, hypothesizing about what they're going to "discover," or relating their personal experiences having to do with the lesson. This time spent prior to the activity is their motivational lead-up for what they are about to do. For many students, this is the time to overcome fears and apprehensions about the unknown, e.g. a scary-looking owl. Not everyone is ready to jump in when the teacher says, "Go." Even if only ten minutes in duration, lead-up time is invaluable.

During lead-up time, decisions must be made about responsibility for group tasks. For example, "I'll be the recorder." "John draws well; he can sketch the parts." "Who wants to label?"

Sometimes it's appropriate for the teacher to select who will do specific jobs. This guarantees that students have an opportunity to practice various roles exercising leadership and responsibility. An efficient way to identify who does what is to assign every student in the group a number. All the teacher has to do is say, "For today, number 1 is the recorder, number 3 is the organizer, and number 5 is the facilitator," and so on. Another way is to post job assignments identifying specific jobs (one for each member of the group) that can be rotated. Possible roles are:

- Facilitator—sees that each group member has the opportunity to share ideas; reviews ground rules (if any) and initiates the discussion; help restart discussion when things bog down

- Inquisitor—asks at least two questions about the subject/topic to reveal the big idea

- Connector—looks for and share connections between the topic and personal experiences

- Illustrator—draws a picture of the most important elements of the topic

- Summarizer/Recorder—summarizes discussions to clarify understandings about content or how to proceed; records events, procedures, conclusions for the group

- Reporter—reads the instructions or information aloud

- Organizer—makes sure the work area is organized and clean

- Quieter—notices when the teacher signals for active listening

Equal opportunity to experience responsibility and leadership is a cornerstone commitment in an ITI classroom. Giving job responsibilities does not, however, mean that only one or two students "do" the activity, work with the firsthand materials, and so on. Everyone is a learner, all must participate in the activity. The jobs assigned to the group are in addition to the job of learning as individuals.

Step 4—The Exploration

Now that students are mentally ready, let them proceed. Let them explore, guide when it is necessary, help them interpret what they find. Shift your role from sage on the stage to guide on the side.

Step 5—Providing Small Group Follow-Up

Can you remember how important it seemed when a teacher gave you personal feedback of an instructive, positive nature? Remember how good it felt and how pleased you were that he/she noticed you personally? Such feedback is critical yet finding time to interact with students more frequently is difficult. Usually students who receive most of our time are those with behavior problems or special needs. To solve this dilemma, limit the time allotted for direct instruction, suggest students ask each other for help ("three before me"), and then take this purloined time to purposefully circulate during the groupwork activity.

"Purposefully circulate" means that you will especially target groups and individuals to reteach, redirect, and/or reenergize. This is the teacher's time to observe, listen, and analyze student responses and to give immediate feedback. This is also a perfect opportunity to acknowledge the use of the Lifelong Guidelines, especially Personal Best as defined by the LIFESKILLS.

Step 6—Capturing the Teachable Moment

The teachable moment is when the student's curiosity is sparked and the teacher can enhance learning by drawing on his/her own knowledge base. It is an opportunity for the teacher to model being an active and competent learner. Taking advantage of teachable moments requires a broad knowledge base and the willingness to extend learning or even digress when appropriate.

In this information age, we're both frustrated and excited by the bombardment of knowledge all around us. To find time to increase your knowledge base, take 20 minutes a day (10 in the morning and 10 in the afternoon or evening) to read about the concepts, significant knowledge, and skills of your theme. Read books, magazines, newsletters, audio cassettes, professional journals, and any other materials that relate. When you are an ITI teacher, your theme will help you assimilate information and hold it organizationally in your mind. Teachers must be active learners committed to mastering how to use information and skills, not just "talk about" them.

Remembering how good it feels to learn—reliving the feeling each day—enables us to recognize when learning is actually taking place in the classroom and to capture the teachable moment.

Step 7—Assessing Learning

Because the Discovery Process is so multidimensional, assessment should be so also. In addition to checking for context, we also need to assess the strength of emotional involvement in learning. How students feel about learning is a big determiner of whether that learning will get wired into long-term memory.

Assessing Emotional Impact

Assessing the emotional impact of a lesson is just as important as assessing content. Feelings while learning something new become the attitudes we hold for the rest of our lives. How often have we heard, "I wasn't good in that when I went to school, so I'm not surprised my child isn't doing well either," or "I've never liked math or science or reading."

A daily journal is one way students can express their emotional responses to what they're learning. After a vigorous lesson such as dissecting owl pellets, it's imperative to allow students to ponder how they feel about what they learned and how this experience will affect learning in the future. Never discount your students' feelings; acknowledge that feelings are a part of being alive and, more importantly, they are the gate keeper to the cognitive domain. Everyone has emotions; unguided or ignored emotions usually hinder learning rather than assist.

If an activity has generated feelings of indignation, outrage, or heightened personal interest and concern, it is time for political action, a time to write letters to the editor, school board, planning commission, Save-the-Whales committee, a chemical company, the President of the United States, local businesses, Sierra Club, and the like. Learning and internalizing information are not enough in today's society. Individuals must realize they have a right and a responsibility to become involved and that their opinions and concerns need to be heard.

Taking action on social issues imparts a sense of importance to lessons learned at school. It provides a real-world context in which to fully explore concepts and skills and gives an audience (and a reason) for exercising a wide range of communication skills.

Assessing Academic Learning

The current "authentic assessment"[1] movement is a pleasant breath of spring across the educational landscape. Brushing aside contrived, trivial, standardized assessments, Grant Wiggins, Fred Newmann, and other authentic assessment leaders admonish us to measure ability to use knowledge—producing knowledge rather than reproducing it. Thus the phrase "authentic expressions of knowledge."

In the ITI model we speak of mastery/competence in terms of performance. There's a large gap between knowing about and knowing how to do. It's the application of knowledge and skills that determines what we can do and measuring what we do with what authentic assessment is all about.

The exploration phase of the Discovery Process is just the beginning and should lead onward to specific demonstrations of what is learned during the Discovery Process. See Chapter 16 for a discussion of assessment in the ITI model.

Step 8—Creating Long-term Memories Through Outreach

Outreach is the purposeful connection of classroom activity to someone or something outside the classroom—a way of applying lessons to reality.[2] Outreach can be planned by contacting a resource person or it can be spontaneous as when students suggest a course of action. Outreach asks the question, "Knowing this information leads me where or to whom?" To have knowledge and skills is to be responsible. Does it demand we take action? In a democracy, if we don't take action to correct problems or social ills, who will? Perhaps the students want to share with other classes or schools, produce a videotape, invite someone in to answer questions, start an information center, or set up a display at the local library or school district office. Educating others is a major responsibility of us all. Outreach demands application of what is studied. It may have long-range effects or short-term impact, but it is an important classroom activity, one which gently prods both the students and the teacher into looking at content in an active, meaningful way.

When looking at outreach, called "political or social action" in the ITI model, we should use the language arts skills of reading, writing, listening and speaking. Outreach activities provide real audiences and a clear sense of purpose. What better environment in which to master these skills? In students' minds it becomes clear that these skills are a means to an important end—the ability to cope in the real world.

The best tools we know to assist you in planning outreach is *Kid's Guide to Social Action: How to Solve the Social Problems You Choose—And Turn Creative Thinking into Positive Action* and *The Kid's Guide to Service Projects: Over 500 Service Ideas for Young People Who Want to Make a Difference*, both by Barbara A. Lewis. These books are filled with practical suggestions for getting involved and vignettes of student political action from around the country. They will assist your students with form, content, addresses, procedures, and presentations. They are comprehensive and written as user's guides. *Enriching Curriculum Through Service Learning*, edited by C.W. Kinsley and K. McPherson, is another fine resource.

Enjoy the moment. Your students certainly will!

Notes

1 According to Fred Newman, as children progress toward authentic expressions of knowledge, "they must hone their skills through guided practice in producing original conversation and writing, through repairing and building of physical objects, through artistic and musical performance." He adds, "A second defining feature of authentic academic achievement is its reliance upon a particular type of cognitive work which can be summarized as *disciplined inquiry*. Disciplined inquiry, in turn, seems to consist of three features: use of a prior knowledge base; in-depth understanding rather than superficial awareness; and production of knowledge in an integrated rather than fragmented form."

2 Leslie Hart admonishes us to remember that that "learning is the acquisition of useful programs." The corollary statement is that information we use is the information that we remember. See Chapter 5.

Appendix C:
Communicating with Parents

Communicating with Parents

Communication with parents and guardians is a completely understated, largely overlooked opportunity for teachers, yet it is one of our most powerful sources of support. Introduce yourself to your parents even before school starts. Let them know that your classroom will be a special experience for their child. Don't wait for the traditional Back-to-School Night in October; it is entirely too late in the fall to serve as a tool for creating an anticipatory set.

Welcome Letter to Students

Begin by sending a letter to their child welcoming him/her to your classroom. In this letter include a personal greeting expressing that you're looking forward to meeting him/her, your commitment to making this year the best ever, and an outline of your plans for the year—the *being there* experiences, the theme, and why you're excited about the year. Also include a request that the child invite his/her parents/guardians to attend a Back to School night held the very first week of school—Thursday night.

Back to School Night

If the first week seems too soon, consider this reality: substitute teachers have less than 60 seconds to establish themselves with students. Four days is more than enough to capture your students' attention and hearts. And, the sooner you communicate with parents, the less time for assumptions or misunderstandings. Your ITI program may be new and different from what they have known in the past, so capture their attention and spread your enthusiasm in the same way you do with your students. Remember, parents are the first and foremost teachers in the children's lives.

At Back to School night, provide a comprehensive information packet such as the one described here. For parents/guardians unable to attend, send the packet home with their child the next day.

Dear Parents/Guardians,

The ITI model (Integrated Thematic Instruction) is an innovative and proven method of implementing in the classroom what we know from current brain research. It also integrates skills and content in real-life ways.

The following pages will introduce you to many of the concepts, terms, and resources which will be used in your child's classroom this year. I am looking forward to working with you to create an extraordinary year for your child.

CONTENTS OF THE PARENT INFORMATION PACKET

1. Recommended Books
2. A Week in the Life of My Child
3. The Power of Emotion in Learning and Performance
4. Lifelong Guidelines/LIFESKILLS
5. Food and its Effects on Learning
6. Yearlong Theme
7. Public Library
8. Research Project
9. Mindmapping
10. Homework
11. Letter to Parents
12. Possible Family Study Trips (aka Study Adventures)
13. Contacting the Teacher

1. Recommended Books for Parents to Read

Character Begins at Home: Family Tools for Teaching Character at Home by Karen D. Olsen and Sue Pearson.

There are hundreds of ideas for nurturing children's character through the Lifelong Guidelines and LIFESKILLS using simple, enjoyable activities at home. Children and youth benefit by hearing and using a common language at home and at school as they develop the social skills of respect and responsible citizenship. This is a great idea for building family/community support.

Human Brain and Human Learning by Leslie Hart.

This is the most significant book on brain research and its implications for the classrooms of America. The term "brain-compatible" was coined by this author. His examples of how learning goes astray inside schools will remind all readers of their own experiences as children. This is the foundation book for Integrated Thematic Instruction, which is based on brain-compatible learning.

Seven Kinds of Smarts: Identifying and Developing Your Many Intelligences by Thomas Armstrong.

Armstrong, a leader in translating the multiple intelligences into practical applications at school and home, provides a clear, understandable overview of the theory of multiple intelligences; a 40-item assessment inventory, and everyday examples of high capability and of the consequences of low capability in each area.

What Kids Need to Succeed by Peter Benson, et al

This book is filled with helpful ideas about how to build support, empowerment, boundaries, expectations, time management strategies, social competencies, and positive values for students in grades 6-12. Offers 900 specific, concrete suggestions.

Punished By Rewards: The Trouble with Gold Stars, Incentive Plans, A's, Praise, & Other Bribes by Alfie Cohn

The more we use artificial inducements to motivate children, the more they lose interest in what we're bribing them to do. Offer practical strategies for parents to minimize bribing children to do a job.

The Over-Scheduled Child by Alvin Rosenfeld and Nicole Wise

Today's parents, with the best intentions, strive to micromanage every detail of their child's life to ensure that the child will give high performances in academic, social, and athletic arenas. This book provides choices to this nonstop pressure for children and parents alike. The authors offer clear, comforting steps to attack this rampant phenomenon, encourage healthier and happier children, and revitalize the parenting experience.

The Ritalin Nation: Transformation of Human Consciousness by Richard DeGrandpre

The author attributes the disturbing prevalence of inattention and hyperactivity in children to the larger psychological consequences of living in a rapid-fire culture. Practical guidelines for charting a hopeful future and moving away from sensory addiction.

The Wonder of Boys by Michael Gurian

The author has the courage to advocate for moral and spiritual values for boys, for teaching boys about sex and love and family. Provides a concrete plan that begins at home but extends deep into the community.

The Right Moves: A Girl's Guide to Feeling Good by Tina Schwager and Michele Schuerger

Start when you are young. What does it take to be totally fit—inside and out? It's a blend of attitude, eating right and exercise. This book will inspire you to take care of your body, get and stay healthy, and believe in yourself.

2. A Week in the Life of My Child

The grid on the next page is for recording the activities of your child for one week. This is useful for you and your child so that you can get a picture of your child's "education" when outside of school. Remember, you are your child's first teacher. Seeing exactly where and on what your child spends his/her time is the beginning step in examining how you might play a more powerful supportive role with your child this year. Also, I would be happy to discuss your child's schedule with you and its possible impact on your child's learning.

The time chart is broken into four sections to help you capture a full 24-hour day overview of seven consecutive days. Record the adult and peer influences your child experiences each day. How much support time are you able to give your child. The more detailed your information, the more valuable it will be.

3. Current Brain Research

The ITI model is based upon the findings of brain research from the past 25 years. Gleaned from many fields and supported by research made possible by high tech instruments such as CAT scans, PET scans, MRI, and fMRI, we can now literally watch a brain in action. For 25 years, the research has provided very consistent findings which are summarized in the ITI model as:

- Intelligence is a function of experiences which cause physiological growth in the brain. Genetics plays a lesser role than generally believed and high levels of sensory input is more important than usually recognized.

- Learning is the result of an inseparable partnership of brain and body. Emotion is the gatekeeper to learning

and performance and movement is key to optimal brain function.

- We have at least seven intelligences. An intelligence is defined as a problem-solving and/or product-producing capability. Each of the intelligences functions from a different part of the brain.

- The brain extracts and creates meaning through a pattern-seeking process. It is not logical and sequential when making meaning (however, it can be very logical and sequential when it is *using* information that it has learned).

- Most useful information is embedded in mental programs; information that does not become embedded in a program for using it in real–world applications is largely forgotten.

Because of these findings, the ITI classroom is dedicated to providing a learning environment with the following bodybrain-compatible elements:

- Absence of threat/
  Nurturing reflective thinking

- Meaningful content

- Movement to enhance learning

- Choices

- Adequate time

- Enriched environment

- Collaboration

- Immediate feedback

- Mastery and the ability to use concepts and skills in real life

	Monday	Tuesday	Wednesday	Thursday	Friday	Saturday	Sunday
BEFORE SCHOOL							
AT SCHOOL							
AFTER SCHOOL							
AFTER DINNER							

Each of these concepts about how the brain works and the bodybrain-compatible elements will be discussed at parent night and in home-school communications throughout the year. We will be spending a great deal of time at the beginning of the year on the role of emotion in learning and how to create an environment notable for absence of threat and enhancing reflective thinking. These are key elements of my classroom management and approach to discipline. Also, these are important areas of a strong home-school partnership. I look forward to working with you to help your child learn and grow.

4. Lifelong Guidelines & LIFESKILLS

Our classroom is practicing Lifelong Guidelines and LIFESKILLS. These differ from regular school rules because they apply to all age groups in all situations, thus the term LIFESKILLS. They form the basis for agreement between teacher and students, and among the students, about behavior and expectations (social and academic). I encourage you to learn about them (ask your child!) and I ask that you reinforce them at home.

Lifelong Guidelines

TRUSTWORTHINESS: To act in a manner that makes one worthy of trust and confidence

TRUTHFULNESS: To act with personal responsibility and mental accountability

ACTIVE LISTENING: To listen attentively and with the intention of understanding

NO PUT-DOWNS: To never use words, actions, and/or body language that degrade, humiliate, or dishonor others

PERSONAL BEST: To do one's best given the circumstances and available resources

LIFESKILLS

CARING: To feel and show concern for others

COMMON SENSE: To use good judgment

COOPERATION: To work together toward a common goal or purpose

COURAGE: To act according to one's beliefs despite fear of adverse consequences

CURIOSITY: A desire to investigate and seek understanding of one's world

EFFORT: To do your best

FLEXIBILITY: To be willing to alter plans when necessary

FRIENDSHIP: To make and keep a friend through mutual trust and caring

INITIATIVE: To do something, of one's own free will, because it needs to be done

INTEGRITY: To act according to a sense of what's right and wrong

ORGANIZATION: To plan, arrange, and implement in an orderly way; to keep things orderly and ready to use

PATIENCE: To wait calmly for someone or something

PERSEVERANCE: To keep at it

PRIDE: Satisfaction from doing one's personal best

PROBLEM SOLVING: To create solutions to difficult situations and everyday problems

RESOURCEFULNESS: To respond to challenges and opportunities in innovative and creative ways

RESPONSIBILITY: To respond when appropriate; to be accountable for one's actions

SENSE OF HUMOR: To laugh and be playful without harming others

5. Food & Its Effects on Learning

There are three books, all very readable, which offer some sound advice and suggestions for feeding children in a healthy manner. I recommend them as a beginning point in understanding the powerful influence food (especially junk food) has upon the chemistry of the brain and, therefore, its ability to learn.

Good For Me! by Marilyn Burns

This is a great book to read with your child. There are also many "things to do" that families will find fun and informational. A quick look at the table of contents gives you an idea of the excitement of this book: Biting In, What's the Use of Food, Anyway?; You Can Hurt Your Stomach's Feelings; The Fizz in Your Diet; The National Meal in a Bun; The Ice Cream Story; Learning to Read Labels; and, Will an Apple a Day Keep the Doctor Away?

Food For Healthy Kids by Dr. Lendon Smith

This provides a thorough look at food, behavior, allergies, and addictions from ages pre-birth to adulthood. Chapter headings include: Hyperactivity and Tension at All Ages; Sugar Cravings—Foods and Moods; Sleep Problems—Foods for Restless Children. Recipes for over a hundred healthy and tasty meals for children are included.

The Body's Many Cries for Water by F. Batmanghelidj, M.D.

Hydration also has a big effect on how the brain functions. Make sure your child drinks at least eight glasses of water a day. Sodas are not a water source; they contain chemicals that cause the body to use its water reserves to dilute and eliminate those chemicals. Numerous health and behavior problems are being attributed to dehydration. See www. watercure.com

6. Yearlong Theme, Key Points, and Inquiries

The basis for Integrated Thematic Instruction is the brain research of the past twenty years. The model was designed to best fit the brain's natural way of learning.

Yearlong Theme and Key Points

Because brain research tells us that the brain learns through seeking out understandable patterns, our curriculum is designed to enhance students' ability to detect and make meaning of patterns. The staff has worked hard at making our key points conceptual because concepts are big patterns and to organize our content around a single, yearlong theme through which all content and basic skills are taught. This is a dramatic departure from the fragmented day during which each subject is taught separately.

Examples of Key Points.

Key points are statements of what is most essential for students to learn—the essential core of knowledge and skills in each of the subject areas included in our yearlong theme. Key points are identified for each day, week, month, and year. They are the content every student needs to learn and be able to apply.

An example of a *conceptual key point* is: In our complex world we use increasingly more and complicated sources of power and machines to help meet our daily needs. Many tools and machines that help us do our work are powered with electricity. Electricity powers machines that help make our homes light at night, keep us warm in the winter or cool in the summer, keep our food cold so that it won't spoil, as well as many other uses. Electrical energy occurs naturally or can be generated and controlled by man.

An example of a *significant knowledge key point* that supports the conceptual key point is: In order for an electrical current to flow, it must have an uninterrupted conducting path. This is called an electric circuit. There are two kinds of electric circuits. A series circuit has only one electrical path, and any break in the path will interrupt the flow of electricity (for example old-fashioned Christmas tree lights). A parallel circuit has multiple paths. A break in one path will not interrupt the flow of electricity in the other paths (for example a string of lights that remain on when one bulb burns out). Knowing the properties, advantages and disadvantages of each kind of circuit can help us to understand why an appliance may or may not work, make decisions about energy conservation and create more complex electrical environments.

A Yearlong Theme. The purpose of the yearlong theme is to provide an umbrella pattern under which everything fits in a way that shows relationships among ideas and thus makes smaller ideas more memorable and retrievable.

The yearlong theme for our classroom is shown below. As you can see, the topics that we will be studying are varied and exciting.

Paste a copy of your yearlong theme here

so that parents can know what's coming next.

Inquiries

Inquiries are the activities your child will do to "learn" the concepts and skills identified in the key points. Inquiries require the application of reading, writing, computing, and best of all, thinking!

The intent is to better provide your child with the capabilities that come with understanding at the level of application and the ability to solve problems in the real world versus rely on rote memorization. The two questions I kept in mind as I was developing curriculum for this year were:

- What do I want students to understand?

- What do I want them to be able to do with what they understand?

These two questions will lead us into higher expectations for student performance, especially in the area of basic skills — reading, writing, and 'rithmetic—because they are basic to doing something in the world outside of the classroom. I look forward to sharing with you the key points and inquiries your child will be studying.

In developing inquiries for both work in class and homework for this class, I have also utilized the conceptual framework of Howard Gardner as presented in his book, *Frames of Mind: Theory of Multiple Intelligences.* Gardner defines intelligence as a "problem-solving and/or product-producing capability" rather than an I.Q. number. He suggests that we are all born with at least seven different, each one operating from a different location in the brain. Each of us develops a propensity for using one or more capabilities in our everyday lives. In the classroom, my goal is to help your child develop all of these areas of intelligence because all are necessary to succeed in life beyond our school years.

Here are some inquiries written for the key points mentioned above. They illustrate the range of problem-solving and product-producing capabilities that can be tapped and nurtured. They are examples of the types of activities your child will be involved in during our course of study.

1. *Design* and *build* a series or parallel circuit that will light each room in your Learning Club's "house." *Discuss* your plan for wiring your house with each other before you begin. *Propose* to each other how the materials will be used and how the electricity will flow through the house.

2. *Diagram* the wiring in your house. *Label* the electrical parts. *Describe* the circuit. *Determine* if it is a series or parallel circuit and *explain* why.

3. *Create* a flow chart that describes what you know about the flow of electricity through a circuit to make something work. *Read* the article "Relay Race" about telegraphs and discuss the sequence of events in the story as well as the sequence of events that enables a message to travel from the sender in one end of the country to the receiver in the other end of the country. *Illustrate* and *describe* the sequence in a step book.

4. By yourself or with a partner, use the measurements for your Learning Club's house to *calculate* the length of wire you will need to complete the circuit of electricity in your house. *Share* your results with the rest of your Learning Club. *Compare* your results with the others in your Learning Club and together *determine* the total length of wire you will need.

INQUIRIES FOR ASSESSMENT:

1. *Design* and *build* a model for an invention that uses electricity to meet a need that could help make life easier in some way or solve an everyday problem.

Diagram your invention and how it should work. *Write* a brief explanation of how the invention is helpful and how it should work. If your invention does not work as you planned it after you build it, *analyze* why you think it did not work and record your analysis in your journal. Be sure to use all of our key points for the week in your invention and your explanations.

2. Edit your research paper first by yourself, then with a partner. Use the rubric to be sure you have included or corrected everything. Rewrite it in its final form. Read it to a partner. Be ready to present it to the class.

As you can see, the inquiries ask students to apply what they are learning to real-world situations. This deepens their understanding, makes learning more memorable, and significantly increases the likelihood that they will remember the knowledge and skills years later. Our assessment inquiries are especially good tests of ability to use knowledge and skills.

To help make this year as rich an experience as possible, I would appreciate any and all support from parents, e.g., serving as a resource person in the classroom, providing materials, generating ideas for possible class study trips, assistance with study trips, etc.

7. The Public Library

Our public library should become your child's favorite place to find information and have questions answered. According to an article published by Northwest Airlines, "There are more than 115,000 libraries serving the American public; libraries employ over 300,000 people and spend almost $3 billion per year on materials and services — less than a dollar a month for every man, woman and child in the United States. America's public libraries circulate more than one billion items per year — everything from books to computer software to children's toys, games, audio cassettes, videotapes, art prints, and films."

It is ironic that some libraries are closing for lack of support in this country. It is the last "free" source of information available to all, regardless of income or education, and deserves to be used and supported. Interestingly, even during a recession, libraries which are heavily used and strongly supported by their communities are never cut from the budget. Libraries which close are eliminated more because public use is limited, not because public funds are limited. Support your library!

The public library is your closest and easiest vehicle to adventure. And, it's free. If your child does not already have his/her own library card, apply for one immediately. We have application cards available at Parent Night. Set a goal of visiting the library twice a week. Teach your child how to browse through the library and how to use the card catalog (or computerized system!).

Check the schedule for special events for children. Most libraries provide a surprisingly wide array of cultural events for children.

Lastly, teach your child how to read public transportation schedules and how to use public transportation. When your child is old enough, teach him/her to go alone. Going to the library will become as typical an adult behavior as turning on TV to watch the news.

8. *Yearlong Research Project*

As part of the Integrated Thematic Instruction model, each child is requested to choose a topic of interest that relates to our theme and to conduct a yearlong research project. Information can be gleaned from the newspaper, magazines, encyclopedias, and museum pamphlets, at all readability levels designed for both children and adults. This is your child's chance to develop practical, everyday information-gathering skills and discover life-long interests.

Resources are as near as the yellow pages of your phone book and Internet and as far away as those listed in the *Encyclopedia of Associations*, a remarkable publication available through your public library. It contains over 30,000 addresses of public and private organizations that have been formed to "get the word out"—information on all subjects. Writing letters to request free information provides a real audience for your child's writing skills. And when the information arrives in the child's mailbox with his/her name on it . . . well, of course, it will be high interest reading material!

The research project articles should be kept in a three-ring binder. Each article is read, highlighted, and at least three facts that your child thinks are interesting or important are mindmapped; the information is then added to the binder which can be easily reorganized as time goes on. Copies of letters sent and answered belong in the binder. At the appropriate time during the year, the teacher will ask for the expertise of your child to be presented to the class. This is the beginning of a lifelong habit of collecting, analyzing, synthesizing, and using information.

The long-term research project is the best "homework" you can do with your child. It provides a point of discussion and analysis. The end products are pride in accomplishing a significant task, deep knowledge, and lifelong learning skills.

9. *Mindmapping*

This year your child will be introduced to a concept called mindmapping—a way of visually representing how concepts and ideas related to each other. Pictures, as well as colors, enhance long-term memory, and retrieval. Mindmapping is a skill and, like other skills, it demands practice in order to do it well. Learn and practice it along with your child. It is a powerful study skill.

Recommended book: *Mapping Inner Space: Learning and Teaching Mind Mapping* by Nancy Margulies.

10. Homework

Homework is best assigned when it has meaning and purpose (from the learner's perspective. It should support and expand the skills, content, and concepts that were presented in the class. It will supplement what has gone on in the classroom that day — something which could not be done at school, either for lack of time or materials necessary to do the job well.

Do not expect your child to bring home "dittos" or "worksheets." Such drills too often kill the joy of learning, and, worst of all, seldom enhance learning. The intent of homework in this class is to give your child practice in using knowledge and skills in everyday life and at real-world standards for acceptability and excellence.

The best homework is the time you spend with your child reading, answering and posing questions, and investigating areas and concepts that will generate a sense of purpose for what your child is learning in the classroom.

11. Letter to Parents

Because your participation in your child's education is so critical to his/her progress this year, I will send you a letter at least twice a month. The letter will keep you up-to-date with happenings in the classroom — what we are currently studying, how you can support your child in mastering the key points for the month, what you might do to assist your child in learning how to apply what he/she is learning to real life (in your home, neighborhood, community), and, lastly, how you might assist the class as a whole — in the classroom or on a study trip.

The letter will typically follow the outline below:

Dear Parents,

We are into our ___ component of this year's theme, and our weekly topics for this month will include:

1.

2.

3.

4.

This week we will be working on inquiries for these key points in our content study:

1.

2.

3.

Our key points in the basic skills area (reading, writing, and mathematics) are:

1.

2.

3.

I invite you to assist your child in understanding those inquiries your child has selected to work on (or that I may have assigned), which support the key points. In particular, I invite you to help your child apply this information to real-life situations.

Your continuing to work with your child on his/her year-long research project is appreciated and makes the efforts all the more worthwhile.

Our resource person for this month (week) will be _____. If you have any additional suggestions regarding resources, especially non-print ones, please let us know.

Our next study trip:_____

Our next learning celebration event: _____

These are special days. Please mark them on your family calendar.

12. Possible Family Study Adventures within a 50-Mile Radius

Parents are not only the first teachers of their children but also the most important. Schools are but a supplement to the educating process of the parents. Your modeling of lifelong learning is the most important gift you can give your child. Make a list of all the possible educational locations within a 50-mile radius of your home (for small towns, increase the radius to 75 or 100 miles; rural areas, 100–300 miles). For example:

- Parks and historical sites
- Museums
- Cultural centers
- Natural environments: lakes, rivers, mountains, oceans, etc.
- Neighboring cities
- Plays and concerts
- Fairs
- Other

Set as your goal at least one study adventure every four weeks. Remember, intelligence is a function of experience. The more experiences children have, the greater is their ability to make connections.

13. Contacting Your Child's Teacher

If you need to contact me, please feel free to call the school and leave a message with the school secretary.

I appreciate your willingness to spend quality time with your child, investing in the role of "first teacher," modeling the behaviors and values of lifelong learners and contributing members of society. Do know that I will be doing everything possible in the classroom to support those goals for your child and I am looking forward to forming a close working partnership with you so that together we can ensure that your child fulfills his/her capabilities.

Sincerely,

Your Child's Teacher

Appendix D:
Age-Appropriate Curriculum

Age-Appropriateness

A young child's brain is not just a "junior" version of the adult brain, an adult brain with less information in it. It processes differently. The human brain unfolds in predictable developmental stages. Each stage is like an ever more complex template laid over the top of the previous one. At each of these stages, the brain is capable of more complex thinking, comparing, and analyzing. Incoming information that requires a level of processing not yet acquired by the brain results in lack of understanding, inability to "get it." When things are "ungettable," students give up and resort to memorization. Over time, when too many things are "ungettable," students slowly learn not to try to understand but merely to memorize and parrot back.

This is a serious issue because it undermines the student's confidence in self as a learner as well as teachers' expectations for student outcomes. Worse, it absolutely kills the joy of learning.

Following is a brief overview of developmental stages based on the work of Larry Lowery, as reflected in presentations to administrators and teachers of the Mid-California Science Improvement Program (MCSIP) and in his book, *Thinking and Learning: Matching Developmental Stages with Curriculum and Instruction.**

Age Three to First Grade:

Comparing the Known to the Unknown

During this stage of life, children learn to understand more words (and the concepts behind them) than they will for the rest of their lives. The child does this through one-to-one correspondences, putting two objects together on the basis of a single property and

_____
* Used with written permission of the publisher, Books for Educators.

learning from these comparisons more than was known before. According to Lowery, the child constructs fundamental concepts about the physical world and its properties (similarity and difference comparisons based on size, shape, color, texture, etc.), about ordinal and cardinal numbers (one-to-one correspondence of varying degrees), about all measures (comparison of known to unknown), and about the use of symbols to stand for meaning (word recognitions).[1]

The major mode of operation at this stage is trial and error. Often, adults mistakenly try to "help" the child in an attempt to reduce or eliminate error or reprimand the child for making an error. This is unfortunate, because the important point here is that the child learns from the situation in either case—erroneous or correct. Whether putting puzzle shapes into the wrong space, learning to dress oneself and getting the shoes on the wrong feet, or falling off a tricycle. For the child, a "no" provides as much information as a "yes."

An important characteristic of this stage is that the child does not yet have the ability to group objects using more than one property simultaneously.[2] For example, pairings made on the basis of size, color, shape, texture, speed, using one property or characteristic to pair them. The three- to six-year-old may also arrange objects by chaining, i.e., the third object in the chain shares an important characteristic with the second object (which was initially chosen to pair with the first object) based on a different characteristic:

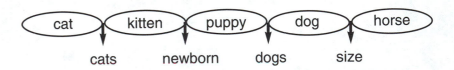

This stage is variously described as: ability to put two objects together on the basis of a single property[3] or learning by one-to-one correspondence. Piaget's description: *pre-operational stage*.

If you take the time to put this information to use and analyze your district's scope and sequence or current textbooks, you're in for a genuine shock and complete surprise. You will find that there is a high percentage of material that is wholly inappropriate. Examples of age-inappropriate topics from a popular, state-adopted science textbook for first grade include: earth as it looks from space, landforms around the world, how water shapes the land, air, and much more!

Second Grade to Third Grade:

Putting Things Together, Taking Things Apart

At this stage a child develops the capability to group all objects in a set on the basis of one common attribute (as compared to putting only two objects together on the basis of a single property). This capacity begins at about age six (late) and is established for most youngsters by age eight.

According to Lowery, "for the first time the student's mental construct is comprehensive and has a rationale or logic to it. . . . Simple rules can be understood and generated by the student if given the opportunity."[4]

At this stage students do less trial and error exploration and are more thoughtful about the actions they impose upon their environment; they create an internal mental structure of those manipulations.[5] An important aspect of students' actions is the rearrangement of the materials with which they work. Students also have the capacity to do things in reverse direction without distorting the concept, e.g., 3 + 2 = 5; 5 - 2 = 3. This is one of the powerful aspects of thinking at this stage.[6]

From an adult's perspective, there is a correct and an incorrect way to put things together or take them apart; the child at variance is thus seen as having done the job "incorrectly." Rather than just judging the task, however, adults should also examine the reason why the student chose that particular response and then focus on the quality of the understanding that is revealed in the answers given.

This stage is variously described as: ability to put all objects together on the basis of a consistent, single property rationale or putting things together and returning things to the way they were.[7] Piaget's term: early concrete operations.

Again, examples of age-inappropriate content from a popular science textbook include the following. For second graders: prehistoric animals and climate changes creating extinction, matter, magnets, light waves, heat transfer, air and air in water, rotation of the earth. For third graders: photosynthesis, particles in matter, changes in matter, forces (gravity, magnetism), energy (work, earth core, earthquakes), forces which shape the land (weathering, water, wind), tilt of the earth produces weather changes, and the solar system. Such topics require an ability to think abstractly which is not possible until the pre-frontal lobes are developed.

Fourth Grade to Sixth Grade:

Simultaneous Ideas

At about age eight to ten, children develop the capacity to mentally coordinate two or more properties or concepts at a time. According to Lowery, when this capacity is in place—which may occur as early as age eight or as late as age ten—students can comprehend place value in math, the need for controlling variables in a science experiment, the use of similies and multiple themes in literature, and can begin to understand the relationships that exist in free trade in social studies.[8] According to Lowery, "as with earlier capabilities, this new one integrates with those preceding it much like a new map of greater abstraction that can be overlaid upon other layers of maps."[9]

At this stage, students enjoy puns and can easily learn about homonyms. In their writing they shift to using multiple descriptors: "an old, bent, tired man." They shift from trial and error thinking to contemplating the effects of comparing two or more situations under different situations.[10] Arrangement of objects now indicates the intersection of multiple properties.

Piaget refers to this stage as late concrete operations; Lowery's term is simultaneity of ideas.

Examples of age-inappropriate content from the same popular science textbook (distributed 1985) are mind boggling. For fourth grade: heat as particle activity, how fossils are formed, ocean floor, causes of tides, ocean currents around the world. For fifth grade: atoms, elements, compounds, molecules, chemical bonding; nuclear fusion; light energy waves; and many other topics which should be moved to junior and senior high. For sixth grade: virtually all areas should be moved to junior and mostly senior high levels.

The irony here is that, for all of America's glorification of youth and childhood, our traditional school curriculum treats elementary students as young adults. Yet for our young adults—high school students—the curriculum for the non-college bound is a re-run of what students were given in elementary school and, thus, is unchallenging and often boring.

So, what does all this mean for an ITI classroom? It means that the closer the curriculum is to the real world, the more likely it will be age-appropriate rather than abstract and calling for mental processing students don't yet possess.

Note: The idea of age-appropriateness is certainly not new. Montessori, Piaget, and countless others have addressed the issue quite clearly. Yet, it just gets pushed aside by tradition when textbooks and state frameworks are being created. A glance through textbooks from the past several decades shows tradition at its most mindless and blind adherence to "the way we've always done it."

The purpose of looking at what is appropriate at each age level is to make thoughtful decisions for less is more. Notice, in particular, the age at which each capacity comes into place. And bear in mind that there will be some students on both ends of each predicted age group. If the mental scaffolding doesn't exist for learning a particular concept, content must be changed to match the stage of intellectual development of individual students. Because some students can understand something doesn't mean that all students at that age can, nor does it mean that such students are less capable.

Notes

1 Lawrence F. Lowery, Thinking and Learning: Matching Developmental Stages with Curriculum and Instruction, (Covington, WA: Books for Educators, 1993), p. 2.

2 Lowery, op. cit., p. 20.

3 Lowery, op. cit., p. 18.

4 Lowery, op. cit., p. 31.

5 Lowery, op. cit., p. 33.

6 Lowery, op. cit., p. 34.

7 Lowery, op. cit., p. 36.

8 Lowery, op. cit., p. 41.

9 Lowery, op. cit., p. 37.

10 Lowery, op. cit., p. 41.

Glossary
Bibliography

Glossary

3Cs of Assessment
A set of criteria for assessing student work used by both students and teachers. The Cs stand for: Correct—conforming to fact or truth, free from error; accurate; Complete—having all parts or elements; the assignment is done to the defined specifications; Comprehensive—of large scope, inclusive, extensive mental range or grasp; reflects multiple points of view, thorough.

Absence of Threat/Nurturing Reflective Thinking
One of the nine Bodybrain-Compatible Elements of the ITI model. See Chapters 1-6.

Adequate Time
One of the nine Bodybrain-Compatible Elements of the ITI model. See Chapters 1-6.

Age-Appropriate
Concepts and/or facts which are understandable (versus memorizable) by students, given the current degree of development of the brain. These biological stages of thinking and learning gained attention through the work of Piaget.

Assessment/Evaluation
A process by which student achievement is assessed. In an ITI classroom the expectation is for mastery of key points by all students on an "A/no credit yet" basis.

"Australia"
A small corner of the room where the students can go to relax, refocus, and reflect. Used to assist students who are highly upset—angry or sad—to reset their emotions so they can return to learning.

Being There
The most powerful input to the brain is being in a real world location that activates all 19 senses, thereby significantly increasing learning (pattern identification and program building).

Bloom's Taxonomy
A model by Benjamin Bloom, et al, originally designed for developing questioning strategies for college exams. In the ITI model, the process verbs characterizing each level are used to develop inquiries.

Bodybrain-Compatible Elements
These are nine conditions that enhance and support powerful learning, the basis for the ITI model. They are: Absence of Threat/Nurturing Reflective Thinking, Meaningful Content, Movement to Enhance Learning, Enriched Environment, Choices, Adequate Time, Collaboration, Immediate Feedback, and Mastery/Application.

Brain-Compatible Learning
Coined by Leslie A. Hart in his book *Human Brain and Human Learning,* it is a key goal of the Kovalik ITI model. A brain-compatible environment is one which allows the brain to work as it naturally, and thus most powerfully, works. Recent brain research has updated this term to "bodybrain-compatible" learning.

Celebrations of Learning
An activity to not only acknowledge accomplishments but to also practice using the knowledge and skills mastered through demonstrating and teaching others, particularly parents.

Choices

One of the nine Bodybrain-Compatible Elements of the ITI model. See Chapters 1-6.

Collaboration

One of the nine Bodybrain-Compatible Elements of the ITI model. See Chapters 1-6.

Common Core of Knowledge

Defined in the ITI model to mean those concepts, significant knowledge, and skills all students are expected to master and that are considered essential to success in life (school and adulthood) and to sustain a democracy and participate in our high-tech society.

Component (monthly)

An integral structure of the ITI model; in a yearlong theme, a component is the framework for one approximately one month of the yearlong theme.

C.U.E.

An acronym describing the three ways information can be presented in order for the learner to readily retrieve it. The "C" stands for creative, the "U" for useful and the "E" for emotional bridge.

Direct Instruction

The 11 to 16 minutes of teacher presentation of a key point which provides the focus of the classroom activities; direct instruction is only one way of orchestrating key points.

Enriched Environment

One of the nine Bodybrain-Compatible Elements of the ITI model. See Chapters 1-6.

Hands-On Experience

A term describing two levels of sensory input: hands-on of the real thing and hands-on of something symbolic or representative of a real thing. Hands-on of symbolic or representational things provides significantly less sensory input, and thus less stimulation of the brain, than does interacting with the real thing.

Immediate Feedback

One of the nine Bodybrain-Compatible Elements of the ITI model. See Chapters 1-6.

Immersion

An environment that simulates as richly as possible the real-life environment being studied, such as transforming a classroom into wetlands or a pond or a period of history to allow students the opportunity to experience or role-play as if they were actually there.

Input, Types of

1. *Being there*, physically being in the real world environment; 2. Immersion—full simulation of the real world environment, includes many real world things; 3. Hands-on of the real thing, (e.g., frog); 4. Hands-on of representation (e.g., plastic model of a frog); 5. Second-hand—pictorial representation, written word (e.g., pictures, videos, or stories about frogs); and 6. Symbolic—mathematics, phonics, grammar (scientific definition of a frog)

Inquiries

A key curriculum development structure in the ITI model, inquiries are activities that enable students to understand and apply the concept, skill, or significant knowledge of a key point. The primary purpose of inquiries is to enable students to develop mental programs for applying, in real-world situations, the key point and wiring such knowledge and skills into long-term memory. Inquiries make learning active and memorable.

Inquiry Builder

A chart that organizes the process verbs of Bloom's Taxonomy of Cognitive Objectives according to five of Howard Gardner's seven intelligences

Inseparable Bodybrain Learning Partnership

Current brain research indicates that the limbic system is part of a larger emotional system involving "information substances" produced and received throughout the body. In other words, the brain talks to the body and the body talks back to the brain. Learning is the result of an inseparable bodybrain partnership.

Integrated

Combining or coordinating separate elements so as to provide a harmonious interrelated whole (as defined by *Webster's Encyclopedia Unabridged Dictionary of the English Language* 1996).

ITI (Integrated Thematic Instruction)

The name given to a bodybrain-compatible, fully integrated instructional model developed by Susan Kovalik. It is a comprehensive model that translates the best of what we know about learning from current brain research into effective teaching strategies and meaningful curriculum.

Key Point

Essential concept, skill, or significant knowledge all students are expected to master (know and be able to use). The primary purpose of key points is to enhance students' ability to detect pattern, i.e., to readily identify the collection of attributes that is essential for understanding the concept, skill, or significant idea of the key point. They also provide a clear focus for the teacher for instructional planning and for orchestration of learning.

Learning, a Two–Step Process

Defined by Leslie Hart as a two-part process: 1. Detecting and understanding patterns—a process through which our brain creates meaning. 2. Developing meaningul mental programs to use what is understood and to store it in long-term memory—the capacity to use what is understood first with assistance and then almost automatically.

Lifelong Guidelines

The parameters for classroom/schoolwide interactions with other students and staff. They are TRUSTWORTHINESS, TRUTHFULNESS, ACTIVE LISTENING, NO PUT-DOWNS, and PERSONAL BEST.

LIFESKILLS

The 18 LIFESKILLS are the day-to-to-day definition of the Lifelong Guideline of Personal Best. The LIFESKILLS are the personal/social parameters for everyone—students and adults. They include: Integrity, Initiative, Flexibility, Perseverance, Organization, Sense of Humor, Effort, Common Sense, Resourcefulness, Problem-Solving, Responsibility, Patience, Friendship, Curiosity, Cooperation, Caring, Courage, and Pride.

Mastery

One of the nine Bodybrain-Compatible Elements of the ITI model. See Chapters 1-6.

Meaningful Content

One of the nine Bodybrain-Compatible Elements of the ITI model. See Chapters 1-6.

Mindmapping

A way to visually represent information, usually as a web or cluster around the main idea with symbols and colors, rather than in traditional outline form.

Movement to Enhance Learning

One of the nine Bodybrain-Compatible Elements of the ITI model. See Chapters 1-6.

Multiple Intelligences

Defined by Howard Gardner as "problem-solving or product-producing capabilities." The first seven intelligences identified by Gardner are: logical-mathematical, linguistic, spatial, bodily-kinesthetic, musical, intrapersonal, and interpersonal. Humans are born with all the intelligences but will develop each according to family and cultural preference, demands of one's environment, and the individual's inclinations and experiences. Gardner has subsequently added an eighth intelligence, naturalist. The multiple intelligences are a key ingredient of inquiries.

Pattern Seeking

A key concept of bodybrain-compatibility; describes the means by which the brain makes meaning from incoming sensory input.

Procedures, Written

Written procedures are an important classroom leadership strategy in the ITI model. They state the social and personal behaviors are expected for commonly occurring events, suchas entering and leaving the room, lunchroom behaviors, and so forth. By describing what social and personal behaviors are expected, these procedures allow students to be successful.

Program Building

A key concept of brain-compatibility describing how the brain stores and uses what it learns. It is defined as "a personal goal achieved by a sequence of steps or actions" which becomes stored in the brain for later retrieval when an action is required. Every goal we accomplish is due to implementation of a program or programs.

Social/Political Action

An integral part of the ITI model which provides students a vehicle for applying what they learn to real-world problems. It assists students in becoming contributing citizens.

Symbolic Input

The most difficult way for the brain to grasp new information such as phonics, grammar, and algebraic equations.

Temperament or Personality Preferences

Based on the work of Carl Jung, Myers and Briggs, and Keirsey and Bates, these four behavior scales strongly affect learning. The behavior areas are: taking in information (sensor or intuitor), decision making (feeling or thinking), lifestyle (judging or perceiving), and orientation to others (extrovert and introvert)

Target Talk

A key instructional tool to teach the Lifelong Guidelines/LIFE-SKILLS. Labels a behavior in context without value judgment.

Weekly Topics

An integral curriculum development structure of the ITI model for dividing each (monthly) component into topics or areas; in the yearlong theme, topics are planned for approximately one week.

Yearlong Research Projects

Topics students choose during the first two weeks of school to become the "expert" on for the class. Students research their project throughout the year and present it to the entire class (and others students as well).

Yearlong Theme

The yearlong theme is the central organizer for integrated curriculum in the ITI model. It is the conceptual organizer for all skills and concepts to be learned.

Bibliography

ABC News Prime Time. *"Your Child's Brain"* with Diane Sawyer. January 25, 1995.

Armstrong, Thomas. *In Their Own Way*. Los Angeles: Tarcher Press, 1987.

Armstrong, Thomas. *7 Kinds of Smart: Identifying and Developing Your Multiple Intelligences*. New York: Penguin Putnam, 1999

Beane, James A. *A Middle School Curriculum: From Rhetoric to Reality*, second edition. Westerville, Ohio: National Middle School Association, 1993.

Bell, Nanci. *Visualizing and Verbalizing for Improved Comprehension: A Teacher's Manual*. San Luis Obispo, CA: Academy of Reading, 1987.

Brady, Marion. *What's Worth Teaching? Selecting, Organizing, and Integrating Knowledge*. Covington, WA: Books for Educators, 1989.

Caine, Renata and Geoffrey. *Making Connections: Teaching and the Human Brain*. California: Addison-Wesley, 1994.

Calvin, William H. *How Brains Think: Evolving Intelligence, Then and Now*. New York: BasicBooks, 1996.

Calvin, William H. *"The Mind's Big Bang and Mirroring,"* unpublished manuscript. Seattle, WA: University of Washington, 2000.

Childre, Doc and Martin, Howard with Beech, Donna. *The HeartMath Solution*. San Francisco: Harper, 2000.

Cohen, Elizabeth. *Designing Groupwork: Strategies for the Heterogeneous Classroom*, Second Edition. New York: Teachers College Press, 1994.

Csikszentmihalyi, Mihaley. *Flow: The Psychology of Optimal Experience*. New York: Harper, 1990.

Cytowic, Richard E. *The Man who Tasted Shapes: A Bizarre Medical Mystery Offers Revolutionary Insights into Emotions, Reasoning, and Consciousness*. New York: Tarcher/Putnam, 1993.

Damasio, Antonio. *Descartes' Error: Emotion, Reason, and the Human Brain*. New York: G. P. Putnam Sons, 1994.

Damasio, Antonio. *"Thinking about Emotion,"* presentation at Emotional Intelligence, Education, and the Brain: A Symposium. Chicago, IL: December 5, 1997.

Diamond, Marion and Hopson, Janet. *Magic Trees of the Mind: How to Nurture Your Child's Intelligence, Creativity, and Healthy Emotions from Birth Through Adolescence*. New York: Penguin, 1998.

Gallese, Vittorio and Goldman, Alvin. "Mirror Neurons and the Simulation Theory of Mind-Reading" in *Trends in Cognitive Sciences*, Vol. 2, 1998.

Gardner, Howard. *Frames of Mind: Theory of Multiple Intelligences*. New York: Basic Books, 1983.

Gardner, Howard. *Intelligence Reframed: Multiple Intelligences for the 21st Century*. New York: Basic Books, 1999.

Gibbs, Jeanne. *TRIBES: A New Way of Learning and Being Together*. Windsor, California: CenterSource Systems, LLC, 2001.

Gibbs, Jeanne. *Discovering Gifts in Middle School: Learning in a Caring Culture Called Tribes*. Windsor, California: CenterSource Systems, LLC, 2001.

Goldberg, Elkhonon. *The Executive Brain: Frontal Lobes and the Civilized Mind*. Oxford: University Press, 2001.

Gopnik, A., A. Meltzoff, and Patricia Kuhl. *The Scientist in the Crib: Minds, Brains, and How Children Learn*. New York: William Morrow and Company, 1999.

Greenspan, Stanley I. with Benderly, Beryl Lieff. *The Growth of the Mind and the Endangered Origins of Intelligence*. New York: Addison-Wesley Publishing Company, 1997.

Hannaford, Carla. *Smart Moves: Why Learning Is Not All in Your Head*. Alexander, North Carolina: Great Ocean, 1995.

Hart, Leslie A. *Human Brain and Human Learning*. Covington, WA: Books for Educators, Inc., 1999.

Healy, Jane. *Endangered Minds: Why Children Don't Think – and What We Can Do About It*. New York: Simon & Schuster, 1990.

Healy, Jane. *Failure to Connect: How Computers Affect Our Children's Minds – And What We Can Do About It*. New York: Simon & Schuster, 1998.

Hermann, Ned. *The Creative Brain*. North Carolina: Brain Books, 1990.

Kagan, Spencer. *Cooperative Learning*. San Clemente, CA Kagan, 1994.

Keirsey, David. *Please Understand Me II: Temperament Character Intelligence*. Del Mar, CA: Prometheus Nemesis Book Company, 1998.

Kohn, Alfie. *Punished by Rewards: The Trouble with Gold Stars, Incentive Plans, A's, Praise, and Other Bribes*. Boston: Houghton Mifflin, 1993.

Kovalik, Susan. *Integrated Thematic Instruction: The Model*, third edition. Covington, WA: Susan Kovalik and Associates, 1997.

Kovalik, Susan J. & Olsen, Karen. *Kid's Eye View of Science*. Covington, WA: Books For Educators, Inc., 1994.

LeDoux, Joseph. "*The Emotional Brain,*" presentation at Emotional Intelligence, Education, and the Brain: A Symposium. Chicago, IL: December 5, 1997.

LeDoux, Joseph E. *The Emotional Brain: The Mysterious Underpinnings of Emotional Life*. New York: Simon and Schuster, 1996.

Lewis, Barbara A. *Kid's Guide to Social Action: How to Solve the Social Problems YOU CHOOSE – and Turn Creative Thinking into Positive Action*. Minnesota: Free Spirit Publishing, 1981.

Lewis, Thomas. *A General Theory of Love*. New York: Random House, 2000.

Lowery, Lawrence F. *Thinking and Learning: Matching Developmental Stages With Curriculum and Instruction*. Kent, Washington: Books for Educators, Inc., 1995.

Margulies, Nancy. *Mapping Inner Space: Learning and Teaching Mindmapping*. Arizona: Zephyr Press, 1991.

Miller, Norma, editor. *The Healthy School Handbook: Conquering the Sick Building Syndrome and Other Environmental Hazards In and Around Your School*. Washington, DC: NEA Professional Library, 1995.

Motluk, Alison. "Read My Mind" in *New Scientist*, p.22. Jan. 27, 2001.

Olsen, Karen D. *Making Bodybrain-Compatible Education a Reality: Coaching for the ITI Model*. Covington, Washington: Books for Educators, 1999.

Olsen, Karen D. *Science Continuum of Concepts, K-6*. Covington, WA: Center for the Future of Public Education, 1995.

Pert, Candace. *Molecules of Emotion: Why You Feel the Way You Feel*. New York: Scribner, 1997.

Ramachandran, V. S. *Mirror Neurons and Imitation Learning As the Driving Force Behind "The Great Leap Forward" in Human Evolution*. www.edge.org/documents/archive/edge69.html

Ratey, John J. *A User's Guide to the Brain: Perception, Attention, and the Four Theaters of the Brain*. New York: Pantheon Books, 2001.

Rivlin, Robert and Gravelle, Karen. *Deciphering Your Senses*. New York: Simon and Schuster, 1984.

Rizzolatti, Giacomo and Arbib, Michael. "Language Within Our Grasp" in *Trends in Neurosciences*, Vol. 21, 1998.

Samples, Bob. *Open Mind, Whole Mind*. California: Jalmar Press, 1987.

Smith, Frank. *Insult to Intelligence: The Bureaucratic Invasion of Our Classrooms*. New York: Arbor House Publishing Company, 1986

Smith, Frank. *to Think*. New York: Teachers College Press, 1990.

Sylwester, Robert. *A Celebration of Neurons: An Educator's Guide to the Human Brain*. Alexandria, VA: ASCD, 1995.

NOTES:

NOTES:

NOTES:

NOTES:

R

Catalog of RESOURCES

Catalog of RESOURCES

Exceeding Expectations:
A User's Guide to Implementing Brain Research in the Classroom
by Susan Kovalik and Karen D. Olsen.. $32.95

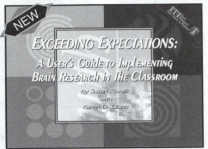

This new book is an absolute essential resource for any educator. Replaces the book entitled, *ITI: The Model.* This is the most comprehensive book available on integration for grades K-6. It describes clearly and succinctly the brain research base which makes ITI (Integrated Thematic Instruction) so powerful for students, and provides practical step-by-step explanations of how to create a bodybrain-compatible classroom. Learn how to develop and imple-

ment a yearlong theme as a structure for integrating all basic skills and content areas. Loaded with curriculum examples, implementation tips, starting points, and timelines. Comprehensive, practical, and insightful. *(400+ pgs.)*

The Way We Were . . . The Way We Can Be:
A Vision for the Middle School
Third Edition, by Ann Ross and Karen D. Olsen........... $27.50

The ITI challenge for middle school educators is to build a conceptual content base, create an environment free of threat, and have sufficient and effective teaching strategies all the while acknowledging the significant changes the students are experiencing. This book provides a range of opportunities for both students and teachers. *(298 pgs.)*

Synergy: The Transformation of America's High Schools
Through Integrated Thematic Instruction
by Karen D. Olsen... $27.50

America's high schools have survived waves of reform efforts unchanged. This book makes the case for achieving true trans-formation rather than merely tinkering with the present system. Describes how to use the ITI model as a vehicle for classroom and schoolwide restructuring. Challenges the very roots of high school calling for radical change and a defined purpose. *(281 pgs.)*

Character Begins at Home:
Using the ITI Lifelong Guidelines & LIFESKILLS in Your Classroom
by Sue Pearson and Karen D. Olsen............................. $27.50

Here are hundreds of ideas for nurturing children's characters through the Lifelong Guidelines and LIFESKILLS using sim-ple, enjoyable activities at home. Children and youth benefit by hearing and using a common language at home and at school as they develop the social skills of respect and responsible citi-zenship. Great idea for building family/community support!

Tools For Citizenship & Life:
Using the ITI Lifelong Guidelines & LIFESKILLS in Your Classroom
by Sue Pearson.. $27.50

Here is the book you've been waiting to have at your finger-tips! For each of the Lifelong Guidelines and LIFESKILLS, you get the description, why to practice it, how to practice it, what it looks like in the real world, what it looks like in school, inquiries to develop, signs of success, and links to related literature to use with students grades K-8. Includes the newest LIFESKILL, resourcefulness. *(283 pgs.)*

Lifelong Guidelines and LIFESKILLS
A wall poster set.. $39.95

The ITI Lifelong Guidelines call for trustworthiness, truthfulness, active listening, no put-downs, and personal best. What is personal best? The LIFESKILLS poster set provides colorful definitions and examples. Set includes a Lifelong Guidelines poster, a Personal Best Clubhouse poster (18" x 22 1/2"), and posters for each of the 18 LIFESKILLS (8 1/2" x 11"). LIFESKILLS include such traits as cooperation, caring, responsibility, initiative, and problem-solving. Artwork by Gwen Pribble is whimsical, action-oriented, and multi-ethnic. Ideal for incorporating character education.

Stage 1 of the ITI Stages of Implementation:
First Things First
(17 min. video)... $79.00

In this video, Joy Raboli takes you through the first steps of setting up an ITI classroom, illustrating each aspect of Stage 1 of the ITI Rubric. Covering the physical layout of the room, beginning curriculum and instructional strategies, how to invite parents into the program, and what you can expect students to accomplish, this is a video that will answer your practical questions.

Can be purchased separately or as a set.

A One-Day Makeover
for Your ITI Classroom
(14 min. video)... $79.00

Join veteran ITI teacher/administrator, Dottie Brown, as she transforms a stark classroom into a bodybrain-compatible learning space. Listen and watch as she analyzes the function for each space and decides how to arrange furniture to meet that need. See the simple strategies she uses so that the classroom promotes cooperation, looks beautiful, is calming and focused, and reflects the topic under study. She did it in one day and so can you!

LIFESKILLS:
Creating a Class Family
(17 min. video)... $79.00

Research conclusively shows that learning is accelerated when the issues of inclusion, mutual respect, and being in communication with each other are resolved and the classroom promotes a sense of community. Join Joy Raboli and Karen Janik and their 60 fifth and sixth graders for a look at what a multi-age class family looks like and how to create one in your own classroom.

Can be purchased separately or as a set.

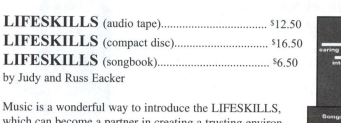

LIFESKILLS (audio tape)................................... $12.50
LIFESKILLS (compact disc)............................. $16.50
LIFESKILLS (songbook)................................... $6.50
by Judy and Russ Eacker

Music is a wonderful way to introduce the LIFESKILLS, which can become a partner in creating a trusting environment that enhances learning. These original tunes and lyrics are whimsical and memorable. Cassette and CD each contain 17 songs. Lyrics booklet includes all 17 songs and has large print ideal for making sing-along copies or overhead transparencies. Created by R&J Productions. Each sold separately.

Spread Your Wings: The Lifelong Guidelines
(19 min. video)... $19.95
(audio tape)... $11.95
(compact disc)... $12.50

With original lyrics, music, and vocals, Jeff Pedersen illustrates the Lifelong Guidelines as he takes us on a walk with students through a zoo. He introduces each song with heartfelt comments about what it means to apply the Guidelines in every aspect of one's life. The Lifelong Guidelines are the cornerstone of interpersonal skills, and are based upon respect for others and self.

Spread Your Wings:
The Eight Ways of Being Smart
(compact disc)...
$6.50

Here's a great way to learn about the Gardner's multiple intelligences—sing them! Jeff Pedersen's latest song for educators and students includes both the vocal and instrumental versions of "Everybody's Smart," an original composition. It's catchy, easy to learn, and has a message kids and adults will love!

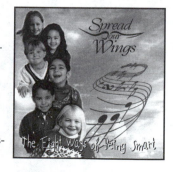

Lifelong Guidelines Mugs

Susan Kovalik & Associates.. $6.00

Like the popular posters you have in your classroom, these mugs offer a daily reminder of the Lifelong Guidelines, with an added bonus —you can fill them up with sixteen ounces of your favorite beverage! They're insulated, and come in an oatmeal shade with green top.

(LIFESKILLS LIVE IT! Design)

(Garden Design)

Lifelong Guidelines & LIFESKILLS T-Shirts & Sweatshirts

T-Shirts.. $17.00*
Sweatshirts... $26.00*

Send the message that you care about how we treat each other—wear a LIFESKILLS T-Shirt! The Lifelong Guidelines are printed over the heart, and the LIFESKILLS, which help you do your personal best, are on the back. The garden design displays the Lifelong Guidelines on the front and LIFESKILLS on the back. The LIFESKILLS LIVE IT! design appears only on the front.

<u>T-Shirt (LIFESKILLS LIVE IT!):</u> white with multi-color design (50/50 Cotton & Poly.)
<u>T-Shirts (Garden Design):</u> yellow haze, mint green & ash gray (Preshrunk 100% Cotton)
<u>Sweatshirts Colors:</u> ash gray only (50/50, crew neck)
<u>Sizes:</u> L, XL, XXL *(please add $1.00 for XXL)*

LIFESKILLS Notecards

Susan Kovalik & Associates.......................... $15.95

These lovely notecards with a garden motif each feature a separate LIFESKILL on a cream background. Use them to write to friends or family, or thank a student or co-worker for good use of a LIFESKILL! Set of seventeen on high quality paper with matching envelopes, suitable for framing.

The ITI Classroom Stages of Implementation:
Assessing Implementation of Bodybrain-Compatible Learning

by Karen D. Olsen and Susan Kovalik.......................... $6.50

Wondering how to assess your progress toward implementing the Kovalik ITI model? What results to expect for students, teachers, and parents? The *ITI Classroom Rubric* describes five stages of implementation from introducing a brain-compatible environment to achieving brain-compatible curriculum encompassing all basic skills and curricular areas. Included at each stage are descriptions of curriculum, instruction, expected results, and indicators. A must for schools implementing ITI, critical for teachers and administrators, ideal for parents and board members. *(14 pgs.)*

The ITI Schoolwide Rubric:

Assessing Schoolwide Implementation of Brain-Compatible Education

by Karen D. Olsen and Susan Kovalik............ $6.50

The *ITI Schoolwide Rubric* is designed to provide both road signs and mileage markers along the road to implementing ITI in an entire school. It describes five stages of training and achievement plus the governance necessary schoolwide in order to provide individual classroom teachers with the support they need and deserve as they work to implement ITI for their students. Includes expected outcomes and their likely indicators. *(56 pgs.)*

Stage 2 of the ITI Stages of Implementation:
Intelligence is a Function of Experience

(14 min. video)... $79.00

Intelligence is a function of experience! Schools need to be able to equalize student experiences in order to increase understanding of content. Follow these 2nd through 8th graders as they engage in a variety of experiences both in and out of the classroom. With a high level of cooperation and commitment to purpose, these students are learning to be responsible, productive citizens.

Curiosity Shop KITS..... $39.95 per kit

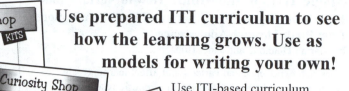

Use prepared ITI curriculum to see how the learning grows. Use as models for writing your own!

Use ITI-based curriculum that fits in with your theme, enriches your teaching, provides quality lessons for substitutes, stimulates curiosity, and expands career awareness! The suggested grade levels are indicated after the title.

A puddle disappears, a cup overflows, and children learn about change!

A Drop of Water
(Grades 4-8) by Ann Ross
Things are changing around us all the time. Here, your students learn to measure that change through very basic scientific methods.

Saving the world and spreading gossip through dots and dashes, zeroes and ones...

I've Got A Secret
(Grades 4-8) by Ann Ross
Explore the world of human communication through secret codes, telegraph messages, and other means. How have they changed the world, and how do they affect your students personally?

Get those fingerprints off the windows & onto paper!

Touching Art
(Grades 1-4) by Patty Harrington
Using their own fingerprints, students can create art as unique as they are. Explore and expand creativity in your students.

Steam shrinks world!

The Train: A Magnificent Machine
(Grades 4-8) by Sr. Patt Walsh
Simple steam experiments, the characters of the westward expansion, humanity's ingenuity in its quest to accomplish work in better and faster ways—these are what your students will explore.

Thumbprint—only one like it in school—leads to capture of good guy!

Young Detectives
(Grades 2-5) by Patty Harrington
The powers of observation lead to exciting discoveries about change when your students are on the case!

Fish gotta swim—we all know that—but how do they do it?

Amazing Fish
(Grades 3-6) by Nicole McNeil-Miller
This hands-on study uses fish to explore form and function and engages students in basic scientific inquiry.

Slips of paper slated to become animals, diamonds, and other items without use of magic!

Super Nifty Origami Crafts
(Grades 3-8) by Judy Eacker
The ancient Japanese art of origami inspires a study of form and function as students make a square of paper evolve from one shape into another and then another.

From ears to hooves, a 1000-pound horse is made of little bits it can't live without!

A Horse Is A Horse, Of Course
(Grades 4-8) by Dean Tannewitz
Specialization is the key to survival for all of us. Learn about a horse's special attributes, how it lives in the wild, and how humans meet its needs when it's domesticated.

Look deep into the jaws of an ant! Bug your teacher!

Amazing Insects
(Grades 1-5) by Pattie Mills
What kind of mouth does an ant have? Is it different than a mosquito's? Why are they different? Form and function are explored through scientific observation and expressed through, art, writing, acting, and more!

I Can Divide and Conquer:

A Concept in a Day by Martha M. Kaufeldt
(55 min. video & handbook)... $59.95

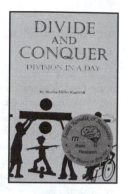

When the learning environment is brain-compatible, something as "hard" as long division—concept and computation—can be mastered in a single day. Follow a fourth grade teacher as she takes fifty fourth, fifth, and sixth graders through an unforgettable day of conquering long division. *(76 pgs.)*

Classroom of the 21st Century

(50 min. video and handbook)... $59.95

Observe an ITI fourth grade classroom where all curriculum content and skills are orchestrated around a yearlong theme. Hear students speak for the power of the model. A comprehensive, 75-page handbook included.

Classroom of the 21st Century

by Robert Ellingsen.. $12.95

How does a dynamic, brain-compatible, thematic classroom function? Here's a step-by-step description of how to weave the basic components of learning around a yearlong theme in order to integrate basic skills and content areas. Illustrates transitional steps from a traditional classroom toward an ITI classroom emphasizing integrating basic skills. *(75 pgs.)*

Stage 3 of the ITI Stages of Implementation:

Creating Conceptual Curriculum
(25 min. video).. $79.00

Join Joy Raboli and Karen Janik to see how a conceptual curriculum is powerful, meaningful, and allows students to predict and generalize. In this video, 5th and 6th grade students learn from guest speakers, "being there" experiences, and skill integration. Watch as they internalize the meaning of responsibility for one's own learning. This is ITI in action!

Jacobsonville: An ITI Micro Society

(30 min. video).. $39.95

Learners have long asked their teachers, "When am I ever going to use this?" Follow students and teachers as they unfold a comprehensive micro-society. In this ITI K-5 school, using information and skills is the goal. From a city government with elected officials to commerce with postal and banking services and a variety of small businesses, students negotiate the business trail (complete with business permits, design, production, marketing, business space rental, and profit margin calculations). A "must see" video!

Making Bodybrain-Compatible Education a Reality:

Coaching for the ITI Model

by Karen D. Olsen... $21.95

Even champions rely on their coaches. This book helps you prepare to be a top-notch ITI coach. It introduces a coaching model designed specifically for ITI coaches that is based on the ITI stages of implementation.*(214 pgs.)*

Human Brain and Human Learning

by Leslie A. Hart
(Revised/Updated 1998)... $21.95

Orchestrating learning that is bodybrain-compatible must be the foundation for what goes on in the classroom. Hart brilliantly explains the biology of learning related to classroom practice and allows the reader to "see" what is necessary for real reform efforts to succeed. The reader comes to appreciate how the brain makes meaning through pattern recognition, prepares to act through mental programs, and responds to emotion. *(402 pgs.)*

Magic Trees of the Mind: How to Nurture Your Child's Intelligence, Creativity, and Healthy Emotions from Birth Through Adolescence

by Marian Diamond and Janet Hopson....................... $13.95

Does rich experience and varied input affect learning? This author proves it beyond a doubt with scientific research. Fascinating and readable, Diamond succeeds in convincing the reader that powerful learning requires interaction with many kinds of resources, experiences doing new things, and rich sensory input to the brain. Educators, including parents are literally helping to build children's brains. *(466 pgs.)*

A User's Guide to the Brain

by John J. Ratey, M.D. $27.50

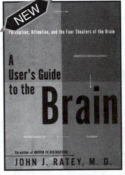

This book explains in lucid detail and with perfect clarity the basic structure and chemistry of the brain: how its systems shape our perceptions, emotions, actions, and reactions; how possession of this knowledge can enable us to more fully understand and improve our lives; and how the brain responds to the guidance of its user. Dr. John Ratey, associate clinical professor of pshychiatry at Harvard University and co-author of *Driven to Distraction*, draws from his own practice, from research, and from every day life to illuminate aspects of the brain's functioning, among them prenatal and early childhood development; the perceptual systems; the processes of consciousness, memory, emotion, and language; and the social brain.. *(404 pgs.)*

Smart Moves:

Why Learning Is Not All in Your Head

by Carla Hannaford, Ph.D... $15.95

Thoroughly supported by scientific research, Hannaford shows why and how the body plays an essential role in learning. Knowledge from the neurosciences and information about how body movement, emotional expression, nutrition, and how the social and physical environment influence learning all are brought together in a remarkable synthesis. *(237 pgs.)*

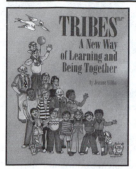

TRIBES: A New Way of Learning and Being Together
by Jeanne Gibbs.. $32.95

Tribes teaches how to build community through the practice of inclusion and influence, a must for successful cooperative learning activities. Specific and practical, you can use these ideas immediately. Designed for elementary grades. *(432 pgs.)*

Thinking and Learning: Matching Developmental Stages with Curriculum and Instruction
by Dr. Larry Lowery.. $12.95

A concise description of the evolving thinking processes of children, this is a handy tool at school and district levels for examining curriculum content and determining what is age-appropriate for our students and, thus, understandable (rather than memorizable). You'll see why textbooks are wildly inappropriate in many areas! *(98 pgs.)*

Environmentally Sick Schools: Students & Teachers at Risk
(90 min. video)... $24.95

This urgent guide for educators and families summarizes distressing, but important information about the ways in which the lives of those inhabiting schools have been drastically affected by environmental exposures. Sensitivity to certain food, mold, or other aspects of the daily school environment can cause illness, change behavior, and affect learning. Increased awareness and knowledge will help you plan responsible improvements.

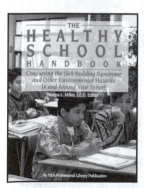

The Healthy School Handbook: Conquering the Sick Building Syndrome and Other Environmental Hazards in and Around Your School
Edited by Norma L. Miller, Ed.D. $24.95

Is your school sick? What is a sick building? Learn how to be alert and aware of indoor environmental conditions and how they can affect the health and learning of students. From price comparisons to medical analysis and aesthetics to immutable biological realities, 22 experts discuss the environment of our schools and what we can and must do to make schools safe and healthy places to be. *(446 pages)*

Discovering Gifts in Middle School: Learning in a Caring Culture Called Tribes
by Jeanne Gibbs.. $32.95

This book presents a lively synthesis of a wealth of research studies and effectively practices which underlie the *Tribes Learning Community* developmental approach for middle level students and their schools. The synthesis draws on relevant literature on cognitive theory, human resilience, constructivism, social-emotional learning, multi-cultural gender equity, reflective practice, and authentic assessment. Placing major emphasis on middle schools becoming responsive to the contextual basis of adolescent development, leads not only to greater achievement and success for students but to a new spirit, energy and the discovery of gifts throughout the whole school community. *(441 pgs.)*

Effective Teaching Effective Learning
by Alice M. Fairhurst and Lisa L. Fairhurst............ $18.95

If you have ever asked yourself: How can I reach more of my students more of the time? Are there simple ways of reaching students who are hard to teach? What makes an exceptional teacher exceptional? How can I increase the effectiveness of my teaching to create more effective learning? Then this is the book for you. The authors draw from their thirty years of combined teaching experience to share practical answers to these very questions. *Effective Teaching Effective Learning* identifies temperament and personality types and offers principles and applications to apply from first grade through college age students to maximize their learning potential. *(328 pgs.)*

The Kid's Guide to Social Action: How to Solve the Social Problems You Choose—and Turn Creative Thinking into Positive Action
by Barbara A. Lewis.. $16.95

Here is an extraordinary source for exploring life beyond the classroom. It provides step-by-step examples of how to initiate and carry out social action projects. Students learn to write letters, create surveys, get TV coverage, and lobby their legislators. Fabulous integration of the language arts skills, social studies, and real life! *(211 pgs.)*

Cooperative Learning

by Spencer Kagan.. $35.00

Applicable to students of all ages and especially upper elementary and beyond, this book provides the theory underlying cooperative learning and the practical strategies for success in applying the theory. Kagan coined the term, "structures," to refer to the many ways in which students can work together productively. Each structure is clearly described and grouped according to function, e.g., thinking skills, communication skills, teambuilding, and so on. Highly practical for cooperative learning beginners and veterans alike. *(368 pgs.)*

Multiple Intelligences in the Classroom

(ASCD Publication)
by Thomas Armstrong.............................. $22.95

In this updated version Armstrong describes how educators can bring Howard Gardner's theory of multiple intelligences into the classroom. Learn how to explore your own intelligences, develop lessons, and conduct assessments using the intelligences with ideas from this valuable resource. *(185 pgs.)*

Multiple Intelligences and the Second Language Learner

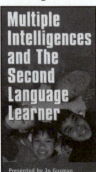

by Jo Gusman (40 min. video)........................... $99.95

Jo Gusman draws on her years of training and experience working with second language learners and her knowledge of Gardner's multiple intelligences to present powerful suggestions for educators. As increasing numbers of students arrive in classrooms speaking English as a second language, teachers must have an expanding repertoire of strategies for ensuring achievement. In her lively style, Jo presents the theory and then takes the viewer to class-rooms to see illustrations of its application. The video reveals insights for faculties who teach diverse populations.

Let's Get Moving:
Movement in the Classroom

(95 min. video with manual)...................... $19.95

Organized movement "wakes up the brain" and enhances student performance in ITI classrooms. Diane Berry's video is an excellent educational tool and visual guide for you and your students to perform exercise movements safely and effectively in the classroom. Shows how to incorporate both high energy and quick energy exercises into your daily routine, promoting physical and mental alertness. Designed for K-6, comes with accompanying handbook.

Lifelines: Songs of Character

(45 min. CD)...................................... $12.00

Jeff Pedersen's original songs add vitality to the school day while reinforcing the LIFESKILLS of perseverance, caring, initiative, curiosity, friendship, sense of humor, and effort. Use the joy and power of music to bring a deeper meaning of these LIFESKILLS to your students. Lyrics for each song are included.

Brain Talk with Barbara Pedersen

6 compact discs................................. $44.95

Invite Barbara's wisdom and experience into your car and heart. This set of six CDs connects the underlying brain research to practical applications on collaboration, classroom management, literacy, and integrated curriculum. Listening is like having Barbara for your personal coach as you implement ITI.

Large Desk Chime............... $45.00
A musical way to call your class together. A 10-inch birds-eye maple frame showcasing eighteen finely tuned chimes.

Science Continuum of Concepts, K-6
by Karen D. Olsen.. $7.95

ITI teachers are encouraged to use science as the basis for all content integration. This amazing K-6 guide identifies the developmentally appropriate conceptual key points, recommended field trips, and expected student performance for each grade level. It is an essential tool for writing integrated curriculum and for making science come alive for students. *(53 pgs.)*

What's Worth Teaching?
Selecting, Organizing, and Integrating Knowledge
by Marion Brady.. $14.95

Brady provides a workable framework for analyzing deficits of traditional curriculum and for creating curriculum appropriate for the 21st century. According to Brady, "The proper subject matter of education is reality." It should be demonstrably applicable to daily experience, universal, and equally valid for every student, as well as being integrated and part of a coherent conceptual structure. This is a "must-read" book for teachers and administrators, grades 7-12. *(147 pgs.)*

What Should We Teach?

A Guide to Community Dialog
by Marion Brady.. $149.95

Meet the rising desire for parental and community involvement in school affairs with a program designed to bring many perspectives to the essential question, "what should we teach?" This program brings together educators, parents, and community activists in a series of weekly small group meetings. Eighteen pocket-size booklets focus the dialog from week-to-week. Each booklet starts with a single idea, but the ideas build and interlock. The set includes 20 complete sets of booklets and a facilitator's handbook. (360 small booklets and 1 Facilitator's Handbook)

"Anchor" Math: The Brain-Compatible Approach to Learning

by Leslie A. Hart.. $16.95

This book is for teachers who find that students respond to math as if it were of another world and had nothing to do with them. It is an informative book for all who teach elementary math and want to greatly increase student achievement. It explores the ways of "anchoring" math to the real world as perceived and processed by a student's mind. A follow-up book to *Human Brain and Human Learning*, it discusses how to teach math in a brain-compatible way. Perceptive, fresh, challenging. Just the tool needed to breathe real life into math and significantly increase student learning. *(148 pgs.)*

Mapping Inner Space: Learning and Teaching Mind Mapping

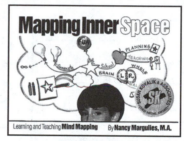

by Nancy Margulies.............................. $32.00

Recipient of the 1992 Susan Kovalik Gold Medal Award for best student resource, this delightfully useful and powerful book is for both adults and children, the experienced mind mapper as well as the first-timer. It will assist students and teachers in using "a revolutionary system for pouring ideas onto paper." Includes many colorful examples. *(123 pgs.)*

The Kid's Guide to Service Projects
Over 500 Service Ideas for Young People Who Want to Make a Difference
by Barbara A. Lewis.. $12.95

Kids. . . pick any topic that interests you, whether it be animals, environment, crime, politics, or another. Use this resource to guide you to simple service projects you can do or to larger projects that may involve groups or communities. With the guidance of this wonderful handbook, you can start making a difference today! *(175 pgs.)*

ORDER FORM

Books for Educators, Inc.
17051 SE 272nd Street, Suite 18 • Covington WA 98042-4959
Call toll free! 888-777-9827 • Fax: 253-630-7215
E-mail: books4@oz.net • Internet: www.books4educ.com
Hours: M-Th, 6:00AM-4:30PM, Pacific Time • Closed Fridays

Organization: _____

Name: _____

Street Address: _____

City: _____ State: _____ Zip: _____

Phone: (_____) _____

E-mail: _____

| **Payment Method**: | ☐ Payment Enclosed — check # _____ |
| | ☐ Visa or MasterCard |

Credit Card # _____ Exp. Date: _____

Authorizing Signature: _____

| **Please Fax or Mail Authorized Purchase Orders** | **FREE Shipping with 25 or More of Same Title** |
| Prices subject to change without notice | Does not apply to *RUSH* Service |

Shipping via UPS: Please specify preferred shipping option below

Regular Service–
Prices listed below.

☐ Regular Ground UPS

$1 - $34.99............... $5.00
$35 - $59.99............. $6.00
$60 - $499.99........... 10% of order
$500 and above....... 5% of order

RUSH Service Options–
Please call for current rates.

☐ 3–Day Service
☐ 2–Day Service
☐ 1–Day Service

Add shipping Charge to Order ➜

QTY	TITLE/DESCRIPTION	PRICE	TOTAL

SUBTOTAL		
AZ Residents Only Add (.056) Sales Tax		
WA Residents Only Add (.084) Sales Tax		
Shipping		
TOTAL		

Thank you!

ORDER FORM

Books for Educators, Inc.

17051 SE 272nd Street, Suite 18 • Covington, WA 98042-4959
Call toll free! 888-777-9827 • Fax: 253-630-7215
E-mail: books4@oz.net • Internet: www.books4educ.com

Hours: M-Th, 6:00AM-4:30PM, Pacific Time • Closed Fridays

Organization: _____

Name: _____

Street Address: _____

City: _____ State: _____ Zip: _____

Phone: (_____) _____

E-mail: _____

Payment Method: ❑ Payment Enclosed — check # _____
❑ Visa or MasterCard

Credit Card # _____ Exp. Date: _____

Authorizing Signature: _____

Please Fax or Mail Authorized Purchase Orders

Prices subject to change without notice

FREE Shipping with 25 or More of Same Title

Does not apply to RUSH Service

Shipping via UPS: Please specify preferred shipping option below

Regular Service–
Prices listed below.

❑ Regular Ground UPS

$1 - $34.99 .... $5.00
$35 - $59.99 .... $6.00
$60 - $499.99 .... 10% of order
$500 and above .... 5% of order

***RUSH* Service Options–**
Please call for current rates.

❑ 3–Day Service
❑ 2–Day Service
❑ 1–Day Service

Add shipping Charge to Order ➡

Thank you!

QTY	TITLE/DESCRIPTION	PRICE	TOTAL

SUBTOTAL	
AZ Residents Only Add (.056) Sales Tax	
WA Residents Only Add (.084) Sales Tax	
Shipping	
TOTAL	

ORDER FORM

Books for Educators, Inc.

17051 SE 272nd Street, Suite 18 • Covington, WA 98042-4959
Call toll free! 888-777-9827 • Fax: 253-630-7215
E-mail: books4@oz.net • Internet: www.books4educ.com
Hours: M-Th, 6:00AM-4:30PM, Pacific Time • Closed Fridays

Organization: _____

Name: _____

Street Address: _____

City: _____ State: _____ Zip: _____

Phone: (____) _____

E-mail: _____

Payment Method: ❑ Payment Enclosed — check # _____
❑ Visa or MasterCard

Credit Card # _____ Exp. Date: _____

Authorizing Signature: _____

Please Fax or Mail Authorized Purchase Orders

FREE Shipping with 25 or More of Same Title

Prices subject to change without notice

Does not apply to *RUSH* Service

Shipping via UPS: Please specify preferred shipping option below

Regular Service–
Prices listed below.

❑ Regular Ground UPS

$1 - $34.99.............. $5.00
$35 - $59.99............ $6.00
$60 - $499.99.......... 10% of order
$500 and above....... 5% of order

RUSH Service Options–
Please call for current rates.

❑ 3–Day Service
❑ 2–Day Service
❑ 1–Day Service

Add shipping Charge to Order ➜

QTY	TITLE/DESCRIPTION	PRICE	TOTAL

SUBTOTAL

AZ Residents Only Add (.056) Sales Tax

WA Residents Only Add (.084) Sales Tax

Shipping

TOTAL

Thank you!

NOTES:

NOTES:

NOTES:

NOTES: